MW01076525

The Wild Turkey

JOHN SIDELINGER

The Wild Turkey

Biology and Management

Edited by James G. Dickson

Southern Forest Experiment Station

STACKPOLE
BOOKS

A National Wild Turkey Federation and USDA Forest Service Book

Published by
STACKPOLE BOOKS
Cameron and Kelker Streets
P.O. Box 1831
Harrisburg PA 17105

Printed in the United States of America

10 9 8 7 6 5 4 3 2 1

Interior layout by Marcia Lee Dobbs
Figures by Donna Ziegenfuss
Line drawings by Bruce Cunningham, Rob Keck, Doug Pifer, and
John Sidelinger

Library of Congress Cataloging-in-Publication Data

The Wild turkey : biology and management / edited by James G. Dickson.
    p.   cm.
    "A National Wild Turkey Federation and USDA Forest Service book."
    Includes bibliographical references (p.   ) and index.
    ISBN 0-8117-1859-X
    1. Wild turkeys.   2. Wild turkeys—Ecology.   3. Wild turkeys—
Habitat.   4. Game bird management.   I. Dickson, James G.
II. National Wild Turkey Federation (U.S.)   III. United States.
Forest Service.
QL696.G254W53   1992
598.6'19—dc20   92-11214
                                                 CIP

Contents

Acknowledgments

David E. Austin
Steve E. Backs
Claudia A. Ball
R. Wayne Bailey
Elizabeth Balko
George F. Barrowclough
David P. Baumann
Samuel L. Beasom
Mike Biggs
Joyce Bond
Peter T. Bromley
Robert T. Brooks
Robert L. Burgess
Joseph J. Campo
Julio Carrera
Jim Clay
John Cominsky
Robert L. Cook
William R. Davidson
Richard DeGraaf
Neal Eichholz
Walter Elling
Ronald Engel-Wilson
Chet Fish
Donald J. Forrester
Garner Fuller
James W. Glidden
Deane Gonzales
Gary Griffen
Jeff G. Groth
Hayden Hauke
Rob Hazelwood
William M. Healy
Gary R. Hepp

Brian Hyder
Paul E. Johns
Ned K. Johnson
Rob Keck
James Earl Kennamer
Mary C. Kennamer
Gwen Kirtley–Perkins
Nancy Koerth
Herb Kothmann
Kenneth L. Kieser
Richard O. Kimmel
Alberto Lafón
J. Larry Landers
Jay Langston
Bruce D. Leopold
John B. Lewis
Terry W. Little
Richard McCabe
M. Mulvey
James A. Neal
James D. Nichols
Oliver H. Pattee
David R. Patten
Danny B. Pence
Paul H. Pelham
Charles Peterson
Fred Phillips
William F. Porter
M. Reneau
Joel Rudy
Leonard L. Rue
Mark A. Rumble
D.C. Saylor
Judith Schnell

L. Schorr
Harley G. Shaw
Henry L. Short
Gene Smith
Glen "Tink" Smith
Mike H. Smith
Dan W. Speake
Martin J. Tarby
U.S. Dept. of Energy and University
   of Georgia, Contract
   DE–AC09–76SR00–819

Matt Vander Haegen
Larry D. Vangilder
Gary West
T. Bently Wigley
Robert Willging
Lovett E. Williams, Jr.
J. Howard Williamson
Gerald A. Wunz
William D. Zeedyk

List of Tables

Chapter 21, Gould's Turkey

JOHN SIDELINGER

List of Figures

Chapter 12, Population Management

Chapter 13, Habitat Analysis and Assessment

Chapter 14, Habitat Requirements

Chapter 15, Florida Turkey

Chapter 18, Eastern Turkey in Midwestern Oak-Hickory Forests

Chapter 19, Rio Grande Turkey

Chapter 21, Gould's Turkey

I

Wild Turkey Background and History

JOHN SIDELINGER

Chapter 1

INTRODUCTION

James G. Dickson
Research Wildlife Biologist
USDA Forest Service, Southern Forest Experiment Station
Wildlife Habitat Laboratory, Nacogdoches, Texas

The goal of this book is to synthesize, summarize, and present in semitechnical style the best available information on the ecology and management of the wild turkey. This book is organized into 4 general sections: (1) introduction, history, and taxonomy; (2) biology; (3) habitat and management; and (4) use and projections for the future. There are 24 different chapters and 24 total authors. Although each chapter has been edited for consistency, there are some different perspectives and conclusions.

There is a need for a semitechnical synthesis and summary of wild turkey information, especially recent information, for managers, scientists, and laymen. Of the previous books on the wild turkey, most contained little or no verified biological information or focused on hunting techniques. It has been more than 20 years since the last broad-coverage summary treatise, *The Wild Turkey and Its Management*.

Meantime, there have been extensive changes in wild turkey range, habitat, and techniques. Now we have substantially more facts and figures. New information covers a broad array of subjects.

In taxonomy, for example, a rare subspecies — the Gould's — has been verified in the United States, there is speculation that *Meleagris gallopavo gallopavo* could remain in its original range or be introduced into South America, and avian taxonomic relationships are being investigated and defined through new objective techniques such as starch-gel electrophoresis and DNA analyses.

Restoration of the wild turkey took quantum leaps with the adaptation of the cannon net and development of effective drugs for capturing wild turkeys. Wild turkeys have been introduced and are thriving in the Midwest, the Northwest, New England, Canada, Europe, and elsewhere. The wild turkey is now found in every U.S. state but Alaska, and old range maps no longer apply. But we still need to focus attention on the futility and potential dangers of releasing pen-reared turkeys.

Effective capture techniques, new technology, and increased research support have brought new information and better management for the wild turkey. We now

Now we have more information to help manage the wild turkey. *Photo by H. Williamson, U.S. Forest Service.*

Radio instrumentation of wild turkeys has revealed much about wild turkey biology. *Photos by L. Williams.*

have effective, long-lived, reliable transmitters that have motion switches and are powered by light. Radio communication with wild turkeys has been a major breakthrough, providing a wide variety of information. We have new quantitative data on behavior, life history, and ecology. Radio-instrumented turkeys have provided information on habitat use by season, sex, and age; seasonal range; and nesting ecology.

Radio instrumentation of turkeys also has produced valuable information on seasonal and long-term population dynamics, on predation, and on the impact of illegal and legal hunting on turkey populations. We have long suspected substantial inroads on turkey populations from illegal hunting, and this impression has been substantiated by several recent studies.

Today we have better equipment and techniques to gather and analyze data. Computers plot turkey loca-

Photo by L. Williams.

Small transmitters enable researchers to track and determine the fate of young poults. *Photo by L. Williams.*

Photo by B. Ericksen.

Restoration of the wild turkey has been successful beyond expectation.

tions and delineate ranges. Multivariate data-analysis techniques such as discriminate-function analysis and cluster analysis help us reach better conclusions about natural relationships in a multivariate world. Vocal repertoires have been defined, and it has been demonstrated that individual turkeys can be recognized by voice (Dahlquist et al. 1990). More comprehensive data are available on aging and sexing turkeys, and a record system for trophy gobblers catalogs valuable information.

Early writings about the wild turkey, such as Mosby and Handley (1943), described optimum habitat as isolated areas where turkeys had persisted during periods of low populations. Since then, experience has shown that turkeys are much more flexible and adaptable. Standards for optimum habitat have changed somewhat, and marginal habitat is now being defined.

Now we know more about wild turkey diseases and are beginning to understand how these affect turkey populations. Also, studies of human-imprinted turkeys have given us insight into turkey behavior and life history.

New information is available on food habits. Several studies have focused on poult food availability and

Through restoration, protection, and habitat management, we now have viable turkey populations in all contiguous 48 states and many other countries. *Photo by National Wild Turkey Federation.*

habits, information that's essential to understanding and providing for that early, critical life phase. Information is being accumulated on the availability and nutritional values of turkey food, and how foods affect survival and productivity.

Information exchange and education on the wild turkey has become prominent through numerous symposiums, workshops, seminars, videos, and magazine articles. New information and emphasis on the wild turkey have resulted in enhanced habitat management in many areas. New hunters have access to a wide variety of training aids and equipment.

There is keen interest by the public in the wild turkey, and no group is more devoted than the turkey hunters. By 1992, the National Wild Turkey Federation had grown to about 70,000 members. Turkey hunting is the fastest growing shooting sport in the United States.

Sportsmen, who have supported the return of the wild turkey, are reaping some of the many benefits. *Photo by G. Wunz, Pennsylvania Game Commission.*

Turkey hunting, long a tradition in parts of the nation, now is being enjoyed by young and old throughout the U.S. *Photo by J. Dickson.*

Where once wild turkeys numbered only in the tens of thousands, now there are some 4 million nationwide. *Photo by J. Kennamer, National Wild Turkey Federation.*

The wild turkey has proved far more adaptable than previously thought. *Photo by L. Williams.*

Turkey hunting has a substantial economic effect. In 1989, it was estimated that spring turkey hunters spent more than $567 million in pursuit of their sport (Baumann et al. 1990). A related industry of turkey-hunting clothes and supplies has developed.

These may be the good old days for turkeys and turkey hunters. Now there is a huntable population of wild turkeys in every state except Alaska. Restoration, information through research, habitat management, and better protection have been successful. There were some 4 million wild turkeys nationwide in 1992. Compare that number with only tens of thousands in the early part of this century. With this book, may we help ensure the wild turkey's future and our enjoyment of this ultimate game animal.

Chapter 2

HISTORY

James Earl Kennamer
Director
Research & Management
National Wild Turkey Federation
Edgefield, South Carolina

Mary Kennamer
Information Specialist
Research & Management
National Wild Turkey Federation
Edgefield, South Carolina

Ron Brenneman
Assistant Director
Research & Management
National Wild Turkey Federation
Edgefield, South Carolina

The wild turkey, native to the North American continent, exists in a variety of habitats throughout its range. The species is tied closely with the early Native American cultures and has an often-misunderstood association with the history of the United States of America.

The once abundant wild turkey, largest native gallinaceous bird found by the European immigrants, declined with colonization and almost reached extinction when the forests fell to the axe and saw as settlers moved west. Wild turkey populations reached their lowest numbers near the end of the 19th century, surviving only in the most inaccessible habitats.

As forest stands regenerated after the Great Depression, the stage was set for the return of the wild turkey. After World War II, active restoration programs and research efforts by state agencies led to wild turkey populations in every state except Alaska. Of these 49, 10 are outside what is considered the wild turkey's ancestral range. In 1991, spring wild turkey hunting seasons were for the first time open in every one of the 49 states having turkey populations. Spring hunting seasons are also held in Ontario and other Canadian provinces as well as in Mexico.

NOMENCLATURE

There was early confusion among the turkey, the guinea fowl, and the peafowl. Even Linnaeus, who proposed the scientific name *Meleagris gallopavo* in 1758, used names reminiscent of the earlier confusion (Aldrich 1967a:14). The genus name *Meleagris* means "guinea fowl," from the ancient Greco-Romans. The species name *gallopavo* is Latin for "peafowl" of Asia (*gallus* for cock and *pavo* for chickenlike) (Aldrich 1967b:23). His descriptions seem to be based primarily on the domestic turkey. Linnaeus further described the Mexican subspecies from a specimen taken at Mirador, Veracruz. It is probably extinct today.

To confuse matters even more, some early authors say the word "turkey" was derived from the bird's call of "turk, turk." A more logical explanation suggests that the Hebrew word *tukki*, which also means "peacock," was applied to the turkey by the Jewish poultry merchants who helped introduce the bird to Europe (Davis 1949).

Over the years, 5 other distinct subspecies occurring in the wild have been named, all native to North America but in different areas.

The eastern wild turkey *(M. g. silvestris)* inhabits roughly the eastern half of the United States. It was named by L.J.P. Vieillot in 1817 using the word *silvestris*, meaning "forest" turkey.

The Florida wild turkey *(M. g. osceola)* was described in 1890 by W.E.D. Scott and was named for the famous Seminole chief, Osceola, who led his tribe against the white man in a war beginning in 1835. This bird is a resident of the southern half of Florida. The specimen used to type (describe) the subspecies is in the Museum of Comparative Zoology at Harvard University in Cambridge, Massachusetts.

The Merriam's wild turkey *(M. g. merriami)* of the mountain regions of the western United States was named by Dr. E.W. Nelson in 1900 in honor of C. Hart Merriam, first chief of the U.S. Biological Survey. The type specimen, collected 76 kilometers (47 miles) southwest of Winslow, Arizona, is in the U.S. National Museum Fish and Wildlife Service collection in Washington, D.C.

The Rio Grande wild turkey *(M. g. intermedia)* of the south-central plains states and northeastern Mexico was described by George B. Sennett in 1879. He said the Rio Grande turkey differed from the other races by being intermediate; hence its name. The type specimen, taken on the Lomita Ranch, Hidalgo County, Texas, is in the American Museum of Natural History in New York City.

The fifth recognized subspecies is the Gould's *(M. g. mexicana)*, which is found in northwestern Mexico and parts of southern Arizona and New Mexico. This subspecies, which currently numbers several hundred individuals in the United States, was first described by J. Gould in 1856 during his travels in Mexico. The Gould's type specimen is in the British Museum. A sixth subspecies *(M. g. gallopavo)* originally inhabiting southern Mexico now is probably extinct. It is the accepted forerunner to the domestic turkey.

The ocellated turkey *(M. ocellata)* is a different species, occurring on the Yucatán Peninsula of southeastern Mexico and possibly in adjacent countries. In color it is much closer to the peafowl than to its 5 cousins to the north. Males have a bronze-green iridescence, long spurs, and no beard. The primary wing feathers are edged in white. The gray tail feathers are tipped with a blue-bronze hue, and there are peacocklike spots on its tail coverts. The blue head has distinct, randomly spaced, round, pinkish growths. Instead of making the familiar gobbling and clucking sounds of the other subspecies, the ocellated turkey makes a whistling noise.

ARCHAEOLOGY

Steadman (1980) proposed that turkeys originated from a pheasantlike stock that became isolated and evolved in the New World. Aldrich (1967a:4) first mentioned the possibility of a link with Asian pheasants but said no fossil remains of these presumed common ancestors had been found (A. Wetmore personal communication, as cited by Aldrich 1967a:4).

A number of now extinct species of the wild turkey have been identified as inhabiting pre-Columbian North America (Steadman 1980). Skeletal evidence found in 1967 in Gran Quivira National Monument, New Mexico, through the combined work of A.W. Schorger, T.W. Mathews, and C.R. McKusick, led Schorger (1970) to

identify it as the Tularosa turkey *(M. g. tularosa)*, a more recently discovered extinct subspecies. McKusick (1980) referred to the Tularosa turkey as the Small Indian Domestic and the *M. g. merriami* as the Large Indian Domestic. The Merriam's wild turkey is now considered a possible feral form of the Large Indian Domestic and is known to have appeared as early as A.D. 500 (McKusick 1980, Rea 1980).

On the basis of the fossil record, Merriam's turkeys lived contemporaneously with the southern Mexico turkey in what are now the contiguous U.S. and Mexican portions of North America, at least as far back as the late Pliocene, 5 million to 1.8 million years ago, before the age of the glaciers (Aldrich 1967a:4).

According to Schorger, the original range of the wild turkey in Mexico went no farther south than to a line from Veracruz on the Gulf of Mexico to Ometepec on the Pacific.

DOMESTICATION

Domestic turkeys had their beginning when eggs from wild birds of Mexico were collected and hatched.

The wild turkey was the progenitor of the domestic turkey, the production of which has become an important economic industry.
Photo by the National Turkey Federation.

The birds were raised for subsequent generations under the control of humans.

The domesticated turkey was widely used by the Native Americans in pre-Columbian culture. Although the wild turkey was undoubtedly an important source of food and textile material for the Native Americans of the forested eastern United States, domestication was not attempted in that region on nearly the same scale as in the Southwest or in Mexico (Aldrich 1967a:5).

McKusick (1980) and Rea (1980) concurred that turkeys may have been introduced to the Southwest United States as domestic fowl along with the macaw from Mexico, as were plant species like corn, beans, pumpkins, and cotton. These turkeys could have become feral (possibly forerunners of the Merriam's wild turkey) sometime between 1350 and 1700, about the time of the breakdown and dispersal of the Anasazi "Cliff Dweller" Culture during the Great Abandonment (Rea 1980).

By 1520 the Spanish conquerors had carried the domestic turkey from southern Mexico to Spain, where it then spread to other parts of continental Europe and to the British Isles. These turkeys were from stock thought to have been domesticated by the Aztecs. The progeny of these original birds, brought from Europe to the first colonies in America, formed the basis for today's commercial domestic turkeys.

According to Wright (1914, as cited by Aldrich 1967a:15), the turkey was established in Europe by 1530 and present in England as early as 1541. Obviously, turkeys were brought to Spain very soon after they were discovered in Mexico by the Spanish explorers, and the birds spread rapidly over Europe.

The domestic turkey arrived in the United States at Jamestown, Virginia, at the time of settlement in 1607 or shortly thereafter (Schorger 1966). A document written in 1584, before English settlements, listed supplies to be furnished to future colonies in the New World. The list included "turkies, male and female" for increase (Hakluyt 1889, as cited by Schorger 1966).

The first turkeys for Massachusetts were apparently sent from England in 1629 (Schorger 1966) for support in the establishment of Boston by the Massachusetts Bay Company. There was no shortage of turkeys for upper-class settlers after the 1630s. By the beginning of the 1700s, turkeys were being raised in large numbers (Schorger 1966).

In the United States domestic varieties of turkeys have been raised from stock brought from Europe—not from native wild birds. A certain amount of crossing, both intentional and unintentional, has happened between domestic and wild birds (Aldrich 1967a:16).

The Suffolk, White, Cambridgeshire Bronze, and Norfolk Black varieties were developed in England. Holland developed a buff-yellow bird with a white topknot that might be an ancestor of the European White Holland (Lavine and Scuro 1984). So much selective breeding, crossbreeding, and linebreeding has been done to produce various strains of turkeys that it is extremely difficult to trace the history of some of them. No early pedigree records exist for the various strains of domestic turkeys.

Before 1900, turkey raising in America was geared to small-scale production and local sales. During the 1920s, large-scale commercial growers emerged, raising turkeys in quantity for shipment to other markets. By the time the United States entered World War II in 1941, raising domestic turkeys had become a major industry.

NATIVE AMERICAN USE

Hunting

The Native Americans used many techniques for hunting or capturing wild turkeys. Unlike the wild turkey of today, the birds were apparently unwary of humans and easily captured. Among the methods used to take wild turkeys were nets, snares, and pens (Morton 1632, cited by Bellantoni 1983; Williams 1643, cited by Bellantoni 1983; Van der Donck 1841, cited by Schorger 1966). Shooting the birds or capturing them by hand on the roost were probably the easiest methods of collection (Dodge 1945, cited by Schorger 1966).

"Some Indian tribes did not consider the wild turkey enough of a delicacy to warrant the attention of their experienced hunters," wrote Mosby and Handley in 1943. Wright (1914, cited by Mosby and Handley 1943) quoted Timberlake, who wrote about the Cherokee country in 1762, that turkeys were pursued by children 8 or 10 years old who were expert at killing with sarbacane, a hollow cane through which they blew a small dart. Mohawk boys of the same age hunted close to their villages while the men ranged farther, "thereby avoiding extinction of animals in their own area and teaching the boys vital skills" (Bruchac 1991:79).

The Chickasaw children were also reported to have killed turkeys with this blowgun. McKenney (1846, cited by Schorger 1966) described the blowgun as a hollow cane 2 or 3 meters (8 or 10 feet) long, through which a foot-long arrow was shot. Turkeys could be killed at a distance of 6 to 9 meters (20 to 30 feet), but only when hit in the head.

Food Source

The wild turkey was a major food of many tribes. At least 7 archaeological sites in Connecticut have been un-

including wild turkeys. Castetter and Opler (1936, cited by Mosby and Handley 1943) found that "as far back as can be remembered many Apache would not eat turkey, quail and dove." The Cheyenne also would not eat turkeys, believing the act would make them cowardly (Kneeling 1910, cited by Schorger 1966).

Clothing

Native Americans throughout North America used turkey feathers to make various types of clothing. One of the most common methods was to attach feathers to some type of cord made from hemp, yucca, mulberry, or basswood that was then woven to form blankets, quilts, dresses, coats, and robes. Native Americans in Florida also made blankets and other coverings from breast feathers (Romans 1776, cited by Schorger 1966), and Pueblo tribes made blankets and other garments from turkey feathers (Hough 1914, cited by Aldrich 1967a:8).

Tools

Native Americans used parts of the turkey to make simple, everyday tools. Archaeological work in New York State has uncovered awls and spoons made from turkey bones (Ritchie 1944, cited by Aldrich 1967a:5).

Native Americans used turkey feathers as fletching and spurs as arrow tips. Champlain (Grant 1907) on his voyage along the New England coast in 1604 first reported the use of feathers on arrows. According to Mooney (1896, cited by Aldrich 1967a:6), the Cheyennes were called the "striped-arrow people" because the barred wing feather of the wild turkey was used to feather their arrows. Captain John Smith reported in 1612 that the spurs of old gobblers were used by Native Americans as tips for their arrows (Mosby and Handley 1943).

Other Uses

In addition to their uses as food, clothing, tools, and weapons, turkeys also were used in ceremonies, as aids in storytelling, and for miscellaneous other uses. Hopis used feathers and bristles from turkey beards to adorn their prayer sticks (Parsons 1939, cited by Schorger 1966). Feathers were also used to make masks and headdresses (see Stephen 1936, cited by Schorger 1966).

The Native Americans of Virginia hung turkey legs from their pierced ears (Strachey 1849, cited by Schorger 1966). Beads and other ornaments were made from tur-

Native Americans used the wild turkey in a variety of ways other than for food. *Photo by National Wild Turkey Federation.*

covered with evidence of turkeys, proving that the Native Americans of that area used them as food (Sherrow 1984). Other tribes that ate wild turkeys were the Navajos in the Southwest (Franciscan Fathers 1910, cited by Schorger 1966) and the Tonkawas of Texas (Sjoberg 1953, cited by Schorger 1966). Buckelew (1925, cited by Schorger 1966) stated that the Lipans ate no other fowl than the wild turkey.

Other archaeological evidence indicates that turkeys were used extensively for food. At the preagricultural Indian Knoll Site in Ohio County, Kentucky, dated by radiocarbon to before 3000 B.C., turkey bones were second in number only to those of deer (Webb 1946, cited by Aldrich 1967a:6).

At the Renner Site near Kansas City, Missouri, dated at or before A.D. 400, turkey bones were more abundant than bison. Only deer and raccoon bones were found in greater numbers (Wedel 1943, cited by Aldrich 1967a:4).

By contrast, customs of some Native American tribes discouraged the eating of certain wild animals,

key leg bones. Moccasins of the Chickasaw high priest were decorated with turkey feathers (Adair 1775, cited by Schorger 1966).

POST-COLONIAL HISTORY

When European settlers arrived on the eastern seaboard, wild turkeys lived in what are now 39 continental states and the Canadian province of Ontario (Schorger 1966). Many important early records are found in Shufeldt (1914), Wright (1914 and 1915), Zimmer (1924), Marsden and Knox (1937), Fluke (1940), Mosby and Handley (1943), Marsden and Martin (1955), and Aldrich (1967). Schorger (1966) includes detailed early references in his extensive bibliography.

Several misconceptions have developed concerning the wild turkey in American history. Contrary to popular belief, Thanksgiving did not become a national tradition under the Massachusetts Pilgrims; nor was the turkey for a fact the pièce de résistance at the famous 1621 meal (Tuleja 1987). Schorger (1966) speculated, "It is doubtful that a turkey became a common adjunct to a Thanksgiving dinner until about 1800."

It is often commonly thought the wild turkey was championed as the symbol to represent the collective states on the nation's seal when the choice was being discussed in the 1770s and 1780s. Apparently that wasn't so. The first "seal committee," formed the same day the Declaration of Independence was signed in 1776, was composed of Thomas Jefferson, Benjamin Franklin, and John Adams. The committee could not reach agreement on a symbol, but a wild turkey was not championed.

By 1782 a third "seal committee" rejected Philadelphia artist William Barton's design of the "Imperial Eagle" of Europe. Subsequently, the design was changed to the bald eagle, native to North America, and the design was adopted by Congress June 20, 1782.

According to Smith (1986), Franklin tired of the variety of bald eagle motifs. In a letter to his daughter, Sarah Bache, in 1784, he noted that the "Order of Cincinnatus" had produced a badge more like a turkey than an eagle. Franklin went on to talk about the bad points of the eagle and the good points of the turkey but never recommended the turkey for the American symbol. In fact, Franklin's comments that the turkey was more respectable than the eagle and a true original native came years after the seal had been selected.

Turkey Sightings

Early records indicate wild turkeys occurred in large numbers throughout their range. Jameson (1909) re-

ported in the 1609–1664 narratives of New Netherland (New York), "Innumerable birds are also found here . . . and possess plumage of great elegance and a variety of colors. In winter superior turkey cocks are taken. . . ."

Lawson, a surveyor in North Carolina, recorded in 1709, "There are great flocks of these [wild turkey] in Carolina. I have seen about five hundred in a flock. . . ." Tregle (1975:276–277), in a French translation of a history of Louisiana from 1774, explained, "the wild turkey . . . is very common all over the colony. They go in flocks, and with a dog one may kill a great many of them." Filson (1784:26) reported that in Kentucky, "the land fowls are turkeys, which are very frequent. . . ." Lewis and Clark, in 1804, saw wild turkeys in western Missouri, Iowa, Nebraska, and South Dakota. On July 1, 1804, near Leavenworth, Kansas, Clark recorded, "Deer and turkeys in great quantities on the bank" (Burroughs 1876:221–223).

Bartram wrote of his 1773–77 travels (Van Doren 1928), "Having rested very well during the night, I was awakened in the morning early, by the cheering converse of the wild turkey-cocks saluting each other, from the sun-brightened tops of the lofty Cupressus *[sic]* disticha

According to early accounts, precolonial old-growth forests supported abundant wild turkeys. *Photo by U.S. Forest Service.*

Unrestricted harvest was instrumental in reducing early wild turkey populations.

and *Magnolia grandiflora*. They begin at early dawn, and continue till sun-rise, from March to the last of April. The high forests ring with the noise, like the crowing of the domestic cock, of these social centinels; the watch-word being caught and repeated, from one to another, for hundreds of miles around; insomuch that the whole country is for an hour or more in a universal shout. A little after sun-rise, their crowing gradually ceases, they quit their high lodging-places, and alight on the earth, where expanding their silver bordered train, they strut and dance round about the coy female, while the deep forests seem to tremble with their shrill noise." The incident discussed probably occurred in northeast Florida, according to landmarks mentioned elsewhere in the text.

DEMISE OF POPULATIONS

As the fledgling nation began to grow, the wild turkey populations quickly began to disappear. Wild turkeys were an important source of food for the pioneers and were hunted year-round without the protection of bag limits. In 1626 Plymouth Colony passed the first conservation law, limiting the cutting and sale of colonial lumber (Urdand 1979:57). Vast virgin forests were being cleared for agriculture and to provide safety borders for

the pioneer villages from the Native Americans. With the turkey's habitat fast dwindling and changing, and under the relentless pressure from market hunters to feed the growing number of colonists (4 million by 1790), the wild turkey began vanishing from much of its original range. Exceptions were some isolated and inaccessible areas, mostly in the southeastern United States. In 1706 the hunting season on deer was limited on New York's Long Island because continued hunting had almost eliminated them (Urdand 1979:95). Could turkeys have been far behind?

As the settlers tamed the wilderness and pushed westward, they eliminated wild turkeys. Connecticut had lost its wild turkeys by 1813 (Table 1). Vermont held out until 1842 (Mosby and Handley 1943). Other states followed. By 1920, the wild turkey was lost from 18 of the original 39 states of its ancestral range and Ontario, Canada (Mosby and Handley 1943).

RESTORATION

Early Recovery

Wild turkey population numbers remained extremely low into the 1900s. The 5 subspecies of wild tur-

Photo by U.S. Forest Service.   *Photo by USDA Soil Conservation Service.*

In the late 1800s and early 1900s, logging and row cropping without proper soil management or reforestation in much of the eastern United States eliminated much wild turkey habitat.

keys in the United States probably declined to their lowest numbers in the late 1930s (Mosby 1975). "In 1937, the wild turkey was in trouble throughout most of its range. . . . In the late 1920s and 1930s there was a scarcity of factual information on existing game bird popula-

Table 1. Last recorded observation of native turkeys prior to recent introductions and range extensions, as compiled by Aldrich (1967a).

State	Locality last seen	Date	Authority
Connecticut	Totoket Mountain, Northford	1813	Merriam (1877)
New York	Sullivan, Rockland, Orange, Allegany and Cattaraugus counties	1844	Eaton (1910)
Massachusetts	Mount Tom	1851	Forbush (1929)
Kansas	Fort Hays	1871	Allen (1872)
South Dakota	Union and Clay counties	1875	Over and Thoms (1946)
Ohio	Wooster, Wayne County	1878	Oberholser (1896)
	Ashtabula County	1880	Hicks (1933)
Nebraska	Fort Niobrara	1880	Bendire (1892)
Wisconsin	Darlington, Lafayette County	1881	Schorger (1942)
Michigan	Van Buren County	1897	Barrows (1912)
Illinois	Bartelso, Clinton County	1903	Felger (1909)
Indiana	Ricknell, Decker Township	1906	Chansler (1906)
Iowa	Lee County	1907	Anderson (1907)

tions in most states because of a paucity of both funds and trained personnel" (Mosby 1937). The World War I period, and the Great Depression, which came a decade later, showed little change in existing populations.

As the small tenant fields and farms of the 1930s and the previously harvested forest areas began to revert to successional types of shrubs and trees, the foundation was laid for the comeback of the wild turkey. Conservation practices slowly improved the landscape for the future of the wild turkey and other wildlife species. Laws enacted early in this century—such as the Lacey Act in 1905 prohibiting the interstate sale of taken wildlife—along with other laws and their enforcement gave needed protection to the remaining wild turkey flocks. Many of our national forests found their beginnings in lands bought by the federal government—much of it marked by eroded gullies and fields devoid of topsoil, indicative of that period. The nation slowly recovered from the Depression until war came again in 1941.

The wildlife management movement had gained credibility with the publication of Aldo Leopold's 1933 book of game-management principles. The Pittman-Robertson Act of 1937 put an excise tax on sporting goods and ammunitions. That money, when matched with state hunting license dollars, provided funds to initiate wildlife recovery programs. As the GIs started returning home in 1945, state fish and wildlife agencies, universities, and federal agencies began to tackle the difficult task of restoring populations of wild turkeys.

One of the first major obstacles was how to capture and move birds from existing flocks for release in other suitable habitats. One early method, which had been used by the Native Americans, was the pole trap. The pole trap was built of long poles about 5 to 13 centimeters

(2 to 5 inches) in diameter. These poles were stacked 5 to 8 high on 4 sides and covered with netting. A trench was dug under one side of the trap and the setup was baited with corn. Modifications included funnel-entrance traps and open-front traps (Baldwin 1947), which improved the chances of capturing birds. Nonetheless, these traps were hard to construct and lacked the flexibility to catch large numbers of wild turkeys. Baldwin (1947) also experimented with a "drop-net" trap that he felt was more effective than the other traps used in the coastal areas of South Carolina.

What eventually made possible the capture of large

Photo by L. Williams.

Photo by National Wild Turkey Federation.

Development of the cannon net was a major factor in capturing and translocating large numbers of wild turkeys for restoration.

numbers of wild turkeys was the cannon net, originally designed to capture waterfowl. This technique allowed states to move wild-trapped birds into new habitats.

The cannon-net technique involves concealing on the ground a net that will be propelled over turkeys by a trapper from a nearby blind. The net is a folded 10-by-20-meter cloth mesh with square openings of 5 centimeters. The net is propelled by 3 or 4 black-powder cannons electrically detonated.

The first wild turkeys known to be captured using this method were in the Francis Marion National Forest in South Carolina in 1951 (Holbrook 1952). The cannon-net delivery was later speeded up by use of rocket projectiles powered by howitzer powder from the U.S. military. The rockets propelled a nylon-mesh net. In the 1960s, sleep-inducing drugs were also used to capture live birds (Williams 1966).

Before the days of early wildlife management, little was known about the biology of wild turkeys or the factors that influenced populations. Mosby and Handley (1943) answered some of the basic questions and ushered in a new era on research and management.

Pen-raised Pitfall

It is highly important to note that recommendations in the 1940s to artificially propagate turkeys for restoration were not biologically sound. Game-farm or pen-raised turkeys are those hatched from eggs taken from wild turkey nests or from hen turkeys raised under human control. Game-farm turkeys are deprived of normal parental influence, so they never develop normal social behaviors, regardless of their genetic wildness.

Early attempts to restore the wild turkey by raising turkeys in captivity were a failure. Turkeys raised in confinement lacked wild characteristics and could not properly raise their young in the wild. *Photo by Ontario Ministry of Natural Resources.*

Although the approach was not new, many agencies and individuals embraced an idea that seemed logical: to mass produce these birds for release. This approach was taken as a shortcut around the difficult problem of capturing wild birds, which are native genetic stock living under the control of the laws of nature.

The pen-raised approach slowed the wild turkey comeback in North America for almost 2 decades. Furthermore, this technique used untold millions of dollars that might have been spent in more wild turkey trap-and-transplant programs, which have proved immensely successful.

A turkey restoration survey from 36 states conducted by Bailey and Putnam (1979) compared the success of both pen-raised (or game-farm) turkeys and wild-trapped birds. About 30,000 wild-trapped birds released on 968 sites resulted in 808 established populations occupying more than 520,000 square kilometers (200,000 square miles) of range. Greater than 330,000 pen-raised birds released on almost 800 sites resulted in 760 failures. Michigan was the only state that reported significant positive results with pen-raised stock. Of 882 game-farm birds released at 13 sites, however, only 3 releases were successful in Michigan. The survey also reported fall hunting was terminated because of overharvest of turkeys with game-farm origin.

The survey reported 6 states that had problems with diseases in game-farm birds. Twenty-three of the 36 states had enacted laws banning or restricting the release of game-farm birds (Bailey and Putnam 1979). In spite of this evidence, today turkey eggs, poults, and adults are advertised and sold under the pretense that they are "truly wild" and therefore suitable for stocking in the wild.

These birds probably fail to survive because of a combination of factors. One cause could be poor genetic quality resulting from the breeding out of wild characteristics during several generations in captivity. Most offspring from first-generation wild birds cannot survive confinement. They die from stress, trying to escape. The few survivors are relatively docile and are able to tolerate the confined conditions. So they reproduce and sustain their population. But birds carrying the characteristics needed for life in the wild are lost under penned conditions.

A second major factor in the poor success of game-farm birds is the failure of poults to learn from a wild hen. Wild hens teach their poults the proper response to predators and other dangers, plus a great deal about food sources, the geography of their home ranges, and social behavior, such as vocalizations and flocking. The pen-raised turkey has no opportunity to learn these important survival mechanisms.

The third big problem involving pen-raised birds is the increase of deadly diseases and parasites under confined conditions. The survivors may become carriers of infectious diseases. L.F. Schorr et al. (1988) evaluated the health of 119 pen-raised wild turkeys and found at least 33 species of parasites. Infectious disease agents isolated or identified were avian pox, *Mycoplasma gallisepticum*, and *Aspergillus fumigates*. Based on their evaluation of disease risks, the investigators concluded that the release of pen-raised turkeys should be discouraged or even prohibited.

Success

Wild turkey populations have increased substantially across the United States since the end of World War II. Trap-and-transplant programs of state game agencies have accelerated this growth since the early 1950s. The support of the private sector and state and federal agencies substantially aided the restoration effort. Combined population estimates nationwide in 1990 showed wild turkey numbers between 3.4 million and 3.5 million birds (Kennamer and Kennamer 1990). Eastern wild turkeys, occupying all or parts of 37 states, totaled better than 2.5 million birds. The Florida wild turkey population is estimated at 75,000 birds. Rio Grande wild turkeys number more than 630,000, and Merriam's greater than 100,000.

The trapping and transplanting of wild turkeys has proved immensely successful in restoring the wild turkey. Where there were once tens of thousands, now there are several million. *Photo by National Wild Turkey Federation.*

Table 2. U.S. wild turkey population estimates by subspecies, 1959–1990.

Year	Source	Eastern	Florida	Rio Grande	Merriam's	Gould's	Total[a]
1959	Mosby 1959	239,134	50,000	102,000	74,675	?	465,809
1970	Mosby 1973	547,500	60,000	—no data available—		?	607,500
1975	Mosby 1975						1,300,000
1980	Bailey 1980	1,162,740	80,000	420,025	84,950	?	1,747,715
1986	Kennamer 1986	1,694,710	80,000	611,360	200,300	90	2,586,460
1990	Kennamer 1991	2,551,500	75,000	636,712	100,750	150	3,364,112

[a] Totals shown may differ from totals in Table 3 because Table 2 does not include categories for hybrids and intergrades.

Wild turkey population estimates by subspecies increased from about 500,000 in 1959 to almost 3.5 million in 1990 (Table 2). All states but Alaska, including 10 states outside the turkey's ancestral range, have huntable populations (Table 3). Information reported by Kennamer and Kennamer (1990) showed population trends up in 35 states, many because of increasing trap-and-transplant efforts. Nine states—Alabama, Arizona, Colorado, Louisiana, Mississippi, Nevada, New Mexico, New York, and Vermont—showed stable populations. Some of these states, like Alabama and New York, for all practical purposes have completed stocking all their suitable wild turkey habitats.

Florida showed a decline, mainly because of habitat loss, and Virginia's population was down from unknown causes. Several states—including Minnesota, Montana, and Wyoming—reported segments of their wild turkey populations down due to several causes.

The primary limitation on wild turkey population levels—besides having all suitable range occupied—was habitat loss. Also acting negatively in some areas were illegal kill, lack of brood and winter habitat, summer droughts, poor mast production, severe winters, predation, and suspected diseases.

Probably no other game bird has had more of an impact on the combined cultures of the inhabitants of North America than the wild turkey. The species has

Cooperation between agencies has helped focus resources toward common goals and has benefited the wild turkey and sport hunters. *Photo by Indiana Department of Natural Resources.*

Table 3. Estimated U.S. wild turkey populations by state, 1959–1990.

	Source				
State	Mosby 1959	Mosby 1970	Bailey 1980	Kennamer 1986	Kennamer and Kennamer 1990
Alabama	54,760	225,000	250,000	350,000	>350,000
Arizona	18,000	35,000	18,000	14,000	50
Arkansas	4,000	30,000	200,000	100,000	100,000
California	2,000	8,000	43,000	100,000	100,400
Colorado	8,000	15,000	15,000	10,400	1,500
Connecticut	—	—	7,000	4,000	6,000
Delaware	—	—	—	200	600
Florida	50,000	60,000	—	70,000	100,000
Georgia	40,000	21,000	40,000	150,000	325,000
Hawaii	—	—	5,000	6,000	—
Idaho	—	—	2,000	—	3,400
Illinois	400	—	10,000	15,000	35,000
Indiana	75	—	10,000	5,000	30,000
Iowa	—	—	30,000	>40,000	>100,000
Kansas	114	750	20,000	45,000	—
Kentucky	1,500	1,930	50,000	13,000	>20,000
Louisiana	2,000	6,500	50,000	18,000	35,000
Maine	—	—	500	700	700
Maryland	2,000	1,000	—	6,000	10,000
Massachusetts	200	150	—	5,000	10,000
Michigan	800	3,700	10,000	15,000	60,000
Minnesota	75	15	8,000	5,000	18,000
Mississippi	20,000	53,000	250,000	350,000	>350,000
Missouri	4,000	12,700	200,000	200,000	400,000
Montana	2,000	—	—	—	—
Nebraska	400	4,000	9,750	25,000	30,200
Nevada	—	—	300	200	900
New Hampshire	—	—	7,000	2,000	2,500
New Jersey	—	—	500	>4,500	5,500
New Mexico	25,000	25,000	—	28,040	30,000
New York	2,500	10,000	50,000	60,000	>65,000
North Carolina	15,000	4,000	12,000	14,000	20,000
North Dakota	7,875	—	6,000	12,000	14,000
Ohio	200	2,100	7,500	>15,800	32,000
Oklahoma	—	—	—	90,000	60,050
Oregon	200	2,000	1,000	—	—
Pennsylvania	40,000	45,000	120,000	150,000	175,000
Rhode Island	—	—	—	750	600
South Carolina	18,000	20,000	35,000	30,000	80,000
South Dakota	5,000	7,000	16,500	20,000	30,000
Tennessee	2,500	5,000	2,400	30,000	60,000
Texas	100,000	575,000	580,000	500,000	582,012
Utah	200	—	1,000	>1,000	>2,000
Vermont	10	—	12,000	15,000	15,000
Virginia	20,000	29,000	100,000	188,000	75,000
Washington	—	2,000	3,000	2,000	5,000
West Virginia	10,000	15,000	45,000	50,000	80,000
Wisconsin	1,000	600	15,000	15,000	60,000
Wyoming	10,000	—	—	10,000	20,150
Total	467,809	1,219,445	2,242,456	2,785,590	3,500,562

directly influenced the lifestyles of both Native Americans plus immigrants and their descendants. Although the wild turkey once was found only in isolated pockets and inaccessible areas, populations now occupy more square kilometers of habitat than any other game bird in North America. The restoration is truly a modern conservation marvel that is a credit to the wild turkey's adaptability to a variety of climatic and habitat conditions, as well as to the great bird's ability to respond well to modern management.

Chapter 3

SYSTEMATICS AND POPULATION GENETICS

Peter W. Stangel
National Fish and Wildlife Foundation
Washington, D.C.

Paul L. Leberg
Department of Biology
University of Southwest Louisiana
Lafayette, Louisiana

Julia I. Smith
Department of Zoology
Museum of Vertebrate Zoology
University of California
Berkeley, California

Wildlife managers are increasingly interested in understanding and maintaining the genetic integrity of wild turkey populations. Populations are now recognized as having distinct biological characteristics that may require specific management programs. The organization of this book into chapters based on regions and subspecies is recognition that wild turkeys are not the same throughout their range. Our goal in this chapter is to describe the evolutionary relationships of turkeys to other birds and to discuss what is known about patterns of morphological and genetic variation in the turkey. We also suggest topics deserving further investigation.

SYSTEMATICS

Interspecific Relationships

Turkeys, together with pheasants, grouse, guinea fowl, and chachalacas, belong to the order Galliformes (from Latin: *gallus*, a cock, and *forma*, form; meaning "cock shaped"). Historically, turkeys have been placed either in their own family, Meleagrididae, or as a subfamily in a much larger family, Phasianidae (Schorger 1966). Pheasants, quail, peafowl, and jungle fowl are all members of Phasianidae.

Currently, turkeys are placed in the subfamily Meleagridinae within the family Phasianidae. This placement is based on evidence from studies of fossils (Rea

1980, Steadman 1980), muscle structure (Hudson et al. 1959), egg white protein mobility (Sibley 1960), amino acid sequences (Jolles et al. 1979), DNA-DNA hybridization (C.G. Sibley personal communication: 1988), and DNA restriction fragments (Helm-Bychowski and Wilson 1986).

Molecular data (Figure 1) suggest that turkeys probably diverged from pheasants about 11 million years ago (Helm-Bychowski and Wilson 1986). This belief agrees well with the fossil record, discussed in detail by Stead-

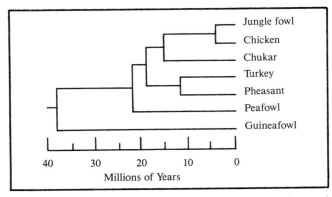

Figure 1. Phylogenetic tree showing relationships among turkeys and other Galliformes based on similarities of DNA sequences (Helm-Bychowski and Wilson 1986). Scale represents the estimated time of divergence of the different groups.

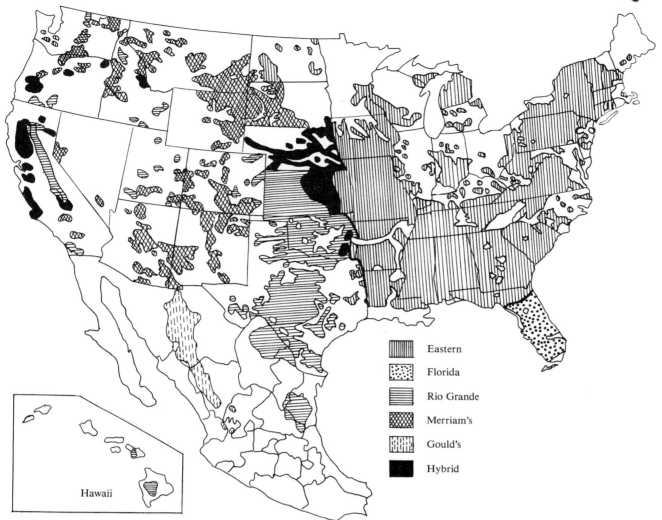

Figure 2. Distribution of the wild turkey subspecies in the United States and Mexico in 1989 (Kennamer and Kennamer 1990, M. Rumble).

man (1980). For example, the fossil *Rhegminornis*, with both pheasant- and turkeylike characteristics, is known from Virginia deposits 16 to 20 million years old. And the earliest true turkey fossil, *Proagriocharis*, dating from 6 to 8 million years ago, was unearthed in Nebraska. Thus, turkeys probably arose 8 to 15 million years ago during the Miocene Epoch.

The oldest fossil turkeys placed in the modern genus *Meleagris* were found in deposits 2 million to 3 million years old (late Pliocene) from Texas and Kansas (Steadman 1980). There are presently 2 species in the genus. The wild turkey (*M. gallopavo*, Linnaeus 1758) occurs widely in the United States and northern Mexico (Figure

2). The ocellated turkey (*M. ocellata*, Cuvier, G. 1820; placed in a separate genus, *Agriocharis*, by some; AOU Checklist 1983) occurs in the Yucatán region of southern Mexico, Belize, and northern Guatemala. No turkeys currently inhabit the intervening tropical rain forests.

Steadman (1980) hypothesized that wild turkeys ranged completely around the Gulf of Mexico during the Pleistocene, when a savannalike corridor connected the areas currently inhabited by *M. gallopavo* and *M. ocellata*. During the late Pleistocene or early Holocene, the climate became wetter, leading eventually to the formation of the rain forest that presently separates the 2 species.

Nomenclature

The scientific name of the wild turkey, *Meleagris gallopavo*, was designated by the Swedish taxonomist Carl Linnaeus (Linnaeus 1758). He based his description on domesticated turkeys imported to Europe from Mexico. The name *Meleagris* can be traced to Greek mythology. When Meleager, son of the king of Caldyon, was killed by a rogue boar, his mourning sisters were transformed into birds called *meleagrides* (Schorger 1966:72). The ancient Greeks also used *meleagrides* to describe guinea fowl. The species name, *gallopavo*, means "chickenlike peafowl." This name reflects uncertainties of early taxonomists about the origin of the wild turkey and its relationship to other Galliformes. Schorger (1966:72) gives an excellent account of discrepancies in early nomenclature for the wild turkey.

Historically, morphological features, such as tail tip and upper covert color, have been used to distinguish subspecies. *Photo by B. Reaves, Texas Parks and Wildlife Department.*

GEOGRAPHIC VARIATION

Intraspecific Variation

Geographic variation in wild turkeys has often been discussed in terms of subspecies. A subspecies is a geographic race of a species that differs from other races in range, appearance, behavior, or genetics. Subspecies differ from true biological species in that they are not necessarily reproductively isolated.

There are 6 recognized subspecies of wild turkey (Figure 2). Subspecies are often viewed as discrete and separate entities, but in the turkey, the exact boundaries of subspecies are subjective. Interbreeding commonly occurs. A zone of intergradation between turkey subspecies can be observed in southern Georgia, Alabama, South Carolina, Mississippi, and northern Florida. Turkeys from these areas have characteristics between those of the eastern and Florida subspecies (Aldrich 1967b).

Detailed descriptions of plumage characteristics of turkey subspecies are available in Aldrich (1967b) and

Schorger (1966). Their accounts are summarized in Table 1. No plumage characteristic perfectly discriminates one subspecies from others. In fact, there is often a wide range of variation in plumage coloration among turkeys from localities within the range of a single subspecies.

Unfortunately, there are few published comparisons of morphologic differences among turkey subspecies. Aldrich (1967b) provides the mean and range for wing, tail, culmen, tarsus, and middle toe lengths for all subspecies, and Steadman (1980) reports 64 skeletal measurements taken from all subspecies except the Mexican turkey. In neither study, however, were the differences in individual characteristics between the subspecies evaluated statistically. Aldrich (1967b) did report significant differences in the ratio of wing-to-tarsus length among subspecies, but did not make direct comparisons of individual measurements.

To better understand size differences, we ranked subspecies from largest to smallest for the average of

Table 1. Comparison of plumage characters of the wild turkey *(Meleagris gallopavo)* subspecies.[a]

Subspecies	Body appearance	Rectrix tips	Upper tail covert tips	Rump
Eastern *M. g. silvestris*	Purplish to coppery bronze	Cinnamon to dark chestnut	Chestnut	Coppery to greenish gold
Florida *M. g. osceola*	Coppery to greenish gold	Cinnamon to light chestnut	Chestnut	Coppery to greenish gold
Rio Grande *M. g. intermedia*	Coppery to greenish gold	Cinnamon or buff	Cinnamon or pinkish buff	Greenish gold to bluish black
Merriam's *M. g. merriami*	Purplish bronze	Buff to pinkish white	Buff to pinkish white	Bluish black
Gould's *M. g. mexicana*	Coppery to greenish gold	Pink to white	Pink to white	Coppery to greenish gold
South Mexican *M. g. gallopavo*	Coppery to greenish gold	Buff to pinkish white	Buff to pinkish white	Bluish black

[a] After Schorger (1966), Aldrich (1967b), and Rea (1980).

each of the measurements evaluated by Aldrich (1967b) and Steadman (1980). Nonparametric analyses (Friedman and Wilcoxen tests) of direct comparisons of individual measurements indicated that Gould's was the largest and the Florida the smallest subspecies, based on average ranks for all measurements (Table 2).

Table 2 suggests consistent size differences among subspecies, but limitations of the data set prevent analysis of 2 important measures of geographic variation:

Table 2. Analysis of differences between subspecies of the wild turkey, based on mean rank of averages of 5 measurements from Aldrich (1967) and 27 measurements from Steadman (1980).[a] Shared letters indicate subspecies that were not significantly different in comparisons among pairs (P > 0.05). The lowest mean ranks indicate the largest sizes.

	Aldrich (1967b)		Steadman (1980)	
Subspecies	Mean rank		Mean rank	
Gould's	1.30	A	1.56	A
Merriam's	3.00	B	2.57	B
South Mexican	3.10	B	—	
Eastern	3.70	B	2.81	BC
Rio Grande	4.40	B	3.35	C
Florida	5.50	C	4.70	D

[a] Steadman (1980) did not measure *M. g. gallopavo.*

shape and the variance of the measurements. Geographic variation in shape may be as important as size for understanding ecological and evolutionary relationships. Aldrich (1967b) found the relationship of wing-to-tarsus length to vary among subspecies. This ratio was greatest in the Merriam's and eastern turkeys, intermediate in Gould's, Rio Grande, and Mexican, and smallest in the Florida. Although Gould's is clearly the largest subspecies for most measurements evaluated, it is intermediate in the ratio of wing-to-tarsus length, suggesting its

legs are relatively short compared with the rest of its body. Additional analyses of subspecific variation in shape will require more extensive morphological data sets.

A second limitation of the data is that there is no way to account for variance of the measurements recorded. To demonstrate the importance of this variation, we evaluated the differences in weight, beard length, and spur length among subspecies. Turkeys used in this analysis were randomly selected from entries by hunters into the National Wild Turkey Federation's "Big Gobbler" program for 1987. Although this data set is biased because only the largest birds are reported, it was the most extensive collection of measurements available to us.

The data in Table 3 demonstrate an important point: The standard deviation, or variation, is relatively large compared with the means of the measurements. For example, the standard deviation in weight of the eastern turkey encompasses the mean weights of all the other subspecies. This large variance resulted in no statistically significant differences in weight or beard length among subspecies.

Spur length did differ significantly among subspecies. The 2 eastern subspecies, Florida and eastern, had the longest spurs. The western subspecies, Gould's and Merriam's, had the shortest. Although results presented in Table 2 and the observations of several biologists (see Schorger 1966, Aldrich 1967b) suggest that size really does differ among subspecies of turkeys, these differences seem minor compared with the variation within subspecies.

We further attempted to quantify geographic variation within the Rio Grande, Merriam's, and eastern subspecies by comparing measurements among those states with a large number of entries in the "Big Gobbler" program. We found no significant differences in any of the measurements among states for the Rio Grande (Texas, Oklahoma, and California) or Merriam's (New Mexico

Table 3. Comparison of male weight, beard length, and spur length for 5 subspecies of the wild turkey.

Subspecies	Sample size	Weight[a]		Beard length[b]		Spur length[b,c]	
		Mean	Standard deviation	Mean	Standard deviation	Mean	Standard deviation
Gould's	5	9.5 (21.0)	1.5	217.5 (8.6)	74.0	11.4 (0.4)	6.6
Merriam's	20	9.4 (20.7)	1.2	235.2 (9.3)	28.9	22.4 (0.9)	5.3
Eastern	120	9.6 (21.2)	1.5	259.1 (10.2)	38.9	28.6 (1.1)	7.4
Rio Grande	30	9.1 (20.0)	1.6	243.0 (9.6)	49.6	27.3 (1.1)	8.2
Florida	10	8.5 (18.7)	0.8	248.5 (9.8)	32.3	33.0 (1.3)	7.5

[a] Kilograms (pounds).
[b] Millimeters (inches).
[c] Mean for right and left legs.

Table 4. Comparisons of weight and beard length for 10 male turkeys from 12 states within the range of the eastern wild turkey. States that are followed by the same letter are not significantly different (P > 0.05).

State	Weight[a]		State	Beard length[b]	
Iowa	11.7 (25.7)	A	Alabama	290.6 (11.4)	A
Missouri	10.2 (22.4)	B	Missouri	288.0 (11.3)	A
Illinois	9.9 (21.8)	BC	Arkansas	275.6 (10.9)	AB
Ohio	9.6 (21.2)	BC	Iowa	265.8 (10.5)	ABC
West Virginia	9.6 (21.1)	BC	Ohio	263.9 (10.4)	ABC
Arkansas	9.4 (20.8)	BC	Virginia	262.9 (10.4)	ABC
New York	9.3 (20.5)	BC	Georgia	262.9 (10.4)	ABC
Virginia	9.2 (20.3)	BC	South Carolina	249.0 (9.8)	BC
Alabama	9.2 (20.2)	BC	Illinois	247.7 (9.8)	BC
Georgia	9.1 (20.0)	BC	Pennsylvania	236.5 (9.3)	C
Pennsylvania	9.0 (19.9)	BC	West Virginia	232.1 (9.1)	C
South Carolina	8.8 (19.3)	C	New York	231.5 (9.1)	C

[a] Kilograms (pounds).
[b] Millimeters (inches).

and Colorado). But we did find that eastern turkeys from the upper Midwest tended to be heavier than those from the Southeast, and beards were longer in the more western states (Table 4).

We consider the available data sets too limited and biased to permit rigorous analysis of geographic variation within or among wild turkey subspecies. If subspecies or populations are to be used as units for management, there is a real need for a comprehensive study (with large sample sizes and many carefully measured characters) examining patterns of morphologic variation in turkeys.

Future attempts to quantify geographic variation in turkey morphology should follow the guidelines established by Zink and Remsen (1986) for the study of size, shape, and color in avian species. Our analyses of morphologic variation among turkeys from different states and subspecies suggest that patterns of variation depend on the variables measured.

Since the morphologic measurements display discordant patterns of geographic variation, the physical differences among turkey subspecies may be better described by analyzing shape differences rather than size differences. This lack of concordance also makes it unlikely that taxonomic designations based on one set of characters (e.g., plumage only) will be good units for examining variation in other characters. Since there is extensive variation among turkeys within subspecies (e.g., eastern), it also is important that future studies attempt to obtain turkeys from throughout the range when comparing differences among subspecies.

Nature of Geographic Variation

The most common explanation for geographic variation in plumage or morphology is that it represents adaptation to local environmental conditions (Aldrich 1967b). For natural selection to occur, individuals with particular traits must have higher survival or reproductive rates (i.e., fitness differences) than individuals with alternate traits. Assuming that the variation has a genetic basis, traits (and associated genotypes) that enable individuals to make a higher-than-average contribution to the next generation will increase in the population. For local adaptation to result in geographic variation, the relative fitness of particular combinations of traits must vary with environmental conditions.

A possible example of adaptive variation might occur in turkeys of the eastern United States. In the eastern subspecies, turkeys are largest in the upper Midwest and smallest in the Southeast. The pattern of increasing body size with latitude, seen in several species of birds and mammals, is called Bergman's rule (Zink and Remsen 1986).

Large animals have a reduced surface area per unit of volume (James 1970). Thus, larger size in the North may aid heat conservation while smaller size in the South may facilitate heat loss. If heat regulation is important for survival and variation in body size has a genetic basis, larger birds would become more common in the North while smaller birds would be more successful in the South. Although there are alternate explanations (McNab 1971), Bergman's rule does provide an interesting example of how variation might be patterned by local adaptation.

Geographic variation may, however, be the result of chance environmental and reproductive factors. According to this hypothesis, variation among individuals is selectively neutral (Kimura 1983). This means that although traits are still subject to selection, alternate forms possess no selective advantage. Because one form is not favored by selection over any other, their survival and abundance is determined largely by chance events.

One scenario for the origination of geographic differences in neutral traits involves the founding of a new population with only a small number of individuals (founder effect, Mayr 1963). These few individuals may represent only a subset of the parental gene pool, and may by chance differ from other such subsets. So populations begun in this way may differ from one another and from the parental population not as a result of selective advantages, but purely as a result of the chance selection of those individuals founding the population.

Although historical evidence is incomplete, Merriam's turkey could have arisen in this way. The fossil record suggests that Merriam's turkey is not native to the American Southwest (McKusick 1980, Rea 1980). Schorger (1966) suggests that about 300 to 100 B.C., Native Americans brought to this area turkeys similar in appearance to Merriam's that had been domesticated and traded in Mexico. By about 500 to 600 A.D. it appears that several wild populations were established from feral birds. These new populations probably gave rise to Merriam's turkey. If this scenario is correct, the differences in size and color between Merriam's and other turkey subspecies may not reflect local adaptation, but rather chance founder effect.

Both the adaptationist and neutralist explanations of geographic patterns focus on the genetic contribution to variation. The environment also has an important influence on development. The relative contributions of genetics and environment to variation in the turkey is largely unknown, but some data exist for other species. For example, latitudinal differences in body shape of red-winged blackbirds are due in part to the environment in which the birds are raised (James 1983).

The dearth of information on the role of selection, chance, and the environment in contributing to geographic variation in turkeys reflects difficulties involved with their study. Each factor interacts in a complex way with the others, and a clear understanding of the processes responsible for variation is elusive.

It is, however, possible to gain some insight into the relative contribution of each. For example, the genetic basis of some traits can be revealed by reciprocal transplants of eggs from one area to another (James 1983). If the resulting offspring acquire characteristics of their foster parents, then environmental factors are probably responsible for differences among regions. Differences between offspring and foster parents would likely be genetic.

An understanding of the genetic basis of a trait and its adaptive significance can contribute to the design of successful stocking programs and the maintenance of desired phenotypes (i.e., subspecies). Moving birds from one region to another will have little effect on traits that are largely determined by environment. After just one generation, translocated birds would exhibit traits similar to those of the native birds.

For traits affected more strongly by genetics, translocation involves greater risks. Introduced birds may fail to survive or attain normal physical, reproductive, and behavioral characteristics because they are not adapted to local conditions. Mixing of different genetic types might also lead to the dilution of local gene pools, lowering survivorship of the entire population. This might also lead to loss of distinctions among populations or subspecies. Such differences are often highly valued as part of the sporting experience.

POPULATION GENETICS

In the previous section, we discussed the importance of understanding how genes influence development of an individual wild turkey. Here we examine the genetic attributes of populations.

The development of molecular techniques over the past 2 decades has provided biologists with new tools to detect genetic variation in wildlife populations. These techniques offer several advantages over examination of more traditional morphological characters. For example, they permit analysis of genes or the direct products of genes, thereby reducing problems associated with analysis of morphological characters that may have been influenced by complex genetic-environmental interactions. With molecular techniques, it is also possible to estimate the magnitude and distribution of genetic variation, information that previously required laborious studies of breeding and heritability.

Genetic variation is important for not only the health of individual organisms but also the evolutionary flexibility of populations and species. Recent studies suggest that in some organisms, individuals with higher levels of genetic variability grow faster, attain larger sizes, and develop more normally than do less variable individuals (reviews in Mitton and Grant 1980; Allendorf and Leary 1986).

In preliminary studies with the wild turkey, we found similar relationships. In 2 different populations, the more genetically variable turkeys weighed more and had larger spurs than the less genetically variable individuals of the same age. Adult turkeys also had higher genetic variability than juveniles in both populations.

Our results suggest that turkeys with higher variability grow faster and have a greater chance of reaching adulthood than do less variable individuals. Genetic variation is also important in an evolutionary sense. Genetic variation is the raw material upon which selection acts. If genetic variability is lost as a result of improper management, a population's ability to adapt to changing environmental conditions could be limited. Ultimately, populations that cannot adapt go extinct. Managers, by surveying genetic variation, may learn something about the genetic health of their populations.

The most widely used technique today for the study of genetic variation in natural populations is starch-gel electrophoresis. Genetic markers identified with electrophoretic techniques have proven useful for studies of population structure, genetic differentiation, and evolutionary history, all of which are important to wildlife managers. Electrophoresis permits the examination of genetic variability in large numbers of individuals in a way that is efficient in both time and cost and is thus well suited for studies of wildlife populations.

Electrophoresis is the process of separating enzymes and other proteins according to their size, shape, and electrical charge. Enzymes are the direct products of genes. Their separation and subsequent interpretation can therefore provide information on the extent of genetic variability within individuals, populations, and entire species. The actual mechanisms responsible for the relationship between heterozygosity, fitness, and evolutionary potential are unclear (Lewontin 1974). We believe, however, that enough evidence on the importance of heterozygosity has accumulated to warrant the consideration of genetic management in wildlife species.

In 1985 we initiated a survey of genetic variability in the wild turkey. We aimed to determine the usefulness of electrophoretic techniques for the study of questions on population and management in this species. Our general objectives were to (1) establish a data base of genetic variation in the eastern wild turkey; and (2) use electrophoretic techniques to investigate potential genetic problems that may arise from establishing or supplementing turkey populations with domestic and game-farm stock. For comparison, we used samples from 3 categories: native (wild), game-farm, and domestic.

We got our native eastern wild turkeys from the Francis Marion National Forest, South Carolina, and the Camp Lejeune Marine Corps Base, North Carolina. Both sites have resident populations of native wild turkeys with no documented history of interbreeding with domestic or game-farm stock. We sampled these sites because the consensus among biologists familiar with them was that they represented eastern wild turkeys of the purest (i.e., nondomestic) stock available. Twenty individuals were collected from the Francis Marion in 1985. From Camp Lejeune, we got 15 in 1985 and 22 in 1986.

Samples from 115 turkeys from 12 game farms in 9 states were acquired in conjunction with a disease study conducted by the Southeastern Cooperative Wildlife Disease Study Unit, Athens, Georgia.

Samples from 82 domestic turkeys (strain Nicholas) were procured from the Louis Rich Company in Newberry, South Carolina.

Three common measures of genetic variation were used in our analysis: heterozygosity, percent polymorphic loci, and mean number of alleles per locus.

Heterozygosity is a measure of the number of loci at which an individual exhibits a polymorphism (more than one allele) and is calculated from the observed frequency of heterozygotes per locus, averaged over all loci.

Percent polymorphic loci is the number of loci in which 2 or more alleles are detected, divided by the total number of loci examined.

Mean number of alleles per locus is the number of different alleles identified at each locus, divided by the number of loci examined.

Genetic Variation in the Wild Turkey

Heterozygosity levels did not differ significantly between the Francis Marion and Camp Lejeune populations ($t_{55} = -1.0295$, $P = 0.31$). Mean heterozygosity for the two populations combined was 2.0 percent (Table 5). This mean value is low relative to the mean heterozygosity levels for birds, but is well within the range of re-

Table 5. Heterozygosity (H) and percent polymorphic loci (P) for some game birds.

Species	H	P	Reference
Wild turkey (eastern)	2.0%	25.0%	Present study
Ring-necked pheasant	2.6	11.1	Gutierrez et al. 1983; Vohs and Carr 1969
Lesser prairie chicken	0.0	0.0	Gutierrez et al. 1983
Chukar	5.2	14.8	Gutierrez et al. 1983
Gambel's quail	3.1	18.5	Gutierrez et al. 1983
Bobwhite	3.4	14.8	Gutierrez et al. 1983
Willow ptarmigan	8.2	26.0	Gyllensten et al. 1979
Phasianidae (14 species)	2.8	18.4	Evans 1987
Birds (86 species)	4.4	24.0	Evans 1987
Vertebrates (551 species)	5.4	22.6	Nevo et al. 1984

ported values (0 to 30.7 percent, Evans 1987). Percentage of loci polymorphic (25.0) is similar to that reported for other birds (range 0 to 71.4 percent), but differs slightly between populations. Mean number of alleles per locus was identical for the 2 populations.

In a general or evolutionary sense, the biological significance of heterozygosity (and other measures of genetic variation) for a species is difficult to interpret. There is no ideal level of heterozygosity for a species. Heterozygosity is simply a measure of genetic variability in one small portion of the organism's genome.

Genetic variability is influenced by a variety of factors including mutation rates, migration rates and patterns, selection, breeding structure, effective population size, and other evolutionary forces. Higher heterozygosity levels in other species do not reflect superiority, but different evolutionary histories. Categorizing these populations of the wild turkey as having low heterozygosity does not imply judgment of the species' genetic status. Rather, it promotes comparison with other populations and species, which may help elucidate the evolutionary forces that have shaped the turkey's history.

For example, one explanation for low heterozygosity is that the Camp Lejeune and Francis Marion populations many years ago experienced a severe reduction in the number of breeding birds. This reduction may have occurred in the early part of this century, when over-hunting and habitat change resulted in isolation of small populations of the wild turkey in parts of its eastern range. Further sampling of other populations of native wild turkeys will allow more conclusive analysis of heterozygosity levels in this species.

Genetic differences between the Camp Lejeune and Francis Marion populations are small. Genetic distance (Nei 1978), a measure of genetic differences between the populations, was 0.002. This value is larger than genetic distances recorded between other populations of Galliformes (D = 0.0007; Gutierrez et al. 1983) but typical for birds in general (D = 0.0024; Barrowclough 1980). Wright's (1978) measure of population differentiation (F_{st}) indicates that of the total genetic variation detected in these populations, only 5.5 percent represents differences between the populations. The remaining 94.5 percent of genetic variation is contained within the individual populations. Evans (1987) reported that for birds in general, about 4.8 percent of the genetic variation represents differences between populations.

Turkeys, like most birds that have been studied, exhibit only small genetic differences between populations. These may be a result of the homogenizing effect of gene flow between the 2 sites. Turkeys can move long distances (Brown 1980). Camp Lejeune and the Francis Marion are about 240 kilometers (150 miles) apart. This distance probably is not a barrier to the movement of turkeys over

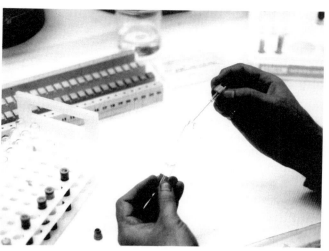

New systematic techniques should clarify genetic relationships. *Photo by National Wild Turkey Federation.*

generations between the sites. On the other hand, if the 2 sites are completely isolated from one another, not enough time may have elapsed since their isolation for genetic differences to accrue. Genetic differences accumulate slowly, particularly if the populations are subject to similar selective forces.

Further analysis of genetic differences among turkey populations will require additional samples from other areas, preferably those for which there are data on dispersal and isolation.

Genetic Variation in Game-farm and Domestic Turkeys

Mean heterozygosity for the game-farm turkeys was 2.3 percent, with a range from 0.4 percent to 7.9 percent. Heterozygosity in the domestic turkey was 0.6 percent (Table 6). There were significant differences in heterozygosity among game-farm samples. Percentage of loci

Table 6. Genetic variability for 28 loci in wild,[a] game-farm, and domestic turkey stocks.

Stock	Sample size	Mean number of alleles per locus	Percentage of loci polymorphic[b]	Percent mean heterozygosity — Direct count (range)
Wild (eastern)	57	1.1	25.0	2.0 (1.7–2.7)
Game-farm	115	1.3	32.1	2.3 (0.4–7.9)
Domestic	82	1.2	14.3	0.6

[a] *M. g. silvestris.*
[b] A locus is considered polymorphic if frequency of the most common allele does not exceed 0.99.

polymorphic and mean number of alleles per locus were lower in domestic (14.3, 1.2) than game-farm stock (32.1 percent, 1.3, respectively).

The range in heterozygosity in game-farm samples may be the result of variability in breeding practices. The birds we sampled varied in appearance. Some resembled the wild phenotype; others were predominantly white. These birds were taken from small commercial operations, hunt clubs, and "backyard" breeders. Information on the origin and maintenance of the stocks sampled is incomplete but represents a diversity of histories. Some sources bred their own stocks. Others bought birds from other breeders or got eggs from nests of wild birds. Several reported crossing wild gobblers with domestic hens.

One breeder's flock was founded with a relatively small number of individuals (less than 13), all of which were closely related. (In this example, a single clutch was taken from a wild brood.) Other flocks were founded by crossing a single wild tom with an undisclosed number of domestic hens, or by using birds from other game farms.

Founding a flock with a small number of individuals, with an unbalanced sex ratio, or with related individuals may result in a genetic deficiency. The genetic variability in such founding individuals is not likely to be representative of the donor population or species as a whole. Maintaining flocks at small sizes and using the same or a smaller number of breeders over generations can further decrease heterozygosity.

Most game-farm breeders are aware of potential problems associated with inbreeding, and they probably try to protect their flocks by introducing new individuals periodically. Our records suggest that wild birds and birds from other breeders are often introduced into game-farm flocks. The introduction of individuals of different genetic backgrounds could quickly (say, in one breeding season) influence the frequency of alleles within a stock, elevating heterozygosity levels. The wide range in heterozygosity levels reflects breeding practices that may lower or raise levels of genetic variability.

One effect of this type of breeding is the accumulation of large genetic differences observed among game-farm samples, compared with those observed between wild populations. The mean F_{st} for the game-farm birds indicates that 16.5 percent of the variation is distributed among populations, triple the level for wild birds. Genetic distance values ranged from 0.000 to 0.012 (Nei 1978). These genetic distances are similar to those reported between species in New World quail (Gutierrez et al. 1983) and are generally an order of magnitude higher than interpopulational comparisons in other birds.

Low heterozygosity in the domestic turkey may be the result of a variety of historical factors. The domestic turkey originated from the Mexican wild turkey, not from the eastern wild turkey. Thus, the large difference in heterozygosity between the wild eastern birds and domestic stock may represent subspecific differences.

Historical accounts of domesticating the wild turkey reveal a series of potential bottlenecks in population size, which may have affected heterozygosity levels. The Mexican wild turkey, domesticated by the Aztecs, was brought to Europe from the New World by early explorers (Mosby and Handley 1943). The domestic turkey was then returned to the United States by early settlers.

Estimates on the number of birds used to establish domestic flocks during these periods are not available, but it seems likely that such a history would result in small population sizes and inbreeding. The domestic turkey may have experienced a bottleneck in numbers during the period in which it underwent domestication by European and American peoples.

Current commercial strategies of breeding domestic turkeys may further reduce heterozygosity. Domestic turkeys are selected for traits that enhance their marketability: growth rate, body size, egg production, and so on. Selection for these traits may result in coincidental reduction in heterozygosity at the loci examined.

Genetic Differentiation among Wild, Game-farm, and Domestic Turkeys

One objective of this research was to investigate the potential genetic impact of introducing domestic and game-farm turkeys into wild populations. We therefore combined all individuals within the domestic, game-farm, and wild categories and looked for differences among the groups. Heterozygosities of the wild and game-farm categories were not significantly different, but both were significantly different from the domestic category. Mean number of alleles per locus and percentage of polymorphic loci were lowest in the domestic stock and similar between wild and game-farm (Table 6).

Wild, game-farm, and domestic turkeys shared variability at only 2 loci (Acp, Aat-2). Allele frequencies were significantly different at both. Four polymorphisms were unique to the game-farm stocks (Mpi-2, Icd-2, Gpi, Pgm), all of which occurred at low frequencies. Wild and game-farm categories shared polymorphisms at 5 loci (Acp, Aat-2, Gpd, Sordh, Tri); wild stock exhibited no unique polymorphisms. Unique polymorphisms in the game-farm stock probably reflect the diverse background of the stocks sampled. These groups were composed of birds from numerous geographic areas and may also include subspecies other than the eastern. There was one rare allele unique to the domestic birds (Aat-2). Genetic distances among the 3 groups were small and identical (0.001), reflecting little overall divergence.

Table 7. Allele frequencies and electrophoretic conditions for polymorphic protein loci[a] resolved from liver samples of wild turkey, domestic turkey, and game-farm turkey.

Enzyme commission number	Enzyme locus	Wild[d]					Game-farm[d]									Domestic	Buffer (pH)
		CL 37	FM 20	IA 10	MO 10	MD 10	PN-I 10	PN-II 10	MN-I 8	MN-II 11	MN-III 7	AL 9	NC 10	GA 10	SC 10	82	
Acid phosphatase (Acp) 3.1.3.2	B	0.194	0.025	0.000	0.000	0.000	0.000	0.050	0.000	0.000	0.000	0.000	0.250	0.050	0.150	0.006	Tris maleate (7.4)
	C	0.806	0.975	1.000	1.000	1.000	1.000	0.950	1.000	1.000	1.000	1.000	0.750	0.950	0.850	0.994	
Aspartate aminotransferase-1 (Aat-1) 2.6.1.1	B	0.014	0.025	0.000	0.000	0.000	0.000	0.000	0.000	0.000	0.000	0.000	0.000	0.000	0.000	0.012	Amine citrate (6.1)
	C	0.986	0.975	1.000	1.000	1.000	1.000	1.000	1.000	1.000	1.000	1.000	1.000	1.000	1.000	0.988	
Aspartate aminotransferase-2 (Aat-2) 2.6.1.1	B	0.014	0.175	0.000	0.000	0.000	0.000	0.000	0.000	0.000	0.000	0.000	0.100	0.000	0.000	0.061	Amine citrate (6.1)
	C	0.986	0.825	1.000	1.000	1.000	1.000	1.000	1.000	1.000	1.000	1.000	0.900	1.000	1.000	0.933	
	D	0.000	0.000	0.000	0.000	0.000	0.000	0.000	0.000	0.000	0.000	0.000	0.000	0.000	0.000	0.006	
Glucosephosphate isomerase (Gpi) 5.3.1.9	B	0.000	0.000	0.000	0.000	0.000	0.000	0.000	0.000	0.045	0.000	0.000	0.000	0.000	0.100	0.000	Tris maleate (7.4)
	C	1.000	1.000	1.000	1.000	1.000	1.000	1.000	1.000	0.955	1.000	1.000	1.000	1.000	0.900	1.000	
Glycerol-3-phosphate dehydrogenase (Gpd) 1.1.1.8	B	0.000	0.050	0.000	0.000	0.000	0.000	0.000	0.000	0.063	0.000	0.071	0.000	0.000	0.000	0.000	Amine citrate (6.1)
	C	1.000	0.950	1.000	1.000	1.000	1.000	1.000	1.000	0.938	1.000	0.929	1.000	1.000	1.000	1.000	
Isocitrate dehydrogenase-2 (Icd-2) 1.1.1.42	B	0.000	0.000	0.000	0.050	0.000	0.000	0.050	0.000	0.000	0.000	0.000	0.150	0.000	0.250	0.000	Tris citrate (8.0)
	C	1.000	1.000	1.000	0.950	1.000	1.000	0.950	1.000	1.000	1.000	1.000	0.850	1.000	0.750	1.000	
Mannose phosphate isomerase-1 (Mpi-1) 5.3.1.8	B	0.000	0.025	0.000	0.000	0.000	0.000	0.000	0.000	0.000	0.000	0.000	0.000	0.000	0.000	0.012	Tris citrate (8.0)
	C	1.000	0.975	1.000	1.000	1.000	1.000	1.000	1.000	1.000	1.000	1.000	1.000	1.000	1.000	0.988	
Mannose phosphate isomerase-2 (Mpi-2) 5.3.1.8	B	0.000	0.000	0.000	0.000	0.000	0.000	0.000	0.000	0.000	0.000	0.000	0.000	0.000	0.050	0.000	Tris citrate (8.0)
	C	1.000	1.000	1.000	1.000	1.000	0.900	1.000	1.000	1.000	1.000	1.000	1.000	0.900	0.950	1.000	
	D	0.000	0.000	0.000	0.000	0.000	0.100	0.000	0.000	0.000	0.000	0.000	0.000	0.100	0.000	0.000	
Phosphoglucomutase (Pgm) 5.4.2.2	B	0.000	0.000	0.000	0.000	0.000	0.000	0.000	0.000	0.000	0.000	0.000	0.000	0.000	0.000	0.000	Lithium hydroxide (8.2)
	C	1.000	1.000	1.000	1.000	1.000	1.000	1.000	1.000	1.000	1.000	1.000	1.000	1.000	1.000	1.000	
Sorbitol dehydrogenase (Sordh) 1.1.1.14	B	0.000	0.075	0.250	0.500	0.050	0.000	0.000	0.000	0.136	0.000	0.000	0.000	0.000	0.200	0.000	Tris citrate (8.0)
	C	1.000	0.925	0.750	0.500	0.950	1.000	1.000	1.000	0.864	1.000	1.000	1.000	1.000	0.800	1.000	
Tripeptide aminopeptidase (Tri)[c] 3.4.11.4	C	0.932	1.000	0.950	0.950	0.950	0.800	0.950	0.938	0.909	1.000	0.944	0.900	0.950	1.000	1.000	Tris citrate (8.0)
	D	0.068	0.000	0.050	0.050	0.050	0.200	0.050	0.063	0.091	0.000	0.056	0.100	0.050	0.000	0.000	

[a] The following loci were monomorphic in all individuals assayed (numbers and acronyms in parentheses): Alcohol dehydrogenase (1.1.1.1; Adh), Lactate dehydrogenase-1&2 (1.1.1.27; Ldh), Malate dehydrogenase-1&2 (1.1.1.37; Mdh), Isocitrate dehydrogenase-2 (1.1.1.42; Icd), Phosphogluconate dehydrogenase (1.1.1.43; Pgd), Superoxide dismutase-1&2 (1.15.1.1; Sod), Glutamate dehydrogenase (1.4.1.2; Glud), Nucleoside phosphorylase (2.4.2.a; Nsp), Creatine kinase-1&2 (2.7.3.2; Ck), Esterase (3.1.1.1; Es; β-naphylacetate substrate), Leucine aminopeptidase (3.4.11; Lap), Aconitase (4.2.1.3; Acon), General protein (Gp).
[b] Enzyme Commission number recognized by International Union of Biochemistry (1984).
[c] Peptidase substrate for tripeptide aminopeptidase was leucylglycylglycine.
[d] Abbreviations are as follows: CL = Camp Lejeune, FM = Francis Marion, IA = Iowa, MO = Missouri, MD = Maryland, PN-I, II = Pennsylvania, MN-I, II, III = Minnesota, AL = Alabama, NC = North Carolina, GA = Georgia, SC = South Carolina.

Management Implications

We found no absolute genetic (fixed-allele) differences among wild, game-farm, and domestic stock. Without such marker alleles, it is not possible to unequivocally identify, for example, the presence of domestic blood in wild stock.

Although there are no fixed-allele differences among wild, game-farm, and domestic turkeys, there are genetic differences among these groups. For example, there are significantly lower levels of heterozygosity in domestic birds and a wide range of values in the game-farm stock. This is potentially important for the management of wild turkeys in areas where domestic and game-farm birds continue to escape or be liberated into the wild. If, as our preliminary studies show, reduced heterozygosity affects vigor in the wild turkey, the low variability in domestic and some game-farm stock would clearly warn against introducing these individuals into wild populations. The release of game-farm stock may increase local abundance of turkeys, and it may even provide an acceptable hunting experience. But the tactic may well degrade the overall genetic resource in wild populations.

Genetic survey data of this type may also be used by biologists to maintain and improve levels of genetic variability in managed populations. For example, newly stocked populations should contain sufficient numbers of unrelated founders in appropriate sex ratios to avoid the loss of genetic variability caused by bottlenecks. Electrophoretic surveys may prove useful in identifying managed populations that exhibit reduced genetic variability because of previous management practices. Such populations might benefit from the influx of new, unrelated individuals to boost levels of genetic variability.

We urge extreme caution in the genetic management of wild turkey populations. Despite great leaps in our understanding of the genome over the past several decades, our knowledge still has many gaps. Some recommendations, like avoiding the release of domestic stock with low variability into the wild, seem uncomplicated. Others, like the manipulations of levels of genetic variability in managed populations, require thorough genetic surveys and a clear understanding of the important management goals.

Wildlife biologists have only just begun to use information garnered from molecular techniques. As our understanding of the genome increases, this information will prove increasingly valuable for the management and conservation of wildlife populations. Molecular techniques, used in conjunction with more traditional management data like habitat quality, offer biologists new tools and approaches to wildlife management.

JOHN SIDELINGER

II

Wild Turkey Biology

Chapter 4

PHYSICAL CHARACTERISTICS

Paul H. Pelham
D.V.M.
Depew, New York

James G. Dickson
Research Wildlife Biologist
Southern Forest Experiment Station
USDA Forest Service
Nacogdoches, Texas

Birds, as a group, are endothermic (warm-blooded) vertebrates. They have feathers, reproduce by eggs, and can fly, although some flightless forms have evolved.

Birds, including the wild turkey, have evolved as flying machines and have special adaptations and characteristics necessary for flight. Size, weight, and shape constraints are requisites for flight. Birds are light, strong, and fast. They are efficient anatomically, energetically, and aerodynamically. Light feathers insulate a bird's body and propel a bird through the air. Wing, leg, and pelvic bones are reduced and are fused for added strength. A bird has no heavy teeth, and its jaw muscles are small. Weight is kept low by means of a reduced skeleton and hollow bones. A bird's relatively efficient respiratory system has large lungs and air sacs. A large keel provides an anchor for the large pectoral muscles, necessary for flight.

Compared with other animal groups, birds have an efficient energetic system. They have a large, 4-chambered heart, high blood sugar, and high body temperature. They eat high-energy food and digest it rapidly. Uric acid is voided rather than the heavier, watery urine. There is usually only 1 functional ovary, and young develop mostly in the egg, outside the mother's body.

The wild turkey is included in a group called gallinaceous birds, which includes grouse and quails. Gallinaceous birds are characterized by strong feet and legs adapted for scratching; short, rounded wings adapted for short, rapid flight; well-developed tail used as a rudder; short, stout beak useful for pecking; and sexual dimorphism (male and female). These group attributes characterize the wild turkey well.

Two indigenous species of turkeys exist in the world today: (1) the ocellated turkey of southern Mexico and Central America; and (2) the wild turkey of the United States and Mexico. There are 5 subspecies (or races) of wild turkey today. The eastern subspecies, having by far the widest distribution, will be used primarily in this chapter's description of the wild turkey. Major differences of the other subspecies are discussed in chapter 3, Systematics and Population Genetics.

Turkey enthusiasts are urged to familiarize themselves with the turkey's external characteristics illustrated in the accompanying anatomical drawing (Figure 1). This information is most useful in determining sex and age in the field.

PLUMAGE (PTILOSIS)

Between 5,000 and 6,000 feathers cover the body of an adult turkey in patterns called feather tracts (pterylae) (Marsden and Martin 1946). Size ranges from tiny, hair-like feathers called filoplumes to the large, stiff, quill-like wing feathers (remiges) and tail feathers (retrices). Feathers of at least 8 different shapes function in the following ways: body covering, insulation, waterproofing, flight, tactile sensation for sensory organ protection, and ornamentation for display and recognition. It is usual for the wild turkey to have 10 stiff primary and 18 or 19 secondary wing feathers. The tail usually has 18 large quill feathers.

The head and upper part of the neck, especially the male's, are scantily feathered. Various-sized protuberances (bumps) of skin, called caruncles, are found on much of this relatively bare head and neck area. The gobbler's caruncles are much more prominent than the hen's.

Feathers are replaced in 4 different molts, resulting in 5 different plumages [natal, juvenal, first basic (post-juvenal), alternate (first winter), and basic (adult), Williams and Austin 1988:51]. Many feathers exhibit a metallic glittering, called iridescence, with varying colors of red, green, copper, bronze, and gold. These colors

Figure 1. External Anatomy of the Male Wild Turkey

KEY

A. Beard.

B. Major caruncles; large and bulbous shaped in the male.

B–1. Minor caruncles.

C. Dewlap.

D. Throat.

E. Beak.

F. Nostril.

G. Eye.

H. Snood; also called a dewbill or leader; prominent in the male.

I. Crown of head; color is white or red in the male, especially during mating season; color is dull gray-blue in the female year-round.

J. Ear opening; covered with bristle feathers.

K. Face; color is important for sex identification.

L. Neck; longer in the male.

M. Shoulder.

N. Back.

N–1. Rump; also called a saddle.

O. Upper major secondary coverts; these form the wing bar, and their size and shape are important for age identification.

O-1. Secondary wing feathers (remiges); they number 18 or 19 and form the wing bay.

P. Upper median tail coverts.

P-1. Upper major tail coverts.

Q. Tail feathers (rectrices); usually number 18.

R. Under tail coverts; major, median, and minor.

S. Primary wing feathers (remiges); 10 in number; usually only the ninth and tenth are visible in the folded wing.

T. Fluff.

U. Abdomen.

V. Metatarsal spur; also called tarsometatarsal spur and tarsal spur.

W. Metatarsus; also called the tarsometatarsus and tarsus; longer in the gobbler.

X. Ankle.

Y. Shank; tibiotarsus and fibula.

Z. Breast; contains the breast sponge in mating season; color of tips of breast feathers are black in the male and tan to brown in the female.

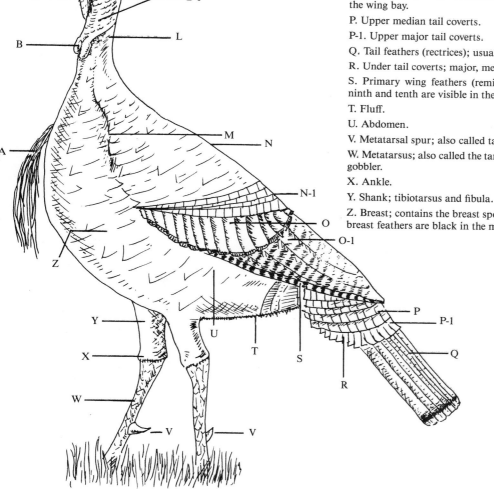

depend on the brightness of light as well as the angle from which the turkey is viewed. Body movements, as well as feather and skin muscles, can affect this iridescence, which is more evident in the gobbler.

The hen's plumage is duller than the gobbler's. She appears generally brownish or lighter in color because of tan to chestnut brown tips of the contour feathers of the breast, midback, marginal coverts of the wing bow, and secondary coverts of the wing bar. Hen coloration is controlled by an ovarian hormone. Gobblerlike plumage develops in hens whose ovaries have been removed (see Lewis 1967).

Feathers in comparable areas of the gobbler are black tipped, giving him a metallic black appearance. In addition, ends of the contour breast feathers of the gobbler are squarish, while the brown-tipped contour breast feathers of the hen are slightly rounded. Male turkey plumage is standard for the species; it develops even in castrated gobblers.

Aberrant Coloration

Several color abnormalities appear in wild turkeys. Melanistic (black), erythritic (red), and albinotic (white) plumages have been reported infrequently in the wild turkey (Williams 1981:30). The smoke gray mutant, an incomplete albino, is the most commonly reported color abnormality. Complete albinos, characterized by pink eyes, appear in domestic turkeys but have not been reported in wild populations.

WEIGHTS

From a birth weight of about 56 grams (2 ounces), a gobbler will multiply his weight by approximately 120 (6.8 kilograms or 15 pounds) in the first year. A hen, in the same time, will reach only about half of that weight (3.4 kilograms or 7 to 8 pounds). As adults, males average 7.7 to 9.5 kilograms (17 to 21 pounds) and females 3.6 to 5.0 kilograms (8 to 11 pounds). Mean weights of the 10 heaviest gobblers recorded in the National Wild Turkey Federation 1990 records were as follows: eastern—14.1 kilograms (31.1 pounds), Rio Grande—11.8 kilograms (26.0 pounds), Merriam's—12.2 kilograms (26.8 pounds), Florida—10.4 kilograms (22.8 pounds), Gould's—10.9 kilograms (24.1 pounds), and Ocellated—5.4 kilograms (11.8 pounds). Adult gobblers in an alert position stand approximately 101.6 centimeters (40

The wild turkey is aptly named. It is the epitome of wariness. *Photo by G. Smith.*

Photo by G. Griffen.

inches) tall. Alert hens stand about 76.2 centimeters (30 inches) tall (Mosby and Handley 1943, Hewitt 1967).

SIGHT, HEARING, TASTE, SMELL

Sight

The wild turkey has excellent vision. The rate of assimilation of detail in the field of vision is very rapid (see Lewis 1967). Sight acuity of the wild turkey is legendary, and all new turkey hunters learn the lesson: Don't move when a turkey is looking. Because its eyes are on the side of its head, a turkey has predominantly monocular, periscopic vision. Though the 3 dimensions of space cannot be clearly perceived (as with stereoscopic vision), the turkey can determine relative distances by a slight turning of its head and viewing an object at different angles. The same head movement allows a 360° field of vision.

Night vision of turkeys is poor, and turkeys are reluctant to leave a roost at night. Rod visual cells of the eye's retina are associated with night vision, and cone cells are associated with colored, day vision. Nocturnal (nighttime) birds, such as owls, have retinas with rods predominating. Turkeys are diurnal (daytime) birds and have a preponderance of cones in the retina (Dukes 1947). Turkeys have a flattened cornea. Turkeys can see colors to some degree. How well color perception is developed is not known, but color changes of the head and neck appendages affect responses from other turkeys.

A translucent inner eyelid called the nictitating membrane constantly sweeps finer particles of dust and other irritants from the eye. Close observation of 8 imprinted adults of both sexes by the first author showed a frequency of 78 to 92 closings per minute of this third eyelid. If a closeup photograph is taken when this eyelid is closed, the eye will appear to have a white film over it. Turkeys often close the outer lids when sleeping.

Hearing

The hearing ability of the wild turkey is acute, although the external ear lacks a flap, or pinna, which concentrates sound waves. Though research has not been done on these auditory capabilities, field observation suggests turkeys hear lower-frequency and more distant sounds than humans.

Taste and Smell

Turkeys probably have a poor sense of taste compared with mammals because turkeys have relatively fewer taste buds. The simple tastes such as salt, sweet, acid, and bitter are believed to be detected by the turkey.

In food selection, color and shape seem to play a more important part than taste and smell. However, turkeys sometimes avoid corn soaked in narcotic and tranquilizing drugs for immobilization if they have had prior experience with such baits.

Smells are interpreted by the olfactory lobes in the forepart of the brain. These lobes are small in the turkey and probably indicate a poorly developed sense of smell. Field observations support this belief. Mothballs in close proximity to shelled corn do not deter turkeys from eating the bait.

MOBILITY

Running

Wild turkeys run well. In heavy cover, running rather than flying is the preferred mode of escape. Even in open cover, heavy gobblers often run rather than fly to escape danger. Powerful legs enable the wild turkey to

Wild turkeys have evolved with predators, and predators have helped to make wild turkeys truly wild. *Photo by J. Whitcomb, Texas Parks and Wildlife Department.*

run at speeds probably greater than 19 kilometers per hour (12 miles per hour) (Mosby and Handley 1943), as well as serve as a catapult, enabling the bird to become airborne in an instant.

Flying

Brood hens encourage their young to fly first at about 8 to 10 days old. Flying enables turkeys to escape danger, roost in trees, and simply change locations rapidly. The lightweight pneumatic skeleton, strong muscles, and powerful wings enable the wild turkey to become airborne easily and quickly. The design of the wild turkey is suitable for short, rapid flight. The ratio of wing area (square centimeters) to weight (grams) is 0.96, among the lowest of all birds (Poole 1938). In adult turkeys, most continuous active wingbeats rarely continue for more than 200 meters (219 yards), but gliding alternated with wingbeats may enable turkeys to cover 1.6 kilometers (1 mile) with little difficulty. Flying speeds up to 88 kilometers per hour (55 miles per hour) have been reported (Mosby and Handley 1943).

The wild turkey is an exceptional flier for short distances. *Photo by H. Williamson, U.S. Forest Service.*

Although it's not normal behavior, turkeys can swim. *Photo by P. Pelham.*

Swimming

Reports (see Lewis 1967) and a personal observation confirm that turkeys as young as 3 or 4 days old can swim for short distances when necessary, although swimming is not a standard mode of travel.

LEGS AND SPURS (METATARSI)

The legs and upper surface of the toes of poults are covered with nonoverlapping keratin scales (scutes), which contain a dark pigment called melanin. As these scales grow, less and less melanin is deposited in the new scale tissue. These scales attain maximum clarity between 1 and 1½ years of age and are similar in color to human fingernails. The red-pigmented tissue layer immediately beneath the scales becomes highly visible, giving the leg of the adult wild turkey its pink or red hue (Williams 1981). Occasionally, this red tissue layer is absent, and then the legs are grayish or white.

The metatarsal spur is at the juncture of the middle and distal (lower) thirds of the lower leg. Both sexes are born with a small button spur, consisting of smooth, shiny keratin. Normally, the spur starts growing in the male soon after birth and can attain a maximum length of about 5 centimeters (2 inches).

The adult spur has a bony core and a keratin covering. With age, the shape gradually changes from round, blunt, and buttonlike to pointed, curved, and sharp. Shape and size of the spur are used as age determinants, especially in juveniles and younger-aged adult gobblers (Kelly 1975, Williams 1981).

Most spurs are black, but some are black and reddish, pink, off-white, or a combination of these colors. Occasional reports describe a hen with spurs or a gobbler that either lacks spurs or has multiple spurs (Williams and Austin 1988).

The eastern and Florida wild turkeys tend to have longer spurs than the western subspecies (Stangel et al. in press). The longest spurs recorded in the National Wild Turkey Federation Wild Turkey 1990 records are 3 eastern gobblers and 1 Florida gobbler, all with spurs of about 5 centimeters (2 inches).

BEARDS

A tuft of stiff, keratinous filaments projecting outward and downward from the lowest part of the ventral midline of the neck is called the beard. The beard usually has been considered a modified type of feather. But feathers undergo molting, and the beard never does. So the beard may not be feathers, but a specialized structure of the skin, growing continuously throughout the life of the turkey. The beard's filaments (or bristles) arise from a featherless, laterally compressed, raised oval of skin

called a papilla (Lucas and Stettenheim 1972). Multiple beards are the result of multiple papillae, each containing bristles and forming a separate beard.

Though the papilla is also present in all females, the beard grows on only 1 to 29 percent of females from different populations (Lewis 1967, Williams and Austin 1988). Hen beards are usually shorter and thinner than gobbler beards, rarely longer than 17.8 centimeters (7 inches).

Most males have a beard that becomes visible beyond the breast feathers at 6 to 7 months of age, even though it emerges from the papilla at 14 to 17 weeks. Gobbler beards grow about 7.6 to 12.7 centimeters (3 to 5 inches) per year, but they begin to wear off from ground friction after about 2 years of age. Taller gobblers tend to grow longer beards because of greater clearance from the ground. Beard thickness depends on the number of bristles.

The 1990 National Wild Turkey Federation Wild Turkey records listed the longest beard as 42.9 centimeters (16.9 inches), from an eastern gobbler taken in

Photo by L. Williams.

Photo by G. Kirtley-Perkins.

The beard of the male turkey projects from the midline of the neck and grows continuously.

A few hens have beards. *Photo by H. Hauke.*

Alabama in 1985. The record multiple-beard gobbler, taken in Wisconsin in 1989, had 8 beards with a total length of 180.2 centimeters (71 inches).

The beard is normally black, with the proximal (closest to the body) one-fourth often grayish black because of a whitish cementlike material adhering to the bristles. The distal (lower) end of beards of juvenile gobblers usually have a reddish or blond tip, but this color disappears in older gobblers as the beard grows and wears off.

Some beards appear to be partially or completely broken off horizontally. In northern climates, this effect can be caused by ice-ball formations from winter feeding in spring seeps and deep snow. In southern areas that have little freezing and snowfall, this cutoff appearance more likely results from lack of black pigment (melanin)

Photo by H. Williamson.

A few gobblers have multiple or truncate beards, and a few are beardless.

Photo by J. Dickson.

in a section of the bristles of some beards, making them brittle and subject to breakage (L. Williams, Jr. personal communication).

THE DEVELOPING POULT

The egg is made up of the ovum (yolk) and a series of layers of albumen, shell membranes, and the shell proper, which surround the yolk as it descends from the ovary down the oviduct. Wild turkey eggs are light buff to pale brown or purple, with brown spots varying in size from fine stippling to coarse, more widely spaced spots. Individual hens tend to lay eggs with consistent size, color, shape, and spotting.

Wild turkey eggs weigh between 64 and 71 grams (2¼ to 2½ ounces) and tend to be larger and more pointed than chicken eggs. The double-yolked eggs that are common in chickens occur infrequently in the wild turkey. Primarily because of moisture loss during incubation, each hatched poult weighs about ⅔ of the original egg weight, or about 45 grams (1.6 ounces).

During the first 3 months, poults will gain about 0.5 kilograms (1.1 pounds) per month. After 3 months, male poults will weigh slightly more than 1.4 kilograms (3 pounds) and females slightly less (Mosby and Handley 1943). Between 3 and 7 months, weight gains are rapid — approximately 0.5 kilograms (1.1 pounds) every 2 weeks.

At about 5 to 6 months of age, the young gobblers weigh 4.1 to 5.0 kilograms (9 to 11 pounds), which is usually more than their mothers. At 7 months of age, average hen weight is about 3.6 kilograms (8 pounds), and immature gobblers weigh about 5.7 kilograms (12.5 pounds). After 7 months, weight gain continues at a slower pace and assumes a seasonal pattern. Total weight of an individual depends on quality and availability of food, energy expended, and genetics.

Adult gobblers normally reach maximum weight just before mating season, when a spongy layer of fat and

The newly hatched poult is covered with natal down. *Photo by P. Pelham.*

Wild turkey eggs vary in shape and color. *Photo by P. Pelham.*

At about 2 weeks old, poults can fly well enough to roost in trees. *Photo by L. Williams.*

Young poults grow rapidly (1-month-old poult). In the first 3 months, they gain about 0.5 kilograms (1.1 pounds) per month. *Photo by P. Pelham.*

blood vessels called the "breast sponge" is most fully developed. This fat layer can account for 10 percent of an adult gobbler's total body weight. Subadults (jakes) do not develop so large a breast sponge; consequently the breast bulge is not nearly so obvious in the young male at this time of year.

At hatching, the poult is covered with natal down that is yellowish with brown markings. At this time, the poult has 7 small primary flight feathers (Williams 1981). Because of rapid growth of these flight feathers, the poult at 8 to 12 days of age can fly up to low branches and bushes. At about 3 weeks of age, the flight feathers are so developed they look too large for the body and extend beyond the tail feathers.

After down replacement, the first body feather coloration is brownish, similar to a young grouse or pheasant. By continuous molting and feather replacement (some complete, some partial), the young turkey goes through 4 plumages and 3 molts by the first winter of life. The young turkey first attains adult-type colored plumage with the first basic (postjuvenal) plumage (third plumage phase) at about 3 months of age. Actually these young turkeys carry some feathers of juvenal, first basic (postjuvenal), and alternate (first winter) plumage from 4 months of age to the first winter of life.

Adult turkeys undergo a complete annual molt, spring through fall (Williams and Austin 1988). Because of continuous molting and feather replacement in a general bilateral (2-sided) pattern, the turkey never has large featherless areas. Nor does it lose the ability to fly when molting, as do some waterfowl.

AGING

Determining age of wild turkeys can be useful to biologists for making decisions on season dates and bag limits, and to hunters for assessing trophy status of gobblers. Age determination of juveniles in the hand can be precise during the first 7 months of life from data on leg length, primary molt pattern, and body weight (Healy and Nenno 1980).

Young turkeys of both sexes, from 5 months of age until their second autumn, can be differentiated from adults by the molting pattern of the main tail feathers (rectrices). Rectrices are molted from the inside outward evenly on both sides of the tail, maintaining bilateral symmetry. During a turkey's first fall, the central 4 to 6 tail feathers will be longer than the others because of the partial molt and replacement with longer feathers. However, the main tail feathers of the adult, when spread in a fan shape, will form a smooth, rounded contour of the outer perimeter. All the young turkey's tail feathers have not been replaced by spring, and this difference between juvenal and adult gobblers is prominent when they are displaying (strutting).

Young turkeys similar in size to adult hens also can be differentiated from adults by field observation of the shape of the greater upper secondary coverts (covert patch or wing bar). This area on adults will form a well-rounded contour. The juvenile coverts will be shorter and form an uneven, less-rounded contour (Powell 1965). This age criterion also holds true until completion of the first annual molt (second fall of life).

Other feathers that distinguish juveniles from adults are the ninth and tenth primary, or only the tenth primary. In the postjuvenal molt in the turkey's first fall, the ninth or ninth and tenth primaries (at the end of the wing) are retained. The others are replaced in the molt. In the juvenile, these feathers are pointed and dark tipped, and they are not white barred near the tip. Adults, by contrast, show rounded tips (or worn tips if they have been strutting), with white barring that extends to the end.

Spur length, body weight, and beard length may be helpful in determining the age structure of gobblers harvested during the spring season. Of these 3 criteria, spur length was the least variable age determinant (Kelly 1975). Spur length could effectively separate 1-year-old from 2-year-old turkeys and 2-year-olds from 3-year-olds ($P < 0.05$) for eastern wild turkeys in Missouri.

Average spur lengths for known-aged gobblers harvested during spring were 1 year old, 6.4 millimeters (¼ inches); 2-year-old, 22.0 millimeters (⅞ inches); 3-year-old, 25.4 millimeters (1 inch); and 4-year-old, 30.2 millimeters (1³⁄₁₆ inches). Published information on Florida turkey spur lengths showed somewhat longer spurs

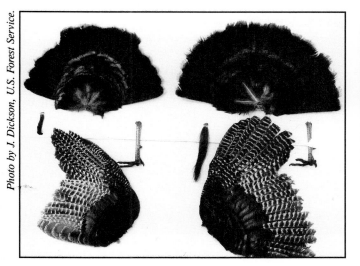

In fall or spring, adult gobblers can be differentiated from immature gobblers by the adult's full fan, full sweep to the secondary coverts, beard longer than 15 centimeters (6 inches), molted tenth primary, and spur longer than 12 millimeters (0.5 inch). Top left: Juvenile left, adult right. Top right: Immature gobblers. Bottom left: Adult gobbler. Bottom right: Adult.

(Williams 1981). Spurs less than 13 millimeters (½ inch) were attributed to gobblers less than 1 year old. One- to 2-year-old gobblers were thought to have spur lengths 19 to 25 millimeters (¾ to 1 inch), 2- to 3-year-old gobblers 25 to 32 millimeters (1 to 1¼ inches), and 3-year-olds and older greater than 32 millimeters (more than 1¼ inches). Recent data analysis has shown radiographs of spur-cap apex lengths were less variable than total spur lengths and could effectively separate 2-year-old from 3-year-old and older gobblers (3.97 millimeters, ⁵/₃₂ inch; Steffen et al. 1990).

Another change that comes with age is leg color.

Young turkeys have dark pigment (melanin) in the scales on the top of the feet and legs that produces a brown to grayish color. They lose this pigment as they age, and legs and feet of turkeys over a year old usually have a pink color and a rougher texture (Latham 1956:18).

A young gobbler's age can be judged by beard development (Williams 1981). The beard grows continuously without molting before reaching the ground and starting to wear off. On young turkeys, the beard tips are amber (blond to reddish). The beard is 1.3 to 6.4 centimeters (½ to 2½ inches) long by the gobbler's first fall, depending on the hatch date. Sometimes the beard is visible on

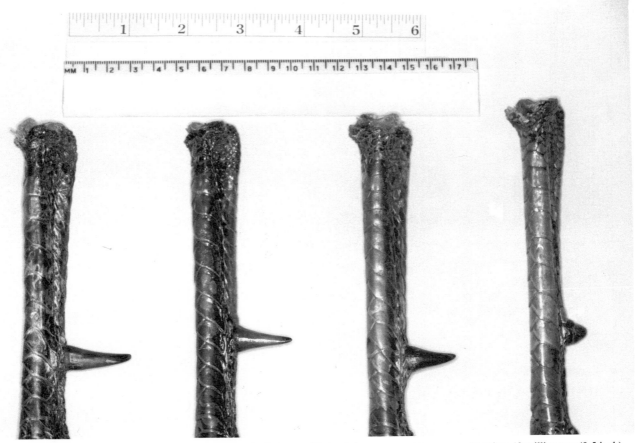

Younger gobblers in the hand can be aged by spur development. Male 1-year-olds (and those younger) have spurs less than 12 millimeters (0.5 inch), 2-year-olds 12 to 24 millimeters (0.5 to 1.0 inch), and 3-year-olds more than 24 millimeters (1.0 inch). Right to left probable ages: 1 year, 2 years, 3 years, greater than 3 years. *Photo by J. Dickson, U.S. Forest Service.*

young gobblers in the field, but often it cannot be seen without parting the breast feathers of a bird in hand. By a gobbler's first spring after hatching, his beard is usually 7.6 to 12.7 centimeters (3 to 5 inches) long and amber tipped. A 2-year-old gobbler's beard is usually still growing and amber tipped, and normally it measures 17.8 to 22.9 centimeters (7 to 9 inches). Three-year-old and older gobblers have longer, black-tipped beards worn off from friction with the ground.

SEX DETERMINATION

Most fall hunting seasons allow the harvest of turkeys of either sex, but a few states permit gobblers only then. Whatever the situation, it is better conservation to harvest a gobbler instead of a hen.

Sex differences become apparent at about 4 months of age because of height, plumage color, and head and neck characteristics. Late-hatched juvenal turkeys during

fall can be difficult to sex in the field (Table 1). A bird in hand is most easily identified if the turkey is laid on its back and the breast feathers checked for black or brown tipping.

It is especially important to distinguish gobblers from hens in the field during the spring season, when only gobblers are hunted. Hens are conspicuous in early spring before continuous incubation, and many will come to a hunter's calling. About 30 percent of 122 turkeys called into range by the first author during 4 years of spring gobbler season in New York were positively identified as hens. A study in Missouri (Kimmel and Kurzejeski 1985) revealed a substantial number of hens were illegally shot during the spring gobbler season. Spring gobbler hunting before peak incubation periods caused substantial hen losses. Population models indicated that the observed levels of illegal hen kill could substantially reduce turkey populations. Carefully controlled spring gobbler seasons are biologically sound if the hunter is properly trained and exercises patience and caution in

Male and female young turkeys in the fall can be difficult to distinguish. Beards of males are just beginning to protrude through the feathers, but male breast plumage usually is obvious. *Photo by P. Pelham.*

A male turkey's beard grows continuously. But the end gets worn off from friction with the ground. *Photo by W. Zeedyk.*

Hunters should exercise extreme caution in distinguishing gobblers from hens. Center bird is adult bearded hen. *Photo by P. Pelham.*

Table 1. Fall sex identification of juvenal turkeys.

Identification feature	Male (jake)	Female (jenny)	Comments
Size	Considerably taller due to longer necks and legs.	Somewhat smaller.	Only useful if both sexes are together.
Body color	Darker or blacker because of black-tipped breast and midback feathers.	Browner in appearance because of brown-tipped feathers.	Perceptions vary with light conditions.
Head and neck	Pink to red skin around eyes, side of face, and throat. More bare skin on back of neck and head. Small, bulbous caruncles may be visible near base of neck; usually red.	Blue-gray head and neck. More feathering on back of neck and head. Bulbous caruncles rarely visible.	*Most useful* identification feature.
Beard	Often not visible because it usually does not protrude beyond breast feathers.	Not visible even in bearded hens of this age.	Generally not very useful.

identifying possible targets. Gobblers look quite different from hens (Table 2). In any season, gobblers are larger than hens, have iridescent black-tipped breast feathers, an almost featherless head and upper neck, and a beard. When gobblers are sexually active, they also can be distinguished by their red, blue, and white head colors, a strutting posture, and drumming and gobbling vocalizations.

Sign left by turkeys also can be useful in sex determination during fall or spring. Gobbler droppings are usually in a rough J or L shape. They are typically straighter, longer, and larger in diameter than hen droppings (Bailey 1956). In West Virginia, immature gobblers in the fall had droppings usually less than 10 millimeters (³⁄₈ inch) in diameter, while droppings of mature gobblers were as large as 16 millimeters (⁵⁄₈ inch) in diameter.

Table 2. Spring turkey sex identification characteristics.

Identification feature	Gobbler	Hen	Comments
Size	1½–2 times as large.	Much smaller.	Valid only when viewed together.
Body color	Appears black, dark, more iridescent.	Appears more brown, less iridescent.	Perceptions can vary as to light conditions.
Head and neck	Usually *white crown*. Blue or red face. Larger, red dewlap. Prominent carunculate skin with *large*, bulbous caruncles. Colors will fade or intensify depending on fear or sexual excitement.	White crown not present. Most of head blue-gray, but dewlap and caruncles often pink or red if excited as in mating season.	Substantial number of hens will show red or pink dewlap and caruncles. Caruncles always smaller. *Best identification feature.*
Feathering	Less feathering on back of neck and head. Bare skin of this area more visible.	Feathering extends farther up neck and head.	Must have a good view.
Beard	Almost always a visible beard *if* breast is visible.	1–29% can have beard.	Can be mistaken for a stick or limb.
Strut	Often displays and struts. Drums while strutting and at other times.	Does not strut or drum, but dominant hen occasionally displays.	Gobbler will not always display, strut, and drum when coming to call.
Snood	Sometimes very prominent and long.	Rarely visible.	Must be close to see.
Vocalizations	Adult gobbles and clucks. Subadults same and may yelp.	Often cuts, clucks, and yelps.	Either sex may come silently to your calling. Both sexes may come together.

Adult hen droppings were smaller (5 to 8 millimeters, 3/16 to 5/16 inches in diameter) and were looped, spiral, or bulbous in shape. Some droppings are not distinctive enough to tell sex. Both sexes void the soft, rounded, flattened, dark brown or black cecal dropping.

Tracks can be used to differentiate turkey sexes. Stride distance and overall track spread is greater for adult gobblers than for adult hens (Williams 1959). In

You can tell gobblers from hens by the sign they leave. Gobbler droppings are usually more a J or L shape than the spiral hen dropping. Gobbler tracks are larger than hen tracks. *Photo by J. Dickson.*

the eastern wild turkey, the distance from the middle toe claw to the back of the heel pad was less than 10.8 centimeters (4.25 inches) in hens, longer in gobblers (Mosby and Handley 1943:108). In an area of eastern and Florida turkey intergrade, Williams (1959) found the lengths of the 5 middle toe pads of hens were less than 5.56 centimeters (2 3/16 inches), and the pad length for gobblers was that much or greater.

GEOGRAPHICAL DIFFERENCES

Over thousands of years, natural selection has produced some physical differences in the wild populations of the various subspecies. Generally, turkeys living in the more moist, deciduous forest regions of the eastern United States have darker plumage, especially of the lower back and tail, than those living in the drier areas of the western United States. Birds of the 2 eastern subspecies have dark chestnut tips on the tail coverts and light chestnut tail tips. The same feathers of the Rio Grande are a light buff color, while the Merriam's and Gould's turkeys are light buff to white in these same areas (tail tips and tail coverts).

Northern birds, as well as those living at higher altitudes, tend to be larger but have relatively shorter feet and legs than those living more southerly, especially at lower altitudes (Aldrich 1967b).

RELATIONSHIP TO DOMESTIC TURKEYS

The domestic turkey originated from the wild turkey of Mexico, probably *Meleagris gallopavo gallopavo*, now thought to be extinct. But, through many generations of selective breeding, the physical conformation of the original ancestor has been drastically changed to a stocky, much heavier bird, suited for rapid growth and adapted to confinement. These conformation changes are perhaps best visualized by comparing a Clydesdale draft horse with a Thoroughbred racing horse. Inherent wildness, essential for the survival of wild turkeys, is lacking in domestic turkeys.

To meet popular demand, domestic turkeys have been developed with much broader, deeper breasts. Legs are shorter and heavier, are set farther apart, and lack the red or pink metatarsal color of the wild turkey. The domestic turkey's neck is thicker and shorter. The head appendages are more pronounced, with larger and heavier caruncles, dewlap, and snood. It is common for gobblers of some domestic varieties to weigh more than 13.6 kilograms (30 pounds) when 6 to 7 months old.

Eight breeds or varieties of various plumage colors are recognized (American Poultry Association 1985). The Bronze variety was the original domestic breed developed, and its plumage color most closely resembles that of the wild turkey.

THE OCELLATED TURKEY

The ocellated turkey of Mexico and Central America is more colorful than the North American wild turkey (Marsden and Martin 1946). It lacks the beard, both sexes have spurs, and body weights of adult gobblers are about half that of the wild turkey.

The main tail and tail covert feathers are more rounded, with a prominent, eye-shaped ocellus in the center of the subterminal band of each feather. These eye-shaped spots are a striking, iridescent purplish blue.

The bare skin of the head and neck of the ocellated turkey is blue, with prominent orange caruncles on the forehead and snood. Smaller orange caruncles are located more sparsely on the rest of the blue head and neck.

JOHN SIDELINGER

The wild turkey (above) has a thicker, longer neck than the domestic turkey.

Chapter 5

BEHAVIOR

William M. Healy
Research Wildlife Biologist
Northeastern Forest Experiment Station
Amherst, Massachusetts

"Under normal conditions, ability of hunters to harvest turkeys is equalled, or exceeded, by the eternally insidious elusiveness of the latter" (Bailey 1959:153). That statement may be criticized for attributing human characteristics to wild turkeys, but it captures the essence of what makes turkey behavior so fascinating.

Animal behavior is a subject that covers a large, diverse array of topics within the fields of biology and psychology (Grier 1984). Several books and monographs focus on wild turkey behavior, including portions of Mosby and Handley (1943), Hale and Schein (1962), Bailey (1967), Bailey and Rinell (1967), Latham (1976), Williams (1981, 1984), and Williams and Austin (1988). This chapter will not summarize all that is known about turkey behavior. Instead, it will give an overview of the life history and behavior of the wild turkey by following the events in a typical year, emphasizing how behavior influences ecological relationships. I will focus on aspects of social organization, vocalization, and learning that have had a great influence on the restoration and management of turkeys and on our ability to see and enjoy wild turkeys.

Behavior studies usually emphasize physical movements of animals in response to specific stimuli, but physiological changes — such as those in hormone levels — may also be included in behavioral studies. There have not been many experimental studies of wild turkey behavior because the bird is so elusive in its own habitat and so difficult to keep in a laboratory. Much of what we know about the wild turkey's sensory capabilities and response to stimuli comes from work with domestic turkeys (Hale and Schein 1962) or must be deduced from knowledge about other species (Dooling 1982).

My ideas about turkey behavior developed when I worked with turkeys I had raised from eggs collected in the wild. I spent 5 summers in the field playing the role of a hen, watching broods use a variety of habitats (Healy and Nenno 1983, Healy 1985). I observed most broods from hatching in spring until October, but one brood followed me until the next March. Grown birds were kept in 3 0.8-hectare (2-acre) wooded pens, and I watched these birds raise their own young both in the pens and as free-ranging, radio-tagged adults (Healy et al. 1975, Healy and Nenno 1978, Nenno and Healy 1979, Healy and Nenno 1985).

Those experiences gave me a unique perspective. Many people helped, and I will refer frequently to human-imprinted turkeys and "our" pens. Edward S. "Sam" Nenno's field skills kept the captive flocks healthy and made the radio-tracking studies possible.

Despite all that is known, much remains to be learned about turkey behavior.

Increasing day length in late winter triggers breeding behavior. Strutting and gobbling can usually be observed on the first warm days in late winter, but breeding occurs after flocks disperse from winter range. *Photo by G. Griffen.*

The gobble of an adult male can be heard for a mile on a calm spring morning. The gobble call attracts hens and occasionally other gobblers. *Photo by G. Smith.*

THE BEGINNING

Breeding Season

I begin discussion of the annual cycle with the breeding season. Breeding behavior is triggered primarily by the increasing daylight hours in spring, but unseasonably warm or cold weather may advance or delay breeding activity. Increased exposure to light causes a rise in the secretion of male sex hormones, which stimulates the development of sexual characteristics and the release of sexual behavior (Schleidt 1970, Lisano and Kennamer 1977b). The first signs of breeding activity are usually the gobbling and strutting of adult males. Breeding begins in February in south Texas but not until April in Vermont and across the northern edge of turkey range.

Courtship activity usually begins while turkeys are still concentrated in wintering areas, often in large flocks. The basic social organization of these flocks is a pecking order (Hale and Schein 1962:556). The pecking order is a linear hierarchy wherein each bird dominates, or pecks, those of lesser social rank. The highest-ranking, or alpha, individual dominates all others in the flock, and the lowest-ranking, or omega, individual is dominated by all others. The organization of large winter flocks is complex: Males and females have separate hierarchies, and there are pecking orders within and between flocks of the same sex.

The most detailed observations of wild turkey social organization were made by C. Robert Watts on the Welder Wildlife Refuge in Texas (Watts 1968, 1969; Watts and Stokes 1971). Watts was able to capture and mark most of the turkeys on the refuge, and he observed them

Wild turkeys occur in flocks and have a pecking order social organization. Male flocks are usually composed of birds that were raised together by 1 or more hens. *Photo by G. Wunz, Pennsylvania Game Commission.*

for several years in the semiopen habitat. Breeding on the wintering ground seems to be a unique characteristic of the population living on this refuge. But the social organization Watts described is probably characteristic of all races, so I will summarize Watts's work.

On the Welder Wildlife Refuge in the brushlands of south Texas, Rio Grande turkeys form winter aggregations composed of flocks of adult and juvenile females, juvenile males, and adult males (Watts 1969). Adult males were permanent residents, but large numbers of females and juvenile males moved to the refuge in winter, doubling the population.

Male flocks were sibling units composed of birds that had been raised together by one or more hens. The pecking order in these sibling units was established by fighting in late fall around the time brood flocks separated into male and female groups. As sibling male groups arrived on the wintering area, a second set of contests determined the rank of sibling units within the winter flock. Siblings fought as units, so larger groups were usually dominant.

Sibling males stayed together for life, but the size of the group decreased by deaths as the birds grew older. Of 32 male sibling groups that lived on the refuge between October 1965 and August 1967, 3 had 4 birds, 3 had 3 birds, 11 had 2 birds, and 15 were lone survivors. Of the 15 lone males, 13 were older than 3.5 years, and 10 of these were older than 4.5 years (Watts 1969:16).

Some breeding took place on the wintering ground, usually by the dominant male of the dominant group. As the breeding season progressed, the female flocks broke into groups of 2 to 5, which dispersed to nest. There was an almost complete shuffling of the female brood flocks, so sibling hens seldom ended up in the same nesting groups. At this stage of the breeding season, every male sibling group had the opportunity to be the only (and thus dominant) group with a specific flock of females. Thus the dominant male of each sibling group had the opportunity to mate after the large winter flocks of hens had dispersed to nest.

Use of traditional display grounds for breeding may be unique to Rio Grande turkeys living in grassland-brushland habitats of south Texas (Watts and Stokes 1971). Rio Grande turkeys living in the 24,300-hectare (60,000-acre) Sandstone Creek Watershed in western Oklahoma gathered into 1 winter flock of more than 300 birds (Logan 1973). Adult males displayed on the winter area, but breeding was not observed until the winter flock had dispersed and separated into flocks of 4 to 7 hens and 2 to 3 gobblers (Logan 1973).

The social organization observed by Watts (1968) on the Welder Wildlife Refuge, which included separate hierarchies for males and females and stable pecking orders within flocks of the same sex, seems to be common to all wild turkey subspecies. Dominant males do the breeding. Juvenile males seldom have the opportunity to breed, and there is good evidence that dominant males can suppress the physiological and behavioral development of subdominants (Lisano and Kennamer 1977a). Small groups of adult males seen strutting and gobbling in unison are probably siblings.

Popular literature frequently refers to the gobbler's territory. Turkeys have home ranges, but not territories. Territories are defended areas, but turkeys fight for dominance, not a piece of real estate. Turkeys are actually at the opposite end of the social spectrum from territorial birds. A territorial bird defends an area with specific boundaries and drives out all members of the same sex. A territorial bird cannot tell one individual from another and reacts instead to specific stimuli. The European robin, a typical territorial bird, will attack a tuft of red breast feathers just as vigorously as it would a real male (Hinde 1970:59). In contrast, pecking-order birds recognize individuals. They share home ranges, but rank has its privileges.

Courtship

The courtship behavior of turkeys consists of highly stereotyped behaviors called "fixed-action patterns" (Hale and Shein 1962). Each behavior pattern is usually elicited by a specific stimulus and is performed at a fixed intensity. In other words, the behavior patterns are per-

formed completely or not at all. An observer is unlikely to see only part of a strut or hear half a gobble.

The characteristic male courtship behaviors are the gobbling call and the strut. The function of gobbling is to call hens for mating (Williams 1984), but gobbling also seems to attract males (e.g., Watts 1968).

Gobbling is the only courtship behavior that can be elicited by several different stimuli, and it even occurs spontaneously in the absence of any outside stimulus (Schleidt 1968). Schleidt (1968) kept domestic male turkeys in soundproof chambers and recorded their gobbling activity through the year. Gobbling peaked in the spring, was absent in the summer, and occurred infrequently during fall and winter. When males are disposed to gobble, almost any sound will trigger it. But at other times, a gobble cannot be stimulated by sound. Overall, the best-known releaser of gobbling seems to be the yelping of a hen (Scott and Boeker 1972).

The frequency and pitch of the gobbling call ensures that it can be heard over long distances in most natural acoustical environments (Williams 1984:52). In most environments sound transmission can be maximized by

The gobbler's strut is a highly coordinated movement that functions as a short-range signal to the hen. *Photo by G. Wunz, Pennsylvania Game Commission.*

Mating sequence clockwise from top left: mounting, treading, and copulation. *Photos by W. Healy, U.S. Forest Service.*

calling from an elevated perch (Dooling 1982:118). So it is not surprising that males often gobble most while on the roost (Hoffman 1990).

The strut is a short-range signal usually directed toward a hen. The strut is a peculiar and highly coordinated movement. The gobbler takes 2 or 3 quick steps, spreads his wings and usually drags the outer primaries on the ground, and emits a low-pitched sound that seems to cause his body to tremble. Williams (1984) calls the sounds a "chump" and "hum" and considers them one call. The sound is often called "drumming," and its low frequency often makes it difficult for us to judge the distance and direction to the source. The hum sound fades rapidly and can usually be heard up to about 60 meters (65 yards) away. But under ideal conditions, the chump sound carries considerably farther. Gobblers usually begin and end the strut from the tail-fanned strutting posture. Gobblers that are with hens strut repeatedly for hours.

A hen signals her receptivity to a gobbler by assuming a characteristic posture. While holding her body horizontal and her neck flexed against her back, the hen walks directly in front of the strutting gobbler and may brush against him. She eventually crouches on the ground. The gobbler approaches slowly in the strutting posture and mounts from the rear.

The gobbler stands on the hen's back and treads slowly with his feet on her sides and around the base of the wings. Treading stimulates the hen to raise her tail and evert (turn outward) the oviduct, while the gobbler lowers his tail. Mating is completed with a brief orgasmic response as the cloacae come into contact. When mating is completed, the gobbler dismounts, and the hen stands and straightens her feathers with a vigorous shaking of the body and wings. If the gobbler is disturbed before copulation has taken place, the hen will remain crouched. The sequence from crouching to copulation can take 4 to 5 minutes. Breeding is promiscuous. Gobblers will mate with as many hens as possible. Gobblers take no part in nesting or parental activities.

The timing of reproduction is controlled primarily by day length, but local weather may advance or delay breeding activity. Nesting was delayed during an unusually cold spring in Missouri (Vangilder et al. 1987), and in south Texas, Rio Grande hens nest earlier when moisture conditions are favorable (Beasom 1970).

Gobbling begins well before mating and can often be heard on the first warm day of late winter. There are normally 2 peaks of gobbling. The first is associated with the beginning of breeding, when gobblers are looking for hens. The second occurs a few weeks later, when most hens are incubating (Bailey and Rinell 1967). In the Piedmont of South Carolina, the primary peak of gobbling occurred in mid-April and the secondary peak in late April (Bevill 1975). In Minnesota, the primary peak of gobbling occurred in the third and fourth week of April and the secondary peak in mid-May (Porter and Ludwig 1980). The peaks of gobbling for Merriam's turkeys in south-central Colorado were also in late April and mid-May (Hoffman 1990).

Exactly what makes a good day for gobbling remains a mystery. No single weather condition accounts for gobbling activity (Scott and Boeker 1972). In South Carolina, the best mornings to hear gobbling were with a clear sky, light breezes, and heavy dew. In Alabama and South Carolina, little gobbling was heard on rainy and windy mornings (Davis 1971, Bevill 1973). In West Virginia, I have heard vigorous gobbling during snow squalls and nothing at all on clear, calm mornings.

Gobbling behavior is extremely variable. The internal motivation of individual gobblers varies from day to day during breeding season. Even during peak periods of gobbling under ideal weather conditions, some males are silent (Hoffman 1990). After intensive study of individual males, Hoffman (1990) made the following generalizations: (1) some males gobble more than others; (2) adults gobble more than subadults; (3) gobbling is more frequent in the morning than in the evening; (4) more gobbling occurs on than off the roost; and (5) more gobbling occurs in the absence of hens than in their presence.

Nesting

The behavior of hens changes dramatically when they begin to nest. Most hens disperse from their winter range and actively avoid other hens while searching for a nest site and laying eggs. The secretive, antisocial behavior of nesting hens contrasts sharply with their usual gregariousness, and it is most evident near the nest. Laying hens may feed with other hens or mate with gobblers, but these social activities take place 0.8 kilometers (0.5 miles) or more from the nest site (Williams et al. 1975). In our pens, the first signs of nesting were a disintegration of the hen flock, pacing the fence line, and avoidance at our approach.

Movements from winter range to nesting sites are best described as a shuffle (Hillestad 1973, Hon et al. 1978). Wintering areas vacated by some hens may be used by others for nesting. Some adult hens return to sites used the previous spring (Hillestad 1973, Hayden 1980). Juvenile hens wander much more widely than adults, usually nesting outside their former home ranges (Ellis and Lewis 1967, Eaton et al. 1976, Hopkins et al. 1980). Except for the Merriam's subspecies, both juvenile and adult hens nest. Generally, the proportion of juveniles and adults nesting and their success rates are similar (see Williams et al. 1972). For some reason, juvenile Merriam's hens seem to nest less frequently than juveniles of the other races (Lockwood and Sutcliff 1985, Lutz and Crawford 1987b). The net result of nesting behavior is a thorough mixing of the population, with a movement of juvenile hens away from their natal ranges.

The nest consists of a shallow depression formed mostly by scratching, squatting, and laying eggs rather than by purposeful construction. Hens use their beaks to place and rearrange twigs and leaves in the nest, but this activity is minimal (Williams et al. 1972, Green 1982).

The hen selects a nest site in low cover or brush. *Photo by M. Rumble, U.S. Forest Service.*

Wild turkeys nest on the ground, and typically there are 9 to 12 speckled eggs in a nest. *Photo by R. Bradshaw, Texas Parks and Wildlife Department.*

Turkey nests have been found in most habitat types that turkeys occupy. Hens seem to select nest sites based on undergrowth characteristics, rather than the general habitat type (Holbrook et al. 1987). In Florida, about 80 percent of nesting hens selected a saw palmetto ecotone (transitional zone) between grazed glades and low oak scrub (Williams et al. 1972). In forested areas, nests characteristically are in places with moderately dense, woody understories that conceal the nest but allow the hen to view her surroundings from ground level.

Nests often are at the base of trees or against fallen logs, and usually within 200 meters (220 yards) of water. Hens frequently use recently logged areas, nesting in slash or beneath downed treetops (Hillestad 1973, Lutz and Crawford 1987b). Hens select sites nearer to a trail, road, or open area than would be expected if hens chose sites randomly (Exum et al. 1985, Holbrook et al. 1987). Trails and open areas presumably are used for access to the nest and as feeding areas during incubation.

Laying and Incubation

Laying a full clutch of 10 to 12 eggs takes about 2 weeks. Laying behavior is variable. Most hens lay 1 egg per day, usually in the middle of the day (Williams et al. 1972, Williams and Austin 1988). Hens seem able to delay laying, in response to disturbance or unusual weather conditions (Healy and Nenno 1985).

Laying hens approach the nest slowly and cautiously. In our pens, laying hens would move away from

the nest immediately if they encountered us or another hen as they approached their nest. Laying hens cover the eggs with leaves, so unincubated clutches are usually at least partially concealed. After incubation behavior starts, hens no longer cover their eggs (Williams et al. 1972, Green 1982).

Early in the laying period hens spend most of their time away from the nest, often feeding and roosting a mile from the nest (Williams et al. 1975). Hens spend more time on the nest as each egg is laid. In Florida, hens stayed on their nests an average of 55 minutes while laying each of the first 5 eggs. Incubation behavior began gradually changing with the laying of the sixth egg, and the length of incubation sessions increased with the laying of each successive egg (Williams and Austin 1988:101). Continuous incubation behavior sometimes begins when the last egg is laid, sometimes the next day (Williams et al. 1972). Some of our hens sat on the nest

Hens cover their eggs with leaves while they are laying the clutch.

After hens begin continuous incubation, they do not cover the eggs when leaving to feed. *Photos by W. Healy, U.S. Forest Service.*

most of the last day of laying, roosted in trees that night, and started incubation the next morning.

Occasionally, hens will roost in trees for the night even after having incubated continuously for several days (Williams et al. 1972). Incubating hens generally sit quietly, moving occasionally to turn eggs, rearrange litter with their beaks, and peck at passing insects (see Williams et al. 1972:102). Turning eggs is accomplished by raising the body and reaching under the breast with the beak. Hens sometimes stand to turn eggs. The frequency of egg turning is variable, but most clutches are turned more than once per hour (Williams et al. 1972, Green 1982).

Most incubating hens leave the nest every day to feed, but they sometimes skip a day (Williams et al. 1972). When they leave the nest, hens usually go directly to water, drink, defecate, and then feed. Incubating hens leave a characteristically large dropping, and I have occasionally found accumulations of these droppings along streams and logging roads. European biologists refer to the droppings of incubating red grouse as "clockers," and they use accumulations of these droppings to help locate nesting hens (Jenkins et al. 1963).

The time a hen spends off the nest varies from day to day. In Florida, feeding recesses averaged 1 hour and 50 minutes (Williams et al. 1972), and in Michigan they averaged 53 minutes (Green 1982). I think weather affects how long hens stay away from the nest. Hens seem to feed longer and in a more leisurely manner on hot than on cold days.

Continuous incubation takes about 26 days (Williams et al. 1972). Among 8 radio-tagged hens in West Virginia, the time from the start of continuous incubation until the brood left the nest varied from 25 to 29 days (Healy and Nenno 1985). Variations in observed incubation periods probably relate to the number of eggs in the clutch, how long the hen spent on the nest while laying, and how long she remained after the poults hatched.

Hatching begins with pipping and ends when the brood leaves the nest. Each poult cracks its own shell from inside by using a hard, sharp spike (called an egg tooth) on the upper beak. Breaking the shell is called pipping, and it takes about 24 hours. Pipping poults rotate within the shell, chipping a complete break around the large end of the egg. When pipping is complete, the poult frees itself from the egg with a few convulsive heaves. Poults are ready to follow the hen within 12 to 24 hours after leaving the egg. The entire process from pipping to departure takes about 2 days.

The social life of the turkey begins before it hatches and is well developed when it leaves the nest. At close range, pipping is audible, both the chipping sounds and a clicking vocalization. Hens respond to pipping sounds

Photo by M. Griffen.

Photo by L. Williams.

Hatching takes about 2 days. The social life of the poults begins with pipping, and the poults are imprinted to the hen before leaving the nest.

with soft clucking calls and with increased inspection and turning of eggs. Vocal communication between the hen and chicks in eggs synchronizes the hatching process and is critical to the survival of the chicks (Hess 1972).

A clutch of turkey eggs placed in a commercial incubator will hatch over a 2- or 3-day period. Hatching time can be shortened so all poults emerge within about 12 hours by playing a tape-recorded clucking call continuously during the last few days of incubation (Healy 1978).

Ecological Implications

Two contrasting social behaviors—winter flocking and spring dispersal—have had a great effect on the management and restoration of wild turkeys. The formation of winter flocks concentrates birds in small portions of their range, providing opportunities for trapping and transplanting them. The tendency to flock also holds small groups of transplanted birds together as effective breeding units. The dispersal of hens for nesting spreads birds into new habitats and allows populations to expand into unoccupied range.

Juvenile hens seem to be the key to range expansion. Juvenile hens often move 2 or 3 times as far as adults and frequently nest outside their former home range (Ellis

and Lewis 1967, Eaton et al. 1976, Exum et al. 1985). Between 1940 and 1969, turkey populations spread northward from south-central Pennsylvania across the contiguous forests of central Pennsylvania at about 8 kilometers (5 miles) a year. That range expansion continued across western New York without any restocking (Wunz 1973:208). The rapid spread of many restored populations is partly attributable to the dispersal behavior of nesting hens.

Dispersal and mutual avoidance of nesting hens may also provide a defense against predators and a mechanism for regulating populations. I observed 2 types of interference among nesting hens in captivity. The first was competition for nest sites. Occasionally, 2 hens would pick the same nest site, and usually the dominant bird would begin incubation on a clutch of mixed parentage. The subdominant hen would renest elsewhere. The second instance resulted in the loss of an entire pipping clutch when the incubating hen was attracted to calls of a young brood passing nearby. The calls of the young poults released brooding behavior in the incubating hen and she followed the brood. The hen's efforts to follow the poults disrupted that brood and resulted in the loss of her own clutch.

Such an event would be improbable in nature. But the fact that the calls of any newly hatched poult will attract an incubating hen makes it advantageous for nesting hens to avoid each other. The role of hen behavior in population dynamics deserves further study.

GROWTH AND DEVELOPMENT

Imprinting and Early Experience

The newly hatched flock must be ready to leave the nest about a day after hatching. The hen has been fasting for a day or more during the process of pipping, and she cannot wait indefinitely. Poults have food reserves in the yolk sac, but their chances for survival decline the longer they delay feeding. So poults must learn quickly to recognize the hen and respond to her calls. Imprinting, a special form of learning, facilitates this rapid social development. Imprinting has profound effects on adult behavior, so I will describe it in detail.

Imprinting forms a strong social bond between the female parent and offspring. Imprinting is characteristic of precocial birds, such as turkeys and ducks, that are down covered at hatching and must feed themselves in order to survive. Lorenz (1937) described the process and called it imprinting to distinguish it from ordinary associative learning. Imprinting occurs rapidly during a brief critical period. Turkeys must be imprinted within 24

Condition of the egg shells reveals the fate of the nest. Eggs that have hatched have largely intact shells, with each shell's large end neatly chipped away. *Photo by P. Pelham.*

Cryptic coloration enables the young poult to escape detection. *Photo by M. Rumble, U.S. Forest Service.*

Turkey poults are precocial. They can follow the hen and feed themselves within a day after hatching. Most behavior patterns—including the strut—are shown in their typical form by poults only a few days old. *Photo by P. Pelham.*

hours after hatching or the process will never occur. Imprinting happens only once, and its effects are irreversible. In essence, the young poult learns to recognize its species, and the lesson is never forgotten. The word "imprinting" describes this learning process, because at times the species image seems to be stamped instantly and indelibly in a young animal's mind. The rapidity with which imprinting takes place is essential for survival.

Most precocial birds, including turkeys, do not have an inborn image of their species. They will imprint to the first creature that provides parental care. It is easy, therefore, to imprint turkey poults to people, or to foster them under a broody hen of another species. Once imprinted, turkeys always respond to the foster parent as if it were a turkey. The behaviors of human-imprinted poults are not changed, but directed to people.

In nature, turkeys imprint to the hen before she leaves the nest. Imprinting has often been associated with following, but it is clear from watching hens and working with poults that they imprint before they can walk and follow.

Imprinting is also essential for the development of normal adult social behavior in wild turkeys. Poults that are raised together in commercial brooders do not imprint and do not show normal parental behaviors as adults. Poults that are imprinted by people prefer people

Hens and their broods spend most of their time feeding, but they will spend some time dusting each day if weather permits. *Photo by G. Wunz, Pennsylvania Game Commission.*

as sexual partners when they mature. But human-imprinted poults, when they cannot interact with people, exhibit normal sexual and parental behavior with their own species.

Poult Behavior

Amazing as it may seem, most behavior patterns exhibited by adults are shown in their typical form by poults only a few days old. Even the strut and sexual crouch are included in this early repertoire!

During the first 6 hours after hatching, poults sleep, rest, and preen. They will give a soft purr call when brooded, and a peep call when jostled or restrained. The peep call consists of 3 or 4 notes ascending in pitch and volume, and it will be heard throughout the summer when poults become separated from the brood flock. Between 6 and 12 hours after hatching, poults are usually completely dry, and they begin standing, walking, and

stretching. Human-imprinted poults will drink and eat mash during this period. Wild poults will venture from beneath the hen and explore the area around the nest (Healy et al. 1975).

Between 12 and 24 hours after hatching, poults become fully coordinated. They can run for several feet. They actively pursue insects and peck vigorously at any small object that contrasts with its background. Imprinting appears to be complete. Poults will follow the hen and will peep loudly if left alone. During this period, human-imprinted poults begin cycles of activity consisting of 20 to 30 minutes of brooding, then 5 to 10 minutes of feeding. Most hens will leave the nest during this period, apparently stimulated by the activity of their poults. Cold, wet weather will delay departure from the nest (Healy et al. 1975, Healy and Nenno 1985).

The hen leaves the nest slowly, clucking almost continuously, stopping frequently, and often turning back toward hesitant poults. This behavior gradually diminishes over the next 2 or 3 hours as poults are integrated into a cohesive flock. Within a few hours, the hen is able to move at a normal walking pace, and poults follow without difficulty. By this time, the flock will form a feeding line: Poults move side by side in loose, arc-shaped lines, pecking at food items as they go. In the lab, 2-day-old poults performed adultlike scratching in mash. But in the field, scratching was seldom seen until late summer, when mast began to fall.

Poults were able to give the putt call before leaving the nest. Putt calls were heard in most broods on the day they left the nest, usually when poults encountered unusual objects on the forest floor. Day-old poults would respond to the hen's trill and putt calls by freezing or darting beneath her.

Sunning behavior was observed in 2-day-old poults. Sunning birds reclined on one side and extended the upward wing and leg to expose a large surface area to direct sunlight. Thus, by the second day off the nest, wild poults are performing most of the characteristic feeding, locomotion, and maintenance behavior patterns.

During the first week, hand-reared poults performed the strut, the female sexual crouch, and the threat display typical of adults. These behaviors seemed to be used in play. Often, the same individual alternately performed male and female sexual patterns in rapid succession, usually when the flock was at rest. Play was often initiated by one bird strutting to a resting poult, and others soon joined the strutting. Strutting, threatening, and crouching would then be done in rapid succession. This sequence of behavior patterns was often followed by hopping and short bursts of running, and then was repeated. The strut included production of the chump and hum. The chump sounded like a puff of air. The hum was inaudible, but the feathers could be seen vibrating (Healy et al. 1975).

Flying developed gradually from the run-flap behavior during the first week. Seven-day-old poults could leap over barriers 23 centimeters (9 inches) high, and their running and flapping looked more like flying. True flight occurred on the eighth day. Thereafter, flying became an important behavior for escape from predators and for following the hen (Williams 1974, Healy et al. 1975).

Individual 3- and 4-day-old poults were seen dusting with hens. By the second week, dusting had become a flock activity. From the second week on, flocks generally spent ½ hour each day dusting, if weather permitted.

The next major development occurs when broods begin roosting in trees for the night. The age at which poults begin roosting in trees varies. It seems to depend partly on nighttime temperature. In Florida, turkeys first roosted in trees at 13 to 17 days of age (Barwick et al. 1970, Williams et al. 1973). In West Virginia, human-imprinted hens with broods began roosting in trees when poults were 21 to 28 days old.

Hen roosting with young poults. Poults begin roosting in trees when they are about 2 weeks old. *Photo by G. Griffen.*

Roosting in trees is an ecologically important event in the brood's development. Roosting in trees occurs at the beginning of a phase of rapid development during which the natal down is largely replaced by juvenile plumage (Leopold 1943a:134) and the diet shifts from predominantly insect to predominantly plant material (Hamrick and Davis 1971, Barwick et al. 1973, Blackburn et al. 1975, Hurst and Stringer 1975, Healy 1985).

This phase of behavioral and physical development is accompanied by a sharp decline in poult deaths and the development of hardiness that is characteristic of the adult. Most poult mortality occurs during the first 3 weeks of life (Glidden and Austin 1975, Everett et al. 1980, Speake 1980, Speake et al. 1985, Exum et al. 1987). Poults that survive the first few weeks to roost in trees have a good chance of surviving until autumn. Roosting in trees helps broods avoid ground predators and probably greatly reduces the chances that an entire brood will be lost in a single attack. Juvenile plumage affords greater protection from the elements than down, and it reduces a poult's dependence on the hen for brooding. Finally, the shift to an omnivorous diet affords the poults more opportunities to meet their nutritional requirements.

Beyond this point, we observed no new behavior patterns until the eighth week. Then broods began to form pecking orders, and true fighting occurred (Healy et al. 1975). Fighting usually began with mutual threatening. The threat posture consisted of an erect stance with the neck extended and the wings held slightly away from the body. From this posture, an aggressive bird could kick, strike with the wing, or peck an opponent. It was also prepared to deflect an opponent's blows.

The threat posture was accompanied by a short, staccato trill or rattle call. Threatening progressed to striking with the wings and kicking. Eventually a bird would grab another's beak or snood, and the birds would entwine their necks and push against each other with their breasts. Fights usually ended when one bird gained the advantage by getting a beak hold on the skin at the back of the opponent's neck. With this hold, the winning bird would force the other's head toward the ground until the loser was able to twist free. Winning birds generally followed losers for some time, threatening to peck and giving a 2-note "phew-phew" call. Fights were usually brief and never resulted in serious injury. Males fought more frequently than females, and fighting behavior continued through summer and into the fall.

By the fourteenth week of age, male and female poults are distinguishable by body size and plumage (Healy and Nenno 1980). As their secondary sexual characteristics become more prominent, males and females form separate pecking orders. The hen, however, remains dominant over all poults until the males leave for good. By autumn, the social order of sibling groups has been established. The young flocks are ready to enter the social organization of the local population.

Hen-Poult Relationships

The hen is the center of the brood flock, and vocal communications keep the poults in orbit around her. In experiments, domestic turkey hens that were deafened when they were poults would incubate eggs normally but killed their own young immediately after hatching. Normal domestic hens presented with silent, dummy poults attacked them after a short time, but dummy poults with speakers emitting recorded peeps were not attacked (Hale and Schein 1962:533). Such experiments have not been performed with wild turkeys, but it is clear that constant vocal communication among hens and poults modifies individual behavior.

Poults that were raised by human-imprinted hens could discriminate the voice of their own hen from that of others, and they showed a strong preference for their own hen. Hens, though, do not recognize the calls of their own poults. Hens respond with equal intensity to the calls of poults in other broods and to tape-recorded lost-poult calls (Kimmel 1983).

The behaviors of separate 4-day-old broods raised by human-imprinted hens in a 0.8-hectare (2-acre) pen illustrate the relationships. Poults in one brood had green leg bands and the other yellow. The broods crossed paths while feeding at 10:40 A.M. Two yellow poults came within feet of the green hen and followed her, but both began peeping rapidly (65 calls per minute). Both hens responded by pacing and calling, and the broods were thoroughly mixed. By 10:50, the hens had separated. One yellow poult followed the green hen. This poult continued to peep, and the green hen responded by calling and turning toward it. The yellow poult fed with the brood, and its peep calling gradually declined. By 11:30, the yellow poult was giving purr calls. It stayed with the green hen and brooded under her that night. The next morning, the yellow and green broods again passed near each other, and the yellow poult returned to its own hen without any reaction from either hen.

Hens do not seem to recognize their own young until they are 8 to 10 weeks old. During the first 4 weeks after hatching, human-imprinted hens did not react to changes in the number of poults with them. Their maternal behavior was the same whether accompanied by one or a dozen poults. When the poults began to develop their own pecking order, hens began to respond to poults with typical adult social behavior (usually threats). This shift in social behavior during the eighth to twelfth week was accompanied by the replacement of juvenile body plumage and the development of secondary sexual characteristics.

The poults I raised could distinguish individual human voices. Human-imprinted poults also showed a strong preference for the person who spent the most time with them. It was always easy for the person who imprinted the brood to call them away from temporary caretakers.

Between the ages of 3 and 8 weeks, broods from different hens readily combine. The hens' responses to each other determine whether multiple broods form. Some human-imprinted hens were aggressive and drove other hens away. Some were social and joined with hens from their winter flock. One radio-tagged, imprinted hen formed a multiple brood with a wild hen and her brood. The numbers of poults and their ages do not seem to matter. Young poults mix with few signs of aggression, even when they differ in age by 2 to 3 weeks.

Once broods begin to establish a pecking order (about 8 weeks of age) formation of a multiple brood is more complex. I think most of the large flocks that are seen in autumn are temporary aggregations of several broods, each with its own pecking order. The broods come together in excellent habitat to feed, form a pecking order among brood flocks, and then go separate ways.

Pecking orders are established by fighting. Vigorous battles among broodmates in late summer will establish a relatively permanent pecking order. *Photo by P. Pelham.*

By 12 to 16 weeks of age, human-imprinted flocks were quite aggressive toward one another. Attempts to combine flocks resulted in pandemonium. Usually older flocks dominated younger ones, but sometimes large groups of younger poults were dominant. I have seen some spectacular displays of calling, running, and flying when wild broods come together in late summer.

Hens are always socially dominant over poults, but hens do not necessarily lead daily flock activities. Hens may lead or follow, responding appropriately to the calls of poults and to other stimuli. From the time poults leave the nest, they start most types of feeding activity. Brooding sessions usually ended and feeding began when poults emerged from beneath the hen, who would stand and follow. Hens continued to follow and feed with poults as long as poults were giving purr calls.

If a poult began peeping, the hen would increase the volume and rate of yelping. If peeping continued, the hen would move toward it. Hens would run toward shrieking poults. As poults became tired or cold, they would give low-volume peep calls. Hens would respond by pausing and calling. If several peeping poults approached, the

hen would crouch to brood and poults would come to her. The leadership role of the hen was most obvious during the first 3 to 4 weeks when poults required brooding. Her leadership became less obvious as poults matured.

Hens clearly led when moving from the nest to brood range and when broods moved to new areas. Broods might move 0.8 kilometer (½ mile) or more in an hour. When hens led, they walked at 3 to 5 kilometers (2 to 3 miles) per hour, and even day-old poults could follow. Small streams were not a barrier (Williams et al. 1973). Down-covered poults floated in water like corks and swam well. Hens might move to new areas after disturbance by people or predators, but some movements seem spontaneous (Hayden 1979a).

Hens led broods when selecting spots for night roosting on the ground, and hens also led for the first few weeks after they started roosting in trees. Later in the summer, poults might fly to roost before the hen.

Feeding poults walked and ran, but broods stayed in the same general area, changing direction frequently and often moving back and forth through an area. The speed of feeding flocks was inversely proportional to the quality of the habitat. Poults literally ran through hardwood stands with open understories and little food. Under these circumstances, hens often took the lead and returned to good feeding areas.

When predators threatened, hens were in charge. Free-ranging human-imprinted hens were seen driving a broad-winged hawk and a red fox away from their broods. One hen even chased a sleeping great horned owl from its perch (Healy and Nenno 1978). Similar instances of Rio Grande hens chasing red-tailed hawks through the air have been reported from the Kerr Wildlife Management Area in Texas (Butts 1977). In one instance, an incubating hen flew from its nest and chased a red-tail that was hunting nearby.

Hens signaled approaching danger with putt calls or a combination of putts and trills. Down-covered poults would dive under cover and sit motionless. They would stay until the hen called them out of hiding. Hiding and freezing was seen in poults as old as 10 weeks. But as poults matured, they were more likely to respond to putting by freezing in an alert posture, watching for the source of danger. Depending on the type of predator and how close it was, the poults might flush or run.

Poults apparently have an innate ability to recognize some potential predators. Poults that I raised responded to snakes and hawks on their first encounter. I do not know how early these responses developed, but poults as young as 14 days reacted appropriately.

Poults usually reacted to snakes by putting, and they behaved like songbirds mobbing an owl. Poults would surround the snake, putting excitedly and stretching forward to see it. Poults would jump or flush if the snake moved, and they continued reacting until the snake moved off.

Bailey and Rinell (1967:97) described a wild turkey hen and 8 poults responding in exactly the same way toward a red fox. The birds walked in a semicircle, necks craned, yelping in a high-pitched tone. This type of behavior seems to reinforce the young turkey's ability to recognize and react to potential predators. Snakes were encountered frequently, and human-imprinted poults became increasingly more alert to their presence as the summer progressed. Maintaining a strong reaction to potential predators would be beneficial when these birds matured and raised their own young, because snakes prey on eggs (Speake 1980) and on young poults (Stringer 1977:24).

Poults were particularly sensitive to objects moving overhead. By the fourth week, poults responded much like adults. They came to attention, often giving a soft whine call when hawks were soaring in the distance. The sudden appearance of a hawk at treetop level would cause the birds to flush into heavy cover.

Poults responded to high-flying airplanes by coming to attention and giving whine calls. Poults occasionally reacted to butterflies and large hovering flies, particularly if they had just been alarmed by hawks, crows, or vultures. This same type of heightened wariness was observed in Rio Grande turkeys that had been harassed by golden eagles (Thomas et al. 1964).

Hens have a remarkably long association with their poults. Most broods stay together 4 or 5 months. Female poults may remain with the hen until the start of the next breeding season. I think the long parent-young association is an important learning experience and is partly responsible for the adaptability of wild turkeys.

Under some conditions, young broods can survive the loss of the hen. Bailey (1955) reported 2 instances of broods surviving without hens in West Virginia. One brood was 3 to 4 weeks old when the hen was lost. The brood survived until October, but the young turkeys did not possess the normal fear of people and automobiles. Although poults have innate responses to some objects, it is clear they also learn from the hen. Poults will approach what the hen approaches, and they will avoid what she avoids.

Daily Activities and Habitat Use

Broods spend most of the day feeding. Time budgets recorded for 2 free-ranging imprinted hens with broods showed that during the first 11 days after hatching, one brood averaged 86 percent of the day feeding and the other averaged 95 percent. These broods walked at a rate of about 200 meters (220 yards) an hour while feeding, but they changed direction frequently and sometimes retraced their steps. So the linear movement in an hour was often quite small. One hen spent from 2 to 32 percent of the day brooding, and the other spent from less than 1 to 14 percent of her time brooding. The largest proportion of brooding-to-feeding activity occurred when a brood of 7-day-old poults fed in a grassy clearing that was wet from nighttime rain. The hen stopped to brood 4 times during the morning for periods of at least 30 minutes. That afternoon when the vegetation was dry, the brood fed without stopping for 3.5 hours. Because of these daily variations, there was little relationship between the age of the brood and the time spent brooding.

Neither brood spent much time dusting, sunning, or preening during the first 11 days. Maintenance behaviors accounted for 1 to 8 percent of the daily activity budget for one brood, but only 2 percent or less for the other. Although I did not record time budgets for broods more than 3 weeks old, I think the figures would be similar for older broods. Throughout the summer, broods probably spend 90 percent of their waking hours feeding.

Poults eat enormous quantities of food. At the average feeding rates I observed, a 2- to 3-week-old poult would eat 3,600 items, mostly small insects, in a day

(Healy 1985). The rapid growth of poults requires a steady intake of nutritious food. Male poults grow from about 0.05 kilograms (1.8 ounces) at hatching in June to 3.5 kilograms (7.7 pounds) by the end of September. Female poults at 4 months weigh about 2.8 kilograms (6.2 pounds) (Healy and Nenno 1980).

During this period of rapid growth, human-imprinted poults always seemed hungry. Poults fed throughout the day, and then they packed their crops during the last 30 minutes before roosting. Fully distended crops were visible on poults of all ages as they settled for the night. In contrast, full crops were never seen during daytime feeding, regardless of what or how fast the birds were eating. The crops of several poults accidentally killed during feeding observations contained just the last few items they had eaten.

I tried on several occasions to see how much natural food a poult would eat, but never found an upper limit. In mid-July, I was making an all-day observation of a 53-day-old brood. At 12:30 P.M., the poults began feeding in a raspberry patch. I picked and fed 19 raspberries to a poult banded red-green, who ate them in rapid succession and immediately returned to feeding with the rest of the brood. In the next 3 minutes, I picked 18 more raspberries, and "red-green" repeated the performance. At that time, I could feel nothing in his crop. During the next 10 minutes, I picked 37 more raspberries, all I could hold in my hand, and again "red-green" ate them in rapid succession and continued feeding with the flock. At that point I gave up. This behavior explains why crops collected from feeding poults seldom contain large quantities of food (Hamrick and Davis 1971, Hurst and Stringer 1975, Stringer 1977).

Human-imprinted and hen-reared broods usually stopped feeding only when they became wet, or they encountered a dusting spot, or the sun had just come out. During the 5 summers that I observed broods, I thought on only a few occasions that broods stopped feeding because they were full.

Poults and hens probably do not need to drink water while they are feeding on insects and succulent plant material (Exum et al. 1985). Broods that I watched in West Virginia frequently fed in and around water. Streams and wooded wetlands were in all the brood ranges, but only rarely were individuals seen drinking. Drinking was never a flock activity during the summer.

The size of a brood's home range increases as poults grow (Hillestad and Speak 1971). Young, down-covered poults have the smallest ranges and the most specialized habitat requirements. For 3 or 4 weeks, poults eat mostly insects, which are generally better sources of protein and energy than plant materials. The best feeding areas contain a rich mixture of forbs and grasses that provide insects and permit poults to move freely (Healy 1985). As poults grow, they use more habitat types and food

sources. By midsummer, poults can move through rank grass and blueberry thickets.

Most broods will range over an area of 100 to 200 hectares (250 to 500 acres) during the summer, but summer ranges are variable even in the same region (Hillestad and Speak 1971, Williams et al. 1973, Holbrook et al. 1987). Part of the variation in brood range size is probably related to habitat quality (Exum et al. 1987). Poults moved slowly where food was abundant, but rapidly where food was scarce. Broods characteristically use small portions of their home range intensively for a couple of weeks and then move to a new center of activity (see Wigley et al. 1986b). These centers of activity may be widely separated, so the daily range is much smaller than the seasonal home range.

Ecological Implications

The process of imprinting, the pecking order social organization, and the prolonged hen-poult relationship have had profound effects on the domestication of turkeys and on the management of wild populations. The process of imprinting greatly facilitated the process of domestication. We will never know how Native Americans first acquired their flocks, but I can easily imagine someone finding a hatching clutch and bringing the poults home. In warmer climates, the poults could have survived with little care, and no cages or pens would have been required to keep the birds around the settlement. When the need arose, however, flocks could have been confined in close quarters because of their pecking order social system. Birds that are truly territorial cannot be kept in groups in confined spaces. They fight until only a single bird survives.

The social processes that promote domestication prevent the production of wild turkeys on game farms. Imprinting is absolutely essential to the normal social development of wild turkeys. Birds that have not been imprinted show serious deficiencies in parental behavior. Long association with the hen also seems essential. The process of hatching eggs in incubators and raising poults in mechanical brooders interrupts social experiences that are the foundation for normal adult behavior in wild turkeys. Even if wild eggs were brought to the game farm each spring, the birds hatched from them and released in the fall would not be behaviorally wild.

FALL AND WINTER

The fall and winter is a period of maintenance and relative stability in wild turkey behavior and habitat use. By early autumn, pecking orders have been established within flocks, and the behavioral repertoire of juveniles is essentially complete. Sexual and parental behaviors will not be seen until spring. The body growth of juveniles ends by the beginning of winter (Healy and Nenno 1980), and most flocks settle into stable winter ranges.

The shift from summer to fall range involves a change in habitat type and often a movement of several kilometers (Eaton et al. 1976). The shift is normally from field to forest habitat. As the area's growing season ends, succulent vegetation and insects become less available in fields and mast becomes more available in the forest. In good mast years, the shift in habitat use can be abrupt.

Young turkeys begin eating acorns as soon as they encounter them in fall. By mid-September poults could swallow even the largest of acorns from red oak and chestnut oak. Turkeys swallow acorns whole and grind them in the gizzard. When human-imprinted poults ate acorns, the grinding and thumping sounds produced by the gizzard could be heard for several meters. By mid-September, poults also crush and grind cherry pits; younger poults digest only the flesh of the fruit and pass the seeds whole. Even after acorns are available, poults continue eating insects, seeming to prefer large ones such as grasshoppers, walking sticks, and caterpillars.

The size of the mast crop usually determines how far flocks move from summer to fall range and the pattern of their daily movements. In southern New York, movements from summer to fall range were about twice as far in years of poor mast production (Eaton et al. 1976). In northern Missouri, in years when mast was scarce, turkeys moved for the winter to river bottoms where row crops were available. When mast was abundant, turkeys did not move from fall range and continued to use woodlots (Kurzejeski and Lewis 1990). In autumn, turkeys wander widely in search of food. By trial and error, flocks will gradually concentrate where food is available.

Mast crops also influence the vulnerability of turkeys to fall hunting (Menzel 1975). In Pennsylvania, large kills usually occur in poor mast years (Wunz 1979, 1986a). When mast is scarce, flocks are drawn to small areas where food can be found, and they frequent fields and farmlands where they can be seen. When mast is abundant, flocks are dispersed through the forest, and the movements of individual flocks are less predictable. Birds do not settle into winter range until snow accumulates and hunting season is over.

In many parts of their range, turkeys concentrate into relatively large flocks and use traditional wintering areas (e.g., Logan 1973, Vander Haegan et al. 1989). The Rio Grande and Merriam's races have the greatest propensity to use traditional roost sites night after night (Hoffman 1968, Watts 1968). Eastern birds may sometimes roost in the same trees for several consecutive nights (Kilpatrick et al. 1988), but generally they use different sites on successive nights (Healy 1977).

By late autumn, male and female juveniles usually have formed separate flocks and have moved into winter range. *Photo by U.S. Forest Service.*

Weather and topography affect the selection of winter night roosts (Tzilkowski 1971). In the mountains of West Virginia, turkeys roosted during fair weather in hardwoods on knolls and at the edges of benches. Though exposed to the elements, these sites offered a good view of the surrounding area and—in case of danger—clear sailing in any direction. White-tailed deer often chose similar sites for bedding. On several occasions, I found where turkeys had roosted directly over bedded deer. In steep country, turkeys often sailed into roost trees from the slope above, rather than fly up from directly beneath the trees.

During winter storms, turkeys roosted in hemlock stands along the edges of major stream valleys. Hemlocks offered good protection from the elements and often were near seeps and springs, which were preferred feeding sites. Some flocks used the same hemlock stands on many occasions during the winter (Glover 1948, Bailey and Rinell 1968:41, Healy 1977).

Turkeys usually select the largest trees available and roost as high in them as they can comfortably perch (see Mackey 1984, Lutz and Crawford 1987a). This tendency was so strong that it was difficult to keep human-imprinted turkeys out of the tops of trees in our pens even by clipping all the flight feathers on one wing. The turkeys would climb leaning branches and leap from limb to limb to get into tree crowns and then gradually work their way to the top. Unfortunately, wing-clipped birds seemed unaware of their limitations and attempted to sail from the roost in the morning as if they were fully capable of flight.

Turkeys have adapted to agriculture. Feed lots, standing corn, and dairy-farm manure spreads have become important feeding areas where winters are severe (Porter et al. 1980, Vander Haegen et al. 1989). Turkeys select agricultural sites bordering woodlots that provide roosting cover. Often they fly directly from roost to feeding sites.

Throughout most of their range, turkeys congregate into large winter flocks in areas that offer shelter from the elements and reliable food sources. *Photo by National Wild Turkey Federation.*

Turkeys respond to snow by restricting their daily movements and selecting favorable habitats. In general, the deeper the snow the smaller the daily range (Glover 1948). As snow depth increases, turkeys seek out areas where snow is melted or blown away, or where trees and shrubs hold food above the snow. In mountainous areas turkeys often move to lower elevations and south slopes where climatic conditions are most favorable (Hoffman 1968, Austin and DeGraff 1975, Wunz and Hayden 1975). Turkeys can scratch through 30 centimeters (1 foot) of snow, but I found that 10 centimeters (4 inches) of snow greatly restricted scratching and caused turkeys to seek bare ground at springs and seeps (Healy 1977).

In areas of extensive forest, turkeys travel and feed along streams and other water courses (Lewis 1963, Healy 1977). In the Northeast, seeps are important winter feeding areas (Bailey and Rinell 1967:288, Wunz and Hayden 1975, Wunz et al. 1983). Groundwater percolating to the surface melts the snow, exposing seeds and providing a rich substrate for invertebrates and plants. In West Virginia, turkeys typically followed small streams from seep to seep. They would probe and scratch in each seep they encountered, and they often followed a major watercourse by alternately working up and down its small feeder streams (Healy 1977).

Turkeys respond to the worst winter weather by spending more time on the roost and flying between roosting and feeding sites (Hayden 1980:264). Glover (1948) observed turkeys roosting continuously for 4 days during a winter storm. Experiments with penned birds indicate turkeys can fast for up to 2 weeks (Hayden and Nelson 1963), which seems to be about the limit for wild birds (Wunz and Hayden 1975:65). Snow depths of 15 to 20 centimeters (6 to 8 inches) limit the turkey's ability to walk, and flocks will begin to travel by flying. Powder snow of 30 to 38 centimeters (12 to 15 inches) will essentially stop all turkey movement on the ground (Austin and DeGraff 1975).

VOCALIZATIONS

Lovett E. Williams, Jr., (1984) provides an excellent description of the voice and vocabulary of the wild turkey. I cannot improve on Williams's descriptions and data, and I have used his names for calls. I will make a few generalizations that provide a behavioral and ecological background for interpreting turkey vocalizations.

The wild turkey's vocabulary consists of 28 distinct calls (Williams 1984). The gobble is given with fixed intensity; the other calls can be given with a range of intensity. Each type of call has a general meaning, but variations in delivery allow transmission of complex messages. For example, the alarm putt may be considered a relatively simple call in number of notes, note length, and

pitch, but variations in alarm putts transmit information about the degree of alarm. In general, the louder the putt the greater the alarm. Depending on its volume, an alarm putt may cause nearby birds to raise their heads and look toward the source or flush instantly.

The information in any type of call is modified by the context in which it is given, the delivery of the call, and the postures and movements of the caller. With our imprinted birds, a poult giving alarm putts and moving toward an object on the ground usually attracted other poults. A poult putting loudly, looking upward, and moving toward cover usually flushed other poults. This type of variation makes it difficult to interpret what we see and hear in the field because the same type of call may produce different responses.

Turkeys can recognize the voices of other turkeys. Individual recognition depends on individual variation. It is reasonable to think of turkey voices as having a degree of variation similar to what we associate with human voices. Individual variation and the ability to distinguish it have several practical implications. Individual male turkeys can be identified from tape recordings of their gobble calls. Dahlquist et al. (1990) used this technique to identify Gould's turkeys and monitor range use by this endangered (only in New Mexico and Arizona) subspecies in southwestern New Mexico. These authors were also able to distinguish tape-recorded gobbles from different subspecies.

Turkey hunters can sound like several turkeys by using several calling devices. Most hunters own several calls and develop elaborate personal myths about which one works under particular conditions. There is biological justification for using several calls, and the knowledge that turkeys recognize individual voices can often be put to good use. A turkey's ability to recognize individual turkey voices implies that it could learn to recognize individual human callers. There was some evidence that wild hens learned to recognize tape-recorded kee-kee calls of lost poults that were played to attract broods (Kimmel 1983).

WILDNESS AND ADAPTABILITY

Turkeys are impressive in their ability to be both wild and adaptable. With equal facility, they can be insidiously elusive or brazenly opportunistic. I will end this chapter with a discussion of wildness and adaptability and a description of some things turkeys learn and remember that relate to these broad aspects of behavior.

A. Starker Leopold (1944), in his classic study, *The Nature of Heritable Wildness in Turkeys*, defined wildness as the inherent behavior patterns and other adaptations that permit the successful existence of free populations. Audubon (1840–44) equated wildness with an instinctive ability to recognize predators, and it is clear that human-imprinted turkeys instinctively recognized some types of predators.

Gerstell and Long (1939) and Leopold (1944) emphasized sensory and physiological capabilities. Keen senses are an obvious component of wildness. The turkey's hearing is considered comparable to human hearing, and the turkey's eyesight is considerably better than human eyesight. But wildness in turkeys seems more than a collection of instincts and keen senses, and Leopold's definition does not distinguish wild turkeys from any other species that maintains a free living population. Perhaps the turkey's wildness is better characterized by the hard stare of an old hen than by scientific prose.

The nature of wildness became more than an academic question when states attempted to restore turkey populations by using artificially propagated birds. Missouri began raising turkeys around 1927 (Leopold 1944), and the Pennsylvania Game Commission opened its wild turkey game farm in 1929 (Gerstell and Long 1939). Differences in behavior between wild and game-farm stock were obvious immediately, and early workers focused on the heritable aspects of wildness. In Pennsylvania, elaborate efforts were made to introduce wild genes into game-farm stock (Gerstell and Long 1939). In Missouri, A. Starker Leopold (1944) was concerned with the damage that might be caused by introducing game-farm genes into wild populations. The debate about game farms and the nature of wildness continued for decades. But eventually it became pointless because of a technical innovation—the cannon net—and the inherent adaptability of wild turkeys.

Perceptions of the turkey had changed during European settlement of North America as the species adapted to changes in the landscape and human activities. In 1892, Charles Bendire reported the following description of turkeys in Florida written by Dr. William L. Ralph: "One can hardly believe that the wild turkeys of today are the same species as those of fifteen or twenty years ago. Then they were rather stupid birds, which it did not require much skill to shoot, but now I do not know of a game bird or mammal more alert or more difficult to approach" (Bendire 1892).

Audubon (1840-44:42) implied that similar changes in behavior were widespread. "Turkeys are still to be found along the whole line of the Allegheny Mountains, where they have become so wary as to be approached only with extreme difficulty." I think Audubon and Bendire were describing the complex interaction between wildness and adaptability that has made the species successful, not a change in wildness or intelligence. The adaptability that these early writers describe has only recently been recognized.

Wild turkeys are far more adaptable than anyone imagined in the 1930s, when populations were at their lowest levels. When modern management began, turkeys were considered specialists requiring large, isolated tracts of mature timber. After all, that is where remnant flocks occurred. Now turkeys thrive in the suburban Northeast, on midwestern farmland, and in intensively managed southern pine forests. Thirty years ago, none of those habitats would have been considered suitable turkey range. Today turkeys are viewed as generalists capable of surviving in many habitat types, including some that have been extensively modified by man (Lambert et al. 1990).

The earlier view of wild turkeys as behavioral specialists was consistent with the fact that individual behavior patterns were stereotyped and usually given at a fixed intensity. It was not recognized that sets of stereotyped behavior patterns could be organized in a way that allowed for flexibility and adaptability.

The overall flexibility in turkey behavior comes from the way simple reactions and behavior patterns are organized in feeding and exploratory activity. Bailey and Rinell (1968:17) succinctly describe turkeys as "'omnivorous opportunists,' that is, they eat whatever acceptable items are available, both plant and animal." Such a diet does not restrict turkeys to any specific habitat type, and turkey feeding activity usually includes a strong component of exploration. Except during the breeding and nesting seasons, turkeys spend most of their time in search of either food items in a particular habitat type, or another habitat type in which to feed.

Feeding turkeys are constantly exploring their environment—walking, observing, and manipulating objects in their beaks. Pecking and manipulating objects in the beak is an important part of their general exploratory activity. Continual exploration enabled human-imprinted poults to find new sources of seed and fruit as soon as they ripened during the summer. Constant exploration allows wild turkeys to use their home ranges efficiently and to change home ranges as seasonal requirements change.

Learning and memory have a role in this behavioral flexibility and the efficient use of habitat. Most of the wild turkey's learning capabilities involve recognizing and remembering either individuals of their own species or features of their own landscape. I found little written about learning and memory, but this aspect of turkey behavior is interesting and has practical application to the study of wild turkeys.

A pecking order social organization requires the ability to recognize and remember individuals. Turkeys recognize each other by head characteristics and voice. Turkeys can recognize large numbers, perhaps hundreds, of individuals and can remember individuals for many months. I kept flocks of 30 individuals that maintained stable pecking orders. And Rio Grande birds formed winter flocks of several hundred, with well-defined hierarchies (Watts 1969). In our pens, adult birds seemed to recognize flock mates after being separated for 6 months. In the fall, juvenile birds were usually treated as strangers if they had been away from the flock more than 2 or 3 weeks. But juvenile birds were changing rapidly in appearance. Their pecking orders were always less stable than those of adults.

Human-imprinted turkeys also recognized individual humans by voice and appearance. Even young poults remembered and responded to us as individuals when we had been away several weeks. One odd aspect of individual recognition indicated persistent memory. Human-imprinted turkeys assigned a sexual identity to us, usually during autumn as the flock pecking order developed. Gobblers who considered me female always strutted to me in the spring. Those who identified me as male were usually threatened when I approached and often attacked with wings and spurs during the breeding season. Hens were more subtle. During breeding season, some hens called and followed me around the pens, and they crouched as I approached. Other hens avoided me or threatened me if I approached too close.

Once a turkey had assigned a sexual identity to us, it maintained that relationship for life. Sexual identification was independent of our actual human sex. Within any brood, some birds would treat me as male and other birds as female.

Wild turkeys learn from each other. The behaviors involved are complex. Some behaviors attract the attention of other turkeys to specific objects. Good examples of behaviors that attract attention are (1) hens feeding poults; and (2) the mobbing of snakes. Hens will knock large insects to the ground and call poults to them (Healy et al. 1975). Mobbing episodes started when one bird spotted a snake, and then they built to a peak through mutual reinforcement.

Among our imprinted poults, much learning occurred by imitation. Turkeys are attracted by the feeding activity of other turkeys. If one poult encounters a concentrated source of food, the rest of the flock are soon aware of it. Poults were strongly attracted by any object in the beak of the hen or another poult. This attraction led to a comic behavior that we called "grab-run." When a poult caught an insect that was too large to swallow whole, it would run from the flock. But other poults would usually see the insect, and a free-for-all chase would develop. The insect would be grabbed by one poult after another until it was finally torn apart.

Although imitative behavior often had comic aspects, it had the practical effect of transferring information about food sources among flock members. By following older birds, younger birds clearly learned not only about their home range but also proper reactions to predators and other hazards.

Turkeys remember the topography of their home ranges. This ability is most obvious when laying hens return daily to their well-concealed nests. I think turkeys usually know just about where they are in their home ranges and have a sense of spatial orientation similar to our own. Human-imprinted turkeys clearly remembered the locations of pens and of preferred food sources. On many occasions, they demonstrated the ability to take a new and direct path from one familiar point to another.

Turkeys recognize changes in their surroundings, particularly in areas they use frequently. Wayne Bailey pointed out this behavior when he was preparing a trap site. Wayne always prepared trap sites with dummy cannons to look exactly as they would when the net was in place. Wayne explained that once turkeys began using the site, they would be frightened by any change in its appearance.

This reaction to change was a nuisance around our pens. If equipment was moved or the site disturbed in areas we visited daily, the turkeys would crane their necks and putt. They avoided the altered spot and sometimes flushed away from it. The response was clearly to the change, not to the object that had been moved or added. Such a reaction might be triggered by moving a log, raking leaves, or moving a wheelbarrow. The alarm response usually subsided within minutes, and turkeys would approach cautiously and explore the area. But on occasion, turkeys were so disturbed by changes such as raked leaves or piled brush that they avoided the area for days.

It seems a paradox that the wild turkey is considered the epitome of wariness and that its domestic counterpart is a symbol of stupidity. The apparent stupidity of domestic turkeys is a result of intense selection against maternal behavior and wariness. Most meat-producing varieties are propagated by artificial insemination. They have been selected for such gross breast development that few adult males can even walk, let alone breed. It is not surprising that such creatures are considered stupid.

The speed and grace of the wild races stand in marked and beautiful contrast to the qualities of their domestic relatives. The wild turkey has been able to adapt to massive changes in the flora and fauna of North America through a unique combination of keen senses, instinctive responses, and specific learning abilities. Given reasonable protection, this handsome and interesting creature will continue indefinitely to share our habitats and enrich our lives.

Chapter 6

FOODS AND FEEDING

George A. Hurst
Professor
Mississippi State University
Mississippi State, MS

Wildlife managers need to know about the type, quantity, and quality of food used by wild turkeys of all ages throughout the year. Among the many factors that affect a turkey population, food is a very important one. The search for nutritious food is a major turkey activity. Studies of turkey food habits (diet), using several techniques and with variable sample sizes, have been conducted for all the wild subspecies. Many lists have been published of the turkey foods identified in crops, in stomachs (proventriculi), in gizzards, in droppings, and through field observations (Davison and Graetz 1957). Major summaries of turkey food habits are available (Schemnitz 1956, Schorger 1966, Korschgen 1967). This chapter presents information on turkey diets by age class, feeding behavior, nutrition, and other topics related to food. Also, this chapter identifies needs for more information.

POULTS

"Unfortunately there is a 'blind spot' in the life of the wild turkey. . . . This is the period following hatching, until the young [poults] reach sufficient size for flight" (Stoddard 1963). Poult refers to turkeys from the moment of hatching to age 4 weeks. Thereafter, the designation is juveniles.

A poult exists on nutrients in its yolk sac for about 3 days. The young turkey greatly increases its body weight during the first 4 weeks (Healy and Nenno 1980) and has a high (28 percent) protein demand during this period (Marsden and Martin 1955).

Food Habits

For a long time, managers have thought insects were an important food for poults (Stoddard 1936, Legion 1946, Wheeler 1948, Schorger 1966, Bailey and Rinell 1968, Latham 1976). Managers were advised to provide preferred-type "insect-catching grounds" (Stoddard 1963).

"Insects are of very great importance to young turkeys, even while confirming data are meager" (Korschgen 1967). Confirming data have been collected. A total of 386 poults that had been adopted by chicken or turkey hens and had fed along edges of fields and in several forest types in Mississippi ate primarily insects (79 percent of dry weight) in their first week after hatching. The percentage of the diet in insects declined each successive week (Table 1). Major insects eaten, in descending order of dry weight, were beetles (Coleoptera), true bugs (Hemiptera), grasshoppers (Orthoptera), and leafhoppers (Homoptera). Plant foods eaten were fruits and seeds of dewberry and seeds of sedges, nut-rushes, and panic grasses (Hurst and Stringer 1975).

Poults that fed in mature pine forests in Mississippi had a ratio of animal-to-plant food of 60 to 40 (4 to 7 days old) and 37 to 63 (8 to 14 days old). In contrast, poults that fed in fields had an animal-to-plant ratio of 79 to 21 (age 3 to 7 days) and 72 to 28 (age 8 to 14 days). Insects were far more abundant in fields than in pine

Table 1. Ratio of animal (mostly insects) to plant foods eaten by wild turkey poults, age 3–38 days, in Mississippi.[a]

Age (days)	Percent	
	Animal	Plant
3–7	79	21
8–14	54	46
15–21	37	63
22–38	13	87

[a] Poults were imprinted on chicken or turkey hens (Hurst and Stringer 1975).

forests. Small beetles, leafhoppers, sedge and nut-rush seeds, dewberries, and blackberries were the main foods (Owen 1976). Human-imprinted poults pecked at or primarily ate insects (leafhoppers, flies, plant bugs) for their first 5 weeks after hatching in West Virginia (Healy et al. 1975).

In Florida, however, 21 wild-raised poults ate mostly (75 percent) plant items such as stargrass seeds, leaves, stems, and huckleberry fruit. Beetles made up most of the animal food (Barwick et al. 1973). Reasons the poult diet was mostly plant food are unknown. Perhaps the sample size was too small, or the poults fed in an area where insects were not abundant (Williams and Austin 1988).

Similarly, 18 poults age 8 to 23 days and adopted by chicken hens fed on a 2-year-old loblolly pine plantation. They ate mostly (94 percent) seeds (nut-rush, sedge, panic grass) and blackberry fruits. Insects accounted for only 6 percent of the total volume. But, in that plantation, insects were scarce and seeds were very abundant (Hurst 1988a).

In slash pine plantations 10 years old or older in south Alabama, 70 droppings from wild poults (less than 4 weeks old) contained 60 percent insects and 40 percent fruit and seeds of blackberry, blueberry, huckleberry, and noseburn (Exum et al. 1985, 1987).

In Pennsylvania, invertebrates accounted for 57 to 99 percent of the total number of items eaten by im-

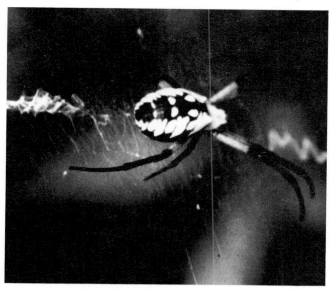

Spider—many different arthropods are consumed by poults. *Photo by G. Wunz.*

printed poults, age 1 to 4 weeks, that fed in several habitats. Insects eaten in food plots were beetles, true bugs, and leafhoppers. Grasshoppers were eaten most often in an old field, while flies and moth larvae predominated in the diet of poults that fed in forests (Nenno and Lindzey 1979).

Diets of 2 human-imprinted broods (up to 4 weeks old) were largely soft-bodied insects (e.g., leafhoppers, plant bugs), on all sites in West Virginia. Most pecks (65 to 95 percent) were to get animal matter. Composition of the poults' diet was similar to sweep-net samples of insects (Healy 1985).

Most studies of poult food habits were based on poults adopted by chickens or imprinted on humans. But 3 wild-raised poults, about 7 days old, had eaten 90 percent animal matter and 10 percent plant matter in Alabama. The most abundant insects in their crops were true bugs and tree- or leafhoppers. By weight, though, grasshoppers were dominant (Hurst 1989a).

Most studies of poult diet have focused on the eastern and Florida wild turkeys. Few such studies have been conducted with the other subspecies. Green vegetation and insects were thought to constitute the essential diet of Merriam's young (Ligon 1946). The crop of one Merriam's poult in New Mexico contained only insects (moths, grasshoppers, leafhoppers, and flies) (Zeedyk 1982). Arthropods, primarily beetles and grasshoppers, were the main items in diets of Merriam's poults in South Dakota (Rumble 1990).

In summary, poult diets consist mostly of insects, and the ratio of animal-to-plant food changes with poult

Grasshopper—an important food for the rapidly growing poult. *Photo by H. Williamson, U.S. Forest Service.*

age. Variations can be expected because of sample type and size, habitat type and vegetative conditions, poult age, and food abundance and availability. Insects or other arthropods seem to be eaten in accordance with their availability and abundance.

Feeding Habits

Williams (1973) said, "A turkey without its behavior is not a whole turkey." Information on poult feeding behavior is limited. Broods of human-imprinted poults were cohesive on the second day and were well synchronized on the third day. Pecking was observed after the first hour of life. The grab-run behavior, in which a poult seizes a food item and then runs to avoid other poults, was noted at 20 to 24 hours of age. A feeding line (a loose arc-shaped line), with poults advancing side by side and pecking at food items, was observed at 3 days of age (Healy et al. 1975).

Poults (broods) adopted by turkey or chicken hens that foraged in fields, forests, or both moved either ahead of or out beside the hen in a loose feeding line, frequently changed positions, fed independently, and ran about pecking. Distance from the hen increased from approximately 3 meters (10 feet) at age 1 week to 6 meters (20 feet) in the second week. Poults pecked at items that moved and that appeared different in shape, color, or luster. Poults examined all plant parts, including the underside of leaves and the surface of ground litter. At first, poults pecked at many nonfood items, but gradually they learned what was and was not edible (Stringer 1977).

Pecking is the fundamental feeding behavior, and it has been classified into 4 categories:

(1) Peck-chase: Poults peck at an item. If it moves, it is chased until it either is no longer visible or is caught and eaten;

(2) Stalk-peck: Poults 4 to 5 days old see an item, move to striking distance—2 to 5 centimeters (1 to 2 inches)—lean forward with an outstretched neck, and swiftly peck;

(3) Jump-peck: Poults 6 to 7 days old see an item on an overhanging plant, jump up, and grab it;

(4) Peck-tug: Poults 1 to 2 days old grab items (often not food) and tug at them. Later, tugging is used to dislodge moth and butterfly larvae and fruits or seeds (Stringer 1977).

Poults seldom scratched, and they were not fed by turkey hens. Most items eaten were small (Stringer 1977, Healy 1985). A poult often grabbed a large item (e.g., field cricket) and vigorously shook its head side to side, immobilizing the arthropod. Insects too large to swallow whole were pecked at, crushed with the bill, picked up, and thrown down until the pieces were small enough to swallow (Stringer 1977).

Competition between poults often occurred, and food was stolen by poults. The grab-run behavior was used to escape from pursuing poults (Stringer 1977).

Poults less than 12 weeks old rarely filled their crops (Healy et al. 1975). But poults less than a week old that fed in clover patches filled their crops to capacity with leafhoppers in approximately 30 minutes (Stringer 1977).

Brood behavior has also reflected contentment or food abundance. Feeding poults communicated almost continuously by chirping (peeping), chattering, or purr-calling. Purr-calling was at its highest frequency during feeding and became very distinctive when poults entered an area with many insects. A lack of food items led to much peeping and chattering. Poults quit foraging and fell in behind the hen (Healy et al. 1975, Stringer 1977). Other behaviors, calls, and hen-brood interactions have been documented (Williams et al. 1973a, Healy et al. 1975). Observations of imprinted and adopted poults (broods) lead to the conclusion that poults gather their own food. Pecking is the main feeding behavior, and poults form feeding lines at a very young age.

Broods began feeding after the dew had dried in the morning, and they fed most of the day, except for a midday inactive period (D.W. Speake personal communication: 1987). Hens with a brood seemed to move in a zigzag pattern while feeding. The overall pattern was movement in a straight line rather than circling or at random. When feeding in a field, hens with broods covered about 91 meters (300 feet) in 15 minutes. The pace was faster in open woods (Stringer 1977). Daily movements of hens with broods at forest-field edge averaged 0.5 kilometer (⅓ mile) (Hillestad and Speake 1970).

Poult feeding rates have been related to food abundance or feeding conditions (Martin and McGinnes 1975, Nenno and Lindzey 1979, Anderson and Samuel 1980, Victor and Tipton 1982, Healy and Nenno 1983, Rogers 1985). While feeding in fields or clearings where invertebrates were abundant, poults stopped to rest, dust, preen, or sun. But poults traveled more rapidly and never stopped to rest while feeding in forested sites, and they may not have gotten enough to eat (Nenno and Lindzey 1979). Poult feeding rates (pecks per minute) were positively related to vegetative conditions (density) and invertebrate abundance (Healy 1985).

Though some data have been gathered on poult behavior and feeding methods, several other areas are not documented and should be investigated: relationships or interactions of insect abundance and availability, habitat types and vegetative conditions, and poult survival rates. Time and energetic costs of gathering required nutrients (insects) and avoiding predation are of paramount importance but have not been studied.

Water

Water is essential for the well-being of poults, but they may not need free (unbound) water (Latham 1976). Poults adopted by chicken hens drank from pools, puddles, ditches, or anywhere water collected, and they did drink dewdrops (Stringer 1977). I have observed wild poults drinking from water-filled ruts along spur roads in pine plantations.

Telemetry data on hens with broods has provided interesting information. In hot and dry (May through July) upland slash pine plantations in south Alabama, hens with broods seldom crossed or came within 100 meters (328 feet) of available water (creeks). Broods remained for weeks in plantations that did not have free-water sources other than dew. Average moisture content of spring and summer poult food items was 72 percent (Exum et al. 1985). Similarly, there was no known free-water source in loblolly pine plantations in hot, dry central Mississippi where broods were raised. In conclusion, poults need water and will use free water from pools, ditches, dewdrops, and so on. But they can also get moisture from succulent insects, forage, and fruits.

Nutrition

Nutritional requirements of domestic turkeys have been reported (Marsden and Martin 1955, Robinette 1968, Warnick and Anderson 1973, National Academy of Sciences 1977). But comparable information on wild poult nutrition is lacking. For both domestic and wild poults 0 to 4 weeks old, energy, protein, amino acid, vitamin, and mineral requirements might be similar. Wild poults, however, likely expend much more energy because they must search for and select a nutritious diet.

Wild turkey poults have a high protein demand (28 percent). Male poults increase their average weight from 75 grams (2.6 ounces) at age 1 week to 364 grams (12.8 ounces) at age 4 weeks (Healy and Nenno 1980). Amino acid levels and patterns in 7 insect orders (e.g., Coleoptera) were similar, and they were like amino acid levels and patterns in wild turkey poult carcasses 1 to 4 weeks old. Poults are what they eat: Their diets match their body composition. A 7-day-old poult weighing approximately 70 grams (2.5 ounces) would have to eat about 12 grams (0.42 ounces) live weight of insects to meet minimum amino acid requirements for just that day (Hurst and Poe 1985).

Poults grow rapidly and are constantly molting (shedding feathers), so protein demand remains high. Poults continue to eat many insects, even though the percentage of animal matter declines during the first 4 weeks after hatching. Protein content averaged 76 percent in spiders, 57 percent in insects, 11 percent in sedge seeds, and 14 percent in panic grass seeds (Hurst and Poe 1985). Protein content of undigested poult foods in droppings was 68 percent. Calcium averaged 2.0 percent, which was above that required (1.2 percent). But the phosphorus level of 0.3 percent was below the required 0.8 percent. Carbohydrates averaged 19 percent, and fat was 5 percent (Exum et al. 1987).

Caloric content of insects averaged 5.3 kilocalories per gram, about 20 to 25 percent greater than that of vegetation (Martin and McGinnes 1975). The average adult insect was 66 percent digestible, and average moisture content of arthropods (insects and other invertebrates) was 65 percent (Stiven 1961). Average metabolizable energy of moisture-free invertebrate food was 3.11 kilocalories per gram. Domestic poults, 0 to 4 weeks old, require 2.80 kilocalories per gram of metabolizable energy (National Academy of Sciences 1977).

Vitamin and mineral requirements for maximum rate of growth for domestic poults have been established, but no such data have been reported on wild poults. There are not enough data to analyze mineral or vitamin values of natural poult diets (Gluesing and Field 1982), and this phase of poult nutrition needs investigation.

Feeding and Brood Habitat

Quantity, quality, and availability of food, as well as feeding conditions (vegetation and weather), affect poult movement and survival (Hillestad and Speake 1970, Putnam et al. 1975, Pybus 1977, Hurst 1978, Hayden 1979a, Hurst and Owen 1980, Pack et al. 1980, Anderson and Samuel 1981, Healy and Nenno 1983, Healy 1985). The relationships of food abundance and feeding conditions to poult survival rate have not been evaluated, however.

High poult death rates (70 to 87 percent) have been reported (Glidden and Austin 1975, Speake 1980, Speake et al. 1985, Exum et al. 1987). Poult mortality has been attributed to cold, wet weather (Wheeler 1948, Powell 1965, Healy and Nenno 1985), but predation is the most probable cause of most poult deaths (Metzler and Speake 1985). Poult survival was directly related to the type of brood habitat selected by successful hens (Everett et al. 1980). Various habitat types have served as brood habitat, but knowledge is lacking on insect abundance and availability and poult survival rates in different habitats.

JUVENILES

Food Habits

Growth rates for juvenile turkeys remain high, but only limited data are available on their diets. When 21 juvenile turkeys 40 to 105 days old fed in mixed field-forest habitats in July to September in Alabama, they ate 73.2 percent plant and 26.8 percent animal matter. Crops contained grass seeds (61.5 percent), with Bahia grass accounting for 48.6 percent. Grasshoppers were the most important (15.5 percent) animal food. Crop volume ranged from 5 to 179 cubic centimeters (0.3 to 10.9 cubic inches) with an average of 54.7 cubic centimeters (3.3 cubic inches) (Hamrick and Davis 1971).

Crop and gizzard contents from poults and juveniles (15 to 164 days old) combined in Florida averaged 72.8 percent plant and 27.2 percent animal foods from April through November. Grass seed was a major food item (17.4 percent), as were acorns, stargrass seeds, arrowhead tubers, panic grass seeds and leaves, and fruit. Animal foods were mostly moth larvae, grasshoppers, and beetles (Barwick et al. 1973).

Availability and utilization of turkey foods were studied in 11 habitat types in Alabama. Droppings from juveniles were collected from June through September, with most from August through September. The 4 most important foods, based on percent volume and frequency of occurrence, were seeds of carpet, Bahia, and crabgrass, and blackberries. Blackberries were most important in June and July, carpet grass in August, and crabgrass in September. The ratio of plant-to-animal food changed from 42 to 54 in June to 84 to 11 in July, perhaps reflecting mixed ages of turkeys. Foods in grassland habitats seemed to be used in proportion to their abundance (Blackburn et al. 1975).

Major foods in droppings of juveniles (4 to more than 8 weeks old) in south Alabama were insects, fruits, green vegetation, and seeds of paspalum and crabgrass (Exum et al. 1987).

From limited data, it looks as if juvenile turkeys have a diet similar to that of adults: approximately 75 to 85 percent plant matter and the remainder animal matter. Important foods were grass seeds, fruits, insects, and green forage.

Feeding Habits

Pecking probably is the major feeding behavior for juvenile turkeys. They began stripping grass seed heads at 6 weeks old, and typical fall feeding behavior was observed at 18 weeks old (Healy et al. 1975). Scratching probably becomes a feeding method in the fall.

Nutrition

Information on nutritional aspects of juvenile wild turkey diets is lacking. Nutritional analyses of undigested foods in juvenile (4 to 8 weeks old) droppings

found these percentages: protein 32, carbohydrates 48, fat 13, ash 6, calcium 0.8, and phosphorus 0.2 (Exum et al. 1987). Nutrient requirements for domestic turkeys 4 to 8 weeks old include 2.90 kilocalories per gram of metabolizable energy and 26 percent protein. In juveniles 8 to 12 weeks old, required energy increases and percentage of protein decreases (National Academy of Sciences 1977).

Juvenile turkeys require water, and some authors noted that they regularly drank from pools or ponds. Because juveniles are more mobile than poults and can get free or metabolic (forage, fruits, insects) water, it should not be a limiting factor.

ADULTS

Food Habits, Eastern Wild Turkey

As with any species, growth in the wild turkey is affected by food quantity, quality, and distribution (spatial and seasonal). Also affected are reproduction, habitat use, and movements.

Naturalists looked at what turkeys ate. In the early 1800s, John J. Audubon said, "The wild turkeys cannot be said to confine themselves to any particular kind of food, although they seem to prefer the pecan-nut and winter grape. . . . They eat grass and herbs of various kinds, corn, berries, and fruit of all descriptions. I have

Adult and young wild turkeys eat ripening blackberries in summer. *Photo by H. Williamson, U.S. Forest Service.*

Table 2. Principal foods of the eastern wild turkey.[a]

Season			
Winter	Spring	Summer	Fall
acorns[b]	acorns	grass leaves	crabgrasses
grass or sedge leaves	grass or sedge leaves	miscellaneous plants	animal foods
corn	oats	blackberries	acorns
grapes	miscellaneous plants	animal foods	grass or sedge leaves
dogwood	bluegrass	bluegrasses	tick trefoils
miscellaneous plants	corn	acorns	miscellaneous plants
sumac fruit	beechnuts	panic grasses	beechnuts
ferns or mosses	sedges	cherries	grapes
animal foods	burdock	crabgrass	cherries
beechnuts	wheat	huckleberries	sheep sorrel
sedges	animal foods	paspalum	panic grass
cherries	chufa	smartweed	grasses

[a] Revised data from Korschgen (1967).
[b] In descending order from highest to lowest volume in crops, stomachs, and droppings.

even found beetles, tadpoles, and small lizards in their crops" (Peattie 1940). Also in the 1800s, "In spring, when fresh vegetation shoots forth, they subsist almost entirely upon it. . ." (Caton 1877, in Bailey and Rinell 1968).

Judd (1905) examined the stomachs and crops of 16 wild turkeys and found they contained 85 percent vegetable matter (fruit 33 percent, browse 25 percent, seeds 20 percent, mast 5 percent, and green vegetation 2 percent) and 16 percent animal matter (insects and other invertebrates). It was thought that turkeys ate acorns, pecans, beechnuts, chinquapin, and other nuts, as well as fruits of black gum, holly, dogwood, and huckleberry in Louisiana (Alexander 1921). Bent (1932) concluded: "Various other kinds of berries, fruits, and insects are doubtless eaten when available, as turkeys will eat almost anything they can find in these lines."

Biologists also have studied what turkeys eat. A total of 3,244 turkey droppings, representing all months, from the Ozark Mountains of Missouri were examined. The year-round diet closely reflected availability of various plants and insects. Plants (78 genera) made up approximately 75 percent, and insects 25 percent, of the annual diet. During spring and summer, many plants were eaten, indicating a "general sampling of vegetation." From April through October, "choice apparently depended upon local abundance and availability." Major foods eaten were leaves and seeds of grasses and sedges, fruits, and acorns. Beetles, grasshoppers, and ants comprised 80 percent of the animals eaten (Dalke et al. 1942).

Crops and gizzards of 537 turkeys, most collected in November and December in Virginia, contained roots, tubers, bulbs, stems, buds, leaves, flowers, fruits, seeds, pods, capsules, and seed heads. These foods represented 80 plant families and 354 species. Animal foods consisted of adults, eggs, egg cases, larvae, nymphs, pupae,

and cocoons of more than 313 species. The bulk of the food eaten (94.7 percent) was plant material, and the "top 10" were acorns; beechnuts; dogwood fruit; seeds and leaves of grasses; corn; the fruit and seeds of grapes, poison ivy, and sumac; and the fruits and leaves of forbs and vines (Mosby and Handley 1943).

As information accumulated on turkey diets, wildlife managers formed opinions on what turkeys preferred. A list of choice, less desirable, and minor plant and animal foods was prepared (Davison and Graetz 1957). Studies of turkey diets using crops and stomachs or droppings (Blakely 1937, May et al. 1939, Good and Webb 1940, Webb 1941, Kozicky 1942, Glover and Bailey 1949) were summarized by Schorger (1966) and Korschgen (1967). Hard mast (e.g., acorns and beechnuts), leaves and seeds of grasses and sedges, other seeds, soft mast, corn, and animals constituted the bulk of the turkey's annual diet (Table 2). Schorger (1966) concluded: "The turkey consumes a great variety of animal and plant foods." Hard and soft mast were major items, when procurable. But succulent plant matter, particularly grasses, was very important. Succulent vegetation was considered essential in the breeding season because it provides vitamins.

Reports on turkey diets made available more recently are presented on a regional basis (Tables 3, 4, and 5).

Northeast. Turkeys ate hard mast (e.g., acorns, beechnuts, black cherry pits, and ash seeds), soft mast (e.g., dogwood and grape), grains (e.g., corn and oats), grass and sedge seeds and leaves, other green forage, and animal matter (Table 3).

In West Virginia, turkeys ate tubers, bulbs, and rhizomes of spring beauty, dogtooth violet, and toothwort gathered by scratching (Bailey and Rinell 1968). Grains

Table 3. Major foods of the eastern wild turkey in the northeastern section of the United States.

Season	Source	State	Foods
fall	crop	WV[a]	oats, corn, grasses, beechnuts
all	crop	WV	hard and soft mast, grasses
fall	crop	PA[b]	acorns, dogwood, grains, grapes, grass, animals
winter	crop	PA	acorns, grapes, corn
fall	crop	PA[c]	beechnuts, tubers, moss, cherry, ash
winter	crop	PA	fern heads, corn, green forage, buds
spring or summer	crop	PA[d]	acorns, grass and sedge leaves, animals
fall or spring	crop or droppings	NY	hard mast (beech, cherry, oak, and ash)
winter	crop or droppings	NY	mast, ferns, sedge leaves, forbs, buds and stems of beech and maple
spring or summer	crop or droppings	NY	tubers, flowers, sedge and grass seeds
winter	observations	MA	corn, barberries, multiflora rose hips, corn silage, grasses

[a] West Virginia = Bailey et al. (1951), Pennsylvania = Hayden (1969), New York = Eaton et al. (1970), Massachusetts = Vander Haegan et al. (1989).
[b] Southern Pennsylvania, oak-hickory forest.
[c] Northern Pennsylvania, beech-maple-cherry forest.
[d] Both southern and northern Pennsylvania.

were significant foods because of emergency feeding programs, or turkeys fed from manure spreads, corn stubble, or silage.

In areas with deep snow, turkeys ate ferns and fern fruiting heads, green forage at springs and seeps, and buds and stems of beech, sugar maple, and hop hornbeam. "When snows are heavy and prolonged, turkeys eat such emergency items as white pine and hemlock needles, lichens, mosses, etc." (Bailey and Rinell 1967).

Midwest. Major foods were hard mast (e.g., acorns, pine and hackberry seeds), grains (e.g., corn, wheat, and milo), grass and sedge leaves and seeds, green forage (e.g., forbs), soft mast (e.g., dogwood and greenbrier), and animal matter (Table 4). "Turkeys are oppor-

Table 4. Major foods of the eastern wild turkey in the midwestern section of the United States.

Season	Source	State	Foods
spring	crop or gizzard	MO[a]	acorns, corn, green forbs, grass and sedge leaves, animals
fall or spring	droppings	IL	corn, acorns, pine seed, grass and sedge leaves, milo
all	droppings	IN	grass and grass seeds, green forage, insects, mast (acorns, dogwood, and greenbrier)

[a] Missouri = Korschgen (1973), Illinois = Lancia and Klimstra (1978), Indiana = Kirkpatrick et al. (1972).

Table 5. Major foods of the eastern wild turkey in the southern section of the United States.

Season	Source	State	Foods
spring	crop	TN[a]	hackberry seeds, wheat, acorns, grass, dogwood, wood sorrel
winter	crop or droppings	MS	pecans, grape seeds, green forage
winter	crop or droppings	MS	acorns, green forage, dogwood
fall	droppings	AL	grass, dogwood, insects, corn, acorns
fall	crop	FL	grapes, grass seeds, corn, forbs, saw palmetto seeds, grass leaves, mast (poison ivy and black gum), animals
all	droppings	AL	green forage, grass seeds, pine seeds, acorns, insects, soft mast (blackberry, french mulberry, and dogwood)
all	crop	MS and LA	hard and soft mast, green forage, wheat and soybeans, invertebrates, tree flowers
summer	droppings	AL	soft mast, grass seeds, green forage, animals
all	droppings	AL	green forage, insects, chufa, acorns, soft mast, grass seeds
all	droppings or observation	LA	hard and soft mast (hackberry, acorns, pecan, swamp dogwood, pepper vine, poison ivy, blackberry), grasses, green forage (oats, wheat, and ryegrass), corn

[a] Tennessee = Tabatabai and Kennedy (1984), Mississippi = Kennamer and Arner (1967), Mississippi = Parker (1967), Alabama = Barwick and Speake (1973), Florida = Barwick et al. (1973), Alabama = Kennamer et al. (1980a), Mississippi and Louisiana = Landers (personal communication: 1989), Alabama = McGlincy et al. (1986), Alabama = Exum et al. (1987), Louisiana = Hyde and Newsom (1973).

tunists, eating whatever acceptable items are most available at different seasons" (Garver 1987).

A total of 101 kinds of plant foods and 35 animal foods were identified from crop and gizzard contents of 698 gobblers harvested in April in Missouri. Hens (sample included 16) ate slightly larger amounts of animal foods. Also, hens ate greater amounts of calcium-rich snails than did gobblers (Korschgen 1973).

South. Turkeys ate hard mast (e.g., acorns, pecan, and pine), soft mast (e.g., dogwood, black gum, poison ivy, grape, french mulberry, blackberry, huckleberry, blueberry, and noseburn), insects, snails, and forage and seeds of grasses (Table 5).

When grass seed and insects became less available, gobblers in Alabama shifted their ranges in the fall from fields and pastures to forests, as mast became available (Barwick and Speake 1973).

Oaks are prime fall and winter food items for wild turkeys wherever they occur throughout their range. Clockwise from above: White oak; Post oak; Live oak; Water oak; Gambel Oak.

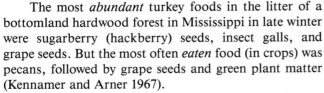

The most *abundant* turkey foods in the litter of a bottomland hardwood forest in Mississippi in late winter were sugarberry (hackberry) seeds, insect galls, and grape seeds. But the most often *eaten* food (in crops) was pecans, followed by grape seeds and green plant matter (Kennamer and Arner 1967).

In an area dominated by loblolly pine plantations in Alabama, green foliage was the most often eaten food,

American beech—an important fall and winter food during good production years in eastern deciduous forests. *Photo by J. Dickson, U.S. Forest Service.*

Dogwood fruit is readily consumed by wild turkeys in fall and winter throughout eastern forests. *Photo by L. Williams.*

Sumac fruit is available to wild turkeys during fall and winter. It can be important when other foods are covered by snow. *Photo by H. Williamson, U.S. Forest Service.*

Clovers are excellent planted food for wild turkeys, winter through spring. *Photo by L. Williams*

Paspalum produces a large seed eaten by wild turkeys when it matures in summer. *Photo by J. Dickson, U.S. Forest Service.*

Panicum is another grass seed commonly eaten by wild turkeys. *Photo by G. Wunz, Pennsylvania Game Commission.*

American beauty-berry fruit and other soft mast are consumed during summer and fall. *Photo by S. Oefinger, U.S. Forest Service.*

Grape is a favorite fall food. *Photo by U.S. Forest Service.*

followed by grass seeds, soft mast, insects, and hard mast. Summer foods were more available in pine plantations, age 1 to 12 years. But foods utilized in the 3 other seasons were most abundant in other habitat types (Kennamer et al. 1980a).

Incubating hens in southwest Alabama ate primarily blackberries (41 percent), other fleshy fruits, grass seeds, green vegetation, and animal matter (14 percent) (McGlincy et al. 1986).

Along the Mississippi River in Louisiana and Mississippi, turkeys ate hard mast (mainly papaw and pecan), soft mast and foliage from forbs (26 species), wheat and soybeans, and invertebrates. During March of 1983, however, when most of the area was flooded, turkeys remained up in the trees and ate flowers from sycamore and cottonwood trees (L. Landers personal communication: 1989).

In Mississippi, I have seen a gobbler's crop full of acorns, one full of galls from wild azalea, one full of rye grass, one full of sedge (*Carex* sp.) leaves and seeds, one full of newly germinated pine seeds, one full of unripe fruit of rusty blackhaw *(Viburnum rufidulum)*, and 2 jakes that had eaten many insects (adults, larvae, and pupae) and green anoles (lizards) (Hurst 1989). One hunter harvested a gobbler in a flooded bottomland hardwood forest and was surprised to find that the gobbler had been feeding on crayfish! A brood hen killed by a great horned owl had eaten 23 periodical cicadas. Another hen ate 21 snails, while other hens had gorged on blackberries.

A variety of planted small grain crops such as this brown-top millet is eaten by wild turkeys during summer and fall. *Photo by L. Williams.*

The wild turkey is an omnivorous feeder, as the contents of these crops illustrate. Top: A varied diet of wheat, corn, and a few beetles during a poor oak-mast year. Middle: Grasses, insects, and clover. Bottom: Jack-in-the-pulpit, insects, and acorns.

In 1984, a biologist and a graduate student sat in a blind in Mississippi, trying to capture wild turkeys on corn that had been treated with an oral drug. At daybreak, 2 dark-eyed juncos flew to the bait site, ate some drugged corn, and were soon flopping about in a drugged state. The observers watched in disbelief as 3 adult gobblers ran to the site. Two of the gobblers seized a junco, tore it apart, and ate the meat. What do turkeys eat? "Everything."

In short, the eastern wild turkey is an opportunistic omnivore, "eating whatever acceptable items are most available at different seasons" (Bailey and Rinell 1967). It does have preferences and does select items, but it consumes a great variety of plant and animal foods. The importance of the same general food types—hard and soft mast; green forage from grasses, sedges, and forbs; seeds from grasses and forbs; agricultural crops; and animal matter—is apparent.

every month, revealed that grass leaves and seeds made up nearly 60 percent of the year's total volume. Other foods were acorns, pine seeds, corn, and the fruit of wax myrtle and gallberry (Schemnitz 1956, Korschgen 1967).

Examination of 548 crops collected throughout Florida from November through January found that turkeys ate almost anything. Acorns were the major food item, but good turkey populations occurred in areas with few, if any, oaks. Cabbage palm fruit, green foliage, grasshoppers, chufa, and many other fruits and seeds were major food items (Powell 1965). Food was seldom a limiting factor for the Florida turkey (Powell 1967).

Long, detailed lists of items eaten by Florida turkeys were published, and an excellent summary is that "the turkey's diet is so broad that a very large sample would be necessary to fully reveal regional and temporal variation" (Williams and Austin 1988).

Food Habits, Gould's Turkey

This turkey ate mostly acorns and other mast in the fall and winter in Mexico. Other major foods in the highlands were juniper, pine, wild cherry, and blackberry. In the lowlands, palms, palmettos, figs, and a variety of other plants provided food. Insects, tender green leaves, and agricultural crops (e.g., corn and wheat) were also eaten (Leopold 1959).

In southwest New Mexico, wild turkey droppings in winter and spring contained grass, acorns, dock and manzanita seeds, and insects (Schemnitz and Zeedyk 1982). In woodlands dominated by oaks, pines, and juniper in southwestern New Mexico and southeastern Arizona, juniper berries were the most important spring food. Newly emerging forbs, however, were heavily utilized. Grasses and insects were the main summer foods. Grass seeds and fruits were the principal fall foods. Dominant winter foods were juniper berries, onion seeds, and manzanita berries during a winter when acorn and piñon production was poor and juniper berries were abundant. Gould's turkeys fed on aquatic vegetation around stock tanks (Potter et al. 1985).

Wild cherry is a regular diet item in the northeastern hardwood forests. *Photo by U.S. Forest Service.*

Food Habits, Florida Turkey

This subspecies has had several intensive studies conducted on its food habits. In 32 crops taken from turkeys from October through February were 114 different foods, but 10 foods made up 92.8 percent of total volume. Pine seeds and acorns accounted for 68.2 percent of all foods eaten. Other major foods were grass seeds and leaves, cabbage palm and black gum seeds, and corn. Analysis of 2,775 droppings, representing

Food Habits, Merriam's Turkey

The diet of this subspecies was described very early. "In winter [turkeys eat] piñon nuts, acorns, and juniper berries; in summer flower buds, grass and other seeds, wild oats, wild strawberries, manzanita berries, rose haws, fruit of wild mulberry and prickly pear, grasshoppers . . . [and] other insects." (Bailey 1928). He also noted that when deep snow covered other foods, the berries of red kinnikinnick became significant.

"Turkeys are omnivorous, taking both animal and plant food in great variety" (Legion 1946). Further, in winter and early spring, acorns, piñon nuts, juniper berries, other nuts (ponderosa pine), seeds of weeds and grasses, and green forage were vital foods. Piñon nuts were considered the "corn" of southwestern forests. Succulent forage and seeds of annuals and grasses were major foods in summer and fall. Grass (blades, fruits, and seeds) and grasshoppers were particularly important in fall and early winter in New Mexico (Table 6).

Dominant foods in Colorado were grass leaves, florets, and seeds; pine seeds; acorns; animal foods (10 percent of yearly total); and forb leaves (Hoffman 1962).

In Arizona, turkeys in 1967 ate from a total of 22 forbs and 44 grasses and in 1968, 24 forbs and 35 grasses. One crop contained 629 piñon pine seeds that weighed 171 grams (6.0 ounces) oven-dry. Another gobbler crop contained 198 grams (7.0 ounces) of acorns. This turkey likes acorns when they are available, but its general diet was highly diversified, substituting less desirable foods when preferred foods were not available (Scott and Boeker 1973, 1975). "This wide use of various plant and animal foods allows turkeys to successfully cope with seasonal and annual variation, in particular food availability, and survive periods of adversity caused by localized food shortage" (Schemnitz et al. 1985).

Is the diet of Merriam's turkey similar to diets of the other subspecies? Yes. It was thought to be an opportunistic feeder, eating a variety of seeds and leaves of grasses and forbs; fruits of shrubs and vines; mast of pine, oak, and juniper; and animal foods such as insects and snails (Zeedyk 1982). The data certainly support this belief.

Food Habits, Rio Grande Turkey

The diet of the Rio Grande turkey was summarized very early: "This turkey feeds on nuts (pecans), acorns, seeds, grain, berries, plant tops, [and] insects" (Simmons 1925). Principal foods were green vegetation; cottonseed cake; acorns; animal matter; skunkberry fruits; and seeds of goatweed, hackberry, cedar elm, mesquite, paspalum, and cacti for turkeys from 3 locations in Texas (Beck and Beck 1955, Korschgen 1967).

Additional studies, all conducted in west Texas, found that this turkey ate grass and forb leaves and seeds, insects, soft mast (e.g., berries from brush), hard mast (e.g., pecans), grains (e.g., corn and sorghum), and prickly pear seeds (Table 7). Similarities in results were noted from macro- and microscopic analysis of crop or fecal materials (Quinton and Montei 1977).

As an indicator of this turkey's diversified diet, 146 crops contained a total of 94 different food items. Animal matter—mostly grasshoppers and beetles—ac-

Table 6. Principal foods of the Merriam's turkey.

Season	Source	State	Foods
all	droppings	SD[a]	kinnikinnick and ponderosa pine seeds, oats, wheat, pine seeds, acorns
spring or fall	droppings	SD	grass seeds (bromus), arthropods, flowers, clover, raspberry
winter	droppings	SD	ponderosa pine and kinnikinnick seeds
spring	crop or droppings	AZ	grasses, forbs, juniper berries
summer			forbs, grasses, animals, fruit
fall			grasses, forbs, soft mast (manzanita, skunkbush, and juniper) hard mast (pine and acorns)
winter			grasses, forbs, acorns, pine seed, fruit, juniper
spring	crop	WA	grass leaves and seeds, forbs, acorns
fall			grass seeds, grasshoppers, pine seed, forb fruit
spring	droppings	NM	forbs, sedges
summer			grasses, rose fruit, juniper, insects
fall			currants, grasses, watercress
winter			grasses, watercress, currants
spring	crop or gizzard	NM	dandelion flowers and leaves, juniper, bluegrass and other grasses, insects, snails.

[a] South Dakota = Peterson and Richardson (1973), South Dakota = Rumble (1990), Arizona = Scott and Boeker (1973, 1975), Washington = Mackey and Jonas (1982), New Mexico = Schemnitz et al. (1985).

counted for an average of 28.7 percent of yearly volume, and dried and green seeds and green leaves of rescue grass averaged 20.3 percent. Annual food utilization averaged 36 percent from grasses, 19 percent from browse, 16 percent from forbs, and 29 percent from insects (Litton 1977).

Insects and the fruits of perennial browse and cacti were preferred. But when these foods were unavailable or scarce, turkeys depended heavily on grasses, grass seeds, and forbs. When conventional foods were lacking, the turkeys ate heavily of rescue grass seed heads and foliage. On marginal range and in a severe winter, rescue grass amounted to 46 percent and California filaree 20 percent of the volume eaten. Ability to utilize grasses and forbs was thought to be a major survival factor on marginal range of west Texas. When prolonged drought eliminated these buffer foods, the turkey population decreased (Kothmann and Litton 1975).

Forty hen crops taken in the spring (February through May) in south Texas contained mainly (48 to 98 percent) plant parts. Green vegetation formed 56 percent of the diet in February, then declined through the rest of spring. Fruits and seeds were important foods throughout the period. Insects and snails contributed little in February or March. But by April 1, insects amounted to

15.3 percent and snails 6.4 percent. By April 24, insects were 29.3 and snails 22.8 percent. Insects declined to 13.5 percent in May, and snails were only a trace. The importance of animal foods as a source of protein and calcium for reproductively active hens was documented (Pattee and Beasom 1981).

In summary, this subspecies is an opportunistic feeder, eating a variety of plant and animal matter, as preferred or available. That turkeys live in semidesert areas and eat prickly pear seeds, gaura, and agarita (cacti) should tell us something about these big birds.

The Turkey in California

Turkeys from several sources have been established in California. Their staple annual food is wild oats. Green grass and forb leafage are important in spring, and acorns are important in the fall (Smith and Browning 1967). Acorns and pine seeds were expected to be major foods for turkeys inhabiting the oak-pine forests (Harper and Smith 1973).

A review of the literature makes apparent that, from Maine to Mexico, in a variety of different habitats, all turkeys eat a great variety of foods, but from the same general types: hard and soft mast, green forage, seeds, agricultural crops, and animal matter.

Feeding Habits

How do turkeys get their food? One would logically expect a species that eats a wide variety of foods to use several feeding methods. In late winter, after the best berries and mast have been eaten, turkeys scratch in the litter for seeds and insects concealed there (Alexander 1921). Turkeys used picking (plucking) and stripping methods to get food in April through November, but scratching was the tactic used most often in winter (Dalke et al. 1942), or fall and winter (Wheeler 1948, Williams 1981). Whole ingestion, picking, stripping, clipping, and scratching were common feeding methods (Korschgen 1967). Turkeys are strong scratchers, digging through deep litter to find morsels. They also scratch into the soil for chufa or other tubers.

Turkeys jump up to grasp an item and pull it down to the ground to eat it. They fly into trees or bushes and eat buds or other plant parts (e.g., leaves, flowers, and fruits) (Wheeler 1948). They wade into water to get plant or animal matter or both. When snow is deep, turkeys follow deer paths and feed where deer have pawed the snow and exposed food items (Schorger 1966). Turkeys fly from tree to tree to reach a feeding area when snow is deep (Mosby and Handley 1943, Ligon 1946).

Table 7. Major foods of the Rio Grande turkey in Texas.

Season	Source	Foods
fall[a]	crop	ironwood berries, prickly pear seeds, insects, corn, pecans, triden seeds, green foliage, sorghum
spring	crop	sorghum, polecat bush berries, cup grass seeds, tall dropseed seeds, prickly pear seeds
spring,[a] summer, and fall	droppings	grass and forb seeds and leaves, berries and mast from brush, insects
winter	droppings	ironwood berries, pecans, triden seeds, insects, bristle grass seeds
all[b]	crop	insects, rescue and other grass seeds and leaves, forbs, fruits of browse and cacti
spring[c]	crop	green foliage, fruits, seeds, insects, snails

[a] Montei (1973), Quinton and Montei (1977).
[b] Kothmann and Litton (1975), Litton (1977).
[c] Pattee and Beasom (1981).

How do turkeys feed when large expanses of their range are flooded? In the Mississippi River Delta, they fly up into the tree crowns and feed on buds, leaves, flowers, and insects (Dalke et al. 1942, Zwank et al. 1988).

The turkey has keen eyesight, enabling it to spot tiny food items. It is highly mobile (can walk, run, and fly), so it can wander over large areas, using several methods to find food. Turkeys often travel in flocks, increasing the chances of finding food.

Feeding Movements

"Feeding movements of turkeys are best described as nomadic within limits, seemingly aimless, yet purposeful in search for food" (Korschgen 1967). Feeding turkeys are seldom still. They continuously move about, pecking or scratching. Turkeys may feed in a small area and then move a considerable distance to begin feeding again. While feeding, the flock might move at a rate of 274 meters (300 yards) to 3.2 kilometers (2 miles) an hour (Mosby and Handley 1943, Lewis 1973).

Turkeys have 2 main feeding periods: (1) soon after leaving the roost in early morning, and (2) in the afternoon (Mosby and Handley 1943, Davis 1949). Turkeys, however, may feed most of the day, depending upon the season, amount of food available, and weather conditions (Mosby and Handley 1943, Wheeler 1948).

A hen with poults (brood) feeds as a unit. But after a week or so, 2 or more successful hens with broods often join together while feeding to form a crèche (multiple-brood flock). Single hens, those in the egg-laying and incubating mode, usually feed alone.

Gobblers, often segregated by age, might or might not feed alone during mating season. Gobblers might not feed much during mating season, living on energy stored in the breast sponge (Williams 1981).

Amount Eaten

Precisely how much food turkeys consume in a feeding period or day is not known. What is known, though, is that the amount varies by sex, age, season, and availability of food. The crop of a wild turkey is expandable. Instances have been reported of crops containing as much as 225 grams (8 ounces) or 386 cubic centimeters (23.6 cubic inches). An average for large crops was 178 cubic centimeters (10.9 cubic inches) (Schemnitz 1956, Mosby and Handley 1943). Several crops of large gobblers contained more than 454 grams (1 pound) (Mosby and Handley 1943). We need to know how much food a wild turkey eats each day under different conditions of climate or weather, different physiological states, and varying food resources (Gluesing and Field 1982).

Nutrition

"While data on food habits are important, listings of food habits in themselves are only a superficial facade of nutritional understanding" (Robbins 1983). Nutritive requirements of adult domestic turkeys have been established, and biologists have documented a strong relationship between nutrition and reproductive success (National Academy of Sciences 1977, Scott et al. 1982).

Some information on nutrition in wild turkeys is available. For instance, a high proportion of wild hens failed to have normal gonadal development during drought years in south Texas. Low rainfall probably resulted in depressed quantity and quality of food. Turkey productivity was correlated to rainfall in the previous fall (Beasom and Pattee 1980). Hatching success and brood survival were influenced by seasonal rainfall patterns, which affected forb abundance in Texas (Kothman and Litton 1975).

In much of the Southeast, a severe summer-fall drought in 1987 resulted in little green forage. In addition, the acorn crop was virtually nonexistent that fall and winter. One result was that turkeys were in very poor condition (low body weights) in the spring. Reproduction was very low (Seiss 1989).

Managers have long believed green forage affects turkey well-being. Wild turkeys of all ages like and require much green food found in areas such as winter cover crops (e.g., oats, wheat, and rye) or recently burned areas (Stoddard 1963). Perhaps turkeys eat new-growth, succulent vegetation in the spring to meet a physiological need (Korschgen 1973) or to get vitamins essential for reproduction (Schorger 1966).

Hens usually can shift spring diets to satisfy reproductive nutritional needs. Rio Grande hens fulfilled their nutritional needs by shifting from forb leaves to forb fruits and seeds, then to animal matter, and then to grass seeds. Turkey hens would not meet nutritive requirements for egg laying by eating just plants; animal matter (insects) is necessary to raise the protein level. Also, calcium and phosphorus levels were met only in April, when high levels of insects are consumed.

Food quality should be considered in future diet studies. Large, bulky foods have been overemphasized, while highly nutritious items that occur in relatively small amounts have been neglected (Pattee 1977, Pattee and Beasom 1981). Nobody has addressed the relationships of soil and site characteristics to the quantity and quality of turkey food and to subsequent population parameters. Foraging strategy and efficiency should become topics for concern as landscapes are altered and demand for turkeys increases. Although wild turkeys have proved more tolerant (i.e., inhabiting environments thought unsuitable for the species), perhaps nutritional limitations are resulting in less than optimal population densities in some areas.

Nutrition of turkey foods. Foods taken from 39 turkey crops in Texas were deficient in energy. These foods seemed low in phosphorus for a breeder or a poult. It was concluded, however, that by consuming a variety of foods, a turkey could get an adequate maintenance diet (Beck and Beck 1955).

In Mississippi, investigators determined the nutritive content and digestibility of 8 fall and winter turkey foods. Utilization coefficients revealed that fat was best utilized, followed by protein and carbohydrates. There was little difference in utilization by adult and juvenile turkeys. The foods most nutritious and highest in utilization of nutrients were spicebush, chufa, and grape (Billingsley and Arner 1970).

Eight common fall and winter turkey foods in New Hampshire had protein levels of 2 percent (apples) to 19 percent (sensitive fern fronds). In fat content, red oak acorns and juniper berries were highest (14 percent). Juniper also had the highest metabolizable energy (4.6 kilocalories per gram) (Decker 1988).

In Alabama, the nutrient composition of turkey foods identified from droppings was similar in summer and spring diets. Protein was highest in poult (less than 4 weeks old) droppings, and calcium was highest in spring (Exum et al. 1987). Nutritive content and digestibility of many potential turkey foods have been determined (Short et al. 1974, Short and Epps 1976, Hayden 1979b). Unknown, however, are the relationships of these values to turkey growth, survival, or productivity. Perhaps an index value of foods—combining nutrient, energetic, preference, consumptive, and cost data—can be developed (Gluesing and Field 1982).

Not well understood is the nutritive role of stuffing or emergency foods. Turkeys, when starving, ate ferns, mosses, beech buds, and other poor foods (Bailey et al. 1951). Sensitive fern was considered a stuffing food, but it had a higher (18.6 percent) crude protein level than corn (8.9 percent) or acorns (5.3 percent) (Mautz 1986).

The importance of turkey basal metabolism, daily energy expenditure, and food intake has been demonstrated. Metabolic costs for thermoregulation (maintaining body temperature) below the lower critical temperature were greater for females than males. Effects of combined low food intake and added thermoregulation costs on reproduction were evident (Gray 1986, Gray and Prince 1987). Relationships of cold temperatures and wind, a problem in Minnesota, are being studied (R. Kimmel personal communication: 1991). Much remains to be learned about wild turkey nutritional requirements and energetics.

Supplemental Feeding

To feed or not to feed wild turkeys is a common debate. Some people would argue that food is seldom a limiting factor in the wild turkey's range. Nonetheless, starvation does occur along the northern periphery of the range during periods of deep fluffy snow (Austin and DeGraff 1975, Wunz and Hayden 1975, McMahon and Johnson 1980, Porter et al. 1983).

Supplemental feeding has been practiced in places for a long time. It did not prevent starvation in some parts of Pennsylvania (Wunz and Hayden 1975). By contrast, supplemental feeding was considered essential in maintaining Merriam's turkeys in mountainous areas of New Mexico during severe winters, deep snows, or no mast (Ligion 1946). Experiments showed that turkeys lived despite having no food for 2 weeks and a 40 percent loss of their body weight (Hayden and Nelson 1963).

Effects of supplemental feeding on reproduction or survival are mostly speculative. Yet reproductive success might increase from correction of some nutritional deficiencies (Beck and Beck 1955). Game-farm turkeys kept on starvation or limited rations laid fewer eggs (Hayden 1963). Captive hens on a supplemental diet laid significantly more eggs (14.4 per hen) than hens fed acorns, green vegetation, and seeds (2.14 per hen) (Gardner and Arner 1968). Also, hens fed a high-nutritive diet began

laying earlier and laid more eggs than hens fed a low-nutrition diet (Billingsley and Arner 1970). Effects of low nutrition on turkey renesting efforts are unknown.

An interesting experiment took place in south Texas. Supplemental feeding with commercial turkey breeder pellets (17.5 percent protein, 2.25 percent calcium, and 0.75 percent phosphorus) resulted in a 270 percent increase in the number of poults versus an area with no such pellets. Areas with pellets had more hens with poults, and the average brood size was higher.

Apparently the increase in poults on areas with supplemental food was the result of 3 factors: (1) more hens laying; (2) earlier start of laying; and (3) later ending of laying attempts. A greater number of hens produced poults on areas with pellets. Poult survival and clutch size were unaffected by feeding (Pattee and Beasom 1979).

Food plots (e.g., wheat, clover, and chufa) for white-tailed deer or wild turkeys are prevalent. Often turkey management is thought to center on planting food plots, an emphasis that can detract from real habitat management. Food plots could be dangerous because chances for poaching, predation, parasitism, and pathogens (disease) are increased. Reliance on automatic, solar-powered, or other types of turkey feeders is even more hazardous. Feeders concentrate turkeys on a very small area. As their droppings accumulate, chances for transmission of parasites and diseases are increased (Stoddard 1963).

Food plots and feeders should be moved frequently and should be placed where they are not visible from roads. Some managers think food plots can be used to hold turkeys on an area where they are protected from poachers (Stoddard 1963).

Relationships of food plots or feeders to turkey population parameters (e.g., density and recruitment) have not been adequately documented. Research should be conducted to provide sound information on the pros and cons of supplemental feeding, including cost-benefit data.

Special Feeding Areas

The importance of seeps, or springs, as turkey feeding areas in the Northeast and the West has been recognized (Glover 1948, Latham 1959, Austin and DeGraff 1975, Healy 1977). Spring seeps were primary feeding places in northeastern mountains during periods of deep snow (Bailey and Rinell 1968). Principal foods were fern fronds, grass blades, rootlets, mosses, seeds, aquatic insects, and watercress (Hayden 1969). Planting and managing for watercress were recommended (Latham 1956,

Healy and Pack 1983, Wunz et al. 1983). In the western United States, vegetation at springs was important for Merriam's and Gould's turkeys during the winter (Schemnitz et al. 1985, Schemnitz and Zeedyk, see chapter on Gould's turkey).

There seem to be special areas throughout turkey range: mature hardwood forests on major rivers or creeks in the Southeast or Midwest, or corn fields in the Midwest. These habitats may be crucial seasonal habitat with energy-rich food.

Competition

Competition for food among turkeys, deer, hogs, and many other species has been discussed (Bailey et al. 1951, Korschgen 1967, Shaffer and Gwynn 1967). But the relationships are unclear. Many species compete for acorns and other mast, but nobody knows whether this competition limits turkey populations over the long term. The variety of foods eaten by the turkey permits it to survive, regardless of competition for specific items (Powell 1967). In subtropical Florida, areas with very high populations of deer and wild hogs and with intensive cattle grazing still supported high turkey populations (Williams 1981). The return of the eastern wild turkey to large numbers in its historic range—and beyond—happened at the same time the deer population was exploding. But the effects of competition in marginal habitat may be severe.

Agricultural Crops

Wild turkeys have readily accepted man's crops, such as corn, wheat, oats, soybeans, peanuts, alfalfa, clover, milo, and sorghum. For the pioneers, crop depredation by wild turkeys was a real problem (Schorger 1966). It is becoming a problem for some southern gardeners and western wheat farmers. The turkey's preference for man's grain was one reason the species was nearly eliminated.

Recently, corn was heavily used and was thought essential to maintain turkeys in southeast Minnesota (Porter 1977). Turkeys in marginal habitats in southern Iowa made extensive use of—and relied on—waste corn for overwintering. Some of the highest turkey densities in the nation now are in this intensively farmed, food-rich area (Little 1980), and grains probably are supporting turkeys in some less suitable environments.

Problems with Studies of Food Habits

In studies of turkey diet, investigators may use crop contents, gizzard contents, and fecal matter (droppings). In some cases, proventriculus (stomach) contents were analyzed.

Crop content analysis is best, but even this method can be biased. Turkeys might shift soft-bodied or succulent items to the gizzard ahead of coarser material (Stringer 1977). Inherent problems (biases) with gizzard and fecal analyses have been recognized (Korschgen 1967, 1973). Succulent (nutritious) foods are processed by the turkey's digestive system more rapidly than more fibrous foods and therefore are underrepresented by standard analyses of food habits (Gluesing and Field 1982). Turkeys are cecal animals and can process large amounts of fibrous foods items (Schorger 1966), thereby complicating food analyses.

Sample sizes are often inadequate and studies too short-term. What turkeys ate one day, one season, or one year may be substantially a reflection of what was then available.

In most studies, no attempt was made to relate foods eaten to foods available. Preference as it relates to availability or nutritional content has not often been determined. Limitations of existing food-habit studies for modeling wildlife-habitat relationships have been noted (Gluesing and Field 1984).

Conclusions

What does the wild turkey eat? Poults are mainly predators, eating insects and other arthropods. At about age 4 weeks, a poult shifts its diet to one similar to that of the adult. Turkeys eat many plant and animal foods, depending on what is available or preferred. Major turkey foods—hard and soft mast, green forage, seeds, grains, and animals—were described in the early 1900s, and later studies have confirmed and elaborated on these observations.

The turkey's feeding methods parallel its diet—varied. Turkeys get food (e.g., tubers) from the soil; seeds, invertebrates, and vertebrates from litter; and several plant parts (stems, leaves, seeds, and fruits) above ground. Turkeys fly into trees to eat flowers and buds. You might call the turkey a scrounger or gleaner, being able to find nourishment from many different sources and by different methods.

The wild turkey is a food generalist, or an opportunistic omnivore, eating whatever acceptable items—plant or animal—are available. "They are as omnivorous as the human race" (Jordan 1898, in Schorger 1966). Food habits vary seasonally, annually, and regionally, and many variables affect food availability (Bailey and Rinell 1968). Turkeys are adaptable to changing food conditions brought about by vagaries of weather, land use, and normal schedules of plant production (Korschgen 1967). The wild turkey might be the master opportunist (Hillestad and Speake 1970). Opportunist—yes; picky—no (Hayden 1969).

Still among our unknowns about the wild turkey are relationships (correlations) of turkey density or recruitment to habitat types or landscape configuration, nutritional planes, and energetic costs. We do not need more lists of what turkeys eat. We need to study interactions between turkey populations and nutritional resources (Robbins 1983). We need to determine whether turkeys compensate for low-quality food or low availability by eating more or by spending more time foraging. We also need to study the effects of food resources on home range size and predation rates (Williams and Austin 1988).

JOHN SIDELINGER

The wild turkey is a food generalist, eating whatever acceptable items are available.

Chapter 7

PHYSIOLOGY

Lytle H. Blankenship
Texas A&M University (Retired)
Uvalde, Texas

Physiology is about the functions of living organisms, how organisms adjust to their environment, and how their functions are regulated. No wild animal exists independently of its environment, and each must cope with the difficulties its environment presents. Many physiological traits are highly sensitive to the environment, causing such organisms as the wild turkey to make adaptations in order to survive in its ever-changing world. Physiology is often structured into the study of various organ systems, including circulatory, digestive and excretory, endocrine, nervous, reproductive, and respiratory. Such systems are presented in this chapter according to how they affect the wild turkey's beginning, growth and development, and survival in its environment.

THE BEGINNING

Factors Affecting Breeding

Most biologists believe the breeding cycle of birds is initiated by increasing light and by the inborn cycle of certain endocrine glands (Figure 1). Other factors that may stimulate or delay breeding by wild turkeys include weather, diet, age, and disease. Light indirectly activates both male and female reproductive organs by stimulating the anterior pituitary through the nervous system. Light may be more effective in activating the sex glands of male birds than of female birds (Bissonnette 1937:247, Bailey 1967:107).

Studies on sexually photoperiodic (affected by duration of periods of light) birds indicate that inherent cycles of the anterior pituitary, gonads, and other glands may depend on pituitary activity to control reproductive and other rhythmic activity. Latham (1956:27) wrote, "Through receptive cells in the eyes, the increased amount of light causes a response from certain endocrine glands. The hormones produced under the stimulus of light cause the testes of the male and ovaries of the hen to begin to enlarge." These hormones (gonadotrophins) ini-

tiate in the male bird the enlargement of the testes and the production of testosterone and millions of spermatozoa. Similar changes occur in the left ovary of hens as ova start to develop. Oviducts in females and sperm ducts in males also enlarge and regress in harmony with the breeding season.

Although internal physiological changes may be occurring, the breeding season is not apparent until the male wild turkey starts to gobble and strut. These activities become more intense as spring breakup of winter flocks progresses and gobblers associate with hens. In Texas, mature gobblers began displaying in early February without any obvious response from hens (Thomas

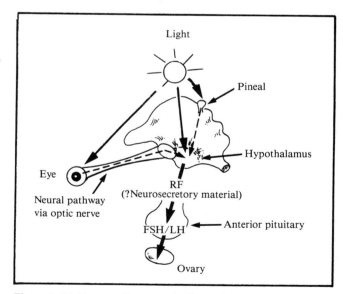

Figure 1. Light may affect reproductive activity through at least 3 possible pathways. Though their relative importance is not entirely known, it seems most likely that the main way is through the eye. In response to light, the hypothalamus produces the releasing factors (RF), which in turn regulate pituitary formation of the gonadotrophins (Gilbert 1971a:320).

et al. 1966:39). This display and subsequent breeding start progressively later to the north. Gobbling and mating may be concurrent, but the peak of mating may occur 2 to 3 weeks after onset of gobbling (Bailey and Rinell 1967a:73). Testosterone is the hormone responsible for sexual behavior in males—i.e., courtship, copulatory behavior, gobbling, and aggressiveness toward other gobblers (Lewis 1967:60). In hens, the hormone that initiates breeding behavior, including broodiness, is prolactin (LTH) (Hohn 1961:97).

As the annual breeding cycle commences, male secondary sexual characteristics become more evident. These traits result from changes in the circulating levels of androgens, especially testosterone, in the wild turkey and most vertebrates. Plasma testosterone levels increase from midwinter to early spring in pen-reared turkeys. The greatest increase (560 milligrams per deciliter) is in the dominant male (Lisano and Kennamer 1977a:184, 187).

Testicular hormones are produced in Leydig (interstitial) cells. Large increases in these cells correspond with the growth and development of the adornments or wattles (snood and caruncles) that cover the head and neck of males. Anatomical changes include increased redness of the caruncles (from a greater blood flow near the skin) and development of a fatty breast sponge. The sponge can equal about 11 percent of a turkey's dressed weight in spring, and it serves as an energy reservoir during the breeding season, since often there is little feeding by the gobbler (Lewis 1967:45).

Despite an increasing photoperiod (length of day) and changes in pituitary hormones, an unusually cold spring could delay reproduction. Low temperature alone may not cause a decrease in sexual activity, but rain, drought, food scarcity, and lack of emerging nest cover could hinder breeding. During drought years, a high proportion of Rio Grande turkey hens failed to show normal gonadal development (Pattee and Beasom 1979:512), possibly the effect of an inadequate diet.

Age also affects mating activities. Many toms less than 1 year old are sexually immature or may be prevented from mating by dominant older males (Leopold

Extended mating behavior depletes a gobbler's energy reserves. *Photo by G. Smith.*

1944:160–161). The lack of mating by young wild gobblers is well documented (Mosby and Handley 1943, Peterson and Richardson 1975). First-year domestic gobblers are vigorous breeders, however, and there has been successful reproduction from releases of a flock of wild turkey hens with a juvenile male.

A sexually mature young domestic tom served 14 to 20 females, while older males served only 8 to 14 on the average (Marsden and Martin 1939:51). Young toms started to produce sperm at 38 to 40 weeks old. Free sperm in 28 percent of the epididymides (efferent tubules of the testis) of subadult wild gobblers suggests that they could breed with hens later in the season (Lewis and Breitenbach 1966:618–620). Spermatocytes probably must reach the secondary stage of development by late April for these toms to be capable of breeding. A 75 percent fertility was recorded for a group of hybrid yearling toms, but none for wild yearling toms (Knoder 1959a).

A gobbler's ability to breed depends on the relationship between the predominant stage of spermatogenesis and testes weight (Lewis and Breitenbach 1966:619). Spermatids were the predominant cell type in testes heavier than 7 grams (0.25 ounces), but not in testes weighing less than 4 grams (0.14 ounces). Average weights of subadult testes ranged from 4.76 grams (0.17 ounces) to 4.98 grams (0.18 ounces). Advanced stages of spermatogenesis were rare in gobblers weighing less than 6.35 kilograms (14 pounds). Since the initial development of testes is induced by androgens, the slow development of yearling toms may be attributable to the lack of these hormones (Leopold 1944:182).

Except for some populations (Ligon 1946:6, Still and Baumann 1991), turkey hens usually mate as subadults. Young Merriam's hens seemed the least likely to succeed in nesting (Lockwood and Sutcliffe 1985:316, Lutz and Crawford 1987b:784). In all subspecies, yearling hens seldom renested if the first nest was unsuccessful, while adult hens were much more successful in nesting and renesting (Glidden and Austin 1975:53–54, Williams et al. 1976:375-376, Lutz and Crawford 1987b:784).

In summary, yearling hens may contribute substantially to production, but yearling males usually do not.

Any disease or parasite that might affect the general state of health and normal physiological process of wild turkeys could hinder their mating. A blood parasite, *Leucocytozoon smithi*, decreases the ability of domestic gobblers to mate and decreases the productivity of hens (Byrd 1959:155, see Johnson et al. 1938; Hensley and Cain 1978:66). Pullorum *(Salmonella pullorum)* can decrease reproduction of domestic turkeys by affecting fertility, egg production, egg hatchability, and poult survival (Hensley and Cain 1978:66), but the disease is not known to occur in wild turkeys. Infection of game-farm wild turkeys with *Mycoplasma gallisepticum* reduced the production, fertility, and hatchability of eggs. These same effects may occur in free-ranging wild turkeys (Rocke et al. 1988:531). Gastrointestinal helminths occur abundantly in wild turkeys from some areas of southeastern United States, but their effects on breeding have not been documented (Maxfield et al. 1963).

Fertilization

The production of sperm and ova are both stimulated by the follicle-stimulating hormone (FSH) of the anterior pituitary. The swelling of testes indicates increased production of spermatozoa. The mean concentration of spermatozoa (millions per milliliter) in adult gobblers is 6,800 (4,800 to 8,200). Munro (1938) inseminated chicken hens with more than 1 million sperm to get fertile eggs. Turkey hens were inseminated similarly for comparable results (Burrows and Marsden 1938:408), although turkey semen is less abundant and thicker. The pH of semen is recorded as 7.0 to 8.0 (Burrows and Kosin 1953) or 7.0 to 8.1 (Altman and Dittmer 1962:164). Best recorded fertilities resulted from pH readings in these ranges.

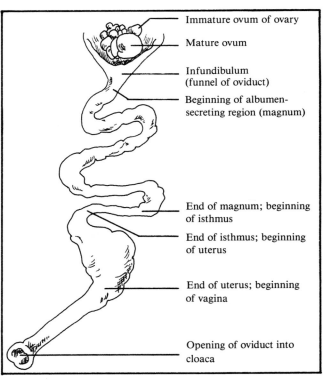

Figure 2. Reproductive tract of the laying hen (chicken). The turkey's tract is similar (after Sturkie 1965:451).

Hormones—FSH and LH (luteinizing hormone)—secreted by the pituitary help prepare the left ovary for egg production (Kennamer 1988a:26). Before breeding season, the ovary consists of many tiny ova, which may be in various stages of development. At sexual maturity, some of the ova—by receiving necessary materials from the blood for yolk formation—develop into mature yolks. At mating, an ovum passes into the infundibulum. There it is fertilized by a sperm that has entered the oviduct and moved slowly through into the infundibulum (Figure 2). Sperm cells may be suspended in fluids of the oviduct as long as a month, waiting for a ripe ovum to be shed. Maturation begins shortly before ovulation and continues as the ovum passes through the infundibulum; the main albumen-secreting area; the isthmus, which secretes shell membranes; the isthmo-uterine junction, which produces a fluid; the uterus for organic shell matrix, a thin albumen, and calcified shell; the vagina; and the cloaca (Matthews and Marshall 1960:213–214). The ovum (egg) remains in the oviduct about 25 to 30 hours after fertilization.

A single breeding (copulation) each spring can fertilize all eggs in a clutch (Cook and Gore 1978:2). The initial fertilization may last through a renesting attempt since crypts in the wall of the upper oviduct serve as sperm reservoirs (Grigg 1957:450). Sperm cells may remain potent for 56 days in a hen's oviduct (Marsden and Martin 1955). With this reservoir of sperm, turkey hens may lay fertile eggs up to 4 weeks after mating, even though hens may be served by toms every day during laying (Bailey et al. 1951).

Fertility can be affected by age, nutrition, health, light, temperature, and season. When males were exposed to extreme cold, the number of spermatozoa was reduced (Burrows and Kosin 1953:140–141). Also, the fertility of semen from males that had a proper environment was significantly greater than semen from males that were partly or totally unprotected from temperature fluctuations. The proper amounts of both heat and light seem essential for optimum production of turkey sperm.

Drought years in south Texas resulted in poor development of gonads and thus low productivity in wild turkey hens (Pattee and Beasom 1979:512). Inadequate diet, especially a diet low in protein, decreased egg production in wild turkeys (Gardner and Arner 1968:257). By contrast, the fertility of Merriam's turkeys was increased by supplemental winter feeding (Spicer 1959). Normally, food is not a factor. Adult turkeys usually increase in weight during winter, reaching a maximum just before mating starts. Even a prebreeding season weight loss of 20 to 30 percent did not affect fertility (Hayden and Nelson 1963:11).

Nesting Cycle

Just as the increasing light and subsequent hormonal production stimulate mating early in the year, they

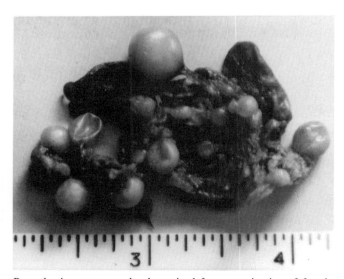

Reproductive status can be determined from examination of female reproductive tract. *Photo by P. Pelham.*

Wild turkey hens normally are in adequate condition to produce a clutch of eggs each spring. *Photo by L. Williams.*

also initiate egg laying. This response enables wild turkeys to reproduce when food for young is most plentiful (Marshall 1961:307). Although light and the corresponding reactions may affect time of laying, egg production usually is not affected (Leighton and Schoffner 1961). In some years, laying may be delayed by abnormal cold (Peterson and Richardson 1975:10). Also, the severity of the preceding winter may affect the physiological condition and reproduction of females in cold climates (Porter et al. 1983). Severe winter reduced the egg-hatching success by younger females. Heavier hens were also affected but nested more successfully. Heavier females in Massachusetts did not have a net productive advantage, perhaps indicating that their physiological condition was not the most important factor affecting productivity, except for renesters (Vander Haegen et al. 1988:132).

Mild conditions that result in high survival and hens in good physiological condition may not always lead to high natality (hatching) and high recruitment (net population increase). Predation, a stabilized population (Vangilder et al. 1987:539), inadequate distribution of water, very low rainfall (Beasom 1973), and the lack of certain nutritional factors may have a greater negative impact on egg production. And though laying is a stress to domestic fowl and may result in death (Romanoff and Romanoff 1949:36), wild turkey hens may not experience such great physical and physiological stress from laying (Lewis 1967:67).

Obviously, diet is important in reproduction. Turkeys fed a supplemental diet rich in protein had a higher egg production than turkeys fed on a diet of common natural foods (Gardner and Arner 1968:256). Egg production in domestic Broad Breasted Bronze breeder hens differed little among hens fed isocaloric (equal calorie) diets with 1.75 percent to 6.25 percent calcium (Jensen et al. 1964:1577–1581). In wild turkeys, laying hens ate more snails or snail shells (calcium source) than nonlayers (Beasom and Pattee 1978:917). Layers also used greater amounts of snails (10.9 percent) than prelaying (3.0 percent) or postlaying (0.8 percent) hens. Inadequate levels of phosphorus affected timing and progress of laying (Pattee 1977). The optimum level of phosphorus should be about 0.6 percent. Adding more phosphorus to a high-calcium diet does not increase the performance of domestic turkey hens (Jensen et al. 1964). Nutritional elements required by wild turkeys for an adequate diet included 0.7 percent phosphorus and 2.2 percent calcium in the breeder stage (Beck and Beck 1955:201).

The end of laying and ultimate clutch size may be caused by the increasing secretion of prolactin. Progesterone stimulates the secretion of prolactin, which suppresses FSH and initiates broodiness. By contrast, estrogen depresses secretion of prolactin (Sturkie 1965). If a nest is destroyed, ovulation again is induced by the cyclic release of LH from the anterior pituitary.

Egg development begins as sexual maturity approaches. Growth and maturation of the ovarian follicle is caused by FSH. The egg, when fully developed, proceeds through the vagina into the cloaca, from which it is laid (Figure 3). The composition of a turkey egg at this point is largely water (Table 1, Gerstell and Long 1939:5). Eggs from wild-mated females were higher in

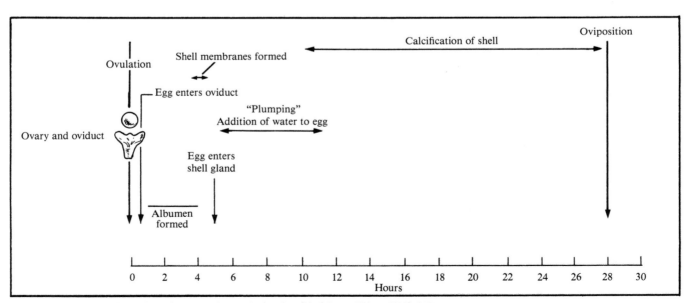

Figure 3. Stages in the formation of the egg after ovulation (modified from Gilbert 1971b:309).

nutrients than eggs from game-farm birds. The higher ratio of nutrients to weight, volume, and density for eggs of wild turkeys may relate to growth, development, and survival of wild birds.

Embryonic Development

Maturation and formation of the first polar body (first maturation division of ovum) occurs in domestic fowl just before ovulation and is initiated by LH (Olsen and Fraps 1944:304). Within a few minutes after ovulation, the egg can be fertilized. After the egg enters the uterus, cleavage progresses through the various stages up to about the 256-cell stage. By the time the egg is laid, gastrulation (early embryo) has occurred. But embryonic development is arrested by cooling of the eggs while the hen is off her nest. Once incubation commences, growth of the embryo is continuous. Embryonic development in the wild turkey is probably similar to that described for domestic embryos (Marsden and Martin 1955:797–800), with hatching occurring after about 28 days.

Hatchability of Eggs

The success of turkey hens in hatching a clutch of eggs may be affected by several factors. Low humidity at nest sites for long periods may cause wild turkey eggs to fail to hatch (Beasom 1970). Higher levels of calcium (2.5 and 3.25 percent) in diets of domestic turkeys depress hatchability (Jensen et al. 1963:605), but levels around 2.0 percent enhance hatchability.

Fertile eggs from captive-reared wild turkey hens infected with *Mycoplasma gallisepticum* had significantly lower hatchability than eggs from control hens (Rocke et al. 1988:528). Age of turkey hens did not seem to affect hatching success significantly (Vander Haegen et al. 1988:130). Hatching times vary somewhat with the latitude and elevation, which may indicate not only a physiological relationship with increasing light but also temperature effects.

GROWTH AND DEVELOPMENT

Hormonal Relationships

Hormones influence reproduction, behavior, body and feather growth, molting, cardiovascular processes, digestion and nutrition, excretion, and pigmentation. Hormones are produced by endocrine glands. These glands are ductless. They secrete their hormones into the bloodstream to be transported to the tissues or organs

Table 1. Percent composition of turkey eggs from game-farm hens crossed with wild gobblers or game-farm males.

Substance	Wild-mated birds	Game-farm birds
water	72.18	74.53
protein	13.42	12.55
fat	11.81	10.47
carbohydrates	1.64	1.53
ash	0.95	0.92
phosphorus	0.25	0.23
calcium	0.11	0.06

they act on. Important endocrine glands in turkeys are the pituitary (hypophysis), thyroids, parathyroids, adrenals, pancreas, gonads (testes and ovaries), and intestine. The pancreas, gonads, and intestine have both endocrine and exocrine functions.

The major endocrine gland is the pituitary; its anterior lobe produces gonadotrophins, adrenocorticotrophic (ACTH), thyrotrophic (TSH), and growth hormone (GH). The gonadotrophins include FSH, LH, and prolactin. The posterior lobe of the pituitary produces oxytocin and arginine vasotocin, which affect the cardiovascular system and uterine contraction. Vasopressin also is present. There is no intermediate lobe in the pituitary of turkeys, but the hormone intermedin has been found in the cephalic portion of the anterior lobe of chickens (Kleinholz and Rahn 1940:157) (Figure 4).

Normal growth and development of domestic turkeys are closely related to thyroidal secretions (Biellier and Turner 1955:1161) (Table 2). As the young grow larger, total secretion increases, but secretion decreases in relation to body weight. Thyroxine secretion rates of young domestic turkeys were correlated with their respective growth rates (Smyth and Fox 1951: 607). Weights for Broad Breasted Bronze increased by 236 percent, Jersey Buff by 246 percent, and crossbreds by 257 percent during a 1 to 3 week growth period, indicating an association between hybrid vigor and thyroid activity.

Changes in behavior and body conformation of males during the breeding season reflected the level of testosterone. Seasonal variations in plasma testosterone level preceded changes in body weight of 3 pen-reared male eastern wild turkeys by 2 to 3 weeks (Lisano and Kennamer 1977a:188).

Thyroid hormones may indicate the physiological status of the eastern wild turkey (Burke et al. 1977:650). Variations in the levels of 2 such hormones, thyroxine (T4) and triiodothyronine (T3) were correlated with seasonal temperature changes and molting. High levels of T4 and low levels of T3 in July and August corresponded to the period of postjuvenal molt in pen-reared turkeys.

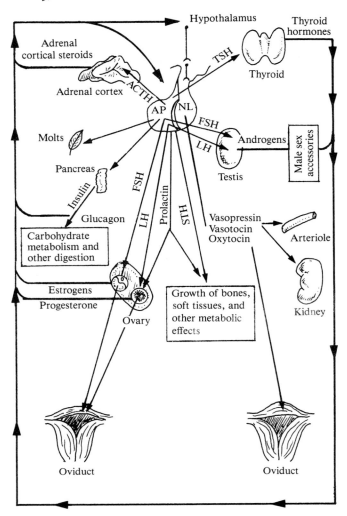

Figure 4. A diagram summarizing some of the main actions of pituitary hormones: AP, anterior pituitary; NL, neural lobe; ACTH, adreno-corticotrophic hormone; TSH, thyroid-stimulating hormone; FSH, follicle-stimulating hormone; LH, luteinizing hormone; STH, somato-trophin (growth hormone) (modified from Turner 1966:44).

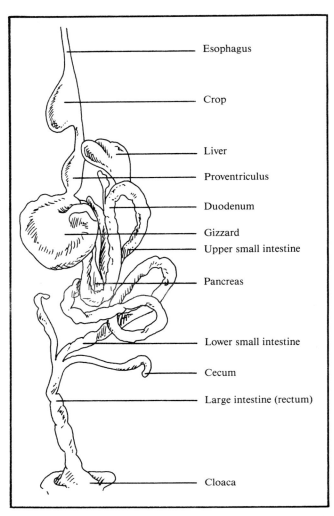

Figure 5. Digestive tract of a chicken. The turkey's digestive tract is similar (after Sturkie 1965:273).

Table 2. Thyroid secretion rates of domestic turkey poults (Biellier and Turner 1955).

Variety	Sex	Age (weeks)	Average body weight (grams/ounce)	Daily d, 1-thyroxine secretion rate in micrograms	
				Poult	Per 100-gram body weight
Broad Breasted Bronze	M	3	315.9/11.0	7.2	2.28
	F	3	304.5/10.7	8.1	2.66
Beltzville White	M	3	350.0/12.3	8.1	2.31
	F	3	325.5/11.5	8.3	2.55
	M	6	950.2/33.5	18.3	1.93
	F	6	783.2/27.6	18.0	2.30
	M	10	2,192.7/77.3	33.4	1.52
	F	10	1,781.6/62.8	29.8	1.67

There was no additional increase in plasma T4 levels just before the breeding season in February and March, but the elevated levels in May to July occurred at the time of summer molt in wild turkeys. Elevated plasma levels of T4 may be necessary for the rapid rate of follicular growth required for feather replacement.

Molting may be associated physiologically with time of breeding and age of sexual maturity. All are regulated through the endocrine system, with the pituitary having primary control (Leopold 1944:176-177). Accordingly, photoperiod is the environmental stimulus that induces molt, while the thyroid hormones control feather replacement (Bissonnette 1937:245). Progesterone may stimulate the growth of new feathers and—together with thyroidal activity—control the number of primaries molted (Shaffner 1954:345, 1955:840). Prolactin too may help in the start of molts (Juhn and Harris 1958:669). In adult gobblers, the start of primary molt is inhibited by early reproductive development and testosterone (Lewis and Breitenbach 1966:621).

Digestion

Nutritional requirements vary by age, sex, and season, although no consistent differences occurred in the use of food among turkeys older than poults (Billingsley and Arner 1970:182, Hurst and Stringer 1975). Wild turkeys take foods that are available, palatable, and capable of supplying physiological needs (Korschgen 1967:150).

Digestive organs include the mouth, pharynx, esophagus, crop, proventriculus, gizzard, small intestine, ceca, large intestine, and cloaca (Figure 5). Turkeys pick up food with the beak and swallow it by raising the head and extending the neck to cause a negative pressure that forces the item downward. The continued passage of food depends upon the motility (spontaneous motion) of the various organs.

Motility is influenced by nerves, food, and hunger (Rogers 1916:555, Ashcraft 1930:105). The vagus, a parasympathetic nerve, is the principal motor nerve for the esophagus, crop, proventriculus, and gizzard. The intestines and ceca may depend for their motility more upon peristaltic waves and segmenting movements than on innervation.

Food passage is more rapid in laying turkey hens (3 hours, 13 minutes) than in nonlaying turkey hens (4 hours, 16 minutes) and more rapid in young turkey hens (2 hours, 27 minutes) than in old hens (3 hours, 52 minutes) (Hillerman et al. 1953:332). The time of food passage differed little between environmental temperatures of 15.5 degrees Celsius (60 degrees Fahrenheit) and 32 degrees Celsius (90 degrees Fahrenheit).

Gastric juices are stimulated when food, especially green foods, enter the proventriculus. The proventriculus contains pepsin (enzyme), and significant digestion probably occurs there. Next, the gizzard, which is used primarily for grinding food, contains pepsin and has an optimum pH of 2 to 3.5. Most of the pepsin probably comes from the proventriculus.

Digestive mechanisms such as enzymes and fermentation continue to act upon food particles through the small intestine and into the ceca. Little or no digestion occurs in the large intestine, except for the ceca, where most crude fiber is digested. Microbial decomposition of cellulose is primarily by fermentation (Beattie and Shrimpton 1958:399). Some water resorption occurs in the large intestine and cloaca.

All parts of the avian alimentary tract are acidic. The gizzard is extremely acidic and the intestines are the least acidic (Farner 1942:445) (Table 3). The pH of the tract is not influenced much by different diets (Winget et al. 1962:1115).

Mixed intestinal fluids contain pancreatic juice, which contributes proteases, trypsin, and probably other enzymes to digestion. Secretin, a hormone formed in the walls of the small intestine, causes an abundant secretion of these pancreatic juices. Trypsin and chymotrypsin have been extracted from the turkey pancreas (Ryan 1965). Digestion by pepsin, trypsin, chymotrypsin, and possibly other proteolytic enzymes occurs in the intestine. Biologists do not know which is the primary enzyme.

Other hormones involved in digestion include ACTH, LTH, and GH of the pituitary; glucagon and insulin from the pancreas; epinephrine and corticosteroids of the adrenal; thyroxine from the thyroid; and several gonadal hormones. Prolactin is considered a significant regulator of avian carbohydrate metabolism (Hazelwood 1965:324). Both ACTH and GH seem to have some effect on blood glucose and liver glycogen in carbohydrate metabolism.

Table 3. Mean hydrogen ion (H+) concentrations of digestive organs of the domestic turkey (4 samples).

Site	Mean	Standard error
crop	6.07	5.99-6.16
proventriculus	4.72	4.55-4.99
gizzard	2.19	1.97-2.66
duodenum	5.82-6.52	5.64-6.69
upper ileum	6.71-6.95	6.56-7.09
lower ileum	6.85	6.71-7.06
large intestine-cloaca	6.46	6.29-6.73
ceca	5.86	5.64-6.06
bile	6.01	5.95-6.14

Alpha cells of the pancreas are responsible for the production of glucagon, which plays a homeostatic (maintaining normal stability) role in avian carbohydrate metabolism by regulating sugar metabolism. Beta cells (islets of Langerhans) are the primary and perhaps only source of insulin, which helps regulate the metamorphosis of glucose into fat. The blood sugar response of domestic turkey poults to administered insulin was hypoglycemia (low blood sugar) if less than 500 units per kilogram were used (Snedecor et al. 1956:355); more administered insulin caused hyperglycemia (high blood sugar).

The corticosteroids (corticosterone and hydrocortisone) of the adrenal cortex increase carbohydrate metabolism in birds. Hydrocortisone and ACTH also induce lipid and protein metabolism alterations in young roosters (Hazelwood 1965:355). Plasma corticosterone increases with stress in eastern wild turkeys (Whatley et al. 1977:192) and consequently alters metabolism.

Thyroxine increases growth of young poults by facilitating the transfer of carbohydrates through the intestinal wall and increasing glucose uptake in peripheral tissues (Hazelwood 1965:358). Thyroidal activity also alters the rate of heat production.

Androgens may influence carbohydrate metabolism, but if so, the effect may be through increasing the number of erythrocytes. Estrogen has an effect on formation of plasma protein, increases lipid synthesis in the liver, and seems to aid the liver in the clearing of certain substances (Sturkie 1965:579–581). Estrogen also tends to protect the liver from certain damages and speeds regeneration when the liver is damaged (Campbell 1957a:339, b:346).

Since heat is a by-product of metabolism, body temperature may rise or fall depending upon food availability and digestion. The amount of heat produced by exercise and by the metabolic activity of the tissue equals the amount of heat lost by the animal to its environment (Whittow 1965:186).

The wild turkey, like all birds, is homeothermic (warm-blooded), so the body temperature needs to remain relatively constant. Body temperature of birds may be affected also by age, size, sex, breed, activity, food, diurnal rhythm, ambient temperature, season, molting, plumage, and nesting habits. The body temperature of domestic turkeys was measured as 41.2 degrees Celsius (106.2 degrees Fahrenheit) (King and Farner 1961:273). The average body temperature of game-farm poults and poults from wild-mated hens was 41.5 degrees Celsius (106.7 degrees Fahrenheit), with a range of 38.7 to 41.6 degrees Celsius (101.7 to 106.9 degrees Fahrenheit) for wild-mated poults up to 48 days old (Gerstell and Long 1939:41).

Metabolism of the eastern wild turkey was measured as a function of temperature during winter and summer (Gray and Prince 1988:133). Basal metabolic rate (BMR) did not differ between sexes within seasons but was higher for juveniles during winter and adults in summer than for adults in winter. Also, metabolic cost for thermoregulation (temperature level where weight loss and physiological response may become evident) below the lower critical temperature (T_{lc}) was greater for females than for males during each season (Table 4). The greater body mass of male turkeys caused them to have a lower T_{lc} than females within each season (Calder and King 1974:259). Adult wild turkeys are heaviest in late winter and lightest in late summer, when changes in lipid reserves result in body mass fluctuations of about 15 percent (Bailey and Rinell 1967:85).

Tests on metabolism of game-farm and wild-mated poults, under forced fasting and varying temperatures, showed that wild-mated birds withstood such hardships as low temperatures and lack of food better than their game-farm counterparts (Gerstell and Long 1939:4). The greatest degree of vigor also occurred in the wild-mated poults. Succeeding age groups of wild-mated poults continued to have a higher BMR, greater physiological resistance over 24 to 72 hours of continuous fasting, and greater heat production than game-farm poults. Wild-mated poults also displayed greater activity. Domestication apparently negatively influences both metabolism and behavior of wild turkey poults, reinforcing the belief that only wild turkeys should be used in restocking programs.

Excretion

Once most available nutrients of ingested food are assimilated, waste products are discharged through the cloaca. Urinary waste products are transported from the kidneys through the ureters into the cloaca, where they are voided with feces. The kidney is primarily an organ of filtration, excretion, and absorption. From the blood, it filters water and substances normally used by the body, as well as removing waste products that are voided in the

Table 4. The estimated lower critical temperature (T_{lc}) of eastern wild turkey in degrees Celsius (degrees Fahrenheit) during fasting studies (Gray and Prince 1988).

Sex	Winter juveniles	Summer adults	Winter adults
Female	15 (59)	19 (66)	11 (52)
Male	11 (52)	15 (59)	7 (45)

urine. Body water, glucose, and other substances are reabsorbed as a conservation measure. Epinephrine, which causes an increase in blood pressure, may cause an increase in urine flow in turkeys and an increase in renal (kidney) blood flow. This hormone stimulates the opening of a renal valve at the junction of the renal and iliac veins.

Circulation

The functions of blood include (1) absorption and transport of nutrients from the alimentary canal to tissues; (2) transport of blood gases to and from the tissues; (3) removal of metabolic waste products; (4) transportation of hormones; (5) regulation of water content of the body tissues; and (6) regulation and maintenance of body temperature (Sturkie 1965:1).

Blood cells. Concentrations of erythrocytes (red blood cells) are 2.24 million per cubic millimeter for domestic turkey males and 2.37 million per cubic millimeter for females (Sturkie 1965:3, from Groebbels 1932). The concentration of erythrocytes may be influenced by age, sex, hormones, season, some minerals, and vitamins.

Leucocytes (white blood cells) consist of 5 types. An average differential white cell count for normal captive wild turkey blood was the following: lymphocytes—50.6 percent; heterophils—43.4 percent; basophils—3.2 percent; monocytes—1.9 percent; and eosinophils—0.9 percent (Johnson and Lange 1939:157). Sex, age, and diet seem not to affect numbers of leucocytes consistently. But environment, hormones, and disease may have either a positive or negative effect.

Androgens cause sexually mature roosters to have more red blood cells than hens (Domm and Taber 1946:258). Thyroxine also exerts control over the numbers of red blood cells in roosters but not in hens. Adrenal hormones can cause a transient lymphopenia (decrease in number of lymphocytes) and leucocytosis (increase in number of white blood cells) in the adult chicken (Shapiro and Schechtman 1949:440).

Hematocrit. The hematocrit (centrifuge that separates blood cells from blood fluid) value was 35.9 percent for domestic turkey hens (McCartney 1952:184), 36.4 percent for 9-month-old females, and 45.1 percent for males (Ringer unpublished, Sturkie 1965:5). The mean hematocrit for pen-reared eastern wild turkey females (40.3 ± 4.1 [standard deviation]) was not significantly different from that of males (41.4 ± 4.3) (Lisano and Kennamer 1977b:159). The mean hematocrit values for pen-reared birds (45.5 ± 3.1) were significantly higher than those for trapped wild birds during winter (41.8 ± 5.4). The difference may have been caused by a lack of food, especially usable iron (Fe), for free-ranging birds. The great differences among values for wild turkey hens and domestic hens could have resulted from genetic differences (Lisano and Kennamer 1977b:160).

The hematocrit (packed cell) volume of domestic turkey blood in 2 instances was found to be 31.9 and 41.2 percent (Rapaport and Guest 1941:269), the 41.2 percent being quite similar to values in wild turkey.

Constituents of Blood

Most information on the constituents of wild turkey blood is based on extrapolations and interpretations of blood parameters for domestic turkey. The available data relate to hemoglobin (Hb); calcium (Ca); phosphorus (P); vitamins A, C, and carotene; plasma glucose; cholesterol; and protein. The data are expressed by sample means ± standard deviations.

Hemoglobin. Hemoglobin values of avian blood may be influenced by sex, reproductive status, age, health, and nutrition. For domestic Bronze turkeys, these levels were 15.0 grams per deciliter for males and 13.9 grams per deciliter for females (Scott et al. 1933:17). Mean Hb levels of blood from the eastern wild turkey were 13.9 ± 2.3 grams per deciliter for males and 13.7 ± 2.3 grams per deciliter for females (Lisano and Kennamer 1977b:160). However, the mean Hb value (15.3 ± 0.1) for all pen-reared wild turkeys differed significantly from that (14.1 ± 1.4) for turkeys trapped in January and February.

Decreasing food availability may have caused the difference, since mean Hb values in March and April (pen-reared birds = 15.6 ± 0.7 and killed birds = 14.0 ± 3.1 grams per deciliter) were not significantly different from the winter values. Age differences were found for Beltsville Small White turkeys. A progressive increase occurred in hemoglobin values from week 1 to week 40 (Wolterink et al. 1947:559). Hemoglobin levels may be useful in monitoring certain physiological aspects of the wild turkey, and thus they may be valuable in management of the turkey.

Plasma glucose. Avian blood plasma transports more than 95 percent of the total blood glucose in the form of d-glucose. Earlier studies on domestic turkeys showed somewhat lower levels of plasma glucose (Scott et al. 1933:17, Rhian et al. 1944:225–228) than reported for wild turkey (Lisano and Kennamer 1977b:163–164). For Bronze turkeys, the plasma glucose means were 191.60 milligrams per deciliter for females and 189.40 for males. For penned and free-ranging wild turkeys, the mean plasma glucose levels were as follows:

	Pen-reared	Trapped	Killed
January–February	375.5 ± 33.1	337.5 ± 48.2	–
March–April	350.8 ± 30.6	–	263.8 ± 83.8

The difference between the glucose levels of penned and trapped turkeys in winter could have been caused by decreased food supplies for the free-ranging turkeys (Lisano and Kennamer 1977b:162). In spring, the difference may have resulted from both food availability and age. The penned juveniles were no more than 11 months old, and most of the harvested gobblers were adults. An age differential in plasma glucose values has not been reported previously for wild turkeys, although Sturkie (1955:575) mentioned it with the chicken, and other investigators have reported such a differential in mammals.

In gobblers at sexual maturity, glucose levels were lower. No differences because of sex were apparent (335.1 ± 57.7 milligrams per deciliter for females versus 336.2 ± 69.9 milligrams per deciliter for males) (Lisano and Kennamer 1977b:163). The higher plasma glucose levels of the eastern wild turkey (Lisano and Kennamer 1977b:164), compared to domestic turkeys, probably result from genetic differences, tameness, and stress. Wild turkeys encounter more environmental and social or behavioral stresses than do most domestic turkeys. The challenges for wild turkeys to endure severe weather, predation, and food shortages require different physiological responses than are required of a protected and sedate domesticated bird.

The importance of other elements of plasma—i.e., nonprotein nitrogen (NPN), uric acid, urea, creatinine, ammonia, and free amino acids—has not been reported for the wild turkey. Adult chickens seem to have higher levels of NPN than immatures. Hens have lower levels than males. And laying hens have lower levels than non-laying ones (Bell and Sturkie 1965:44).

Uric acid in plasma may be influenced by sex and reproductive state. Nonlaying chickens had higher levels than layers (Bell and Sturkie 1965:45). Starved birds had abnormally low levels of uric acid, which normally constitutes 60 to 80 percent of the total nitrogen in urine of birds. Uric acid must be voided properly, or its increase in blood (uricemia) can cause death in birds and mammals (Bell and Sturkie 1965:45).

Domestic turkeys and other species can suffer from visceral gout, characterized by deposits of uric acid on serous surfaces of kidneys, lungs, and other organs (Siller 1959:1319). Chickens with elevated urea levels are known to suffer from paralysis, tumors, respiratory disorders, and parasites (Howell 1939:573). Little variation has been shown in urea levels (2.23 to 2.83 milligrams per deciliter) of chickens of different sex or age, whether fed or starved, laying or nonlaying (Bell et al. 1959:355).

Urea levels of domestic turkeys were 4.9 (hens) and 4.7 (toms) milligrams per deciliter (Kirshner et al. 1951:875).

In female and male turkey blood plasma, creatine of 2.5 and ammonia of 2.8 milligrams per deciliter have been reported (Kirshner et al. 1951:875). Hurst and Poe (1985) gave levels of essential (10) and nonessential (8) amino acids in the whole body of wild turkey poults, but they did not separate blood from other body parts. Domestic turkeys had amino acid means of about 18.8 (hens) and 21.1 (toms) (Kirshner et al. 1951).

Plasma proteins. A chief function of plasma proteins is to maintain normal blood volume and normal water content in tissues by a colloidal osmotic pressure. Proper balance can be influenced by changes in body temperature, stress, and other factors. Plasma protein composition in the domestic turkey was 66.5 percent serum albumin, 7.9 percent alpha globulin (often shown as alpha$_1$ and alpha$_2$), 14.4 percent beta globulin, and 11.2 percent gamma globulin (Lynch and Stafseth 1954:54).

The total plasma of domestic turkeys was 3.96 to 4.91 grams per deciliter (Lynch and Stafseth 1954), while the plasma protein percent was 4.54 for males and 4.8 for females (Rhian et al. 1944:225–226). Overall means for the eastern wild turkey were 4.7 ± 0.5 grams per deciliter (males) and 4.6 ± 0.5 grams per deciliter (females) (Lisano and Kennamer 1977b:165). A range of 4.85 to 6.01 grams per deciliter was determined for the same species (Martin et al. 1981:801).

The level of plasma protein was fairly stable from mid-November to early February (5.29 ± 0.15 grams per deciliter). The level reached a peak of 6.01 ± 0.22 in early May and then declined to 5.30 ± 0.18 by mid-June. The higher levels in breeding season could result from higher estrogen levels, which coincide with longer periods of daylight (Mukherjee et al. 1969:2081–2086).

Age also affected total plasma protein levels (Lisano and Kennamer 1977b:165). The value for pen-reared poults 6 weeks old was 3.6 ± 0.4 grams per deciliter, but it rose to 4.6 ± 0.2 grams per deciliter for birds 14 months old. Mean values for males (4.7 ± 0.5) varied little from those of females (4.6 ± 0.5). No difference appeared between levels of protein in pen-reared and wild-trapped birds, but a difference was found between pen-reared (4.8 ± 0.8) and killed (5.4 ± 0.8) turkeys, primarily because the killed birds were older.

Plasma lipids. Plasma lipids include total cholesterol, total fatty acid, phospholipids, and total lipids. Plasma cholesterol increased with age in male and female Broad Breasted Bronze domesticated turkeys from 8 weeks (148 milligrams per deciliter) to 16 weeks (249 milligrams per deciliter), and then leveled off (Speckman and Ringer 1962:49). Values for White Holland turkeys were 115.0 ± 11.5 milligrams for adult males and 133.0 ± 32.1 milligrams for hens (Kirshner et al. 1951).

Higher values but similar differences were shown between sexes of wild turkeys: 123.2 ± 26.7 for toms and 159.8 ± 38.1 for hens (Lisano and Kennamer 1977b:161). These differences between sexes apparently are genetic. Plasma cholesterol levels of pen-reared, trapped, and harvested wild turkeys followed similar patterns related to age, sex, and season.

Increases in plasma cholesterol levels of females were obvious from January (157.8 milligrams per deciliter) to February (182 milligrams per deciliter) and through the breeding and egg-laying seasons. A greater demand for cholesterol, which constitutes egg yolk, occurs in laying hens. Cholesterol levels for wild turkey hens increased from 138.5 ± 8.1 milligrams per deciliter in November to 191.0 ± 18.9 milligrams per deciliter in early March to 112.1 by mid-June (Martin et al. 1981:801).

Mean plasma cholesterol for males was 134.3 ± 20.5 milligrams per deciliter in February, decreasing to 87.8 ± 14.0 in May. This period coincided with the breeding season and the development of a breast sponge, which took some of the plasma cholesterol.

Metallic elements. Values for 2 of the major metallic elements, calcium and phosphorus, have been reported for domestic turkeys. Calcium was listed as 11.7 milligrams per deciliter for males and 11.1 for females (Scott et al. 1933:17), with means ranging from 9.25 to 25.5 milligrams per deciliter (December 1943 to May 1944) for turkey hens and 6.9 to 10.5 for toms (Paulsen et al. 1950:15). Bronze turkey hens had calcium values of 20.9 and 20.2 milligrams in June and 12.4 milligrams in August (Rhian et al. 1944:225).

Males require less calcium than females; there is a great demand for calcium by egg-laying hens. Although thick-shelled eggs are strongly hereditary, a deficiency of calcium in the diet results in a progressive thinning of the shell and a complete cessation of laying, probably the result of an inhibition of gonadotrophin secretions (Taylor and Stringer 1965:485–486). A large volume of snail shells (10.5 percent) has been reported in Rio Grande turkey diets during the egg-laying season (Van Norman 1989:24). Snails occurred about 9 times more in laying hens than in prelaying or postlaying birds (Beasom and Pattee 1978:917).

Inorganic phosphorus levels in domestic turkey plasma were 4.20 milligrams per deciliter for females and 3.66 milligrams for males (Scott et al. 1933:17). Mean values of 4.41 to 7.09 milligrams per deciliter for hens and 3.22 to 5.56 for toms were reported by Paulsen et al. (1950:15). For normal Bronze turkey hens, the values were about 3.8 milligrams per deciliter in June and 3.64 in August (Rhian et al. 1944:225).

Vitamins. Small amounts of various vitamins seem necessary for normal physiology of animals. Blood plasma values of Vitamin C were given as 0.950 milligrams per deciliter for 48 Broad Breasted Bronze turkey hens and 0.876 for 12 White Holland hens, for a mean of 0.935 ± 0.357 milligrams per deciliter (Rhian et al. 1944:225, 228). Values for toms were 0.550 for mid-June and 0.558 for mid-August. Mean values for Vitamin A in hens varied from 0.086 milligrams per deciliter in June to 0.158 in August and in toms, from 0.125 to 0.145. Carotene mean values for hens on 3 different dates in June were 0.225, 0.345, and 0.414 milligrams per deciliter and 0.475 in August. Toms had carotene levels of 0.329 and 0.421 in June and 0.200 in August.

Blood Pressure

After sexual maturity, both blood pressure and atherosclerosis tend to increase with age. Systolic pressure has been related to increased levels of cholesterol in the abdominal aorta of the domestic turkey (Speckman and Ringer 1962:40). The systolic blood pressure of the adult Jersey Buff turkey was 12 percent to 15 percent higher than for a young poult (Weiss and Sheahan 1958:209). Adult Broad Breasted Bronze turkeys had higher blood pressures than adult Jersey Buffs (Ringer and Rood 1959:395), indicating that some genetic differences may exist between varieties and probably between wild and domestic turkeys.

Male domestic turkeys have significantly higher blood pressure than their female counterparts (Weiss and Sheahan 1958:209, Ringer and Rood 1959:395). The systolic pressure (197.8 millimeters HG) of an 8-week-old Broad Breasted Bronze male increased about 50 percent to 296.7 millimeters HG at 22 weeks. Systolic pressure in females of the same age rose 36 percent, from 189.3 to 257.3 millimeters HG. The diastolic pressure changes for males were 164.2 to 222.0 and for females, 158.2 to 200.0 millimeters HG. Pulse pressures changed from 33.3 to 74.7 for males and 31.2 to 57.3 for females.

Sex hormones alter blood pressure of turkeys and chickens (Sturkie and Ringer 1955:53). Estrogen suppresses the pituitary output of gonadotrophins, so pituitary hormones may help control blood pressure through a vasodilating effect on blood vessels. Oxytocin lowers blood pressure through vasodilation. The depressing effect of vasotocin is more variable.

An increase in the epinephrine during stress causes a marked elevation of systolic blood pressure. Consequently, turkeys nearing sexual maturity may be inclined—if atherosclerosis is present—to rupture a weakened aorta when exposed to stress. Wild turkeys may be subjected to more stress than domestic birds. Yet atherosclerosis may not be as frequent, because of less available food and greater activity of wild turkeys. Also, adrenals are usually larger in wild animals and probably release more epinephrine under stress.

Cardiac Output

Cardiac output is influenced by heart rate, volume per stroke, and the amount of venous blood returning to the heart. These factors in turn are affected by sex, exercise, temperature, and metabolic state (including starvation). The mean cardiac output of male Broad Breasted Bronze turkeys was given as 231 milliliters per kilogram[0.73] per minute, with mean carotid end points for systolic pressure at 301 millimeters HG, mean diastolic pressure at 206 millimeters HG, and pulse pressure at 95 millimeters HG (Speckman et al. 1961:1460).

Heat-adapted chickens have a much lower cardiac output than those adapted to winter temperatures (Vogel and Sturkie 1963:1404). Starvation also lowers cardiac output. These factors would affect wild turkeys as well, since stresses related to temperature and lack of food are encountered more frequently by wild birds.

Heart Rate

Adult turkeys have lower heart rates than younger ones, and males have lower heart rates than females. The heart rate of domestic male poults decreased from 288 at 8 weeks to 198 at 22 weeks (Ringer and Rood 1959). For female poults of the same ages, the decrease was from 283 to 232. The sex difference in heart rates developed at about the age when production of gonadotrophic hormones began. Adult male Bronze turkeys had a heart rate of 147 beats per minute (Speckman et al. 1961:1460).

Availability of food also may affect heart rates in the wild turkey. After 24 hours of fasting, game-farm poults registered heart rates of 345 beats per minute while wild-mated poults registered 348 beats per minute (Gerstell and Long 1939:40). After a 72-hour fast, the heart rate of game-farm poults decreased by 11.7 percent while the wild poults showed a 9.4 percent decrease.

At night compared to day, birds generally have not only decreased activity but also a lower heart rate. During daytime, exercise such as walking or even eating is known to increase heart rates of domestic birds. Similar exercises probably affect the wild turkey more significantly, since it has a larger heart and slower heart rate than the domestic turkey (Lewis 1967:63).

Respiration

Respiration in birds varies, depending on body size, sex, temperature, stress (including excitement), and flight. Male domestic turkeys have a respiratory rate of 28 per minute and females a rate of 49 (Kaupp 1923:36). (In contrast, the canary's respiratory rate is as high as 100 per minute.)

Hatching of embryos can be impaired if incubating eggs cannot respire adequately. The rate of gas exchanged in avian embryos in natural and artificial incubation depends on the resistance to diffusion offered by the shell and its membrane (Christensen et al. 1982:1756). Extreme egg sizes (larger in domestic than wild turkeys) may decrease respiration, so larger eggs could be detrimental to hatchability. The number of pores per egg has not changed through domestication and artificial selection, but those pores are spread across a 32 percent greater surface area. One pore in wild turkeys serves an area of 0.6 square millimeters (0.0093 square inches), and 1 pore in domestic birds serves an area of 0.9 square millimeters (0.01395 square inches). Respiration for domestic turkey embryos may be more difficult than for wild turkey embryos.

Respiration rates declined after young were hatched, but then increased as turkey poults became older (Table 5). Overall, the rates of 57 wild-mated poults varied from 54 to 106, with an average of 74.0 per minute. Respiration (and body temperature as it affects respiration) and other physiological processes were important because they provided some indication of the internal condition of birds (Gerstell and Long 1939:8). Turkeys, like most birds, are panting animals, and this activity—as a function of the respiratory system—helps to regulate body temperature, as does gular flutter.

Nervous System

An organism becomes an operational entity through the correlation and integration of all other systems by way of the nervous and endocrine systems (Figure 6). Behavior in the turkey is a response to stimuli that act upon the nervous system (Bailey 1967:93), and hormones—by their action on the central nervous system—also influence the behavior of wild turkeys (Lewis 1967:60).

Leopold (1944:183–190) discussed the impact on wild behavior attributable to the larger size of the eastern wild turkey's brain, pituitary, and adrenals in compari-

Table 5. Respiratory rates (respirations per minute) of different-aged game-farm poults (GF) and poults from wild-mated hens (WM) (Gerstell and Long 1939).

| Poults | Average respirations per minute | | | | |
	30 hours	54 hours	78 hours	5–9 days	15–19 days
GF	46	43	40	43	52
WM	45	45	45	48	51

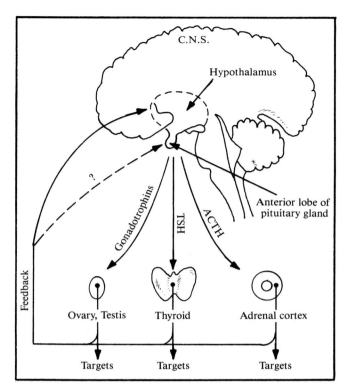

Figure 6. A diagram illustrating the reciprocal relationship among the central nervous system and certain endocrine glands. Ovarian, testicular, thyroidal, and adrenocortical hormones in the blood act back upon the anterior pituitary, with the hypothalamus as the probable intermediary, to adjust the output of hormones in accordance with the organism's needs (Turner 1966:48).

son with domestic varieties. He used as an example the "freezing" response in wild turkey chicks, which is induced by a nervous stimulus transmitted to the brain through the ear or eye. Because this is a fear reaction, the sympathetic and the central nervous systems probably receive the stimulus. When the sympathetic system is stimulated, it receives a "shot" of adrenaline, the size of which depends on the size of the adrenal glands as well as on the strength of the stimulation.

Wildness in turkeys is tied in with the functioning of the central and sympathetic nervous systems and with secretions of pituitary and adrenal glands (Leopold 1944:190). The pituitary is stimulated through the nervous system to release corticotropic hormones, which stimulate the adrenals to release adrenaline. The differences between wildness and domesticity, 2 heritable physiological complexes, result primarily from differences in form and function of the nervous and endocrine systems in the individual turkey.

In reproduction, light first stimulates the pituitary through the nervous system. Gonadotrophins are released to initiate breeding, including gobbling activities. Both light periodicity and air temperature (Marshall

1961:309) may stimulate the nervous system before any other physiological process is initiated. The endocrine system, in conjunction with the nervous system, almost completely controls an organism's response to internal and external stimuli that may be received through the skin as well as the eyes (Romanoff and Romanoff 1949).

Light probably initiates molting in wild turkeys (Lewis 1967:53) by first stimulating the nervous system. The light stimulus, acting through the nervous system, activates the pituitary to produce thyrotropic hormones, which govern the activity of the thyroid (Bissonnette 1935:170–180) and thus control feather replacement.

Behavior

Since, as Leopold said, "the nervous and endocrine system jointly exercise almost complete control over the functioning of an organism, the possible effects of differences in development of these two systems upon behavior are obvious" (Leopold 1944:189). The relationship of the 2 systems is reciprocal. The nervous system exerts regulatory control over endocrine glands, and hormones from these glands act back upon the nervous system to affect psychologic and behavioral characteristics of the species (Turner 1966). For example, the actual process through which turkeys go to roost at night and leave a roost in the morning is controlled by the daily light cycle. This decreasing and increasing light cycle probably stimulates the anterior pituitary, thus regulating the turkey's activity.

Gonadotrophins and gonadal hormones are largely responsible for reproductive behavior. Of these, testosterone is responsible for aggressive behavior of gobblers. Prolactin, secreted by the pituitary, initiates broodiness and incubation in hens.

Epinephrine initiates quick responses to various stresses such as predators, humans, and weather. This wariness and response to stress may account for survival of the wild turkey under extreme conditions. Other hormones may have a direct or indirect effect on the normal behavior of turkeys.

SURVIVAL

It is remarkable that the wild turkey has been able to thrive in spite of continual and severe pressure from the environment and from predators. Survival of the wild turkey depends upon both intrinsic and extrinsic factors. Wild turkeys usually breed in late winter or spring, avoiding the more adverse weather and food shortages earlier in the year. The turkey, being alert and wary, disappears quickly when danger threatens. Young poults will hide or freeze, in contrast to domestic counterparts, which scatter. This inherent behavior and physiology of the wild turkey help it survive in a hostile world.

Age

Longevity and breeding age are important to the viability of a population. The overall mortality rate of the wild turkey is about 70 percent during the first 2 weeks of life (Williams and Austin 1988:151–153). Expected longevity is much longer after this critical early phase. The average longevity of the Florida wild turkey was given as 18 months, but some wild turkeys have lived as long as 9, 12, and 14 years (Mosby and Handley 1943:175, Ligon 1946:7, Powell 1965:16, Lewis 1967:69). Although yearling toms usually do not breed, some yearling hens breed freely in a normal population of wild turkeys. The young raised by yearling hens may enhance viability of a wild turkey population in critical years.

Condition

The physiological condition of the wild turkey hen, as influenced by severity of the preceding winter, was a major factor affecting productivity in a northern turkey population (Porter et al. 1983:281). Heavier females were more likely to nest and to have greater productivity than lighter females. The lighter hens may have lacked energy reserves to lay and incubate a second clutch. Hens could lose significant amounts of body weight during winter without affecting fecundity as long as they regained the weight prior to laying (Prince and Gray 1986:47). For toms weighing less than 6.35 kilograms (14 pounds), advanced stages of spermatogenesis were rare (Lewis and Breitenbach 1966:619).

Fat tissues compose 25 percent of winter body weights in adults and 15 percent in juveniles (Prince and Gray 1986:42). The breast sponge alone on gobblers may weigh as much as 0.9 kilograms (2 pounds) (Bailey and Rinell 1967:85). The increased winter lipid reserves might

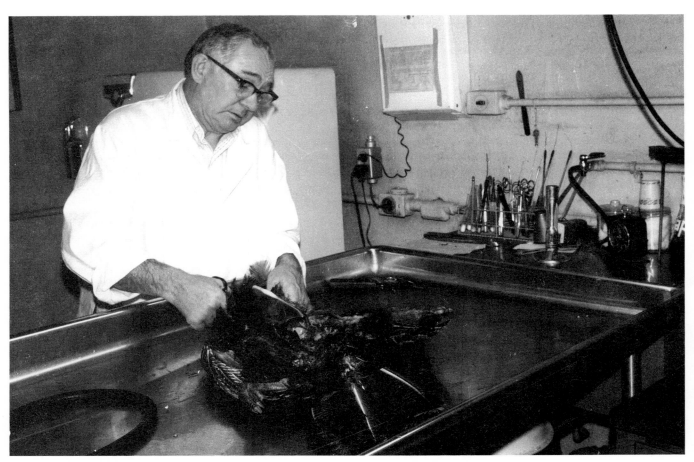

Postmortem of turkey thought to have starved in severe winter. *Photo by G. Wunz, Pennsylvania Game Commission.*

serve as an energy reserve and as added insulation, thereby improving survival chances (Gray and Prince 1988:136, Oberlag et al. 1990:666). Body weight losses of 35 percent in adult wild turkeys and 25 percent in juveniles could result in death, although some wild turkeys may lose a third of their body weight without any permanent effects (Mosby and Handley 1943:97, Hayden and Nelson 1963:10). Juveniles and adults within each sex have equal thermoregulation costs per unit of body weight at low temperatures, but adults have a survival edge due to greater adipose and muscle tissue reserves (Prince and Gray 1986:45). The T_{lc} was lower for both sexes and all ages in winter (Gray and Prince 1988:136, Oberlag et al. 1990:665). Biochemical changes associated with acclimatization (Dawson et al. 1983a:353, b:755, Marsh et al. 1984:469), or better insulation provided by plumage and fat reserves (Pohl 1971:185–193, Mortensen and Blix 1986:8–13), or a combination of these probably cause the reduced T_{lc} in winter birds. Physiologically, the age, sex, and corresponding body conditions correlate closely with survival potential of wild turkeys.

Stress

Typical stimuli that elicit stress include pain, fear, cold, blood loss, anoxia, exposure to environmental contaminants, emotional tension, and intraspecific competition (Kirkpatrick 1980:111–112). Many stress indices involve adrenal gland characteristics. For example, changes in the corticosterone level in peripheral blood of the domestic turkey reflect the severity of stress (Brown 1976:538–542). Consequently, levels of plasma corticosterone in eastern wild turkeys have been used to measure the degree of stress to which wild birds are exposed (Whatley et al. 1977:191–193). Some of these stress factors were loss of habitat, changes in food availability, and overpopulation.

Weather. When birds are exposed to ambient temperatures below their critical temperature, their heat production increases to a maximal value, designated "summit metabolism," that may be 3 to 4 times greater than normal (Sturkie 1965:253). Birds respond by shivering to increase heat production. They maintain a normal body temperature as long as physiologically possible (Kendeigh 1934). As thermogenetic fatigue sets in, body temperature falls until the bird dies.

Physiological differences occur in the ability of sexes to withstand climatic severities. Turkey hens survive longer (15.2 days) than males (11.3 days) when exposed to severe cold and heat in fasting conditions (Latham 1947:148). Although males may have greater fat reserves,

females need relatively less food, a significant difference when food is limited but mobility is not (Oberlag et al. 1990:666).

Up to 60 percent of a turkey population succumbed to severe winters in north-central Pennsylvania. But usually a population recovered in a breeding season, indicating some birds survived by adapting to the severe cold (Wunz and Hayden 1975:67, 69). The effects of snow on food availability and turkey mobility may be more important to survival than temperature alone (Oberlag et al. 1990:666).

Studies on basal metabolism and energetic cost of thermoregulation in wild turkeys provide insight into how they often survive stress and differences that result from age and sex (Gray and Prince 1988). Evidence exists that young turkeys, especially males in the northern part of their range, grow little after the onset of cold weather. This state is important to survival since growth during winter would require a winter molt to provide protection for the increased surface area, and energy reserves would be depleted by molting (Bailey and Rinell 1967a:85).

Nutrition. Wild turkeys normally can survive extended periods of time without much food. These birds are opportunistic feeders and will survive where other species may not (Van Norman 1989:77). Drought or overgrazing that reduce ground cover or food supplies and expose poults to high ground temperatures decrease survival (Markley 1967:227). Drought also suppressed gonadal development in a high proportion of Rio Grande turkey hens (Pattee and Beasom 1979:512). So nutrition must be considered important in promoting or suppressing poult survival.

Disease. Wild turkey populations usually are free from disease or have adapted to naturally occurring diseases. Occasionally, diseases may be detrimental. For example, pullorum infections do not occur frequently, but they can result in losses through reduced egg production, lower hatchability, and higher poult mortality (Hensley and Cain 1978:66). Of greater concern is the threat of deadly diseases introduced into nonresistant wild turkeys by the release of pen-raised turkeys as a propagation technique (Kennamer 1988b:22–23). Diseases seem to thrive and spread more easily under conditions that concentrate birds. Penned birds may survive because of built-up resistance, but also they may become carriers of diseases potentially threatening to wild birds.

Capture. Capturing, even with minimal handling, can cause stress to turkeys. As indicated by the mean and standard error, trapped wild turkeys had much higher levels (6.28 ± 0.78 milligrams per deciliter) of plasma corticosterone than pen-reared (2.13 ± 0.11) or killed (1.96 ± 0.13) wild turkeys (Whatley et al. 1977:192). When biologists used alpha-chloralose to anesthetize turkeys, little stress occurred, and plasma glucose levels did not rise (Donahue et al. 1982:472–473). This drug or others may be used to reduce stress in birds being handled (Williams and Austin 1988:27–36).

Special Senses

Although considered separately from the nervous system by many investigators, the 4 special senses of sight, hearing, smell, and taste are each controlled through sensory perceptions. These special senses are clearly relevant to survival of wild turkeys.

Sight. The wild turkey has a lower threshold for discerning movement and has a wider field of vision than man, a combination that often proves frustrating to hunters. Quoting Pumphrey (1961:58), "A bird with a single glance lasting perhaps a second takes in a picture which a man could accumulate only by laboriously scanning the whole field piece by piece with the most accurate portion of his retina." Pumphrey also states that the bird's picture is flat and that man, with his slow, binocular search, can acquire more information about relative distances. A bird would get similar information by successive glances from different places. This difference in perceiving distance may partly account for a turkey's inability to land easily in a tree at night. Discerning shape becomes more difficult as the bird gets closer to a landing site. With its flat perception, the turkey's eye may not be able to sort out distinct images at night as well as in daytime.

In vision, light entering the eye is refracted by the cornea, aqueous humor, lens, and vitreous humor to form an inverted image at the retina. On the retina of diurnal birds such as turkey are "areae" within which is usually a depression forming a pit (fovea). Within and near the fovea, where cones are the densest, is the place of maximum optical resolution. Some birds have 2 foveas, but turkeys only have a central one (Kare 1965: 410–411).

Turkeys readily detect momentary color changes in head adornment of gobblers, and they can distinguish between grains of white and yellow corn (Lewis 1967:67). The high density of cone cells allows all diurnal birds to have color vision.

Hearing. The ability to discriminate among frequencies within the range of birds as a group seems similar to that of man (Kare 1965:426). The hearing of many birds has its highest sensitivity between 1,000 and 3,000 cps (cycles per second). Some owls have their highest sensitivity around 6,000 cps. A human being's limits are about 16,000 to 20,000. A wild turkey's hearing may be as acute as that of humans, but turkeys probably can detect higher and more subtle frequency variations than people.

Smell. The poorly developed olfactory system in the turkey does not allow for a well-developed sense of smell (Lewis 1967:68), and field experience supports this conclusion.

Taste. Wild turkeys probably distinguish the 4 primary gustative qualities typical in man: sweet, sour, salty, bitter (Portman 1961:42). However, young chickens were indifferent to sugar solutions of up to 25 percent (Kare and Medway 1959:1119). Gallinaceous and other birds use salty water to some degree (Kare and Beily 1948:751, Hamrum 1953:872, Bartholomew and Mac-Millan 1961:505), but young chickens would not take salt solutions beyond 0.9 percent.

Birds have a wide range of tolerance for acidity and alkalinity in drinking water (Kare 1965:437). Turkeys can detect and avoid drugs such as methoxymol with which they have had previous experience, perhaps by smell or touch, but presumably through taste (Williams and Austin 1988:34).

CONCLUSION

The wild turkey is the epitome of wildness but also is quite adaptable to environmental conditions. Its biological processes are supported by physiological systems honed by centuries of natural selection. But even in this age of advanced technology and increased interest, we still lack basic biological and physiological information about the wild turkey.

Since physiology is about the functions of living organisms and how they interact with their environment, we cannot manage a species effectively until essential information is available for the wildlife manager.

Chapter 8

POPULATION INFLUENCES: DISEASES AND PARASITES

William R. Davidson
School of Forest Resources
and
Southeastern Cooperative
Wildlife Disease Study
College of Veterinary Medicine
The University of Georgia
Athens, Georgia

Emily Jo Wentworth
Georgia Department of Natural Resources
Game and Fish Division
Gainesville, Georgia

Wild turkeys have been the subject of intensive and highly successful restoration and management programs during the past few decades. These successes were accompanied by rising interest in many aspects of the wild turkey's biology, including numerous studies on diseases and parasites of wild turkeys (Maxfield et al. 1963, Prestwood 1968, Prestwood et al. 1973, 1975, Forrester et al. 1974, 1980, Hon et al. 1975, Davidson et al. 1985, Rocke and Yuill 1987). These and other publications have disclosed that wild turkeys are susceptible to many infectious and noninfectious diseases.

This chapter summarizes the information on disease and parasitism among wild turkeys, focusing mainly on diseases potentially significant at the population level or on parasites easily detected by casual observation. Detailed consideration of each agent is beyond the scope of this book. But the reader is referred to the original sources cited in the text, for additional details.

INFECTIOUS DISEASES

Avian Pox

Avian pox is an infectious, contagious viral disease of birds, including both wild and domestic turkeys. Avian poxviruses belong to the genus *Avipoxvirus* in the family Poxviridae and include numerous strains that vary in virulence and host range. In much of the earlier literature, the term "fowlpox" was used for poxvirus infections in turkeys, chickens, and other birds. Now, however, the broader term avian pox is preferred because fowlpox virus has been designated as a specific strain of avian poxvirus.

Avian pox is a very common viral infection that produces clinical disease among wild turkeys, especially from the eastern United States. For example, Davidson et al. (1985) reported that avian pox accounted for approximately 25 percent of the diagnoses in wild turkeys found sick or dead in 8 southeastern states.

The distribution of avian poxviruses in wild turkeys is incompletely known, although infections have been reported from Alabama, Arkansas, Florida, Georgia, Mississippi, South Carolina, Tennessee, Texas, Virginia, and West Virginia (Powell 1965, Davis 1966, Prestwood 1968, Prestwood et al. 1973, Forrester et al. 1980, Akey et al. 1981, Davidson et al. 1985). Avian poxvirus infections probably occur to some extent in much, if not all, of the range of the eastern subspecies and possibly in portions of the ranges of other subspecies.

Information on the annual prevalence of poxvirus infections is not available, although infections are known to occur annually in a substantial proportion of wild turkey populations in some areas in Florida (D.J. Forrester personal communication: 1988). Davidson et al. (1985) reported cases of clinical disease due to avian pox in 12 of 13 years in 8 southeastern states. Collectively, the observations from Florida and the diagnostic case accession data from the Southeast suggest that the prevalence of avian pox infections in the southeastern United States is relatively high, although it undoubtedly varies greatly by year and by location.

Poxvirus infection of epithelial tissues results in proliferative, wartlike growths. These lesions are most frequent on unfeathered areas such as the feet, legs, eyelids, and margins of the bill and in the mouth or upper respiratory tract (Davidson and Nettles 1988). Lesions often spontaneously regress 6 to 12 weeks after initial infection.

The prognosis for infected birds depends primarily on the severity and location of lesions. The diphtheritic or "wet" form of pox, where lesions occur in the mouth or trachea, usually results in higher rates of morbidity and death than the cutaneous or "dry" form, where lesions occur on the skin. Lesions in or surrounding the eyes also may result in debilitation or death.

Clinical signs of avian pox may include emaciation, weakness, respiratory distress, and blindness. These signs may be totally absent in birds with only mild lesions or in birds whose lesions do not impair feeding, respiration, or vision. Turkeys that become debilitated due to avian pox are vulnerable to predation, as evidenced by the ease with which they are caught by people. Probably many sick birds are removed by predators before they are detected by people (Davidson and Nettles 1988).

Avian poxviruses are transmitted by a variety of means including (1) contact of the virus with abraded or damaged epithelium (surface layer) of the skin, eyes, upper respiratory tract, and oral cavity, or (2) mechanical inoculation of the virus into epithelial tissues. Among wild turkeys, mechanical transmission by blood-feeding arthropods is probably the most important route of transmission. Previous studies have demonstrated the importance of mosquitoes as vectors of avian poxviruses among wild turkeys in Florida (Akey et al. 1981). Mosquitoes and other blood-feeding arthropods are termed mechanical rather than biological vectors because the virus does not replicate within the arthropod. Rather, the arthropod simply takes the virus from one bird and transfers it to another bird.

The mosquitoes *Culex nigripalpus* and *Wyeomyia vanduzeei* were demonstrated to be vectors of avian poxviruses isolated from wild turkeys and to mechanically transmit the infection to a high proportion of turkeys exposed by experimentally interrupted feeding (Akey et al. 1981). The temporal distribution of *C. nigripalpus* populations and the fact that *C. nigripalpus* was documented to be an experimental vector led Akey et al. (1981) to conclude that *C. nigripalpus* was an extremely important factor in the occurrence of avian pox in wild turkeys in Florida. Under experimental conditions *C. nigripalpus* transmitted virus up to 4 weeks after feeding on infected turkeys.

Mosquito transmission in Florida was demonstrated throughout much of the year. But the majority of infections occurred during peaks in mosquito activity in late summer and fall (Forrester unpublished data in Akey et al. 1981:597). Annual prevalence of poxvirus infections among wild turkeys seemed to depend on precipitation patterns. There is a critical relationship between rainfall and mosquito population levels. Other potential sources of transmission among wild turkeys include ingestion or inhalation of particles of virus-containing scabs that are shed into the environment, such as in dusting areas (Davidson and Nettles 1988).

Diagnosis of avian pox is relatively easy. The lesions are usually external and prominent. Other infections, however, may resemble pox, and suspected pox cases should be confirmed by laboratory examinations. An easy and reliable method for confirmation is histopathologic (tissue) examination of lesions that have been fixed in 10 percent neutral buffered formalin. Microscopic examination of lesion sections usually reveals characteristic inclusion bodies (aggregates of virus particles) in the epithelial cells. An alternative method of confirmation is by isolation of the virus from fresh, frozen, or even air-dried lesion material. The scabs that often develop over and around pox lesions may contain large amounts of virus, and virus in these scabs will remain infective without preservation.

Control of avian pox among wild turkey populations is not practical with current technology. Prevention can be accomplished in some situations by preventing virus introduction via infected birds. One example is to cull birds with lesions during restocking programs.

Viral Neoplasms

Neoplasms (tumors) of presumed or confirmed viral origin have been reported infrequently in wild turkeys. Busch and Williams (1970) reported a "Marek's disease–like condition" in 2 wild turkeys from Florida. Subsequently, a herpesvirus, with similarities to the herpesviruses associated with Marek's disease of chickens and viral neoplasms of domestic turkeys, was isolated on 2 occasions from wild turkeys in Florida (Colwell et al. 1973, Grant et al. 1975). Then Davidson et al. (1985) reported a single case of a lymphoproliferative disease in a wild turkey, which was very similar to the neoplastic disease described by Busch and Williams (1970). Colwell et al. (1973) reported serologic evidence of antibody against a herpesvirus in 22 of 46 wild turkey serum samples from Florida, and Grant et al. (1975) isolated herpesvirus from 5 of 10 wild turkeys from Florida. The available data suggest that a herpesvirus capable of inducing neoplastic tumors is widespread in Florida wild turkeys, yet the virus so far has not often been associated with clinical disease.

Other Viral Diseases

Wild turkeys undoubtedly are susceptible to infection by many of the viruses that produce disease problems in domestic turkeys. Most of these diseases, however, either are not known in wild turkeys or have been reported only rarely.

For example, Domermuth et al. (1977) surveyed 211 wild turkeys from Florida and Texas for antibodies to hemorrhagic enteritis virus (HEV) of turkeys but failed to find any evidence of exposure to this agent. Similarly, Nettles et al. (1985), Rocke and Yuill (1987), and Davidson et al. (1988) collectively tested 682 wild turkeys from 9 states and found no evidence of infection by avian influenza (AI) viruses. A total of 620 wild turkeys from Texas have been tested for Newcastle disease (ND) virus, with uniformly negative results (Trainer et al. 1968, Trainer 1973, Hensley and Cain 1979). Surveys such as these suggest that the epidemiologic factors necessary for maintaining several important or potentially important viral diseases of commercially produced domestic turkeys do not occur among wild turkey populations. One factor that may be very critical is the difference between the frequent bird-to-bird contact in confined domestic turkey flocks and the infrequent contact among widely scattered flocks of wild birds.

Serologic evidence indicates that wild turkeys, as well as many other species of birds and mammals, may be exposed to certain endemic arthropod-borne viruses (arboviruses). For example, Trainer (1973) noted a substantial number of wild turkeys with antibodies to western equine encephalitis (WEE) virus and St. Louis encephalitis (SLE) virus in Texas, where both viruses are endemic and circulate periodically. Conversely, he found very low prevalences of antibodies to California, Venezuelan, and Eastern equine encephalitis viruses, which normally do not occur in this geographic region (Trainer 1973). These encephalitis viruses have not been associated with clinical illness in wild turkeys. Additionally, Trainer (1973) reported antibodies to vesicular stomatitis (VS) virus, suspected to be arthopod-borne, in wild turkeys in Texas during a 1965 VS outbreak in cattle and horses.

Mycoplasmosis

Mycoplasmosis is the term for disease produced by any of several species of organisms in the genus *Mycoplasma*. The best known avian mycoplasmas are *M. gallisepticum* (MG), *M. synoviae* (MS), and *M. meleagridis* (MM). These species are better known than others because of the disease problems they produce in domestic poultry. There are many other species of *Mycoplasma*,

including *M. iowae* and *M. gallopavonis*, to which both domestic and wild turkeys are susceptible. By far the most important species is *M. gallisepticum*, which causes infectious sinusitis and reproductive problems in domestic turkeys (Lancaster and Fabricant 1988). In recent years, MG has been the subject of considerable attention by wildlife agencies involved in wild turkey restoration programs (Amundson 1985, Davidson 1987).

Mycoplasma gallisepticum (MG). Turkeys, chickens, and other galliform birds are the most frequent hosts of MG. Infection in turkeys may lead to clinical disease characterized by respiratory distress and swollen infraorbital sinuses. Swollen sinuses contain purulent (pus) to caseous (cheesy) exudate, and there may be plaques of yellowish exudate on the air sacs. In severe cases, the bird may have a diffuse inflammation of the air sacs, with large amounts of exudate. Infection also may suppress reproductive performance.

Infected birds, especially chickens, may show no (or only very mild) clinical signs, but such birds may be chronic carriers and shedders of MG organisms. The organisms may be transmitted by contact with infected individuals, or by vertical transmission through the egg (Yoder 1980). Evidence of MG is not uncommon among backyard domestic poultry and pen-raised gamebirds, but it has been found only rarely in free-ranging wild turkeys (Davidson 1987).

Clinical infectious sinusitis has been reported only 3 times in free-ranging wild turkeys, and 1 of these cases involved semiwild turkeys. Davidson et al. (1982) reported the first cases from semiwild turkeys on Cumberland Island, Georgia. Jessup et al. (1983) confirmed MG in a single flock of wild turkeys in California, and Adrian (1984) reported MG in wild turkeys from Colorado. In the Colorado situation, MG and other diseases were more common in populations of wild turkeys with histories of poor population performance than in more vigorous populations in other areas. In each of these reports, the case histories included contact with domestic poultry, which circumstantially suggests that infections originated from domestic poultry.

Jessup et al. (1983) were able to isolate MG from domestic Bronze turkeys on a farm adjacent to the one where infected wild turkeys were found. Eight years after the disease was diagnosed in semiwild turkeys from Cumberland Island, Georgia, by Davidson et al. (1982), Luttrell (1989) found a high prevalence of seropositive free-ranging chickens from the same site. At least 1 of the seropositive chickens was reported to have been alive at the time of the original diagnosis of the disease in wild turkeys.

Antibodies to MG have been reported in native wild turkeys from California (Jessup et al. 1983), Colorado (Adrian 1984), Missouri (Amundson 1985), Texas

(Hensley and Cain 1979, Rocke and Yuill 1987), and Wisconsin (Amundson 1985, Rocke 1985). Generally, reports of antibodies in native wild turkeys have involved a low percentage of seropositive birds. The available serologic evidence does not particularly support a contention that MG occurs frequently in wild turkeys. For example, Davidson et al. (1988) failed to detect antibodies in 322 wild turkeys from 7 eastern states and concluded that wild turkeys were not important in the epidemiology of MG in this region. The situation in the western United States, where other subspecies of wild turkeys occur, may be somewhat different. Rapid plate agglutination (RPA) tests occasionally disclose seropositive birds. The interpretation of these serologic reactions remains uncertain in the absence of confirmatory isolation of MG organisms.

Salmonellosis

Salmonellosis is an infectious, contagious bacterial disease of many species of wild and domestic birds. Salmonellosis may be caused by any of several species in the genus *Salmonella*, including *S. pullorum* (the causative agent of pullorum disease), *S. gallisepticum* (the causative agent of fowl typhoid), and *S. typhimurium* (the causative agent of enteric and systemic salmonellosis). Also, less common species of *Salmonella* may cause a variety of diseases. Infection by any of these bacteria could be termed salmonellosis. The most important, however, are pullorum disease, fowl typhoid, and enteric and systemic salmonellosis, and they are best discussed separately because of their different clinical syndromes and their different implications for infected birds.

Pullorum disease and fowl typhoid are reportable diseases of domestic poultry and are the subjects of strict prevention and control programs by the domestic poultry industry and regulatory agencies. Currently, no evidence suggests that either pullorum disease or fowl typhoid occurs in wild turkey populations in the United States. Antibodies to *S. pullorum* were reported in 6 of 249 (2 percent) wild turkeys from Texas, but *S. pullorum* was not isolated from these turkeys. In the absence of confirmatory isolation, seroreactors (birds that produce antibodies) can only be considered as suspect (Snoeyenbos 1984).

Enteric and systemic salmonellosis due to *S. typhimurium* has been reported infrequently in wild turkeys. Howerth (1985) reported a single case of salmonellosis due to *S. typhimurium* in an emaciated adult female found in a weakened condition in Dallas County, Alabama. Gross lesions included multiple, small, yellow-white foci scattered throughout the liver and large cores of caseous (cheesy) debris within ulcerated ceca (a pair of pouches connected to the intestine). A subsequent case of salmonellosis also due to *S. typhimurium* was confirmed in an emaciated adult male wild turkey from adjacent Wilcox County, Alabama (SCWDS unpublished data). Lesions in the second case were similar to those in the first.

Two additional suspected cases of salmonellosis due to *S. typhimurium*, one from Telfair County, Georgia, and one from Nelson County, Virginia, have been diagnosed (SCWDS unpublished data). *Salmonella* organisms were isolated in both of these cases, and both cases had necrotizing (killing living tissue) or ulcerative lesions in the intestines or ceca. White et al. (1981) isolated *Salmonella* organisms from 18 of 411 (4 percent) wild turkeys from Florida that were examined between 1969 and 1979. *Salmonella typhimurium* was the most frequent organism isolated. But in no instance was clinical disease associated with infection. Hensley and Cain (1979) reported serologic evidence of *S. typhimurium* infection in less than 5 percent of 174 eastern and Rio Grande wild turkeys in Texas. Rocke and Yuill (1987), however, isolated no *Salmonella* organisms from 511 Rio Grande wild turkeys from 5 areas in Texas.

Available information suggests that wild turkeys occasionally may be infected with *S. typhimurium* and that such infection may lead to clinical disease characterized by necrosis and ulceration of the cecal mucosa and by multifocal necrosis of the liver. This combination of lesions may superficially resemble histomoniasis, so differential diagnosis is important. Diagnosis of salmonellosis is based on gross and microscopic lesions found in intestine, ceca, liver, and other organs, combined with isolation of the organism from fresh tissues. Generally, intact sections of intestine and visceral organs, especially liver and spleen, are best for isolation of the bacteria. Preservation of tissues in 10 percent buffered formalin is preferred for histologic examinations.

Coligranulomalike Diseases

Coligranuloma and similarly appearing disease processes are characterized by granulomatous (chronically inflamed and with granulation) nodules in the visceral organs and have been reported occasionally in wild turkeys in the southeastern United States (Prestwood et al. 1973, Davidson et al. 1985). Coligranuloma is caused by infection with *Escherichia coli*; the similar, coligranulomalike diseases are caused by a variety of other bacteria. Coligranulomalike diseases diagnosed have been due to infection with *Fusobacterium nucleatum*, *Streptococcus* sp., and various other bacteria (Davidson et al. 1985, SCWDS unpublished data).

Escherichia coli is part of the normal bacterial flora of the gastrointestinal tract of many species of animals and is spread naturally by the fecal-oral route. Most infections are totally asymptomatic. At times, however, pathogenic strains of *E. coli* may produce disease. Animals become infected by exposure to contaminated foods, water, and other environmental sources. The impact of coligranuloma and similar diseases on wild turkey populations is unclear, although evidence does not suggest these infections are responsible for significant mortality.

Avian Chlamydiosis (Ornithosis)

Avian chlamydiosis is caused by the intracellular bacterium *Chlamydia psittaci* and is a systemic, contagious disease of birds and mammals, including man (Page and Grimes 1984). Ornithosis is an important zoonotic (communicable from lower animals to man) disease, and human cases acquired from various birds have been well documented. At one time, the disease was known as psitticosis because of the frequent association of the organism with psitticine birds (parrot family). This association led to the lay name "parrot fever."

There have been numerous outbreaks of chlamydiosis in U.S. domestic poultry since 1960, and most have occurred in turkeys (Page and Grimes 1984). Clinical disease has not been reported in wild turkeys despite some instances where wild turkey flocks occurred adjacent to domestic poultry experiencing the disease (Hensley and Cain 1979). Several serologic surveys have been conducted on wild turkeys from Texas and have demonstrated a very low level of exposure to *C. psittaci* (Glazener et al. 1967, Trainer et al. 1968, Trainer 1973, and Hensley and Cain 1979). Although wild turkeys probably are fully susceptible to infection by *C. psittaci*, current evidence suggests that wild turkeys are infected very rarely with this agent and that wild turkeys do not play a significant role in perpetuating this disease.

Other Bacterial and Rickettsial Infections

Illness or death of wild turkeys has been attributed to a variety of other bacterial infections in individual or sporadic cases. For example, Davidson et al. (1985) reported that, in addition to those noted above, confirmed or suspected bacterial infections accounted for approximately 7 percent (7 of 96) of the wild turkey case accessions from southeastern states over a 12-year period. Included in that report were a *Fusobacterium nucleatum* septicemia, a suspected *Clostridium* necrotic enteritis, a *Bacillus*-induced bumblefootlike condition, and 3 cases of mixed species bacterial septicemias (Davidson et al. 1985, SCWDS unpublished data).

Since that report, the SCWDS diagnostic laboratory has diagnosed other bacterial infections including a *Clostridium perfringens*-induced necrotic enteritis, a *Staphylococcus*-induced bumblefoot, and 2 cases of air sacculitis and pneumonia, probably caused by coliform bacteria (SCWDS unpublished data). Hatkin et al. (1986) reported a case of listeriosis, caused by *Listeria monocytogenes*, in an emaciated wild turkey from Lauderdale County, Mississippi. Whether these rather infrequent reports truly represent the significance of various miscellaneous bacterial diseases among wild turkeys or merely reflect a lack of reporting sporadic cases is unclear. Davidson et al. (1985) suggested that bacterial diseases may be a more frequent cause of mortality than is generally recognized.

A rickettsial agent identified as *Aegyptianella pullorum* on the basis of ultrastructural morphology has been isolated by subinoculation of blood from Rio Grande turkeys in Texas into domestic poults (Castle and Christensen 1985). Twenty-four of 300 turkeys tested were found infected. All previous reports of *A. pullorum* have been from domestic fowl in Africa, Asia, or Europe where the agent has been associated with severe clinical disease (Castle and Christensen 1985). The isolate from Texas did not cause disease in the domestic poults, and its significance as a pathogen (disease-producing agent) is uncertain. Unfortunately, serologic tests were not available to compare the Texas isolate with the Old World isolates of *A. pullorum*.

Aspergillosis

Aspergillosis is a mycotic (fungal) disease caused by species in the genus *Aspergillus*, notably *A. fumigatus*. Aspergillosis may occur as a primary disease or as a secondary infection when hosts become weakened from other factors. Although the fungus may invade many organs, most often it is associated with respiratory tract infections. Primary disease due to *A. fumigatus* very often appears as a pulmonary infection characterized by firm, white nodules in the lungs and white plaques on the air sacs or on the surface of visceral organs. In advanced cases, the fungus may form moldlike colonies on visceral surfaces.

The fungus is ubiquitous in the environment and will grow on many types of organic material. Consequently, aspergillosis is considered an environmental pathogen, and transmission among hosts is not an important means of disease spread (Locke 1987). The disease occurs commonly in a variety of wild birds, especially waterfowl, but has been reported only once in wild turkeys (Davidson et al. 1985). This single case had typical respiratory involvement, with numerous discrete plaques in the lungs and air sacs.

Other Mycoses

Two other fungal infections have been reported in wild turkeys. Candidiasis due to *Candida* spp. was noted in the upper digestive tract (oral cavity, esophagus, and crop) in several wild turkeys examined by Davidson et al. (1985). This condition was considered a secondary or incidental finding and was not listed as a direct cause of sickness or death. Infections were reported to be more common in turkeys with avian pox infections of the oral cavity.

The second miscellaneous fungal infection was invasion of the feather shafts of wild turkeys from St. Tammany and St. Helena Parishes, Louisiana, by several species of fungi (Davidson et al. 1989). The condition involved only the tail feathers, which were broken, frayed, and split. Fungi were isolated from the feathers, demonstrated within the disrupted feather sheath and pulp, and transferred to normal feathers, on which they also were invasive. This condition was not considered to

A sick poult. Many different diseases and parasites afflict the wild turkey. *Photo by L. Williams.*

be particularly detrimental to the birds. Yet the tails of severely affected birds were not desirable mementos for successful turkey hunters.

PARASITES AND PARASITIC DISEASES

Wild turkeys are host to a wide range of parasites, including protozoans, trematodes, cestodes, acanthacephalans, nematodes, and arthropods (Tables 1 to 5). Most wild turkeys are infected by several species of parasites at some point during their lives, but these infections usually are not intense enough to produce clinical disease or death. These subclinical infections are common and should be considered normal, although their subtle impacts are not clear and merit further study.

Some species of parasites, such as *Histomonas meleagridis* — the causative agent of histomoniasis — are exceptions to this generalization and can produce disease and mortality in wild turkeys. The severity of many parasitic infections often not only depends upon the number of parasites present but also can be influenced by other variables such as the age or overall health of the host.

The following summarizes parasitic infections in wild turkeys by phylogenetic group, with emphasis on parasite species considered to have significant pathogenicity.

Protozoans

Histomoniasis (blackhead disease). Histomoniasis is caused by the protozoan parasite *Histomonas meleagridis* and is a disease of many galliform birds. Often the disease has been called infectious enterohepatitis, or blackhead disease. The preferred term, however, is histomoniasis (Reid 1967). Histomoniasis appears frequently in the scientific, semitechnical, and popular literature on diseases of wild turkeys. Confirmed primary accounts of histomoniasis in wild turkeys in the scientific literature are relatively few (Stoddard 1935, Mosby and Handley 1943, Thomas 1964, Prestwood et al. 1973, Hurst 1980, Davidson et al. 1985). Other reliable accounts of histomoniasis, either confirmed or suspected, can be found in various wildlife agency reports or other publications (for example, Snyder 1953, Roberts 1956, Bailey and Rinell 1968).

The primary accounts of histomoniasis in the literature involve only single or very few turkeys. It is probable that many cases remained unreported by publication in the belief that the occurrence of histomoniasis in only a few birds did not merit reporting. Nonetheless, histomoniasis is considered a more important mortality factor than indicated by reports in the literature (Hurst 1980, Davidson et al. 1985). For example, it was diagnosed in 12 percent of the sick or dead wild turkeys examined from 8 southeastern states during a 13-year period (Davidson et al. 1985).

Histomoniasis is characterized by necrosis and ulceration of the cecal mucosa and by focal necrosis in the liver. The combination of swollen, inflamed ceca with yellow caseous (cheesy) cecal cores along with discrete foci of necrosis in the liver is considered characteristic for histomoniasis. Variations in the severity and appearance of lesions, however, are not uncommon, and cecal lesions without liver involvement occur occasionally. The histomonads invade the cecal mucosa, producing necrosis, ulceration, and hemorrhage, which are accompanied by extensive inflammation and the development of caseous cecal cores. Histomonads from the cecal lesions commonly gain entry to small veins and are carried by the portal venous blood to the liver. In the liver, the histomonads continue reproducing and cause focal areas of necrosis and intense inflammation (Reid 1967).

The mode of transmission of *H. meleagridis* is unusual: The vector is the nematode cecal worm *Heterakis gallinarum*, which also infects the ceca of many species of galliform birds. The histomonads, in addition to infecting the ceca of the bird, also infect the female heterakid nematodes and may eventually be incorporated within the heterakid eggs. The delicate protozoans, which do not survive exposure to the environment, are transmitted from bird to bird within the protective covering of heterakid eggs in the feces of infected birds.

When the histomonad-bearing heterakid eggs are ingested by a suitable host and then hatch, the histomonads are released in the ceca, where they reproduce by repeated division. In addition, birds may acquire both heterakids and histomonads by consuming earthworms, which can serve as transport hosts of heterakid larvae by ingesting heterakid eggs in the soil. Earthworms can acquire and store large numbers of heterakid larvae and, in this capacity as transport hosts, are an important means of transmission, especially in the field (Reid 1967).

Different species of galliform birds vary greatly in their susceptibility to clinical disease due to *H. meleagridis*. The course of *H. meleagridis* infection in different host species spans the entire spectrum from a total tolerance of the protozoan without lesions to severe disease with a very high death rate (Lund and Chute 1972a). Unfortunately, turkeys, either wild or domestic, almost invariably develop severe clinical histomoniasis after infection (Reid 1967, Lund and Chute 1975). Chukar partridge, peafowl, and ruffed grouse also are prone to severe disease (Lund and Chute 1971a, 1972b).

At the opposite end of the spectrum are species such as ring-necked pheasants, chickens, and jungle fowl, in which infections are largely subclinical (Lund and Chute 1972b, 1972c, Kellogg et al. 1978). Pheasants, chickens, and jungle fowl serve as reservoirs of the parasite for more susceptible species such as wild turkeys. Bobwhites, guinea fowl, and Hungarian partridge occupy intermediate positions. Clinical disease is common, but with moderate rates of disease and death (Lund and Chute 1971b, 1972a, 1972d, Kellogg and Reid 1970).

Diseased avian hosts may die and be lost as a source of infection. Furthermore, lesions within diseased ceca of infected hosts have a great bearing on the subsequent transmission of histomonads. In diseased ceca, the survival of the heterakid nematode vector is extremely poor. Often, heterakid populations in diseased birds are totally eliminated. Thus, individual birds or species in which severe cecal lesions develop usually are not important sources for transmission (Lund and Chute 1974). In contrast, hosts in which cecal lesions are absent or minimal continue to support heterakids, which in turn produce large numbers of histomonad-bearing eggs (Lund and Chute 1972a, 1974).

These epidemiologic factors are important considerations in the prevention and control of histomoniasis under field conditions. They serve as the basis of the old axiom of poultry producers: "Do not raise chickens and turkeys together" (Reid 1967). The same factors form the basis for the recommendations not to introduce carrier species into habitats occupied by wild turkeys and not to use contaminated chicken litter as fertilizer on openings or pastures frequented by wild turkeys.

Coccidiosis. Coccidiosis is caused by infection with cyst-forming, protozoan parasites that typically invade the intestinal tract of hosts and produce disease when intense infections cause significant tissue damage. In wild turkeys, coccidia in the genus *Eimeria* occur, including at least the species *E. adenoides, E. dispersa, E. gallopavonis, E. meleagridis, E. meleagrimitis,* and *E. subrotunda* (Prestwood et al. 1971, Doran 1978). Most of these species are restricted to occurrence in turkeys, either wild or domestic, although *E. dispersa* occurs naturally in other galliform birds such as bobwhites (Reid et al. 1984).

Clinical coccidiosis has not been reported in free-ranging wild turkeys. But in domestic turkeys, coccidiosis is a disease of young poults (Reid et al. 1984). Studies have not been conducted to adequately assess the significance of coccidial infections in young wild poults. Subclinical infection with species of *Eimeria* are common in wild turkeys from the eastern United States (Prestwood et al. 1971, 1973).

Lesions associated with coccidiosis vary, depending on the species of coccidia and the severity of infection. Frequent lesions include edema (fluid), hyperemia (bloody congestion), focal necrosis, or hemorrhages in the intestinal wall, which may result in diarrhea, stunted growth, or death. Coccidia develop within the epithelial cells that line the digestive tract. Eventually coccidia produce cystlike structures, the oocysts, which are shed in the feces. Once in the environment, each oocyst develops to the infective stage by producing several individual single-celled organisms called sporozoites within the oocyst. When a host bird ingests the oocyst, the sporozoites are released in the intestinal tract and subsequently invade the epithelial cells. A process follows that ultimately results in the production of oocysts. Because the development in the intestinal epithelium involves a series of replications by the parasite, several hundred to several thousand oocysts can result from an infection by a single oocyst (Reid et al. 1984).

In domestic poultry, clinical coccidiosis tends to be a disease problem when large numbers of birds are confined to limited space. That combination leads to rapid contamination of the facility with large numbers of oocysts. The much lower density and greater mobility of wild turkeys undoubtedly reduce the frequency and intensity of their exposures to oocysts. Except in unusual circumstances, opportunity for the development of severe infections and clinical disease is probably limited.

In fact, exposure of domestic poultry to small numbers of oocysts—which results in mild subclinical infection followed by development of immunity—is one means of preventing coccidiosis (Reid et al. 1984). This method of biological control of coccidiosis in poultry suggests that the mild infections commonly found in wild turkeys may be beneficial in maintaining immunity and thus protection from coccidiosis.

Toxoplasmosis. Toxoplasmosis is caused by infection with the protozoan *Toxoplasma gondii*, an intracellular, cyst-forming, coccidian parasite. Domestic cats and wild felines are the only definitive hosts for *T. gondii*, but virtually all vertebrates can serve as intermediate hosts. A feline definitive host sheds in its feces the oocysts, which are infectious for intermediate hosts. The life cycle is completed when felines prey upon intermediate hosts with parasites in their tissues.

This parasite also can be transmitted to other predators or scavengers that consume infected intermediate hosts. And the parasite can be transmitted across the placenta to fetuses. Most infections with *T. gondii* do not result in clinical disease, although the infected host may harbor the organism in tissue cysts for life. In some cases, animals experiencing the first exposure to *T. gondii* or animals that are immunosuppressed due to other diseases or factors may develop clinical toxoplasmosis. In such cases, the disease is often a disseminated, multiorgan syndrome characterized by focal necrosis and inflammation.

There is a single report of fatal systemic toxoplasmosis in a wild turkey (Howerth and Rodenroth 1985). The adult female turkey from Union County, Georgia, had marked severe pneumonia and an enlarged and mottled spleen. Organisms identified as *T. gondii* by electron microscopy were found in numerous tissues and were associated with areas of necrosis and inflammation. The authors concluded that, although *T. gondii* infections may be fairly common in wild turkeys, only rarely does clinical toxoplasmosis occur. They believe also that toxoplasmosis probably is not an important cause of death for wild turkeys.

Protozoan blood parasites. Wild turkeys are hosts to 4 genera of blood parasites: *Haemoproteus, Leucocytozoon, Plasmodium,* and *Trypanosoma*. All 4 are transmitted by blood-feeding arthropods. Species of *Haemoproteus, Leucocytozoon,* and *Plasmodium* occur within erythrocytes (red blood cells), but parasites in the genus *Trypanosoma* occur extracellularly (outside the cells) in the blood. *Haemoproteus* and *Leucocytozoon* infections have been reported frequently from wild turkeys in many regions of North America. Reports of *Plasmodium* and *Trypanosoma* are less frequent. Efficient detection of these species depends upon subinoculation of blood into susceptible experimental poults, however, and this technique has seldom been employed. Current known distribution of *Plasmodium* and *Trypanosoma* should be considered minimal, and it probably is reliable only for studies in which subinoculation techniques were used.

Haemoproteus meleagridis is a widely distributed blood parasite of wild turkeys (Table 1) (Cook et al. 1966, Roslien and Haugen 1970, Eve et al. 1972a, 1972b, Stone et al. 1972, Forrester et al. 1974, Stabler et al. 1974, Noblet and Moore 1975, Castle et al. 1988). For many years, important aspects of the biology and significance of *H. meleagridis*, including both its arthropod vector and developmental stages in the turkey, were unknown.

Although some of the earlier literature speculated on the potential pathologic significance of *H. meleagridis*, most researchers have considered the parasite nonpathogenic. Studies by Atkinson and coworkers (Atkinson et al. 1986, 1988a, Atkinson and Forrester 1987) have shown that the presumption of nonpathogenicity is not totally accurate. Experimental infections with domestic poults revealed that *H. meleagridis* undergoes a stage of replication in the skeletal and cardiac muscle of turkeys, which may lead to episodes of lameness and depression about 3 weeks after infection (Atkinson et al. 1988a). In addition, Atkinson and Forrester (1987) reported a single death of an emaciated adult wild turkey that was attributed to *H. meleagridis* infection. In this case, numerous small (1 to 2 millimeters) cysts throughout the skeletal

Table 1. Protozoans reported from wild turkeys in the United States.

Species	Location in host	Vector	Geographic distribution
Eimeria adenoides	Intestine	None	AL, AR, MS, WV
Eimeria dispersa	Intestine	None	AL, AR, MS, WV
Eimeria gallopavonis	Intestine	None	AL, MS, WV
Eimeria meleagridis	Intestine	None	AR, MS, PA, WV
Eimeria meleagrimitis	Intestine	None	AL, AR, MS, WV
Eimeria subrotunda	Intestine	None	MS, WV
Eimeria sp.	Intestine	None	AL, WV
Haemoproteus meleagridis	Erythrocytes (red blood cells), muscles	Midges	AL, AR, FL, GA, IA, MI, MS, ND, NY, PA, SC, TX, WV
Histomonas meleagridis	Ceca, liver	Cecal worms, earthworms	AL, AR, FL, GA, IA, KY, MI, MS, NY, PA, SC, TN, TX, VA, WV
Leucocytozoon smithi	Leucocytes (white blood cells), liver, spleen	Blackflies	AL, AR, FL, GA, MI, MO, MS, NY, PA, SC, SD, VA, WV
Plasmodium hermani	Erythrocytes, bone marrow	Mosquitoes	FL
Plasmodium kempi	Erythrocytes	Mosquitoes	IA
Plasmodium sp.	Erythrocytes	Mosquitoes	TX
Toxoplasma gondii	Numerous organs	None	GA
Trichomonas gallinarum	Ceca	None	PA, Southeast
Trichomonas sp.	Mouth, crop, esophagus	None	PA
Trypanosoma sp.	Blood	Unknown	WV

musculature were associated with severe inflammation and degeneration of muscle tissue.

Field studies in Florida have disclosed that several species of biting midges in the genus *Culicoides*, in particular *C. edeni* and possibly to a lesser extent other species, serve as biologic vectors of *H. meleagridis* (Atkinson 1988, Atkinson et al. 1983, 1988b). The parasite was transmitted year-round in southern Florida; in more temperate northern Florida, transmission was interrupted during winter (Atkinson et al. 1988b). During some periods, exposures to *Culicoides* populations for only 24 hours resulted in 100 percent prevalences in experimental turkeys. An estimated 2 percent of the *C. edeni* were infected with *H. meleagridis* in southern Florida where the higher prevalences occurred (Atkinson 1988, Atkinson et al. 1988b).

Traditionally, *H. meleagridis* has been most often detected by examining stained blood films. If, however, *H. meleagridis* is suspected as a cause of sickness or

death, sections of all major tissues—including skeletal muscle—should be preserved in 10 percent neutral buffered formalin for histopathologic examination.

Leucocytozoon smithi is a widely distributed blood parasite of wild and domestic turkeys (Table 1) (Byrd 1959, Eve et al. 1972a, 1972b, Stone et al. 1972, Forrester et al. 1974, Noblet and Moore 1975). The parasite is transmitted by blackflies (buffalo gnats) in the genera *Simulium* and *Prosimulium*, specifically *S. occidentale*, *S. meridionale*, *S. congareenarum*, *S. slossonae*, *S. jenningsi*, and *P. hirtipes* (Noblet et al. 1972, Greiner and Forrester 1979, Pinkovsky et al. 1981).

When an infected blackfly feeds on a susceptible turkey, the infective stages (sporozoites) of the parasite are injected into the bird. Subsequently, the parasite undergoes replication in tissues including the liver, spleen, bone marrow, and kidney. These stages (schizonts and megaloschizonts) may produce substantial tissue damage, leading to disease characterized by loss of appetite, depression, and weakness. Eventually, gametocytes, the stages infective for the blackflies, are produced and enter circulating red blood cells. The gametocytes are thus available for transmission to blackflies.

Leucocytozoonosis is considered a relatively devastating disease in domestic turkeys. By inference, it has been listed as a potential cause of death for wild turkeys (Eve et al. 1972a, 1972b). Currently, however, there are no confirmed instances of death caused by this parasite in wild turkeys. Many of the effects of *L. smithi* infection in domestic turkeys are rather subtle and may increase vulnerability to other mortality factors rather than causing death directly. Infected turkeys serve as chronic carriers of the protozoan, and during the spring, carrier birds often suffer a relapse. That leads to high intensities of circulating parasites, which coincide with emergence of the blackfly vectors.

This synchronization of the intensity of parasites circulating in the blood with the appearance of the vector ensures optimum opportunity for transmission (Alverson and Noblet 1977). In many areas, the prevalence of infection is very high, frequently approaching 100 percent. Most often, infection with *L. smithi* is diagnosed by detection of parasites in stained blood slides. But when leucocytozoonosis is suspected as a cause of sickness or death in wild turkeys, formalin-fixed visceral organs are critical to the diagnostic process.

Wild turkeys are hosts for at least 2 species of true malarial parasites in the genus *Plasmodium*. *Plasmodium hermani* was first reported by Telford and Forrester (1975) from wild turkeys in Florida. Later, Christensen et al. (1983) reported *P. kempi* from wild turkeys in Iowa. Both species were found only by subinoculation of blood from wild turkeys into domestic poults, which were then monitored for parasitemias. Since these initial reports, additional work has focused on the use of subinoculation methods for detecting malaria. Castle et al. (1988) reported detection of a species of *Plasmodium* very closely related to *P. vaughani* in wild turkeys from Texas. In all of these cases, the parasites could not be detected by examination of blood slides alone. So all prior reports of blood parasites based solely on blood slide examinations must be considered suspect in their reliability for detection of *Plasmodium* organisms.

As with other species of true malarial parasites, all 3 species are transmitted by mosquito vectors. *Culex nigripalpus* is considered a very important vector of *P. hermani* in Florida (Young et al. 1977, Forrester et al. 1980b), although other culicine mosquitoes such as *C. salinarius* and *C. restuans* also may be involved in transmission (Nayar et al. 1981a, 1981b). *Plasmodium kempi* may be transmitted by *C. tarsalis*, *C. pipiens*, or possibly *C. restuans*, although *C. tarsalis* appears to be the more effective vector (Christensen et al. 1983). Exten-

sive field studies have been conducted only on *P. hermani* in Florida, and in this work, exposure of experimental turkeys to mosquito bites in naturally endemic areas resulted in prevalences of infection greater than 50 percent during peak populations of *C. nigripalpus* in late summer (Forrester et al. 1980). Although a high transmission rate occurred, the prevalence of naturally infected mosquitoes in the area was quite low (3 infections were produced from 9,747 wild-caught mosquitoes) (Forrester et al. 1980b).

Experimental transmission studies demonstrated that bobwhites were susceptible to infection by *P. hermani* (Nayar et al. 1982). Later, Forrester et al. (1987) demonstrated naturally acquired *P. hermani* infections in wild bobwhites from an area in Florida known to have *P. hermani* in wild turkeys. Although these studies confirm that *P. hermani* can also occur in bobwhites, Forrester et al. (1987) indicated that *P. hermani* was primarily a parasite of wild turkeys and that bobwhites were only occasional hosts.

The effects of *Plasmodium* infections on wild turkeys are not completely understood, although experimental infections in domestic poults suggest a potentially detrimental effect (Forrester et al. 1980b). When poults were infected with *P. hermani* alone, the effects were minimal. But when poults were infected with both *P. hermani* and avian poxvirus, there seemed to be a strong synergistic action that led to clinical disease and death. The dual infections were more severe than either agent alone and resulted in stunted, weak poults and an increased death rate (Akey 1981, Wright 1986). These results may be very important to actual field situations where *C. nigripalpus*, the major vector of *P. hermani*, also is the major vector of avian poxvirus (Akey et al. 1981). Under natural conditions, wild poults would be expected to be commonly infected simultaneously with both agents.

Trematodes

Wild turkeys harbor at least 19 species of trematode parasites (Table 2). Trematodes are parasitic flatworms, often called flukes. Trematodes found in wild turkeys are not considered highly pathogenic and have not been associated with clinical disease. Flukes may infect many different organs, including the intestines, liver, bursa, oviduct, and kidneys. Most of the flukes found in wild turkeys are inconspicuous and often difficult to find because of their small sizes and obscure locations in the host. One species that may be detected relatively easily is the liver fluke *Athesmia heterolecithodes*. This species infects the bile ducts of the liver and when numerous enough may obstruct the flow of bile. This blockage

Table 2. Trematodes reported from wild turkeys in the United States.[a]

Species	Location in host	Intermediate hosts	Geographic distribution
Ascocotyle sp.	Intestine	Snails, ?	FL
Athesmia heterolecithodes	Liver	Snails, arthropods	AL, WV
Brachylaima virginianum	Intestine	Snails	AL, AR, FL, LA, MD, MI, MS, NC, SC, TN, VA, WV
Cotylurus flabelliformis	Intestine	Snails	AL, AR, FL, MS, NC, TN, VA
Cotylurus sp.	Intestine	Snails	IL
Echinoparyphium recurvatum	Intestine	Snails, tadpoles	AL, AR, FL, LA, MI, MS, NC, OK, SC, TN, WV
Echinostoma revolutum	Intestine	Snails, amphibians, fish	FL, MI, MN, SD
Leucochloridium sp.	Intestine	Snails, ?	MS
Postharmostomum gallinum	Intestine	Snails	NC
Prosthogonimus ovatus	Bursa, oviduct	Snails, dragonflies	FL, MS
Psilotornus audacirrus	Intestine	Snails, ?	AL
Renicola hayesannieae	Kidney	Unknown mollusks	MS
Rhopalias macracanthus	Intestine	Snails, ?	GA
Stomylotrema vicarium	Cloaca	Snails, ?	FL
Strigea elegans meleagris	Intestine	Snails, ?	FL, MI, TX
Strigea sp.	Intestine	Snails, ?	AL, AR, LA
Tanaisia zarudnyi	Kidney	Snails	AR, MS
Tanaisia sp.	Kidney	Snails	FL
Zonorchis sp.	Liver	Snails, ?	FL
Zygocotyle lunata	Ceca	Snails, cyst on vegetation	AR, FL, MI, OK

[a] Table adapted from Kingston (1984).

results in enlargement and fibrosis of the bile ducts. Prominence of the fibrotic, yellow-stained bile ducts is a clue that *A. heterolecithodes* may be present. Close inspection of affected livers usually reveals the long, slender, brown and white flukes in the bile ducts.

All of the trematodes found in wild turkeys require a snail as the first intermediate host. A second intermediate host, usually an invertebrate, is often required. Suitable second intermediate hosts vary among the fluke species. Because these parasites require a snail as first intermediate host, wild turkeys from areas with large amounts of rainfall or surface waters have a greater diversity of trematode species. Wild turkeys inhabiting more arid regions generally have lower numbers and fewer species. None of the flukes are considered detrimental to wild turkeys, and their presence does not seem of particular importance to the level of the turkey population.

Cestodes

Wild turkeys are hosts for at least 13 species of cestodes, all of which occur as adult forms in the intestinal tract (Table 3). Cestodes are often referred to as tapeworms because they are flat, segmented, and ribbonlike. Wild turkeys frequently have large numbers of tapeworms, and these parasites are often detected by hunters when they eviscerate turkeys. The worms periodically break, and portions (segments) pass in the feces, where they are easily observed in fresh droppings.

Although many of the tapeworms of wild turkeys are readily detected, none of them are considered highly pathogenic. In rare cases, very heavy infections may interfere with the passage of food through the intestine. And cestodes may compete with or interfere with the absorption of nutrients by the host (Reid 1984). Nevertheless, in the absence of other complicating factors, such problems are generally not considered to significantly affect the health of wild turkeys.

All tapeworms found in wild turkeys require an intermediate host for completion of their life cycle. Eggs or segments containing eggs are shed in the feces, and these eggs are infectious for the first intermediate host, most commonly terrestrial invertebrates such as ants, beetles, or slugs. Larvae develop to the infective stage in this intermediate host, and wild turkeys become infected by consuming it. Because young poults rely on invertebrates as a source of high-protein food during growth, poults acquire tapeworm infections early in life. For example, Hon et al. (1978) first detected *Metroliasthes lucida*, a common tapeworm of wild turkeys, in poults only 8 to 14 days old.

Table 3. Cestodes reported from wild turkeys in the United States.[a]

Species	Intermediate hosts	Pathogenicity	Geographic distribution
Amoebotaenia cuneata	Earthworms	Mild	MS, WV
Davainea meleagridis	Unknown	None reported	AL, AR, FL, MD, MI, MS, TN, VA, WV
Davainea proglotina	Snails, slugs	Mild to moderate	WV
Drepanidotaenia watsoni	Unknown	None reported	AR, LA
Hymenolepis cantaniana	Beetles	None reported	GA, TN, VA
Hymenolepis carioca	Flies, beetles	None reported	AL, AR, FL, GA, KY, MI, MS, TN, VA
Hymenolepis sp.	Unknown	None reported	IL, NC
Imparmargo baileyi	Unknown	None reported	WV, CA
Liga braziliensis		None reported	TX
Metroliasthes lucida	Grasshoppers	None reported	AL, AR, FL, GA, IL, KY, LA, MS, NC, OK, SC, TN, TX, VA, WV
Raillietina cesticillus	Beetle	Mild	FL, MD, NC
Raillietina georgiensis	Ant	None reported	AL, FL, GA, KY, MS, TN
Raillietina ransomi	Unknown	None reported	AL, AR, FL, GA, LA, MD, MS, NC, PA, TN, VA, WV
Raillietina williamsi	Unknown	None reported	AL, AR, FL, GA, IL, KY, MD, MS, NC, TN, TX, VA, WV
Raillietina sp.	Unknown	None reported	CO

[a] Table adapted from Reid (1984).

Acanthocephalans

Acanthocephalans are nonsegmented parasitic worms, often called thorny-headed worms. They are parasites in the intestines. Members of the genus *Mediorhynchus* have been reported rarely from wild turkeys. Prestwood et al. (1973, 1975) reported *Mediorhynchus* spp. from wild turkeys in Arkansas, Mississippi, and West Virginia. Huggins and Dauman (1961) found *M. grandis* in South Dakota. Hon et al. (1975) found *M. papillosum* in Florida. These infections were considered to represent accidental infections (Huggins and Dauman 1961, Hon et al. 1975). Acanthocephalans, because of their infrequent occurrence, are not considered a serious threat to wild turkey health.

Nematodes

Wild turkeys are host to a large variety of parasitic nematodes (roundworms), including representatives of at least 25 species (Table 4). Summaries of the species found, their geographic distribution, and their signifi-

cance as pathogens have been presented (Maxfield et al. 1963, Prestwood et al. 1973, 1975, Hon et al. 1975, Castle and Christensen 1984, Schorr 1988).

Although most nematodes infecting wild turkeys inhabit the gastrointestinal tract, they also become parasites in many additional locations, including the trachea, lungs, heart, body cavity, subcutaneous tissues, and eyes. Nematodes that parasitize sites other than the gastrointestinal tract all require an invertebrate intermediate host of some type. By contrast, many of the gastrointestinal nematodes have direct life cycles (do not require an intermediate host) (Ruff 1984).

Of the many species of nematodes that have been reported from wild turkeys, a few can be termed characteristic of the parasite fauna of wild turkeys. These characteristic species occur over wide geographic areas and usually are very prevalent. Included in this group are *Ascaridia dissimilis, A. galli, Capillaria caudinflata, C. obsignata,* and *Strongyloides avium* in the intestines; *Heterakis gallinarum* and *Trichostrongylus tenuis* in the ceca; *Capillaria contorta* in the crop and esophagus; *Dispharynx nasuta* in the proventriculus (front part of the stomach); *Cyrnea colini* in the proventriculus and giz-

Table 4. Nematodes reported from wild turkeys in the United States.[a]

Species	Location in host	Intermediate hosts	Pathogenicity	Geographic distribution
Aproctella stoddardi	Body cavity	Unknown	None to mild	FL
Ascaridia dissimilis	Intestine	None	None reported	AL, AR, FL, GA, IL, KY, LA, MD, MI, MS, NC, PA, SC, TN, VA, WV
Ascaridia galli	Intestine	None	None to mild	FL, IL, MD, NC
Aulonocephalus pennula	Ceca	Unknown	None reported	FL
Capillaria annulata	Esophagus, crop	Earthworm	None to mild	MD, MI, MS
Capillaria bursata	Intestine	Earthworm	None reported	MD, TN
Capillaria caudinflata	Intestine	Earthworm	None reported	AR, KY, MD, MI, MS, NC, TN
Capillaria contorta	Esophagus, crop	None	None to moderate	AR, MI, MS, PA, VA
Capillaria obsignata	Intestine	None	None to moderate	AL, AR, FL, GA, MI, MS, TN, VA
Capillaria tridens	Intestine	Unknown	None reported	AL, LA, SC, WV
Chandlerella sp.	Skin	Unknown	None reported	FL
Cheilospirura spinosa	Gizzard	Grosshopper	None to mild	FL
Cheilospirura sp.	Gizzard	Unknown	None reported	PA
Cyrnea colini	Proventriculus	Cockroach	None to mild	AL, AR, FL, GA, MS, VA
Cyrnea neeli	Proventriculus	Unknown	None reported	AL, FL
Cyrnea sp.	Proventriculus	Unknown	None reported	AL, AR, FL, MS, NC, WV
Dispharynx nasuta	Proventriculus	Pillbug	Mild to severe	AL, FL, MS, WV
Gongylonema ingluvicola	Esophagus	Beetle, cockroach	None reported	AL, WV
Heterakis gallinarum	Ceca	None	None reported	AL, AR, CA, CO, FL, GA, IL, KY, LA, MD, MI, MS, NC, PA, SC, SD, TN, TX, VA, WI, WV
Heterakis sp.	Ceca	None	None reported	AR, LA, MS, NC, WV
Oxyspirura turcottei	Eye	Unknown	None reported	WV
Oxyspirura sp.	Eye	Unknown	None reported	AR, MS
Singhfilaria hayesi	Skin	Unknown	None reported	AL, AR, FL, MS
Splendidofilaria sp.	Heart	Unknown	None reported	FL
Strongyloides avium	Ceca	None	None to mild	FL
Strongyloides sp.	Ceca	None	None to mild	AL, AR, FL, MS, SC, WV
Syngamus trachea	Trachea	None	Mild to severe	AL, AR, MI, MS, PA, WV
Synhimantus sp.	Gizzard	Unknown	None reported	FL
Trichostrongylus tenuis	Ceca	None	None reported	AL, AR, FL, GA, LA, MD, MI, MS, NC, SC

[a] Table adapted from Ruff (1984).

zard; and *Syngamus trachea* in the trachea. The remaining species are found only as incidental parasites or in restricted geographic areas.

Most species of nematodes have not been associated with disease problems in wild turkeys and do not appear to be of any critical danger to health at the population level (Maxfield et al. 1963, Prestwood et al. 1973, 1975,

Hon et al. 1975, Castle and Christensen 1984). A small number of species, however, have considerable pathogenic potential and merit consideration as factors that could threaten wild turkey health.

One such species is *Heterakis gallinarum*, the common cecal worm of wild turkeys. Although *H. gallinarum* itself has not been shown to cause significant disease in wild turkeys, it is critically important as the vector (carrier) of histomoniasis, or blackhead disease. Histomoniasis, an important disease of wild and domestic turkeys, produces a high death rate among infected birds (see *Histomoniasis* elsewhere in this chapter). Because of its role as a vector of histomoniasis, the occurrence of *H. gallinarum* in wild turkeys is an important consideration for the health of wild turkeys.

The prevalence of *H. gallinarum* in wild turkeys, however, is much higher than the observed occurrence of histomoniasis. This difference suggests that even though wild turkeys are commonly exposed to *H. gallinarum*, they are not being exposed to virulent strains of *Histomonas meleagridis*, the causative agent of histomoniasis. This aspect of wild turkey biology needs further investigation and clarification.

A second nematode that merits consideration as a health problem in wild turkeys is the proventricular worm *Dispharynx nasuta*. When present in sufficient numbers, *D. nasuta* can produce considerable sickness and death in a diverse range of avian species (Ruff 1984). *Dispharynx nasuta* has been considered a potential pathogen by several investigators who have examined large numbers of wild turkeys (Prestwood et al. 1973, 1975, Hon et al. 1975, 1978, Rickard 1985). These studies have revealed that prevalences and intensities of *D. nasuta* are higher in poults than in older turkeys, a situation similar to *D. nasuta* infections in other species of birds (Bendell 1955, Ruff 1984).

Working in Florida, Hon et al. (1975, 1978) provided the most detailed findings on the ecology and pathogenicity of *D. nasuta* in wild turkeys. Infections occurred almost exclusively in young poults, peaking at an 89 percent prevalence of infection in August and virtually disappearing by November. This seasonality of infection was believed to possibly be influenced by 2 factors: (1) consumption of sow bug *(Chaetophiloscia floridana)* intermediate hosts was reduced when poults began to shift to a diet of almost exclusively plant material in the early fall; and (2) either an age resistance or acquired immunity, or both, may have developed as the poults became older (Hon et al. 1978).

In addition, the acquisition of *D. nasuta* was related to fluctuating water levels on the study site that at times forced the poults to move from cypress-dominated lowlands, which supported high densities of sow bugs. In years of summer flooding, the intensities of *D. nasuta* infection were lower (Hon et al. 1978). Hon et al. (1975, 1978) also provided evidence indicating that *D. nasuta* was maintained on the site by a combination of larvae overwintering within sow bugs and persistence of low-intensity infections in a wide range of avian species.

Hon et al. (1975) noted that the occurrence of highest poult mortality during the first 4 weeks of life coincided with the highest prevalences (virtually 100 percent) and intensities (about 5 to 7 worms per bird) of *D. nasuta*. The death of 1 young poult was attributed, at least in part, to *D. nasuta* infection (Hon et al. 1975). Although there is evidence supporting the idea that *D. nasuta* is highly pathogenic in the young of various species of birds (Cram 1928, Bendell 1955), the true significance of this parasite to wild turkeys is unclear. The potential of *D. nasuta* as a pathogen in young poults suggests that further investigation of its significance in mortality is desirable.

A third species of nematode with the potential to produce sickness or death in wild turkeys is *Syngamus trachea*, the tracheal worm (Ruff 1984). This species has long been associated with clinical disease in young domestic poultry, especially prior to development of modern confinement rearing practices, and in pen-raised game birds, particularly pheasants (Ruff 1984). Infections most often lead to clinical disease when they occur in young birds. These large, red nematodes and the inflammation they cause may occlude (block) the trachea, resulting in respiratory difficulty or suffocation (Ruff 1984).

According to accounts from domestic poultry and pen-raised game birds, the concentration of birds over a period of years on a site where the young have access to the ground can increase infection intensities and clinical disease problems. Contact with the ground is important since earthworms are important, but not essential, as sources of infective larvae. Reports of *S. trachea* in wild turkeys are not frequent (Prestwood et al. 1973, 1975) although they do extend across a wide geographic area. Infections are more frequent in young poults. The real significance of this parasite to wild flocks is not clear, although it does not seem to hold as much potential for producing disease as do other parasitic nematodes such as *D. nasuta*.

Arthropod Parasites

Wild turkeys are host to a large number of species of external arthropod parasites (ectoparasites), including various ticks, mites, lice, and louse flies (Table 5). In addition, there are records of wild turkeys being attacked by several species of blood-feeding arthropods, such as various mosquitoes (Forrester et al. 1980b, Akey et al. 1981), midges (Atkinson et al. 1983), and blackflies (Noblet and Moore 1975, Pinkovsky et al. 1981). Although the number of arthropod parasites is quite large and diverse, comparatively little is known about their significance to wild turkeys. These arthropods could affect health of the host by directly causing injury or by serving as vectors of other diseases.

Table 5. Arthropods reported from wild turkeys in the United States.

Phylogenetic group Species	Location on host	Pathogenicity	Geographic distribution
Ticks			
Argas miniatus	Skin	None reported	Southwest
Ambylomma americanum	Skin	Mild to moderate	AL, MS
Ambylomma cajennense	Skin	None reported	AR, MS
Rhipicephalus sanguineus	Skin	None reported	MS
Mites			
Knemidocoptes mutans	Leg scales	Mild to moderate	TX
Megnina cubitalis	Feathers	None reported	MD
Megnina sp.	Feathers	None reported	AL, MS
Neoschongastia americana	Skin	None to mild	AL, MS
Lice			
Chelopistes meleagridis	Skin, feathers	None to mild	AL, AR, AZ, MS, OK, PA, SD, TX, VA, WV
Goniocotes sp.	Skin, feathers	None reported	VA
Goniodes meleagridis	Skin, feathers	None reported	VA
Lipeurus gallopavonis	Skin, feathers	None reported	VA
Menacanthus stramineus	Skin, feathers	None to mild	AL, AR, MS, OK, SD, VA, WV
Menacanthus sp.	Skin, feathers	None reported	TX
Oxylipeurus corpulentus	Skin, feathers	None to mild	AL, AR, MS, TX, WV
Oxylipeurus polytrapezius	Skin, feathers	None to mild	AL, AR, AZ, FL, MO, MS, NC, OK, SD, TX
Flies and Louseflies			
Lynchia americana	Skin, feathers	None reported	AL, AR, MS, WV
Olfersia sp.	Skin, feathers	None reported	AL, VA
Ornithoctona erythrocephala	Skin, feathers	None reported	MS

Ticks. Wild turkeys have been reported as host to only a few species of the ticks that occur within the United States. The lonestar tick *(Amblyomma americanum)* has been reported most frequently (Cooley and Kohls 1944, Bishop and Trembley 1945, Kellogg et al. 1969). Species reported less commonly include *A. cajennense, Argas miniatus* (Bishop and Trembley 1945), and *Rhipicephalus sanguineus* (Kellogg et al. 1969). None of these authors reported harmful effects from tick infestations. Jacobson and Hurst (1979) reported that wild turkey poults acquired significantly lower *A. americanum* infestations when foraging on areas subjected to recently prescribed burning than on unburned areas. This work suggests that prescribed fire may have some potential for reducing infestations.

Mites. Three types of mites have been found on wild turkeys: the scaly-leg mite *(Knemidokoptes mutans)* (Thomas 1964), the chigger mite *(Neoschoengastia americana)* (Kellogg et al. 1969), and the feather mite *(Megninia cubitalis)* (Gardiner and Wehr 1949, Kellogg et al. 1969). Both scaly-leg mites and chigger mites have been associated with minor lesions in wild turkeys. Thomas

(1964) noted a single "obviously diseased" Rio Grande wild turkey with scaly-leg mite infestation in a group of 330 turkeys trapped in Sutton County, Texas. Thomas did not describe the specific lesions found. But scaly-leg mites typically burrow beneath the epithelium of the leg scales, producing thickening of the leg skin and the formation of crusty scabs on the legs (Loomis 1984).

Chigger mites were reported to produce small, craterlike lesions on the skin of wild turkeys (Kellogg et al. 1969). The craters, which were 3 to 5 millimeters (0.1 to 0.2 inches) in diameter, contained as many as 40 *N. americana.* Feather mites have been found commonly on wild turkeys in the southeastern United States but have not been associated with any damage to the host (Kellogg et al. 1969, Prestwood et al. 1973).

Lice. The most frequent arthropod parasites of wild turkeys are lice *(Menacanthus stramineus, Chelopistes meleagridis, Oxylipeurus corpulentus,* and *O. polytrapezius).* They have been reported from many regions (Clay 1938, Emerson 1951, Hightower et al. 1953, Carriker 1954, Keler 1958, Kellogg et al. 1969, Prestwood et al. 1973). Lice have not been associated with specific disease syndromes in wild turkeys, and wild birds commonly are infested without any obvious harm to their health. In general, however, very heavy infestations of lice are often characteristic of hosts that have other disease problems. Extreme infestations of lice on sick or dead wild turkeys should be a clue to look for additional disease problems.

Louse flies. Three species of louse flies have been reported from wild turkeys: *Lynchia americana, Ornithoctona erythrocephala,* and *Olfersia* sp. (Kellogg et al. 1969). The most frequently encountered species was *L. americana*. None of these species were associated with any disease conditions (Kellogg et al. 1969). Because louse flies often fly from shot birds onto hunters, inquiries about their identity are fairly frequent.

Other blood-feeding arthropods. Many types of blood-feeding arthropods feed upon wild turkeys as well as other hosts. Turkeys, like other wild and domestic animals, are subject to the nuisances of mosquitoes, midges, gnats, and blackflies. The direct effects of these insects on turkeys through blood loss and annoyance are not known. But these insects transmit infectious disease agents such as avian poxvirus and parasites such as *Plasmodium, Leucocytozoon,* and *Haemoproteus*. So these pests represent disease potentials beyond direct damage such as blood loss. Details on the status of these insects as vectors of diseases are provided in appropriate sections of this chapter.

NONINFECTIOUS DISEASES AND MISCELLANEOUS CONDITIONS

Toxicoses

Toxicoses have been reported rarely in free-ranging wild turkeys. The few reports can be categorized into poisoning by 2 types of toxicants: agricultural pesticides and heavy metals. Clawson (1959) reported the circumstances surrounding an experimental application of dieldrin and heptachlor for control of fire ants *(Solenopsis saevissima)* in an area of Wilcox County, Alabama, inhabited by wild turkeys. After the pesticide applications in March 1958, the frequency of adult turkey sightings on the area declined sharply, and the reproductive success on the area for the subsequent nesting season was estimated to be essentially zero.

From the data presented, it is unclear whether immediate mortality or reproductive loss was more important in suppressing the population for the 2-year period following application, but both events were strongly suspected to have resulted from the pesticide applications.

The second report involving pesticide toxicosis that produced detectable mortality was an instance of organophosphate poisoning due to 0,0-diethyl 0 [p-(methylsulfinyl) phenyl] phosphorothioate (Dasinit, Chemagro Corp., Kansas City, MO 64120) described by Nettles (1976). In this instance, a small group of wild turkeys from Sapelo Island, Georgia, was killed when the birds consumed dead and dying mole crickets on a golf course that had recently been treated with the pesticide. In this case, the pesticide had not been applied according to label directions. Bridges and Andrews (1977) surveyed wild turkeys in Illinois and detected only sublethal concentrations of 13 different agricultural pesticides, which generally reflected their level of use in various locations.

Unpublished records of the Southeastern Cooperative Wildlife Disease Study contain 5 instances of poisoning by pesticides, including Dasinit, diazinon, and famfur. Case files show that these incidents involved both accidental and intentional (directed at other species) poisonings, but the number of turkeys killed was small in all cases. These reports suggest that wild turkeys can be hurt or killed by pesticides. But, considering the amounts of pesticides applied, such instances are infrequent.

The second type of toxicosis noted was a poisoning by heavy metals, and in particular, lead poisoning (Stone and Butkas 1978). In this case, a single wild turkey with classic lead poisoning was diagnosed from Chemung County, New York. The bird was severely emaciated, the vent was stained with greenish feces, and the gizzard contained 4 worn lead pellets. The diagnosis was confirmed by chemical analysis of lead concentrations in the liver: more than 17 parts per million (wet weight). The source of the ingested pellets was not determined.

Such instances are apparently rare; they infrequently appear in the literature. The probable rarity of subclinical or undetected instances of heavy metals toxicosis is supported by the work of Scanlon et al. (1979), which failed to find any evidence of abnormal exposures to heavy metals in wild turkeys from 19 counties in Virginia.

Capture Myopathy

Capture myopathy, also commonly called overexertion syndrome or white muscle disease, has been recognized for decades in wild mammals (Chalmers and Barrett 1982). It almost invariably occurs in recently captured animals.

The basic circumstance of capture myopathy involves exertion of major muscles beyond the body's ability to supply oxygen. This condition eventually leads to the onset of anaerobic (without oxygen) respiration to meet the muscles' respiratory needs. If anaerobic respiration is prolonged, its production of lactic acid can result in metabolic acidosis. In addition, the overexertion of muscles beyond the capacity of the body to meet their respiratory needs leads to hypoxia (insufficient blood oxygen) and muscle death, followed by the release of toxic metabolites from necrosing muscles. These metabolites may result in kidney damage, and the muscle damage causes lameness.

The disease has been reported only recently in wild turkeys (Davidson et al. 1985, Spraker et al. 1987). Davidson et al. (1985) noted that a syndrome of overexertion, heat prostration, and shock accounted for 12 of 31 (39 percent) capture-related deaths in a series of wild turkeys from the southeastern United States. Spraker et al. (1987) found gross or microscopic lesions characteristic of capture myopathy in 20 of 60 (33 percent) wild turkeys captured by various methods in Colorado.

Clinical signs of capture myopathy vary, depending on the severity of metabolic acidosis and muscle or kidney damage and on the duration of the condition. Often the first signs noted are reluctance to move about, lameness, or depression. In mammals, myoglobinuria (muscle proteins in the urine) with dark, coffee-colored urine occurs after kidney damage. But this condition has not been reported in the few cases of capture myopathy noted in avian species.

The common gross lesions of capture myopathy are small to large areas of pale muscle tissue in the major muscle groups. Spraker et al. (1987) noted "small to large, patchy, pale, white-streaked areas" in breast, wing, and leg muscles of wild turkeys with capture myopathy. These lesions were often bilateral but not symmetrical. In some cases, muscle bundles had ruptured, resulting in surrounding areas of hemorrhage.

Wild turkeys captured by any method (for example, rocket nets, drop nets, or oral tranquilizers) often struggle violently during the procedure. Struggling also may occur in transport boxes. This struggling can lead to capture myopathy. Clinical signs often develop 24 to 72 hours after the overexertion. In other words, these signs may occur after the birds have been released in many trap-and-transplant operations.

This delayed manifestation is suggested both by data of Spraker et al. (1987), in which clinical signs were not noted during short intervals of captivity, and by case history data from turkeys examined by Davidson et al. (1985), in which some lame turkeys with typical capture myopathy lesions were recovered at release sites several days after release (SCWDS unpublished data). This evidence suggests some transplanted wild turkeys may succumb shortly after release. Lame or debilitated birds also may be more vulnerable to predation. Every effort should be made to minimize the amount of struggling and exertion during capture, and to monitor turkeys after release.

Capture myopathy should be considered a distinct possibility in any failed stocking attempt in good habitat, especially when there is suspicion of high mortality shortly after release.

Other Miscellaneous Conditions

A limited number of other miscellaneous pathologic conditions have been reported from wild turkeys. Davidson et al. (1985) noted 4 cases of crop impaction among 108 wild turkeys submitted for diagnostic examination by wildlife agency personnel in the southeastern United States. All 4 turkeys were emaciated and had greatly distended, food-impacted crops. In the most severely affected bird, the crop contents accounted for 1/3 of the total body weight. In all cases, material in the crops was mainly if not completely coarse vegetation. The condition was similar to crop impactions noted in domestic turkeys (Peckham 1984). The etiology (cause) of this condition is not known, although evidence from domestic turkeys indicates there may be a hereditary predisposition to development of the condition (Peckham 1984).

Davidson et al. (1985) reported a single instance of aortic rupture as the cause of death of a live-captured wild turkey. A similar condition is well documented in domestic turkeys. The role of various contributing factors such as nutritional components is not clear, however, (Peckham 1984). Aortic atherosclerosis also has been reported in both pen-raised (Manning and Middleton 1972) and wild turkeys (Bolden et al. 1980) and may be related to spontaneous aortic rupture. A single instance of melorheostosis, a rare proliferative bone disorder, has been noted in wild turkeys (Davidson et al. 1985).

Doster (1974) reported 3 cases of suffocation in rocket-netted turkeys when the birds inhaled whole kernels of corn. Davidson et al. (1985) reported 8 similar cases of inhalation of bait (corn or wheat) with subsequent suffocation among 31 capture-related mortalities. One of the cases reported by Davidson et al. (1985) involved the use of oral tranquilizers rather than rocket nets as the capture method.

PEN-RAISED TURKEYS AND DISEASE PROBLEMS

Virtually any modern text or technical bulletin on wild turkey management admonishes the reader not to consider pen-raised or game-farm turkeys for restocking programs, usually for 2 major reasons: (1) pen-raised turkeys are considered genetically inferior, and interbreeding with existing native wild turkeys results in genetic pollution of the native wild turkey gene pools

(Lewis 1987); and (2) pen-raised turkeys have been considered a potential means of introducing diseases that could spread to native wild populations (Lewis 1987).

The concept of genetic inferiority was demonstrated in a rather straightforward manner by Leopold (1944). He showed that pen-raised turkeys or hybrids did not have the heritable wildness of native wild turkeys and thus did not survive well in the wild. In contrast, evidence supporting the concept of disease introduction has been less clear and largely circumstantial. For example, Powell (1965) implied that release of pen-raised turkeys in Volusia County, Florida, initiated a decimating outbreak of avian pox in native wild turkeys. Although the events described by Powell (1965) suggest that his conclusions might be correct, the actual source of the poxvirus was not confirmed.

The continued release of pen-raised turkeys in the private sector, along with the scarcity of data on the disease potentials of this practice, led Schorr (1988) to investigate diseases of pen-raised turkeys. Three disease-related considerations were identified and evaluated: (1) diseases that might be introduced into native populations of wild turkeys or other wild species; (2) diseases that might cause high mortality among pen-raised turkeys after release; and (3) diseases that might be of potential significance to the domestic poultry industry.

The study involved examination of 119 pen-raised turkeys from 12 counties in 9 states, acquired in a way that simulated buying for release by private individuals. The turkeys were examined for a wide range of avian pathogens and were found to be infected with at least 33 species of parasites and 7 infectious disease agents. Although many of the parasites were not considered significant, the presence of active infections by avian poxvirus, *Mycoplasma gallisepticum, Histomonas meleagridis,* and *Syngamus trachea,* along with serologic evidence of possible *Salmonella* infections, were considered potential threats to native wild turkeys and domestic poultry. These pathogens also were considered capable of causing substantial mortality among pen-raised turkeys during confinement or after release. Schorr (1988) emphasized that the pathogens found in this rather small-scale study represented a minimum of what was present and that because of the dynamic state of diseases, the situation could be expected to be constantly changing, with some diseases declining and others increasing. Schorr (1988) concluded that "pen-raised wild turkeys harbor parasitic and disease agents that could jeopardize the health status of wild populations when infected birds are released" and recommended that the practice of "uncontrolled release of pen-raised wild turkeys . . . be discouraged or prohibited."

Wild turkeys—the subject of intensive and successful restoration programs—frequently suffer from diseases introduced by pen-raised stock.

Chapter 9

POPULATION INFLUENCES: PREDATORS

James E. Miller
National Program Leader
Fish and Wildlife Extension Service
U.S. Department of Agriculture
Washington, D.C.

Bruce D. Leopold
Associate Professor
Department of Wildlife and Fisheries
Mississippi State University
Mississippi State, Mississippi

THE PROCESS OF PREDATION

Predation on the wild turkey has been well documented through personal observation and early studies (see Blakely 1937, Mosby and Handley 1943, Dalke et al. 1946, Ligon 1946, Wheeler 1948, Davis 1959). Most avid hunters, photographers, land managers, biologists, and landowners who spend considerable time in habitats containing wild turkeys have either witnessed predation, seen attempts by predators, or found remains of turkeys apparently killed by predators.

For example, a biologist, while counting grouse in Indiana, saw a mass of feathers fall from the sky. Upon investigation, he discovered a great horned owl atop a hen turkey (S. Backs personal files: 1988). In Montana, a biologist observed Merriam's hen nests destroyed by black bears (R. Hazelwood personal files: 1988).

The fact that the wild turkey is preyed upon by a wide variety of predators is rarely questioned. These diverse predators include large mammalian carnivores such as the cougar and bobcat, omnivores such as the raccoon, avian predators such as hawks and eagles, several species of snakes, and occasionally an armadillo or feral hog (Table 1).

There has been considerable interest in predators and the process of predation for quite some time (Errington 1946, Holling 1959, Rosenzweig and MacArthur 1963, Connell 1970, Sanderson 1972, and many others). By definition, a predator is an animal whose survival depends on capturing and consuming other animals. But the process of capture, escape, and survival is poorly understood. This is because, except in simple ecosystems, the relationship between predator and prey is very complex, affected by a broad range of interacting biotic and abiotic factors including habitat quality, animal behavior, presence or absence of other animal species, and climate.

Predators can depress or regulate prey populations (Errington 1943, Mech 1970), maintain community stability (Connell 1970, 1972, Paine 1980), increase vigor of a prey population by eliminating sick or unfit individuals (Markley 1967, Lindzey and Wanless 1973, Williams 1981), or maintain prey wildness (Leopold 1944, Hornocker 1970, Leopold 1989). A discussion of the impact of predators upon a specific prey species (the wild turkey) entails not only an evaluation of the predator-prey interaction but also an evaluation of all environmental factors that may affect that interaction.

Predation theory is based on studies (many in the laboratory) of systems between a single predator and a single prey. Many of these theories, however, have applications today. To understand predation and its role on turkey population dynamics, it is important to review not only the theory itself but also the research evaluating this theory.

Lotka (1956) and Volterra (1928) developed the simplest model, which predicted that a single predator-prey

Table 1. Species of predators of the wild turkey.

Mammals	Birds	Reptiles
bobcat or lynx	broad-winged hawk	rat snake
coyote	crow	eastern coachwhip
cougar	goshawk	pine snake (bull snake)
dogs	great horned owl	king snake
fox (red and gray)	golden eagle	
opossum	red-tailed hawk	
raccoon	raven	
skunk		
rodents		
fisher		

Other species that have been reported to depredate nests or turkeys include armadillo, bald eagle, black bear, mountain lion, badger, groundhog, wild or feral hogs, feral house cats, ringtail, rock squirrel, eastern screech owl, short-eared owl, magpie, and a variety of other snake species.

system would cycle. Field studies support predator-prey cycles, but primarily in northern environments (tundra and boreal forest). These studies include the classic lynx-snowshoe hare interaction (Elton and Nicholson 1942, Keith 1963), the grouse-great horned owl (Rusch et al. 1972), the jackrabbit-coyote (Wagner and Stoddart 1972), and many others (microtine rodents *[Microtus]*, for example).

Solomon (1949) proposed the concept of numerical and functional responses in predation. Numerical response refers to an increase in predator numbers (density) as a result of more prey. Functional response refers to an increase in rate of predation (prey consumed/predator). Additionally, Holling (1959) incorporated the concept of "search image" coined by the ethologist Tinbergen (1960, as cited in Curio 1976:58–68), implying that predators must learn what the available prey is before actively searching for and killing it.

Additional studies, involving a diverse array of species, examined predator-prey interactions in the laboratory and field and provide a sound basis for examining any form of predation (Errington 1946, Huffaker and Kennett 1956, Huffaker 1958, Rosenzweig and MacArthur 1963, Connell 1970, 1972, Bergerud 1971, Paine 1980, Duebbert and Kantrud 1974). From these studies, plus many others (see Errington 1946, Taylor 1984, also see above), several basic components of predation become apparent. These components of predation will be a recurrent theme throughout this chapter's discussion of turkeys, their predators, and the process of predation:

(1) Simple predator-prey systems (1 predator, 1 prey) may be cyclic (particularly in northern environments);

(2) Stability of predator-prey systems is a function of diversity. The more prey species (buffer species), the less likely a predator will significantly impact any single prey species (demonstrated in terrestrial as well as aquatic systems);

(3) Refugia (places for prey species to hide) are important in ensuring stability of predator-prey systems (particularly for simple predator-prey systems);

(4) Prey species with a high biotic potential (ability to reproduce and survive) are seldom regulated by predators; the numerical response by predators can rarely equal or exceed that of such prey species; and

(5) Predators often are beneficial to animal-plant communities and aid in community stability.

Many factors affect these components. Bailey (1984) provides an excellent summary. According to Bailey (1984), these factors include the following, with special reference to wild turkey biology (in brackets):

A. **Factors affecting number of predators relative to prey numbers:**

1. **Numerical response of predators to prey abundance.** As prey density increases, density of predators increases through immigration and improved predator reproduction and survival. [Enhancing habitat for turkeys, such as by including more pastures and open fields, generally increases habitat quality for other prey species (e.g., rodents), thereby attracting predators and possibly increasing predation rate on turkeys.]

2. **Prey diversity.** Greater prey species diversity reduces likelihood that predator population may decline if density of a specific prey species significantly declines. [Even under low turkey densities, predators may remain abundant if alternate (buffer) prey species are available, possibly exasperating attempts to increase turkey numbers.]

3. **Biotic potential and longevity of prey and predator.** This is a complex interaction. The greater the rate of the predator's increase, the more likely the predator may control its prey. This rate is a function of the prey's rate of increase, however. If the prey species has a greater rate of increase compared with the predator, prey numbers will generally exceed predator numbers and regulation (impact) by the predator is unlikely. [Turkeys have large clutch sizes and are long-lived, so the impact of predation is reduced under moderate turkey densities.]

4. **Geographic concentrations of predators.** Specific areas may attract and concentrate prey species and thus predators. [Developing food plots for turkeys, as well as baiting, may concentrate turkeys and increase likelihood of predation.]

5. **Intrinsic regulation of predator numbers.** Many predators are territorial, and thus their numbers may be limited through behavioral interactions rather than prey abundance.

6. **Competition among predators for prey.** If predator species are diverse, then competition for prey may be great. The result can be poor predator nutrition, which limits predators' reproduction and survival. Conversely, if there are few predator species (as may be brought about by predator control) this may actually enhance remaining predator populations. [Predator control to enhance turkey populations may actually enhance predator species and increase predation rates on turkeys.]

B. **Factors affecting prey's vulnerability to predation:**

1. **Habitat quality.** Habitat that provides excellent cover from predators or poor visibility by prey to detect predators affects an animal's likelihood to predation. [Turkeys prefer open habitats; habitats that are too dense are not commonly used by turkeys.]

2. **Decreased animal quality at higher prey densities.** As prey populations reach or exceed the habitat's long-term carrying capacity, more animals become weakened from decreased nutrition, disease, and parasites, increasing predation rates of prey species. [Turkey populations that are very dense have greater disease incidence, leading to predation or allowing smaller predators that do not normally attack turkeys to be able to attack and kill turkeys.]

3. **Dispersal of subordinate prey animals into poor habitats.** Subordinate individuals forced to disperse into unknown areas are more prone to predation as they lack knowledge of critical habitat features (e.g., escape cover). [Dispersed juvenile turkeys are more likely to be killed by predators, or introducing turkeys into habitats with high predator densities may result in high mortality of the attempted transplant.]

4. **Adaptability of prey.** Many prey species have adapted predator-evasion strategies to enhance survival. Predators continually evolve better means to hunt and capture prey, however. [The large body size of turkeys, especially gobblers, precludes attack by many small- to medium-sized predators. Also, roosting in trees at night prevents access by many terrestrial predators.]

5. **Mutual defense.** At certain prey densities, groups of prey aid in predator detection and thus reduce predation rate. [The flocking behavior of turkeys increases the chances of sighting a stalking predator.]

6. **Prey learning.** If attacks by predators are frequent, prey may avoid areas where attacks, or even the attacking species, are common. [When a nest is destroyed, the hen generally moves long distances in a short time.]

C. **Predator behavior and changes in behavior in response to changes in prey vulnerability and abundance:**

1. **Concentration of predator effort.** Locations where predators are repeatedly successful in capturing prey may cause them to hunt those areas intensively. [Locations where gobblers strut, as well as where hens nest, may be searched more intensively by predators once several successful kills are made. Predators may develop a temporary search image for these sites.]

2. **Predator learning.** Predators may gain experience in killing specific prey species, particularly if the species is abundant. [Animals acquiring a taste for eggs may form a search image for nests, or the habitat they are found in, and the associated smells of a nest, such as a wet hen on a nest.]

3. **Predator group facilitation.** If a predator becomes more abundant and is a social predator, group sizes may increase, and thus they become more efficient in killing prey. [Groups of dogs are more likely than a solo dog to encounter a nesting hen or a hen with poults.]

4. **Concentration of predator effort on alternate prey species.** If prey species diversity is high (more buffer species), then predator effort is not concentrated on any single prey species. [Predation on the wild turkey is generally a random process as there are many other prey species to encounter.]

The foregoing discussion, although somewhat theoretical, covers points that are important for management of any wildlife species, including the wild turkey. The examples provided indicate clearly that basic concepts of the process of predation, derived from a diverse array of animal species, apply to the wild turkey and its management.

Now we will attempt to integrate these basic concepts of predation into the wild turkey's situation by discussing possible predators and evidence for predation throughout the turkey's life cycle. Then we'll look at the wild turkey in relation to predators and predation as the subject applies to wild turkey management.

PREDATORS

The wild turkey, throughout its life, faces a diverse array of predator species, which vary in their mode of search and capture. Many species can be considered true predators or carnivores. They actively search for and kill living prey. Mammals that prey on the wild turkey include the mountain lion, bobcat, lynx, and fisher. Predatory birds include hawks, owls, and eagles. All snakes fall into the predator group.

Many predators of turkeys, however, are more generalists (omnivores), consuming as much nonprey matter (such as plants, seeds, carrion, and insects) as meat secured from stalking and killing prey. These omnivorous species include such mammals as coyotes, gray and red foxes, and rodents and such birds as ravens and crows. Notorious omnivores (which are coincidentally the most significant nest predators) include opossums, raccoons, and skunks.

Finally, some known predators such as feral dogs and cats should not be considered wild, but under certain conditions may be as harmful to turkeys as their wild counterparts or even more harmful. Regardless of the predator species, it is important to note that most turkey predators (carnivore and omnivore alike) are opportunistic: They detect prey by sight, sound, or smell during their normal travels and searches for food, and their capture of wild turkeys is usually incidental to pursuit of any suitable prey.

Wild turkey ground nests and young poults are vulnerable to a number of predators. Clockwise from top left: Rat snakes; Crows; Raccoons; and Skunks.

In general, we do not have adequate data on wild turkey or predator populations, but some general trends have been apparent within wild turkey range. In spite of losses to predators, wild turkey numbers have increased from tens of thousands in the early 1900s to about 4 million in 1990 (Kennamer and Kennamer 1990), and their range has been extended more northerly and westerly than historic range.

Predator populations also have changed. Most large carnivores have diminished. Such species as the gray wolf of northern states, red wolf of southern states, grizzly bear, and cougar can no longer maintain viable populations in much of their historic range. But among many of the more adaptable predators of wild turkeys—including coyotes, hawks, owls, raccoons, crows, skunks, snakes, rodents—population densities may be as high or higher today in historic and expanded turkey range.

Increased urbanization has resulted in habitat loss or degradation and in more feral cats and dogs, which may be more harmful to some species of wildlife than native predators.

There may be a number of reasons for this increase in some predators, such as less hunting and trapping, urbanization, adaptability (especially true for the coyote), habitat change, and reduction in some of the larger predators that preyed on smaller predators of the wild turkey.

THROUGH THE YEAR

Predators kill substantial numbers of wild turkeys. For example, in a survival study of 74 eastern wild turkeys in Texas, 24 birds were documented to have died

Many raptors and carnivores such as these kill young and adult wild turkeys. Clockwise from top left: Great horned owls; Bobcats; Coyotes; and Mountain lions. *Photos by L. Rue, III.*

A coyote or dog killed this wild turkey. *Photo by D. Reid, Ontario Ministry of Natural Resources.*

This wild turkey was probably killed by a great horned owl. *Photo by G. Hurst.*

during the study period, and 14 of these were suspected to have died from predation (Swank et al. 1985). In northern Missouri, predation accounted for 55 percent of hen mortality (33 of 60 radio-marked hens), mostly in spring (Kurzejeski et al. 1987).

In another study, predators, principally bobcats, coyotes, and owls, accounted for 76 percent of radioed adult gobbler and 90 percent of hen mortality in about a 1-year period (L. Vangilder personal communication: 1990). Less severe predation rates have been reported for West Virginia, where approximately 14 percent of radio-equipped hens (of 149) were killed by predators including foxes (5 percent), bobcats (less than 1 percent), and dogs (less than 1 percent), avian predators (2 percent), and the rest by unknown predators (Pack and Taylor 1991).

In a study of predation on wild turkeys in Alabama (Speake 1980) on 4 study areas from 1973 to 1979, only 5 gobblers (less than 1 percent) were killed by predators, and all were subadults. Two additional unsuccessful attacks by golden eagles on gobblers were observed. Three of these gobblers were killed by bobcats in September, 1 by a golden eagle in December, and 1 by a gray fox in March. Hens also were subject to a low predation rate for most of the year, except during the nesting and early brooding season, when 1.4 percent (April), 5.1 percent (May), and 3.9 percent (June) of all hens instrumented were killed by predators. In 12 cases of predation where the predator could be directly identified, bobcats killed 6 hens, gray foxes 3, dogs 1, and a golden eagle 1.

In addition to increases in predation during spring, Speake (1980) also noted an early fall (September and October) increase in predation on hens and juveniles.

Hens were most vulnerable to predation during incubation and the first 2 weeks after poults hatched. Similar predation observed throughout the year for adult turkeys in Mississippi by Phalen (1986), Seiss (1989), and Palmer (1990) included raccoon, great horned owl, bobcat, skunk, opossum, and unknown canid species, possibly coyote, feral dog, or gray fox.

In a study of the ecology of wild turkeys in an intensively managed pine forest area in Alabama (Exum et al. 1987), 22 of 84 juvenile and adult birds radio-tagged over a 3-year period were documented to have been killed by predators. Only 5 of the 22 were gobblers; 17 were hens. All but 1 were killed by mammalian predators.

Similar predation rates for juveniles and adults were reported in a New England study, where hen mortality was 23 percent in the prenesting period, 5 percent in the nesting period, and 8 percent in the postnesting period (Thomas 1989). The main predators were the coyote, fox, and fisher. In western Massachusetts (Vander-Haegen et al. 1988), predation was the dominant cause of mortality for adult and yearling hens (75 percent), with survival the lowest during the period of dispersal from winter flocks through the nesting season.

Nesting hens, nests, and young poults are particularly vulnerable to predation (Glidden and Austin 1975, Speake 1980, Vangilder et al. 1987). Overall, about half of all nests are lost to abandonment or predation, and more than half of all poults die within 2 weeks of hatching, mostly to predation.

Speake (1980) found that 53 of 119 nests (45 percent) were lost to predators. In 40 of these 53 nests preyed on, the predator was identified. Species causing the most predation on nests were raccoons, followed by dogs, opossums, crows, snakes, skunks, and gray foxes. Bobcats also killed 3 incubating hens, but the bobcats did not eat the eggs. Of 18 poults monitored, 6 were killed by predators within 2 weeks of instrumentation. Overall loss rate of 41 poult groups with instrumented hens averaged 75 percent.

Deaths of wild turkey poults were documented from radio-tagged hens and poults on 2 northern Alabama study areas (Speake et al. 1985). Of 400 poults hatched, 279 died. Of these, cause of death was established for 136 poults, of which 111 were documented losses to predators: 51 percent to mammals, 20 percent to avian predators, 8 percent to reptiles, and 21 percent to undetermined predators. Of the 111 wild turkey poults taken by predators, free-ranging dogs took 32, raccoons 14, and bobcats and gray foxes 11. Broad-winged and red-tailed hawks took 21 poults, and a screech owl a single young turkey. Gray rat snakes were the only reptile to prey on young poults.

More than 92 percent of all poult mortality that was monitored by telemetry occurred within 15 days of hatching. High nest losses and high poult losses attributed primarily to predation substantially affected the reproductive success of wild turkeys on these study areas.

Other studies have substantiated high rates of nest loss and poult mortality from predation throughout the eastern United States. Exum et al. (1987), in their study in Alabama, reported that of 32 radio-tagged poults, 15 were killed by predators before they were 4 weeks old. Eleven of these were killed by mammalian predators, 4 by avian predators.

In New Hampshire, Thomas (1989) reported that 18 of 40 nests were destroyed by predators. Poult mortality was 90 percent because of severe spring weather and predation. Vander-Haegen et al. (1988) reported that predation on eggs or the female accounted for most (92 percent) of nest losses and was the most significant influence on productivity. In Mississippi, Seiss (1988) monitored 105 radio-equipped hens and reported that of the 12 nests monitored, mammals accounted for 25 percent of nest destruction, with raccoons destroying the majority (17 percent) and unknown mammals 8 percent.

Artificial, or dummy, nests have been established to assess nest predation. Predation rates on these artificial nests were higher than on those of wild hens but provide some interesting data. Of 107 dummy nests in a variety of nesting sites in Alabama, 85 percent suffered predation from raccoons, skunks, opossums, snakes, crows, foxes, and other predators (Davis 1959).

A similar dummy nest study monitored by automatic cameras (Pharris and Goetz 1980) was conducted in the Land Between the Lakes area of Kentucky and Tennessee during the spring of 1978. A previous study on this area had shown that nests of all 11 radio-instrumented adult hens were destroyed by predators over a 2-year period, and predator damage to 55 percent of 80 artificial nests was observed (Wright 1975). During the 1978 study, 129 dummy nest sites were established. Predation rates in both experimental and control nests in this study varied from 58 percent to 94 percent, averaging 80 percent for all nest sites. Raccoons destroyed 49 percent of these dummy nests, opossums 20 percent, skunks 16 percent, and gray fox 5.6 percent.

Baker (1978) monitored 350 dummy nests in Texas and found that striped skunks and raccoons were major nest predators (55 percent), while coyotes and armadillos were minor (6 percent). Although armadillos and feral hogs have been suspect as predators of wild turkey nests, studies have not implicated either as serious predators. But they disrupted some nests (Henry 1969, Kennamer and Lunceford 1973, Williams et al. 1980).

Most western turkey populations probably also experience high predation rates. Three studies of Rio Grande turkeys in Texas verified high predation. Cook (1972) reported that out of 121 nests, 74 (61 percent) were destroyed by predators or deserted. Of the 74 nests, predators, including snakes, skunks, raccoons, bobcats, and crows, destroyed 53 (71 percent). Reagan and Morgan (1980) found high nest predation, with 56 percent of radio-monitored incubating hen nests destroyed by predators. Of 43 clutches of eggs (including renesting attempts), 24 were destroyed by predators, and only 10 of the 43 (23 percent) were successful in hatching poults. Mammals destroyed 13 nests (including 1 destroyed by a rock squirrel), and 11 were destroyed by snakes. Ransom et al. (1987) reported that all (100 percent) of the 17 nests monitored were destroyed by predators and 1 renesting attempt was also destroyed by a predator. They attributed most of the nest losses to raccoons, while predators (bobcats and coyotes) were responsible for 58 percent of adult hen mortality.

Predation, of course, occurs at other times of year. Wild turkey populations in northerly latitudes suffer high mortality, including predation, during extended periods of deep snow (Porter 1978, McMahon and Johnson 1980, Miller 1983). Porter (1978) reported that, although predation was the *direct* cause of more than 70 percent of winter deaths, the extent of mortality was related not to predator population levels but to severity of winter stress on the birds. Additionally, Porter (1980) stated that areas of severe snowfall but abundant corn (food plots) resulted in higher survival rates (lower predation rates) than locations with little or no available corn.

Predation rate of wild turkeys is also affected by turkey behavior, which is a function of time of year. In open areas where vocalizing gobblers display, they seem particularly vulnerable to predators. In the spring, many people have observed successful and unsuccessful predator attempts on vocalizing gobblers by coyotes, bobcats, and foxes. Glazener (1967b) reported predation on gobblers in the spring, and Ligon (1946) noted observations of coyotes and other mammalian predators successfully attacking mature gobblers during other seasons.

PREDATOR CONTROL

The control of predators is somewhat controversial, and its effectiveness is debated. Several studies provide sufficient evidence that predator control should be applied with caution.

For example, Knowlton (1972) reported that in areas of low predator control, average litter size of coyotes was 3.65, contrasted with an average litter size of 6.56 on areas with intensive predator control. Connolly and Longhurst (1975), using simulation, reported that a 70 to 75 percent reduction in coyote population annually would be required to maintain coyote populations at ½ an area's carrying capacity for coyotes. Further discussion and review of predator control principles and ecology is provided by Berryman (1972), Hornocker (1972), McCabe and Kozicky (1972), and Connolly (1978).

Studies about the effect of predator control on wild turkey populations are equally controversial. Many studies have demonstrated that predator control can enhance turkey production in the short term. Merriam's turkey restoration success was directly related to the degree of predator control in areas of high densities of coyotes and bobcats (Lignon 1946). In a more recent study of Rio Grande turkey populations in Texas, on areas where predator control for coyotes, bobcats, and other small, predatory furbearers was initiated and compared with areas with no predator control (Beasom 1974a), reproductive success (poults per hen) and total poult production were significantly higher on the areas where predators were controlled than on check areas.

In eastern wild turkeys in Alabama, Speake (1980) found a significant difference between treatment (predator control) areas and check (no predator control) areas in poults-per-hen ratios each year of the 5-year study. On predator control areas, 55 percent of the hens were accompanied by poults, in contrast to only 24 percent of the hens on check areas.

The conclusions were that (1) predator control had a beneficial effect on hatching success; (2) predation did not seem to cause a significant loss of adult wild turkeys, except on hens during nesting and brooding season; (3) intensive control of nest predators can increase turkey production; (4) such control measures probably would produce higher fall populations on areas where populations are well below carrying capacity of the habitat; (5) intensive predator control is expensive; and (6) even though predation takes a heavy toll on nesting hens, nests, and poults in Alabama, the wild turkey apparently can sustain these losses and usually maintain or increase fall populations.

Several studies, however, have concluded the opposite about predator control: It is not effective. MacDonald (1960–64) and MacDonald and Jantzen (1967) found no significant increase in Merriam's turkeys with intensive predator control, and it was not cost-effective. In a study of Florida turkey nesting, 59 percent nesting success occurred with no predator control, compared with 72 percent nesting success on the study area with predator control (Williams et al. 1980). With nests lost from predation, however, there was substantial renesting, and no definite conclusions could be made about the benefits of predator control.

Differing results from these studies confirm that wild turkeys and their predators are components of dynamic and complex natural ecosystems that differ from location to location and from animal community to community. Predator control may be effective in the short term locally where populations are severely depressed or recently introduced, where predator populations are very high, and where predators can be limited cost-effectively. Alternative measures such as sport hunting and trapping of predators could be implemented to reduce identified wild turkey predators before control measures are intensively pursued. In most cases, the investment of efforts and resources to maintain quality habitat are probably more effective than predator control in increasing turkey productivity.

SUMMARY

Potential predators of the wild turkey are found throughout the landscape, making predation an important component of any turkey's life cycle. Larger predators, such as the bobcat, coyote, fox, and eagle, kill adult hens and even gobblers. Losses of adult turkeys, however, generally do not significantly affect turkey population dynamics. In contrast, smaller predators, including skunks, raccoons, opossums, and snakes, are the primary nest and poult predators and may affect turkey populations. But the debate continues on whether this impact is significant (Markley 1967, Williams 1981).

The wild turkey has flourished (coevolved) in the presence of predators. Reflecting the evolutionary impact of predators are many characteristics of the wild turkey: large clutch sizes, large body size, flocking behavior, and night roosting in trees. This evolutionary view is supported by studies that have demonstrated that high turkey densities are achievable even with high predator densities.

The adaptations by turkeys to predation do not take account of losses by hunting as well as habitat degradation or loss. When natural (such as predation) and man-made (hunting, habitat change) mortalities are combined, predation of nests and poults may have a significant impact on the turkey population's rate of increase. Whether predation significantly impacts a turkey population is a function of many interacting variables. Some of these variables are hunting pressure (including poaching), habitat availability and management, climatic variables (e.g., winter severity), and disease.

The interactive nature of the various mortality factors requires investigation to evaluate whether predation, and other natural mortality, is additive to (is intensified by) or compensatory (is replaced by) hunting mortality (Nichols et al. 1984). Additionally, no known predator reported in the literature actively seeks exclusively turkeys as food. Most predator-turkey encounters are random. It is difficult to examine a random process compared with studying, for example, mountain lion predation of deer. Predator learning, however, may play an important role if predator-turkey encounters are common, as may exist with the raccoon (Johnson 1970) and perhaps other egg-consuming predators.

The degree of predation (and thus its impact upon turkey populations) varies by season, location, and patterns of land use. Glazener (1967) and Markley (1967) stated that predation may significantly impact turkey populations when (1) populations are low (especially during turkey introductions); (2) nesting cover is poor; (3) food and/or water scarcity forces turkeys into unfavorable range; (4) number of other prey species (buffer) is low; (5) birds are exposed to severe weather for prolonged periods of time; and (6) predator populations are abnormally high—usually as a result of man's actions. It should be noted that these 6 conditions are true for predation in general, a position supported by the literature.

Predator control remains controversial. But it may be warranted under specific situations such as when introducing turkeys to former range (Clark 1985). This control should continue only until a viable turkey population is established. Studies have shown that viable turkey populations can generally withstand predation (Powell 1967, Shaffer and Gwynn 1967) and that often in the long term, predator control is ineffective and not cost-justified. Studies concerning other wildlife species (that are also ground-nesting) generally agree, including ring-necked pheasants (Chesness et al. 1968, Trautman et al. 1974), turkeys and also deer (Beasom 1974b), water-

fowl (Balser et al. 1968), and bobwhite quail (Guthery and Beasom 1977).

Two reports that examined predator control (Leopold 1964 and Cain 1972) warrant review before implementing any predator control program. Furthermore, the Wildlife Society's position on predator control (as cited in Robinson and Bolen 1984:270) is cautious and supports only programs that are the minimum required and are justified. The Wildlife Society encourages use of efficient, safe, economical, and humane methods of control (as well as research to improve control methods) and encourages federal and state regulation of control programs.

An alternative to predator control is maintaining quality habitat. Fine habitat is important in wild turkey management and has been demonstrated to have an impact on predation rate of turkeys. For example, providing adequate herbaceous cover allows hens and poults to better escape detection by predators (Beasom 1970, Glidden and Austin 1975, Everett et al. 1980, Metzler and Speake 1985, Thomas 1989). In addition, density of vegetation (and thus habitat structure) affects predation rates either by providing the hen and poults with more cover (Beasom 1970, Speake 1980, Speake et al. 1985) or perhaps by not being suitable for predators because of low prey abundance (e.g., rodents) (Seiss et al. 1990). Such habitat conditions would reduce the probability of predator-turkey encounters.

The concept of managing habitat to minimize predator-prey encounters is not new (such as for pronghorn-coyote predation examined by Barrett 1981, and others). Baker (1978) found significant differences in rate of dummy nest predation, depending on the type of grazing system, pasture deferment time, plant community, and degree of coyote exclusion. And Palmer (1990), studying adult hen-habitat relationships in Mississippi, found that hens used bottomland hardwoods throughout most of the year because fields and pastures were not abundant. Use of bottomland hardwoods, however, was associated with a high predation rate on adult hens and nests. Palmer suggested improving upland pine stands by increasing density of hardwoods, particularly hard mast producers, to lure turkeys away from the predator-rich bottomland hardwood forests. The concept of managing habitats with predation in mind should be investigated further, especially when considering predator control. Perhaps management should be directed at creating conditions for minimizing predator-turkey encounters while simultaneously enhancing nesting and brood habitat.

Predation of the wild turkey is indeed a complex process, and examining the process will require more complex (and expensive) research designs. Innumerable studies have indicated that predation plays an important role in wild turkey dynamics. But an equal number have demonstrated the reverse (see Bailey and Rinell 1967b).

This discrepancy is not surprising, especially when we consider that predation of wild turkeys (adult gobblers, hens, nests, and poults) is a result of the very complex interaction between the population dynamics of the turkey itself, of perhaps 1 or 2 large predators (e.g., coyote and bobcat), of perhaps 3 or 4 small predators (e.g., fox, opossum, raccoon, and skunk), of all the alternate prey species of these predators, as well as of man's actions (e.g., farming and timber harvest), variations in climate, and responses of vegetation to all of these factors.

Research so far has centered on examining the wild turkey and its predators (a natural history approach). It is time for research to examine the process of predation of the wild turkey. To examine such a complex system

requires long-term, multispecies research programs. Besides, management objectives should be clearly defined and closely aligned with the dynamics of the specific turkey populations. The implication is that the turkey populations should be monitored annually for rates of survival (and thus mortality) and productivity. Predator populations should be monitored as well as changes in land use (and thus habitat quality) and how these actions affect turkey predation.

The wild turkey has existed and survived with predators and predation for thousands of years. Management should center as much on managing man's impact upon turkey populations as on managing predators of the turkey. A recurring theme in most studies of turkey ecology is that proper management of habitat and the people utilizing that habitat does more good for the resident turkey population than the predators do harm.

It's time to research the effects of predation on the wild turkey.

Chapter 10

POPULATION INFLUENCES: ENVIRONMENT

William M. Healy
Research Wildlife Biologist
Northeastern Forest Experiment Station
Amherst, Massachusetts

I don't recall anything unusual about the spring and summer weather of 1969, but the fall kill of 129 wild turkeys on the 8,094-hectare (20,000-acre) Middle Mountain area in West Virginia was memorable. That harvest was 3 times greater than any recorded in the previous 18 years, and the fall turkey population was estimated at 782 birds, or 10 per square kilometer (25 turkeys per square mile)! Middle Mountain is in the heart of West Virginia's turkey range—the oak-and-hickory-covered ridges of Pocahontas and Greenbrier counties. It was also the site of most of R. Wayne Bailey's pioneering turkey research, so a good deal was known about the local population.

At that time, the West Virginia Department of Natural Resources and the Northeastern Forest Experiment Station were studying the effects of forest management on wildlife and on hunter behavior. We had been trapping and banding turkeys and interviewing most of the hunters using the area. The bumper turkey crop was *the* topic of discussion during many of the 1,265 interviews we conducted in 1969, as it was among the biologists working on the project. That group of biologists included R. Wayne Bailey, James C. Pack, and Jack Ward Thomas—all experts on turkey biology.

We concluded the population increase was real but temporary. Fall turkey harvests were 24 in 1967, 40 in 1968, 129 in 1969, and 30 in 1970. Gobbler counts and brood counts substantiated the dramatic increase in 1969. Habitat change and hunting were ruled out as causes for the fluctuation in turkey numbers. The habitat had been undisturbed, and hunting pressure was similar in all years of the study.

The consensus was that variations in weather were responsible for the changes in turkey numbers. Clearly, 1969 had been a good year for turkeys. But the particular aspect of weather that was responsible (and how it operated) remained a matter of speculation. In this chapter, I aim to synthesize what is known about the influence of environment on the abundance and distribution of wild turkeys.

I will examine 2 aspects of the environment that influence turkey populations: weather and climate. Weather refers to local and short-term atmospheric conditions at a specific time and place. Climate deals with average weather conditions of a region over a period of years (Markley 1967:226). Both weather and climate have profound effects on wild turkey populations.

I will begin by describing the climatic conditions that limit the distribution of turkeys in North America. Then I will consider how annual variations in weather affect local populations. Because wild turkeys have been restored to most of their ancestral range—and in some cases established beyond those limits—we can draw some definite conclusions about climate and turkey distribution. In contrast, the crystal ball used for predicting annual fluctuations in turkey numbers is still mostly clouded. Nevertheless, what biologists have learned about weather effects on local populations is fascinating and worth pursuing.

CLIMATE AND DISTRIBUTION

Precipitation is apparently the ultimate climatic factor limiting the distribution of wild turkeys in North America. Temperature seems to play a secondary role. The northern limit of distribution is set by a zone where deep, fluffy snow cover persists through most of the winter. The western boundary for the eastern, Rio Grande, and Merriam's subspecies occurs where there is insufficient precipitation to support the growth of trees.

It is not clear from the literature what sets the southern limit of the Mexican subspecies in Central America. So no definite conclusions can be drawn about the effects of climate on the southern limits of turkey distribution.

Snowfall and Northern Populations

From southern Maine westward to Michigan and Minnesota, deep and persistent snow cover establishes the northern limit of the eastern wild turkey. The northern boundary of turkey range ebbs and flows with the severity of the winter. Schorger (1942:179–180) traced the expansion and contraction of the northern limits of turkey range in Wisconsin during the 1800s in response to winter weather. This environmental tug-of-war can be seen today where turkeys have been reestablished at the northern limits of their ancestral range.

Nineteen wild turkeys were introduced into Fulton County in the southern Adirondacks of New York in the mid-1960s. This release resulted in a self-sustaining population that was carefully monitored from 1966 through 1973 (Austin and DeGraff 1975). The area, in the transition zone between the heavily forested Adirondack Mountains to the north and the agricultural lands of the Mohawk Valley to the south, is at the northern limit of historical turkey range in New York. The average survival of the wild turkeys over 5 mild or average winters ranged from 71 to 100 percent. The survival over the 2 severe winters was 55 and 58 percent, or about 20 percent less than in mild winters. Biologists believe the additional mortality was caused by the direct and indirect effects of deep snow and cold temperatures.

The severe winters of 1969–70 and 1970–71 had average snow depths of 38 to 76 centimeters (15 to 30 inches) for January, February, and March. Deep, powder snow averaged from 30 to 61 centimeters (12 to 24 inches) during a 6-week period from late December to mid-February. Snow cover exceeded 2.5 centimeters (1 inch)

Fluffy snow deeper than 30 centimeters (12 inches) stops turkey movement. *Photo by M. Vander Haegen.*

for more than 4 months, and it was deeper than 30 centimeters (12 inches) for better than 3 months.

Tracking birds on snow indicated that a powder snow of 15 to 20 centimeters (6 to 8 inches) limited daily movements of flocks. Powder snow deeper than 30 centimeters (12 inches) stopped nearly all turkey movement on the ground. Despite periodic harsh winters, this population persists. But it has never expanded its range to the north.

The relationship between snow depth and survival can also be seen on the Allegheny Plateau in north-central Pennsylvania (Wunz and Hayden 1975, Wunz 1981). Turkeys did not inhabit the original forest, which was 40 percent coniferous, but turkeys occupied the second-growth hardwoods during the late 1940s and early 1950s as populations expanded northward through Pennsylvania. Over a 19-year period (1963–1981), turkeys died from starvation in 7 harsh winters. Turkeys starved when powder snow greater than 30 centimeters (12 inches) deep persisted for longer than 2 weeks.

Winters were defined as severe when the number of days with a minimum temperature of −13 degrees Celsius (9 degrees Fahrenheit) plus the number of days with snow deeper than 15 centimeters (6 inches)—some days counting twice—totaled more than 130. On the average, 1 in 5 winters was rated severe, and 1 in 3 winters was harsher than usual (index about 100 harsh days). After severe winters, populations usually recovered within a year. But populations depressed during a series of 3 severe winters took 2 years for recovery to begin. Most of the deaths occurred on the upper third of the study area, where powder snow persisted for weeks.

In severe winters, part of the population usually shifted range to lower elevations. The range usually expanded into the upper elevations during the following summer. During average or mild winters, birds usually remained at high elevations.

Snow limits the movements of turkeys and their access to food. Starvation and predation are usually the causes of death during periods of deep snow and cold temperatures. The survival of turkey populations in southeastern Minnesota near the northern limits of turkey range in the upper Mississippi Valley illustrates the ability of turkeys to withstand climatic extremes if they have ample food.

Two populations, living about 80 kilometers (50 miles) apart, were studied during 2 winters that differed in severity (Porter et al. 1980). In 1976–77, a mild winter with little snow, survival exceeded 75 percent on both ranges. In 1977–78, survival was near 90 percent in the northern population, but less than 35 percent on the southern range. Birds in both populations occupied home ranges of about 100 hectares (247 acres) in hardwoods on south slopes or deep ravines. The home ranges

Emaciated turkey. Deep, powdery snow can result in turkey deaths when it persists for more than 2 weeks. *Photo by G. Wunz, Pennsylvania Game Commission.*

of the northern population included small fields of standing corn adjacent to the hardwoods used for roosting. The corn remained available through the winter. On the southern range, though, mast was unavailable. The persistent fruits on shrubs were consumed during February. Despite similar weather conditions, survival of the 2 populations differed, depending on the availability of food above the snow.

The exact tolerance of healthy, adult wild turkeys to cold has not been established. Schorger (1966:331) cites a report of 2 "domesticated" wild turkeys freezing to death on their roost in a barn in Hancock County, Maine, when the temperature dropped to −36 degrees Celsius (−33 degrees Fahrenheit). He also reports that 2 wild turkeys survived roosting in a tree on a game farm at Teduc, Alberta, when the temperature was −31 degrees Celsius (−24 degrees Fahrenheit). The lethal low temperature would depend partly on body size and fat reserves of the individual bird.

Energy requirements of wild turkeys increase in direct proportion to the decrease in temperature below a critical minimum value (Gray and Prince 1988). The estimated lower critical temperatures in winter ranged from 7 degrees Celsius (45 degrees Fahrenheit) for adult males to 15 degrees Celsius (59 degrees Fahrenheit) for juvenile females. The lower the temperature, the greater the stress on the turkey. Most experiments, natural and planned, have combined the effects of cold and fasting.

Northern populations routinely survive prolonged periods of subfreezing temperatures. If food is available,

Wild turkeys can withstand severe weather if food is available. Standing corn and dairy farming provide important sources of food for northern populations. *Photo by G. Wunz, Pennsylvania Game Commission.*

Northern turkeys can usually find food as long as the snow is packed or crusted. Persistent fruits of shrubs and vines are particularly important when snow is deep. *Photo by G. Wunz, Pennsylvania Game Commission.*

In the mountains of the Northeast, seeps (where groundwater flows to the surface) are the turkey's primary feeding places during deep snow. *Photo by W. Healy, U.S. Forest Service.*

the effects of cold seem negligible. Turkeys in western Massachusetts that wintered on agricultural land and had access to waste grain did not lose weight and had an average winter survival of 93 percent (Vander Haegen et al. 1988). Northern populations usually can withstand 2 weeks of fasting at ambient winter temperature before significant numbers of turkeys die. Turkeys can usually recover from a 30 percent loss of body weight, and a turkey usually does not die until it loses more than 40 percent of its weight (Hayden and Nelson 1963).

My own observations and the writings of most investigators indicate that starvation is usually the ultimate cause of death during harsh winter weather. Starvation predisposes birds to other causes of death, and predation is often the immediate cause among starving turkeys. Gerstell (1942:19 in Shorger 1966:330) examined 5 wild turkeys found dead in southern Pennsylvania in February and March 1936. Two were found coated with ice immediately after a severe ice storm. The others died during periods of high wind and low temperatures. The birds apparently died of exposure; their crops contained corn and green food. Such cases must be rare.

Wherever deep snow occurs regularly, turkeys respond by restricting their range to special habitats that permit access to food in spite of snow. In New England, key winter habitat is associated with dairy farms and their manure spreads, silage, and corn stubble. In Minnesota and other parts of the Midwest, standing corn is important. Seeps, springs, and small streams provide access to food all across the northern range and at higher elevations in the eastern mountains.

The northern limit of the eastern wild turkey seems to be set by the condition, depth, and duration of snow cover. Powdered or fluffy snow is most detrimental. Turkeys cannot scratch through more than 15 centimeters (6 inches) of powder, nor can they walk far if the depth exceeds 30 centimeters (1 foot). Northern turkeys can usually find food as long as the snow is packed or crusted. They can scratch through a foot or more of packed snow and can walk over it to where food is available. Winter mortality is rare in the Lake Erie snowbelt of northwestern Pennsylvania and western New York. Snow there is deep but seldom fluffy (Wunz 1981).

Temperature has less effect than snow condition and depth on wild turkeys. Temperature and snow, however, always act together on northern turkey populations. Snow cover cannot persist without freezing temperatures.

In the Northeast, the limiting snow line corresponds with the transition zone between oak-hickory forest types to the south and the spruce-fir, maple-beech-birch, and aspen-birch forests to the north. In parts of New England, New York, Pennsylvania, and Michigan, turkeys have extended their range beyond the limits of the oak

Lack of trees, rather than an absolute shortage of water, limits the distribution of turkeys in the Central Plains and West. Turkeys occupied 1.4 million hectares (3.5 million acres) of scrub mesquite in west Texas after power lines were erected. *Photo by H. Kothmann, Texas Parks and Wildlife Department.*

forest—usually where human activity provides special winter habitats. Northern red oak, a key species for northern turkey populations, occurs well into the maple-beech-birch forest and beyond the range of the wild turkey. In that zone (where deep snow accumulates and the oaks yield dominance to aspens, beeches, and maples), the tree-roosting, ground-feeding wild turkey relinquishes the forest to the snow-roosting, treetop feeding ruffed grouse.

Water and Trees, the Western Boundary

South of the snowbelt, the range of the eastern turkey ends where forest gives way to prairie and brushland. The western limit of Rio Grande turkey range is where open expanses of prairie and brushland begin. Similarly, the range of Merriam's turkey ends where western mountain habitats of ponderosa pine-oak forest change to desert, prairie, and sagebrush.

In the Central Plains and the West, the lack of trees, rather than an absolute shortage of water, limits the distribution of turkeys. In west Texas, the Rio Grande turkey was formerly restricted to the Edwards Plateau and major flood plains of the Colorado, North, Middle, and South Concho rivers. Recently, wild turkeys have expanded into 1.4 million hectares (3.5 million acres) of scrub mesquite prairie on the high plains. Kothman and

Litton (1975:159) describe the process: "During the 1950's, internal combustion engines which powered thousands of oil well pumps in the Permian basin were replaced by electric motors to reduce maintenance and noise. This conversion resulted in a maze of power transmission lines and poles. Considered a necessary eyesore, these man-made structures created an artificial forest of wooden and metallic 'trees' that turkeys readily utilized as roost sites above the reach of natural predators."

Haucke (1975) also reports the widespread use of transmission lines for roosting in the mesquite-grasslands of south Texas. The turkeys seemed to prefer natural sites over artificial roosts but readily adapted to roosting on camp houses, corrals, and windmills where trees were scarce. Pen-raised turkeys introduced to treeless Matagorda Island off the south Texas coast readily accepted artillery observation towers and transmission lines as roost sites. Turkeys occupying these treeless areas fed on insects, fruits of perennial browse, forbs, and grasses (Kothmann and Litton 1975). The absence of roost sites sets a limit on the distribution of turkeys in west Texas. In this semiarid country, trees are more valuable as roost sites than as sources of food.

The original distribution of the eastern turkey included narrow extensions into the prairies along larger, tree-lined streams (Schorger 1966:44). According to Schorger (1966), the eastern turkeys did not occur where the annual rainfall was below 64 centimeters (25 inches), and the Rio Grande turkey was confined to areas of Texas where the annual rainfall was from 51 to 76 centimeters (20 to 30 inches). Treeless expanses of prairie, desert, and shrub steppe also limited the distribution of Merriam's turkeys. The ancestral range of *M. g. merriami* included the ponderosa pine-oak forest of the intermountain region at elevations of 1,800 to 3,000 meters (6,000 to 10,000 feet) from central Colorado south almost to the Mexican border (Ligon 1946). Extensive ponderosa pine forests occur to the north and west of Merriam's range, but these forests are separated from turkey range by the deserts of Nevada and sagebrush steppe of Wyoming and Idaho (Harlow and Harrar 1958:107, Plate 7). Turkeys have been successfully introduced to these ponderosa pine forests.

Precipitation limits the distribution of Gould's and Rio Grande turkeys in Mexico, except perhaps at the southern extreme of the range. Both races occur primarily in the temperate, pine-oak vegetation zone: Gould's turkey in the northwestern mountains (Sierra Madre Occidental) and the Rio Grande turkey in the northeastern mountains (Sierra Madre Oriental). Most of the range of these 2 races is bounded by mesquite-grasslands (Leopold 1948:394, Figure 1, Leopold 1950, Figure 1). The southern edge of the range, however, is bounded by a complex of vegetation types, including tropical deciduous forest, tropical evergreen forest, cloud forest, and desert. The

Mexican turkey *(M. g. gallopavo)* did extend its range into the tropical deciduous forest (Aldrich 1967b:43) but was apparently absent from some parts of the pine-oak uplands (Leopold 1948). It is not clear to me what climatic factor limited the southern distribution of wild turkeys in Mexico.

WEATHER AND PRODUCTIVITY

Annual fluctuations in the abundance and productivity of turkey populations are the rule. The dramatic increase I described at the start of this chapter occurred in a healthy population that had persisted since precolonial times and occupied primary range. Similar fluctuations have been reported from most parts of wild turkey range (e.g., Jonas 1968, Kennamer et al. 1975, Beasom and Pattee 1980, Porter et al. 1983).

Annual fluctuations in the abundance of game birds have been the subject of intensive study in many parts of the world for many years (Siivonen 1957, Brittas 1988). Unraveling the causes of annual fluctuations would provide a basic understanding of the species population dynamics. Short-term fluctuations in turkey numbers, in addition to having theoretical significance, are of practical importance to wildlife managers and hunters. If annual changes in the abundance of turkeys are caused by weather, then population changes could be predicted and seasons, bag limits, and hunting plans adjusted accordingly.

Among population biologists, there are 2 schools of thought on regulating animal abundance (Smith 1974:328). One school emphasizes factors that depend on the density of the population itself. Social competition for food and space are key factors in density-dependent theories. The other school emphasizes the role of environmental factors that are independent of population density. Weather plays a central role in density-independent theories (Figure 1).

No simple mechanism will explain the population dynamics of wild turkeys. We know turkey populations respond to weather, social pressure, and many other factors. Which factors are important depends on which population we consider. I will begin by examining the effects of weather on the reproduction of Rio Grande turkeys because the relationships between rain and reproduction have been well established in the semiarid lands of Texas.

Rainfall and Productivity in South Texas

Dramatic fluctuations occur in the annual productivity of the Rio Grande turkey in south Texas. In years of normal precipitation, productivity is good. But in

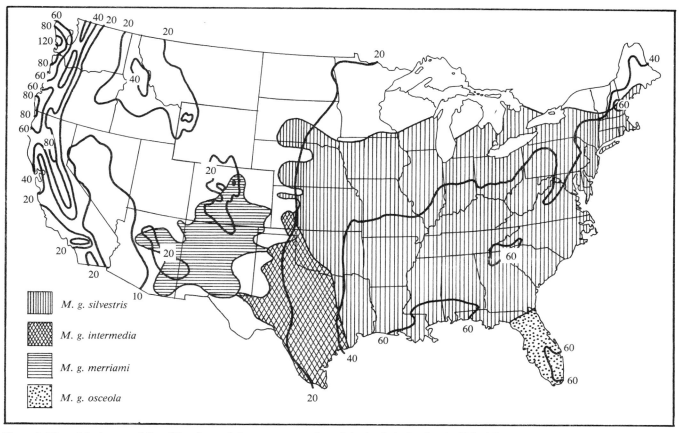

Figure 1. The original range of the wild turkey and the average annual precipitation in inches for the United States.

In years when previous rainfall was abundant, lush vegetation provides food and cover for Rio Grande hens, and poult production is good. *Photo by B. Reaves, Texas Parks and Wildlife Department.*

drought years, there may be almost no production of young turkeys (Baker et al. 1980, Beasom 1970, 1973). The most important rainfall occurs during the tropical storm season in August and September. Rain during the breeding season is of secondary importance. Rain during early fall affects turkey reproduction the next spring through its influence on soil moisture and subsequent vegetation growth (Figure 2).

In this region, new growth of vegetation in the spring depends on adequate soil moisture storage. Heavy rainfall during tropical storms in September recharges soil moisture to capacity. Little of this moisture is lost over winter. So when the spring growing season begins, the new growth of vegetation responds favorably. Rainfall after February occurs when potential evaporation is relatively high (and moisture loss elevated), so the benefit to plant growth is reduced (Beasom 1973:81–83).

Rain affects the nutrition of hens and the amount of predation on nests and incubating hens. Ample autumn rain will stimulate the growth of grasses and forbs early the following spring, thus improving the quantity and quality of food for adults and the amount of concealing cover for nests. In moist years, almost all hens are reproductively active, and the peak of hatching occurs 1 to 5

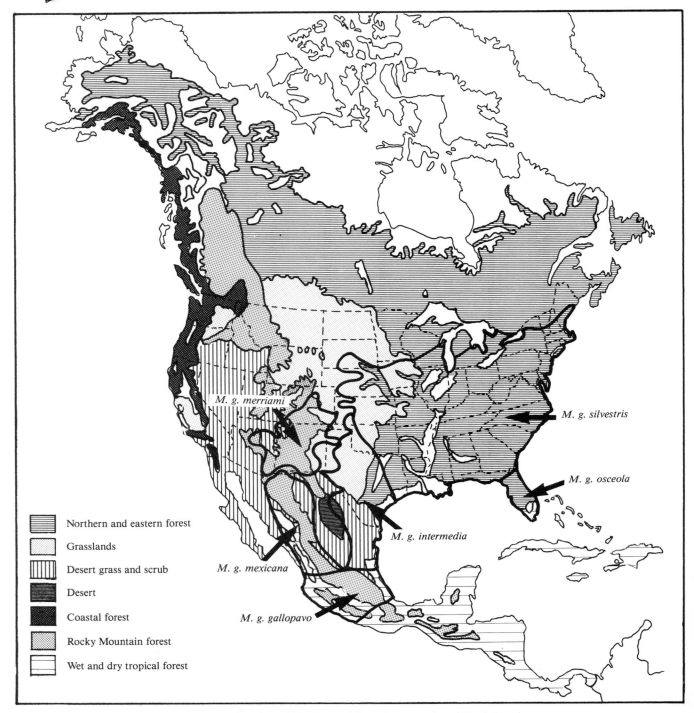

Figure 2. The original distribution of the subspecies of the wild turkey and the major vegetation of North America.

Legend:
- Northern and eastern forest
- Grasslands
- Desert grass and scrub
- Desert
- Coastal forest
- Rocky Mountain forest
- Wet and dry tropical forest

M. g. merriami
M. g. silvestris
M. g. osceola
M. g. intermedia
M. g. mexicana
M. g. gallopavo

weeks earlier than in dry years. In drought years, as many as 40 percent of the hens never lay eggs.

Beasom and Pattee (1980) used the ratio of poults per hen as a measure of productivity. They were able to account for more than 97 percent of the annual variation in poult-hen ratios with models based on (1) soil mois-

ture storage and total precipitation during the previous fall; and (2) precipitation during the breeding season. That is as strong a relationship as we ever see in field ecology.

Pattee and Beasom (1979) tested the effect of nutrition on reproduction by feeding 2 populations of Rio

Grande turkeys during late winter and early spring. Both populations were monitored for a year before the feeding began. Then one population was fed the first year only, and the other population was fed the second year only. Each population was the control group for the other. Fed populations had about 230 percent more hens with poults than control populations in both years. Poults hatched earlier and over a longer time period on the fed area than on the control area. The fed populations produced substantially more poults than the control populations in both years.

The survival of poults did not seem to be affected by rainfall. Poult survival was similar in wet and dry years (Beasom 1973:184) and in fed and unfed populations (Pattee and Beasom 1979). Predation in dry years seemed to be associated with nest destruction. Beasom (1973: 182) conducted intensive predator removal experiments and found substantially greater productivity where predators were removed. During dry years, predator removal could mean the difference between almost complete failure or relatively high reproductive success. In wet years, however, reproductive success was high without predator removal.

Before leaving our considerations of the Rio Grande turkey, I must stress the importance of local conditions in assessing the effects of weather on wild turkeys. Beasom (1973) studied 4 areas that differed in soil and vegetation type but were only 48 to 64 kilometers (30 to 40 miles) apart. On 3 areas with mesquite and live-oak vegetation, turkey populations responded positively to increased rainfall. On the scrub-oak area, turkeys were influenced negatively by rainfall. The low-lying scrub-oak area flooded after tropical storms and remained largely covered with water during the 2 nesting seasons when reproductive success was good on the other 3 areas. In other words, the same weather conditions had exactly opposite effects on turkey populations in the same region. Extreme local variation in effects of weather seems to be a general phenomenon in turkey populations.

Spring Weather and Eastern Wild Turkeys

Most early writers describe turkey poults as very sensitive to chilling and wetting (Audubon 1840–44, Judd 1905, Bent 1932). The idea that low temperatures and heavy rainfall during the hatching and early brood-rearing period reduce poult survival is generally accepted (Markley 1967). But, because nests and poults are so hard to observe, the influence of weather has been difficult to measure.

In 1976, my colleague E.S. "Sam" Nenno suggested we might be able to measure the effects of weather on poult survival directly by radio tracking human-imprinted hens. We had been raising turkeys from eggs

collected in the wild and using the poults to study brood habitat. In this endeavor, we literally took the role of the hen. The effects of the early imprinting experience were permanent. Through their adult lives, the birds treated us as if we were turkeys. Yet they exhibited normal breeding and brood-rearing behavior in 0.8-hectare (2-acre) forested pens.

The idea was simple. In early February, we would attach radio transmitters to the hens and pull their clipped wing feathers. (It had been necessary to clip the feathers on a wing to keep the birds from flying over the 2.4-meter [8-foot] fence.) The birds would grow new flight feathers. And at the time of spring flock breakup, the turkeys would disperse from the pens to nest. We would track the birds and observe them daily through nesting and the first month of brood rearing. Weather data were available from a permanent station located next to the pens. Our aim: to learn enough to be able to predict fall populations on the basis of the previous fall's population and the temperature and precipitation during May and June. The plan almost worked.

We tracked 16 hens through the nesting seasons of 1977 and 1978 on Chestnut Ridge in north-central West Virginia (Healy and Nenno 1985). Weather during the laying period did not affect the hatching of eggs. All clutches were exposed to freezing temperatures at least once before incubation began. In 1978, 2 successful nests were exposed to freezing temperatures 6 times during the laying period, and 4 centimeters (1.5 inches) of snow fell on April 22 while each nest contained 9 eggs. The snow melted within 24 hours, both hens continued to lay, and both began incubating on April 25. One hen hatched 7 of 11 eggs after 25 days of incubation. The other hatched all 16 eggs after 29 days of incubation.

Latham (1958) suspected that freezing temperatures during egg laying could kill the embryos and result in hens hatching partial clutches. Unincubated eggs resist freezing. We found unincubated eggs survived overnight lows of −4 degrees Celsius (25 degrees Fahrenheit) (Healy and Nenno 1985). Hens cover eggs with leaves during the laying period, providing further protection from freezing. Freezing of unincubated eggs is probably rare.

Weather caused some poult deaths, but not the way we expected. The most severe storm occurred on June 9, 1977. Rainfall measured 3.7 centimeters (1.4 inches) between midnight and 5:30 the next evening. Temperatures ranged from 7 to 11 degrees Celsius (45 to 52 degrees Fahrenheit). Four broods were under observation at the time. Two broods aged 3 and 6 days suffered no mortality. A 12-day-old brood lost 7 of 9 poults, and a 15-day-old brood lost 5 of 11 poults.

The younger broods survived the storm intact because they still had energy reserves in the yolk sac and were able to fit completely beneath the hen when brood-

In West Virginia, poults less than 10 days old were able to survive heavy rainstorms because they could brood completely under the hen and had some food reserves in the yolk sac. *Photo by W. Healy, U.S. Forest Service.*

Two-week-old poults died during prolonged cold rains because they could not brood beneath the hen. *Photo by W. Healy, U.S. Forest Service.*

ing. The older birds had depleted their yolk sac food reserves, and their quail-sized bodies would not fit entirely beneath the brooding hen. All broods were active during the storm when poults initiated feeding activity.

The deaths occurred in the afternoon after the broods had been exposed to more than 12 hours of rain and low temperatures. The older poults became progressively wetter during the day, and their activity seemed to contribute to wetting their hens. By late afternoon, some poults were soaked. They stopped following their hens and collapsed during feeding movements. During this period, plumage of the hens was soaked, bare skin showed at the base of the wings, wing tips were dragging, and the hens were shivering. Hens roosted on the ground for the night around 6:40 P.M., and poults roosting with them survived.

We thought the youngest poults would be most susceptible to wetting and chilling. The loss of poults 12 and 15 days old was unexpected. This age-specific effect complicated our efforts to predict fall populations because both weather and brood age would have to be built into a model.

The storm also illustrated the importance of threshold values. Turkey populations are adapted to the average weather conditions of their region. Weather must deviate substantially from the average — and do so for some time — before it affects populations. None of the 4 broods would have had poults die if the storm had lasted only 12 hours.

One other storm deserves mention. It illustrates the importance of luck (technically, the stochastic nature of weather events). On June 14, 1977, a thunderstorm produced 1.1 centimeters (0.4 inches) of rain between 1:45 and 4:30 P.M.; temperatures ranged from 14 to 22 degrees Celsius (57 to 72 degrees Fahrenheit). Broods aged 8, 11, and 21 days suffered no mortality. A 1-day-old brood lost 8 of 11 poults. The brood had hatched the previous day, and the thunderstorm struck abruptly shortly after the new birds left the nest. Apparently the sudden downpour disoriented and scattered the brood.

In sum, spring weather in West Virginia caused mortality of turkey poults. Weather after hatching was an important cause of poult mortality in 1977 but not in 1978. In 1977, 21 of 43 deaths were attributed to weather; in 1978, only 1 of 16 deaths was attributed to weather. The combination of low temperature (7 to 11 degrees Celsius; 45 to 52 degrees Fahrenheit) and rain for more than 12 hours caused deaths. Poults survived periods of low temperature (0 to 18 degrees Celsius; 32 to 64 degrees Fahrenheit) lasting up to 48 hours. In most cases, rain accompanied by mild temperatures (16 to 24 degrees Celsius; 61 to 75 degrees Fahrenheit) produced no mortality. There was no simple connection between mortality and daily temperature and precipitation.

Spring weather is less important for southern populations than for northern populations and birds living at high elevations in eastern mountains where weather is usually severe. Few poults are lost to rain in the warm, temperate, rainy climate of the Cumberland plateau in northeastern Alabama (Speake and Metzler 1985, Speake et al. 1985). Speake et al. (1985) used an innovative approach to studying mortality and habitat use. Soon after radio-instrumented hens hatched clutches, the researchers captured the poults by hand and attached 2.7-gram (0.09-ounce) transmitters. The miniature radios lasted 4 to 5 weeks and did not affect survival.

From 1979 to 1983, Speake et al. (1985) radio-tagged 162 of 335 poults in 34 broods and got data on mortality for another 45 poults in 4 broods. "Direct losses to rain occurred only once when an entire brood was lost during a 12.5-centimeter (4.9-inch) rain" (Speake et al. 1985: 474). The biologists believed loss to excessive rain probably did not occur after poults began roosting in trees. The poult death rate was almost 70 percent, and predators were responsible for most losses. Exposure, starvation, flooding, and birth defects accounted for 18 percent of the losses (Speake et al. 1985:473).

In Florida, 12 broods were unaffected by rain during hatching and the first weeks of life (Williams et al. 1973a). Heavy rains fell while several broods were hatching, and all broods experienced at least a moderate to heavy rainfall before they were 2 weeks old. Two broods lost poults about the time they were known to have crossed water-filled ditches or streams within a few hours of leaving their nests. Williams et al. (1973a) suspected that summer rains affected populations only when they caused flooding.

Spring weather can affect other aspects of reproduction besides poult survival. In the dense, stable turkey populations of northern Missouri (20 to 30 birds per square kilometer of timber; 52 to 78 per square mile), variation in nesting chronology and overall reproductive success is attributable to variation in spring weather (Vangilder et al. 1987). A late spring may substantially reduce hen success by lowering the renesting rate. In the particularly cold and late spring of 1984, the start of nesting was delayed 3 or 4 weeks. The renesting rate in 1984 was only 14 percent, compared with 40 to 75 percent in other years. Because the initial nesting attempt was so late, many hens may have entered the period of photo refractivity (when day length no longer stimulated gonadal development) by the time the first nest was lost. If so, they were physiologically incapable of renesting.

Spring weather and annual productivity are clearly related. In northern populations, cold, wet weather probably causes poult deaths on a recurring basis. In warmer southern climates, poult mortality from weather probably occurs only during floods and other natural disasters. Throughout the eastern turkey's range, spring weather has a direct effect on the timing of reproductive events, and consequently an indirect effect on the rate of renesting and on the nutrition of hens and poults. Spring weather no doubt also influences the health of predators that eat turkeys, so the relationships are complex.

I am no longer optimistic we can develop models that will accurately predict fall populations in the northeastern United States on the basis of spring weather. Too many other factors are involved, and local and random effects of weather make regional population predictions imprecise. The overall relationship between spring weather and eastern wild turkey populations is clearly described by Bailey and Rinell (1968:32). "As average temperature and rainfall deviate from normal (either above or below) brood production decreases. The greater the departure from normal, the greater the reduction in fall population."

Winter Weather and Northern Populations

Winter weather has a direct effect on populations by killing wild turkeys in some years. Severe winters can also dampen reproduction the following spring by influencing the nutrition and physical condition of hens. The relationships between maternal nutrition and the production and survival of young have been demonstrated for many species, including people.

Moss et al. (1975) were among the first to relate nutrition to breeding success in a wild population of gallinaceous birds in their study of red grouse on the moors in northeast Scotland. The ecosystem on the moors is relatively simple. The dominant plant—heather—makes up over 90 percent of the birds' spring diet. Annual variations in breeding success were correlated with the number of days the heather had been growing before hens finished laying, and also with the density of heather. Even in this ecosystem, however, population changes could not be predicted from environmental factors, and population changes were the result of complex interactions among density-dependent and environmental factors (Watson et al. 1984).

Links between rainfall, nutrition, and reproduction have been demonstrated for the Rio Grande turkey in south Texas (Beasom 1973, Beasom and Pattee 1980). We might expect that severe winter weather would affect the nutrition and reproduction of eastern turkeys, but such a relationship has been surprisingly difficult to demonstrate.

In southeastern Minnesota, the winter body weights of hens were positively related to their reproductive success. Porter et al. (1983) studied reproductive performance during 3 years: 1975, 1977, and 1978. Two years, 1975 and 1978, had prolonged periods of deep snow and average death rates of 30 to 40 percent. The degree of winter severity depends on the combination of food, cover, and weather in a specific location.

To account for these local effects, Porter et al. (1983) used body weight and survivorship within flocks as indi-

Winter severity depends on the combination of food, cover, and weather. In Minnesota, flocks wintering in woodlots adjacent to standing corn survived and reproduced well. *Photo by W. Porter.*

ces to winter severity. Hens were heaviest in December and lightest in March. Weight loss was greater in some flocks than in others in all years. Birds that weighed less than 3.5 kilograms (7.7 pounds) in late February and March did not survive to the breeding season. Hens weighing more than 4.3 kilograms (9.5 pounds) were more likely to survive to breed (100 versus 70 percent) and more likely to attempt nesting (100 versus 71 percent) than hens weighing less than 4.3 kilograms (9.5 pounds). Between light and heavy hens that nested, there were no differences in clutch size, nesting success, and hatching success. But the number of female poults surviving until late summer averaged 4.3 for heavy hens and 2.6 for light hens.

Reduced flock survivorship was also correlated with reduced reproductive performance among females that survived to breed. Yearling females from flocks with poor winter survivorship (less than 75 percent survival) had lower hatching success than yearling females from flocks with good winter survival. Porter et al. (1983) suggested that the primary effect of winter weather was related to the ability of the hen to hatch eggs and rear young. Nutritionally stressed females had the energy reserves necessary to lay and incubate a clutch of eggs but not to care for the poults.

In the Northeast, there seems to be little relationship between winter severity and reproduction the following spring. On the Allegheny Plateau in north-central Pennsylvania, dramatic population increases often occurred after severe winters (Wunz and Hayden 1975). Reproductive performance was independent of the number of birds surviving the winter. In West Virginia between 1955 and 1966, many of the largest fall harvests occurred after winters of unusual severity (Bailey and Rinell 1968:46).

Hens can recover quickly from the stress of winter starvation. Hayden and Nelson (1963) subjected 50 hens to alternating periods of complete starvation and half rations from January 4 to March 20. The birds were kept in outdoor pens with no shelter in north-central Pennsylvania. A control group of 50 hens was fed normal full rations.

From January 4 to 25, the experimental birds lost weight on a half-ration diet. Then they were given no food from January 26 to February 9. Nine hens died during this period, and the surviving hens lost an average of 30 percent of their initial weight. From February 10 to 28, the experimental hens were fed half rations. They gained weight, but they averaged 0.8 kilograms (1.8 pounds) lighter than control hens.

The second starvation period extended from February 29 to March 8. Nine more experimental birds died, and the average body weight dropped to 2.5 kilograms (5.5 pounds). From March 9 to 20, the birds again got half rations. None died, and the average body weight increased to 2.7 kilograms (6.0 pounds). Birds were put on full rations at the end of the experiment. The surviving experimental hens had suffered an average weight loss of 30 percent. The maximum loss for a surviving hen was 43 percent of initial body weight.

In the mountains of Pennsylvania and West Virginia, turkeys often winter on lower slopes where springs and seeps are abundant. Snow melts faster on this southern exposure. *Photo by G. Wunz.*

Control hens gained weight during the experiment, and they started laying eggs on March 27. The experimental hens started laying eggs on April 7, 12 days later, but only 18 days after being put back on full rations. Control birds averaged 16 eggs per hen compared with 11 eggs per hen for experimental birds. Fertility, hatchability, egg weight, and poult weight were not different for experimental and control birds. There is no way to know how well these hens would have done raising broods, but it is clear that hens can recover from starvation rapidly if they get ample food.

There is no reason to believe wild turkeys are exempt from the general laws of animal nutrition. Yet several factors make it difficult to measure the impact of weather on the nutrition and reproduction of wild populations. First, winter severity, as measured by snow depth and minimum daily temperatures, can be independent of nutrition. Porter et al. (1980, 1983) showed that in Minnesota, birds wintering near standing corn were in good physical condition regardless of the weather. The same type of habitat effect has been demonstrated in western Massachusetts, where snow depth has little impact on flocks residing on dairy farms that make food available in manure spreads (Vander Haegen et al. 1988).

Second, severe weather in January and February may have little impact on food resources in spring. A harsh winter followed by an average or mild spring may have no effect on reproduction. Finally, population estimates are usually made for large management units, yet intensive studies (for example, Porter et al. 1983) show that a finer scale of measurement may be necessary to detect the effects of weather.

DISASTERS AND DIGRESSIONS

Hurricanes, freak snowstorms, and floods occasionally take their toll of wild turkeys (see Jonas 1968, Hartman and Wunz 1974, Kennamer et al. 1975). The impact of these unusual storms generally is less than we imagine during the storm. Individual turkeys are remarkably tough, and wild turkey populations are resilient.

Hurricane Agnes struck the Northeast in June 1972. Pennsylvania was particularly hard hit. Rain fell almost continuously for 5 days. Up to 46 centimeters (18 inches) of rain fell in eastern sections of the state. Flooding and property damage were extensive. In south-central Pennsylvania, turkey sightings dropped from 1,518 poults in 1971 to 526 in 1972 (Hartman and Wunz 1974). Statewide, the impact was less dramatic. The storm's effects were minimal in western sections of Pennsylvania. Throughout the state, turkey habitat is on ridges and mountains, so turkey populations escaped much of the flooding (Figure 3).

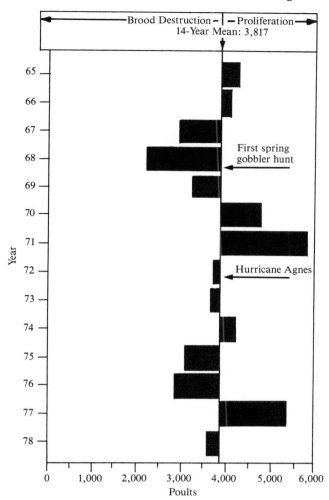

Figure 3. Variations in total brood counts in Pennsylvania show the dilemma of drawing inferences about weather and turkey populations. Hurricane Agnes caused widespread destruction in June 1972, yet brood counts were near the long-term average.

Examining the long-term trends in statewide brood counts will put the effects of Hurricane Agnes into perspective. Brood counts have been conducted in Pennsylvania annually since 1953 (Wunz 1978a, Wunz and Shope 1980). The July and August counts are correlated with the subsequent fall harvest, providing a good measure of population trends. During the 14 years from 1965 to 1978, there were 5 years in which brood counts increased from the previous year and 8 in which counts decreased. The relative annual increases on brood counts ranged from 5 to 81 percent; decreases ranged from 1 to 41 percent. In only 3 years did the counts change by less than 10 percent from the previous year.

The year of Hurricane Agnes, 1972, had the largest relative decrease—41 percent lower than 1971. But, the highest count in the series was in 1971, and relative annual increases of 30 to 44 percent were observed in 1969, 1970, and 1971. So 1972, with a statewide count of 6,397 poults and hens, was slightly above the 14-year average of 6,316.

Much to the chagrin of Arnie Hayden and Jerry Wunz, Pennsylvania wild turkey biologists, the lowest brood count occurred in the summer of 1968, after the state's first spring gobbler hunt. That was the third successive year of declining brood counts. The hunt had nothing to do with the low count, but critics of spring hunting were skeptical.

The next 3 years showed the wisdom of adopting the spring hunt. Brood counts and populations increased dramatically in all years. As we now know, Hurricane Agnes arrived in 1972, interrupting this geometric increase and probably saving Pennsylvania from a plague of turkeys!

Jonas (1968) described how the unusual spring of 1967 affected Merriam's turkeys on the 26,305-hectare (65,000-acre) Long Pines area in southeastern Montana. That year was the wettest on record in 64 years. The most unusual event was a 94-centimeter (37-inch) snowfall on May 1. The snow melted within 10 days and produced substantial flooding. June had 22.71 centimeters (8.94 inches) of rain, about 3 times the average for that month. The heavy snow delayed or interrupted egg laying and incubation for most (but not all) birds. Only 16 percent of the young turkeys observed were from eggs under incubation before May 10, 1967, compared with 81 percent in other years. Considering the depth of snow in early May,

it is remarkable that any hens were able to start or continue with incubation during that period.

My guess is the surviving nests were in blowdowns or similar situations that provided overhead cover. Fewer hens and fewer poults were observed in 1967 than in other years. Poult-to-hen ratios were slightly lower, and there seemed to be less renesting in 1967 than in other years. Yet reproduction was not a complete failure.

Bottomland hardwoods between the Mississippi River and the levees are flooded regularly, yet this habitat supports some of the highest densities of wild turkeys in North America (Kimmel and Zwank 1985). Like other populations, turkeys living in bottomland hardwoods exhibit annual variations in productivity (Kennamer 1970, Kennamer et al. 1975). Kennamer et al. (1975) studied populations on 18,616 hectares (46,000 acres) in the Mississippi delta from 1968 to 1972. During these 5 summers, the ratio of hens with poults to hens without poults ranged from 6.79:1.0 to 0.25:1.0.

The total number of poults seen, the number of poults seen per day, and other indices of productivity showed similar annual variations. The lowest production was in the year with the highest flood stage, but there was no simple pattern between flooding and reproduction. Flooding apparently had to reach a certain stage before there was an effect, and the timing and duration of flooding were also important. Rainfall during May and June had no adverse effect on productivity.

Zwank et al. (1988) studied habitat use by hens on 2,550 hectares (6,301 acres) of bottomland hardwoods on Point Lookout, Louisiana. The area is usually flooded every spring. During major floods, all but about 60 hectares (148 acres) of Point Lookout is inundated. During 1983 and 1984, flooding prevented successful nesting on the area. Hens spent most of their time in trees and did not move beyond the levees to nest. It is not clear what maintains these populations in years of reproductive failure.

Bottomland hardwoods along the Mississippi River are flooded regularly, but this habitat supports some of the highest densities of turkeys in North America. *Photo by J. Neal, U.S. Fish and Wildlife Service.*

CONCLUSIONS

Turkey populations thrive across a broad range of climatic conditions. Precipitation seems to be the most important climatic factor affecting their distribution. In North America, turkeys are limited by extremes: deep, persistent snow cover at one end and insufficient rain to support the growth of trees at the other. Temperature plays a secondary role, but precipitation and temperature are usually correlated. This is especially so at the edge of the turkey's range where climate tends to be hot and dry or cool and moist.

The original range of the wild turkey extended from southern Maine westward to South Dakota and south to central Mexico. Several subspecies have been introduced beyond the limits of their original range. Populations of Rio Grande and Merriam's turkeys have been established in the mountains of California. Merriam's turkeys have been introduced to ponderosa pine habitats in North Dakota, Wyoming, and Montana north of their ancestral range. Eastern turkeys from Vermont have been stocked in West Germany (Wunz et al. 1985), and healthy populations of Rio Grande turkeys live on 4 Hawaiian Islands (Gonzalez 1982). It seems likely that turkeys can survive in temperate and subtropical climates worldwide.

Weather fluctuations contribute to annual changes in turkey abundance. In some habitats and with some populations, weather variables explain most of the annual variation in turkey productivity (Beasom and Pattee 1980). It is difficult to generalize from individual studies because the effects of weather are profoundly modified by local conditions, and many other factors influence turkey populations. Despite these difficulties, we can make some generalizations.

First, weather conditions must usually pass some threshold before they affect turkey populations. For example, in the Northeast, deaths occur in winter when deep, fluffy snow persists for more than 2 weeks. In West Virginia, young poults began to die from exposure after 12 hours of cold rain. Shorter storms had little effect. In much of the South, rain apparently does not affect poults until it causes flooding. In general, weather must deviate substantially from the average for some time before it affects wild turkey populations.

Second, the loss of young poults to exposure has probably been overemphasized. Weather conditions that delay breeding and nesting seem to have greater impact. The mechanism through which weather influences breeding chronology and reproductive output varies among populations. In south Texas, rainfall and soil moisture influence plant growth and in turn the nutrition of hens and the amount of cover for nests. In dry years, hens eat poorly and their reproductive development is retarded. Fewer hens nest, and nesting begins later and ends earlier than in moist years. Winter and early spring weather probably influences the nutrition and physical condition of northern populations. In Missouri, cold, wet spring weather delays breeding and reduces poult production, primarily by reducing the rate of renesting. In the Mississippi bottomlands, flooding often delays nesting; in some years it prevents any nesting. Rainfall after hatching, however, is not correlated with poult survival in Mississippi bottomlands.

Finally, the amount of variation in populations attributable to weather varies among regions and in some regions from year to year. In general, the effects of weather are greatest along the fringes of the turkey's range. The closest link between weather and populations occurs for Rio Grande turkeys in semiarid south Texas. Northern populations seem to respond to weather thresholds, so the influence of weather is large in some years and minor in others. In my West Virginia study, weather accounted for about 50 percent of poult mortality in one year, and 6 percent in the next. Southeastern populations seem least influenced by weather. Floods are important in bottomland habitats, but overall predation seems more important.

Chapter 11

POPULATION DYNAMICS

Larry D. Vangilder
Wildlife Research Biologist
Missouri Department of Conservation
Columbia, Missouri

Population dynamics, as the term is used in this chapter, refers to changes in the size of a group of wild turkeys inhabiting a specific area. These changes in the size of a turkey population are the result of 3 processes: (1) birth (reproduction); (2) death (mortality); and (3) immigration and emigration (movement).

In most wild turkey populations, reproduction occurs only during the spring and summer (usually May, June, July, and August). Mortality and movement can occur almost anytime. The effects of movement on the size of a wild turkey population are difficult to determine. In most cases, the boundaries of an area where a group of turkeys lives are defined arbitrarily by the investigator.

For example, "the turkey population" may refer to all turkeys living in the state of Missouri or to only turkeys living on a 52-square-kilometer (20-square-mile) study area in Adair County, Missouri. Movement will have little effect on the population of a large area. On a small area, however, movement may have a considerable effect. Mayr (1970) defines a local population as "a group of individuals so situated that any two of them have equal probability of mating with each other and producing offspring." In reality, isolating or studying a group of wild turkeys that fits this definition is difficult, if not impossible.

In this chapter, I will focus mostly on reproduction and mortality, and how these processes affect populations. A wild turkey population can be characterized by not only the processes that affect it but also by its size and sex and age structure. Population size is just the total number of birds that inhabit an area. The sex and age structure of a population refers to the number of males and females of each age. These population characteristics depend on, and are a function of, reproduction, mortality, and movement.

Knowledge of the rates of reproduction, mortality, and movement is critical to understanding the population dynamics of wild turkeys. If we know the initial size and sex and age structure of a population, we can fully describe the dynamics of that population through time, provided the age- and time-specific rates of reproduction, mortality, and movement can also be determined.

Unfortunately, measuring the rates of reproduction, mortality, and movement, or determining the size and sex and age structure of a wild turkey population is, in practice, very difficult.

In this chapter, I will review the information available on populations of wild turkeys, mainly the eastern subspecies; more information is available for the eastern subspecies than for the others. I will also outline methods for determining population parameters, discuss a population model that combines estimates of reproduction and mortality, and discuss gaps in our current knowledge of wild turkey population dynamics.

REPRODUCTION

The reproductive process can be broken down into a number of components or parameters (Vangilder et al. 1987) including nesting and renesting rates, first nest and renest success rates, and hen success rate (Table 1). With current technology, estimates for most of these parameters can be acquired only through the use of radiotelemetry. Before the use of radiotelemetry techniques became common, only overall estimates of nest success were available. Mosby (1967:117, 136) reported on nesting studies of *M. g. silvestris* in the 1940s and 1950s and concluded that nesting success averaged 35 to 40 percent. Schorger (1966:268) also reported that success of wild turkey nests was about 35 percent. These estimates were based on nests that were located at various stages after the eggs were laid and were computed as the proportion of these that were successful. The estimates included both first nests and renests, and the estimates

Table 1. Definitions.

Nesting rate	Proportion of hens that attempt to nest.
First-nest success	Proportion of first nests from which at least 1 live poult hatches.
Renesting rate	Proportion of hens that were *not* successful on their first nesting attempt that attempt to renest.
Renest success	Proportion of renests from which at least 1 live poult hatches.
Hen success	Proportion of hens that have a successful nest (hatch at least 1 live poult) in 1 of their nesting attempts.

provided by these studies were almost surely biased because of the method of calculation (see Hensler and Nichols 1981).

Radio transmitters for wildlife were developed in the early 1960s (Cochran and Lord 1963, Slagle 1963) and were first applied to wild turkeys in 1965 and 1966 (Ellis 1966, Williams and Austin 1988:43). Because wild turkeys are difficult and expensive to trap, the number of radio-marked individuals in most studies has been small, and the studies have been of short duration (less than 5 years). These studies, however, have provided information on reproductive parameters where none had been available.

Nesting Rate

Estimates of nesting rates for the wild turkey (Table 2) indicate that in most years a high proportion of adult hens attempt to nest. The mean nesting rate for adult hens ranged from 75 to 100 percent in 10 studies. Data from these studies show that juvenile hens may have a lower nesting rate, especially juvenile Merriam's hens. Estimates of nesting rates for juvenile eastern hens ranged from 55.5 to 100 percent in 6 studies, while the range for juvenile Merriam's hens was from 7.7 to 30.8 percent. In Iowa, the nesting rate of eastern juvenile hens was extremely variable among years, ranging from 0 to 75 percent (Jackson et al. unpublished data).

The nesting rate of hens in most of the studies listed in Table 2 was determined by frequent (daily) monitoring of radio-marked hens. A pattern of localized movements over a period of several days indicated a nesting attempt. Because nests of hens that do not reach incubation are seldom actually seen by the investigator, using localized movements to indicate a nesting attempt may result in an overestimate of the true nesting rate. On the other hand, other researchers did not record a nesting attempt unless a hen actually reached incubation and the nest was found. This procedure almost certainly underestimates the nesting rate. Nests of hens destroyed by predators or abandoned before incubation begins are not included.

The wild turkey hen nests on the ground and lays about 10 eggs. Almost all the eggs have living embryos. This high productivity is necessary for population viability. *Photo by W. Healy, U.S. Forest Service.*

Renesting Rate

The renesting rate varied considerably among studies and among years within studies for both juvenile and adult eastern hens (Table 3). The renesting rate of adult eastern hens varied from 32 to 66.7 percent in 6 studies. For juvenile hens, the renesting rate varied from 12 to 70 percent. In most studies, juvenile eastern hens exhibited a lower renesting rate than did adult hens. In 2 studies of Merriam's turkeys, juvenile hens did not attempt to renest. Schemnitz et al. (1985) reported a 27 percent renesting rate for Merriam's hens in New Mexico, but did not differentiate adult and juvenile renesting.

Williams and Austin (1988) reported that Florida hens losing nests after continuous incubation had begun then renested at a lower rate (28 percent, 27 of 93 hens) than did hens losing nests during the laying period (57 percent, 17 of 30 hens).

Nest Success

Success of first nests ranged from 30.7 to 62.0 percent and renests from 0 to 72.7 percent in 5 studies of eastern wild turkeys (Table 4). Considerable variation was also evident among years within studies for both first nests and renests. Average overall nest success of Mer-

Table 2. Nesting rate of wild turkey hens.

State	Subspecies	PS[a]	Adult			Juvenile		
			Mean	Range	N[b]	Mean	Range	N[b]
Missouri[1]	Eastern	E	100.0	—	4	100.0	—	4
Massachusetts[2]	Eastern	E	100.0	—	2	81.0	—	2
Iowa[3]	Eastern	E	97.0	72.0–100.0	8	42.0	0.0–75.0	8
New York[4]	Eastern	E	90.0	83.3–94.4	2	100.0	—	2
Minnesota[5]	Eastern–Merriam's	E	96.0	—	3	88.0	—	3
Texas[6c]	Eastern	N	87.5	79.0–96.0	3	—	—	—
Pennsylvania[7]	Eastern	E	96.7	—	2	55.5	—	2
New Mexico[8]	Merriam's	E	75.0	—	5	7.7	—	5
Oregon[9]	Merriam's	E	100.0	—	2	30.8	—	2
New Mexico[10]	Merriam's	E	76.0	—	4	11.0	—	4

[1] Vangilder et al. 1987.
[2] Vander Haegen et al. 1988.
[3] Jackson et al. unpublished data.
[4] Glidden and Austin 1975.
[5] Porter et al. 1983.
[6] Campo et al. 1984.
[7] Hayden 1980.
[8] Lockwood and Sutcliffe 1985.
[9] Lutz and Crawford 1987b.
[10] Schemnitz et al. 1985.
[a] Population status. E = established; N = within 5 years of original release.
[b] Number of years during which data were collected.
[c] Data from the first 3 nesting seasons after release. Data were not separated according to age.

riam's hens in New Mexico was 31 percent in a 4-year period (range 22 to 38 percent) (Schemnitz et al. 1985).

Williams and Austin (1988) used the Mayfield (1961) method to calculate success of 171 Florida turkey nests. They assumed the laying period was 12 days long and the incubation period 27 days. The daily probability of survival for a nest during the laying period was 0.963 and during the incubation period was 0.988. The probability of a nest to hatch was 0.457 ($0.963^{12} \times 0.988^{27}$).

Hen Success

Hen success rate is a function of first-nest success, renesting rate, and renest success. It is the proportion of hens that are successful (hatch 1 or more live poults) in at least 1 nesting attempt. Hens that do not attempt to nest are not included in the calculation of hen success. In several studies listed in Table 5, the authors did not know whether a hen attempted to nest unless the hen reached incubation. For these studies, I assumed all hens attempted to nest in order to calculate the tabular value of hen success. The footnotes for these studies provide values for hen success based on the assumption that hens that did not reach incubation did not attempt to nest.

Mean hen success in 8 studies of eastern wild turkeys ranged from 38.3 to 82.8 percent for adults and from 15.4 to 61.0 percent for juveniles. Within studies, success of adult eastern hens also varied considerably among years. In Iowa, for example, adult hen success ranged from 12.9 to 50.0 percent, while juvenile hen success ranged from 0 to 60.0 percent (Jackson et al. unpublished data).

The data for eastern wild turkeys also indicate that juvenile hens tend to be less successful than adult hens.

Nest destroyed by mammalian predator. Normally nest success is low. Only about half of all nests are successful in producing poults. *Photo by P. Pelham.*

Table 3. Renesting rate of wild turkey hens.

State	Subspecies	PS[a]	Adult			Juvenile		
			Mean	Range	N[b]	Mean	Range	N[b]
Missouri[1c]	Eastern	E	44.8	14.0–75.0	4	—	—	—
Massachusetts[2]	Eastern	E	57.1	—	2	33.3	—	2
Iowa[3]	Eastern	E	32.0	4.0–86.0	8	12.0	0.0–19.0	8
New York[4]	Eastern	E	66.7	50.0–75.0	2	33.3	0.0–40.0	2
Minnesota[5]	Eastern–Merriam's	E	57.1	—	3	70.0	—	3
Texas[6d]	Eastern	N	47.4	0.0–100.0	3	—	—	—
Florida[7]	Florida	E	44.0	—	14	22.0	—	14
New Mexico[8]	Merriam's	E	34.6	—	5	0.0	—	5
Oregon[9]	Merriam's	E	0.0	—	2	0.0	—	2

[1] Vangilder et al. 1987.
[2] Vander Haegen et al. 1988.
[3] Jackson et al. unpublished data.
[4] Glidden and Austin 1975.
[5] Porter et al. 1983.
[6] Campo et al. 1984.
[7] Williams and Austin 1988.
[8] Lockwood and Sutcliffe 1985.
[9] Lutz and Crawford 1987b.
[a] Population status: E = established; N = within 5 years of original release.
[b] N = number of nesting seasons during which data were collected.
[c] No difference in renesting rates between adult and juvenile hens.
[d] Data from the first 3 nesting seasons after release.

In north Missouri, adult hens were more successful than juvenile hens in 1 of 4 years (Vangilder et al. 1987). In Iowa, adult hens were more successful than juvenile hens in 7 of 9 years (Jackson et al. unpublished data).

Mean hen success in 2 studies of radio-marked Rio Grande turkeys ranged from 25.0 to 28.6 percent for adults and 0 to 12.5 percent for juveniles. Among years within studies, hen success was extremely variable.

Beasom and Pattee (1980) reported that Rio Grande hen success (as determined by the percentage of hens observed with poults) was extremely variable (Table 5). On their Santa Gertrudis study area, no hens were observed with poults in 1971. In 1972, however, 93 percent of the hens were observed with poults. These extreme fluctuations in productivity seemed to be related to the amount of autumn rainfall.

Table 4. Nest success for wild turkey hens.

State	Subspecies	PS[a]	First nest			Renest		
			Mean	Range	N[b]	Mean	Range	N[b]
Missouri[1]	Eastern	E	30.7	14.3–47.4	4	30.0	0.0–60.0	4
New York[2]	Eastern	E	35.9	23.1–42.3	2	50.0	0.0–62.5	2
Minnesota[3]	Eastern–Merriam's	E	62.0	—	3	72.7	—	3
Texas[4]	Eastern	N	44.6	40.0–45.8	3	44.4	0.0–50.0	3
Iowa[5]	Eastern	E	38.0 Ad. 56.0 Jv.		8	52.0 Ad. 0.0 Jv.		8

[1] Vangilder et al. 1987.
[2] Glidden and Austin 1975.
[3] Porter et al. 1983.
[4] Campo et al. 1984.
[5] Jackson et al. unpublished data.
[a] Population status: E = established; N = within 5 years of original release.
[b] N = number of nesting seasons during which data were collected.

Table 5. Hen success for wild turkeys.

State	Subspecies	PS[a]	Adult Mean	Adult Range	N[b]	Juvenile Mean	Juvenile Range	N[b]
Missouri[1]	Eastern	E	40.0	19.4–65.0	4	29.6	0.0–100.0	4
Massachusetts[2]	Eastern	E	68.0	—	2	33.0	—	2
Iowa[3]	Eastern	E	38.3	12.9–50.0	8	55.5	0.0–60.0	8
Alabama[4c]	Eastern	E	58.8	36.4–50.0	3	15.4	0.0–20.0	3
New York[5]	Eastern	E	48.1	20.0–65.7	2	50.0	33.3–55.5	2
Alabama[6d]	Eastern	E	45.9	33.3–66.7	3	46.7	42.9–66.7	2
Minnesota[7]	Eastern–Merriam's	E	64.0	—	2	61.0	—	2
Virginia[8e]	Eastern	E	40.0	—	1	—	—	—
Texas[9f]	Eastern	N	51.8	45.5–70.0	3	—	—	—
Georgia[10g]	Eastern	E	50.0	30.0–90.0	3	—	—	—
Pennsylvania[11]	Eastern	E	82.8	—	2	100.0	—	2
Mississippi[12]	Eastern	E	37.5	16.7–75.0	5	—	—	—
West Virginia[13g]	Eastern	E	35.0	—	5	—	—	—
Florida[14g]	Florida	E	59.3	—	14	—	—	—
Texas[15h]	Rio Grande	E	25.0	0.0–50.0	2	0.0	—	1
Texas[16i]	Rio Grande	E	28.6	0.0–42.9	4	12.5	0.0–37.5	4
New Mexico[17]	Merriam's	E	46.2	—	5	50.0	—	5
Oregon[18]	Merriam's	E	75.0	—	2	25.0	—	2
New Mexico[19g]	Merriam's	E	43.0	—	4	—	—	—
Alabama[20gj]	Eastern	N	57.0	30.0–82.0	4	—	—	—
Mississippi[21gj]	Eastern	E	44.5	28.2–87.2	5	—	—	—
Texas[22gjk]	Rio Grande	E	27.0	0.0–93.0	10	—	—	—
Texas[22gjl]	Rio Grande	E	17.7	1.0–70.0	10	—	—	—

[1] Vangilder et al. 1987.
[2] Vander Haegan et al. 1988.
[3] Jackson et al. unpublished data.
[4] Exum et al. 1987.
[5] Glidden and Austin 1975.
[6] Everett et al. 1980.
[7] Porter et al. 1983.
[8] Holbrook et al. 1987.
[9] Campo et al. 1984.
[10] Hon et al. 1978.
[11] Hayden 1980.
[12] Hurst 1988.
[13] Pack et al. 1980.
[14] Williams and Austin 1988.
[15] Ransom et al. 1987.
[16] Reagan and Morgan 1980.
[17] Lockwood and Sutcliffe 1985.
[18] Lutz and Crawford 1987b.
[19] Schemnitz et al. 1985.
[20] Gardner et al. 1972.
[21] Kennamer et al. 1975.
[22] Beasom and Pattee 1980.
[a] Population status: E = established; N = within 5 years of original release.
[b] N = number of nesting seasons during which data were collected.
[c] Assumes all hens attempted to nest. Seven hens did not reach incubation (1 adult, 6 juveniles). Excluding these hens, success for adult and juvenile hens was 60.1 and 28.6 percent, respectively.
[d] Assumes all hens attempted to nest. Six hens did not reach incubation (4 adults, 2 juveniles). Excluding these hens, success for adults and juvenile hens was 58.6 and 63.6 percent, respectively.
[e] Four of 10 hens successfully hatched poults. Data were not separated according to age of hens.
[f] Data from the first 3 nesting seasons after release. Data were not separated according to age.
[g] Data were not separated according to age of hens.
[h] Assumes all hens attempted to nest.
[i] Assumes all hens attempted to nest. Excluding hens that did not reach incubation (3 adults, 20 juveniles), hen success was 33.3 percent for adults and 40.0 percent for juveniles.
[j] Based on percentage of hens observed to have 1 or more poults. Not based on radiotelemetry information.
[k] Santa Gertrudis study area.
[l] Encino study area.

Table 6. Clutch size for wild turkey hens.

State	Subspecies	PS[a]	First nest			Renest		
			Mean	SE	N[b]	Mean	SE	N[b]
Missouri[1]	Eastern	E	10.65	0.27	69	8.50	0.34	28
Alabama[2]	Eastern	E	10.30	–	–	10.30	–	3
New York[3]	Eastern	E	12.6	–	23	11.86	–	7
Alabama[4]	Eastern	E	10.8	–	–	8.0	–	–
Minnesota[5]	Eastern–Merriam's	E	11.8	0.30	39	10.9	0.68	7
Michigan[6]	Eastern	N	12.7	–	3	10.2	–	3
Iowa[7]	Eastern	E	9.4 Ad.	–	8	9.1 Ad.	–	8
			8.8 Jv.	–	8	7.0 Jv.	–	8
Texas[8]	Rio Grande	E	10.3	0.47	24	8.9	0.63	9
New Mexico[9]	Merriam's	E	8.5	–	–	9.5	–	–

[1] Vangilder et al. 1987.
[2] Exum et al. 1987.
[3] Glidden and Austin 1975.
[4] Everett et al. 1980.
[5] Porter et al. 1983.
[6] Grenon 1986.
[7] Jackson et al. unpublished data.
[8] Reagan and Morgan 1980.
[9] Lockwood and Sutcliffe 1985.
[a] Population status: E = established; N = within 5 years of original release.
[b] N = number of clutches.

Clutch Size

Clutch size was larger in first nests than in renests in 6 of 7 studies of eastern wild turkeys. Clutch size ranged from 10.3 to 12.6 eggs in first nests and from 8.0 to 11.9 eggs in renests (Table 6). In Missouri, clutch size of adult hens did not differ from that of juvenile hens (Vangilder et al. 1987). Jackson et al. (unpublished data) found, however, that mean clutch size of first nests of adult eastern hens (9.3, sample of 131) was larger than that of juvenile hens (8.7, sample of 18) in southern Iowa.

Williams and Austin (1988) found that clutch size of first, second, or third nests of the same Florida hens did not differ. In addition, clutch size of early (before May 1), middle (May 1 to May 20), and late (after May 20) nests did not differ. Adult hens, however, had slightly larger clutches (mean of 10.5, sample of 132) than did juvenile hens (mean of 10.0, sample of 32). Williams and Austin (1988) reported that clutch sizes of Florida hens were smaller than those of eastern hens in Alabama, Virginia, and Missouri.

Lutz and Crawford (1987b) reported a mean clutch size of 10.9 eggs for Merriam's hens in Oregon, with no difference between adult and juvenile hens. Average clutch size was 8.6 eggs for Merriam's nests in New Mexico (Schemnitz et al. 1985). Cook (1972) reported a mean clutch size of 10.3 eggs for nests of Rio Grande hens.

Green (1982) and Lewis (1962) reported mean clutch sizes of 14.8 (14.3 excluding 1 suspected dump nest) and 13 eggs, respectively, for eastern turkeys of game-farm origin in Michigan. Grenon (1986) found that first nests of wild-trapped turkeys released in Michigan had an average of 12.7 eggs.

Fertility and Hatching Success

Egg fertility and hatching success are generally very high. In most studies, hatching success was effectively defined as the proportion of eggs (whether fertile or infertile) that hatch in successful nests. Therefore, hatching success, by this definition, takes account of egg fertility, embryo viability, and partial predation.

Hatching success was greater than 80 percent in a number of studies of eastern, Merriam's, Florida, and Rio Grande turkeys (Table 7). Fertility was only slightly higher than hatching success in most studies. Age of hen did not seem to have much influence on fertility or hatching success, but some seasonal differences have been revealed. In Texas, Cook (1972) found that early nests (before July 5) contained significantly more fertile eggs (91 percent) than did later nests (83 percent). Glidden and Austin (1975) found that 95 percent of eggs were fertile in first nests while 85 percent were fertile in renests. This difference, however, was not significant. Hatching success was 71.5 percent in a study of Michigan birds of game-farm origin (Green 1982).

On a heavily hunted area in Alabama, 3 of 14 hens laid infertile clutches in a year (Exum et al. 1987), suggesting that a "shortage of breeding gobblers existed."

Table 7. Fertility and hatching success for wild turkey hens.

State	Subspecies	PS[a]	Fertility[b] Mean	Hatching success[c] Mean	Range	N[d]
Massachusetts[1]	Eastern	E	—	84	—	2
Iowa[2]	Eastern	E	—	85	44–100	8
New York[3]	Eastern	E	93	90	—	1
Alabama[4]	Eastern	E	95	92	—	2
Minnesota[5]	Eastern–Merriam's	E	—	80	—	2
Pennsylvania[6]	Eastern	E	98	80	—	2
Iowa[7]	Eastern	N	88	84	—	1
Florida[8]	Florida	E	—	89	—	14
Texas[9]	Rio Grande	E	90	90	—	4
Texas[10]	Rio Grande	E	—	89	—	1
New Mexico[11]	Merriam's		66	—	—	4
New Mexico[12]	Merriam's	E	88	87	—	5

[1] Vander Haegen et al. 1988.
[2] Jackson et al. unpublished data.
[3] Glidden and Austin 1975.
[4] Everett et al. 1980.
[5] Porter et al. 1983.
[6] Hayden 1980.
[7] Little and Varland 1981.
[8] Williams and Austin 1988.
[9] Cook 1972.
[10] Ranson et al. 1987.
[11] Schemnitz et al. 1985.
[12] Lockwood and Sutcliffe 1985.
[a] Population status: E = established; N = within 5 years after release.
[b] Fertility = (number eggs fertile/clutch size) x 100.
[c] Hatching success = (number eggs hatching/clutch size) x 100 for successful nests.
[d] N = number of years during which data were collected.

Schemnitz et al. (1985) reported a low egg fertility rate of 66 percent for Merriam's hens in New Mexico. During the first 2 years of their study, egg fertility was only 48 percent and the eggs in 5 of 6 abandoned nests were completely infertile. Investigators did not, however, attribute the low egg fertility to low gobbler densities. Instead, they suggested that weather, nutrition, or the spring gobbler hunt may have disrupted or delayed the breeding cycle.

Poult Mortality

The proportion of poults dying during the first 14 days after hatching ranged from 56 to 73 percent in 7 studies of eastern wild turkey broods (Table 8). In 6 studies, poult mortality 4 weeks after the hatch ranged from 53 to 76 percent. In general, most poult mortality occurs during the first 2 weeks. Speake et al. (1985) was able to identify the cause of death for wild turkey poults (sample of 279) in Alabama in 49 percent of the cases. Predation accounted for the death of 82 percent of the 136 poults for which the cause of death was known. Exposure, starvation, flooding, and birth defects accounted for the others.

Life in the wild begins. Many perils may threaten these poults during their life. Overall, only about half of all poults survive their first 2 weeks of life. *Photo by P. Pelham.*

Table 8. Poult mortality for wild turkeys 2 weeks and 4 weeks posthatching.

State	Subspecies	PS[a]	2 weeks			4 weeks		
			Mean	Range	N[b]	Mean	Range	N[b]
Missouri[1]	Eastern	E	—	—	—	61.9	41.3–69.7	4
Massachusetts[2]	Eastern	E	62	—	2	—	—	—
Alabama[3]	Eastern	E	64	—	5	—	—	—
New York[4]	Eastern	E	57	—	1	76	—	1
Alabama[5c]	Eastern	E	73	—	2			
Alabama[6]	Eastern	E	71.3	—	5	—	—	—
Minnesota[7]	Eastern–Merriam's	E	—	—	—	53	—	3
Texas[8]	Eastern	N	55.8	35–88	3	55.8	35–88	3
Georgia[9]	Eastern	E	—	—	—	74.0	69.8	2
Iowa[10]	Eastern	N	60	—	1	74	—	1
Florida[11]	Florida	E	64	—	14	—	—	—

[1] Vangilder et al. 1987.
[2] Vander Haegen et al. 1988.
[3] Speake et al. 1985.
[4] Glidden and Austin 1975.
[5] Everett et al. 1980.
[6] Speake 1980.
[7] Porter et al. 1983.
[8] Campo et al. 1984.
[9] Hon et al. 1978.
[10] Little and Varland 1981.
[11] Williams and Austin 1988.
[a] Population status: E = established; N = within 5 years after original release.
[b] N = number of years during which data were collected.
[c] Data from 1976 and 1977 only.

In Alabama, average poult mortality in 21 broods (up to 8 poults per brood were radio instrumented) was 75.1 ± 6.5 percent (standard error). Broods were followed for up to 64 days (Metzler and Speake 1985).

Glidden and Austin (1975) reported 100 percent mortality of poults (50 of 50) hatched by juvenile hens, at 28 days posthatch. Poults hatched by adult hens had 65 percent mortality (70 of 107). By 36 days posthatch, overall poult mortality was 86 percent.

In a study of human-imprinted eastern wild turkey hens and their poults in West Virginia, Healy and Nenno (1985) found that in 1 year (1977), 49 percent (21 of 43) of the poult deaths were weather related. Brood survival is related to brood habitat characteristics (Everett et al. 1980, 1985, Metzler and Speake 1985), but the relationship between predation rates and habitat characteristics is not clear.

POSTFLEDGING SURVIVAL RATES

Survival (or mortality) rates important to understanding the dynamics of a wild turkey population include age-specific annual and seasonal rates of survival (mortality), and cause-specific mortality rates. Before the development of radiotelemetry in the early 1960s, only annual estimates of survival (mortality) were available. These estimates were derived from composite dynamic life table analysis of band (leg or wing) recovery data or from age ratios of a sample of trapped or shot birds. Two such studies (Bailey and Rinnel 1965, West Virginia; and Powell 1965, 1967, Florida) of leg-banded juveniles were summarized by Mosby (1967). His analysis showed a

Without adequate low cover, poults are especially vulnerable to predators. *Photo by G. Wunz, Pennsylvania Game Commission.*

Poults that survive the early, perilous period have a significant life expectancy. *Photo by L. Williams.*

mean life expectancy of 1.3 to 1.6 years and average annual mortality rates of 76 percent (West Virginia) and 60 percent (Florida). Lewis (1980) reported results of 15 years of band recovery data. Because there were no clear population trends, Lewis (1980) used the pooled age-ratio data from turkeys trapped in winter over 15 years to estimate mortality on a Missouri study area. The data suggested an average annual mortality rate of 52.4 percent.

Although these studies provided some of the first estimates of wild turkey mortality rates, these rates were not age-, sex-, or time-specific. Since the initiation of these studies, investigation of band-recovery models has shown that the composite dynamic life table method provides invalid estimates of mortality unless some very restrictive assumptions can be met (Burnham and Anderson 1979, Anderson et al. 1981). The properties of the life table model have been described by Anderson et al. (1985): "The critical underlying assumptions of the life table model are invalid and the estimators of the model parameters are sensitive to these model failures, thus rigorous inference about the survival rates of ringed bird populations or their age-specific dynamics is impossible." Caughley (1974) has also outlined the dangers of using age-ratio data to estimate mortality.

Future studies of wild turkey survival rates based on recoveries of leg or wing bands *must* use modern methods of band-recovery analysis (Brownie et al. 1978, 1985) if valid estimates are to be derived. Unfortunately, the sample sizes required by these modern methods are so large that their use to estimate mortality of wild turkeys will be impractical in most, if not all, cases.

Another closely related way to estimate survival rates (as well as population size in some cases) is through the analysis of mark-recapture or mark-resighting information. Most of these methods are based on the Jolly-Seber model. The theory, methodology, and application of the Jolly-Seber model have been discussed by Seber (1982, 1986), Brownie et al. (1985:170–175, 1986), Brownie and Pollock (1985), and Pollock et al. (1985, 1990). For certain experimental applications, the release-recapture models recently developed by Burnham et al. (1987) may prove useful.

Gribben (1986) used a number of different methods in analyzing mark-recapture data to provide population and survival estimates for wild turkeys on the Tallahala Wildlife Management Area in Mississippi. Although he was able to provide some estimates of population size and survival, in most cases he did not have the large samples of banded and recaptured birds necessary to produce reliable estimates. Because his estimates of population size were not very reliable, Gribben (1986) concluded that a change in population size of less than 40 percent for males and 60 percent for females could not be detected using capture-recapture analysis.

A mark-resighting study of wild turkeys similar to studies done by Stromborg et al. (1988), Hestbeck and Malecki (1989), or Krementz et al. (1989) on other species of birds could provide relatively precise estimates of survival, especially in situations where large numbers of birds can be easily captured and marked (e.g., Rio Grandes in Texas or Merriam's in South Dakota) or where resighting probabilities are high.

The most reliable estimates of survival (mortality) can be made by using radiotelemetry. Transmitters are now available that change pulse rates when the transmitter does not move for a certain period of time (usually 4 to 8 hours). These transmitters allow rapid investigation of the death of radio-marked birds.

Two methods have recently been used to estimate survival rates from radiotelemetry data: (1) the Heisey-Fuller method (Heisey and Fuller 1985); and (2) the Kaplan-Meier method (Kaplan and Meier 1958). The Heisey-Fuller method is a modification of the Mayfield

Many different predators kill wild turkeys, but we still don't understand the long-term relationships of wild turkeys and their predators.

technique of estimating nest success (Mayfield 1961). A refinement on how data from animals whose fates are unknown should be handled in Heisey-Fuller analyses of survival has been presented by Vangilder and Sheriff (1990).

The use of the Kaplan-Meier method in wildlife applications has been presented by Pollock et al. (1989) and specifically for wild turkeys by Kurzejeski et al. (1987). A recent paper presents the use of a staggered-entry design (entering animals into the analysis as they are radio marked) (Pollock et al. 1989).

These 2 methods avoid the biases associated with survival rate calculations based on simple percentages (Heisey and Fuller 1985). Much of the survival rate information from radiotelemetry published to date has been based on percentages, and animals whose fates were unknown (radio contact was lost) were usually totally excluded from the analyses. In future studies of wild turkey survival using radio transmitters, either the Kaplan-Meier or the Heisey-Fuller method should be employed to calculate survival estimates. These methods provide unbiased estimates of survival with associated estimates of variance. Reliable estimates of survival can be made if at least 50 radio-marked turkeys are alive throughout the periods of interest.

Annual Survival Rates

Three studies of eastern wild turkeys have used either the Kaplan-Meier or the Heisey-Fuller method to calculate annual survival-rate estimates from radiotelemetry studies (Iowa, Mississippi, Missouri; Table 9).

Average annual survival-rate estimates for hens for the 3 studies were similar (range: 0.540 to 0.583 or 0.548 to 0.620). Variation in annual survival rates among years within studies was quite high, however. Among years, annual survival-rate estimates varied from approximately 45 to 70 percent. In Missouri, the variation among years was statistically significant. The annual survival rate in 1987 (0.693) was higher than in either 1984 (0.445) or 1986 (0.452) (Vangilder unpublished data).

Most other estimates of annual survival (Table 9) are based on data pooled across years, study areas, or both. Campo et al. (1984) reported a minimum survival rate (including only those known to be alive at the end of the year) of 0.71 for 14 eastern gobblers and 0.58 for 24 hens, 1 year after release in Texas. Corresponding maximum survival rates (1-known [includes only those birds known to be dead] mortality rates) were 0.86 and 0.96. For another release of 25 hens, the minimum survival rate was 0.60 (maximum survival rate of 0.84).

Porter (1978) in Minnesota and Vander Haegen et al. (1988) in Massachusetts found that survival-rate esti-

Table 9. Annual survival rates of wild turkeys.

State	Subspecies	Sex–age	PS[a]	Annual survival rate	Range	NI[b]	NY[c]
Texas[1d]	Eastern	Gobblers	N	0.710(0.140)[e]	—	14	1(1979)
Texas[1d]	Eastern	Hens	N	0.580(0.040)[e]	—	24	1(1979)
Texas[1d]	Eastern	Hens	N	0.600(0.160)[e]	—	25	1(1980)
Texas[2f]	Eastern	Gobblers and hens	N	0.676(0.108)[e]	—	74	2
Massachusetts[3g]	Eastern	Jv. hen	E	0.570	—	13–53	3
		Ad. hen		0.750	—	—	—
Mississippi[4h]	Eastern	Jv. & ad. hens	E	0.540(0.36–0.73)[i]	0.42–0.67	26–35	4
				0.620(0.44–0.81)[j]	0.45–0.81	26–35	4
Minnesota[5k]	Eastern–Merriam's	Jv. & ad gobblers	E	0.643	—	23–47	5
		Jv. hens	N	0.394	—	15–91	5
		Ad. hens	E	0.574	—	15–91	5
Virginia[6l]	Eastern	Jv. & ad. gobblers, hens	E	0.150	—	32	1
Michigan[7m]	Eastern[n]	Jv. & ad. gobblers	E	0.627	—	—	3
		Jv. & ad. hens		0.742	—	—	—
Alabama[8o]	Eastern	Jv. & ad. gobblers	E	0.632	—	38	3
		Jv. & ad. hens		0.725	—	51	—
Iowa[9p]	Eastern	Ad. gobblers	E	0.383(0.065)[q]	0.159–0.635	—	9
		Jv. gobblers		0.333(0.056)[q]	0.078–0.635	—	9
		Ad. hens		0.583(0.027)[q]	0.469–0.715	—	9
		Jv. hen		0.568(0.071)[q]	0.193–1.000	—	9
Missouri[10r]	Eastern	Jv. & ad. hens	E	0.548(0.039)[s]	0.445–0.693	23–74	6
Texas[11t]	Rio Grande	Jv. & ad. hens	E	0.726	—	31	2

[1] Campo et al. 1984.
[2] Swank et al. 1985.
[3] Vander Haegen et al. 1988.
[4] Hurst 1988.
[5] Porter 1978.
[6] Holbrook and Vaughan 1985.
[7] Kulowiec 1986.
[8] Everett et al. 1980.
[9] Jackson et al. unpublished data.
[10] Vangilder unpublished data.
[11] Ransom et al. 1987.
[a] Population status: E = established; N = within 5 years after release.
[b] NI = number radio marked at beginning of year.
[c] NY = number of years during which data were collected.
[d] Percentage method used to calculate *known* survival and mortality rates. Animals whose fates were unknown (censored animals) were excluded from the analyses. Percentages calculated after each 6-month period after release.
[e] Figures in parentheses are *known* mortality rates.
[f] Similar to above. Calculated from months after release. Censored observations were excluded.
[g] Survival rates calculated using bird-months (1 bird alive 1 month) and by percentage method for certain periods. Three years of data combined for each month's calculated survival rate. Sample size by month varied from 13 to 53 birds. Censored observations were excluded.
[h] Sample size for each year ranged from 26 to 35. Total sample size for 4 years combined was 125. Survival rates were calculated using the methods of Pollock et al. (1989a). Minimum and maximum survival rates were calculated by assuming all hens for which radio contact was lost died or by assuming all hens for which radio contact was lost lived. A survival rate that included censored animals until radio contact was lost was not provided. This estimates would be somewhere between the minimum and maximum estimates provided and would be the best estimate of survival assuming that death and censoring were independent events.
[i] Minimum survival rate (95 percent confidence interval). All years combined.
[j] Maximum survival rate (95 percent confidence interval). All years combined.
[k] Monthly mortality rates were calculated by the percentage method. Data for January to April included years 1975, 1977, and 1978, while data for May to December included years 1974, 1976, and 1977.
[l] Mortality rates for 2 periods (September to February and March to August) were calculated by the percentage method. The survival rate was calculated by multiplying the survival rates (1-mortality rate) for each period together. Censored observations were excluded.
[m] Mortality rates calculated by percentage method. Censored observations were excluded.
[n] Population of game-farm origin.
[o] I used simple percentage to calculate survival rate: hens [1 − (14/51)], gobblers [1 − (14/38)]. The authors provided no estimates of annual survival.
[p] Heisey-Fuller method used to calculate survival rates. Censored observations are included up until the time of disappearance as suggested by Vangilder and Sheriff (unpublished ms.).
[q] Standard errors are based on among year variation (sample = 9).
[r] Kaplan Meier method used to calculate survival rates with staggered entry design (Pollock et al. 1989).
[s] Standard error is based on among year variation (sample = 6).
[t] Daily and annual survival calculated using methods of Trent and Rongstad (1974). Field research only conducted January to August. Daily rate expanded to calculate annual rate from these months. Assumes daily survival rate is constant throughout the year. Censored observations were excluded.

mates for adult hens were greater than those of juvenile hens. In some years, a difference in estimated survival rate between juvenile and adult hens was also apparent in Iowa (Jackson et al. unpublished data).

Data on annual survival rates of gobblers are very limited. Campo et al. (1984) reported a minimum survival rate of 0.720 during the first year after being released into a new area. Porter (1978) reported a survival-rate estimate of 0.648 for juvenile and adult gobblers in 2 Minnesota populations. In Alabama, the survival-rate estimate for adult and juvenile gobblers was 0.632. In Iowa, on a heavily hunted area, gobbler survival rates were 0.383 for adults and 0.333 for juveniles (Jackson et al. unpublished data).

Cause-Specific Mortality Rates

Cause-specific mortality rates can be calculated from radiotelemetry data by using either the Heisey-Fuller (Heisey and Fuller 1985) or Kaplan-Meier (Pollock et al. 1989) method. These rates provide an idea of the relative contributions of the various causes of mortality to the overall mortality (survival) rates. If, however, more than 1 agent of mortality was acting on the population being studied, and these agents are not independent, the cause-specific mortality rate for 1 agent (say predation) is not an estimate of what the mortality rate would be if all other forms of mortality except predation were absent (see Heisey and Fuller 1985:671).

Vangilder (unpublished data) estimated cause-specific mortality rates using the Heisey-Fuller method for radio-marked wild turkey hens in Adair County, Missouri, in 5 different years (Table 10). Across years, estimates of mortality rates due to specific causes varied considerably, both among and within years. Across years, mortality rates due to predation ranged from 4.2 to 31.1 percent, from poaching 1.4 to 37.3 percent, and from fall harvest 1.9 to 10.9 percent. In 1 year, the mortality rate from poaching was higher than from any other form of mortality. Using the Kaplan-Meier method, Kurzejeski et al. (1987) calculated a survival rate of 0.610 with predators as the only source of mortality on eastern hens in 1984 in Adair County, Missouri.

Pooled monthly mortality rates (percentage method) of radio-marked wild turkey hens and gobblers in Alabama were calculated by Speake (1980) across 7 years and 3 study areas. The annual rate of mortality from predation was 19.1 percent for hens and 10.9 percent for gobblers.

Causes of Death

In the studies examined, most deaths of wild turkeys were caused by predators (Table 11) (see chapter on predation for more information). Poaching was also an important cause of death in some studies. In Missouri, an estimated 4, 25, and 9 percent of hens alive on April 1 during 3 years (1981, 1982, and 1984) were illegally killed during the spring gobbler season (Kimmel and Kurzejeski 1985). Illegal hen kill was higher during years when spring gobbler season began before peak incubation

Table 10. Cause-specific mortality rates of wild turkey hens in Adair County, Missouri. Rates were calculated using program MICROMORT (Heisey and Fuller 1985) with censored observations included as described by Vangilder and Sheriff (1990).

Year	Cause of mortality			
	Predators	Poaching	Harvest	Other
1981–82	0.042	0.042	0.096	0.048
1982–83	0.080	0.373	—	—
1984–85	0.311	0.206	0.019	0.019
1985–86	0.191	0.014	0.022	0.058
1986–87	0.284	0.031	0.109	0.031

periods in Missouri (Kimmel and Kurzejeski 1985, Kurzejeski et al. 1987) and in Iowa (Jackson personal communication).

During 7 spring seasons in Adair County, Missouri (including the 3 studied by Kimmel and Kurzejeski 1985), the average known illegal hen kill was 5.2 percent of hens alive just prior to the opening of the 14-day spring season (sample of 305 radio-marked hens pooled across 7 years). When figures include deaths from unknown causes and hens with which radio contact was lost during the spring season, the rate of illegal hen kill was 8.2 percent (Vangilder unpublished data). Kimmel and Kurzejeski (1985) thought that the use of 5.1-by-15.2-centimeter (2-by-6-inch) colored patagium tags to mark hens might have constituted a bias favoring illegal kill during the 1981, 1982, and 1984 seasons. These tags were not used to mark hens from 1985 to 1988. Indeed, the rate of illegal hen kill (both known and possible) was significantly higher during 1981, 1982, and 1984 than during 1985 to 1988 (12.2 versus 1.9 percent for known illegal loss, 13.3 versus 5.8 percent for possible illegal loss). The data for 1981, 1982, and 1984, however, were strongly influenced by the data from 1982, when 6 of 20 hens were killed illegally (Kimmel and Kurzejeski, 1985, reported 5 of 20).

The known illegal harvest rate of hens during early springs (2.1 percent over 3 years) was significantly lower than during late springs (7.9 percent over 4 years) (P < 0.05) when normal plant growth and wild turkey breeding were delayed (Vangilder unpublished data).

In Florida, *possible* illegal hunter kills accounted for 14 and 18 percent of the radio-marked hens alive at the beginning of a 16-day spring gobbler season on 2 study areas (Williams and Austin 1988:200). *Known* illegal kill accounted for 2 and 6 percent of the hens on the 2 study areas. Williams and Austin (1988:173) also reported a 63 percent illegal loss of radio-marked Florida hens during gobblers-only fall seasons on the Fisheating Creek Wildlife Management Area.

Illegal kill has also been considered a significant mortality factor in Alabama (Fleming and Speake 1976)

Table 11. Number (N) and cause (percent) of death of wild turkeys.

| State | Sex and Age | Nᵃ | Cause of death | | | | | | | Subspecies |
			Predators	Poaching	Disease	Starvation	Harvest	Other	Unknown	
Massachusetts[1]	Ad. & jv. hens	16	75	0	6	0	0	6	12	Eastern
Texas[2]	Ad. & jv. gobblers/hens	24	58	4	0	0	17	4	17	Eastern
Alabama[3b]	Ad. & jv. gobblers/hens	26	85	15	0	0	0	0	0	Eastern
	Poults	17	88	0	0	0	0	12	0	Eastern
Minnesota[4]	Ad. & jv. gobblers/hens	75	68	0	0	9	0	0	23	Eastern–Merriam's
Michigan[5]	Ad. & jv. gobblers/hens	23	61	22	4	0	13	0	0	Eastern[c]
Alabama[6]	Ad. & jv. gobblers	14	29	7	0	0	50	7	7	Eastern
	Ad. & jv. hens	14	71	21	0	0	0	7	0	
Minnesota[7d]	Ad. & jv. gobblers/hens	8	100	0	0	0	0	0	0	Eastern
Missouri[8]	Ad. & jv. hens	153	67	21	0	0	6	1	5	Eastern
Texas[9b]	Ad. & jv hens	11	64	0	9	0	0	18	9	Rio Grande

[1] Vander Haegen et al. 1988.
[2] Swank et al. 1985.
[3] Exum et al. 1987.
[4] Porter 1980.
[5] Kulowiec 1986.
[6] Everett et al. 1980.
[7] McMahan and Johnson 1980.
[8] Vangilder (unpublished).
[9] Ransom et al. 1987.
[a] Number of deaths.
[b] Researcher-induced mortality excluded.
[c] Population of game-farm origin.
[d] One bird injured by rocket net is excluded.

and on Land Between the Lakes in Kentucky (Wright and Speake 1975). On Land Between the Lakes during the 1974 spring gobbler season, 63 percent (5 of 8) of radio-marked hens disappeared in a heavily hunted area, but none of 10 radio-marked hens disappeared or died in an area closed to hunting (Wright and Speake 1975).

Harvest Mortality

Although not evident from the studies cited in Table 11, legal harvest can also be a major mortality factor.

Spring gobbler harvest. During the first hunting season for gobblers on the Saugahatchee Area in Alabama (March 20 to April 26, 1971), 51 percent of the estimated (by direct count) gobbler population was harvested (Gardner et al. 1972). Weaver and Mosby (1979) reported that during Virginia's 1976 spring season, an average of 16.8 percent of the estimated (calculated from flock counts of hens and juveniles) adult gobbler population was harvested.

On 2 study areas in Alabama (Thomas and Scotch Wildlife Management areas), 5 of 14 (37.5 percent, 10-day season) and 1 of 5 (20 percent) of the radio-instrumented gobblers were shot during the 1978 spring gobbler season. One of 14 (7 percent) and 1 of 5 (20 percent) were also believed lost to crippling (Everett et al. 1978).

Everett et al. (1980) reported that 7 of 16 (43.8 percent) radio-marked adult gobblers were killed during the 1978 spring season on the Thomas WMA. None of 4 juveniles was shot.

In Mississippi, on the Tallahala Wildlife Management Area, direct-recovery rates of marked gobblers by spring turkey hunters ranged from 15.0 percent (3 of 20) in 1987 to 40.0 percent (16 of 40) in 1986. Across the 6 years of the study (1984–1989), 29.1 percent (55 of 189) of gobblers marked the winter before the spring hunting season were harvested by spring turkey hunters during the 40- to 45-day season (Palmer et al. 1990).

Williams and Austin (1988:201) reported that 12 of 35 (34 percent) of radio-marked gobblers were shot during the 16-day spring hunting season on the Lochloosa study area in Florida. In addition, 3 of the 35 were lost to crippling, bringing the total loss to 43 percent (15 of 35).

On a study area in central Missouri from 1965 through 1969, an average of 18.7 percent of marked adult and juvenile gobblers were recovered during the first spring hunting season after banding (Lewis and Kelly 1973). During the same study from 1965 through 1979, 12.3 percent of the marked juvenile gobblers were recovered during the first spring hunting season after banding (Lewis 1980) and 19.1 percent of the marked adult gobblers were recovered (J. Lewis personal communication).

In Adair County, Missouri, 17.2 percent of marked adult gobblers were recovered during the first spring hunting season after banding over 7 years (Vangilder unpublished data).

On Land Between the Lakes in Kentucky, 32.4 (11 of 34) of banded adult gobblers and 11.1 percent (11 of 99) of juvenile gobblers were recovered during the first spring season after banding over 7 years (1984 through 1990) (G. Wright personal communication).

The data on recovery rates for adult and juvenile gobblers suggest that the adults are more vulnerable to spring harvest than are the juveniles. This differential vulnerability is probably related to behavior of both the wild turkey and the hunter. In most instances, the adult gobblers do most of the gobbling, a trait that allows a spring turkey hunter to walk to within a few hundred yards and attempt to call in the gobbling bird.

Fall hunting mortality. From 1955 through 1964, Bailey and Rinell (1968:36–37) banded and released 1,721 turkeys in August and September on the Rimel-Neola areas. The direct-recovery rate of bands during the fall hunting season averaged 18 percent and ranged from 15 to 23 percent in years when at least 100 turkeys were banded before fall season.

From 1949 through 1963, 3,550 turkeys were banded and released on the Fisheating Creek Wildlife Management Area in Florida (Powell 1965). First-year band returns averaged 24 percent, but the reporting rate was not given (mandatory checking evidently was not required).

Another study of fall harvest on the Fisheating Creek WMA was conducted from 1968 through 1974 in response to declining turkey harvest (Williams et al. 1978, Williams and Austin 1988). During 3 years (1968, 1969, and 1974) either sex was legal during the 7-week fall season. But during the other 3 years (1971, 1972, and 1973) gobblers only were legal. Under either-sex hunting, 83 percent of radio-marked males and 89 percent of radio-marked females were harvested. Under gobblers-only regulations, 74 percent of radio-marked males and 63 percent of radio-marked females were harvested (Williams and Austin 1988:168–175). Turkey populations on this area were supplemented prior to nesting season by the release of 355 wild-trapped birds during the course of the study.

In Iowa, on a heavily hunted study area, the average annual survival rate of radio-marked turkeys during 4 years before the start of fall hunting was higher than during 5 years after the start of fall hunting (Table 12). Hunter densities averaged 14.1 hunters per square kilometer of forest (36.5 per square mile), and harvest averaged 4.3 turkeys per square kilometer of forest (11.7 per square mile) (Little et al. 1990).

In Missouri, legal fall harvest accounted for an average of 4.4 percent of radio-marked hens alive the day before the 14-day season opened (204 radio-marked hens pooled across 9 years) (Vangilder unpublished data).

Excluding 3 years when fewer than 10 hens were radio marked before the season, the harvest rate was 4.8 percent (187 radio-marked hens pooled across 6 years). During these 6 years, the harvest rate varied from 2.6 to 14.3 percent.

Early studies of hunting-removal rates (as a percent of the population removed) for fall either-sex seasons have been reviewed by Mosby (1967) and Weaver and Mosby (1979). Most of the studies reviewed by these authors calculated prehunt population size by the personal interview, map-plot technique (Mosby and Handley 1943). So the accuracy and confidence limits of these estimates are unknown. Fall either-sex hunts removed from 5.2 to 46.0 percent of the population. During the fall 1975 either-sex season in Virginia, an average of 14 percent of the estimated fall population was removed (Weaver and Mosby 1979).

Seasonal Survival Rates

Survival rates of eastern hens during summer (June 1 to August 31) and winter (December 1 to March 13) were higher than in spring (March 14 to May 31) and fall (September 1 to November 30) in Adair County, Missouri, in 1984 (Kurzejeski et al. 1987).

For eastern hens in Mississippi, Hurst (1988) reported minimum survival rates (pooled across 5 years) of 0.95 for winter (January 10 to March 20), 0.80 for nesting (March 21 to June 29), 0.90 for brood rearing (May 30 to August 7), 0.95 for postbrood rearing (August 8 to October 16), and 0.75 for fall (October 17 to December 25). Although differences were not statistically significant, point estimates of survival were lower during the nesting period and during fall.

Speake (1980) concluded that eastern hens in Alabama were most vulnerable to predation while incubating and during the first 10 to 14 days of the brood-rearing period. His calculated monthly mortality rates from predation were higher in May (5.1 percent) and June (3.9 percent) than in all other months (3.0 percent or less).

Table 12. Effects of fall hunting on wild turkey survival rates on a heavily hunted area in southern Iowa (Little et al. 1990).

Sex and age	4 years before fall hunting	5 years after fall hunting	P[a]
adult gobbler	0.493	0.281	0.08
juvenile gobbler	0.399	0.169	0.07
adult hen	0.639	0.576	0.07
juvenile hen	0.644	0.434	0.12

[a]P = probability that difference is significant.

In northern climatic extremes, turkeys don't fare well when deep, dry, fluffy snow covers the ground for extended periods. *Photo by W. Healy, U.S. Forest Service.*

Everett et al. (1980) found that in north Alabama, 9 of 10 hens killed by predators were killed during the nesting season.

At northern latitudes in wild turkey range, winter survival rates have been reported lower than during other seasons. During a 3-year study, Porter (1978) reported monthly mortality rates of 7.3, 16.5, and 16.5 percent during January, February, and March for juvenile and adult hens in Minnesota. On Porter's (1978) south study area, where waste grain was not available, 50 percent of adult hens and 80 percent of juvenile females died during a winter of prolonged deep snow. During the Minnesota study, mortality was also high during the nesting and brood-rearing period (May, 10.3 percent; June, 8.3 percent). Winter losses during severe winters were estimated at 45 percent in New York (Austin and DeGraff 1975) and more than 50 percent in Pennsylvania (Wunz and Hayden 1975).

Mortality rates of eastern wild turkey hens in western Massachusetts were low during winter (December 1 to March 31, 7 percent) and during the postnesting period (end of incubation to August 31, 7 percent) (Vander Haegen et al. 1988). Vander Haegen et al. (1989) found that 5 flocks of wild turkeys studied in western Massachusetts centered their activities on dairy farms during winter, and that during periods of deep snow they restricted their movements to an area of less than 20 hectares (49 acres) and fed largely on grain in spread manure. Winter survival was high (93 percent) (Vander Haegen et al. 1988). Most deaths occurred during the nesting season (April 1 to end of incubation). Monthly mortality rates were 7.6 percent in May, 12.8 percent in June, and 5.1 percent in July (Vander Haegen 1987).

In Virginia, peaks in eastern wild turkey mortality were associated with the spring and fall hunting seasons (Holbrook and Vaughan 1985).

POPULATION MODELING

The previous pages on reviews of the literature have provided estimates of survival and reproductive rates from a number of studies and across a number of years. Survival and reproductive rates were often found to be both age-specific and time-specific. It is very difficult, if not impossible, to determine what separate estimates of survival and reproductive rates mean in terms of population size and age structure.

A population model is a way of mathematically combining survival- and reproductive-rate estimates to produce projections of population size and age structure through time. For a specific combination of survival and reproductive rates, a model may tell you whether a wild turkey population will grow, decline, or remain stable. A model may be useful in determining the effects of varying death rates (e.g., harvest mortality) on population size and age structure. A model may also be useful in pointing out deficiencies in data on certain parameters or in our understanding of how population parameters are interrelated.

The results from a population model, however, are only as good as the assumptions that go into the conceptualization of the model. Some of these assumptions (and so the validity of the model) may be tested by comparing the results of a model to what happens in the real world. For example, if we have estimates of survival and reproductive rates, population size, and age structure, the results of the population model (using estimates of survival and reproductive rates as input) should approximate estimates based on observation of population size and age structure. Unfortunately, good estimates of the size of a wild turkey population are difficult (and often impossible) to get.

The Missouri Model

Vangilder and Kulowiec (1988) developed a 2-age-class (jv and ad) accounting style microcomputer program to model the dynamics of a Missouri wild turkey population. The input parameters required for this model are those that can be estimated from a radio-marked sample of wild turkeys (Table 13). The parameter values are consistent with the preceding review of available literature. In the following discussion of the conceptualization and assumptions of this model, I describe the model and how it works. I also point out deficiencies in our understanding of wild turkey population dynamics.

The Missouri model uses 1 day as its basic unit for calculating natural mortality. At the end of each model day, the model multiplies the current size of each sex and age segment by its corresponding daily mortality rate and subtracts these products from the current size of each segment.

The user may input data for a specified number of data years and run the model not only for those data years but also for a number of years beyond. The parameter values for years beyond the actual data years are randomly generated from a uniform distribution within the 95 percent confidence interval around the mean of

Grain crops can help flocks survive during extended periods of snow-covered ground. *Photo by D. Reid.*

Table 13. Data requirements for the Missouri wild turkey population model.

1. Productivity.
   a. Age-specific nesting rates.
   b. Age-specific first-nest success rates.
   c. Age-specific first-nest clutch sizes.
   d. Age-specific hatchability rates.
   e. Age-specific renesting rate.
   f. Age-specific renest success rates.
   g. Age-specific renest clutch sizes.
   h. Age-specific renest hatchability rates.
   i. Sex ratio of poults at hatching.
2. Natural mortality.
   a. Poult mortality rates from hatching to end of summer season.
   b. Age-specific daily mortality rates for each of 4 seasons.
3. Hunting mortality for spring and fall season.
   a. Actual number of birds harvested or proportion of population taken (proportion of male population for spring hunting season, proportion of total population for fall hunting season).
   b. Proportion that each sex or age class comprises of the total harvest input above.

each parameter value for the data years, thereby adding a stochastic (random) element to the model.

Long-term field studies of survival and reproductive rates have shown that these survival and reproductive rates fluctuate considerably from year to year. To date, much of this variation seems random. For example, hen success fluctuates widely from year to year in apparent response to random fluctuations in weather conditions (temperature and spring phenology [Vangilder et al. 1987]) or rainfall (Beasom and Pattee 1980). Natural mortality rates also fluctuate widely and apparently at random.

In a long-term study over a number of years, parameter estimates should begin to encompass the entire range of values that occur in nature. Because of the model's stochastic nature, each run provides only 1 possible long-term population outcome. Only a number of runs of the model with the same input data set will give the modeler an idea of the possible results that 1 input data set can produce. For example, 100 runs of the same input data set may show that the population after, say, 35 years past the data years increased slightly in 50 runs and decreased slightly in 50 runs. In this simulated population, births and deaths are, on average, approximately balanced.

An important assumption of the stochastic feature of the model is that true parameter values vary independently. For example, it would be a violation of this assumption if high annual survival rates were associated with low hen success. Indeed, parameter values for survival and productivity probably do not vary independently, but no studies of wild turkeys that I am aware of have demonstrated functional relationships among any of the parameter values.

Another important feature of this model is that it allows both a spring and fall hunting season of any reasonable length. The model is flexible in that it allows the input of either (1) a proportion of the population to be harvested or (2) the number of individuals to be harvested.

Harvest mortality is one of the few influences on wild turkey population dynamics that is under direct control of resource managers (through appropriate harvest regulations). One of the questions asked most frequently by resource managers is how varying levels of spring or fall harvest affect population size under a given set of survival and reproductive rates.

Perhaps the most important assumption of this part of the population model is that hunting mortality is added to natural mortality. An alternative would be to assume that hunting mortality is compensated for (partly or completely) by a decrease in nonhunting mortality rates after the hunting season.

Under the hypothesis of additive mortality, the annual survival rate should decline linearly as the hunting mortality rate increases. The nonhunting mortality rate after the hunting season should be independent of hunting mortality, and therefore also independent of density.

Under the hypothesis of compensatory mortality, the annual survival rate is independent of the hunting mortality rate until some threshold hunting mortality rate is reached. Nonhunting mortality after the hunting season (when the hunting mortality rate is below the threshold) decreases and therefore is somehow density dependent. Nichols et al. (1984) listed 3 ways to distinguish the compensatory mortality hypothesis from the additive mortality hypothesis:

(1) Annual survival rates are not related to hunting mortality rates (as long as hunting mortality is below some threshold);

(2) As the hunting mortality rate increases, the nonhunting mortality rate after hunting season decreases;

(3) As population size at the end of the hunting season increases, the nonhunting mortality rate after the hunting season increases.

The hypotheses on additive and compensatory mortality have received much attention, especially among waterfowl biologists (Anderson and Burnham 1976, Rogers et al. 1979, Nichols and Haramis 1980, Conroy and Eberhardt 1983, Nichols and Hines 1983, Burnham and Anderson 1984, Burnham et al. 1984, Nichols et al. 1984, Caswell et al. 1985, Johnson et al. 1986, Trost 1987, Krementz et al. 1988, USFWS 1988b). Most, but not all, of these studies generally supported the compensatory mortality hypothesis. All the studies just cited, however, were correlational rather than experimental. In other words, harvest rates were not manipulated but were allowed to vary naturally through time.

Pollock et al. (1989c), during a long-term band recovery study of northern bobwhite quail, found evidence that late-winter hunting mortality (10 days, from February 7 to February 21) was additive to natural mortality. Average annual mortality rates were 81.3 percent for males and 85.7 percent for females. The average annual kill rate was 29.8 percent.

For northern bobwhites on the Carbondale Research Area (CRA) in Illinois, Roseberry (1979) and Roseberry and Klimstra (1984) demonstrated through regression analysis of total fall-to-spring mortality on harvest rate that hunting mortality was somewhere between being completely compensated for by a reduction in natural mortality and being completely additive to natural mortality. Mortality was density-dependent (see Anderson and Burnham 1981 and Roseberry 1981 for a discussion of methodological problems).

The functional relationships among annual survival rates, hunting mortality rates (for either the spring or fall hunting season), and population density are unknown for any wild turkey population (as well as for any exploited animal population). The data on survival rates of wild turkeys before and after instituting fall hunting in an Iowa study area (Little et al. 1990), however, has provided some insight into the question of additive versus compensatory mortality (Table 12) in wild turkeys. Although no corresponding control area was studied where fall hunting was prohibited, their data suggest that fall hunting mortality was additive. Average annual survival rates declined 21 to 23 percent for adult gobblers, juvenile gobblers, and juvenile hens and 6 percent for adult hens after fall hunting was instituted. Harvest levels averaged 4.3 turkeys per square kilometer (11.2 per square mile).

In general, spring hunting mortality of gobblers has been assumed to be completely additive to nonhunting mortality. Nonhunting mortality rates of gobblers are generally believed to be low and therefore allow little room for any compensatory mortality process. These ideas, however, have never been tested.

Another implicit assumption of this model is that recruitment (summer gain) is not related to population size (i.e., recruitment is independent of density and therefore is not related to harvest mortality). If recruitment was density dependent, increasing harvest (by reducing the breeding population) would increase recruitment.

For northern bobwhites, the rate of recruitment was found to decrease (curvilinearly) with an increasing ratio of breeding density to carrying capacity on the CRA in Illinois (Roseberry and Klimstra 1984:119).

Experimental evidence for density-dependent recruitment does not exist for wild turkey populations. Some authors have hypothesized that density-dependent

recruitment exists, based on comparisons of recruitment in relatively stable wild turkey populations with recruitment in rapidly expanding populations (Vangilder et al. 1987, Vander Haegen et al. 1988).

Newly reintroduced populations of wild turkeys do seem to grow exponentially (e.g., Speake et al. 1969), and in general, newly introduced populations of animals tend to grow exponentially. Some examples of exponential growth for some mammal populations can be found in Eberhardt (1987). Populations do not, however, continue to grow exponentially. To incorporate density-dependence in our model, the functional relationships between recruitment and population density for a wild turkey population must be known.

For large mammals, density-dependent recruitment is well established (e.g., see Fowler and Smith 1981, Clutton-Brock et al. 1982, McCullough 1979, 1984) and the relationship between recruitment and population size (density) has been incorporated into "black-box" stock recruitment models (e.g., McCullough 1979, 1984). The size of wild turkey populations is very difficult, if not impossible, to estimate with any accuracy or precision in most regions with current census techniques. Evidence for density-dependent recruitment may depend on the development of better population estimation techniques.

In summary, because neither the process of density-dependent mortality (and therefore compensatory harvest mortality) nor density-dependent recruitment has been demonstrated for wild turkey populations, these processes have not been incorporated into our model. And because density-dependent processes are not incorporated in the model, the growth rate of a simulated population does not decrease as population size increases. Over the range of wild turkey densities found in much of the United States, the effects of density-dependent recruitment may indeed be negligible.

When simulating the effects of harvest (spring or fall) on wild turkey populations, the assumption that hunting mortality is additive is obviously the most conservative. In view of the large annual variation in survival rates and hen success noted previously, a conservative approach seemed most reasonable. The large variation observed in survival and reproductive rate estimates for wild turkey populations—and the apparent relationship of this variation to environmental variation—suggests that environmental stochasticity (randomness) may swamp any density-dependent population responses that might exist (McCullough 1984). Because the effect of a large amount of environmental stochasticity is to make a population more vulnerable to overharvest, conservative harvest strategies should be used.

Simulated spring harvest. Parameter estimates for this simulation were obtained for 6 data years from radiotelemetry data gathered in Missouri (hens) and

Iowa (gobblers) (Vangilder unpublished data, Jackson et al. unpublished data). One 40-year run of the model was made at each of 6 levels of spring harvest (10 to 60 percent of the male population). The same set of random numbers was used to generate parameter values for the 34 years past the data years for each run, thereby allowing direct comparisons of the results. Adult gobblers were assumed to be approximately 2 times more vulnerable to harvest than juvenile gobblers.

The range of spring harvest values encompassed the range of values reported from other studies earlier in this chapter (see "Spring gobbler harvest"). A fall harvest of 5 percent of the total population was incorporated into each run. Starting population size was 5,820, and average recruitment was 1.55 poults per hen. The results (Table 14) demonstrate that increasing spring harvest (1) decreases the average percent of adult gobblers in the population prior to the spring hunt, (2) decreases the average percent of adult males in the harvest, and (3) decreases annual survival rates of adult and juvenile gobblers. In 9 of 40 years, at a 60-percent gobbler harvest, the spring season harvested all the adult gobblers.

The proportion of adult and juvenile gobblers that died from natural (nonhunting) causes decreased slightly as harvest rate increased. The observed decrease in the proportion dying of natural causes was because adult and juvenile gobblers that die from harvest in the model are no longer available to die from nonhunting causes. This effect (called "competing risks" in the survival literature) probably occurs in nature and is not responsible for compensatory mortality but may complicate tests of compensatory mortality hypothesis (Nichols et al. 1984).

At each level of spring harvest, population size increased because reproductive rates were high enough to offset annual mortality and because reduced gobbler densities were assumed not to affect reproductive rates of hens (i.e., each gobbler was assumed to mate with more than 1 female). If, however, the spring gobbler season begins before mating activity and if gobbler harvest levels are very high, some hens may possibly lay infertile clutches. In fact, some evidence exists to this effect (Exum et al. 1987).

The reduced number of adult gobblers in the prespring hunt population at high levels of harvest may also reduce hunting quality by reducing gobbling activity and by increasing the proportion of juvenile gobblers in the harvest.

Simulated fall harvest. The same parameter values for the 6 data years used for the spring harvest simulation were also used for this fall harvest simulation. Investigators made 25 40-year runs of the model at each of 4 levels of fall harvest (5 to 20 percent of the total population) because a principal aim was to determine whether the population would increase or decrease, given stochasticity of survival and reproductive rates. In that regard, a different set of random numbers was used to generate parameter values for the 34 years past the data years for each run of the model

During the fall season, juvenile gobblers, juvenile hens, and adult hens were 2.33, 2.00, and 1.33 times more vulnerable than adult gobblers. The proportion of juveniles in the model's harvest also increased as production increased. These relationships were empirically determined from Missouri's harvest data.

Table 14. Results of a wild turkey population model with varying levels of spring harvest.

Spring harvest (percent of male population)	Average percent adult gobblers in prespring hunt population	Average percent adult gobblers in harvest	Annual survival rates				Population size year 40
			Adult gobbler		Juvenile gobbler		
			Natural	Natural & hunting	Natural	Natural & hunting	
10	31	76	0.734	0.618	0.623	0.536	23,317
20	26	70	0.738	0.523	0.625	0.500	21,190
30	21	65	0.743	0.420	0.628	0.460	19,689
40	17	59	0.748	0.306	0.631	0.415	18,616
50	13	52	0.754	0.181	0.634	0.364	17,803
60	10	45	[a]	[a]	0.638	0.308	17,205

[a] In 9 of 40 years no adult gobblers were alive after the spring season ended.
Data years: 6
Simulation years: 34
Total years: 40
Starting population size: 5,820
Average recruitment: 1.55
(Poults surviving to fall/hens alive at start of fall)
Fall harvest: 5
(percent of total population)

Table 15. Results of a wild turkey population model with varying levels of fall harvest. Tabular values are the average of 25 runs (each run for 40 years) of the model at each level of fall harvest. Starting population size for each run was 5,820.

Fall harvest (percent of total population)	Average spring population size				Average survival rates				Average recruitment rate	Number of runs where population increased
	1990	2000	2010	2020	ADM	ADF	JVM	JVF		
5	13,595	21,935	57,822	127,466	0.524	0.610	0.505	0.596	1.63	25
10	5,758	6,584	7,665	9,098	0.510	0.579	0.468	0.550	1.61	17
15	3,276	2,085	1,439	909	0.498	0.551	0.434	0.508	1.61	0
20	1,765	564	210	63	0.484	0.523	0.399	0.466	1.61	0

A 20 percent spring harvest was incorporated in each run. At a 5 percent fall harvest, population size increased in all 25 runs (Table 15). In 40 years, the simulated population increased to an average of 127,466. A 5 percent fall harvest had little effect on population growth. At a 10 percent fall harvest, the population increased in 17 of 25 runs and average population size at year 40 was 9,098. At 15 and 20 percent fall harvests, the population declined in all 25 runs and average population size was 909 (15 percent harvest) and 63 (20 percent harvest). Obviously, effects on population growth began at a 10 percent fall harvest and were quite severe at 15 percent and 20 percent fall harvests.

The Suchy Model

Suchy et al. (1983) used a deterministic accounting model to simulate the effects of fall harvest on Iowa turkey populations under both the additive and compensatory mortality hypotheses. They assumed constant annual fecundity and survival rates. Survival rates were about 60 percent for hens and 50 percent for gobblers. Poult mortality was 56 percent. At a 10 percent fall harvest rate, they found that it took 6.5 years for the population to decline 25 percent under additive mortality. Under the compensatory mortality hypothesis (threshold rates were 5 percent for females and 16 percent for males), at a 10 percent harvest rate, the population declined 25 percent only after 73.6 years. At a 15 percent fall harvest rate, the time until a 25 percent population decline was 3.3 years under the additive hypothesis and 6.2 years under the compensatory hypothesis.

Both the Missouri model and the model of Suchy et al. (1983) indicate that population growth may still occur at sustained fall harvests below 10 percent.

In both models, *sustained* fall harvests greater than 10 percent resulted in rapid declines in population. Lobdell et al. (1972) used a stochastic model to simulate the effects of fall and spring hunting on wild turkey populations. They assumed that (1) annual mortality ranged

from 45 to 75 percent (mean of 60, standard deviation of 5); (2) there was no differential mortality among sex and age classes; (3) recruitment (juvenile-to-adult female ratio) in the fall ranged from 2.275 to 3.775 (mean of 3.025, standard deviation of 0.25); (4) fall hunting did not result in differential mortality among sex and age classes and removed 10 to 40 percent (mean of 25, standard deviation of 5) of the population; and (5) fall hunting was completely compensated for by a decrease in nonhunting mortality. The 3 parameters—total annual mortality, recruitment, and fall harvest—were allowed to vary stochastically about the means (random variates selected from a normal distribution of 3 standard deviations either side of the mean).

Their simulated population (starting size of 1,000, adult to juvenile of 40 to 60, male to female of 50 to 50) ranged from approximately 550 to 1,150 over the 100 years of the simulation. Population size was below 1,000 from about year 20 through year 85 of the simulation.

Under the hypothesis of complete compensation, their simulated population was able to withstand fall harvests ranging from 20 to 35 percent, a level much higher than the level observed to cause population declines in the previously discussed models.

The discrepancy among the models arises not only from the different assumption about harvest mortality (additive, compensatory with a threshold, or completely compensatory) but also from the values input for recruitment. Lobdell et al. (1972) average value for recruitment (juvenile-to-adult hen ratio) was 3.025. They found that a value of 3.000 resulted in a 40 percent decline in population over 100 years. They derived their value from an examination of the sex and age of hunter-killed turkeys in the fall, but they did not assume that juveniles were more vulnerable than adults. So their values for recruitment were probably too high.

The Missouri model used the input of field-collected radiotelemetry data on reproductive parameters. The model then calculated a recruitment rate (juvenile-to-adult hen ratio) at the beginning of the fall season (September 1). On average, this value for recruitment (1.61 to

1.63, see Table 15) was much lower than the value used by Lobdell et al. (1972). Average fecundity in the Iowa model (Suchy et al. 1983) was 2.8 poults per adult female and 0.8 poults per juvenile female *before* the effect of poult mortality. These values would no doubt result in much lower values of recruitment than would the value used by Lobdell et al. (1972).

CONCLUSIONS

Despite many years of investigation, the population dynamics of wild turkey populations are still not well understood. Density-dependence (in either mortality or recruitment rates) has not been demonstrated for wild turkey populations. The effects of exploitation on wild turkey populations are also not well understood. The relationship between hunting mortality and annual survival rates needs to be studied in several wild turkey populations across a number of years to determine whether hunting mortality is additive to natural mortality or compensated for by a decrease in natural mortality.

Almost no data exist on survival of poults from 4 weeks posthatch to winter. Mortality of young during this period may be highly variable.

Recent telemetry studies have shown that both natural mortality and reproductive rates are quite variable and that this variation may be related to stochastic environmental events. This variation requires a conservative approach to population management. Given the survival and reproductive rates measured in the Midwest, a spring harvest of less than 30 percent of the male population and a fall harvest of less than 10 percent of the total (both male and female) population should allow continued population growth.

Almost no data exist on poult survival from 4 weeks posthatch to winter.

Chapter 12

POPULATION MANAGEMENT

Eric W. Kurzejeski
Wildlife Research Biologist
Missouri Department of Conservation
Fish and Wildlife Research Center
Columbia, Missouri

Larry D. Vangilder
Wildlife Research Biologist
Missouri Department of Conservation
Fish and Wildlife Research Center
Columbia, Missouri

The development of wild turkey trap-and-transplant techniques was the foundation of the successful restoration of all subspecies. Most states have completed or are within the final phases of turkey restoration. Increases in both the range and population densities of wild turkeys have led to increased numbers of turkey hunters. Biologists once concerned primarily with restoration now face decisions on managing hunter numbers, on hunting quality, and most important, on the impact of increasing harvests on turkey populations.

In this chapter, we will review the present knowledge of (1) restoration; (2) population monitoring techniques; (3) harvest strategies; and (4) potential strategies for providing quality hunting. For some subspecies of wild turkey, information is abundant. For others, fewer data are available. Some information in this chapter was solicited by questionnaires from biologists in all states within the North American range of the wild turkey. We appreciate their assistance.

RESTORATION

In a recent book, *Restoring America's Wildlife*, John Lewis thoroughly described the history of wild turkey restoration programs in the United States. We summarize some of the material presented by Lewis (1987) in his chapter "Wild Turkeys: A Success Story," but we refer readers to this text for a more detailed account of early restoration programs.

At the North American Wildlife Conference in 1949, Dr. Henry Mosby delivered a paper titled "The present status and the future outlook of the eastern and Florida wild turkey." In this paper, Mosby reported that the ancestral range of the eastern and Florida wild turkey had been reduced by over 80 percent and that populations

remained in only 17 states. Of these states, 5 reported that turkey populations were at dangerously low levels, and officials in only 3 states thought numbers were increasing. Mosby (1949) thought that management of habitats on public lands could be a major factor in halting turkey population declines. He perceived, however, that private lands—because of human impacts—offered little habitat value. Mosby also perceived that livetrapping of turkeys showed some promise as a means of acquiring a source of birds. But he concluded that trap-and-transplant programs would not, in themselves, stop the decline of the eastern or Florida subspecies.

The old-growth, precolonial forests had abundant wild turkeys, but extensive logging eliminated much habitat and helped reduce populations. *Photo from Missouri Department of Conservation.*

Exploited land was rarely reforested by early loggers. *Photo by U.S. Forest Service.*

At the same time, C.H. Walker (1949b) published a report describing the status of Merriam's and Rio Grande wild turkeys in parts of the West. He indicated Merriam's turkeys were increasing their range in Arizona and Colorado but were declining in New Mexico. Introduced populations, outside the historic range, were increasing. South Dakota, Wyoming, and Montana released Merriam's turkeys captured in other states and got phenomenal population growth. In the Black Hills, a release of 29 turkeys increased to an estimated 5,000 to 7,000 birds in 10 years (Petersen and Richardson 1973). In Wyoming, McDonald and Jantzen (1958) reported the initial release of 15 birds from New Mexico in 1935 had grown to more than 10,000 turkeys by 1958.

In Montana, Merriam's turkeys were released in the mid-1950s. Biologists observed such rapid population growth that they instituted a hunting season in only 4 years (Jonas 1966). Walker (1949b) painted a similar picture for Rio Grande turkeys in Oklahoma, where numbers were increasing. In Texas, however, he noted populations were declining. Trap-and-transplant programs in the Southwest were responsible for population establishment and range expansion of the Rio Grande subspecies.

Problems with Game-farm Turkeys

One problem that continued to plague restoration of the eastern and Florida subspecies in the 1940s and 1950s was the release of game-farm-reared turkeys as a substitute to wild-trapped birds. Because wild turkeys were limited in numbers and in distribution and were notoriously hard to capture, it is no surprise that game-farm-reared turkeys were suggested as a solution. But the repeated failures of game-farm stock to establish viable populations suggested this approach was flawed.

A 1942 Missouri study demonstrated the differences in the heritable wildness between native wild turkey and

The propagation of game-farm turkeys was an expensive experiment that failed. *Photo by R. Cady.*

hybrid (or game-farm) turkeys and put an end to the release of game-farm birds in that state (Leopold 1944). Leopold showed that the adaptability that allowed hybrid turkeys to be successfully raised in captivity precluded their survival in the wild. Wherever game-farm birds were released near existing wild populations, hybridization and disease (Markley 1967) posed a real threat to the few remaining wild birds, likely setting back restoration.

In Arkansas, James et al. (1983) examined turkey population growth on 9 release sites. Four sites were stocked with wild-trapped turkeys and 5 received "Pennsylvania strain" game-farm birds. All of the birds were released from 1957 through 1961. Wild-trapped birds showed dramatic population increases averaging an estimated 225 percent over 3 years. Game-farm birds did not increase on any study area. In fact, they decreased sharply on 3 of the sites. Similar work in Pennsylvania (Wunz 1973) suggested that game-farm turkeys had lower survival, reproduction, and propensity to establish populations than did wild-trapped birds. In Massachusetts (J. Cardoza 1982) and Michigan (Rusz 1987), it has been suggested that winter feeding may play an important role in the maintenance of game-farm stock. When artificial winter feeding of a flock of game-farm birds was halted

in Massachusetts in 1968, the population declined sharply—from 113 to 30 birds. The remaining population never expanded its range (J. Cardoza, Massachusetts Dept. of Wildlife Conservation personal communication, cited in Rusz 1987).

The work of Leopold and of others who followed did not result in the halt of stocking game-farm turkeys everywhere. These studies did, however, inspire wildlife managers to look for ways to use wild-trapped turkeys to restore populations.

Developing Capture Techniques

Trapping methods used to capture turkeys in the West were not successful on eastern wild turkeys. Several trap designs successful in the West (roll-front, open-front, drop-front, slide-front, and drop-net) were used in early attempts to capture eastern turkeys in South Carolina (Baldwin 1947). Baldwin reported limited success with some of these traps but said, "In general it would appear that turkeys of the southwestern brush areas are more likely to enter open-front traps than those of the eastern forests."

The development of the rapidly propelled net greatly accelerated the trap-and-transplant strategy. *Photos by M. Vander Haegen.*

The drop-net trap captured large numbers of wild turkeys in some western parts of wild turkey range. *Photos by C. Lange (left) and D. Seaton, Winfield Courier (right).*

The capture of eastern and Florida turkeys by using walk-in traps was time-consuming and expensive. Besides, it did not provide enough birds for restoration programs. In 1948, a cannon-projected net trap was developed by Dill and Thornsberry (1950) on Swan Lake National Wildlife Refuge in Missouri. The inventors of the cannon-net trap intended it primarily for capturing waterfowl, but they believed that it offered a practical and economical means for trapping large numbers of any species of birds tending to flock together. This breakthrough in trapping technology made it possible to capture enough eastern and Florida turkeys for large-scale restoration programs. Cannon nets were first used to trap turkeys in the early 1950s on the Francis Marion National Forest in South Carolina (Holbrook 1958) and in Missouri (Sadler 1954). Later modification in cannons, nets, and charges improved the method's overall effectiveness for capturing turkeys.

A later development in trapping technology was the recoilless cannon or rocket. Hawkins et al. (1968) used the first rocket-net trap to capture deer in southern Illinois. Since then, improvements have been made in the method. Many biologists now shoot the net out of a trapezoid-shaped box (Wunz 1987b). The box keeps the net dry and free of snow and ice. The box is easy to camouflage, and the bait is put out farther from the box (6 meters; 20 feet) than it is from a cannon net (3 meters; 10 feet). So turkeys seem less likely to be spooked by a rocket-net box than by a cannon-net set. Rocket-propelled nets are therefore faster, catching a higher proportion of the birds attracted to the bait. Basic considerations and recommendations for trapping wild turkeys, along with a summary of previous literature, appear in Bailey et al. (1980).

Various anesthetic drugs have been used to capture wild turkeys. Williams (1966) was an early investigator in developing drug-capture techniques for wild turkeys. As with any capture method, there are risks. Perhaps the major problem in capturing turkeys with drugs is the possibility that partially drugged birds may wander off in a seminarcotized condition before they can be recovered. The primary advantages of this technique are (1) tranquilizers do not require the preparation or clearing of a bait site; (2) the cost is lower than for cannon-net equipment; (3) fewer people are needed at a bait site; and (4) vandalism is nonexistent (Williams and Austin 1988).

Only capture of wild turkeys from the wild and release in the wild has been successful over the long term. *Photo by B. Ericksen.*

A variety of drugs have been successfully used to capture wild turkeys. The most common are alphachloralose and tribromoethanol. These drugs generally produce narcosis in 10 to 40 minutes. The duration of anesthesia varies from 4 to 40 hours, depending on dosage (Williams and Austin 1988). Because of the long time turkeys are under anesthesia, holding boxes and a facility in which to keep birds are necessary.

How Many Turkeys in Each Release?

The number of wild turkeys used in transplanting programs has varied considerably through time and from state to state. In West Virginia, Gilpin (1959) reported a population was established from a release of only 2 adult males and 4 hens. Another West Virginia release, 5 gobblers and 4 hens in 1953, resulted in an estimated population of 60 to 80 birds by fall of 1964. In Arkansas, 4 releases of wild birds were made during the early 1950s, resulting in the successful reestablishment reported by Preston (1959). Restoration efforts in Missouri were initiated in 1954, using wild-trapped turkeys. Between 1954 and 1958, 6 releases were made in Missouri with a normal stocking rate of 12 birds (4 male and 8 female) (Lewis 1961).

Low numbers of turkeys were used in early restoration efforts. For one thing, there was the desire to make every bird count or try to stock as many areas as possible. Besides, low population densities in source areas made trapping difficult. As trapping success improved and turkey densities increased, the tendency was to increase the number of turkeys in each release. In Missouri, the mean number of turkeys used per release in the 1960s and 1970s was 20 (8 gobblers and 12 hens). As a rule, a release of that size resulted in a huntable population after 5 breeding seasons.

Across the nation, stocking rates have varied considerably. For releases of eastern turkeys, numbers range from 9 birds for some releases in Mississippi and Oklahoma to from 30 to 56 in West Virginia (Kennamer 1986). The number of Merriam's and Rio Grande turkeys per release is generally larger. In New Mexico, 66 birds were released at a single site (Kennamer 1986a).

More recently, some states have tried block stocking (Iowa, Texas, Kentucky) by releasing groups of birds at a number of sites within a release area. In Iowa, all potential release sites within a habitat block (county-sized area) are stocked at the same time, even though site quality may vary (Little 1980). As many as 5 releases have been made in an area with no more than 6 kilometers (3.7 miles) between sites. Under this strategy, the popula-

How many poults survive is a key to how well wild turkey populations fare. *Photo by L. Williams.*

The hen, her nest, and her young poults largely determine population success. *Photo by G. Wunz, Pennsylvania Game Commission.*

tions in the release area can generally be hunted in 5 years.

In east Texas, a similar strategy is being used to accelerate turkey restoration (Campo and Dickson 1989). Release sites are distributed at intervals of 12.8 kilometers (8 miles) within turkey management units, the smallest of which is a county. Fifteen birds are liberated at each site. Each block stocking is expected to result in 12,950 hectares (32,000 acres) of occupied range in 3 years.

Supplemental stockings—or interplantings—(Backs and Eisfelder 1990) have been used to rehabilitate low-density turkey populations in Indiana. Populations at some release sites exhibit limited growth or initial growth and a subsequent decline. Backs and Eisfelder (1990) suggest population isolation as a causal factor. They caution, however, that habitat quality should be ruled out as a factor suppressing populations before supplemental releases are considered. They recommend supplemental releases of 8 to 10 hens if the area has gobblers, or they recommend a normal complement of 11 hens and 4 adult gobblers if the density of gobblers is unknown. Recommended spacing of releases is at least 8 kilometers (5 miles) apart.

The costs of turkey restoration programs vary greatly. In Kansas, relocation of Rio Grande turkeys costs as little as an estimated $12 per bird. But in the same state, eastern wild turkeys cost $400 per bird (Kennamer 1986a). Most states estimate costs at from $300 to $500 per bird.

Improvement of capture techniques certainly played an important role in wild turkey restoration, but many other factors hastened the success of such programs. Better habitat conditions, because of improvements in forest management on both the state and federal levels, proved vital to restoration success. Better law enforcement—plus a ground swell of public support for conservation measures in general—also contributed substantially. These factors, plus the wild turkey's adaptability to habitats previously thought unsuited, made possible the remarkable restoration success.

POPULATION SURVEYS AND INDICES

The need for improved techniques to count wild turkey populations has been a concern of biologists for decades (Mosby 1949, Mosby 1967, Lewis 1973, Wunz and Shope 1980). Accurate estimates of animal population size are important tools, allowing wildlife managers to evaluate the effects of habitat conditions, habitat management practices, and harvest regulations. Many techniques have been used to get estimated counts of wild turkey populations. These procedures include mark-recapture, line or strip transects, and direct enumeration (flock counts).

Another aspect of population monitoring involves surveys that result in an index to population parameters (reproduction and density) rather than an estimate of population size. Indices are often used to monitor population trends at state and regional levels. Methods include brood surveys, gobbling counts, and a number of hunter or cooperator surveys.

Mark-Recapture Methods

Mark-recapture techniques start with the trapping and marking of individual birds. Subsequent recapture is through resighting or harvest. In Texas, DeYoung and Priebe (1987) evaluated the use of the mark-recapture technique for Rio Grande turkeys. They marked 83 birds with patagial (on skin between shoulder and forepart of wing) tags and recaptured individuals (resighting) along 8 vehicle routes—each 16 kilometers (10 miles) long—that dissected the study area. The estimated population size (278 ± 28 [standard error]) on the 5,700-hectare (14,085-acre) study site was the lowest of the 3 methods tested. (The others were line and strip transects.)

These authors concluded that the mark-recapture technique has applications for estimating population size in detailed research studies but that it is impractical for large-area management uses. Major factors affecting the practicality of the technique were cost and effort required to derive the estimates. In addition, the ability of mark-recapture methods to provide unbiased estimates of population size requires that a number of important assumptions be met. DeYoung and Priebe (1987) cautioned that the assumption of equal probability of recapture (resighting) for marked and unmarked birds was not met, because the road network did not allow them to uniformly sample their study area.

In Mississippi, Gribben (1986) evaluated the ability of the mark-recapture technique to determine differences in population size of eastern wild turkeys. His conclusions based on 469 captures of 349 individual turkeys over 3 years were the following:

(1) Capture-recapture techniques are costly and time-consuming;

(2) Capture of turkeys is too difficult to result in the necessary sample sizes needed for detailed population studies;

(3) Capture-recapture methodology is not an appropriate method for estimating population structure.

While the precision of the estimator is affected by the biologist's inability to capture and recapture a sufficient number of individuals, Gribben (1986) did suggest the method is of some use in setting management objectives.

Line and Strip Transects

In the brush country of south Texas, a variety of line- and strip-transect methods were used to estimate densities of Rio Grande turkeys. Beasom (1970) used both helicopter and vehicle routes to determine turkey densities on a 971-hectare (2,400-acre) area. Vehicle routes provided estimates of 166 ± 47 (standard error) and 101 ± 11 birds per 405 hectares (1000 acres) in each of 2 distinct habitat types. Helicopter counts resulted in lower estimates of 56 birds in the first area and 51 in the second (no standard errors provided). Evaluation of the techniques was not a priority objective of this study (Beasom 1970), so no conclusions were presented on the merits of either method as a census technique.

Line and strip transects were compared by DeYoung and Priebe (1987) in south Texas. They concluded that the strip transect, using vehicle routes, was too variable over time and did not meet the assumption that all individuals in the fixed-width transect were sighted. The line-transect method resulted in larger standard errors. Nonetheless, these authors thought the line-transect method should be further evaluated because it compensated for differences in observability along survey routes and had the greatest potential for broad application.

Wild turkeys usually congregate into large flocks during fall and winter. *Photo by P. Pelham.*

Direct Count

In both northern and southwestern parts of the nation, direct counts are used for population census. Winter counts based on cooperator data are used in Michigan's northern lower peninsula to determine population size of winter flocks (Weinrich et al. 1985). Landowners and other selected individuals (e.g., postal carriers and wildlife agency personnel) throughout the turkey range are interviewed and asked to report the number of birds observed in each flock. Estimates of population size are correlated with the following spring's harvest. The census required the efforts of 6 to 8 people for a 2-week period to collect data from cooperators. The validity of this technique is related to the fact that winter weather restricts movements of turkey flocks in this portion of the range and that supplemental foods (e.g., silage and corn cribs) attract birds, resulting in greater visibility.

Direct counts are used in Texas to estimate populations of Rio Grande turkeys. Cook (1973) compared density estimates at winter roosts compiled by both cooperating landowners and biologists. In western parts of the Rio Grande's range in Texas, data collected from landowners were similar to those derived from biologists counting birds at the same roosts. Landowner estimates were 7 percent higher than those provided by biologists. In the eastern portions of the range, landowner estimates were 203 percent greater, with the difference being attributed to movement of flocks to different winter roosts and subsequent double sampling. Where roost sites are stable, censusing Rio Grande turkeys by landowner contacts may provide accurate data. Banding studies to monitor the mixing of flocks and movement among roost sites may allow improvement of this technique in areas where roosts are inconsistently used.

Population Indices

Several indirect methods are used to monitor annual trends in a turkey population's size, reproductive success, and distribution rather than provide a count or estimated numbers. While lacking the precision of quantitative estimates of density, these methods and the resulting indices they produce may provide valuable and easily gathered data on which to base management recommendations. Indices of turkey population status and reproduction are used to evaluate statewide and regional trends. In particular, brood surveys are correlated with fall harvest (Wunz and Shope 1980, Vangilder unpublished data,

Wunz and Ross 1990). Brood survey results have also been found to correlate with the proportion of juvenile gobblers in the subsequent spring's harvest in Missouri.

Cooperator brood surveys are used by some state agencies to evaluate annual production. In Missouri, a brood survey card is mailed to landowner cooperators in June, July, and August. Cooperators are asked to report the number of poults, hens, and broodless hens observed each month. A poult-to-hen ratio is derived from these data. The ratio is correlated with the proportion of juveniles in the fall harvest and with the percent of juvenile males in the following spring's harvest. The survey sample size (2,000 cooperators) allows for examination of population trends by region of the state.

Production indices are valuable in assessing population status and in evaluating harvest strategies. Pennsylvania acquires production data from field officers (Wunz and Shope 1980). Biologists then use the total number of hens and poults observed as a production index. Over 26

Frequently a locked gate and controlled human access are critical to protecting wild turkey populations. *Photo by G. Wunz, Pennsylvania Game Commission.*

years of data collection, the production index was found to be significantly correlated with fall harvest.

Another indirect survey technique that provides an index to turkey numbers is the use of hunter reports to monitor annual change. In Minnesota, Welsh and Kimmel (1990) found that reports from a randomly selected group of antlerless-deer hunters provided cost-effective means to detect annual population fluctuations. Reports from turkey hunters (Kennamer 1986) also have been used as a way of indexing population change. Hunter surveys may offer an advantage over landowner-cooperator observation surveys: A number of potential survey participants can easily be defined, and data can be collected over a shorter period of time (length of hunting season).

Survey methods using observational techniques are often applied to intensive study areas. Most surveys involve repeated observations along specific routes within established time periods. Speake (1980) got both production and age and sex data in Alabama by counting turkeys on a 24.1-kilometer (15-mile) route that was run 2 or 3 times weekly from June through August.

Production estimates on Rio Grande turkeys in Texas were derived by Beasom (1970) and Beasom and Pattee (1979) using similar procedures. Survey routes were run during specified time periods: morning (dawn to 10 A.M.) and evening (4 P.M. to dark). Data were obtained on poult-to-hen ratios, brood size, and percentage of hens with poults.

In Arizona, Shaw (1973) used standardized morning and evening survey routes to establish an annual production index for Merriam's turkeys. Route length ranged from 16 to 27 kilometers (10 to 16.8 miles). The greatest number of observations were in the first 3 hours of daylight. Shaw's (1973) recommendation was to establish, as

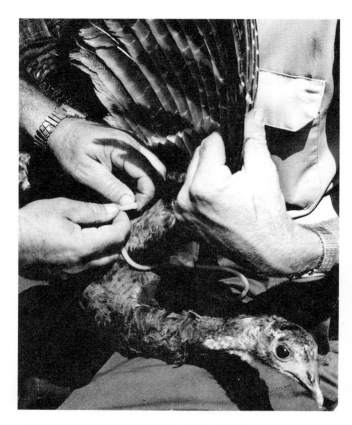

Valuable information about wild turkey population size and structure can be gathered at check stations. *Photo by E. Kurzejeski, Missouri Department of Conservation.*

Radio instrumentation of wild turkeys has provided much information useful for managing populations. *Photos by L. Williams.*

a basis for assessing production, long (64-kilometer; 40-mile) routes that should be run only during the 3-hour early morning period. He also suggested only a single survey (no route repetitions) to eliminate the bias of repeated counts of individuals.

Smith (1962, cited in Shaw 1973) provided confidence limits for hen-to-poult ratios based on the number of total observations (1 observation equal to 1 sighting of hens or poults, alone or in any combination), using data from the White Mountains in Arizona. With 200 observations, the 95 percent confidence interval was ±14 percent of total observations. When only 50 observations occurred, the 95 percent level was ±56 percent of total observations. The point is that the accuracy of this technique changes with the number of hen-to-poult observations. As observations decline, so does reliability. Shaw (1973) concluded the technique was adequate to detect year-to-year changes of 20 percent at the 80 percent confidence level.

Bartush et al. (1985) evaluated the utility of brood survey routes on northwestern Florida wildlife management areas as a means of developing a cost-effective method for inventory of wild turkeys. Recommendations for standardizing and conducting survey routes are the following (Bartush et al. 1985:179):

(1) Establish 32-kilometer (20-mile) routes on low-traffic roads, based on an area size no greater than 24,300 hectares (60,045 acres). Larger areas should have 2 or more routes for each additional 12,150 hectares (30,023 acres);

(2) Run surveys twice weekly between June 25 and August 15. Alternate starting points on consecutive counts;

(3) Start surveys 2 to 3 hours before sunset, and complete them no later than 30 minutes before sunset.

Kimmel and Tzilikowski (1986) evaluated the use of a tape-recorded poult distress call as a means of estimating reproduction. The call was played to radio-marked hens with and without broods. Of the hens with broods, 67 percent responded by moving toward the taped calls. Hens without broods never responded. Response time and the probability that the hen and brood would move toward the tape player decreased as poults aged. They concluded that taped calls were useful for luring broods into open areas where visibility of poults would be optimum. This method, when used with vehicle routes, could result in more precise enumeration of brood size.

Gobbling Counts

Gobbling counts have been used as an indication of both turkey density and distribution (Scott and Boeker 1972, Porter and Ludwig 1980). In recently introduced turkey populations in Minnesota, Porter and Ludwig (1980) found that extensive surveys of gobbling activity were useful for monitoring range expansion and trends in population growth. They also found a good correlation between hunter success rates and gobbling counts in zones open to hunting.

Constraints on survey methods to control sources of extrinsic variation were (1) standardized techniques; (2) careful selection of listening positions; (3) appropriate weather conditions for surveys; and (4) a large sample of simultaneous survey records. With this technique, the authors suggested they could monitor changes in abundance between years on areas of approximately 900 square kilometers (349 square miles). But they were unable to evaluate how the technique may perform when applied to smaller study sites.

In Arizona, Scott and Boeker (1972) evaluated gobbling counts as an index to Merriam's turkey population size. They found daily gobbling activity highly variable. The highest counts of gobbling (total number of gobblers), however, were correlated with the observed adult hen-to-gobbler sex ratio on the study area. These authors suggest gobbling counts have the utility to monitor breeding population status, but they caution about use of the technique without supporting information from other areas. In Colorado, Hoffman (1990) monitored gobbling intensity of individual Merriam's turkey gobblers over time. He concluded that gobbling varied greatly among individuals and with the chronology of breeding activity. This finding suggests that gobbling routes may be of limited use as a population measure. On the Tallahala Wildlife Management Area in Mississippi, Palmer et al. (1990) attributed the lack of correlation of gobbler population size and gobble counts to variation in gobbler body condition. The investigators suggested that gobbling activity was reduced after winters that had food shortages.

The Past and the Future

Over the past 2 decades, improvements have been made in the development, refinement, and application of techniques to estimate turkey numbers. Observational survey techniques seem to have the greatest potential for evaluating population status and reproduction in the more open habitats occupied by the Merriam's and Rio Grande subspecies. Brood surveys provide reliable indices to annual reproduction for all subspecies. Quantitative estimates of density are still difficult to get. Techniques such as mark-recapture and line transect—while valuable methods of population measurement—have limited applicability to monitoring turkey populations because the nature of the wild turkey prevents the capture or observation of sufficient numbers to derive accurate estimates. Except under rare situations such as winter flocking in northern Michigan and traditional roost sites in Texas, direct counts have limited feasibility. The future ability of researchers and managers to provide for more detailed evaluations of the impacts of both habitat management practices and harvest regulations on turkey populations requires the means to detect changes in population size. As in 1967, when Mosby cited the need for improved turkey census techniques, development of reliable techniques is still a major obstacle limiting our ability to improve the management of the wild turkey resource.

MONITORING HARVESTS AND HUNTING PRESSURE

Most state wildlife management agencies attempt to estimate the annual wild turkey harvest and the amount of effort expended by turkey hunters. The most common method of gathering these data is from mail surveys of permit buyers. In states without a separate turkey hunting permit, the sample is drawn from small-game license buyers. In those states requiring a turkey permit, a random sample of individuals who buy turkey licenses is surveyed. A major factor delaying the collection of survey information is the time needed to get names and addresses of license buyers from permit vendors. This information must then be entered on a computer, and finally the survey materials are mailed. The process can take up to a year to complete. Because of these delays, turkey season survey data are not available in some states for 12 to 18 months after the season closes.

Mail Versus In-Person Survey

In states where turkey hunters are required to apply for permits, surveys can be conducted in a more timely fashion. Names and addresses of hunters are available before the season begins. A questionnaire can be mailed to hunters promptly when the season ends and recollections are fresh, thereby reducing some of the possible survey biases.

Surveys do provide a variety of data on both harvest and hunting pressure. Common statistics include the number of turkey-hunting trips, hunter success rates, specific dates hunted (distribution of hunting pressure), and age (adult and subadult) of turkeys harvested. Surveys can also be used to gather information on hunter interference rates and other data related to hunter experiences.

Estimates derived from hunter surveys may be affected by 1 or more of the following problems (1) suc-

cessful hunters tend to respond at a higher rate than unsuccessful hunters (nonresponse bias); (2) hunters may report harvesting more birds than they actually did (brag bias); (3) surveys do not permit the collection of some biological data (e.g., most hunters do not carry scales to weigh birds but would guess if asked); (4) sample size may be inadequate to provide regional or county information; (5) the results usually are not available before the regulation setting for the next year's season, nor available to the public in a timely fashion; and (6) the delay in sending survey material to hunters can result in a bias because hunters may not remember the actual number of days hunted or other requested details.

Some states use mandatory in-person checking of harvested turkeys as an alternative to harvest surveys. The advantages are that check stations (1) provide a count of legally harvested birds; (2) provide harvest data at the county or regional level; and (3) permit collection of a variety of biological data (e.g., turkey's age, sex, and weight). Disadvantages of mandatory checking that are often cited are cost and hunter inconvenience. While hunters may have to travel some distance to check in a bird, their participation in the collection of data necessary to manage the turkey resource should not be considered an inconvenience. Mandatory-check-station costs are often justified by the quality of information they provide for managers.

The Missouri Department of Conservation evaluated costs associated with producing turkey harvest estimates from postseason mail surveys as compared with check-station statistics. Determining harvest estimates of ± 5 percent at the 95 percent confidence interval for each of Missouri's 114 counties would require surveying 99.2 percent of spring turkey permit buyers (based on 1985 sales of spring turkey permits).

Cost of the survey at 1985 postage rates was estimated at $70,450. Obviously the cost at today's postal rates would be even greater. If the resolution was reduced to estimating turkey harvest in only the 8 zoogeographic regions within the state, the cost would still have exceeded $60,000. Additional costs of data entry and analyses were not included in the estimate.

Getting the same level of reliability for fall turkey harvest data would result in an additional $35,000 in survey costs. Costs of maintaining mandatory spring and fall turkey check stations in Missouri average $40,000 annually (R. Glover, Missouri Department of Conservation, personal communication). Therefore, costs for mail surveys and subsequent data entry and analyses can be greater than those for check stations.

Considering the added benefits of timely collection and availability of harvest and age-ratio data, mandatory check stations may be preferable over mail surveys to collect harvest data. If, however, hunting-pressure estimates that include unsuccessful hunters are the goal, then a separate mail survey must be conducted in addition to maintaining check stations. Mandatory checking generally provides harvest data of higher resolution than do mail surveys, but the choice of which method to use depends on each state's population-management objectives.

SEASONS AND HUNTING REGULATIONS

Spring Turkey Seasons

Throughout the United States, spring seasons vary from 7 days in parts of Kentucky to 46 days in Georgia. Bag limits vary from 1 gobbler in many states to 6 in Alabama. Because turkeys are polygamous, spring gobbler seasons are thought to have little negative impact on turkey populations. While polygamy does ensure that most hens will be bred even if some males are harvested, the contention that spring harvests do not affect long-term population levels is not necessarily true. A season structure that results in the harvest of a high proportion of males obviously reduces the density of gobblers. This condition can affect both age structure and population density of males in subsequent years.

Liberal spring harvests in conjunction with several years of low reproduction can result in a decline in the proportion of adult males in the population in subsequent years (see Population Dynamics chapter). Other factors that may affect gobbler density are the length of the spring season, opening dates, bag limits, and hunter densities. Spring seasons can also result in substantial losses of hens by illegal kill (Kimmel and Kurzejeski 1985, Little et al. 1990), and this problem is likely greater during longer seasons.

Arkansas data (R. Smith, Arkansas Game and Fish, personal communication) indicate that the spring season's length and timing in relation to breeding chronology may affect gobbler densities. Spring turkey harvest in Arkansas was around 4,500 birds from 1978 through 1983 (range 4,096 to 4,703). In 1984, the spring season was shortened from approximately 5½ weeks to 4 weeks by moving the opening date from April 1 to around April 10. This regulation aimed at providing the opportunity for dominant gobblers to breed more hens before harvest and moving hunting pressure closer to the second peak of gobbling, which occurs as hens begin incubation.

After these regulation changes were enacted, spring turkey harvests increased every year but 1990. Harvest in 1984 was 4,509 birds compared with 8,144 in 1988 and 8,355 in 1991. Although it cannot be proved that the increased harvest was the result of the regulation changes, the strategy may have been effective in allowing a rapid increase in the proportion of adult males in the population.

Conventional wisdom holds that when spring seasons open before hens are receptive to gobblers, the gobblers are more vulnerable to hunters' calls. By opening the spring season later and reducing its length, managers could increase the proportion of males in the population. So the timing and length of the spring season are critical for population structure.

Of course, factors other than season length can result in harvest increases: (1) increased hunting pressure; (2) increases in occupied range; and (3) increases in hunter success. The harvest increase in Arkansas from 1984 through 1991 is likely the result of a shorter season combined with other factors. In any event, the old adage that "spring harvest has no effect on population growth" may not always be true.

Spring turkey seasons are generally set according to the reproductive chronology of the wild turkey and hunting opportunity, tempered by a strong measure of tradition. Several philosophies exist on the timing of spring seasons. Some states attempt to schedule their seasons so the second peak of gobbling activity (Figure 1) occurs midway through the season. This peak arrives when hens become less responsive to gobblers, either late in egg laying or during incubation. Biologists reason that opening the season during this period should result in less disruption of breeding, in a reduction of illegal hen kill, and in increased responsiveness of gobblers to hunters' calls (Hoffman 1990). Setting the season to coincide with the second gobbling peak makes for a relatively short season.

Other states have spring gobbler seasons open through the entire breeding period, providing a long hunting season. Often these states have a liberal bag limit and no limit on hunter numbers. Some states with long seasons have a limit on hunter numbers and divide the hunting season into segments, thereby controlling hunter numbers and harvest pressure.

In many states, tradition may play a strong role in season structure — especially if the opinions of hunters are solicited. In northern Missouri, a study of breeding chronology of eastern wild turkeys showed the median date for hens to start incubating first nests is May 4 (Figure 2). However, the 2-week spring season concludes as early as May 1 and no later than May 7. A survey of turkey hunters (Vangilder et al. 1990) indicated 39.9 percent of hunters in north Missouri thought the season was timed just right, 26.3 percent thought it was too late, and only 16.4 percent thought it was too early. Though the spring season could be adjusted to coincide more closely with peak incubation, hunters seem to be comfortable

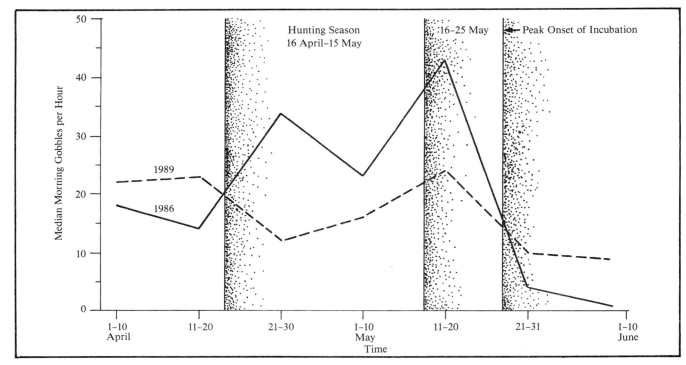

Figure 1. Chronologic distribution of gobbling activity of adult male Merriam's wild turkeys in Colorado and New Mexico (Hoffman 1990).

with the current dates. Because the traditional season dates seem preferable to a majority of hunters, a change seems unwarranted.

Spring seasons, then, tend to fall into 2 categories: (1) those that are conservative, with either a short season or a quota on licenses and a reduced bag, and (2) those that are liberal, with long seasons, higher bag limits, and

no limit on hunters. Neither approach is necessarily better than the other. Season lengths and bag limits in each state should, in part, depend on the goals of turkey population management and on hunter preferences.

Biological and ecological factors should also be considered in evaluating season formats. Examination of data from states that report both spring harvest and

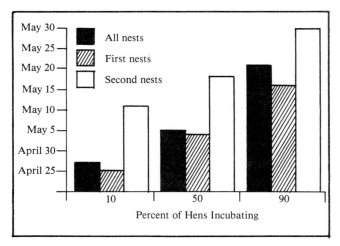

Figure 2. Reproductive chronology of wild turkey hens in Adair County, Missouri, from 1981 to 1988.

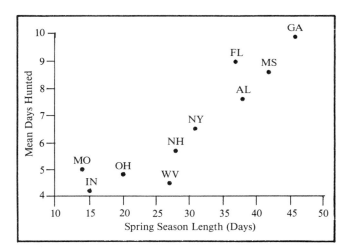

Figure 3. The mean number of days hunted versus season length for spring gobbler seasons in 10 states.

Table 1. Hunter effort, season length, and bag limits for spring eastern wild turkey seasons by state or province.

State or province	Kill per 1,000 trips	Kill per hunter	Average number days hunted	Season length	Bag limit	Year
Alabama	127	0.971	7.62	38	6	1988
Arkansas	NR[d]	NR	NR	NR	NR	NR
Connecticut[a]	43	0.151	3.50	21	2 or 1[b]	1988
Florida	—	—	9.00	37		1987
Georgia	49	0.484	9.90	46	2	1987
Illinois[a]	61	—	—	24	2	1988
Indiana	46	0.194	4.20	15	1	1988
Iowa[a]	135	0.450	3.34	28	2	1988
Kentucky	—	0.139	—	14 or 7	1	1988
Louisiana	50	0.379	7.58	8–37	3	1986
Maine[a]	23	0.071	3.11	21	1	1988
Maryland	NR	NR	NR	NR	NR	NR
Massachusetts[a]	—	0.037	—	19	1	1988
Michigan[a]	64	0.307	4.76	38	1	1988
Minnesota[a]	88	0.281	3.20	33	1	1988
Mississippi	109	0.933	8.59	42	3	1987
Missouri	70	0.352	5.03	14	2	1988
New Hampshire	20	0.116	5.70	28	1	1988
New Jersey[a]	37	0.118	3.20	33	1	1988
New York	23	0.150	6.46	31	2	1986
North Carolina	—	—	—	28	2	1988
Ohio	37	0.179	4.80	20	1	1988
Oklahoma	—	—	—	37	1–3	1988
Ontario[a]	40	0.160	4.00	12	1	1988
Pennsylvania	—	0.071	—	29	1	1987
Rhode Island	NR	NR	NR	NR	NR	NR
South Carolina	—	0.230[c]	—	31	5	1988
Tennessee	NR	NR	NR	NR	NR	NR
Vermont	—	0.122[c]	—	31	2	1988
Virginia	NR	NR	NR	NR	NR	NR
West Virginia	21	0.095	4.47	27	2	1985

[a] Permit sales are limited.
[b] Two on private land, 1 on state land.
[c] Harvest per permit sold.
[d] NR = not reported.

effort (hunter-trip) data for eastern wild turkeys revealed that harvest varies from 20 to 135 birds per 1,000 hunting trips (Table 1). Days hunted (effort) increases with increasing season length (Figure 3), and harvest increases with effort (Figure 4). Spring harvests varied from 0.07 to 0.97 birds per hunter (Table 1). Longer seasons tend to result in more effort by hunters and, therefore, increased harvests. The wide variation in harvest per 1,000 trips and harvest per hunter among states is undoubtedly the result of many factors, including variation in population size, season length, bag limits, hunting traditions, and methods of data collection.

To examine the relationship between the percentage of adults in the spring harvest and the season's length, we attempted to get from each state the adult-to-juvenile ratio in the spring harvest. Only 12 states could provide such information. Except for West Virginia, there was a tendency for states with longer spring seasons to harvest a lower proportion of adults (Table 2), but the correlation coefficient ($r = 0.78$, 5 d.f.) is not significant ($P = 0.04$).

Biologists in many states suspect that season length can affect the proportion of adult gobblers in harvests of subsequent years. In Missouri, population modeling has shown that harvesting more than 25 percent of adult gobblers each spring will result in a shift in the age structure in favor of juvenile males.

It has been suggested that under a liberal spring season format, a higher proportion of males are harvested and hunter opportunity is maximized. The result is said to be greater annual fluctuations in spring harvests and a lower ratio of adult gobblers in the harvest. By contrast, conservative seasons restrict harvest opportunity. Annual fluctuations in harvest are smaller, and the proportion of adult gobblers in the harvest is generally greater.

An analogy most sportsmen can relate to is trophy-deer management. To produce adult bucks requires restrictive harvests on younger bucks. Similarly, a conservative turkey season structure generally results in a larger proportion of gobblers surviving the hunting season.

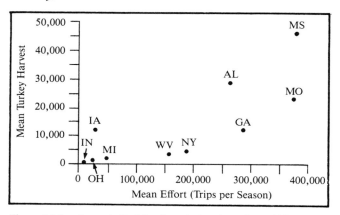

Figure 4. Mean harvest of wild turkeys during the spring gobbler season versus mean hunter effort (trips) for 10 states. Mean harvest and mean hunter effort for each state were calculated from data available for spring seasons from 1979 to 1988 (maximum sample of 10 years).

Table 2. Mean percentage of adult gobblers in spring harvest for selected states, 1979–1988.

State	Percentage of adults	Range	Season length (days)	Number of years
Arkansas	57.0	42–81	28–39	9
Illinois	52.2	39–64	a	10
Indiana	66.6	53–79	15	10
Iowa	67.5	56–74	a	10
Maryland	56.1	50–61	30	10
Michigan	55.3	43–71	a	3
Missouri	69.2	55–88	14	10
New York	50.4	40–66	31	10
Ohio	60.9	51–82	20	10
Oklahoma	62.9	–	16–38	10
South Carolina	56.0	45–72	31	10
West Virginia	71.2	54–92	27	10

a Hunters may not participate the entire season.

While some of the birds are lost to natural mortality during any year, conservative harvest regulations tend to shift the age ratio of males to favor older age classes (i.e., increased proportion of adult gobblers). Under a liberal season, adult gobbler densities are generally lower, and spring harvest depends more on annual reproduction. In springs following years with good reproduction, the total harvest increases because a large number of juvenile gobblers are available. In years following low reproductive success, harvests tend to decline because of a decrease in the total number of available males. In states with conservative seasons, spring harvest levels can be stabilized even after poor reproduction because the density of adult gobblers tends to be higher or more stable.

In general, the effects of spring season length and bag limits on wild turkey populations are not clearly understood. There is little doubt that many factors, acting synergistically, often affect age ratios and population density. Hunter selectivity and habitat quality may also change age ratios in the harvest.

Under this hypothesis, states with longer seasons, unregulated hunter numbers, and liberal bag limits tend to be heavily forested and most are located in the South and Southeast. They have large total turkey populations, but turkeys are well distributed over the extensive forest habitats, resulting in lower densities (birds per square kilometer). Because turkeys are widespread, hunter interest and numbers are high. But because of low turkey densities, hunters hear fewer birds on any morning and tend to harvest any legal bird (adult or juvenile tom). In addition, because of the liberal limit, the harvest of a juvenile tom does not preclude taking an adult bird later in the season.

In contrast, states with shorter seasons tend to be those that have high turkey densities per square kilometer of occupied range. Hunters hear multiple gobblers on many mornings and know that the chances of successfully taking an adult tom are good. The reduced bag limit, combined with the high number of gobblers, tends to result in greater selectivity toward adult birds. So selectivity and turkey density, not season length, may result in the observed level of juveniles or adults in the harvest. Under this hypothesis, the proportion of adults and juveniles in the harvest does not reflect the proportion of adults and juveniles in the population.

We want to stress that regardless of the approach, liberal or conservative, the effects of season structure are not absolute. On lightly hunted private lands, seasons and bag limits will have little impact on gobbler numbers. But in heavily hunted areas, such as state and federal lands, liberal seasons have an even greater impact on turkey density and hunting quality. Wildlife managers may need to consider separate season structures on areas that receive intense turkey-hunting pressure if their goal is to maintain a high proportion of adult gobblers.

The most efficient means to examine the effects of spring harvest on gobbler densities is through population modeling. If rates of survival and reproduction are known, biologists can test various management scenarios by using simulated populations (see Population Dynamics chapter). Similar efforts toward understanding population dynamics of wild turkeys and the role of harvest are under way in many states. These studies should, in the next decade, permit added refinement of harvest regulations and the ability for states to establish population-management objectives.

Fall Turkey Seasons

Fall turkey regulations generally allow the harvest of birds of either sex, and season lengths vary widely. In eastern states with a fall turkey-hunting tradition, hunter numbers in fall exceed those in spring. For example, Pennsylvania had 280,000 fall turkey hunters in 1987 compared with only 206,000 spring hunters. In many states where fall turkey hunting has only recently been permitted, spring hunters greatly outnumber fall hunters.

Fall seasons have a greater potential than spring seasons to affect wild turkey populations. This is particularly true in years of poor reproduction, when a much higher proportion of the harvest can be adults (Little et al. 1990). Population modeling has recently been used to evaluate the effects of simulated levels of fall harvest on turkey populations. Using a model developed in Missouri, investigators found that population growth stabilized when the fall harvest reached 10 percent of the population. At a 15 percent harvest level, populations showed declines (see Population Dynamics chapter). Suchy et al. (1990) used radiotelemetry data from Iowa to model fall harvests. They concluded that fall harvests in small areas of public land with easy hunter access may reduce turkey densities substantially, particularly the densities of males. Their modeling indicated that a fall hen harvest of 15 to 20 percent would substantially reduce spring population densities.

Studies in Missouri (Vangilder unpublished data), have shown that less than 5 percent of marked hens were taken during a 2-week fall season on private lands with 3.8 to 5.0 hunters per square kilometer (10 to 13 per square mile) of timber. In southern Iowa, Little et al. (1990) observed hunter densities on heavily hunted public land that averaged 14.1 hunters per square kilometer of forest (36.5 per square mile), resulting in a fall harvest mortality rate that ranged from 11 percent for juvenile males to 24 percent for juvenile females. It seems clear that resource managers should attempt to determine the proportion of the fall population being harvested under existing regulations. Only through long-term population dynamics studies can a sound basis be established for setting fall seasons. When season formats must be set without knowledge of the potential long-term impacts on turkey populations, then conservative bag limits and season lengths are warranted if managers aim to have the population maintain itself or grow.

Harvest regulations are usually established according to input from 3 areas: (1) biology of the species, (2) public comment, and (3) administrative or legislative concerns. Biological information may include harvest and harvest trends, age ratios, nesting chronology, and gobbling counts. Additional facts and figures important in setting regulations are turkey-hunting pressure, hunter success, research findings, and hunter interference rates. Hunter density data are used to establish the number of quota permits in states such as Wisconsin and Massachusetts. In Iowa, when hunter interference rates exceed

33 percent in a particular zone, the recommendation is that license quotas be reduced to improve hunting quality (Jackson 1988).

Important in the regulatory process are the opinions of turkey hunters. Information from turkey hunters may be gathered through attitude surveys or by direct contact with special interest groups. Unsolicited comments also are received and considered. An attitude survey based on a random sample of turkey hunters is the best way of assessing the preferences and desires of the turkey-hunting public (Vangilder et al. 1990). Unsolicited comments, or comments from vocal minorities, often unduly influence regulations—especially when attitude survey data are not available. The concerns of the state agency administration or commission, or of the state legislature often are extremely influential in the regulations process. These concerns may or may not always be in the best interests of the resource or the resource user.

QUALITY HUNTING

Since 1975, spring turkey hunter numbers in New York have risen 134 percent. Similarly, turkey hunter numbers have risen 77 percent in Mississippi and 50 percent in Missouri. More so today than ever before, state wildlife agencies must deal with increasing hunter numbers and the effects on turkey populations. These agencies must also deal with the impact of regulation changes on hunting quality. Many regulations aimed at improving hunting quality also affect population management. Hunter quotas are an excellent example. Enacted to reduce hunter interference rates, quotas also affect harvests and therefore turkey populations. Similarly, regulations governing shot size, gauge restrictions, baiting, and even hunter orange all can have impacts on both harvest and populations. The management of turkey populations and turkey hunters are highly interrelated.

The term "quality" most often relates hunter density to turkey population density. Williams and Austin (1988), in a survey of Florida turkey hunters, concluded, "Many factors contributing to a good hunting experience are directly related to the density of the turkey population while those factors most often cited as degrading to the hunting experience were things that can be directly attributed to human activities, many of which can be dealt with through regulations." Furthermore, they suggested a "large standing population of turkeys may be as important as a large annual harvest." They added, "Management procedures that permit hunters to enjoy their hunting, whether they kill a turkey or not, may be more important than management procedures that are designed for maximum harvests."

A number of techniques have been used by states to limit hunter numbers. In states with limited turkey range

Managing hunters has become an important part of managing the wild turkey resource. *Photo by E. Kurzejeski, Missouri Department of Conservation.*

or ongoing restoration programs, hunters often must apply for permits within zones open to hunting. And, as in Iowa, multiple seasons may be held in each zone (Little 1980). In 1974, when turkey hunting was initiated in Iowa, 450 permits were distributed over 3 zones. Each zone had 2 7-day seasons. The primary management objective was to maintain a quality hunting experience. By 1979, 8 zones—each with 3 seasons (7, 7, and 11 days)—were opened to hunting. Hunter density in the southern zones in 1979 was estimated at 1 hunter per 0.9 square kilometer (2.3 per square mile) of forest (Little 1980) across all 3 seasons. Despite the ability of quota permits to regulate hunter numbers, ⅔ of the hunting pressure and harvest in Iowa that year occurred on only a third of the total habitat in 4 of the 8 counties open to hunting.

Estimates of hunter density on public lands ranged from 9.4 to 10.1 per square kilometer (24 to 26 per square mile) of forest compared with 1.8 to 4.9 (4.6 to 12.6) on "heavily hunted" private lands. Obviously the distribution of hunters within zones, and particularly on public lands, cannot easily be regulated through quota permits.

In 1987, Iowa separately zoned larger public hunting areas in an attempt to maintain quality spring gobbler hunting (Jackson 1988).

In Florida, Williams and Austin (1988) set a quota of 1.2 hunters per square kilometer (3 per square mile) on a state wildlife management area, with an objective of minimizing "annoying encounters between hunters." They monitored hunter satisfaction through mail questionnaires and oral interviews. In 2 years, only 5 percent of respondents indicated there were too many turkey hunters on the 10,000-hectare (24,700-acre) area.

In Wisconsin, turkey permits are also issued by quota. With an objective of limiting hunter interference, quotas are aimed at maintaining a density of 0.7 hunters per square kilometer (2 per square mile) of forest. In fall 1989 and spring 1990, quotas were raised experimentally in zone of southwestern Wisconsin to accommodate hunting pressure of 1.5 hunters per square kilometer (4 per square mile) of forest (Kubisiak et al. 1991). An evaluation of hunter and landowner attitudes indicated similar acceptance of both degrees of pressure.

In Missouri, spring turkey hunter densities range from 0.7 to 1.9 per square kilometer (2 to 5 per square mile) of forest in the southern parts of the state and from 3.8 to 5.8 hunters per square kilometer (10 to 15 per square mile) of forest in agricultural northern Missouri. An attitude survey conducted in 1988 (Vangilder et al. 1990) provided insights into hunter perceptions of hunter density and the actual number of times hunters were interfered with by other individuals.

A majority of hunters in Missouri indicated they perceived "many hunters" in the woods but hunter density "was not a problem." When asked how many hunters, other than those in their party, they encountered while spring turkey hunting, 72 percent of respondents indicated they encountered less than 4 hunters; 25 percent of the total saw none. The perception among Missouri spring turkey hunters that other hunters "are not a problem" may arise partly from the 30 percent hunter success rate and the density of gobblers.

As Williams and Austin (1988) suggested, many of the negative attributes of spring turkey hunting—particu-larly hunter densities and turkey densities—can be dealt with through regulations. Opening the spring gobbler season on a weekday has been used by some states as a method of distributing hunting effort without limiting permit sales. In Missouri, the spring season traditionally opens on Monday. Hunting pressure, as measured by the proportion of trips each day, indicates most pressure occurs on opening day and subsequent Saturdays.

Because Missouri turkey seasons have not opened on a Saturday, it is not possible to compare hunter effort in such a format. But the fact that the percentage of trips on the first Saturday of the season is only slightly less than the percentage on opening day suggests that a weekend opening date would increase hunter densities.

Another way of reducing hunter density during Missouri's spring season is to regulate the bag limit within the season structure. Hunters are permitted to harvest 2 birds, but only 1 may be taken during each week of the 2-week season. Typically, 65 percent of the Missouri spring harvest and 60 percent of trips occur the first week of the season. If a 2-bird bag were permitted at any time

Ensuring wild turkey population success and providing a sporting hunt are management objectives. *Photo by G. Smith.*

during the season, it is likely that higher hunter densities would occur in the early part of the season.

Reducing Hunting Accidents

Many regulations have been enacted to address aspects of quality other than hunter density. Most states prohibit the use of rifles for spring turkey hunting. The rationale is that the effective range of a shotgun requires a hunter to call the bird into range. In addition, the prohibition of rifles discourages road hunting and lessens the chance for severe accidents.

In New Jersey, hunters are required to carry a calling device, and it is not legal to attempt to stalk turkeys. Requiring hunters to have a call in possession encourages use of calls, thereby placing emphasis on traditional hunting techniques. The regulation against stalking is by admission "difficult to enforce." It is viewed, however, as a way of encouraging safe and ethical turkey hunting.

Both spring and fall turkey seasons are plagued with an alarming number of mistaken-for-game accidents. Consequently, a number of turkey-hunting regulations exist that are aimed at reducing the potential for hunting accidents. One of the more common regulations is the restriction on shot size. Another safety-oriented regulation requires a turkey hunter to affix a small yellow safety sticker to the shotgun's receiver. The sticker reads, "Be Safe." While nobody can evaluate the effectiveness of such a requirement, it is an excellent example of how wildlife agencies can emphasize turkey-hunting safety.

The wearing of hunter orange has reduced deer-hunting accidents. But because of hunter orange's potential negative effect on turkey-hunting success, only one state has adopted regulations requiring its use by turkey hunters (Pennsylvania). Studies indicate it is possible to call in and harvest turkeys while wearing hunter orange (Witter et al. 1982, Eriksen et al. 1985). But hunters participating in these studies indicated they felt hunter orange decreased their success. If hunter acceptance of using orange is low, then laws requiring its use while turkey hunting may result in a lack of compliance. If compliance remained low, then enactment of such laws would do little to reduce accident rates.

Most states rely on aggressive turkey hunter education and awareness programs as their attempt to reduce turkey-hunting accidents. Mandatory hunter education programs with modules on turkey hunting will probably be most effective because they will reach a majority of turkey hunters.

Tradition's Influence

Some regulations, enacted in an effort to maintain quality or tradition, continue to be sources of controversy among wildlife professionals and sportsmen. For instance, baiting and decoys are legal and accepted practices in many states. In other states, however, both are illegal under the contention they are unethical.

Federal laws for decades have prohibited the hunting of migratory birds over bait. Harvesting waterfowl or doves over baited areas is viewed as an unfair advantage for hunters. Baiting of wild turkeys, where legal, can be a successful method of providing opportunities for harvest, even during the spring season. The practice of baiting exemplifies the impact that regulations can have on ethical questions. In states where baiting of turkeys is legal, the practice is often widely used and accepted among sportsmen. These same sportsmen might find the baiting of waterfowl unacceptable, even if it became legal. Similarly, where baiting of turkeys is illegal, the general perception among hunters is that the practice constitutes an unfair advantage.

The definition of ethical hunting behavior will always be one of a personal nature. Wildlife agencies can and do direct the sportsman's thinking on ethics through the regulatory process. But the question of what constitutes the ethical pursuit of wildlife will continue to be strongly guided by what is traditionally acceptable.

Most states estimate the costs of wild turkey restoration programs at from $300 to $500 per bird.

III

Wild Turkey Habitat and Management

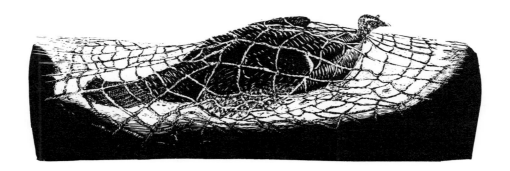

Chapter 13

HABITAT ANALYSIS AND ASSESSMENT

William F. Porter
Faculty of Environmental and Forest Biology
College of Environmental Science and Forestry
State University of New York
Syracuse, New York

"When a manager asks himself whether a given piece of land is suitable for a given species, he must realize that he is asking no simple question, but rather he is facing one of the great enigmas of animate nature." — Aldo Leopold, *Game Management*

When we're out in rural or wild areas with people interested in turkeys, we will often hear comments such as "This is exceptional habitat," or "This area is not suitable for wild turkeys." Such opinions refer to the perceived potential for an area to support a higher population than is typical of the region, or not to support a population at all.

Without doubt, turkey biologists and experienced hunters can walk through an area and judge its relative suitability for wild turkeys. What features do they look for? By what process do they draw their conclusions?

Habitat modeling is an attempt to identify these features and mimic the mental processes of assessment. Models are abstractions of a more complex system or process (Figure 1). The intent in developing habitat models is to provide a means for any competent biologist, even one having no experience with wild turkeys, to accurately assess an area's habitat suitability.

An important motivation for developing habitat models was the National Environmental Policy Act of 1969. This law requires an assessment of the likely effects of all federally funded projects on wildlife habitat, as well as on other natural resources.

When assessments show that projects will significantly affect wildlife habitat, ways to reduce the harm must be examined. Because such action may add substantial costs to the project, assessments of likely impact must be capable of withstanding challenges. What's needed is an objective, reliable, and justifiable assessment procedure.

Habitat assessment models are based on habitat analysis. This chapter describes how biologists identify environmental characteristics that are important to the wild turkey. Analytical techniques presented here emphasize traditional habitat preference, and more recent regression and multivariate statistical analyses. Then the chapter describes habitat models used today in assessing habitat for wild turkeys.

Two basic approaches to modeling are presented: (1) the Habitat Suitability Index models (Schamberger and Farmer 1978, U.S. Fish and Wildlife Service 1981, Schamberger and Krohn 1982) and (2) the Pattern Recognition models (Williams et al. 1978). My intent is to provide an overview for wild turkey enthusiasts, managers, and administrators, with the hope that it will enhance their communication with biologists who use these techniques.

HABITAT ANALYSIS

The foundation for habitat models is the ecological study of habitat relationships, *habitat analysis*. The goal is a comprehensive understanding of the biological and physical features, their interactions, and the mechanisms by which they influence wild turkey survival and repro-

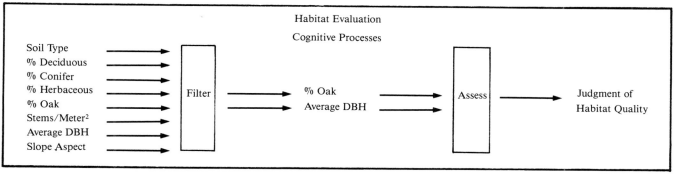

Figure 1. Hypothesized model of the cognitive processes by which habitat assessments are made from examinations of a multitude of environmental features.

duction. As I will discuss, this analysis provides the ecological integrity of the habitat assessment models.

Our approach frequently begins with a correlation of patterns of habitat characteristics that allow reliable prediction. Once these correlative patterns are identified, we begin to formulate and test hypotheses about the underlying causal relationships.

Habitat analyses are built on 2 sets of variables and a single key assumption. One set of variables is obviously habitat characteristics; the other set of variables is attributes of the wildlife population. The assumption is this: The wildlife population, specifically in its attribute we measure, is responding to habitat conditions.

The procedure seems straightforward. It is not. Great care must be exercised in selecting variables for analysis and in applying the assumption.

Habitat Variables

Selecting habitat variables is more complex than you might suspect. As Whitmore (1981) observed, biologists are prone to measure a large array of characteristics as a substitute for thinking. Two criteria need to be applied in selecting variables for measurement:

1. Is there any logical reason or empirical evidence to suggest the characteristics are ecologically meaningful to the survival and reproduction of the species?
2. Can the characteristic be readily measured with a sufficient degree of precision (in the statistical sense)?

Consider the first criterion. If we measure the wrong habitat characteristics, we waste time and money; even the most sophisticated analysis will not succeed. This is a difficult criterion because there is no way to know beforehand which characteristic is right or wrong.

When we consider data collection in the field, the greatest costs are generally associated with travel time to the sample plot, not the time spent at the plot measuring.

So it is important to think carefully about the rationale for each variable and not proceed with a "shotgun" approach.

Ideally, the biologists should be able to state a hypothesis about the potential ecological relationship between each chosen habitat characteristic and the species. However, if we are to err, we should err by measuring too many characteristics at each sample plot, rather than too few.

The second criterion is easier to satisfy. The measurements of some characteristics are confined to a relatively narrow range of values. Measurements of some variables by different people result in consistent values. However, other characteristics are naturally highly variable or prone to measurement error.

Noon (1981) suggests a rule of thumb: To be valuable, 90 percent of the sample observations for a specific characteristic must fall within 10 percent of the mean value. Achieving this goal is possible because in calculating a standard deviation for a mean, we divide the sum of the differences between our observations and sample mean by the number of observations.

$$s = \sqrt{\Sigma (X_i - X)^2 / n - 1} \qquad (1)$$

Where:

X_i represents individual sample values;

X is the sample mean;

n is the number of observations.

As the number of observations grows, the standard deviation becomes smaller. With sufficient samples, we reduce the range of values within plus or minus 2 standard deviations (90 percent) of the mean. In cases where natural variation is high, thousands of samples may be needed, many more samples than feasible. If preliminary sampling suggests such a situation, serious consideration must be given to rejecting the characteristic or measuring it in a different way.

Wildlife Population Response Variables

Wildlife response, ideally, is measured in terms of population density, reproduction, or physiological vigor. Suppose our primary interest is in identifying the habitat characteristics of areas that most influence population densities of wild turkeys. The measurement of density can be an absolute estimate or an index of relative abundance. A difference in density between 2 sites suggests differences in habitat quality.

We proceed by measuring a variety of habitat features and identifying those that are dissimilar in the 2 areas. Note the implicit assumption: Population density at both sites is reflecting some habitat feature that we can and will ultimately measure.

Failure of the assumption that density is responding primarily to current habitat conditions can lead to problems in the analysis. For instance, Figure 2a displays populations at 2 sites at their ecological carrying capacity. Site A is capable of supporting a higher population than Site B. If our population survey technique is sound, the difference will be apparent in the measurement. Figure 2b, however, shows the same 2 sites when the assumption is violated. The population in A is not at carrying capacity. It may be recovering from a crash induced by severe weather, or it may be low because of high rates of predation or hunter harvest. Regardless of the cause, if we were unaware that the population was well below ecological carrying capacity, our conclusions about habitat conditions would change, perhaps radically.

An alternative to population density is to use some measure of physiological condition as the response parameter. This tactic has intuitive appeal because physiological condition seems more directly linked with habitat conditions. Within ecological regions, healthier turkeys are associated with better habitat conditions.

Health can be measured in a number of ways, including body growth rates, body mass at a given age, age of first reproduction, fat deposits, and blood chemistry. The difficulty with physiological indicators is that they, too, are influenced by position of the population on the growth curve. With increasing intrapopulation competition for resources as the population grows to its maximum, decline in physiological parameters is expected. So comparing the fat deposits of turkeys from Sites A and B could lead to erroneous conclusions.

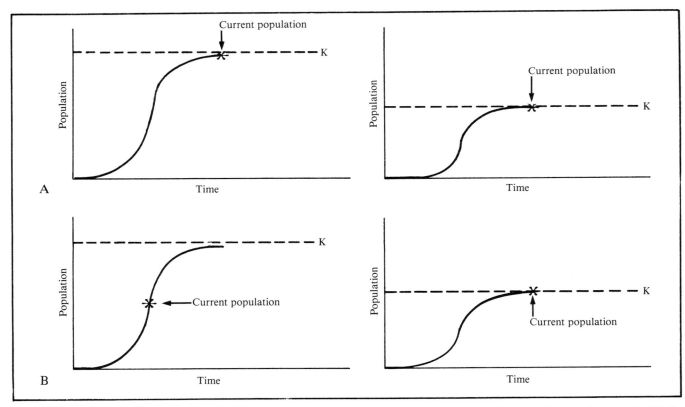

Figure 2. Population density is not an infallible indicator of habitat quality. If populations on 2 sites are both at ecological carrying capacity (K), the indicator is sound. However, populations may not be at K, and unless we know the true position of the population relative to K, inferences would be in error.

If we can support the assumption that all populations are at the same relative position on the growth curve, modern habitat analysis is a logical extension of the 2-site scenario. Measurements are taken at a series of sites and examined, using statistical techniques such as correlation and regression.

Correlation and Regression Analysis

When we take a series of measurements on population or habitat variables, we likely will observe some variation. If we can assume this variation is distributed normally (most of the measured values cluster around a mean, with progressively fewer values at the extremes of the range), we can submit these measurements to parametric statistical analyses.

Correlation analysis measures the intensity of linear association between variables and identifies general patterns. It answers the following question: Do the measurements on the population and habitat characteristics taken from across the sites show similar trends in variation (direct correlation) or opposite trends (inverse correlation)? Correlation analysis allows the user to quantify these trends and determine whether they are likely to be real or something we would expect to occur in random measurements.

While correlation analysis seeks only patterns of variation, regression analysis allows the examination of hypothesized cause-and-effect relationships. Wildlife population variables typically are defined as *dependent* on the habitat variables. The population characteristics vary only as a response to the independent habitat variables. Regression analysis, in its simplest form, includes a population (dependent) variable and a habitat (independent) variable, in mathematical form:

$$Y = B_0 + B_1 X_1 + e \qquad (2)$$

Where:

Y is the population (dependent variable);

X is the habitat (independent variable);

B_0 is a mathematical constant representing the intercept point on the Y axis;

B_1 is the slope of the line relating Y and X;

e is the variation in Y that is not related to X.

We know that populations frequently respond to many habitat variables. We can extend the regression technique to include multiple habitat variables using the mathematical form:

$$Y = B_0 + B_1 X_1 + B_2 X_2 + e \qquad (3)$$

X_1 represents the first habitat variable, and B_1 is its slope; X_2 is the second habitat variable, and B_2 is its slope. We can add as many habitat variables to this equation as we like, as long as our sample size is greater than the number of independent variables.

Multiple regression is valuable because it gives us means to sort out unimportant variables. Using stepwise regression, we can determine which habitat variables are contributing to improvements in predicting the dependent variable. A *significance level* (i.e., a statistical test) is applied to provide a standard rule for including or excluding a particular variable. Those variables excluded are considered unimportant to determining habitat condition and are dropped from further analyses.

Multiple regression also provides an indication of the relative importance of each variable. If the habitat variables are standardized so that the differences in variation due to scale of measures (e.g., some in meters, others in kilometers) are removed, the *B* coefficients provide an indication of the relative importance of the habitat variable. The larger the *B* coefficients, the more important the variable. If the sign of the *B* coefficient is negative, the relationship between the variable (in combination with others in the equation) and the dependent variable is considered to be inverse.

In addition to resting on the assumption that the measurements for each variable come from a normal distribution, regression analysis requires 2 key assumptions. First, all of the independent variables are assumed to be measured without any error. For example, if our sampling units are townships and one habitat variable is percent of the township in forest, we must be certain that percent forest has been measured accurately in each township. Second, we must assume that the habitat variables vary independently of one another; the correlation among them is statistically insignificant. The application of regression analysis and the importance of these assumptions are explained in more detail in references such as Sokal and Rohlf (1981) and Zar (1974).

Ideally, the application of regression analysis should be done in 2 stages. In the first stage, random subsets of the data are drawn and used to formulate the regression equation. The resulting equation represents a hypothesis for testing. The evaluation is conducted with the balance of the data.

Multivariate Statistical Analysis

Because of the importance of the assumption that habitat variables are to be independent, we need a means of identifying any intercorrelation among variables and minimizing it. Anyone who has ever done habitat analysis knows that habitat variables often are highly intercorrelated. Multivariate statistical techniques provide a procedure for objectively identifying habitat attributes that are statistically independent.

Factor analysis is a multivariate technique that is particularly helpful for exploring a data set that has many variables and extensive intercorrelation. The objective in factor analysis is to structure the variation for all variables by creating new variables called *factors*. Each factor is a linear combination of a selected subset of the original variables. Each subset is composed of variables that are intercorrelated, and each factor has the distinction of being statistically independent of all others.

We can describe the characteristics of each factor in terms of those variables that are highly correlated with it and use the factor in other statistical analyses. Also, we can draw a single variable that is highly correlated with each factor (and no other) and use it in subsequent analyses. In either case, we have objectively reduced the data set by identifying unique variation in the data and eliminating the variables that add no information. Because eliminated variables are correlated with retained variables, most of the original information content is still available for subsequent analyses.

A second multivariate technique useful to habitat analysis is discriminant function analysis (DFA). While regression analysis seeks to predict the value of a dependent variable as a continuous function of a set of independent variables, DFA is designed to classify an observation (such as a given site) into discrete categories (e.g., utilized versus nonutilized habitat).

DFA has intuitive appeal because we suspect that wildlife populations respond, simultaneously, to a multitude of variables. Univariate statistical analysis allows us to examine differences between utilized and nonutilized habitat based on a single variable (e.g., abundance of oak trees more than 30 centimeters [12 inches] in diameter at breast height). This examination may result in poor discrimination between areas being used and those not being used by turkeys because oak trees aren't the only characteristic turkeys require.

A bivariate approach is designed specifically to enhance discrimination by incorporating 2 variables, such as abundance of oak trees and the percent of the area in grass (Figure 3). Multivariate DFA is simply an extension of this approach to include 3 or more habitat characteristics in the analysis.

As an example, Lazarus and Porter (1985) used factor analysis and discriminant function analysis to develop a model to classify nest sites and random sites to their respective categories. A total of 120 variables were hypothesized to potentially influence nest site selection. Measurements for each variable were taken at nests and random points in the study area. Factor analysis identified a set of statistically independent variables in the

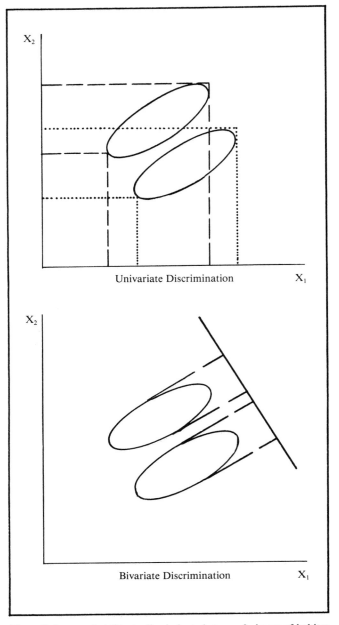

Figure 3. Increased ability to discriminate between 2 classes of habitat conferred by a bivariate approach to analysis (National Wild Turkey Symposium 5:72).

data set, and one original variable was drawn from each factor for further analysis. The habitat variables retained from factor analysis were submitted to DFA, and the procedure identified variables most helpful in classifying the sites. From the 120 original variables, factor analysis and DFA identified 4 variables that could classify nest and non-nest (random) sites with at least 89 percent accuracy. These 4 variables formed the basis for several hypotheses on ecological cause-and-effect relationships.

Photo by L. Williams.

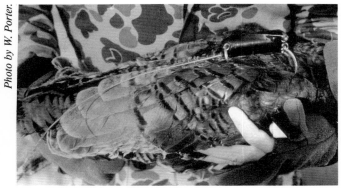

Photo by W. Porter.

Radio instrumentation of wild turkeys has provided much useful information for management.

Locating instrumented turkey during a study of brood habitat in clearings. *Photo by G. Wunz, Pennsylvania Game Commission.*

While multivariate statistics is not a new field, it only recently has become part of the standard battery of analytical tests in habitat studies. The popularity of multivariate statistics is traceable to its increasing availability on microcomputers, as well as to the intuitive similarity to habitat concepts. As a result, while stringent assumptions are stated in most texts describing multivariate statistics, the robustness of the techniques (i.e., degree to which they will tolerate deviations from the assumptions) is still uncertain. Capen (1981) provides a comprehensive overview of the application of these techniques in wildlife studies and should be consulted concurrently with an appropriate statistical text (e.g., Morrison 1976) during the design phase of any habitat investigation.

Behavioral Response Variables and Preference Analysis

Within the past 2 decades, biologists have given increasing attention to a completely different response variable, behavior. The expense and difficulties of getting good population data led to exploration of alternative approaches. With the advent of transistors and the subsequent miniaturization of radio transmitters, biologists began to pursue radiotelemetry as a means of acquiring good information on behavior. By the early 1970s, reliable equipment was available at reasonable costs. The number of telemetry studies on wild turkeys escalated rapidly.

Radiotelemetry has several distinct advantages in behavioral studies. Radio equipment used on wild turkeys allows the biologist to locate an individual, anytime of the day or night, from a distance of 1.5 to 5 kilometers (1 to 3 miles), depending on terrain. Because each transmitter operates on its own individual frequency, the biologist can distinguish among many birds in an area that carry them. Radio signals provide information on location and on whether an individual is active (i.e., moving or not). A considerable amount of information can be gained with no need for the biologist to see the animal (and be seen), and potentially alter its behavior.

What are the effects of the radio tag on a wild turkey's behavior and reproduction? The question is a matter of frequent concern. Research has shown that radio packages normally have no effect on survival, dispersal, growth, and reproduction (e.g., Johnson 1971, Greenwood and Sargeant 1973, Nenno and Healy 1979). Observations of radio-tagged wild turkeys showed that attachment of the device altered behavior initially but that behavior returned to normal within 3 to 8 days.

There are 2 approaches to using radiotelemetry data in habitat preference analysis. The most common approach involves classification of the study area into relatively homogeneous vegetation cover types. Telemetry is used to record a sample of locations for each radio-tagged bird through a time interval (e.g., month, season, or year). The number of locations occurring in each cover type represent the relative amount of time a turkey spends there.

In traditional preference analysis, this distribution of *observed* use is compared with the distribution of use *expected* if the turkey were simply moving through the cover types randomly (i.e., showing no preference). If a turkey spends proportionately more time in a cover type than expected, we conclude this type is preferred. But if the observed use is less than expected, we conclude the type is avoided.

Several statistical procedures have been applied to assess objectively whether observed use differs from expected use. Most common is the Chi-square goodness-of-fit test, a nonparametric analysis (e.g., Zar 1974) that takes the form:

$$X^2 = \Sigma \ \{(O_i - E_i)^2 / E_i\} \qquad (4)$$

Where:

　O_i is observed use of cover type i;

　E_i is expected use of cover type i.

There are several other forms of this basic test. Most widely used is that of Neu et al. (1974), which provides a confidence interval around the estimate of observed use for each habitat type and tests for differences from expected use.

Computers help store and analyze data. *Photo by W. Porter.*

Measurements at nest site. We now have quantitative data on nesting sites and nesting success.

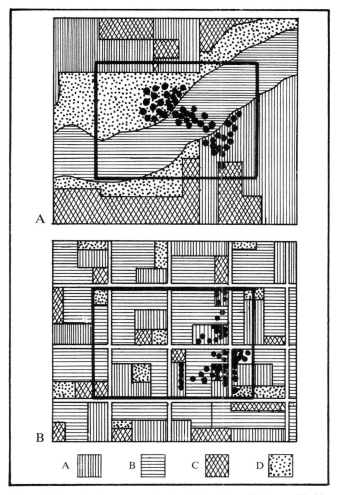

Figure 4. Example of an aggregated habitat pattern. Patterns of habitat dispersion can have a significant impact on habitat preference analysis (see Porter and Church 1987).

The observed-versus-expected approach has 2 important limitations. First, the statistical comparisons are sensitive to the dispersion pattern of cover types. Delineation of study-area boundaries (or alternatively, home-range boundaries) defines the proportional distribution of cover types on the study area, and thus determines the values for *expected* use. Where cover types are arranged in an aggregated pattern (Figure 4), small changes in delineation of study-area boundaries can have dramatic effects on the statistical analyses.

Porter and Church (1988) showed that unless the dispersion of cover types occurs in a statistically regular pattern (Poole 1974:105), any change in study-area boundaries may reverse conclusions about preference and avoidance. Because study-area boundaries are generally defined somewhat arbitrarily (based on logistical rather than biological rationale), inferences about preferences are suspect. Similarly, home-range boundaries depend on the technique used for delineation. There are many techniques. Which is the correct one is generally open to debate.

The traditional approach fails to include any measures of juxtaposition and interspersion of cover types. These characteristics are critical to habitat for wild turkeys. For example, nests frequently occur along edges between forest and open field cover types where vegetation 0 to 1 meter tall is well developed. Broods use old fields (for feeding) that are close to forests (for protection). (See chapter 14, Habitat Requirements.) The importance of edges and combinations of cover types is not readily discerned by examining preference and avoidance of individual cover types.

The second approach to preference analysis focuses exclusively on observed use. It involves dividing the study area into units, or cells, of equal size. Habitat characteristics such as areal coverage by each cover type, diversity of cover types, length of edge between forest and field cover types, and average diameter of trees can be measured for each cell. The use of each cell is determined by the number of telemetry locations occurring within it. Only those cells in which at least 1 telemetry observation occurs are included in analyses. This approach obviates the need to define *expected* use. The analyses are conducted by using regression and multivariate statistics.

A key decision that must be made before doing the study is the size of the cell. The principal criteria are (1) to maximize the number of cells that can be entered in the analysis (maximize sample size) and (2) to maximize the variation in habitat characteristics and distribution of use across the cells.

As cells become larger, within-cell variation in habitat generally increases. But as cells become larger, fewer cells contain an increasing proportion of observations and thus the total number of cells containing at least a single telemetry observation declines.

As cells decrease in size, the variation in habitat characteristics, such as number of cover types or amount of edge, declines. The range of values for number of telemetry observations also declines.

What is the optimal size? It depends on sizes and dispersion patterns of both habitat and movements. Extreme cell sizes (too large or too small) can seriously limit the analysis.

An optimum size must be sought through a consideration of several different cell sizes. Modifications to cell size can be accomplished easily with computerized systems, or various sizes can be tested by manually adjusting cell sizes and observing effects on habitat characteristics and use.

There is no single, correct procedure for habitat analysis. A great deal of forethought is essential to decisions on selecting the variables, measurement technique, sample size, cell size, and specific statistical tests. Exploring the data with lots of different analyses is important, however. This approach, combined with thinking, can lead to identifying previously unseen relationships.

Finally, the most important step is to tease the ecological implications and management applications from the test results. Any good computer analyst can feed the data in and get the test results out. The secret is in recognizing the patterns that emerge, the support or refutation of a hypothesis, and the germ of a new hypothesis. This step is a dialectical synthesis of statistical data with our current understanding of ecological relationships to form a new description or explanation. One application is the creation of a habitat assessment model.

HABITAT ASSESSMENT

Multivariate analysis helps us conceive of habitat as a complex of biological and physical gradients that influence the ability of a species to survive and reproduce. Along each gradient are points at which conditions are more suited to meeting the requirements of the wild turkey for survival and reproduction. The relationship between habitat suitability and a series of gradients might be depicted as a cloud of points (Figure 5). Suitability of a given environment depends on a combination of features. The combination of gradients A and B can be displayed graphically, and the area of overlap can be thought of as defining a region that meets both habitat criteria.

Ideal habitat conditions occur at a single point or cloud of points where the suitability for both gradients is at the optimum. This point cloud is theoretical. In reality, we may have thousands of acres on which conditions match it. In these areas, we can expect wild turkeys to accumulate all the energy and nutrients necessary to survive, and we can expect them to have sufficient additional resources to reproduce at the maximum rate.

As we move away from the optimum, suitability declines. Habitat conditions are classified as *marginal* when turkeys are unable to accumulate sufficient energy to reproduce in most years. Conditions are defined as *unsuitable* where turkeys are unable to even survive through a year. Habitat requirements are generally described by many gradients. Defining the region of suitability is a mathematical extension of this graphical approach into more dimensions.

Habitat Suitability Index Method

The U.S. Fish and Wildlife Service adopted a procedure to reflect this idea and called it the Habitat Suitability Index (HSI). In the HSI system, gradients are variables and their suitability is assigned a relative value associated with its quality. For ease of use, suitability index (SI) values always range from 0 to 1.0. A value of 0 (zero) represents habitat conditions unsuited to survival and reproduction, and 1.0 represents the ideal condition. In an assessment, an SI value is determined for

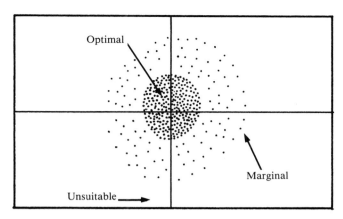

Figure 5. Two dimensions of habitat and the cloud that defines suitable habitat simultaneously on both dimensions. Habitat conditions can be classified as unsuitable, marginal, and suitable. Only suitable conditions permit survival and reproduction with consistency.

each geographical region that is ecologically homogeneous (Schamberger and Farmer 1978, Schamberger and Krohn 1982, U.S. Fish and Wildlife Service 1981).

In the HSI approach, the interaction of the gradients, or variables, is represented as simple mathematical equations in which suitability index values are added or multiplied. This tactic has the advantage of allowing additional information to be readily incorporated. For instance, we know that the presence of one feature can compensate for the absence of another. So we might portray requirement for a given combination of features as:

$$H = (A + B)/2 \qquad (5)$$

Where:

H is habitat condition;

A is SI value for gradient A;

B is SI value for gradient B.

Dividing the sum of the SI values by 2 gives an average *(arithmetic mean)* of the values, accommodating the compensatory relationship and keeping the mathematical result between 0 and 1.0.

We also know that some environmental gradients are more important than others to the determination of habitat conditions. This reality can be incorporated into the mathematical model by giving numerical weight to a particular gradient, as in the example below:

$$H = (A + 2B)/3 \qquad (6)$$

Here B is considered twice as important as A. Dividing by 3 gives us the arithmetic mean, maintaining the value for H within the 0–1.0 range.

Some features may be absolutely critical. If the HSI value for a given gradient is 0, the habitat is unsuitable. This is represented by a multiplicative relationship:

$$H = (A \times B)^{1/2} \qquad (7)$$

Here both A and B are critical. If the SI for either is 0, H is 0 and the site is judged unsuitable. When both A and B are greater than 0, but less than 1.0, the product becomes smaller than either A or B and more difficult to interpret. Taking the square root (raising to the ½ power) alleviates this problem by providing the *geometric mean*.

For example, assume we wish to assess the impact of timber harvest of all oak trees from 100 hectares (250 acres) of a 1,000-hectare (2,500-acre) management area. To do this, we compare the suitability of an area before and after cutting. For the sake of simplicity, assume our model contains just 3 variables and the HSI curves are as shown in Figures 6a–c. The equations reflect needs for food and cover:

$$H_f = (O + G + S)/3 \qquad (8)$$
$$H_c = \{3(O) + S\}/4 \qquad (9)$$

Where:

H_f is habitat conditions for food;

H_c is habitat conditions for cover;

O is percent of area with oaks greater than 25 centimeters (10 inches) diameter breast height;

G is percent of area in grassland;

S is percent of area in shrubland.

Taking values from Table 1 and using Equations 8 and 9, we can generate a suitability score for the area prior to timber harvest:

Food value is $(0.8 + 0.9 + 0.5)/3 = 0.73$

Cover value is $(3 \times 0.8 + 0.5)/4 = 0.72$

The HSI approach assumes the lowest value is the limiting factor, so the overall value for this management area is 0.72.

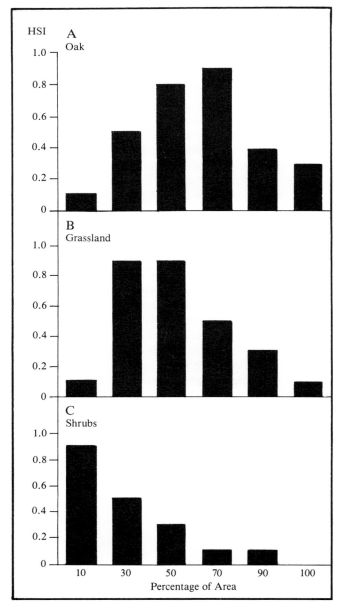

Figures 6a–c. HSI curves are hypotheses of the relationship between habitat suitability and an important environmental feature (Schroeder 1985).

Table 1. Values for illustration of Habitat Suitability Index (HSI) assessment technique under a treatment converting 25 percent of the area from oak to shrub cover type.

Variable	Pretreatment		Posttreatment	
	Area	HSI	Area	HSI
oak	50 percent	0.8	25 percent	0.5
grassland	25 percent	0.9	25 percent	0.9
shrub	25 percent	0.5	50 percent	0.3

Now assume that 5 years after cutting the oak, the area is occupied by shrubs. This changes the area's suitability:

$$\text{Food value is } (0.5+0.9+0.3)/3 = 0.57$$
$$\text{Cover value is } (3\times0.5+0.3)/4 = 0.45$$

Thus the new value is 0.45, and our assessment suggests that a marked reduction in habitat quality will occur with the treatment.

This system for habitat evaluation relies on a comprehensive understanding of the ecology of the species. The models require answers to 4 essential questions:

1. Which environmental gradients constitute important habitat characteristics?
2. What is the relationship between habitat suitability and the range of values on each gradient?
3. What is the interaction among habitat characteristics?
4. Are some habitat characteristics more important than others?

Pattern Recognition

While the approach used in developing HSI models emphasizes understanding, other methods of assessment emphasize prediction. The most common of these approaches is Pattern Recognition, or PATREC. The PATREC procedures are drawn directly from the medical profession.

Physicians look for an array of symptoms associated exclusively with a specific disease. Regardless of the physiological relationship between each symptom and the disease, the fact that the symptoms and the disease coincide allows diagnostic prediction. When there is sufficient confidence in the prediction, a treatment can be prescribed.

Rarely can physicians be certain that a particular symptom is a predictor of a particular disease. In most instances, confidence in the predictive value of a symptom is expressed in statistical probability. Confidence increases with the addition of several symptoms because diseases sharing only a single symptom can be eliminated. Physicians search for key symptoms by comparing those people who ultimately prove to have the disease and those who do not.

Predictive approaches to habitat assessment attempt to discern patterns of habitat characteristics that are associated with high and low wildlife populations. Biologists search for environmental patterns that coincide with high and low populations. Through many comparisons,

Table 2. Relationships among habitat measurements and habitat conditions illustrating the application of Pattern Recognition in habitat assessment. High and low population values represent the proportion of sample units likely to be associated with a given habitat condition.

Variable	Measurement centimeters (inches)	Condition	High population	Low population
average DBH	<5 (<2)	unsuitable	0.1	0.6
	5–40 (2–16)	marginal	0.4	0.3
	>40 (>16)	optimal	0.5	0.1
percentage of oak	<10	unsuitable	0.2	0.8
	10–35	marginal	0.3	0.1
	>35	optimal	0.5	0.1

they can determine the probability that a given habitat characteristic will coincide with either population level (Table 2).

In its simplest form, a PATREC model is developed through a 3-step process:

1. Biologists identify areas that support high and low populations for a species such as the wild turkey;
2. They identify a set of environmental gradients that vary independently of one another, and they determine the position of the tract of land on each gradient through measurement;
3. They look for patterns in these sets of gradients by estimating the probability of encountering a particular condition in a location where the population is high or low.

A more complex extension of this approach to a predictive model is to incorporate Bayesian statistics. This area of statistics improves our predictions by including information from other sources. In practice, this technique is illustrated by assuming a large geographic region divided into units, or cells, such as square miles. A biologist answers a series of questions:

1. What is the highest population that can be expected to persist in a given area, long-term? What is the lowest (nonzero)?

This approach provides the *high-density standard* and *low-density standard* and allows calculation of a midpoint population level.

2. What percent of the area within the geographic region supports populations higher than the midpoint density?

This approach provides the *prior probability* that any randomly selected square-mile unit in the region would contain a high-density population.

Calculating the value for (1.0 − *prior probability [High]*) gives the prior probability of encountering

a low population density in a randomly selected square-mile unit, or *(prior probability [Low])*.

3. What is the possible range of values on the gradient for each habitat characteristic? Are there subranges of the variable that are known to confer optimal, marginal, and unsuitable habitat conditions?
4. For each habitat characteristic, what percent of the square-mile units having a high population also have a measurement for the characteristic that falls in the optimal range? Marginal range? Unsuitable range? (The relative frequencies in the 3 ranges must total 1.0.)

This procedure is repeated for all habitat characteristics at low population densities.

As an example:

Assume the high-density standard =

7.7 turkeys/kilometer^2 (20 turkeys/mile^2)

Assume the low-density standard =

0.8 turkeys/kilometer^2 (2 turkeys/mile^2)

Assume the prior probability$_{HIGH}$ = 0.6

prior probability$_{LOW}$ = 0.4

We go out to a particular square-mile unit and measure a sample of trees. The average DBH (diameter at breast height) is 17.6 centimeters (6.9 inches), and the percent of trees that are an oak species is 84.

Calculation 1

High population = 0.6 × (0.4 × 0.5) = 0.120

Where:

0.6 is the prior probability for a high density;

0.4 is the value for the condition class containing 17.6 centimeters (7 inches) at high density;

0.5 is the value for condition containing 84 percent at high density.

Low population = 0.4 × (0.3 × 0.1) = 0.012

Calculation 2

The probability that the square-kilometer or square-mile unit (land-area units are arbitrary, so either will do) will contain a high population density is calculated:

0.12/(0.12 + 0.012) = 0.91

Where:

0.12 is the high-population value;

0.012 is the low-population value.

The probability that the square-mile unit will contain a low population density is calculated similarly:

$$0.012/(0.12 + 0.012) = 0.09$$

Calculation 3

The predicted population on the area is computed:

$$7.7 \times 0.91 + 0.8 \times 0.09 = 7 \text{ birds/kilometer}^2$$
$$20 \times 0.91 + 2 \times 0.09 = 18 \text{ birds/mile}^2$$

Evaluating Assessment Models

There are 5 principal criteria for determining the relative merit of these or any habitat assessment models: precision, accuracy, resolution, cost, and ecological integrity.

Precision (in the statistical sense) and cost are relatively easy to test. Precision refers to the ability to get 2 or more observers to measure an attribute and arrive at the same value. Cost is obviously a function of the time, salary, travel, and supplies necessary to get the measures and run the calculations. But tests of accuracy, resolution, and ecological integrity are more troublesome.

Examination of accuracy involves comparing predicted habitat conditions to actual conditions as verified by population levels. To conduct such a test requires 2 important assumptions: (1) population levels are responding solely to measurable habitat conditions; and (2) densities are at biological maximum or ecological carrying capacity (Caughley 1979).

If populations are not responding to the habitat variables we measure, or are at a density lower than maximum for the ecozone, then the population will not be representative of true habitat conditions. We know that predation, competition, and the effects of weather are not generally measured, yet they influence populations. For wild turkeys, legal and illegal harvest may have the greatest impact on population dynamics. The validity of our 2 assumptions is therefore questionable at best.

Perhaps more important, tests of accuracy and resolution require a good estimate of actual population size. For wild turkeys, as for most wildlife populations, data on population size are very expensive to gather. Harvest statistics offer an avenue and can provide an index (relative measure) or a direct estimate. Use of harvest data, however, is not simple (e.g., Caughley 1977) and requires good data on harvest and unit of hunter effort. Few states have these data available.

In habitat assessment, resolution is important in 2 contexts. Resolution refers to the assessment's ability to distinguish between 2 conditions. Higher resolution indicates an ability to identify progressively smaller differences in habitat condition.

The key question is this: What level of resolution is ecologically meaningful? Is the difference between 0.6 and 0.7 important? What about 0.72 and 0.73? Few studies have examined this question. Bayer and Porter (1988), examining forest-dwelling songbirds, found that even the best models could produce consistent results only when broad classes of HSI values were used (0, 0.1 to 0.5, and 0.6 to 1.0).

Resolution also refers to the size of geographic units for the assessment. In assessing habitat for wild turkeys, should we examine compartments (100 to 1,000 hectares, 250 to 2,500 acres) because they are a standard unit on national forests, or townships (9,000 hectares, 22,000 acres) because they are standard for statewide data bases? Layman and Barrett (1986) suggest that units for testing should be smaller than the home range of the animal. Or we might consider the area occupied by a population deme (i.e., an area in which all individuals have an equal probability of encountering all other individuals for breeding). This is an area that has only recently begun to receive attention from researchers, and few concrete guidelines exist.

Ecological integrity is the most difficult criterion to evaluate. Ecological relationships form the core of HSI models. Yet to defend the mathematical relationships portrayed in these models requires a comprehensive understanding of interactions among habitat, behavior, and population dynamics. Such an understanding does not exist for the wild turkey or any other vertebrate. The evaluation is limited to an assessment of the degree to which the model corresponds to existing ecological theory and empirical data.

Applications of HSI and PATREC habitat evaluations to wild turkeys are few, but those available conclude that resolution is the most immediate concern. Schroeder (1985) developed a Habitat Suitability Index for the eastern wild turkey. The HSI curves and equations represent a good synthesis of our knowledge but require adjustment to fit local situations. Kurzejeski and Lewis (1985) applied PATREC model to an assessment of Missouri turkey habitat, using harvest statistics to estimate population levels. Statewide applications seriously underestimated populations and were judged unsuccessful, but evaluations of smaller, ecologically homogeneous regions were successful. Regional models were significantly improved by including seasonally important habitat characteristics.

There is rapid integration of habitat assessment models with geographic information systems (GIS). Habitat is inherently spatial, and biologists often work with maps that show roads, vegetation types, and management history. If we divide a map of a management area into cells of uniform size (such as already described for Pattern Recognition), we can begin to attribute a series of characteristics to each cell. Instead, we may wish to divide our area into cover types or compartments of irregular shape. A GIS is simply a way to keep track of the data for each cell or compartment.

Geographic information systems offer 2 key advantages to habitat assessment.

First, they allow easy sorting and display of characteristics. A biologist can establish a series of criteria and display all the areas that meet them. For instance, we might wish to display all cells that contain both forest dominated by oak and open areas in pasture. With modern computer programs, a data base can be established and such a display can be accomplished in a matter of a few keystrokes.

Second, GIS allow examination of proximity variables. Habitat assessment models (especially HSI) frequently contain variables characterizing the distance between 2 habitat types (e.g., distance from a forested area to the nearest open field).

The most sophisticated programs allow integration of vegetation-succession models. These systems depict changes in vegetation through time under different assumptions about how vegetation management regimes (e.g., silviculture, agriculture, and fires) and succession will interact to change habitat quality (Steblein and Porter 1989).

Examples of using GIS in habitat assessment are increasing. In the turkey literature, Williamson and Koeln (1980) provide an excellent example of how habitat assessment can be done in a GIS. Donovan et al. (1987) describe a system for evaluating brood habitat. An overview of integrating GIS concepts to resource management is provided by Walsh (1985), Berry (1986), Burroughs (1986), and Devine and Field (1986).

In summary, we now have techniques available that enable us to identify what's important to wild turkeys. We also have procedures that allow us to assess objectively and quantitatively how suitable a piece of land is for wild turkeys, and to examine the effects of management actions on habitat condition.

There remains a gap, however, between our knowledge and the true relations between the wild turkey and its habitat. As Stephen Fretwell (1975) has observed, because of this gap, the final ingredient in applying habitat analysis and assessment is the wisdom of experienced biologists.

A gap remains between our knowledge and the true relation of the wild turkey to its habitat.

Chapter 14

HABITAT REQUIREMENTS

William F. Porter
Faculty of Environmental and Forest Biology
College of Environmental Science and Forestry
State University of New York
Syracuse, New York

BACKGROUND

Restoration of the wild turkey is a foremost success story in wildlife management. The achievement is a sterling example of the value of coordinating wildlife research and management.

Success of the management programs can be attributed to the exceptional adaptability of this species. Also critical to the success, however, have been not only the accelerating research into the habitat requirements of this species in the past 2 decades but also the rapid transfer of this knowledge to wildlife managers.

Unusual circumstances shaped the original ideas of biologists about the habitat requirements of the wild turkey. Research began in earnest in the 1940s, when turkey populations remained only in areas of extensive timberland. These areas supported turkeys because topography made them inaccessible and kept legal and illegal hunting to a minimum. Inaccessibility also made logging and agriculture difficult, so these areas remained forested.

As a result, biologists began to associate the wild turkey with big timber. A minimum of 10,000 hectares (25,000 acres) of mature forest land was a common criterion for evaluating turkey habitat. Shaw (1959:100) concisely summarized opinions on habitat requirements at the first wild turkey symposium: "A wild turkey needs one thing for sure, lots of timberland and not much human disturbance."

Three significant advances brought about a major reassessment of this conventional wisdom during the 1960s and 1970s.

First, development of cannon- and rocket-netting techniques for livetrapping in the 1950s had resulted in successful transplants of wild turkeys into areas from which they had been eliminated. These transplants were so much more successful than those of game-farm stock that conservation agencies generally abandoned game-farm propagation in favor of livetrapping programs.

Second, vastly improved law enforcement and increased public interest in seeing turkeys resulted in a reduced illegal kill and allowed these transplanted populations to grow. In many areas, populations grew exponentially, doubling every year in the first 5 to 10 years.

By the late 1960s, transplant programs and population growth filled what was then considered good range, and wildlife managers began experimenting with transplants in other areas. Populations took hold in Washington and Oregon, well beyond historic distribution of the wild turkey. Perhaps more important, turkey numbers began to grow in agricultural areas where forest cover was extremely limited. These areas previously had been considered unsuitable for wild turkeys.

Third, the expansion into unconventional habitats prompted an explosion of research during the 1970s. Biologists were keen to understand habitat characteristics critical for the wild turkey. Coincident with the transplant programs, technological advances in radiotelemetry allowed biologists to investigate habitat requirements in much greater detail. Regional comparisons of turkey populations with broadly defined landscape patterns were complemented by behavioral studies of turkeys and their use of narrowly defined habitat types.

In the 1980s, biologists began to synthesize the findings of this research into a modern approach to assessing habitat quality. With the passage of the National Environmental Policy Act in 1969 came the need for objective, quantitative evaluations of habitat condition. Biologists borrowed techniques developed in computer science, engineering, and sociological and medical research to construct mathematically based habitat evaluation models.

Extensive cleared land is not suitable wild turkey habitat. *Photo by J. McConnell, USDA Soil Conservation Service.*

Because of the wealth of information available on the wild turkey, it was among the first species to receive this kind of attention.

This chapter provides a summary of what we have learned about the habitat requirements of the wild turkey in the past 2 decades. From the extensive data base, I have attempted to draw the patterns that constitute common denominators across the range of this species, from Florida to Oregon. For the layman, I hope this chapter will provide insight that will enrich the experience of seeing the wild turkey. For the scientist, it will provide some hypotheses to stimulate thinking.

GENERAL REQUIREMENTS

Directly or indirectly, moisture seems to be key to determining the ability of the wild turkey to survive and reproduce. Distribution of the species in the South and East is bounded by the coastal wetlands. The wild turkey is largely cursorial (ground dwelling and ground feeding) and is not well adapted to marsh environments. In the

North, distribution is limited by persistent deep snow (more than 25 centimeters, 10 inches), which restricts movement and feeding ability. In the West, dry conditions that limit access to water and food (and preclude the development of trees suitable for roosting) set limits to the wild turkey's distribution.

More specifically, suitable habitat includes 2 key ingredients. Regardless of the nature of the environments or subspecies, turkeys must have a combination of trees and grasses. Trees provide food, daytime resting and escape cover, and—most important—nighttime roost sites. Grasses provide food for adults and are especially important to poults as environment in which they can efficiently forage for insects. The annual home range of wild turkeys varies from 150 to 550 hectares (370 to 1,360 acres) (Brown 1980) and contains a mixture of these cover types.

How much woodland and grassland is optimal? The proportional distribution of vegetation cover types has been central to reassessing the habitat requirements of the wild turkey. Early research suggested that ideal habitats were composed of woodlands with grassy openings,

The nesting hen (look for the eye) is usually well concealed by low vegetation. *Photo by W. Healy, U.S. Forest Service.*

and quantitative estimates of 5 to 10 percent in grass are common (e.g., Hillestad and Speake 1970, Bailey 1973, Dellinger 1973, Donohoe and McKibben 1973, Holbrook 1973, Dickson et al. 1978).

Experiences in west Texas and the upper Midwest during the 1970s and 1980s cast new light. With the extension of rural electrification into west Texas and the development of concrete livestock watering ponds, turkeys colonized the region (Kothmann and Litton 1975). In the upper Midwest, studies in Minnesota began to show that extensive forest cover was not necessary for turkeys. Townships with as little as 15 percent forest cover were supporting viable populations (Hecklau et al. 1982). In Iowa, the potential of many counties was reevaluated several times as trap-and-transfer efforts succeeded in areas of increasingly limited forest cover. By 1980, Iowa had populations averaging 8 to 12 birds per square kilometer (21 to 31 per square mile) in areas where stands of timber more than 400 hectares (1,000 acres) are rare (Little 1980).

These findings do not seem to reflect recent adaptations by the species. In fact, a rereading of accounts by early explorers suggests that high densities of wild tur-

keys lived in the coastal plains of the South and in the tall-grass prairies of the Midwest. Common to these areas are trees and grass in plant communities influenced by fire. Both the coastal plains from Texas to Georgia and tall-grass prairie regions of Iowa, Missouri, Illinois, and Indiana were in constant transition from grassland to savanna to forest, depending on what the fires did. When fires burned frequently, grass predominated; when they burned less frequently, trees invaded the areas.

These are highly productive environments for turkeys, providing a rich diversity of food resources. Also in these environments, the species is easily exploited by man. Wild turkey populations were rapidly eliminated after the introduction of firearms. It is easy to understand why biologists more than a century later would not think open environments suitable habitat for the wild turkey.

Today, because of the wild turkey's protection from overexploitation, the full range of habitat tolerance is open to exploration. The wild turkey, once viewed as a wilderness species, adapts well to a wide diversity of environments. The next habitat factor tested will likely be density of human population. Reports of turkeys in sub-

Fairly dense, low vegetation is appropriate brood habitat. Young poults forage on the invertebrates and plant parts found here. *Photo by L. Williams.*

urban areas are increasing. Possibly turkeys will respond to suburban environments as did ring-necked pheasants, Canada geese, white-tailed deer, and raccoons, becoming abundant in some locales.

BREEDING AND NESTING HABITAT

What is ideal nest habitat for the wild turkey? The key elements have long eluded biologists. Wild turkeys are known to nest in areas as dissimilar as mature oak forests and alfalfa hayfields. Nests are frequently found at the base of trees and in logging slash, shrub cover, and herbaceous vegetation. But in the 1980s as a result of radiotelemetry studies, researchers began to recognize a pattern.

The characteristic common to habitat immediately surrounding the nest of the wild turkey is lateral cover. Lateral cover obscures horizontal vision. Many studies, from Alabama to Oregon, describe forest stands in which turkey nests were found in areas having an open overstory and well-developed understory. Turkeys often nest in small openings in the forest, or along forest roads and edges between forest and open field. Nests occur in power-line rights-of-way (ROWs) through forests, and in fields of herbaceous vegetation close to forests. All these nesting habitats are environments with well-developed vegetation 1 meter (1.1 yards) above the ground.

This pattern is consistent across the wild turkey's range. For example, in Alabama, 37 percent of nests were found in utility rights-of-way, even though such habitat was only 0.6 percent of the area. Wild turkeys nested in

ROWs only when average vegetation height exceeded 25 centimeters (10 inches). Overall, 73 percent of the nests in the study area occurred in habitats with well-developed herbaceous and shrub vegetation (Everett 1982).

In Minnesota, nest sites occurred in parklike forest areas with an average of 40 percent canopy closure, 0.9 woody stems per square meter (0.8 per square yard), and 20 to 30 percent cover by forbs, or in open fields near forest edges (Lazarus and Porter 1985).

In Oregon, nest habitat had high shrub density and visual obstruction at 0.5 meters (0.5 yards). Most nests were found in Douglas fir that had been selectively cut or thinned to less than 50 percent of the original stocking. Slash and shrubs provided lateral cover (Lutz and Crawford 1987b).

The occurrence of a well-developed overhead cover—a canopy layer at 0.5 to 3.0 meters (0.5 to 3.4 yards)—at the nest is a less-prominent pattern. Studies in Georgia (Hon et al. 1978), Oklahoma (Logan 1973), and New Mexico (Goerndt 1983) all report immediate overhead canopies of from 50 to 90 percent cover associated with many nests. Minnesota studies showed that 80 percent of successfully hatching nests were associated with overhead cover, but only 25 percent of the unsuccessful nests had overhead cover (Lazarus and Porter 1985). A tree or other guard object adjacent to the nest is widely reported, but this factor has not been evaluated quantitatively.

Another pattern that may be emerging is a preference for sites described as mesic (having moderate soil moisture). Minnesota and New Mexico studies have demonstrated that turkeys choose mesic slopes most frequently for nesting (Jones 1981, Goerndt 1983, Lazarus and Porter 1985), although they sometimes use xeric (dry) sites with good vegetation cover. Whether the mesic condition provides an important microclimate for the female

and eggs, or is simply correlated with greater development of vegetation in the 0 to 1.0 meter (0 to 1.1 yards) stratum, needs examination.

Finally, Lazarus and Porter (1985) suggest that wild turkeys may select nest sites partly because of proximity to brood cover. The data show that females establishing nests early in the spring tend to place them in woodland areas distant from brood cover. But nests established later in the season are closer to brood cover (Figure 1).

Woodland sites provide denser lateral cover early in the spring. But as lateral cover develops with growth of herbaceous vegetation in the fields, females nesting later (or renesting) selected open-field sites. These open fields are subsequently used for rearing broods. Theoretically, broods hatching closer to suitable brood-rearing habitat would have higher probabilities of survival (Figure 2). This hypothesis has yet to be tested elsewhere.

BROOD-REARING HABITAT

During the first eight weeks after the hatch, there are 3 essential ingredients for brood habitat.

First, poults need an environment that produces insects and in which they can efficiently forage.

Second, they need habitat that permits frequent foraging throughout the day.

Third, poults need an area that provides enough cover to hide them but allows the adult female unobstructed vision for protection from predation.

All these ingredients must occur within a relatively small area. Weekly home ranges average less than 30 hectares (75 acres), and total summer home ranges are about 100 hectares (250 acres) (Speake et al. 1975, Porter 1980).

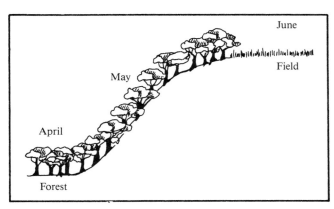

Figure 1. Turkeys in Minnesota show a progression from woodland to open field for nest sites, with early nests occurring in woodlands and late nests or renests occurring in open field (Lazarus and Porter 1985).

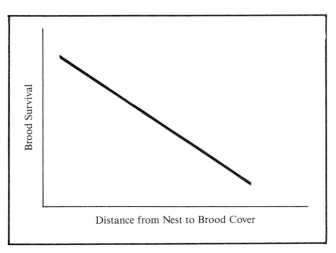

Figure 2. Hypothesized relationship between nest proximity to brood cover and poult survival.

Photo by D. Baumann.

Photo by E. Kurzejeski, Missouri Department of Conservation.

Grassy openings are important for year-round habitat suitability. Insects and other foods are abundant there, and these openings are used for strutting areas.

Patterns in the wild turkey's brood habitat are the most consistent of any habitat relationship. The key to brood habitat is herbaceous vegetation interspersed with forest. Here are some examples:

Ideal turkey brood habitat in Pennsylvania consists of forested sites with grassy understories, or savannas adjacent to mature forest (Hayden 1979a).

Adult females with broods using old fields in Alabama have the highest poult survival rate (Metzler and Speake 1985).

In Texas, broods use riparian woodlands and savannas (Baker 1979).

Broods less than 4 weeks old in South Dakota use south-facing woodlands with a 50 percent canopy closure and grass- or forb-dominated understory (McCabe and Flake 1985).

Brood habitat in New Mexico is described as grassy openings in mixed conifer forests, meadows, and aspen glens (Schemnitz et al. 1979).

In Minnesota, broods spend the first week in forest vegetation and make increasing use of fields beginning the second week. Peak use occurs during the seventh week, when broods spend as much as 60 percent of the daytime in open fields (Porter 1980). Ideal habitat in Minnesota is characterized by a field-to-forest ratio of 4 to 1.

Herbaceous vegetation is key because it provides an ideal foraging environment for young poults. Hurst and Poe (1985) estimate that turkey poults require 9 to 12 grams (0.3 to 0.4 ounces) of spiders and insects each day to meet protein requirements for growth. Insect abun-

Summer brood roost. Wild turkeys prefer certain tree and stand characteristics for roosting. *Photo by L. Williams.*

dance is greater in open fields than in forest habitats, particularly when the fields are not mowed (Hurst 1978, Hurst and Owen 1980). Foraging efficiency of poults is highest in areas with standing crops of grass cover of 600 to 3,000 kilograms per hectare (530 to 2,700 pounds per acre) and is lower in all forest types except those of the very best sites (Healy 1978, 1981). Heavier vegetation supports more insects, but poults have difficulty moving through it.

The height of vegetation is another key feature. Porter (1980) observed extensive use of alfalfa fields by broods and hypothesized that these fields provided excellent protection from predators. The vegetation is 30 to 70 centimeters (12 to 28 inches) tall, allowing adult females to see predators at long distances and also allowing poults to hide. Exum (1985) and Songer (1987), working in different plant communities, reached the same conclusion: Vegetation height is one of the most important features.

Nevertheless, turkey broods are seldom found far from tree cover. Trees may be important for 2 reasons.

First, microclimate is critical to heat regulation in young poults. Healy and Nenno (1985) report that cold, wet conditions when poults are 12 to 15 days old are an important factor in poult deaths. At this age, the poults have consumed the energy reserves of the yolk sac and are becoming too large for the hen to efficiently brood. Trees provide shade from heat and shelter from rain.

Second, trees provide escape cover once poults can fly (10 to 12 days after hatching). Broods will venture away from trees, and I have observed adult females with poults more than 5 weeks old in hayfields farther than 300 meters (330 yards) from the nearest tree cover but adjacent to corn approximately 1.5 meters (5 feet) tall. Upon being disturbed, the broods immediately retreated into the corn. This example may serve to support the following basic hypothesis: Thermal and predator cover are all that are necessary.

The emerging pattern for brood habitat is that of a parklike environment. Investigations in Alabama, Georgia, West Virginia, Mississippi, Michigan, Minnesota, Texas, Arizona, Utah, and Oregon all describe brood habitat as consisting of complete ground cover of forbs and grasses with average heights of approximately 50 centimeters (20 inches), and 10 to 50 percent overhead or nearby tree cover. This pattern fits the description of a savanna and suggests a hypothesis: Savannas constitute the best habitat condition for broods.

Under natural conditions, most savannas are a product of fire. The value of fire in maintaining brood cover is receiving increasing attention. Highest mortality for turkeys occurs during early brood rearing, and any increase in insect abundance could lead to survival of more poults. The underlying relationship may be that increased insect abundance reduces the need to move about (which is energetically expensive) or promotes more rapid growth (larger poults are less prone to hypothermia), or both. Pattee (1977) demonstrated that an increase in available protein, phosphorus, and calcium can significantly increase the production and survival of young to late summer.

Fire promotes production of food resources. It increases the amount and vigor of seed-producing grasses and forbs. It does likewise for legumes important to adults and to young in late summer (Buckner and Landers 1979). Fire also increases total animal food available during the first 3 years after burning (Hurst 1978).

Fire can enhance the structural characteristics of vegetation. In the Southeast, for instance, succession in the understory of pine forests moves through a grass-and-herb stage to perennial herbs and shrubs and finally to trees. Prescribed burning in pine forest reduces mat-forming perennial herbs and woody plants (Buckner and Landers 1979). This strategy can produce a vegetative environment that is optimal for poults because it allows easy movement and increases food resources.

Disturbances and variable habitat conditions are common throughout the range of the wild turkey. It's reasonable to hypothesize that the wild turkey is adapted to taking advantage of periodic, highly favorable reproductive conditions. Fires, like mild winters in the North and wet winters in the Southwest, provide conditions conducive to maximum reproduction. Such events are episodic and unpredictable.

Studies in environments as dissimilar as West Virginia, Texas, and Minnesota show that unfavorable conditions can adversely affect nesting success and poult survival without hurting adult survivorship (Beasom 1973, Porter et al. 1983, and Healy and Nenno 1985).

The wild turkey lives long (adults frequently survive more than 6 years) and has a high innate capacity for reproduction. When conditions are favorable, more than 90 percent of females nest, producing an average of 5 females per female in the population. When 40 percent of young survive to breeding age (higher rates are common in good years), the finite rate of growth is more than 2.0 (i.e., the breeding population more than doubles in a single year) (Pattee 1977, Porter 1978).

FALL AND WINTER HABITAT

Wild turkeys seek 2 key habitat ingredients for the fall and winter: food and roosting cover. During the fall, food is critical to continued growth of young and the building of fat deposits by young and adults. For most of the winter, at least in northern latitudes, growth is halted and turkeys are on a sustaining or declining energy supply. Food is critical. But, in many regions, protection from adverse weather is equally important.

Vegetation used by turkeys during fall and winter is highly varied. In southern latitudes where snow does not persist for weeks, hardwood stands containing a diversity of tree species—interspersed with softwoods and field edges—are important. Turkeys increase their use of forested cover during the fall and winter and decrease their use of open areas. This pattern is prevalent from Virginia to Texas (e.g., Speake et al. 1975, Kennamer et al. 1980a, Campo 1983, Holbrook 1984).

Mast (pine seeds, acorns, and other fruits) is the principal food during fall and winter. Habitat value increases with the proportion of mast-producing species in the forest and their degree of maturity. Forest types, ranked according to acorn yields (highest to lowest) in Virginia are mixed oak, oak-pine, cove hardwood, and

Spring seeps provide foraging areas in northern habitat when snow covers the ground. *Photo by G. Eckert.*

mixed pine (Forsythe 1978). Green vegetation is also an important food, however (Kennamer et al. 1980b), so there's a need for forested areas to be interspersed with herbaceous growth.

In areas where snow exceeding 15 centimeters (6 inches) covers the ground for 2 to 16 weeks, the wild turkey needs additional habitat resources. In the mountainous environments of the Northeast and West, spring seeps are an important source of food (Healy 1981, Goerndt et al. 1985). The seeps provide invertebrates, mast, and green vegetation. Because such water does not

Excellent wild turkey habitat usually is well watered. *Photo by G. Smith.*

Small agricultural crops interspersed with woodlots make excellent habitat. Top left: Cornfield in pine stand in the Southeast. Top right: Soybean stubble with adjacent riparian zone in Kansas. Above: Field-forest mixture in Missouri.

freeze, it provides a microenvironment that allows foraging throughout the winter. Optimal conditions occur on south-facing areas with less than 20 percent gradient and where seeps are spread out, covering more than 15 square meters (18 square yards).

Where agriculture is prominent, a mix of cropland and forest cover seems to be highly suitable habitat. In the North, turkeys make extensive use of corn (Porter et al. 1980, Crim 1981, Clark 1985, Kulowiec and Haufler 1985, Kurzejeski and Lewis 1985). Corn, compared with acorns, is higher in protein, lower in fats, and similar in carbohydrates (Crim 1981). Turkeys can feed on corn while it is standing, when it's on the ground after picking, and when it's residual in manure spread from dairy-farm operations. My own observations suggest standing corn is superior because the structure of the rows provides protection from avian predators such as golden eagles.

In the South, chufa is an important resource. The plant produces tubers that are easily scratched out by turkeys, particularly when chufa is grown on sandy soils. Both in the North and South, optimal fall and winter conditions may be a 1 to 1 mix of forest cover and agricultural land (Little 1980).

Historically, turkey populations along the northern and southern edges of their range have fluctuated with food resources. Acorns and beechnuts constitute an irregular and unpredictable food resource. Studies in very diverse environments show that adverse food conditions can hurt not only winter survival but also reproduction (Beasom and Pattee 1980, Porter et al. 1980, 1983).

In Minnesota, deep snows restrict movements and prevent turkeys from exploiting widely dispersed food resources. Because corn is a much more reliable and concentrated food resource, agriculture in northern regions may be the foundation for these turkey populations.

In Texas, adequate rainfall is critical to vegetation growth that supplies nutrients (protein, phosphorus, and calcium) essential for reproduction (Pattee and Beasom 1979).

Experiments with free-ranging turkeys show that supplementing natural foods with crops and artificial feed can reduce winter deaths and can enhance reproduction. This knowledge has led to a series of management programs to offset the periodic severe winter. Fields of standing corn, shrub plantings, and spring-seep management seem to be far more effective than feeding stations (Porter et al. 1980, Crim 1981, Healy 1981, Clark 1985, Kulowiec and Haufler 1985, Kurzejeski and Lewis 1985).

The difficulty with feeding stations is that they tend to be supplied only in severe winters. Turkeys often fail to find these feeding stations. When they do, the feeding stations concentrate birds and this density increases risk of predation and spread of disease. The key is to provide consistent food resources (all winter, every winter), spread over relatively large areas (1 to 3 hectares, 2.5 to 7.5 acres).

The second characteristic critical to winter habitat is roosting cover. Roost habitat is necessary throughout the year. In general, characteristics of roost sites do not seem to be highly specific. Perhaps the best evidence to support this belief comes from the use of artificial structures (power poles and lines) in Texas (Kothmann and Litton 1975). The essential feature is a horizontal spreading structure 10 to 30 meters (30 to 100 feet) above the ground.

An additional feature, however, physiography, may be important to roost sites in regions where winter temperatures are frequently below freezing. Winter roosts tend to be in areas protected from prevailing winds. Reports from Pennsylvania, Minnesota, Arizona, New Mexico, and Colorado indicate that roosts tend to occur on northeasterly slopes (Hoffman 1968, Boeker and Scott 1969, Tzilkowski 1971, Porter 1978, Goerndt 1983). Turkeys roost most frequently on the upper third of the slope (Mackey 1972, Goerndt 1983, Porter unpublished data). This location in ravines and small river valleys may provide an advantage in maintaining body temperature. Such a site protects turkeys from prevailing winds and allows them to be above the cold-air drainage. Where conifers are available on these slopes, turkeys use them, further reducing the energy required to maintain body temperature.

SUMMARY

That the wild turkey is a highly adaptive species has become increasingly clear over the past 2 decades. Individual subspecies have adapted to regional environments, and the specific conditions that contribute to habitat suitability vary from region to region. Still, there are general patterns in the data that suggest fundamental habitat requirements common across the range of the species. These patterns reflect our best scientific evidence to date. An important direction for future research will be the close examination of these emerging patterns. A synthesis of our current knowledge of the wild turkey suggests 7 hypotheses that warrant examination.

1. The key to nesting habitat is lateral cover and cover types with well-developed herbaceous or woody vegetation at 0 to 1.0 meter (0 to 3 feet) above the ground.
2. Moisture conditions at mesic sites provide an important microclimatic characteristic for nests.
3. Close proximity to brood cover is an important criterion in selection of nest sites by female wild turkeys.
4. The keys to brood cover are food and thermal cover, and savannas are the best brood-rearing environment.
5. Ideal brood-raising conditions are episodic and unpredictable. The wild turkey is an opportunistic breeder, adapted to widely fluctuating environmental conditions.

Photo by L. Williams.

Photo by G. Wunz, Pennsylvania Game Commission.

Photo by R. Williams, USDA Soil Conservation Service.

Photo by J. McConnell, USDA Soil Conservation Service.

Many different vegetation types make appropriate wild turkey habitat. Opposite page, clockwise from top left: Florida turkey cypress-oak scrub habitat; Eastern wild turkey oak habitat in Pennsylvania; Eastern wild turkey mature pine habitat in the southern Coastal Plains; Eastern wild turkey bottomland hardwood habitat; clockwise from above: Rio Grande turkey oak-juniper savanna habitat in the Rolling Plains of Texas; Merriam's turkey ponderosa pine habitat in the Black Hills, South Dakota; Gould's turkey oak-savanna habitat in Chihuahua, Mexico.

6. Roost trees on northeast-facing slopes and that allow turkeys to roost above cold-air drainage are important in regions of cold winter weather.
7. This species is not restricted to wilderness environments, and even suburban environments provide suitable habitat.

Finally, the hypothesis that the wild turkey has evolved in a widely fluctuating environmental condition has important implications to habitat management. In assessing habitat suitability, biologists tend to focus on deficiencies. However, a critical characteristic may not be consistently deficient. But when the deficiency occurs, the result may be such a decline in turkey abundance that the population cannot recover in a single normal breeding season. Prudent management may require annual effort and investment for conditions that occur only once or twice a decade. Good examples of this strategy are the technique of leaving corn standing through the winter as an alternative during years of poor mast production, the development of shrub planting, and spring-seep management.

Chapter 15

FLORIDA TURKEY

Lovett E. Williams, Jr.
Florida Wildlife Services, Inc.
Gainesville, Florida

The wild turkey *(M. g. osceola)* in Florida closely resembles the eastern subspecies *(M. g. silvestris)*. It is said (Scott 1890) to be smaller than *M. g. silvestris*, but there is so much overlap among specimens that size is useless as an identification character.

M. g. osceola can best be distinguished by its darker wings. The white bars of the primary wing feathers are narrower than the black bars and are irregular and broken along their length. The secondaries are also darker in *M. g. osceola* than in *M. g. silvestris*. *M. g. osceola* can be distinguished from *M. g. intermedia, M. g. mexicana,* and *M. g. merriami* (all of which range in the western United States and Mexico) by the brown tips of its tail feathers and major tail coverts. The same feathers of the 3 western subspecies are white, or nearly so.

The Florida wild turkey occurs only in the peninsula of Florida (Figure 1), where the fall population is estimated to be 80,000 to 100,000. There is a zone (Figure 2) from South Carolina through southern Georgia, northern Florida, southern Alabama, and coastal Mississippi, to the "Florida" parishes of Louisiana, in which wild turkey specimens are intermediate between *M. g. silvestris* and *M. g. osceola* in color markings (Aldrich and Duvall 1955).

Turkeys thrived in north-central Florida after they were eliminated from the plantations of southern Georgia. Herbert Stoddard (1963) thought southern Georgia was restocked by natural expansion of northern Florida turkey populations when southern Georgia farmland became reforested after the Civil War. If such natural movement occurred, that—along with the transplanting programs of the Florida Game and Fresh Water Fish Commission—has probably advanced the genes of *M. g. osceola* somewhat northward in recent years.

CLIMATE

Although the Florida peninsula lies in the temperate

The white bars of the primary wing feathers of *M. g. osceola* are narrow, which makes the wings darker than those of *M. g. silvestris* or the other subspecies. *All photos in this chapter by L. Williams.*

zone, the climate borders on subtropical because of the surrounding ocean waters. The median date of the first subfreezing winter temperature inland at Lake Okeechobee is December 25, and the median date of the last winter freeze is January 23. In some years, it is not cold enough in the southern reaches of the Florida turkey's range to kill the summer vegetation. The mean annual rainfall in the Florida peninsula is 128 centimeters (50 inches) to 140 centimeters (55 inches), with over half of

214

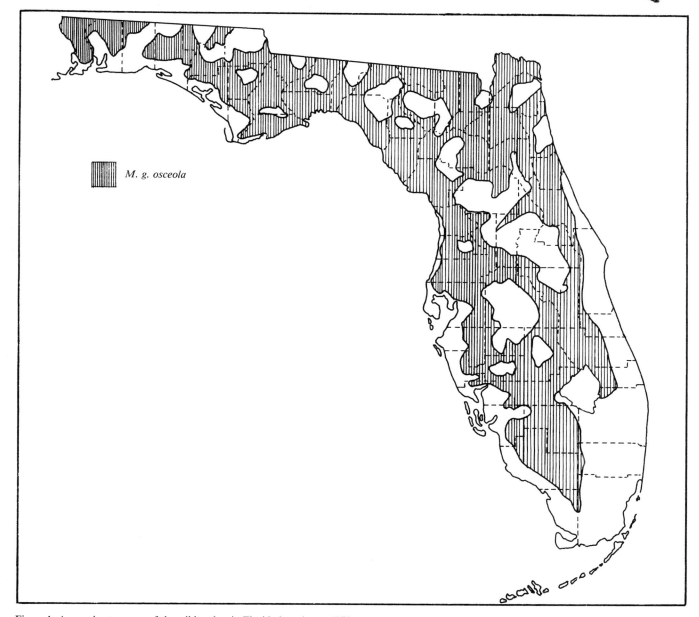

M. g. osceola

Figure 1. Approximate range of the wild turkey in Florida based on a 1973 survey.

it occurring in summer (National Oceanic and Atmospheric Administration 1978).

In the northern range of the Florida turkey, at Gainesville, the mean annual temperature is 22.2 degrees Centigrade (72 degrees Fahrenheit). The median date of the first frost is December 6, and the median date of the last frost is February 14. Central Florida gets killing frosts every winter, but snow is rare anywhere in the range of the Florida turkey. Dry air nearly always accompanies subfreezing winter temperatures. Wild turkeys are probably never seriously stressed by cold weather in Florida.

HISTORY

When the Old South was a land of cotton plantations, Florida was a wilderness of poor soils, waterlogged land, hot climate, high humidity, hostile Native Americans, and hordes of mosquitoes. That combination discouraged human settlement. The antebellum plantation culture of the 1800s touched only a few Florida counties, and they were along the Georgia line.

Florida was the last state east of the Mississippi River, except Wisconsin, to become a state. The army did not gain the upper hand in the Seminole Wars until 1857,

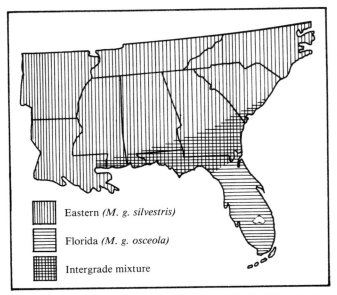

Figure 2. The zone of intergradation between *M. g. osceola* and *M. g. silvestris* (Aldrich and Duvall 1955). Turkeys in this zone are not typical of either *M. g. osceola* or *M. g. silvestris* in coloration.

and it never did make the tribe surrender. While the wild turkey was being killed out of the industrial North and parts of the plantation South, Florida had a virtually unexploited wild turkey population. In 1860, Florida had more turkeys than people.

Florida grew in population very slowly in the first half of the 20th century. Human numbers did not reach 1 million until the 1920s. Cattle roamed unfenced until 1948, and train engines had cowcatchers in front even after that. Free-range hog ownership, reminiscent of the open-range cattle grazing of the Old West, was widely practiced and was legal until the 1960s. There was no land ownership ethic in Florida, as there was in the rest of the South. Very little acreage was posted against trespassing before about 1950. Most land was considered wild regardless of its ownership.

Much of the hunting by Florida residents during the early 1900s was for subsistence. Sport hunting as we know it today occurred, but it was not the rule. Few early Florida hunters could call turkeys effectively, or even tried. Turkeys were hunted either by shooting over bait or by locating flocks at favorite roosting places and shooting the birds out of the trees. Both methods were effective, and a couple of hunters sometimes killed large numbers of turkeys in a single hunt. Fortunately, there were only a few hunters and much wild land.

By the 1940s, the state was becoming more heavily settled. The improving road system and private automobiles were providing access to wild areas. Remote tracts no longer provided secure refuge for game.

By the end of World War II, the Florida wild turkey was being seriously overhunted. A turkey population that once probably exceeded a quarter million was reduced to only 26,000. When a statewide survey was conducted in 1948, 18 Florida counties were essentially without wild turkeys (Newman and Griffin 1950).

The Florida Game and Fresh Water Fish Commission was formed in 1943 to replace an older and more politically oriented game department. Much to its credit, the new commission's staff attempted to resist strong pressures to stock pen-reared turkeys; they stocked fewer than 1,000 semidomestic turkeys before initiating a statewide restoration program in 1949, as recommended by Newman and Griffin (1950), using wild-trapped stock. Between 1950 and 1969, approximately 5,500 wild turkeys were trapped from Lykes Fisheating Creek Refuge and other south-central Florida tracts.

Some of the wild-trapped turkeys were captured in connection with research studies, and many were transplanted in public hunting areas that already had wild turkey populations. But most were released in vacant turkey habitat, establishing new wild turkey populations.

After all large public tracts had been restocked, releases were made on a few large private tracts that lacked wild turkeys. Florida completed its wild turkey restoration program in 1969. It thereby became the first state to restore wild turkeys to all suitable habitat within its borders. At that time, the statewide fall turkey population was an estimated 100,000. In some years, however, there might have been 150,000 or more. Populations fluctuate annually, and the estimates may have been inaccurate.

For a brief period in the 1970s, the Florida Game and Fresh Water Fish Commission permitted the supervised trapping and sale of wild turkeys from certain private properties. The stock was trapped by agency biologists to be sold by the landowner for release on private property where commission biologists considered stocking justified. This tactic eased some of the pressure from private wildlife managers to use pen-reared turkey stock. Biologists found it easier to say no to pen-reared turkeys while pointing to a source of genuine wild stock.

Unfortunately, these sales ended in 1976 and have not been resumed. The demand is still high in Florida for real wild turkeys to use in stocking private property. Pen-reared turkeys are being released every year on private property in a misguided attempt to establish wild populations.

Florida has a tradition of liberal regulations on turkey hunting. In the 1940s, there was an open season practically throughout the state from mid-November through early January. Then during the 1950s, a 2-week spring gobblers-only season was added in northern Florida. Later it was extended statewide. Recently there has been a fall hunting season of 8 to 9 weeks in most counties, timed to coincide with the fall deer season. There also has been a 5-week spring gobblers-only season. There is now a liberal either-sex fall archery-only season and a 3-day either-sex muzzle-loader-only season. A bag limit of 2 wild turkeys of either sex per day and 3 per season was in effect for several years. It was changed during the 1970s to 1 per day and 2 birds of either sex during the fall season, plus 2 males in spring—for a total of 4 turkeys annually. Regulations vary among the public hunting areas, counties, and regions, and substantial changes are made almost every year.

Taking turkeys over bait is prohibited. But deer and other resident game can be legally baited for hunting, and turkeys are shot when they are attracted to baited blinds intended for other species. Shooting during the fall season begins at a half hour before sunrise and ends a half hour after sunset. Spring gobbler hunting has traditionally ended daily in early afternoon. There are no restrictions on firearms and ammunition for taking turkeys. Hunting from unbaited blinds and use of decoys are legal; turkey-hunting dogs and electronic devices are not.

There has been no turkey tagging system since one was tried briefly and discontinued in the 1950s. Florida has no effective system for checking the annual statewide turkey harvest. A mail survey is used to estimate the annual harvest on private land, but its accuracy is questionable. A hunter needs a standard resident or non-resident hunting license plus a special turkey permit to hunt turkeys in Florida. The revenue is earmarked by act of the legislature for turkey research and management.

HABITAT

The Florida peninsula ranges in elevation from sea level to 99 meters (325 feet) in the central highlands near Lake Wales. Slight differences in elevation affect hydrologic conditions and strongly influence the vulnerability of the vegetation to fire. Only a few inches in elevation separate the dry pinelands, which burn easily and frequently, from hardwood swamps, which are virtually fireproof.

Florida's vegetation reflects the state's mild climate, long growing season, sandy soils, and general wetness. Many trees are broad-leaved evergreens, shedding their leaves in spring rather than fall. The woods are green most of the year. Plants and cold-blooded animals have only a relatively brief period of winter dormancy. The sandy soils do not produce especially tall trees, but where soil moisture is favorable, the tree and shrub cover is luxuriant despite low soil fertility.

Vegetative cover types occur in small units with edges, ecotones, and ecological gradients so prominent

that it is sometimes difficult to distinguish the type from the ecotones. The pattern of interspersed cover conditions is favorable to wild turkeys. The turkeys have their year-round needs met in relatively small areas, with no distinct habitat preferences based on sex or age class.

The extreme interspersion of cover types with their many ecotones and transition zones makes it difficult to describe Florida turkey habitat. Davis (1980) classified Florida's landscape into 26 broad "ecological communities" based on vegetation. I will discuss only those of particular interest in turkey habitat management and will use the well-established vernacular names that correspond closely to the terminology of Davis (1980).

Fire

There is a continuing struggle in the Florida landscape between the plant associations that tolerate fire and those that do not. The plant cover that occurs on dry, sandy sites—mainly pine woods, palmetto prairie, and oak scrub—tends to burn regularly and has done so for thousands of years. This pattern has led to associations of plants and development of genetic adaptations that not only enable the plants to tolerate occasional woods fires but actually invite and accommodate fire by producing highly combustible vegetation.

When such a plant association burns, its fire-tolerant members are able to survive, but the plants intolerant of fire are killed. In this way, the fire-type plant association is cleansed of invader species. As long as fire recurs at intervals, the same associations of plants persist.

At the other extreme are communities easily killed by woods fires, like most hardwood forests. These associations either grow in wetlands or have heavy overhead foliage that shades the ground level and prevents the growth of vegetation that would produce fuel for fires. In effect, they are nearly fireproof.

Between fire dependence and fireproofness there are communities that burn from time to time and have intermediate tolerances to fire. Sand pine scrub is destroyed by fire. But the small oaks and other adapted plants sprout from roots, and the pine seeds germinate profusely on bare mineral soil.

What determines which type of plant association—fire or nonfire—will occur on a site? Soil moisture is largely responsible. Hammocks are mostly on soils with limestone deposits near the surface or on reasonably moist soils. Scrub vegetation is on dry, sandy soils. Pine flatwoods and palmetto prairie are mostly on acidic, sandy sites with a shallow hardpan. Once either the fire or nonfire type of plant association gains a foothold, it tends to expand along its borders into the domain of the other. Thus the edges of hammocks and pine woods are

A live oak hammock in south-central Florida. Cattle grazing keeps the ground cover well cropped. This is an excellent component of Florida wild turkey habitat.

A typical Florida hardwood hammock with overstory dominance shared by live oak and sabal palmetto. Hammocks of this type are heavily used by wild turkeys.

constantly under attack from encroachment by the other type. So vegetative "climaxes" with their considerable stability do not occur in the Florida peninsula in the popular sense, but some communities are somewhat older, or more stable, or both than others.

Hardwood Hammocks

Hardwood hammock is a type of broad-leaved evergreen forest that occurs only where soil moisture, heavy shading by the vegetation, or fire barriers prevent forest fires. Soil moisture levels vary from hammock to hammock. There are hydric hammocks on wet soils along watercourses, mesic hammocks on moist soils of the uplands, and xeric hammocks on excessively drained soils. Very dry sites do not support hardwood hammocks unless natural fire barriers or human intervention protects them from fire.

Florida hammocks on moist soils are usually dominated by live oak and contain other hardwood trees such

as red mulberry, laurel oak, water oak, hackberry, red maple, red bay, and southern magnolia. Many hammocks in southern Florida are entirely live oak, while others share dominance with sabal palmetto and other trees.

Most Florida hammocks, whether they occur on moist or dry soils, are similar in general appearance and in plant species composition. Hammocks have a relatively open vegetative structure at ground level that is preferred by turkeys, and all produce hard mast and other fruit and seeds that are the choice foods of turkeys in fall, winter, and spring. The cover of hammocks provides shade, resting places, escape cover, and nesting cover and is an important component of good turkey habitat in Florida.

Pine Woods

Slash pine and longleaf pine woods are the most widespread upland forest type in Florida. Extensive, level

Longleaf pine and turkey oak woods in central Florida—good fall, winter, and spring wild turkey habitat when associated with swamps, creek bottoms, and stands of hardwood timber. Like many such stands, this one has been heavily logged, leaving only a few young longleaf pines.

Longleaf pine woods in central Florida with wire grass ground cover. When the ground cover is burned regularly by gentle fires, the understory is open and attractive to summer broods.

expanses of pine woods are called flatwoods; small isolated stands are called pine islands. Flatwoods soils are acidic, sandy, poorly drained, and low in fertility. Pine is sometimes mixed with hardwoods where pine seed sources occur near hammock soils. Older pine trees are found in hardwood stands that are in transition from pine to hardwoods because fire has become too infrequent to perpetuate a pure pine stand.

Longleaf pine woods. Longleaf pine and wire grass woods occur on moderately drained to well-drained upland soils. The turkey oak and blue jack oak that often occur in association with longleaf pine are fire tolerant and deciduous. Hot fires will damage and retard the oaks, but most Florida longleaf pine acreage is burned with only mild back fires and have a vigorous oak component.

The longleaf pine, wire grass, and turkey oak association is a good component of turkey habitat. There is satisfactory fall and winter hard mast and some food-producing herbaceous cover. Heaviest turkey use is in winter and spring. Productivity is low, however, in very large expanses of longleaf pine woods. Yet excellent tur-

key populations and productivity occur where longleaf pine and turkey oak are associated with stream bottoms, hammocks, or cypress swamps.

Most of Florida's longleaf pineland was heavily logged or cleared for agriculture during the early 1900s. Because longleaf pine regeneration is not practiced on a significant scale, longleaf stands have dwindled to mere remnants and are being widely replaced by slash and sand pine plantations, which are much less suitable as habitat for wild turkeys.

Slash pine woods. Slash pine flatwoods, the other major type of pine flatwoods, occur on poorly drained, sandy soils. Saw palmetto, gallberry, fetterbush, and other shrubs and grasses generate considerable fire fuel. The fires during dry periods get so hot that even the green vegetation burns. The understory survives the fire (by virtue of extensive underground root systems and other adaptations) and springs up to produce fuel for a new hot fire. Slash pine itself is not as fire tolerant as longleaf pine and is severely damaged by hot fires. Few oaks occur in slash pine woods, except runner oaks, which survive by underground stems.

The understory of natural slash pine woods, unless burned regularly, becomes overgrown with dense vegetation and will not support good wild turkey populations. Even when burned, large homogeneous expanses of slash pine flatwoods are marginal turkey habitat because of low mast production and dense understory vegetation.

Most forest managers avoid burning slash pine woods altogether because of the danger of damaging young pine trees. This strategy results in long periods of fire exclusion and fuel buildup. When fire does occur, it destroys most trees, large pines included.

Slash pine woods in central Florida. Unless burned frequently, the understory becomes choked with saw palmetto and other brushy shrubs and is unattractive to wild turkeys.

Because of the severity of fires in slash pine flatwoods, few hardwood trees occur therein except in swamps. Even the swamps sometimes experience extensive damage from head fires, that is, fires running with the wind. The major tree species in the flatwoods swamps are cypress, sweet bay, red bay, red maple, water oak, and black gum.

Swamps that occur in the pine flatwoods tend to become densely vegetated around the edges due to profuse sprouting of fire-damaged hardwoods. But the larger swamps are open inside and sometimes virtually without ground cover, because of heavy shading and frequent flooding. Smaller swamps that are burned entirely through by fast-moving head fires usually contain pond pine (a prime indicator of infrequent but very hot fires) and have an extremely dense shrub layer. Neither the entirely open nor the densely vegetated swamps are useful to turkeys except to roost over or escape into.

Slash pine has been widely planted in old fields and on sites that were formerly mesic hammock, upland pine and hardwood, or longleaf pine and turkey oak. Many of these plantations of the mid-1900s regenerated a component of oaks—primarily turkey oak, live oak, sand live oak, water oak, and laurel oak, depending on the site—and are becoming excellent fall and winter turkey habitat. Unfortunately, the pine in these stands is now being harvested, and the hardwoods are being destroyed by intensive cultivation methods, resulting in complete degradation as forest wildlife habitat.

Oak Scrub

Where sandy soils are coarse, deep, and situated well above the water table, vascular plants are stressed for lack of water during periods of the year and for lack of nutrients most of the time. This results in vegetation that is short and woody (e.g., scrub oaks, scrub hickory, and other dwarf shrubs). This cover is called oak scrub or merely scrub. When sand pine is present, the association is called sand pine scrub. The vegetation is much like that of the back dunes of sandy, coastal regions.

Oak scrub, despite its dependable acorn production, is not used by wild turkeys, except around the edges. The

Oak scrub in south-central Florida. Florida scrub is too dense to be used by wild turkeys except around the edges. Most central Florida scrub contains a sparse overstory of sand pine.

vegetation is too dense at turkey level. Hens use the transition zone along the edge of the scrub for nesting, but they nest also in many other cover types.

Prairie

Treeless savanna, called palmetto prairie or dry prairie, occurs extensively in south-central Florida on drier sites where cattle ranchers burn the prairies. Fires are so frequent and so hot that pine cannot survive. Except for the absence of pine, the vegetation is almost identical to south Florida slash pine and longleaf pine flatwoods. When pine does occur, it is mainly in small islands that happen to be protected from intense fires by natural landscape features.

Although turkey hens nest in the edge of the dry prairies, their nests are usually within 200 meters (219 yards) of adjoining woods. The tree cover in prairies is too sparse and the ground cover too dense to invite regular turkey use.

Palmetto prairie in southern Florida. Because of sparse tree cover, dense ground cover, and poor food production, Florida prairies are not attractive to wild turkeys except in spring, when the edges are used for nesting.

A creek bottom in north-central Florida—a deciduous wetland cover type that is an excellent component of wild turkey habitat.

Wetlands

Florida wetlands types are difficult to delineate because of the intergrading conditions that exist in the flat landscape among ponds, lakes, sloughs, glades, marshes, and swamps. Wetlands seldom burn except during drought.

Bottomland hardwoods. The hardwood swamps that lie along moving watercourses are small examples of river bottoms. Although the vegetation is similar to that of upland hardwood hammocks, the soils of these hardwood wetlands are alluvial and more fertile. Also, there is a large component of deciduous trees including hackberry, black gum, sweet gum, red maple, cypress, swamp chestnut oak, and American hornbeam. And usually present are broad-leaved evergreen trees such as live oak, laurel oak, water oak, American holly, and sweet bay.

Bottomland hardwoods cover produces the same foods as hardwood hammock and similar cover struc-

A flag pond in southern Florida with sandhill cranes foraging in the background. Turkey broods feed in flag ponds during the dry season.

Typical cypress pond in southern Florida. This pond is a favorite wild turkey roosting place. Most Florida turkeys roost in cypress trees.

A slough in southern Florida. A Florida slough supports grasses, sedges, and semiaquatic forbs, which produce attractive conditions for turkey brood foraging during periods of low surface water in spring and early summer.

ture; it serves the same purposes as an important turkey habitat component.

Ponds. Ponds are small, shallow, semipermanent lakes that are named for their principle emergent vegetation (i.e., flag pond, cypress pond, gum pond, pop ash pond, saw grass pond). Many shallow ponds are too wet or too densely vegetated to serve wild turkeys in any known way. Shallow flag ponds, however, have fertile organic soil and are dominated by lush semiaquatic and emergent herbaceous vegetation such as pickerel weed, arrowhead, maiden cane, and sedges. When such ponds are alternately flooded and burned, they are good summer brood habitat. Large cypress ponds are favorite wild turkey roosting places.

Sloughs and glades. In southern Florida, sloughs are shallow wetlands that occur where the surface is so flat that during the rainy seasons, water moves slowly over a broad area without forming distinct channels. Even during dry seasons, the soils of sloughs are wetter than the surroundings. The semiaquatic vegetation is less likely to be seriously damaged when wildfires sweep through.

Unforested sloughs resemble meadows in dry seasons, and in wet seasons are like shallow marshes or lakes. Sloughs, although unforested, are much more attractive to turkeys than are prairies. Sloughs produce a variety of buds, seeds, succulent vegetation, and insects and do not have the dense vegetation of prairies. A favorite spring food of Florida turkeys are the tubers of pennywort, which are exposed by the rooting of wild hogs in the dry sloughs.

Florida sloughs that are less drought stressed usually have a shallow, creeklike channel and contain water-tolerant trees such as cypress, ash, and gum and are called strands. Turkeys roost in forested strands and feed heavily on vegetation and small invertebrates in adjacent unforested sloughs, especially during the warm seasons.

Glades are similar to unforested sloughs and marshes. The Everglades of the southern tip of the Florida peninsula is a large saw grass marsh-glade-slough complex. Large glades are not suitable as turkey habitat because they lack trees. The greater Everglades region has only scattered populations of wild turkeys, associated with pine islands.

The Big Cypress Swamp. Northward from the marshes of the Everglades, the land slopes gradually upward and is seasonally drier, supporting open stands of slash pine, sabal palmetto (cabbage palm), and cypress, with small hardwood hammocks where sand and organic soil occur above the bedrock. The western part of this region, called Big Cypress Swamp, contains ponds,

Cypress woods in southern Florida. When dry, which is the normal condition in spring and early summer, cypress woods have ideal ground cover density and tree cover for wild turkeys.

Inside a bayhead, or forested swamp, in southern Florida. Most bayheads have vegetation too dense and too wet to be attractive to wild turkeys except for roosting.

sloughs, marshes, pine islands with cabbage palm, and many miles of stunted cypress and slash pine. The wild turkeys in the Big Cypress Swamp inhabit the larger islands and surrounding cypress, and are—except for the few small flocks in the wooded fringes of the Everglades—the southernmost populations of wild turkey in Florida. North of the Big Cypress, from the Gulf to the Atlantic, the terrain is higher and drier, more forest cover occurs, and turkeys are more abundant and widespread.

Cypress woods. Low-lying terrain along watercourses, in shallow ponds, and around the edges of lakes is usually forested with cypress. These swamps and cypress heads are used by turkeys in wet seasons for roosting and in dry seasons for escape, feeding, nesting, and brood rearing.

Bayheads. Where surface water collects in deep organic depressions, often from subsurface seepage off sandy hills, junglelike growths of woody shrubs, vines, and ferns develop. Any large trees are probably broad-leaved evergreens such as sweet bay, red bay, and loblolly

bay. These forested swamps are called bayheads. The shallow water and thin ground cover protect bayheads from frequent and damaging fires, although they are subject to peat fires during excessively prolonged dry periods. Turkeys seldom use this dense cover except for temporary escape from excessive hunting pressure and for roosting.

Habitat Requirements

Food is critical to wild turkey survival and reproduction, but the location of food supplies seems one of the least important determinants of habitat utilization by turkeys in Florida. A more compelling factor is the structure of the cover. Turkeys do not occur in large numbers where tree cover is too sparse or where understory vegetation is too dense.

Habitat structure and food supplies are not necessarily good predictors of wild turkey populations in Flor-

Mystic Warriors by Brian Jarvi. Wild turkey-related items, such as art, help enthusiasts enjoy the wild turkey more and have become a substantial industry.

Gobbler (left) and hen (above). The sexes of the wild turkey are quite distinctive (see chapter 4, Physical Characteristics).

Florida turkey.

Eastern turkey.

Rio Grande turkey.

Merriam's turkey.

Gould's turkey.

Ocellated turkey, a closely related species.

Insects, such as this grasshopper, are high in protein and are essential for the rapidly growing young poults.

Red mulberry fruit is a choice food of the eastern wild turkey in the Northeast.

Blackberry and dewberry fruits are readily consumed during summer where they occur in wild turkey range.

Dandelion is a regular spring food for the Merriam's turkey.

Large, mature grass seeds, such as this *Paspalum*, are eaten by wild turkeys in summer.

Oak acorns are the most important winter food throughout the range of the wild turkey.

Fruits of a variety of shrubs, such as this American beautyberry, are eaten by wild turkeys as they ripen from summer through fall.

Dogwood fruits show up consistently in the fall diet of the eastern wild turkey throughout its range.

Wild grapes are a preferred fall food throughout a wide area.

Sumac fruit is a regular fall and winter food, especially when winter snows cover other foods on the ground.

Hen and nest. It takes about 28 days of incubation for the poults to hatch.

Hatching poults. It takes about 2 days for all the poults to hatch.

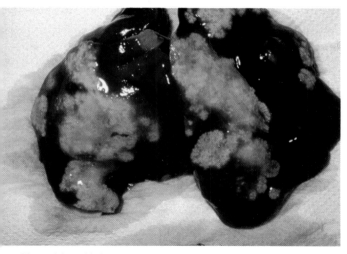

Liver with multiple granulomas from a wild turkey with coligranuloma caused by the bacterium *Eschrichia coli*. This disease has been diagnosed sporadically among wild turkeys in the Southeast.

Multiple granulomas and areas of necrosis in the liver of a wild turkey with a septicemia caused by the bacterium *Fusobacterium nucleatum*. Several other diseases, including histomoniasis or coligranuloma, appear similar to this, making laboratory tests important in identifying which disease is present.

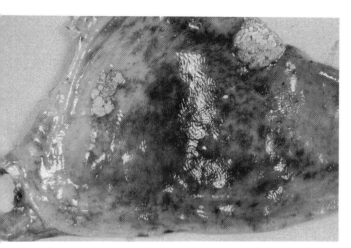

Necrotic enteritis with ulceration of the large intestine of a wild turkey caused by the bacterium *Clostridium perfringens*. This disease has been diagnosed rarely in wild turkeys.

Split and broken tail feathers from a wild turkey caused by invasion of several species of fungi. This condition was seen for several years in wild turkeys from floodplain areas in Louisiana and may be related to periodic flooding, which promotes fungus growth.

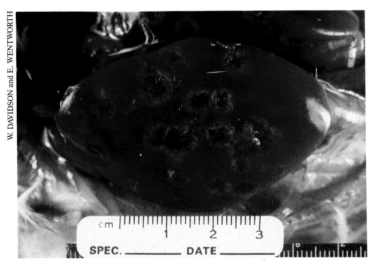

Histomoniasis, also known as "blackhead disease," is nearly always characterized by multiple discrete areas of necrosis and fibrosis in the liver. It is devastating to turkeys, with the mortality rate among infected turkeys being very high, usually well over 75 percent.

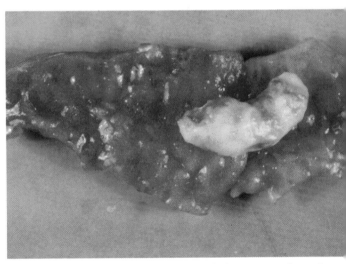

Necrotic cecal cores in turkeys with histomoniasis are present in nearly all cases. When present along with liver lesions, they are considered strong presumptive evidence for a diagnosis of histomoniasis. Other galliform birds, especially chickens, pheasants, and junglefowl, are reservoirs for histomoniasis. For this reason efforts should be made to prevent their contact with wild turkey populations.

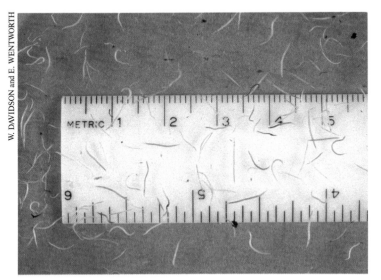

The cecal nematodes, *Heterakis gallinarum*, are required for the natural transmission of *Histomonas meleagridis*, the causative agent of histomoniasis. Turkeys become infected with histomoniasis by ingesting *Heterakis* eggs from the soil or by eating earthworms, which can store *Heterakis* larvae in their bodies.

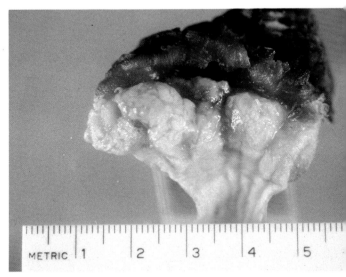

The proventricular nematode, *Dispharynx nasuta*, may cause tissue proliferation and inflammation leading to obstruction of the proventriculus in wild turkeys, especially young poults. This nematode also occurs in many other species of wild birds.

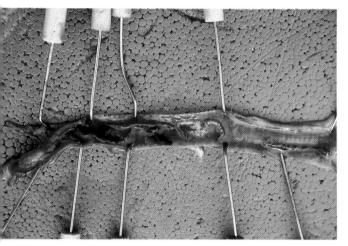

The gapeworm, *Syngamus trachea*, may produce mechanical obstruction of the trachea in young turkey poults, resulting in death due to suffocation. Mortality from *S. trachea* is not thought to be common among wild poults.

Wild turkeys commonly have infestations of lice, and either lice or their egg masses are readily visible upon close inspection of the feathers and skin. Many other types of external parasites occur on turkeys, but these external parasites are not health risks to people. They do occasionally crawl onto successful turkey hunters.

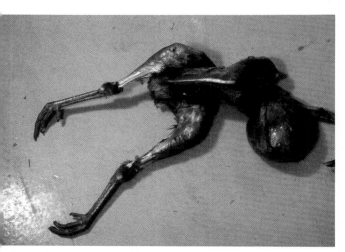

Impaction of the crop with coarse ingesta has been noted on a few occasions in wild turkeys from the southeastern United States, but the cause of this condition is not known. In one case, the crop contents accounted for a third of the body weight.

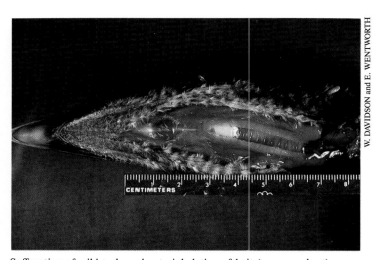

Suffocation of wild turkeys due to inhalation of bait (corn or wheat) during capture operations has been reported infrequently. It should be considered a possibility with any birds that die during capture and handling, especially if death occurs immediately after capture and there is no indication of injury.

The Legacy Continues by Zettie Jones.

ida. These factors are often overshadowed by the effects of hunting. Marginal habitat hunted conservatively will have a higher and more productive wild turkey population than outstanding habitat that is overhunted.

Although scientific data are lacking, field experience suggests that approximately 25 to 30 percent tree cover within a stand is the minimum threshold for Florida turkey habitation. But the size and density of trees that wild turkeys require are affected by the level of human intrusion. The less disturbance and hunting pressure, the more heavily turkeys will use sparsely timbered cover. This relationship between cover and human disturbance has been observed repeatedly on heavily hunted public lands and suggests that dense timber for escape cover is especially important in hunted areas.

Turkeys avoid dense understory vegetation when foraging, regardless of overstory character, probably because of the high risk of attack by mammalian predators. Consequently, wild turkeys do not occupy marshes, bayheads, oak scrub, densely vegetated forest clearcuts, unburned pine woods, or other dense cover that has limited lateral visibility at the turkey's eye level. Turkeys prefer cover that allows good visibility out to about 40 meters (44 yards) (author's personal observations).

A typical wild turkey nest in low saw palmetto cover in south-central Florida.

The wild turkey's requirement for forest cover and the bird's aversion to dense understory vegetation suggest that avoiding predation is more critical than finding food in the everyday life of the Florida turkey. The resourceful wild turkey can usually find food wherever cover requirements are met.

Important turkey habitat components in Florida include cypress forest, bottomland hardwood, and hardwood hammocks associated with small sloughs, glades, shallow ponds, small, improved cattle pastures, and grassy forest openings. Mixed-pine and hardwood uplands, although not an extensive cover type in the peninsula, are also excellent. Longleaf pine wood with turkey oak is good turkey habitat when associated with streams and swamps.

The habitat component most important to Florida wild turkey productivity is spring and summer brood range. The most productive brood habitat is on moist, fertile soils where much of the sunlight reaches ground level and permits grasses, herbs, and other low-level plants to grow vigorously, supporting populations of insects and other arthropods during spring and summer. Good brood cover is open enough for lateral visibility by the brood hen and not too high for the hen to see over when standing. Broods do not regularly use even excellent herbaceous cover farther than about 100 meters (328 feet) from forest cover. So small openings are used more fully than large ones.

One excellent natural brood cover type is cypress woods. When not flooded, it has variable canopy densities and contains pockets of organic soil producing patches of lush understory vegetation adjacent to heavily shaded spots. It also has ample trees for escape cover. Small, cattle-grazed or mechanically mowed clearings on moist soils adjacent to any type of heavy timber are also good brood habitat. Expansive forested conditions are too shaded and therefore poor in producing spring and summer food. Completely unforested conditions are unsatisfactory for lack of escape cover. Especially dry soils do not produce the vigorous vegetative growth necessary for producing seeds and arthropods.

Habitat Management Goals

Habitat management, using the best natural conditions as the model, should be directed toward fostering suitable vegetative structure. Suitable structure is more important than plant species composition, and there is no reason to plant selected wild plant species not already present. Agricultural plantings of certain types might be beneficial, but no research findings support the practice. Many agricultural operations conducted to benefit wild

Typical Florida wild turkey nesting habitat. There is ample walking space, and the hen can see over the surrounding vegetation when standing. This is a favored nesting cover of the Florida wild turkey.

turkeys provide only fall and early winter foods and are probably not cost-effective.

The most critical factor affecting wild turkey population size may be the amount and quality of spring and summer brood range. When less than 20 percent of the landscape is in open fields, and the adjoining woods is mature, more openings should be created and maintained. Up to 30 percent of the landscape should be in fields, improved pasture, sloughs, shallow ponds, and similar covers that produce summer turkey foods at ground level.

Whenever possible, hardwoods should be favored over pine in forest management, and older pine stands should be favored over closely planted stands. Hardwood logging should be minimized, and conversion from hardwood to pine should be avoided.

My observations suggest that a ratio of 20 to 80 open areas (fields, sloughs, and grassy glades) to forest is a suitable year-round mix. Although Florida turkeys tolerate large openings, the acreage in the middle of fresh clearcuts larger than about 12 hectares (30 acres) remains relatively unused by turkeys. In effect, the middle of a large clearcut is useless to turkeys. Further, a forest clearcut in Florida serves as an opening for only about a year. Thereafter, a clearcut has become too dense for turkeys and is used only around the edges, primarily for nesting.

Fire should be used at optimal frequency. Most of the understory and ground cover in pine woods should be burned every 2 to 3 years, but a few large patches should be left unburned each year as nesting cover. Two-year-old burns are favored nesting cover.

In a pine woods burning program, care should be taken to "ring out" (protect from burning) any young stands of oaks. Water oak and upland laurel oak will make a respectable hammock and begin producing significant acorn crops when 12 to 15 years old. That addition would improve the carrying capacity of any tract dominated by pine.

Although the effects of cattle grazing on wild turkey populations have not been studied, moderate to heavy grazing seems beneficial in all types of Florida turkey cover. A wide variety of cover types and cover treatments should be encouraged.

Where suitable cover exists for escape and for brood rearing, no special provisions are needed for roosting sites. And if surface water is ever needed, it is readily available in Florida wild turkey habitat.

FOODS

Two Florida studies of turkey food habits have been published (Schemnitz 1956 and Barwick et al. 1973), and I have made a number of personal observations and notes on crop contents and feeding of Florida turkeys since about 1960. Nothing suggests anything unique about the diet of the Florida turkey. Like the other turkey populations, the Florida turkey has a widely varied diet and does not pass up the opportunity to eat almost anything with food value that it can find and swallow.

In one study (Barwick et al. 1973), the spring foods of 21 wild poults 1 to 14 days old were identified and measured by examining stomach and crop contents. Star grass seed heads made up 75 percent of the diet by volume and occurred in 85.7 percent of the specimens. Twenty-five percent of the crop and stomach contents by volume was animal matter, entirely insects. Star grass occurs widely in the natural ground cover of unshaded sites associated with saw palmetto and wire grass and would be widely available to broods using prairie edges and other natural open places.

In a sample of 54 summer poults 2 to 24 weeks old from 2 study areas, grass seeds, acorns, and star grass seed pods made up the bulk of the diet. Acorns of the black oak group, such as laurel oak and water oak, are available well into the summer. Even after they sprout, turkeys dig them up. The animal foods eaten by the same group of poults was 27 percent of the diet by volume.

In a sample of 8 adult Florida wild turkeys taken in summer at Fisheating Creek, wild grapes, grass seeds, and butterfly pea flowers were the most important plant items, and butterflies and moths were the most important animal items (Barwick et al. 1973).

These studies and general observations of turkey feeding behavior suggest that insects and seeds from spring plants are the most important components of the wild turkey's diet in spring, with grass seeds becoming increasingly more important from middle summer to fall. Other important spring and summer foods are the many types of flower blossoms and seed pods, succulent leaves and stems, summer fruits and berries, and small terrestrial insects and other arthropods. Obviously, summer foods are those produced at ground level rather than in the forest canopy or by shrubs. Those foods underscore the value of herbaceous openings in turkey habitat.

Acorns of several species top the list of fall and winter foods, followed by grass seeds and the seeds of such trees and shrubs as pine, sabal palm, gallberry, wax myrtle, hackberry, and dogwood (Schemnitz 1956, author's files).

Providing food has been a focal point of most wild turkey management, despite the dearth of available information. Data are needed that will address some of the following questions: Is food a limiting factor in typically structured wild turkey habitat? When food is a limiting factor, can that lack be remedied by artificial feeding? If so, what are the best foods? What is the relationship between the productivity and health of turkey popula-

tions and the availability and nutritional value of the foods they eat? Are the supplies of certain preferred foods exhausted by turkeys each season? Are some foods produced in excess of the turkey's needs? To what extent do competing wildlife species consume turkey foods, and of what importance is such competition to turkey productivity? Will easily available food sources influence seasonal movement, and if so, how strongly? What correlations exist between heavy dependence on artificial food sources and predation rates? Is poult survival higher where brood food is abundant?

The answers to questions such as these would be the kind of information that is badly needed for more intensive wild turkey management than is now possible.

MATING AND NESTING

In southern Florida, turkeys gobble during warm periods in January, but this vocalizing precedes mating by several weeks. Spring breakup of gobbler flocks occurs during late February and early March. It is usually mid-March before the hen flocks dissolve and hens begin to associate with adult gobblers.

The mating season (Figure 3) of the wild turkey in Florida is not much earlier than for the eastern turkey in the other southern states. Laying is mainly in April, and major hatching is in May rather than in March and April as reported previously (Bailey and Rinell 1967a). Although the latitudinal effect on mating has not been carefully measured in the Florida peninsula, differences from south to north are not noticeable except for the vigorous

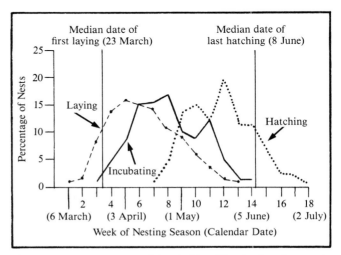

Figure 3. The mating season of the Florida wild turkey based on yearly samples from 1968 to 1982.

premating-season gobbling that usually occurs in southern Florida.

Recent radio-tracking studies in Florida have produced information on many aspects of nesting not yet studied in other regions. The observed behavior is probably not peculiar to the Florida wild turkey.

Nesting

The hen lays her eggs in a shallow, scratched-out place on bare soil. The nest is not prepared until the first egg is about to be laid. The hen remains at the nest an average of 1 hour (extremes from 0.2 to 2.0 hours) as she lays each of the first 5 eggs. Laying is mainly in midday. Before leaving the nest, the hen places over the eggs a few dry leaves picked up in her bill from beside the nest. This debris accumulates during the laying period to become the lining of the nest.

After laying her first egg, the hen skips one day. Sometimes the hen skips another day after the second egg. But with the laying of the third or fourth egg, laying becomes a daily event. After laying the sixth egg, the hen begins sitting on the nest about 1 hour longer each day. This routine gradually initiates incubating behavior. The notion that a turkey hen lays her clutch without incubating until after all eggs are laid is not correct. By the time the last egg is laid, she has done approximately a full day of incubating.

Overnight incubating behavior of the hen begins with the laying of the last egg, or sometimes with the next to last. A few hens roost in trees an additional night after laying the final egg, returning to the nest the next morning to begin continuous day-and-night incubating.

The eggs hatch after 25 or 26 days of continuous incubating, rather than the 28 days traditionally stated. This briefer period may result partly from the warmer Florida climate where this study was done. But another factor is the embryonic development that occurs when the hen sits during the laying period. The widely quoted 28-day incubating period (see Mosby and Handley 1943) is evidently based on the embryonic development of eggs in artificial incubators and does not take into account the incubating behavior of the hen during the laying period, which shortens the period of continuous setting by at least a day.

Studies in Florida indicate that the wild turkey has little, if any, hatching synchronization as reported in the northern bobwhite (Vince 1969). Hatching requires nearly 2 days from the first pipping to leaving the nest.

Clutch Size

In a study of 179 completed Florida wild turkey nests, average clutch size was 10.3 eggs. The mode was 10 (Figure 4). Clutches of yearling hens averaged 10.0 eggs, while adult clutches averaged 10.5. The small difference was statistically significant at the 10 percent level of confidence. Clutch size may be slightly smaller in Florida turkeys than in populations farther north, as is true of other birds that lay large clutches (Welty 1982), but data available from other regions do not reveal a large difference (Table 1).

Nesting Habitat

The vegetation was analyzed near 236 nests on study areas in north-central and southern Florida (Williams and Austin 1988). The hens preferred to nest in dense ground cover, but they usually could see over the top of the surrounding cover when they stood at the nest. Hens

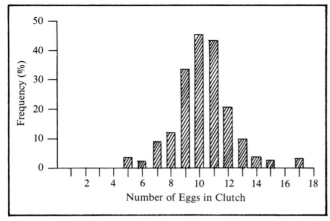

Figure 4. Frequency of distribution of clutch sizes in 179 incubated wild turkey nests on study areas in north-central and south-central Florida.

Table 1. Mean clutch sizes reported for the wild turkey.

State	Number of nests	Average number of eggs	Reference
Alabama	32	9.8	Everett et al. 1980
Florida	179	10.3	Williams and Austin 1988
Mississippi	12	11.6	Schumacher 1977
Missouri	25	11.1	Dalke et al. 1946
Pennsylvania	11	12.7	Kozicky 1948
Texas	71	10.3	Cook 1972
Virginia	27	11.3	Mosby and Handley 1943
Virginia	34	12.3	McDowell 1956

showed a strong preference for nesting on dry, sandy soil in the transition zone between palmetto prairie and oak scrub. This zone is never flooded, and water does not puddle in the sand, even during the heaviest rains. Many nests were in other dense cover, sometimes including herbaceous growth in cypress woods and various woody and herbaceous plant cover in pine woods. Contrary to widespread belief, very few nests were in low places that could be easily flooded by heavy spring rains.

Hens are well concealed on their nests in Florida cover. They will tolerate a man's (and presumably a predator's) approach within 2 meters (6.6 feet) without flushing. This tolerance lessens the risk that spring turkey hunters might accidentally flush nesting hens. I have observed that hens on less-concealed nests are prone to flush more readily.

Nesting Success and Predation

Sixty percent of 171 nests monitored in Florida were successful. Not all, however, were observed from their very beginning, a flaw that could bias the results. To avoid this bias, the Mayfield (1961) method, which takes into account nest survival on a per-day basis, was used. Calculated that way, the proportions of nests surviving was 63.8 percent during the laying period, 70.8 percent during the incubating period, and 45.2 percent during the entire nesting period. This is the true success rate, lower than the 60 percent recorded overall on a per-nest basis. The loss rate per day was twice as high during the 14-day laying period as during the incubating period.

By trapping predators and examining predator field sign at nests hit by predators, it was determined that the major nest predators were the raccoon in the cypress woods and the striped skunk and spotted skunk in drier upland sites. Other identified nest predators were the opossum, gray fox, and domestic dog. Crows destroyed only a single nest of the 248 under observation. The eggs disappeared from a few nests without evidence of the predator involved.

Potential nest predators that were not known to take turkey eggs in the Florida study included the feral hog, which has been reported to depredate turkey nests (Barkalow 1942, Blakey 1937), and the armadillo, which has previously been reported not to take turkey eggs (Kennamer and Lunceford 1973). Both of these species were abundant on the Florida study areas.

Hens brooded their poults during hatching and for several weeks after leaving the nest. Broods were tracked by radio in rainy weather, but no poult was known to die from exposure to cold or wet weather. When turkey poults were observed while rain fell, none was seen holding its head to the sky, as has been widely supposed.

Poults can fly well at 11 to 12 days, but they do not roost in trees until approximately 14 days old (Barwick et al. 1971). During the ground-roosting period, broods suffer a predation rate exceeding 70 percent (Williams and Austin 1988). A similarly high level of poult predation was observed in Alabama (Speake 1980). Raccoons, red-shouldered hawks, and gray foxes were implicated in the Florida studies; owls, snakes, broad-winged hawks, bobcats, and dogs were suspected in Alabama (Speake et al. 1985). Such a wide array of predators poses a serious obstacle in considering possible remedies to high poult predation. More knowledge about the relationship between habitat structure and turkey vulnerability to predation would be useful.

Flock Structure

The age and sexual makeup of Florida wild turkey flocks are rigid. The family flock, composed of the brood hen and young of both sexes, is the initial social unit. Many summer brood flocks include 2 or 3 family flocks.

In late fall, the immature males leave the family flocks and form their own loose social units. Some young males attempt to associate with adult males in winter but are rebuffed by the older birds. After mating season is over, a few yearlings are incorporated into the social structure of adult male flocks. But many yearling flocks remain intact, and they mature as adult male flocks composed of a single age class.

The family flocks, as well as flocks of hens that were unsuccessful in nesting, remain segregated from other turkeys as described by Watts (1969) for Texas populations of wild turkey. Thus, in summer there are 3 types of turkey flocks, and in winter there are 4. This segregation by age and sex is seldom violated except during the mating season, when turkeys of both sexes and all ages are sometimes seen together.

Molt

In molting pattern, Florida and eastern turkeys are similar but not identical. The postjuvenal molt of the wing is more extensive in Florida, and the tail molt is not as orderly as in *M. g. silvestris* (Leopold 1943a). The season of molting is longer in Florida, lasting about 6 months per individual and 9 or 10 months for the population. The molting differences between *M. g. osceola* and *M. g. silvestris* probably reflect the mild Florida climate and longer warm season available for replacing plumage.

It was once thought that the 2 most distal juvenal primaries of the eastern and Florida wild turkey are retained in the first winter plumage (Petrides 1942,

Table 2. Number and percentage of 125 juvenile turkeys in first winter (alternate) plumage that retained juvenal primaries 9 and 10, 10 only, or neither 9 nor 10 (Williams and Austin 1988).

Sex	Retained numbers 9 & 10	Retained only number 10	Retained neither number 9 nor 10
Males	2 (5%)	30 (73%)	9 (22%)
Females	7 (8%)	60 (71%)	17 (20%)
Total	9 (7%)	90 (72%)	26 (21%)

Leopold 1943). After reporting that, Petrides (1945) modified his view by saying that juvenile Florida wild turkeys tend to molt the number 9 primary during the postjuvenal molt.

More recently, it has been observed (Williams and Austin 1988) that 72 percent of young Florida turkeys molt number 9 (retaining only the number 10) and 21 percent molt both 9 and 10, retaining no juvenal primary in the "first winter plumage." Only about 7 percent of Florida turkeys retain juvenal primaries 9 and 10 during their first winter (Table 2). Dan W. Speake (personal communication: 1975) observed that turkeys in Alabama shed primary number 9 before their first winter, as do about 72 percent of Florida turkeys. This molting condition probably extends well into the range of the eastern wild turkey beyond Alabama and may apply to wild turkey populations in the western United States.

The latest evidence indicates that a significant proportion of juvenile wild turkeys cannot be identified correctly by the traditional distal primaries character. So the configuration of the greater upper secondary covert patch (Williams 1961) is a better feature for identifying juveniles than are the juvenal primaries. For a more complete description of the molt of *M. g. osceola*, see Williams and Austin (1988).

Voice

Preliminary studies of the Florida wild turkey's voice indicate at least 28 calls (Williams 1984). While there is presently no reason to think that the voice of the Florida wild turkey is substantially different from that of other populations, studies in other regions could be illuminating.

Wild turkey vocalizations have important social functions that begin even before hatching. The hen's voice is crucial to the imprinting process (Lorenz 1937) and for controlling poult defensive behavior during the early days of life. Some characteristics of the Florida turkey's calls as analyzed from sonograms made from recordings in the wild are given in Table 3.

Table 3. Characteristics of 11 selected calls of the Florida wild turkey.

Name of call[a]	Usual number of notes	Peculiar quality, if any	Rhythm Beat	Rhythm Notes per second	Rhythm Length of notes (seconds)
lost whistling	3	musical	waltzlike	2.5	0.20
kee-kee	3	musical	uneven	2.5	0.10–0.15
kee-kee-run	4–10	variable	uneven	3.3	0.05–0.10
tree yelp (hen)	3–5	nasal	even	6–7	0.08
plain yelp (hen)	4–7+	—	even	6–7	0.08–0.10
lost yelp (hen)	8–20+	raspy	even	6–7	0.10–0.15
assembly yelp	6–10+	variable	even	variable	0.12–0.20
plain cluck	1–3	staccato	uneven	1	0.04
loud clucking	4–10+	staccato	uneven	3–7	0.04
alarm putt	1+	staccato	uneven	1	0.04
cackle	10–15	excited	uneven	5	variable

[a] Based on Williams 1984.

PROBLEMS

Habitat Loss

In Florida, wild turkey populations have been a by-product of timber- and rangeland. Timber and cattle, however, are not as profitable as the more intensive forms of development and are being phased out. The economic developments of choice are those that attract and accommodate tourists and a larger resident human population.

The most serious inroads into upland wildlife habitat are being made by new housing and apartments, ranchette subdivisions on wild lands, trailer parks, new and expanded highways, new and enlarged airports, industrial areas, shopping centers, tourist attractions, phosphate mining, garbage disposal, and the many other support facilities required by more than 12 million residents and additional millions of tourists and winter residents. Although not to the liking of most Florida conservationists, the philosophy of intensive development is supported by Florida government, and state environmental agencies can do nothing to stop growth of the human population.

Recent Florida growth management legislation is designed to accommodate future growth. But because the legislation has unintentionally slowed construction of housing developments in parts of central and southern Florida, it is coming under attack from the state's growth and development forces. If development continues to be curtailed, there are signs that the legislation may be amended so that development can regain its rapid pace.

Many environmental problems directly affecting human health and welfare have gained front stage far in front of wildlife and hunting—pesticides and heavy metals in food and water, oil drilling in the Gulf of Mex-

ico, water shortages and excesses, commercial over-
fishing, beach erosion, and eutrophication of lakes, to
name a few.

Efforts to save wildlife habitat from development
include state acquisition of a few of the wild tracts that
are left, attempting to impede urban development
through use of regulatory devices such as the endangered
species laws, and attempting to legally define wetlands
into the public domain. There are, of course, many other
activities being lobbied and pursued by conservation interests in Florida, but they do not promise much for the
wild turkey and other wildlife.

Most Florida wetlands, including those with cover
types that are valuable as turkey habitat, have experienced some degree of drainage. Many large swamps and
marshes have been purposely dried up altogether since
the late 1800s. The support given wetland protection by
state government is, like growth management legislation,
intended to accommodate the development of Florida by
providing an endless supply of water for additional residents, tourists, and agriculture.

The state of Florida has a sizable land acquisition
program, but dry land is very expensive. To date, much
emphasis has been on preserving wetlands. Meanwhile,
several types of wild uplands (i.e., old-growth longleaf
pine flatwoods, upland oak hammock, and oak scrub)
have been nearly eliminated. The Florida wild turkey
would benefit from more emphasis on buying large,
wild, upland wooded tracts of types seriously underrepresented in public ownership.

Is Florida overpopulated? That depends on your
perspective and values. Wildlife conservationists and
hunters consider Florida already seriously overpopulated. But it is a wild paradise in the sun for the new-
comers from the even denser centers of the North, for
many tourists visiting the man-made features and attractions, and for younger urban dwellers and foreign immigrants seeking their fortunes here. They are now in the
majority, and it is their interests that the state of Florida
will pursue in the future.

Management Needs

Although turkey hunting interests are pressing for
an accelerated Florida wild turkey management program, the available knowledge provides few dependable
management options. And there is no more vacant habitat to stock in Florida. We will have to find ways to make
better use of existing turkey populations.

Management to increase turkey productivity would
be an appropriate objective to offset creeping habitat
losses. Unfortunately, the land management practices
widely used to ostensibly increase turkey productivity
have not been tested in Florida or anywhere else. It re-

mains to be seen how the carrying capacity of wild turkey
range can be increased by direct manipulation. The necessary research has not been done.

There is neither a census method for turkeys nor any
suitable substitute. This lack seriously impedes tests of
the efficacy of potential management procedures. If you
can't count the birds accurately, how can you tell if a
procedure is working? Research is needed here, too.

Despite the critical importance of proper turkey harvest management, the subject has received little serious
attention. In one Florida study (Williams and Austin
1988), crippling losses of 20 percent were measured during spring gobbler hunting on a public hunting area. That
loss is greater than any known management procedure
can offset. But there is little information on arms and
ammunition efficacy in turkey hunting.

Although there are a number of restrictions on arms
and ammunition for taking deer and other game, it is
legal in Florida to shoot wild turkeys with virtually any
firearm that is used for any other kind of game. The .22
rimfire rifle and lesser firearms—as well as high-powered
deer rifles and buckshot or slugs in shotguns—are legal
for taking wild turkeys in Florida. When such arms and
ammunition are used on wild turkeys, crippling losses
are high.

Although either-sex turkey hunting is allowed in
Florida, nothing is known about the proportion of hens
that can be harvested without adversely affecting population productivity. Previous studies indicated serious overharvest of hens on one Florida study area (Williams and
Austin 1988), and hens are probably being overharvested
on other public areas. This is not to suggest that fall
hunting should be ended in Florida. Fall turkey hunting
can be done without excessive harvest of hens. But adequate research, management, and public educational
programs will be required to plan and carry out such
hunting. Florida needs to make more efficient use of the
diminishing hunting opportunities it has without dis-
carding present opportunities such as fall turkey hunting.

What About the Future?

A few seasons of good turkey productivity—coupled with the benefits of better protection and better harvest management—could result in temporary upswings
in harvest levels in Florida. But the long-range trend will
be downward. Improvements can be made in current and
near future uses of the wild turkey resource by resuming
a substantial wild turkey research and management program in the Florida Game and Fresh Water Fish Commission, emphasizing harvest management and population productivity enhancement.

Chapter 16

EASTERN TURKEY IN EASTERN OAK-HICKORY AND NORTHERN HARDWOOD FORESTS

Gerald A. Wunz
Wildlife Biologist
Pennsylvania Game Commission
Milroy, Pennsylvania

James C. Pack
Wildlife Biologist
West Virginia Department of
Natural Resources
Elkins, West Virginia

No other wild turkey range has such varied habitats, landforms, and histories as the oak-hickory and northern hardwood forests of the eastern United States. These 2 forest ecosystems, extending from New England seacoasts to southern Ontario into midwestern prairies and south to western Tennessee and northern Alabama, originally covered nearly 777,000 square kilometers (300,000 square miles) in 20 states. These forests embraced all of the Blue Ridge, Ridge and Valley, Appalachian Plateau, and Interior Low Plateau physiographic provinces and portions of the Central Lowlands, Piedmont Plateau, Coastal Plain, and New England provinces (Fenneman 1938). The varied climates, soils, aspects, and terrains in these forests span 3 life zones (Canadian, Alleghenian, Carolinian) and contain perhaps the most diverse and abundant biota found anywhere outside of the tropics.

ENVIRONMENT

Climate

The climate of this region is temperate and mainly continental. It has warm, humid summers and moderate-to-cold winters that are locally influenced by latitude (35° to 45°) and elevations that vary from sea level to 1,800 meters (6,000 feet) in the southern Appalachians and northern New England. Precipitation is fairly evenly distributed during each month of the year, averaging 114 centimeters (45 inches) but varying from 76 centimeters (30 inches) on the leeward side of some mountains to nearly 254 centimeters (100 inches) on the highlands of the southern Appalachians.

Average snowfall varies from 13 centimeters (5 inches) that lasts 5 days on the ground in the South to more than 254 centimeters (100 inches) that covers the ground for 120 days on snowbelt uplands to the south and east of Lakes Erie and Ontario. The forest regions seem more closely related to distribution of snowfall than to annual precipitation, presumably because of the associated temperature. The oak-hickory forest is generally limited to areas with less than 127 centimeters (50 inches) of snowfall (Lull 1968).

Physiography

At the heart of these 2 major deciduous forest regions that extend more than 1,610 kilometers (1,000 miles) from southwest to northeast are the Appalachians, among the oldest mountains on earth. The Appalachians include the Blue Ridge, Ridge and Valley (both true mountains), and Appalachian Plateau physiographic provinces. Cataclysmic folding formed these mountains. Subsequent erosion of the folds exposed a variety of strata that slowly uplifted and weathered, leaving hard sandstone ridges and valleys of shale and limestone. The resulting mosaic of soils ranged from excellent (derived from limestone) to infertile (from acid shales and sandstones).

The Appalachian Plateau, which flanks this mountain range on its western side, includes the Cumberland

The darker eastern and Florida subspecies inhabit the humid eastern U.S. forests. *Photo by L. Williams.*

Plateau on the south and the Allegheny Plateau on the north. The plateau is higher (1,200 meters, 4,000 feet) on its eastern side, decreasing to 180 meters (600 feet) on its western and northwestern edges. There it joins the Interior Low Plateau and the plains of the Central Lowlands. More recently uplifted than the Appalachian Mountains, the Appalachian Plateau has been deeply dissected by stream courses that have left narrow, steep-sided valleys. Plateau soils were derived from horizontal strata of mainly sandstone and shale. Consequently they are not as varied as the mountain soils, tend to be podzolic, and are generally less fertile.

Through much of the Appalachians, the rugged terrain and poor soils discouraged permanent settlement. Although denuded of nearly all of its original forest through logging or clearing for farming, 65 percent of the

Appalachians has remained forest or reverted to forest. Agriculture is now limited mainly to the limestone valleys of the Ridge and Valley area and to the flat tops and narrow valley bottoms of the plateau. Numerous mining and manufacturing communities were established in the plateau area to exploit oil, gas, iron, and especially forests and coal. As the minerals and original forests were depleted, many small towns were abandoned. But a number of the larger towns and cities persist as commercial centers that maintain a large human population in parts of the plateau.

Most of the large towns and cities, however, are in the gentler terrain of the other physiographic regions covered by the 2 forest type groups featured in this chapter. The northeast coastal area, where colonists first settled in numbers and cleared most of its forests, remains the

The juncture of eastern mountains and open valleys is good wild turkey habitat. *Photo by J. Pack.*

most densely populated part of the United States. It extends from Virginia to southern Maine and is referred to as the East Coast Megapolis.

Most of today's agricultural lands are on the plains of the Central Lowlands in Ohio, Indiana, northern New York, and southern Ontario. Also containing farm areas

are parts of the Interior Low Plateau in western Tennessee and Kentucky, the Piedmont Plateau and Coastal Plains from Maryland to New Jersey, and the glaciated northern Allegheny Plateau from Ohio into New York. Only remnants of forest remain (less than 40 percent) as woodlots or waterway corridors in the farming areas. Much of New England was cleared for farming during colonial times, but soils in most of this heavily glaciated region were too thin and rocky to sustain farms. Most of the area's farms have reverted to forest. New Hampshire is now 84 percent forested and Vermont 73 percent.

The total area occupied by the 2 forest ecosystems historically constituted only 8 percent of the nation's land area. Today, some 80 million people (35 percent of the total U.S. population) share living and recreational space with wild turkeys on the remaining 417,000 square kilometers (161,000 square miles) of forested habitat (Table 1).

Forest History

The eastern oak-hickory forest ecosystem extends from western Tennessee and Kentucky northeastward in an unbroken band up to 500 kilometers (300 miles) wide for 1,610 kilometers (1,000 miles) to the New England coast. The northern hardwood forest borders the oak-hickory forest in a similar, but narrower, band to the north, extending from southwest Indiana to western

Table 1. Human populations and forestland in states included in the eastern oak-hickory and northern hardwood forest ecosystems.

State	Number of people per square kilometer (square mile)	Square kilometers of oak-hickory or northern hardwood forest ecosystems[a] (square miles)	Percent of state forested
Connecticut	248 (642)	7,500 (2,900)	60
Delaware	117 (304)	1,300 (500)	30
Indiana	58 (150)	16,100 (6,200)	30
Kentucky	35 (90)	46,100 (17,800)	49
Maine	13 (34)	9,800 (3,800)	76
Maryland	153 (397)	10,100 (3,900)	41
Massachusetts	268 (694)	10,400 (4,000)	59
New Hampshire	38 (99)	9,600 (3,700)	81
New Jersey	362 (937)	5,200 (2,000)	40
New York	136 (353)	55,700 (21,500)	56
North Carolina	43 (111)	16,600 (6,400)	62
Ohio	101 (261)	25,900 (10,000)	34
Pennsylvania	101 (261)	64,700 (25,000)	58
Rhode Island	342 (886)	1,500 (600)	60
Tennessee	42 (109)	51,800 (20,000)	50
Vermont	20 (53)	9,300 (3,600)	77
Virginia	50 (130)	25,900 (10,000)	70
West Virginia	31 (80)	50,000 (19,300)	80
Total	95 (245)	417,500 (161,200)	57

[a] USFS State Forest Statistics, 1976–1985.

Table 2. Area of major forest types within the oak-hickory and northern hardwood ecosystems.[a]

State	Oak hickory		Northern hardwood		Other types	
	square kilometers	square miles	square kilometers	square miles	square kilometers	square miles
Connecticut	3,000	1,160	1,240	480	3,240	1,250
Delaware	260	100	0	0	1,040	400
Indiana	5,930	2,290	6,470	2,500	3,780	1,460
Kentucky	29,140	11,250	5,440	2,100	11,760	4,540
Maine	850	330	2,380	920	6,680	2,580
Maryland	4,710	1,820	800	310	4,790	1,850
Massachusetts	2,430	940	1,530	590	7,980	3,080
New Hampshire	1,300	500	3,210	1,240	5,050	1,950
New Jersey	1,550	600	1,290	500	2,330	900
New York	7,380	2,850	30,430	11,750	17,960	6,940
North Carolina	15,540	6,000	650	250	390	150
Ohio	15,800	6,100	5,440	2,100	4,690	1,810
Pennsylvania	30,410	11,740	25,540	9,860	11,860	4,580
Rhode Island	730	280	50	20	880	340
Tennessee	38,330	14,800	2,410	930	12,510	4,830
Vermont	600	230	5,830	2,250	2,950	1,140
Virginia	24,610	9,500	340	130	1,040	400
West Virginia	27,840	10,750	10,830	4,180	8,370	3,230
Total	210,410	81,240	103,880	40,110	107,300	41,430

[a] USFS Forest Statistics, 1976–1985.

Maine and occupying a position between the deciduous and boreal forests. Other than outliers of northern hardwoods in the higher elevations of West Virginia, western Maryland, southwestern Pennsylvania, and the southern Appalachians, the border between these 2 major forest types generally coincides with the southward limit of continental glaciation. In the transition zones, where the 2 forests overlap, oak-hickory types usually occupy the warmer and drier south-facing slopes, and northern hardwoods grow on north-facing slopes. The proportions of these 2 major forest types in the 18 states in the oak-hickory and northern hardwood regions are listed in Table 2.

Unfortunately, we have little qualitative and quantitative information on these forests in their pristine condition. Accounts from early explorers and travelers leave the impression that these forests were largely extensive stands of old-growth timber, broken only occasionally by meadowlike openings that were either natural prairies and glades or made by Native Americans for their villages and primitive farming. In total, these openings probably did not amount to more than 10 percent of the forest area, except perhaps in isolated pockets of prairie in Indiana, Ohio, and Kentucky.

Apparently the understory was usually lush, but Mosby and Handley (1943) reported the forests in the Shenandoah Valley and other limestone valleys were "open and parklike," believed to be largely a result of extensive burning there by the Native Americans "to keep down the underbrush and to hunt game." Braun (1950)

found indications that much of the eastern deciduous forest had been burned by Native Americans prior to settlement by Europeans. These settlers also used burning on a much larger scale to clear land permanently for farming.

Logging of the original forest was piecemeal at first. Through time, however, the water-accessible forests along the northeastern seaboard and larger rivers were nearly eliminated. Large-scale logging did not begin until after the mid-19th century, when railroads and steam-powered logging technology made it possible to penetrate all but the most remote and inaccessible timber stands. By 1925, nearly all of the original forest land in this vast region had been cut over.

The resulting great accumulation of logging debris fueled searing wildfires that repeatedly burned over some areas. In general, fires were probably less frequent in northern hardwood regions than in the drier oak-hickory forests. Regardless, consequences of fire in both ecosystems were changes in forest composition that favored the resprouting and fire-resistant species (such as oaks) and diminished fire-susceptible seedlings (such as white pine and hemlock).

Northern Hardwood Forests

Tree species commonly found within the northern hardwood ecosystem are sugar maple, red maple, American beech, yellow birch, and black cherry. Common associate species that occur in this type are eastern hemlock, white pine, sweet birch, white ash, basswood, white oak, and northern red oak. The climax species seem to be American beech, eastern hemlock, and sugar maple. Throughout the entire northern hardwood forest region, American beech is the most widely distributed species and is usually present in all ages and sizes (Hough and Forbes 1943).

Northern hardwood forests that grow on the central lowland and lake plains region from Indiana to southern Ontario and northwestern New York are mainly a beech-sugar maple association. Because of the gentler terrain and better soils, much of this region is farmed and urbanized. Most of the remnant forest area presently exists as woodlots. The northern hardwoods in the Appalachians, New England, and most of New York are composed of a northern hardwood association of hemlock and white pine. Braun (1950) reported the average number of canopy species in the beech-maple forest was 9.5, compared with the 11.5 average counted in stands of hemlock-white pine northern hardwoods, or 15.7 in the mixed-mesophytic forests or oak-hickory forests to the south.

Although northern hardwood forests are considered less diverse than oak-hickory, Hough (1936) found 25 tree species, 20 shrubs, 4 club mosses, 24 ferns, and 66 herbaceous plants from a 1,652-hectare (4,080-acre) tract of climax forest in northwestern Pennsylvania. Lutz (1930) found 19 tree species, 25 shrubs, 3 club mosses, 10 ferns, and 45 herbaceous plants on a 49-hectare (120-acre) tract of climax forest in the same region. Hobblebush and mapleleaf viburnums were usually the most common shrubs, but these and other shrubs and herbaceous plants have been greatly reduced or eliminated from the understory through long-term overbrowsing by white-tailed deer in portions of this ecosystem (Forbes et al. 1971). Also, most understory species that grow in northern hardwood forests seem to be more palatable to deer or susceptible to browsing damage. Striped maple is often the only shrub able to survive.

Oak-Hickory Forests

The oak-hickory ecosystem is usually composed of forest types represented by various oak species, singularly or in combination with other oaks or hickory, yellow poplar, basswood, buckeye, red maple, black walnut, black locust, sweet gum, and black gum as associates. Before the American chestnut blight, *Endothia parasitica*, the eastern oak-hickory forest was mainly an oak-chestnut association, a climax type in which northern red oak, American chestnut, and yellow poplar were the most frequent dominants. This forest was further diver-

Lush understory develops in unbrowsed forest. *Photo by G. Wunz, Pennsylvania Game Commission.*

Fire can be used to control plant succession and vigor. *Photo by G. Wunz, Pennsylvania Game Commission.*

sified by a climax association of mesophytic cove hardwoods and by altitudinal and aspect variations that also included species more commonly associated with northern hardwood forests. The word "mesophytic" refers to a moderately moist environment in which the majority of plant species thrive best (Sinnot 1946).

This mixed mesophytic forest region, which is at the heart of the oak-hickory ecosystem, was described by

Small openings in oak-hickory stands can produce grassy brood habitat. *Photo by G. Wunz, Pennsylvania Game Commission.*

Braun (1950) as the most complex and oldest association of the Deciduous Forest Formation—from which all other climaxes of the deciduous forest have arisen. This forest attains its greatest diversity of plant species in the southern Appalachians, where as many as 20 tree species may share the canopy, 10 species may occupy the midstory, and 20 shrubs may grow in the understory. Barber

Reproduction in northern hardwood stands can be severely restricted from browsing by white-tailed deer. *Photo by G. Wunz, Pennsylvania Game Commission.*

(1984) identified 54 species of native trees, shrubs, and vines on a 0.4-hectare (1-acre) plot in the Cumberland Plateau of eastern Kentucky. Common understory species in the oak-hickory ecosystem are hollies, greenbrier, grape, blackberry, mountain laurel, rhododendron, blueberry, and huckleberry. Braun (1950) referred to the herbaceous layer as exceedingly luxuriant. This plethora of plant species diminishes somewhat in the portions of the oak-hickory forest to the west and north of the southern Appalachians, but the diversity remains considerable throughout the area of this forest ecosystem.

Until recently, deer populations have not been as high in most of the oak-hickory forests as in some northern hardwood forests. The exception is in Pennsylvania, where decades of overbrowsing have reduced the diversity of oak forest understories to less-palatable ericaceous heath species such as huckleberry, blueberry, and mountain laurel, often in dense stands.

TURKEY HISTORY

Before colonists arrived from Europe, wild turkeys were endemic throughout all of the oak-hickory forest region and all but the northern third of the hardwood forest region that lies in the northern parts of New England and New York. In Ontario, turkeys ranged north to the Canadian Shield and Georgian Bay of Lake Huron.

The old-growth forests of the Northeast supported very abundant wild turkeys before exploitation. *Photo by U.S. Forest Service.*

But also within this historic range were certain places turkeys seldom or never lived, such as the conifer-clad uplands of the higher mountain ranges or plateaus in the Appalachians, the Adirondacks in New York, and the Green Mountains in Vermont. The largest such vacant area was an 80-by-322-kilometer (50-by-200-mile) area on the Allegheny Plateau of north-central Pennsylvania. Although this area was covered mostly with northern hardwoods, in addition to hemlock, the severe winter climate apparently discouraged habitation by turkeys.

Unfortunately, there are no accurate estimates of precolonial turkey densities. But many historical accounts in the early days of settlement agree that turkeys were abundant and seem to have been particularly numerous in the Ohio Valley (Aldrich 1967a). The northeastern United States was the first area to be colonized intensively, and turkey populations suffered from unregulated hunting. Even worse was the destruction of much forest habitat by settlers in relentless land clearing.

By the end of the 19th century, from central Pennsylvania south, the wild turkey was gone from all but the most remote mountains and plateaus of the Appalachians. Wild turkeys were gone from all of New England, Canada, New York, Ohio, Indiana, Delaware, and New

Jersey. The only outlier population remaining was between the Cumberland and Tennessee rivers in western Kentucky.

After the turn of the last century, 2 major events occurred in this region that would have a profound effect on the welfare of the wild turkey: (1) Economics forced a human migration from depleted forest and farms to urban industrial and commercial centers, allowing the abandoned land to revert to forest; and (2) equally important was the blooming of a conservation ethic, that is, the will to restore and protect turkeys and other wildlife resources.

Because of scarce remnant flocks, lack of effective trapping methods, and preoccupation with game farms, early restoration efforts usually were with pen-raised turkeys. Some 284,000 pen-raised turkeys were reported released by wildlife agencies in 13 states in this region. Additional thousands were released by individuals and sporting clubs. The Pennsylvania Game Commission alone had stocked 219,320 of these birds (Wunz 1986b).

Essentially all releases of pen-raised turkeys, regardless of their origin or pedigree, were failures. An assessment of all turkey releases (Bailey and Putnam 1979) showed only 215 of these birds or their progeny were estimated to have survived at the time of the survey in these 13 states. In comparison, they reported that 5,117 wild-trapped turkeys were relocated to 169 release sites, of which 145 resulted in established populations. By 1980, the last state-operated turkey farm closed.

Today, more than 500,000 wild turkeys (about a sixth of the total U.S. population) occupy nearly 310,800

Brood habitat in *Carpinus-Crataegus* stand, Allegheny Plateau, north-central Pennsylvania. *Photo by G. Wunz, Pennsylvania Game Commission.*

square kilometers (120,000 square miles) of the states in these 2 forest ecosystems. This is a tenfold increase over the 50,000 turkeys that Mosby (1949) had compiled for the 7 states in this region that still had turkeys in the 1940s (Table 3). All states in the region now have established populations, and annual harvests have increased to more than 85,000 turkeys (Table 4). The restoration efforts are now more than two-thirds complete, with less than 129,500 square kilometers (50,000 square miles) of potential range remaining unoccupied (Table 5).

Most land in these regions is privately owned. Only 9 percent of the occupied range is public land, ranging from 2 percent in Delaware to 22 percent in Pennsylvania (Table 6). Initial restoration efforts were centered on public lands, but nearly all future range expansion must be on private lands. Recent trends indicate turkey populations continue to increase in 15 of these states, are stable in 2 (New York and Vermont), and are decreasing in only 1 (Virginia) (National Wild Turkey Federation 1986).

HABITAT RELATIONSHIPS

Wild turkeys in the eastern part of their range live in a wide variety of forest situations and are exposed to a wide range of human-altered environments. So determin-

ing their actual habitat needs has been difficult. Although various research studies have fallen short of defining specific habitat requirements (Wunz 1982), some habitat preferences were revealed that generally seem to apply across regions.

Foremost is the observational evidence that turkeys apparently do best in habitats that contain a large variety of successional stages and species, ranging from pioneer herbaceous plants to old-growth, mast-producing trees, and where human intrusions are minimal and conservation ethics are favorable.

Forest Succession

By natural succession, vegetation is in a constant state of ecologic change. It matures through stages over time. These stages have differing utility as seasonal wild turkey habitat.

For example, the first forest successional stage of grass and forbs provides brood habitat. The second stage, resulting from invasion of these herbaceous openings by pioneer shrubs and trees, may continue to furnish brood range. This stage may also provide winter habitat, particularly if groves of conifer roosting trees for thermal cover are nearby and the trees and shrubs retain their

Table 3. Turkey population estimates from the 1940s to 1988 for the states included in the eastern oak-hickory and northern hardwood forest regions.

State	Year				
	1940[a]	1958[b]	1968[c]	1979[d]	1988[e]
Connecticut	0	0	0	1,000	6,000
Delaware	0	0	0	0	450
Indiana	0	75	0	5,000	20,000
Kentucky	1,000	1,500	1,900	3,000	20,000
Maine	0	0	0	125	600
Maryland	90	2,000	1,000	2,000	8,000
Massachusetts	0	200	150	1,200	5,000
New Hampshire	0	0	0	1,000	1,500
New Jersey	0	0	0	400	4,500
New York	0	2,500	10,000	25,000	60,000
North Carolina	10,000	15,000	4,000	6,000	17,000
Ohio	0	200	2,100	6,000	30,000
Pennsylvania	12,000	40,000	45,000	100,000	150,000
Rhode Island	0	0	0	0	600
Tennessee	5,000	2,500	5,000	8,400	30,000
Vermont	0	10	0	8,000	15,000
Virginia	20,000	20,000	29,000	65,000	124,000
West Virginia	6,000	10,000	15,000	25,000	70,000
Total	54,090	93,985	113,150	257,125	562,650

[a] Mosby 1949.
[b] Mosby 1959.
[c] Mosby 1973.
[d] Bailey 1980.
[e] Fall populations.

Table 4. Total annual turkey harvest, spring and fall, in the states included in the eastern oak-hickory and northern hardwood forest systems.

State	Year				
	1940[a]	1958[b]	1968[c]	1979[d]	1988[e]
Connecticut	0	0	0	0	328
Delaware	0	0	0	0	0
Indiana	0	0	0	48	300
Kentucky	0	0	17	50	750
Maine	0	0	0	0	11
Maryland	25	511	360	175	1,590
Massachusetts	0	0	0	0	557
New Hampshire	0	0	0	0	90
New Jersey	0	0	0	0	390
New York	0	0	1,050	2,462	6,725
North Carolina	3,000	3,294	220	208	600
Ohio	0	0	20	265	2,000
Pennsylvania	3,772	16,156	17,300	34,300	43,346
Rhode Island	0	0	0	0	5
Tennessee	0	77	214	295	1,200
Vermont	0	0	0	882	1,300
Virginia	6,067	2,060	4,707	9,735	16,835
West Virginia	430	1,173	1,700	3,676	9,465
Total	13,294	23,271	25,558	52,096	85,487

[a] Mosby 1949.
[b] Mosby 1959.
[c] Mosby 1973.
[d] Bailey 1980.
[e] Fall populations.

Table 5. Occupied and unoccupied turkey range in the states in the eastern oak-hickory and northern hardwood forest regions.

State	Occupied range 1979[a]	Occupied range 1988	Unoccupied range 1988
Connecticut	500	3,200	200
Delaware	0	100	400
Indiana	2,000	11,000	5,000
Kentucky	1,000	2,000	20,000
Maine	40	600	Unknown
Maryland	1,100	1,800	1,200
Massachusetts	1,100	2,700	1,000
New Hampshire	1,000	3,000	1,000
New Jersey	180	2,300	0
New York	20,000	21,300	0
North Carolina	5,500	11,000	3,200
Ohio	1,600	6,200	700
Pennsylvania	15,000	25,000	0
Rhode Island	0	400	100
Tennessee	2,100	10,000	3,500
Vermont	3,000	5,000	0
Virginia	25,000	30,800	0
West Virginia	16,000	21,000	3,000
Total	95,120	156,900	39,300

[a] Bailey 1980.

Table 6. Ownership of commercial forestland in states in the oak-hickory and northern hardwood forest region.

State	Percentage of public land[a]
Connecticut	8
Delaware	2
Indiana	9
Kentucky	8
Maine	4
Maryland	10
Massachusetts	13
New Hampshire	14
New Jersey	17
New York	6
North Carolina	9
Ohio	6
Pennsylvania	22
Rhode Island	8
Tennessee	10
Vermont	10
Virginia	11
West Virginia	10

[a] USFS Forest Statistics, 1976–1985.

fruit during the winter. Unfortunately, these early stages of succession can be short-lived on some sites, where dense stands of rapidly growing tree saplings shade the understory.

The pole-timber stage that follows is characterized by trees too young to produce significant amounts of mast, but their dense canopies shade out too much light to permit growth of adequate densities of herbaceous vegetation and shrubs. The pole stage is the poorest of all forest habitats, but it must be tolerated as part of forest maturation.

Mature stands of mast-producing trees, with canopies sufficiently open to allow some understory shrubs and herbaceous growth, are considered the heart of eastern turkey habitat.

Human Populations

The effects of human populations on wild turkeys can be as varied as they are profound. In West Virginia, for example, Bailey and Rinell (1968) reported turkeys were unlikely to succeed where roads are more than 0.6 kilometers per square kilometer (1.0 mile per square mile) and people number more then 23 per square kilometer (60 per square mile). In Pennsylvania, a turkey population has been self-sustaining for the past 18 years on a study area with a road system and a human density 3 times greater (Wunz 1985a). On the Land Between the

Lakes Recreational Area in western Kentucky and Tennessee, turkeys avoided areas with foot trails used by some 125 people per week (Wright and Speake 1975). Turkeys on heavily used Presque Isle State Park in Pennsylvania (a peninsula in Lake Erie) abandoned open woods but stayed in a 121-hectare (300-acre) area of early succession forests with brushy understories where, despite foot trails, the turkeys were less visible and less likely to be disturbed by people (Wunz 1971). Although people's attitudes toward turkeys differed geographically, they have generally improved over time. The fact remains that lower human populations and less access to turkey range generally resulted in less poaching, less chance of legal overharvest, less destruction of habitat, and less harassment by people and free-ranging dogs.

Forests and Foods

Formerly, the usual concept of ideal turkey woods in the Appalachians was a remote and large expanse of mast-producing hardwood forests. The protection afforded turkey flocks by the remoteness was probably more important to their survival than the age of the forest.

Since then, turkeys have been found to tolerate even small pole-timber stands if acceptable food sources are available. The mature forest may remain as the heart of turkey habitat, but the more reliable, year-round, food-producing potential of some pioneer shrubs and trees interspersed with small herbaceous clearings or crop fields can also be important components. This potential

Planted shrubs provide important food, especially during winter. Clockwise from top left: Red mulberry; Japanese barberry; Autumn olive; Asian crab apple. *Photos by G. Wunz, Pennsylvania Game Commission.*

is particularly valuable during years of poor crops of hard mast, such as acorns and beechnuts, or where deep snow covers all foods on the ground during severe winters.

Dogwood, cherry, black gum, crab apple, hawthorn, grape, huckleberry, and blackberry are examples of shrubs and small trees that produce soft mast, some of which retain their fruit until it drops or is eaten during the winter. The herbaceous plant communities in the forest or in the clearings are consistent producers of foods in the forms of seeds, green vegetation, tubers, bulbs, and invertebrate animals. Insects and spiders, especially, provide essential nutrients for growing poults.

Cover

Beyond requiring nesting cover for hens, wild turkeys ordinarily are not thought of as needing cover. They generally avoid dense understories and ground vegetation. Yet there are times when turkeys seek out cover and it appears necessary. Overhead and ground cover in the form of sparse-canopied trees and herbaceous vegetation seem to be the preferred habitat of hens with broods. Turkeys also used timber-cutting slash and dense understory as cover in which to escape from avian predators and especially from hunters during the fall (Wunz 1989b). On Presque Isle Park and other study areas, tur-

Planting of autumn olive on this clearing edge will enhance habitat. *Photo by G. Wunz, Pennsylvania Game Commission.*

keys normally avoided feeding in forests near well-traveled roads and areas of human activity unless terrain or dense roadside vegetation formed a visual barrier. Without this cover, large acreages adjacent to roads through open-understory forests may be useless for turkeys.

Water

The need for free water, in addition to water supplied in foods, by turkeys in the Northeast is not clear. Healy (1981) found little use of water by broods of imprinted birds, but the work of Rogers (1985) with imprinted poults in the dry Ridge and Valley section of eastern West Virginia suggested water may be very important and could influence habitat selection.

Some radio-tagged brood hens monitored on dry mountain tops and slopes in similar habitat in south-central Pennsylvania were not known to have moved near any source of free water during the early part of brood

rearing, apparently getting adequate moisture for their poults in their food. After midsummer in this region, it is common for turkeys (even those using lowlands where water is available) to move to upper slopes and mountain tops to feed on blueberries and huckleberries (Pack et al. 1980, Ross and Wunz 1990).

Apparently the use of water by turkeys is governed by its availability and the ability of their foods to supply it. In the moister environments, characteristic of the northern hardwood ecosystem, water seems of little concern. But in some of the drier sites more common to oak-hickory forests, the relative scarcity of water and less moisture in foods could detract from habitat quality, especially in dry summers.

Forest Openings

Researchers as early as Mosby and Handley (1943) recognized that openings of herbaceous vegetation in eastern forests are commonly used by turkeys, especially

Openings are important in forest habitat. Top: One use is by displaying gobblers. Bottom: Openings also provide invertebrates eagerly consumed by young poults. *Photos by G. Wunz, Pennsylvania Game Commission.*

hens with broods, and may be essential habitat components. On an intensively managed study area in western Virginia, a large increase in turkeys that was associated with land management activities and increased law enforcement protection was attributed largely to the clearings that were created (McGinnis and Ripley 1962).

In Tennessee, however, no consistent relationship was found between the amount of openings and the turkey population (Lewis 1964). Study areas in Alabama and Kentucky, reported by Speake et al. (1975), also showed inconsistencies. Areas of 5, 7, and 24 percent in openings all had high turkey densities of about 12 per square kilometer (30 per square mile), while 1 area with 15 percent in openings carried only 1 turkey per square kilometer (2.7 per square mile).

A 20-year study on 3 areas in central Pennsylvania indicated turkey populations appeared to have increased in response to clearings created to simulate the spacing and amount of permanent herbaceous openings that would result from log landings in normal timber-harvest procedures common to that region (Wunz 1990). The fact that populations increased where these clearings amounted to a maximum density of less than 0.3 percent of the forest area suggests that goals of at least 5 percent specified in most forest management plans (Healy 1985) may be unrealistic in practice but desirable to assure significant benefits for wild turkey production.

Although clearings are obviously important in turkey range, the optimum amount and distribution in particular situations has yet to be determined. The optimum ratio of open land to forests in farming regions is also uncertain. A survey of some of the best habitat in 10 states in these 2 ecosystems showed the amount of open land in turkey range varied from 10 to 40 percent (Pack 1986a).

A comparison of the percentage of forest land to turkey harvest data in West Virginia indicated turkey harvests peaked where range was 30 percent open (West Virginia Department of Natural Resources Plan 1974). Little (1980) suggested 50 percent of open land might be optimum in Iowa.

Turkeys in western Pennsylvania tolerated farmland that had only 26 percent forest, where they occupied woodlots as small as 51 hectares (125 acres) (Wunz 1985a). Turkeys have been restored successfully in similar habitats in Ohio (Clark 1985) and Indiana (Miller et al. 1985). These studies also showed that turkeys avoided open fields except for brood hens in the summer and for feeding in croplands during the winter. Flocks spent 75 percent or more of their time in wooded cover that comprised less than 30 percent of the total area. Even turkey broods that ranged on the edges of large forested tracts in Pennsylvania study areas used open fields less often than they were available. No more than 3 percent of the telemetry locations were in agricultural fields (Hayden 1982, Ross and Wunz 1990).

These findings may seem contrary to the impression of high turkey densities reported from some fragmented habitats where large proportions were open land, especially cropland. Yet intensive winter census work in northwestern Pennsylvania showed that estimates of turkey populations based on casual observation in such habitats are likely to be exaggerated (Wunz 1989c).

The eastern turkey, despite long-term and radical changes in its environments, remains basically a creature of the forest, seeming to be insecure away from its cover. It seems that no more open land is essential than the amount needed to provide grasses and forbs for a varied and reliable food source of greens, seeds, or invertebrates. It appears logical that these needs could be met in most eastern forests by devoting about 10 percent of the acreage to widely distributed permanent herbaceous openings, in addition to the temporary openings that result from timber harvest and other activities.

SEASONAL HABITAT

Spring Courtship

No clear habitat preferences have emerged from studies of turkeys after winter flocks break up in the spring for nesting. The impression that gobbling males use certain sites year after year seems to relate to the location of adequately large roost trees and to their aspect. Gobblers apparently prefer points, or "noses," of ridges, where they can see or be heard for greater distances. The use of traditional strutting grounds or meeting places that may be attributed to other turkey subspecies or to other regions does not seem to be inherent in eastern turkeys in these 2 ecosystems. The nearest relationship with particular habitat types during courtship is that turkeys seem to prefer woods with open understory or small clearings or field edges. They avoid habitats where their vision is greatly reduced by understory vegetation and where there is repeated disturbance from people.

Nesting

In these 2 forest ecosystems, wild turkey hens nest in a variety of habitats. These range from dense shrub cover to open-understory forests, but preferences for certain cover types are evident. Everett et al. (1985) found 81 percent of nests were in upland and stream-bottom hardwoods in dense patches of greenbrier and huckleberry in northern Alabama. Pack and Igo (1981) in West Virginia and Wunz (1978b) in Pennsylvania noted understories of ericaceous shrubs (laurel and huckleberry) were common nest sites in oak-hickory habitat. Raybourne (1974) in Virginia found nests in brushy clearcuts. In northern Pennsylvania's dairy-farm woodlot habitat, Hayden (1980) found nests in a variety of habitats ranging from uncut hay and reverting weed fields to clearcuts. Nests of 64 hens in western New York habitats, composed of nearly 75 percent northern hardwood forest and brushland, were present more frequently in moderately dense understory woods than in reverting fields in various stages from rank grass to small trees (Glidden 1977 a,b).

Generally, shrub understory cover for nesting sites is abundant in oak-hickory forests, but the sparsity of shrubs in some northern hardwood stands appears to cause hens to use weed fields, clearcuts, tops from felled trees in forests, and various other available cover. Preferred and more successful nesting sites seem to be in extensive (rather than isolated) stands of brush and herbaceous vegetation, but most nests are near the edge of this dense cover.

Brood Range

A variety of habitats are used by hens with broods: pastures and hayfields, abandoned fields, wildlife clearings, energy transmission rights-of-way, and natural glades or savannas in various stages of succession or invasion by stands of pioneer tree species. Anderson and Samuels (1980) and Rice (1986) found that broods used reclaimed surface mines planted to legumes, grasses, shrubs, and small trees. Brood-rearing habitat usually is associated with forest clearings, but Pack and Igo (1981) and Ross and Wunz (1990) found that hens can also raise broods successfully in forests that lack clearings if midstories and ground stories provide adequate food and cover.

Particularly for early summer brood habitat, cover structure seems as important as ground vegetation types. Brood hens prefer cover that is near or under trees. One preferred habitat, particularly in northern hardwood forests that have sparse understory cover, is a partial overhead canopy formed by orchardlike stands of pioneer small tree species (aspen, locust, hawthorns, and such) that allow sufficient sunlight to develop a moderately dense, herbaceous ground cover. Pack et al. (1980) found that broods preferred similar herbaceous ground cover under white oak sawtimber stands in West Virginia.

As poults mature and herbaceous ground cover increases during the summer, broods may venture farther into openings to feed, but they seldom stray far from the overhead cover of trees or shrubs. The diet of poults is primarily insects during the first month. As summer progresses, the young turkeys eat more green vegetation, seeds, berries, and other soft mast (Healy 1981).

Fall and Winter Habitat

By midautumn, most turkeys in eastern forests are feeding mainly on hard mast, and they usually range over a large area of forest to feed. But during years when these mast crops are scarce, wild turkeys tend to restrict movements and concentrate at localized food sources. Turkeys adapt to failures of hard mast by eating lesser foods on the forest floor, such as ferns, bulbs, tubers, and spore heads of club moss. Turkeys may also range into crop fields or feed on seeds of grasses and forbs in clearings.

These patterns of behavior and feeding generally extend through the winter, but they can be altered by terrain and weather. When the mountaintops and plateau tops are snow covered and foods are hard to find, turkeys usually move to lower elevations. The snow on valley bottoms and lower slopes, particularly those facing south, is not so deep and is likely to be packed or crusted enough to support a turkey's weight. Here they can walk and find sustenance in spring seeps that are free of snow. They can pick fruits and seeds that remain on shrubs and vines. Or they can feed in farm fields on standing corn, on waste grain, or where barnyard manure has been spread (Wunz and Hayden 1975).

All of these food sources can be important to the welfare of turkeys during severe winters. But in remote northern hardwood forests at higher elevations, where the effects of winter are worse and there is no help from agriculture, spring seeps may be the sole source of turkey food essential for survival. Turkeys feed in these relatively warm seepage areas on tree seeds, fern spore heads, insects and other small animals, and especially on green vegetation (Healy and Pack 1983, Wunz et al. 1983).

Beech stands provide an important but erratic food source during winter. *Photo by W. Healy, U.S. Forest Service.*

Acorns, such as from these white oaks, are an important food in the mountainous oak-hickory forests. *Photo by H. Williamson, U.S. Forest Service.*

What about turkeys living on broad, high plateaus or in flat terrain at the northern edge of occupied range? They face hardship and possible death every severe winter (Austin and DeGraff 1975, Wunz 1987d). One such area is the Allegheny Plateau of north-central Pennsylvania. Turkeys historically did not inhabit this area, probably because of the prolonged periods of deep-powder snow that persisted under the shading and microclimatic effects of the pristine forest (Wunz and Hayden 1967). Today turkeys occupy this plateau, but they live a precarious existence in severe winters. As much as 60 percent may die (Wunz and Hayden 1975).

Conifers provide winter shelter. *Photo by W. Healy, U.S. Forest Service.*

Turkeys have become established more than 161 kilometers (100 miles) north of historic range limits in New York and Vermont and into Quebec. The extent of this northward expansion seems highly dependent on farming. Walski (1987) attributes the relative lack of expansion by turkeys in New Hampshire to the small amount of farmland there and its progressive abandonment.

In this region, turkeys roost most of the year in any large tree where night overtakes them. In winter, they usually roost in conifer groves, apparently selected for their heat-retention and windbreaking qualities, situated in valley bottoms or on the lee side of hills. Turkey movement is more restricted during winter where snow accumulates, so turkeys may roost repeatedly in the same groves. During periods of deep-powder snow, turkeys may be forced to stay in roost trees unless food sources such as spring seeps and trees with persistent fruits are nearby. In such an inactive state, turkeys can survive 2 weeks with no food intake. Gerstell (1942) and Hayden and Nelson (1963) found that turkeys could lose 40 percent of their body weight before dying.

The availability of food seems to influence winter flocking behavior. Where winter foods are abundant and localized, especially as a result of farming operations or artificial feeding of grain, turkeys are apt to congregate in large flocks. But in more extensive forest habitats at high elevations, or near the northern edge of turkey range when foods are naturally scarce or under deep snow, winter flocks usually have fewer than 10 birds.

FOREST MANAGEMENT

Habitat managers generally agree: Mature, mast-producing forests with appropriate amounts of brood range (and, for northern turkey populations, winter-survival range) is just about ideal habitat for wild turkeys. In commercial forests, timber-harvest strategies and natural succession must be considered in attaining and maintaining these habitats. Managing habitat for wild turkeys in the northern hardwood and oak-hickory forest ecosystems is seldom separable from timber management or other economically motivated activities. The profound effect that forest management practices can have on eastern turkey populations emphasizes the importance of cooperation between forest and wildlife managers in planning. This rapport is made easier by the increasing receptiveness of foresters to multiple-use principles that may enhance their professional and public image.

For long-term planning, the first step needed is an inventory of timber size class, forest cover types, forest understory, diversity, openings, nearby agricultural ac-

Fall flock foraging in a black cherry stand in the northern hardwood forest. *Photo by W. Healy, U.S. Forest Service.*

tivities, and key wildlife habitat areas. Planning should include knowledge of roads, energy, and any mineral and real estate developments on or adjacent to the area that can usurp or make even the best nearby turkey habitats untenable. The area of the land must be considered. Four hundred hectares (1,000 acres) is usually necessary to meet all the habitat needs of turkeys, but smaller tracts can also be made more attractive to turkeys if they are adjacent to acceptable turkey range.

Forest Management Systems

Providing quality habitat for turkeys requires retaining or creating key components of their environment. Brood-rearing and winter habitats may have to be managed by means other than commercial forest practices, but the bulk of wild turkey range will involve some form of timber management. Foresters may choose to manage for uneven-aged stands (which result from selection-type harvest methods) or even-aged stands (which are usually attained by clear-cutting).

Uneven-aged management. Both single-tree selection and group selection are reproduction methods of uneven-aged management. Group selection generally involves cutting all trees in areas of up to 0.8 hectares (2 acres). Regulation of cut is based on some form of volume control, and 0.2 hectares (0.5 acres) is frequently recommended as the minimum size. Single-tree selection is also acceptable forest management. But diameter-limit cutting, where only trees larger than a certain size are cut, can result in removing the highest-quality trees (known as high-grading) and leaving a less-productive forest.

Uneven-aged management, which results in forest stands composed of trees of all ages, has a distinct advantage: It can eliminate the 30- to 40-year period of low food production that occurs in a stand harvested with even-aged methods. Liscinsky (1984) and Drake (1987) reported that increased crowns that result on trees remaining after selection cutting may yield as much mast as the original stand before cutting. But significant understory or herbaceous ground cover is not likely to develop unless the overstory is adequately opened.

If deer or livestock are present in large numbers, sufficient forage may not be produced to prevent their overgrazing of tree and shrub regeneration and herbaceous vegetation of value to turkeys. If overgrazing occurs, the result is likely to be the increase of trees, shrubs, and herbaceous vegetation (such as ferns and ericaceous shrubs) that are less palatable to these herbivores (Hough 1965, Marquis and Brenneman 1981, Wunz 1987c) and are of low value to turkeys.

Preservation or enhancement of key turkey habitat components, such as glades or spring seeps, may require select cutting to remove competing trees. In practice, the single-tree selection method tends to favor species tolerant of shade and competition from other trees, like beech, which is a preferred food for turkeys. But not all tolerant species are favored by turkeys. The tendency is to cut the best trees, and single-tree selection tends to eliminate oaks, black cherry, and white ash. To avoid such high-grading of a forest stand, more work and expertise are required to properly choose trees for the single-tree selection method of harvesting.

Even-aged management. In contrast to the selection method, the objective in even-aged management is to grow a stand of trees that are essentially the same age, and a forest of different age classes. An even-age management system is generally considered easier to plan and control. For large-scale production of timber, most forests will eventually be managed by some form of even-aged management, which involves clear-cutting. Clear-cutting to regenerate forest stands generally is not regarded as a practice harmful to turkey habitat in the oak-hickory and northern hardwood regions, where the silviculture objective is usually to regenerate a variety of intolerant (to shade and competition) and tolerant tree species rather than short-rotation softwoods.

Dellinger (1973) cautioned that even-aged management applied from only a silvicultural standpoint could devastate wildlife habitat, but agreed with Zeedyk (1969) that with certain constraints, this management option offers more possibilities for improving habitat than uneven-aged silviculture. Clear-cutting, for example, can promote regeneration of the less shade-tolerant commercial trees that are valued by turkeys (oaks, ash, and black cherry) as well as fruit-bearing small tree, shrub, and vine species.

Clear-cutting also has the potential to restart the successional cycle and increase diversity by providing the full sunlight required for most plant species to grow. Comparing treatments made 20 years earlier in northern hardwoods, Lang et al. (1982) found up to 4 times more tree species in clearcuts than in thinned stands ranging from 30 to 80 percent removal of trees. Also, since most even-aged management compartments (about 400 hectares, or 1,000 acres, each) are well within the size of the annual home range of most turkey flocks (Brown 1980), the scheduling of cutting to balance age classes in each compartment, as proposed by Roach (1974), should stabilize food production as effectively as uneven-aged management.

The long-term food gaps characteristic of most even-aged-managed stands may be partly alleviated by leaving some specimens, especially large ones, of trees valued by turkeys (oak, ash, cherry, black gum, and such) that by their growth form or site would be less susceptible to windthrow in clearcuts. Marquis et al. (1984) found that up to 2.3 square meters per hectare (10 square feet per acre) of basal area (area of total tree stems at breast height) could be left standing without hindering regeneration of the stand. The food base can be further diversified and enhanced by saving and avoiding logging damage to indigenous shrubs and small trees, such as hawthorns, crab apples, dogwoods, hornbeams, and the like.

Bulldozing a clearing. Habitat manipulation can improve habitat suitability. *Photo by National Wild Turkey Federation.*

Clear-cutting Size

Clear-cutting in large blocks, more than 12 hectares (30 acres), is generally considered detrimental. The degree of damage depends on the location of the cut and on what consideration is given to the remainder of the habitat available to turkeys.

The rationale given for large clearcuts was usually based on economics or yield or, where deer were abundant, on the need to provide enough forage for some of the seedlings and sprouts to escape browsing and regenerate the stand. Marquis (1987), however, found no significant relationship between regeneration success and individual opening size and concluded that the effects of browsing on 4 clearcuts of 10 hectares (25 acres) were nearly the same as on a large one of 40-hectares (100-acre).

Projected timber harvest models by Roach (1974) showed timber yield losses of less than 3 percent if a 40-hectare (100-acre) timber sale was divided into 5 separate 8-hectare (20-acre) cuts spaced as far apart as economically feasible for the logger to operate within a management compartment of some 400 hectares (1,000 acres).

Turkey Use of Clearcuts

Turkey use of most clearcut sites seems to follow a similar chronology, except for variations in regrowth rates of trees that may be influenced by latitude, altitude, forest type, site, and deer or livestock grazing. During the first 10 years, use of clearcuts by turkeys is limited generally to nesting cover (Raybourne 1974, Pack et al. 1980) and to herbaceous vegetation on the edges by broods. When some overhead cover develops, possibly within 5 years, broods venture farther into the clearcut to feed in the herbaceous vegetation remaining, especially in access roads and log landings (where logs are assembled for loading onto trucks) (Wunz 1989b). After 10 years, shade from the growing tree saplings limits herbaceous vegetation to the landings and small areas that have not yet regenerated into tree growth. Clearcut sites are least productive during the 20- to 40-year sapling and small pole stages, when understory plants are less abundant and the trees are not yet producing mast. Fifty years after the cut, mast production increases and persists until the stand is cut.

Strips of mature trees 45 to 91 meters (50 to 100 yards) wide should be left standing along streams or as corridors. Such strips in Virginia were used by nesting hens, and the adjacent edges of clearcuts were used as brood range (Holbrook et al. 1985). In Mississippi, streamside zones of hardwoods in short-rotation pine

plantations were used extensively by turkeys year-round (Burk et al. 1990).

A long and narrow 40-hectare (100-acre) clearcut without such travel lanes separated a stream bottom forested with conifers from an adjacent south-facing mountainside on a Pennsylvania study area. Turkeys abandoned this winter range for 10 years until the cut area had grown enough to provide access and cover. After 10 years, the revegetated clearcut was used by turkeys as escape cover during the fall hunting season and nearly year-round to feed on fruits and in herbaceous vegetation in the landings and access roads (Wunz 1989b).

Perpetuating the Forest Habitat

Most managers still consider mature forests the heart of eastern turkey habitat. Their recommendations may call for maintaining as much as 50 to 75 percent of the forest in mast-producing condition. To attain this goal, managers must preserve the remnant fragments of old-growth timber and increase rotation lengths up to 100 or more years. Long rotations increase the proportion of saw-log to mast-producing trees. For example, a 100-year rotation would eventually result in a forest composed 50 percent of mast-producing trees. Under a 150-year rotation, some 75 percent of the forest would be in this stage. Existing forests on steep or wet sites, considered inoperable for logging equipment, should be allowed to become old-growth stands. So should stream-course protection corridors.

Unfortunately, most eastern hardwood forests are in a state of unbalanced age class distribution because of massive clear-cutting of original forests in a relatively short period during the late 1800s and early 1900s. To attain a sustained yield regime in such forests, Roach (1974) proposed balancing age classes by cutting some stands before maturity (100 to 110 years in his example oak forest) and allowing other stands to go 30 years or more beyond maturity.

The eventual result would be to stabilize the forest economically and also its capability to produce wildlife—in other words, to level off the feast-and-famine cycles that are certain to continue if these stands are cut only at maturity.

Maintaining Oak-Hickory Forests

Overstory trees of particular value to turkeys in the eastern oak-hickory forest are 8 species of oaks (white, post, chestnut, black, blackjack, scarlet, northern red, and southern red), as well as black gum and hickories. In the northern part of this ecosystem, the important oak species are limited to northern red, white, chestnut, black, and scarlet. Maintaining this desirable oak component, however, has become increasingly difficult on some sites. The problems include outbreaks of defoliating insects, overbrowsing by deer (Gottshalk 1986), a tendency for oak forests in the North on good sites to regenerate into northern hardwoods (Crow 1988), and the practice of harvesting without considering oak regeneration development.

Clear-cutting, shelterwood cutting, and group selection are practices recommended for regenerating oak-hickory stands. Generally single-tree selection is not promoted, and group selection does not appear to regenerate oaks on good sites. Regardless of the system, advanced oak regeneration, either in the form of seedlings or in the potential for stump sprouts, is required prior to removing the overstory. Sanders et al. (1984) developed guidelines to periodically monitor and evaluate the adequacy of regeneration.

If oak regeneration is lacking, a shelterwood type of treatment has been recommended if cutting was completed within 3 years after a good oak mast year (Wolf 1988). Sanders (1988) suggested killing nonoak trees of up to 5 centimeters (2 inches) in diameter at breast height and reducing the overstory to 70 percent stocking when using the shelterwood method.

The trees left uncut should be dominant and codominant oak and other important mast trees, preferably uniformly spaced. The shelterwood treatment may be best because of mast production and the presence of an overhead canopy that turkeys prefer. In the southern Appalachians, Loftis (1988) found that shelterwood cuts with removal rates of 50 percent of the basal area on good sites were excessive and this resulted in increases of yellow poplar and birch, both inferior species for turkeys. He recommended removing 30 to 40 percent of the initial basal area of the trees below the main canopy with herbicides, leaving the main canopy intact for at least 8 to 10 years.

After a timber stand has become established, thinning practices may be used to put volume growth on trees, increase mast, and stimulate desirable understory development. Beck and Harlow (1981) pointed out that thinning in the early pole stage may have the greatest benefit for forage and that thinning in the midstory encourages herbaceous vegetation. Everett et al. (1985) suggested that thinning could create a less abrupt ecotone between openings and the surrounding forest by increasing herbaceous vegetation and woody cover to provide escape cover and a greater variety of habitats for turkeys.

In the plans for thinning, seed production biology should be considered. Because large trees produce more mast than small trees (Tubbs et al. 1987) and individual trees vary in seed production, it is best to mark trees for harvest during the fall to save the best mast producers. Thinning encourages crown development by removing competing trees. Dominant and codominant trees with full and rounded crowns produce the most mast and are less likely to develop excess branching on their trunks. Dioecious trees like white ash, in which both male and female trees are necessary for mast production, should be left uncut in groups. To assure good pollination with both dioecous or monoecious species, trees saved should be grouped or at least relatively close to one another.

In thinnings, do not remove dogwoods, witch hazels, hornbeams (hop and American), apples, persimmons, crab apples, viburnums, and hawthorns. These noncommercial trees and shrubs are important to turkeys and seldom compete with overstory trees.

In oak-hickory stands, marking guidelines should favor oaks, northern red and white oak in particular, because they produce mast more consistently than others (Beck 1977). A good rule is to have 1 of 3 potential oak crop trees in the white oak group. Turkey biologists generally recommend that 50 to 60 percent of the leave trees be mast producers. Some hickories, white ashes, cherries, cucumbers, and black gums should also be left for diversity.

Healy (1981) recommended maintaining a 60 to 100 percent stocking level for wild turkeys. In mixed-oak sites with 60 to 80 site-quality indices, Dale and Hilt (1986) suggested thinnings may be initiated as early as age 40 to a residual stocking of 40 percent and a second thinning to 60 percent. Keep in mind that heavy thinnings on poor sites may result in a dense, woody understory. Because turkeys are usually reluctant to enter exceedingly dense vegetation (Bailey and Rinell 1967b, Holbrook and Lewis 1967, Kennamer et al. 1980), prudent turkey habitat management is to thin lightly until further research determines the best tree-stocking levels for turkey habitat. Large overmature trees that are left when a stand is cut and regenerated can be exceptionally valuable as perhaps the only mast producers in these young stands. Their indiscriminate removal during thinning would result not only in reduced food production but also in possible damage to adjoining trees.

Covert and Michaels (1975) and Pack et al. (1980) found in steep, mountainous terrain that turkeys prefer gentle slopes. So mistakes in thinning and regenerating stands on ridgetops, coves, and benches will likely do more damage to turkey habitat than mistakes on other areas.

Maintaining Cove Hardwoods

Cove (mixed) hardwoods are usually limited to small hollows or indentations in mountainsides where a

Mountain cove hardwood habitat in West Virginia. *Photo by J. Pack.*

moist environment promotes vegetation that is usually unique in the surrounding oak-hickory forest. Beck (1986) pointed out that the cove hardwood types apparently develop with minimum care. Because of the hard and soft mast produced by the variety of species that grow there (cucumber tree, basswood, beech, black locust, oaks, hickories, black gum, spicebush, holly, grape, and herbaceous plants), such areas are frequently used by turkeys.

Turkeys are also attracted by the abundant herbaceous vegetation in cove hardwoods (Healy 1985). Kirkham and Carvell (1980) found that thinning in cove hardwood sites, especially the removal of large crowned yellow poplar, results in an understory of many herbaceous species and some woody shrubs and tree seedlings. Carvell (1980) reported that removing less than 20 percent of the basal area resulted in an increase of herbaceous plants on moist sites in West Virginia. But heavy thinnings (more than 35 percent removal) reduced the amount of herbaceous vegetation because of heavy invasion by woody plants. Light thinnings in cove hardwoods, as in oak-hickory forests, seem best for turkey habitat.

Cove hardwoods have been regenerated by a variety of methods from clear-cutting to single-tree selection. Generally speaking for turkey habitat, oaks and other mast-producing species should be favored by reducing dominance of yellow poplar and birch. Underplanting oaks (Johnson et al. 1986) or applying the Loftis (1988) Shelterwood technique (mentioned earlier under oak-hickory management to increase oaks) seems promising for use in cove hardwood stands.

Planting is expensive. So is using herbicides. Leaving some oaks in the stand or oak seed trees when regenerating a stand will increase the chance of seedling development in the future or at least provide oak mast until the trees die.

Maintaining Northern Hardwoods

The most important northern hardwood trees for turkeys are beech, black cherry, northern red oak, and white ash. Recommended rotation rates are similar to those for oak-hickory forests. Most northern hardwoods desirable for turkeys are intolerant species and are best regenerated by shelterwood and clear-cutting methods. Clear-cutting in strips has been used successfully for white ash and, by exposing more edge, is probably beneficial to turkeys.

Black cherry tends to dominate northern hardwood regeneration because of its longer-lived seed, the nearly constant presence of its seedlings on the forest floor, its low preference as deer browse, and its rapid growth rate. Despite the use of cherry as turkey food and its valued addition to increase variety in turkey habitat, there is evidence linking low turkey densities to cherry monocultures that occurred naturally or through intentional management for its considerable commercial value (Wunz 1989b).

Guidelines prescribed by Marquis (1988) involved gathering data on specific overstory, understory, and site variables that should favor the turkey-food-producing species and avoid monocultures. To retain diversity in the regenerated stand, 75 to 200 trees of tolerant species per hectare (30 to 80 per acre) that are from 8 to 25 centimeters (3 to 10 inches) in diameter at breast height should not be cut.

Of these tolerant species (sugar maple, American beech, and eastern hemlock), sugar maple is the least important for turkeys. Thinning guidelines call for maintaining 60 to 80 percent densities and limiting each thinning to no more than a 35 percent reduction. Densities in the 60 to 70 percent stocking range increased understory densities of both trees and herbaceous vegetation. The tendency toward high-grading can be controlled by limiting the total cut to a third above the merchantable diameter at breast height and two-thirds below.

Improving Forest Habitat Diversity

Whether managers are regenerating a forest stand or applying other practices such as thinning or timber stand improvement, one of their goals should always be to maintain forest vegetation diversity. Midstory and understory trees such as hop hornbeam, serviceberry, and flowering dogwood are still being sacrificed as competitors in some improvements of timber stands.

German foresters tolerate midstory and understory species because they have ecological benefits to commercial tree growth by enhancing the soil and reducing excessive branching of crop trees (Wunz et al. 1985). Saving all remnants of food-producing small tree and shrub species, in addition to not cutting some tolerant tree species in clearcut sites, can add considerable plant diversity to the stands.

To improve diversity in future forests, managers have tried underplanting shrub seedlings before sites are clearcut. Nearly as successful and far less costly was broadcasting a variety of tree and shrub seeds in planned clearcut sites prior to cutting. The logging activity covered the seeds, and the slash protected some of the seedlings from browsing deer (Wunz and Lang 1981). Of the 35 species seeded, 25 (ranging from black cherry and black locust to barberry and viburnums) germinated and grew. Failures of some species were mainly the result of the low viability of the available seed, incompatible sites, excessive deer browsing, or a prolonged time between seeding and the start of logging.

INTENSIVE HABITAT MANAGEMENT

A comparison of turkey movement studies by Brown (1980) showed annual home ranges are smaller on superior habitat areas that carry high densities of turkeys. This finding supports the thesis that turkey carrying capacity is linked to the area required to meet their annual habitat needs and suggests that all necessary habitat components should, insofar as possible, be provided within a forest management compartment.

Forest management for turkeys is extensive management in which the entire forest habitat eventually would be enhanced to varying degrees. On the other hand, intensive habitat management usually does not have the advantage of most or all of the cost being borne by an economic endeavor like logging. Since intensive habitat management can be costly, it must be confined to relatively small areas or to habitat components, such as brood habitat or winter range, that are critical to wild turkey productivity or survival.

Brood Habitat

Prescribed burning. This habitat management tool, which has been used to improve turkey habitat in other regions (Stoddard 1963, Lewis et al. 1964), has

been slow to gain acceptance by managers in eastern oak-hickory and northern hardwood forests. Fire has been used to temporarily control laurel and rhododendron in the southern Appalachians (Hooper 1969).

The finding of DeSelm et al. (1973) was that fire increased grass and legumes in a Tennessee forest. Pack et al. (1988) evaluated fire and thinning, finding that woody vegetation was reduced and herbaceous vegetation was increased to improve brood habitat in oak forests of West Virginia. The objective of these fires was to improve and increase herbaceous vegetation on the forest floor, not to kill or severely affect the quality of dominant trees.

Photo by G. Wunz, Pennsylvania Game Commission.

Photo by J. Pack.

Top: Brood habitat can be established on rights-of-way or in other openings. Bottom: Also by thinning and burning forest stands.

Currently, prescribed burning is practiced in hardwood habitats on federal and state forests in West Virginia and Virginia, and it is used to improve vegetation for turkeys in clearings in Kentucky, North Carolina, and West Virginia. Managers have found burning plans and desired weather conditions recommended by Mobley et al. (1978) valuable guides.

Natural openings. Old relic clearings have originated from such causes as fires, beavers, logging, mining, habitations, and farming. Since they are already open or partially so, costs in maintaining these spaces are considerably less than for creating new clearings. Periodic mowing, the cutting of invading trees, prescribed burning, and chemical treatments have all been used successfully.

Another recommendation: Leave some of the fruit-producing small tree and large shrub species (such as hawthorns, crab apples, mulberry, holly, and witch hazel) in orchardlike stands to provide overhead cover for turkey broods. Depending on crown size, leaving these trees at intervals of 4 to 6 meters (13 to 20 feet) will usually allow sufficient sunlight for herbaceous vegetation to grow on the ground for cover and food.

Creating clearings. Forest openings have been created by fire, herbicides, cutting, or bulldozing. An evaluation of these methods in both forest types in Pennsylvania showed bulldozing was the best method to establish long-lasting herbaceous openings (Wunz 1987a). Clearings in which the soil was properly prepared and seeded still have good stands of grass after 15 years without any maintenance.

Attempts to make permanent clearings by cutting or using herbicides were short-lived; trees and shrubs reinvaded the sites. Seeding wildfire sites with grasses was the least expensive method of all, but results were unpredictable. More research is needed.

Costs for removing, killing, or cutting trees and shrubs were similar whether for bulldozing, using herbicides, or cutting with chain saws. The costs of bulldozing also included removal of wood debris from the site, which is necessary for proper soil preparation and seeding.

Enlargement of existing log landings or other small openings was more economical than creating new ones, but even more practical would be specifying log landings of 0.2 to 0.4 hectare (0.5 to 1 acre) in timber sale con-

Log landings converted to a grass-and-legume clearing improve year-round habitat. *Photo by G. Wunz, Pennsylvania Game Commission.*

tracts. Costs of liming, fertilizing, and seeding to create a pasture-hayfield type 0.4-hectare (1-acre) opening in previously cleared log landings was $250 (1987 costs) compared with $550 for a clearing that required bulldozing.

Because of the high cost of making clearings specifically for wildlife, most clearings will be the result of economic endeavors (logging, mining, oil and gas wells, or energy transmission rights-of-way). Since nearly all of these forest areas will be cut eventually, opportunities for creating openings are greater with logging (via log landings and temporary access roads) than with other land-use activities.

For example, the projected amount of log landings at the end of the rotation in these 2 forest regions, based on their present average size of 0.2 hectare (0.5 acre) and a density of 1 per 10 hectares (1 per 25 acres) of timber sale, would be 2 percent of the forest. Most government agency forest management plans call for at least 5 percent of a forest in permanent herbaceous openings (Healy 1985). To help attain this goal, either the landings should be enlarged or their numbers increased. More openings usually should prove the better option. The greater distribution of clearings, resulting from more landings, should reduce costs of skidding logs and would provide more poult-rearing sites and increase opportunities for broods harassed by humans or predators to move to less disturbed habitat.

Size of openings that have been made in these 2 forest regions varies from 0.2 to 4 hectares (0.5 to 10 acres). State and federal agencies with the most experience in managing clearings recommend 0.2 to 0.8 hectares (0.5 to 2 acres).

To assure adequate sunlight, clearing size should be based largely on a ratio of the width of the opening to the height of surrounding trees. Considering the effects of increased shading as these trees mature, a width-to-height ratio of 2 to 1—or about 45 meters (150 feet) wide (the dimensions of a 0.2-hectare or 0.5-acre clearing)—is minimal. Larger existing openings or fields should be divided into smaller units by planting hedgerows of shrubs and small tree species to provide travel corridors and cover for turkey broods.

Costs can be saved on some fertile sites where indigenous grasses and forbs may seed naturally to establish the dense sod of a prairie-type plant community that is necessary to thwart invasions of unwanted vegetation. But most forest soils are acidic and infertile, and clearings are usually invaded by tree regeneration, ferns, ericaceous shrubs, or low-quality grasses unless soils have been improved with amendments and seeded to grasses and legumes.

The potential for increasing the productivity and longevity of a clearing usually justifies the additional cost of preparing the soil and seeding. Kalmbacher (1976) and Wunz (1984) found high rates of amendments were unnecessary and that moderate applications of lime (2.2 to 4.5 metric tons per hectare, or 1 to 2 tons per acre) and fertilizer (236 kilograms per hectare, or 300 pounds per acre of 15–10–10 or similar analysis fertilizer) were adequate to establish and sustain grass and legume mixtures, even in poor soils.

Also, preparing a well-tilled seedbed and planting persistent species of grasses and legumes have proved indispensible for long-lasting, low-maintenance pasture-type clearings (Wunz 1984). Selecting species to plant is particularly important and should be based upon combined criteria of persistence and wildlife value. Not only must the plant be able to produce greens, seeds, invertebrates, or cover, but also its palatability as forage for competing herbivores must be considered.

White clover, for example, is a favored food of various animals, including wild turkeys. Where deer are abundant, clover may be so severely overgrazed that it soon fades from the clearing. The wise choice there would be to seed with another legume, such as bird's-foot trefoil, that is less preferred by deer and other wildlife but still produces insects and invertebrates for turkey poults. The dual role of legumes in not only producing foods and invertebrates but also fixing atmospheric nitrogen makes them a necessary component of plant mixtures in clearings.

The keys in choosing species to plant are to strike a practical balance between palatability and persistence while also selecting those plants that provide enough cover to conceal turkey broods but are not too dense to hinder their movements through it. This combination of factors eliminates the tall grasses with dense upper foliage, and some aggressive vine-type legumes like crown vetch. But some of these legumes, such as flatpea, produce seeds eaten by wildlife and may still have value for turkeys when planted on eroded or rough sites.

Species planted in clearings in states north of the Mason-Dixon line are usually the cool season grasses (tall and red fescues, orchard grass, and Kentucky bluegrass), bird's-foot trefoil, and white clover. Annual species are seldom used. In states to the south, orchard grass, bluegrass, Korean lespedeza, various clovers, annual grasses, and small grains are planted. The legumes are usually planted in mixtures with grasses. Seeding rates vary from 22 to 56 kilograms per hectare (20 to 50 pounds per acre) of mixtures comprising about a third legumes and two-thirds grasses.

The objective in maintaining a permanent pasture-type clearing is to stop, or at least slow down, natural succession. The high cost of making and maintaining these clearings dictates that they be made to last as long as possible without care. The longevity of a clearing depends on selecting sites and soils where clearings are most likely to succeed, preparing a proper seedbed by scraping off shrub or fern root mats and duff to expose the mineral soil, adding moderate amounts of lime and fertilizer, and seeding persistent species of grasses and legumes. Some clearings with such a background have lasted, as of this writing, 15 years with no care (Wunz 1987a).

The tendency is to overmaintain clearings by fertilizing more often than needed. Then plants grow too tall and dense for young poults. To avoid the need for frequent mowing, apply fertilizer to maintain only a moderate stand of grass. Mowing should be needed only to control invading woody species and undesirable herbaceous plants. Where deer are abundant, usually enough of them are attracted to herbaceous forage to retard invading woody plants and control the density of herbaceous vegetation (Wunz 1987c).

The most used maintenance method in states of these 2 forest regions is routine mowing (varying from annual to once each 5 years). Prescribed burning to control vegetation in clearings (especially natural and old field types) is not widely practiced, but interest in its use is increasing. Use of chemical herbicides is even more restricted because of environmental policies. In some situations, chemicals may be the most cost-effective method for control of undesirable vegetation in brood habitat.

Roads and rights-of-way. Pipelines, power lines, well sites, access roads, and reclaimed surface mines offer opportunities for brood range, especially the linear types of habitat. Management of most of these sites is similar to that for clearings. But the small or narrow openings on well sites or access roads may require planting shade-tolerant species such as red fescue or orchard grass. Removing trees from road shoulders (called "daylighting") to provide more sunlight is a common maintenance practice to dry out roads. It also allows herbaceous vegetation to grow on the roadsides and can add significantly to linear brood habitat. On these roadsides, however, some shrubs and small tree species should be kept for overhead cover.

Access roads and trails are often used by turkeys as travel lanes and for feeding, especially if herbaceous vegetation is present, but humans also use these travel lanes. Aversion of wild turkeys to roads and trails frequently used by people has been documented (Wunz 1971, Wright and Speake 1975, Michael 1978, Pack and Igo 1981) and shows the need to close as many access roads as possible. A forest road through part of a study area lacking conventional brood habitat was frequently used by broods after it was gated (Wunz 1989b). Gating of roads also restricts illegal hunting and overall hunting pressure (Holbrook et al. 1985, 1987).

A survey of some top turkey habitat in 10 states of these 2 forest ecosystems showed 60 percent of the states

Gated forest road provides brood habitat in this oak stand. *Photo by G. Wunz, Pennsylvania Game Commission.*

had less than 1 kilometer of open public roads per square kilometer (less than 2 miles per square mile) (Pack 1986a). Only one state reported more public road than 1.9 kilometers per square kilometer (3 miles per square mile). So it seems prudent to manage in ways that reduce unnecessary human-turkey contacts by restricting roads, especially those open to public travel. The policy should be to encourage temporary roads for timber harvesting that can be seeded to herbaceous cover, gated or tank-trapped, and abandoned until the next cutting cycle. This strategy is preferable to public roads that require frequent maintenance.

Trees and shrubs in clearings. Evidence that turkey broods feel more secure under some overhead cover (Healy 1981) is reason to consider planting food-producing shrubs and small tree species as orchards or as edges in clearings. Evaluations of 38 species planted in these 2 forest ecosystems in Pennsylvania showed Asian crab apples, Washington hawthorns, autumn olive, Japanese barberry, and multiflora rose were the most hardy and

Habitat improvement projects can benefit wild turkeys, as well as people. *Photos by G. Wunz, Pennsylvania Game Commission (left) and T. Hyde (right).*

Sportsmen volunteers planting trees and shrubs for turkey winter food. *Photo by G. Wunz, Pennsylvania Game Commission.*

Opening the canopy over a seep in this oak stand will encourage vegetative growth. *Photo by G. Wunz, Pennsylvania Game Commission.*

adapted to grow in both forests. Mulberry, unusual in producing fruit early enough for growing poults, and black locust were adapted only to oak sites (Wunz 1989a). Where deer are abundant, all except barberry may require fencing unless they are at least 2 meters (7 feet) tall when planted.

Winter Range

Intensive management of winter habitats should be of little concern except at the highest elevations of the Appalachians and from central Pennsylvania northward. But where fluffy snow accumulates and persists for long periods, turkeys may starve and populations may become depressed. Providing corn or other small grains in cribs or hoppers, called turkey feeders, has proved not to be a long-term solution (Wunz 1987d). Most annual food plot

plantings of grains and greens are costly, are sometimes used extensively by other wildlife, and frequently are covered by deep snow. Other long-term solutions through experimental improvements to winter habitats, such as food-producing shrubs and trees, thermal cover, and spring seeps, are being assessed.

Spring seeps. During periods of deep snow, spring seeps may provide the only place some turkey flocks can walk and feed. The literature is replete with the importance of spring seeps to turkeys in northeastern forests (Glover 1948, Latham 1956, Walls 1964, Bailey and Rinell 1967b, Wunz 1978c, Healy and Pack 1983).

Seeps are most abundant, are most important, and respond best to management in the northern hardwood ecosystem on the Allegheny Plateau. Ecological studies

Seeps provide important foraging areas for wild turkeys and also deer when winter snow covers most foods. *Photo by G. Wunz, Pennsylvania Game Commission.*

showed the biomass of animal life was negligible but that green vegetation was increased dramatically (7-fold) after tree canopies were removed. But during a severe winter when this forage was most needed by turkeys, deer denuded all green vegetation and most of the turkeys wintering there died (Wunz et al. 1983).

Canopy removal or thinning should be in conjunction with commercial timber sales. Management should focus on seeps on southern aspects and lower slopes, or on seeps in known winter concentration areas. All logging debris and slash should be removed from seeps, and logging equipment should be prohibited from entering seeps. Haul roads need to be at least 50 meters (165 feet) downstream and the same distance uphill from the head of the seep. Uncut travel corridors should be left to connect mature forests to high-quality seeps in large clearcuts.

Thermal and roosting cover. In northern states, turkeys usually spend winters in or near conifer groves in valleys or on lower hillsides. Under conifers, snow usu-

ally is not so deep as elsewhere. Turkeys may be able to scratch and find some feed. Thermal cover is especially important to turkey survival when they may be forced to stay in these roost trees during extended periods of severe weather and deep snow. Conifers should make up at least 10 percent of the forest. But more important than extent of the groves are their locations and their closeness to other components of winter range. These groves should be in bottoms or on lower slopes and within short flying distance of food sources.

Where no natural conifer groves grow, winter range may be enhanced by planting conifer seedlings in remote valleys at higher elevations where turkeys are stressed in severe winters. The size of plantations needed to provide sufficient thermal cover seems to be about 2 hectares (5 acres). Best species to plant are usually those native to the area.

Nine of 11 species planted in northern hardwood sites in northern Pennsylvania showed good initial survival, but only Scotch pine and white spruce could sur-

Fruit-producing trees and shrubs are also important in snow-covered winter habitat. *Photo by National Wild Turkey Federation.*

vive and grow into adequate stands without being fenced from deer. The cost of fencing conifer plantations as winter cover may be difficult to justify unless the potential contribution of conifer seed in the diet of turkeys is also considered.

Winter food plantations. In some northern hardwood forests, where winter foods are scarce and turkey densities are low, plantations of food-producing small trees and shrubs may create or enhance winter range and prevent periodic starvation. Species should be hardy and consistently abundant producers of fruit that persists on branches during winter. Of 39 species tested, those best meeting these criteria were Washington hawthorn, Asian crab apples, autumn olive, multiflora rose, and Japanese barberry (Wunz 1989a). The best of the shrub species for the purpose are usually exotic ornamentals. Unfortunately, long-term horticultural experiments needed to improve native species have been neglected.

As insurance against late frosts that may cause fruit failures for most species, at least 4 species should be planted. A plantation of 0.8 to 1.2 hectares (2 to 3 acres) may satisfy the food needs of a turkey flock. But to make certain there is also enough extra to feed competing wildlife species and guard against the chance of fruit failures, at least a 2-hectare (5-acre) plantation may be needed. If possible, it should be near a conifer grove. Although most of these species are vigorous enough to tolerate some deer browsing, fencing may be necessary to assure success.

Natural shrub communities. The value of naturally occurring shrub communities for turkeys is often overlooked or underestimated. During the most severe winters on record in West Virginia (1977 and 1978), frequent reports told of turkeys concentrating in hawthorn and crab apple thickets. In northeastern states, turkeys also use these thickets as both brood and winter ranges, and they may subsist during winter on the persistent fruits of such shrubs as exotic barberries and rose.

In addition to encouraging naturalized exotic shrubs, managers should locate and include in their plans communities of such important native fruit-producing species as scrub oak, grape, greenbrier, dogwood, and viburnum. Mast surveys showed that these shrubs and vines are more consistent food producers than overstory

Table 7. Turkey population density estimates in occupied range of states in the eastern oak-hickory and northern hardwood forests (fall 1987).

State	Turkeys per square kilometer (square mile) of occupied forested range
Connecticut	0.7 (1.9)
Delaware	1.2 (3.0)
Indiana	0.6 (1.7)
Kentucky	3.9 (10.0)
Maine	0.4 (1.0)
Maryland	1.7 (4.4)
Massachusetts	0.7 (1.9)
New Hampshire	0.2 (0.6)
New Jersey	0.8 (2.0)
New York	1.1 (2.8)
North Carolina	0.6 (1.6)
Ohio	1.9 (4.9)
Pennsylvania	2.3 (6.0)
Rhode Island	0.6 (1.5)
Tennessee	1.2 (3.0)
Vermont	1.5 (4.0)
Virginia	1.2 (3.0)
West Virginia	1.6 (4.1)

trees (Uhlig and Wilson 1952). And Nixon et al. (1970) found that their fruit production was 3 times greater in the open than in the forest.

Grapevine communities, which furnish a preferred and valuable fall and winter food for turkeys, may be managed by deferring the cutting of trees that support them and by removing surrounding trees that shade them. Old grape tangles have been rejuvenated by felling into a pile the trees with vines. When growing in regenerating clearcuts, grapevines are particularly valuable because their climbing keeps up with tree growth. This ability enables grapevines to survive and provide food during the sapling and pole stages after most species of fruit-producing small trees and shrubs have been greatly reduced or eliminated by shading or browsing.

Scrub oak, blueberries, and huckleberries are probably the easiest and cheapest communities to manage. Scrub oak can be revitalized on a prescribed burning rotation of 12 to 15 years, and blueberry and huckleberries on a 3-year rotation. When fire could not be used in New Jersey, food production of scrub oak and chinquapin has been improved by using a combination of thinning and herbicides to eliminate low-yield shrubs. Then, the high-yield shrubs that remained were cut and allowed to sprout (Wolgast 1973).

Forests that lack understory shrub communities are likely to regenerate into similar forests. Residual seed or new seed sources for most shrub species are no longer there. A successful tactic is to underplant seeds and seedlings of shrubs before such sites are clear-cut (Wunz 1983).

HARVEST AND POPULATION MANAGEMENT

The 18 states in these 2 forest ecosystems have only 20 percent of the total occupied wild turkey range and 17 percent of the total turkey population, but these states have 55 percent of all spring turkey hunters (National Wild Turkey Federation 1986). Because of this high recreational demand and the comparatively low turkey densities (Table 7), perhaps nowhere else in wild turkey range is knowledge of their habitat, knowledge of population trends, and the control of hunting more critical.

Inventory Methods

All states in this region have conducted some habitat and population inventories. Each state has done pretransplant range surveys to select release sites, and 7 have done broad-scale surveys of habitats. In addition, forest statistics are available from U.S. Forest Service timber surveys for every state. Three states have evaluated brood and winter habitats, and 8 have inventoried mast crops.

Most states conduct summer brood or winter concentration counts or rely on harvest data or estimates by field personnel. A few states use landowner estimates and gobbling counts or collect legs and wings from hunters for sex and age ratios. Three states use track counts to survey study areas or extrapolate population estimates to larger areas.

Spring Hunting

Fall hunting is traditional in most states of this region in which wild turkeys were never wiped out (North Carolina, Virginia, West Virginia, Maryland, and Pennsylvania). And fall hunting was adopted in New York, where huntable populations were restored in the 1950s and 1960s. Beginning in the 1960s, spring gobbler seasons came into vogue in these states, especially where newly restored populations had not expanded enough to withstand either-sex fall hunting. New Jersey and Vermont opened spring seasons as early as 4 years after the first wild-trapped turkeys were released.

Now all this region's states and Ontario have spring turkey hunting. Even turkeys in some urbanized and densely populated northeastern states have shown remarkable tolerance to restricted habitats and to spring hunting.

The reputation that spring seasons are biologically safe has made this harvest universally acceptable to managers of turkey populations. Few controls seem needed

Sport hunters have supported and are enjoying the return of the wild turkey. *Photo by G. Wunz, Pennsylvania Game Commission.*

other than restrictions to maintain hunting quality. As turkey populations grow, or managers gain experience, the tendency has been to liberalize hunting opportunity and bag limits. Only 6 states in this region issue permits to control hunter numbers. Bag limits vary from 1 to 4 gobblers per season, and season length is from 2 to 6 weeks, averaging 3.5 weeks. The total spring harvest for this region is nearly 40,000 turkeys by more than 440,000 hunters (Table 8). Almost half of these hunters are in Pennsylvania.

Fall Hunting

Unlike spring hunting, fall hunting requires more controls simply because the most important component for reproduction of the population, hens, may be legally harvested in either-sex seasons. The indication is that many hunters cannot distinguish sex of turkeys during the fall, sometimes even with the bird in hand, so the proposal of male-only fall seasons is unrealistic. Methods used by managing agencies in the region to control the

turkey kill have been to regulate the number of fall hunters by a permit system and to restrict bag limit, weapon allowed, and timing and length of season. The permit option, usually used by states starting fall seasons, can be expensive to administer. The other choices are favored because they usually involve little more than declaring a regulation.

A conservative trend in regulating fall hunts is evident in the cautious adoptions by states with more recently restored turkey populations, and in the decreases of season length in some traditional fall hunting states. The tendency in some heavily hunted states is to time turkey seasons to coincide with hunting for game-farm species, but to avoid concurrent seasons with deer or other forest game. The objective is to reduce pressure on turkeys. Shortened or earlier seasons have reduced the likelihood of tracking snows that may result in excessive harvests.

In 1989, 11 states in this region allowed fall hunting, but 4 restricted hunters to bows. Bag limits are 1 bird each season in most states; no state allows more than 2. Season lengths range from 1 to 8 weeks, averaging 4. The

Table 8. Turkey harvest and hunting pressure in spring and fall season in states included in eastern oak-hickory and northern hardwood forests.

State	Spring			Fall		
	Number of hunters	Harvest	Hunters per square kilometer (square mile)	Number of hunters	Harvest	Hunters per square kilometer (square mile)
CT	2,140	318	0.3 (0.7)	450[b]	10	0.04 (0.1)
DE	NOS[c]	NOS	NOS	NOS	NOS	NOS
IN	1,275[a]	300	0.2 (0.4)[a]	NOS	NOS	NOS
KY	5,000	750	1.0 (2.5)	NOS	NOS	NOS
ME	450	11	0.3 (0.8)	NOS	NOS	NOS
MD	10,500	1,010	2.2 (5.8)	8,500	580	2.7 (7.1)
MA	10,000	557	1.4 (3.7)	NOS	NOS	NOS
NH	900	90	0.2 (0.4)	300[b]	4	0.04 (0.1)
NJ	3,900	390	0.7 (1.7)	NOS	NOS	NOS
NY	50,000	4,775[a]	0.7 (1.7)	45,000	3,812	1.7 (4.5)
NC	6,500[a]	600	0.2 (0.6)[a]	NOS	NOS	NOS
OH	16,000	2,000	0.2 (2.6)	NOS	NOS	NOS
PA	226,000	15,000	3.5 (9.0)	300,000	28,346	5.8 (15.0)
RI	200	5	0.2 (0.5)	NOS	NOS	NOS
TN	11,000	1,139[a]	0.5 (1.2)[a]	NOS	NOS	NOS
VA	63,900	5,400	0.8 (2.0)	135,084	11,435	1.4 (3.7)
VT	5,000	500	0.4 (1.0)	6,000	800	0.5 (1.2)
WV	50,000	6,526	0.9 (2.4)	44,000	2,939	1.9 (4.9)
Total	442,775	39,371		539,334	47,926	

[a] 1983–85 data, all others 1987–88 data.
[b] Bow only.
[c] NOS = no open season.

approximately 540,000 fall hunters in this region take almost 50,000 turkeys annually (Table 8).

Nearly 60 percent of these fall hunters are in Pennsylvania. There the pressure of 6 hunters per square kilometer (15 hunters per square mile) of occupied turkey range open to fall hunting is more than twice that of any other state. Overharvest has been a concern. The long-term custom of opening the turkey and game-farm seasons on the same date and avoiding seasons concurrent with big game has dissipated some hunting pressure.

In addition, a management area concept was started with 2 areas in 1960 and increased to 4 in 1981. Since 1985, Pennsylvania has been divided into 9 basic ecological management areas. Each is based on its amount or composition of forest habitat, potential to support turkeys, road network or land ownership for hunter access, and human population or urbanization. The goal is to limit harvests in each area, consistent with that area's ability to support and produce turkeys. The method is to establish minimum-length seasons for each management area, based on the above-listed criteria. There is an option to extend seasons on short notice in any area if this tactic can be justified by results of summer brood counts (Wunz and Ross 1990b).

West Virginia, a state with heavy pressure from squirrel hunting and archery deer hunting, traditionally had concurrent squirrel, archery, and fall turkey seasons.

Experiments in separating these seasons since 1983 resulted in a significant decline in fall hunting pressure on turkeys when the turkey season opened 1 to 2 weeks after the start of squirrel season and 1 week after the start of deer archery season (Pack 1988). In addition, the total annual harvest (fall and spring) suggests a trend of a growing turkey population.

Similar control methods are being tried or considered in other states of the region. Also, indications that food shortages concentrate turkeys and cause them to be vulnerable to overshooting (Menzel 1975, Wunz 1978a, Pack 1986b) suggest that mast surveys should be considered in addition to brood production data in setting fall hunting seasons.

PROJECTIONS FOR THE FUTURE

The wild turkey prognosis for these 2 ecosystems during the next decade is still bright, mainly because almost 130,000 square kilometers (50,000 square miles) of these forests remain to be occupied by turkeys. But eventually the increasing trend in turkey populations that we have enjoyed will meet not only increased demands for hunting but also conflicting land uses. Perhaps the best basis for long-term projection is in the statistics of the Forest Resource Inventories that have been periodically conducted in each state by the U.S. Forest Service (1976–1983). These data show that increases in forest acreage occurring in recent decades — because of cleared land reverting into forest — have come to an end in most states. Turkey living space has become obviously finite.

The good survey news on the future of turkey habitat was that the forests were maturing and growth was expected to continue to exceed cutting rates for some time. Neither is it expected that large-scale conversion of hardwoods to softwoods would occur in these forests as has happened in Piedmont and Coastal Plain forests of the southeastern states. But according to projections of the U.S. Forest Service (1984) and Zinn and Jones (1987), hardwood consumption will grow substantially by the year 2000 to satisfy growing domestic and foreign markets.

That could be the year of change for turkey habitat. The timber maturity and increased markets will result in more harvesting, which begets intrusions and developments in the forest. At some point we will no doubt see loss or degradation of turkey habitat. This forecast follows Bailey's (1980) prediction that turkeys may prosper nationwide for several years, but populations will inevitably peak and decline because of continuing loss of habitat.

Habitat losses should be less in the mountainous areas, where rugged terrain is a hindrance to development. In level terrain, where forest habitats are already limited and fragmented, losses could be serious. Also, as human populations and economies increase, some of these forests again may be cleared for agriculture, energy extraction, or transmission lines.

But the greatest threats seem to be urbanization, homes, recreation developments, and other human intrusions (Donahoe 1990). Unfortunately, these developments are usually in the lowlands of valleys that often are habitats critical to turkeys for rearing broods or for winter survival.

The Forest Resource Survey information suggests that habitat losses will be greatest in forests on the eastern slopes of the Appalachians and in southern New England that are nearest the east coast megapolis corridor. In the past decade, coastal states from Maryland to Massachusetts have lost from 8 to 14 percent of their forests, largely to urbanization. In New Jersey, the most densely human populated state, the present 6,000 square kilometers (2,300 square miles) of turkey range may drop to less than 3,900 square kilometers (1,500 square miles).

In the next 30 years, forests and habitats will probably change least on the western side of the Appalachians (particularly in West Virginia), on the Cumberland Plateau of eastern Kentucky and Tennessee, in the more mountainous areas of the Allegheny Plateau in Ohio, Pennsylvania, and New York, and in the St. Lawrence

In the Northeast, turkey habitat will be lost to land uses supporting demands of a high human population. *Photo by U.S. Fish and Wildlife Service.*

Valley of New York. Although the forest areas of Vermont, New Hampshire, and southern Maine may not decrease, further encroachments by real estate and recreational developments are expected. In the past decade, forests increased from 5 to 16 percent in Ohio, New York, and West Virginia and changed only slightly in the other states.

Unless acceptable alternatives are found to replace fossil fuels, surface mining will probably increase on the Cumberland and Allegheny plateaus and in other coal-producing areas from Tennessee to Pennsylvania. We can expect more intrusions and disturbance into habitats for gas and oil wells and access roads as other domestic and foreign energy sources diminish or become unavailable. But reclaiming these energy extraction sites can be an opportunity for the innovative manager to improve habitat.

Although the problem of conversion from hardwoods to softwoods may never be significant in these forests, there is concern for monoculture management of certain economically popular hardwoods — such as black cherry (Tilghman 1989) — that will sacrifice habitat diversity. Forest managers in the future may also observe degradation of turkey habitat in some areas where succession or timber-harvesting practices result in increases of less desirable tree species such as red and sugar maples and birch.

Insects and diseases undoubtedly will continue to affect wild turkey habitat. The historic and tragic loss of such a valuable food species for turkeys as American chestnut, from the chestnut blight, may be followed by

The forces of nature as well as man have always affected northeastern forests. The chestnut blight eliminated a dominant species throughout, the gypsy moth now is reducing oaks, and dogwood anthracnose is reducing flowering dogwood (shown here), an important fall and winter food. *Photo by M. Kennamer, National Wild Turkey Federation.*

other such problems to key food plants. Diseases already are apparent in beech (Anonymous 1986) and flowering dogwood (Hibben and Dougherty 1988), and even in multiflora rose (Amrine and Hindal 1988). Insect plagues, such as the oak leaf roller *Archipis semiferanus* or the gypsy moth *Lymantria dispar* have killed some oak trees and reduced oak in forest stands from New England to Pennsylvania.

The gypsy moth, which has received considerable attention from the news media, was introduced into America from Europe in the late 1860s. Despite intense control and eradication programs, it has spread from New England southwest into West Virginia and Virginia. The fear of enormous problems caused by the gypsy moth and the existence of vast areas of susceptible oak forests to the south and west of the current infested area indicate that the moth will be a concern in the future.

Oaks are affected most. But Gansner and Herrick (1987) found that in states where the gypsy moth has been around for a long time, oaks now account for only a slightly smaller percentage of the total hardwood inventory than they did before the infestation. The combined oak-growing stock volume has actually increased by 23 percent. Oak sawtimber volume is up 32 percent, and its quality has improved. By 1985, 7 years after moth defoliations, growth had offset most of the timber loss in Pennsylvania.

No doubt habitats will change as the gypsy moth spreads, but the overall effects on turkey populations in New England and Pennsylvania have not been apparent. One Pennsylvania study found no turkeys until the spring after the year of an almost complete defoliation that occurred during the early brood-rearing period of turkeys. But during previous summers, turkey broods used the edges of localized infestations often enough to suggest they may have fed on the immature larvae (Ross and Wunz 1990). Also, evidence from tracks in the snow indicated turkeys have fed on gypsy moth egg masses that were laid on tree trunks.

Tree kill on some sites has resulted in a temporary increase of herbaceous understories, which benefit turkey brood habitat and spring grazing areas, or increase food-producing shrubs and midstory trees. The negative side, however, has been the relatively high kill of chestnut oaks on ridgetops. These trees often had produced acorns during years when frost eliminated mast in adjacent lowlands. In addition, the understory and ground cover of ericaceous shrubs that usually grow on such poor sites often become too dense for turkeys. On more productive sites, oaks that die are apt to be replaced by such turkey food producers as black cherry, beech, and black gum or nonfood producers like red maple, sugar maple, yellow poplar, or birch.

Perhaps an even greater threat to turkey habitat than the gypsy moth itself are forest owners on the advancing edge of infestations who panic and cut stands prematurely and indiscriminately, believing the forest will be wiped out. Gottschalk (1987) has developed guidelines for silvicultural alternatives to minimize gypsy moth impacts. One suggestion is to reduce tree species preferred by the gypsy moth (mostly oaks) to less than 20 percent of the stand. This tactic could have a damaging impact on turkey habitat.

Forest managers should keep in mind the history of gypsy moth infestations. The moths will surely spread south and west regardless of efforts to stop them, and they will reduce both the forest's oak component and the frequency of good acorn crops.

Severity of subsequent defoliations, however, will probably decline. The end result may be a more diverse habitat. Even remaining residual oaks may produce more acorns as crowns enlarge. In any event, we will still have a forest, and we need to remember Campbell's (1979:42)

remarks: "Systematic change is occurring constantly in any living landscape, but we often think of the forest around us as a sort of mausoleum—static and unchanging."

Donahoe (1990), who considers land-use management the key to the wild turkey's future, laments that the concept of planning and zoning has not been accepted by the public. Also, the increasing antihunting movement, perhaps already more prevalent in the heavily urbanized northeastern states than elsewhere, will complicate management and could eventually reduce financial support from hunters. Other threatening conflicts are the increasing demands from other outdoor recreational uses, such as hiking or trails for off-road vehicles, in this heavily urbanized region. It seems the second generation of turkey managers may face challenges that surpass those that confronted the pioneer managers in restoring the bird.

Although broad strategies already may have been set for managing turkey populations in most states, refinements will always be needed in inventories and harvest tactics to meet current situations. As more and more private land becomes closed to public access, the fact that so little land in this region is publicly owned will further complicate ways of maintaining quality hunting. Historically, most of this region has resisted fee hunting, but the concept appears to be growing. Wigley and Melchoirs (1986) suggested means for state agencies to compensate landowners for allowing the public to hunt on their property.

There will no doubt be fewer places for turkey hunting. So the carrying capacity for turkeys must be increased in the range that remains. So far, the surface has barely been scratched in learning and applying proven methods of habitat management. In finding ways to hold and improve this habitat, the field is wide open for those who follow us. Bailey (1980) said it better: "If our management efforts are supported by all that can be mustered in human intellect, foresight, and determination, old *Meleagris* will be around for a long time."

Chapter 17

EASTERN TURKEY IN SOUTHERN PINE-OAK FORESTS

George A. Hurst
Professor
Mississippi State University
Mississippi State, Mississippi

James G. Dickson
Research Wildlife Biologist
USFS, Southern Forest Experiment Station
Nacogdoches, Texas

The eastern wild turkey historically has been associated with productive southern forests. Accounts of early travelers revealed wild turkeys were abundant throughout the South in precolonial times (Mosby and Handley 1943).

Through unregulated market and subsistence hunting and habitat destruction, the wild turkey in the South was decimated in the late 1800s, reaching its lowest level around 1930. State wildlife agencies, using Federal Aid in Wildlife Restoration funds (Pittman-Robertson Act 1937), began providing some protection. These agencies also attempted restoration of turkeys through releases of pen-raised, semiwild turkeys. The release programs failed.

Beginning about 1950, with the advent of capturing wild turkeys by cannon net, the highly successful trap-and-transfer program began in earnest. Through great efforts of turkey trappers throughout the South, better protection, and improved habitats, the wild turkey has been restored (National Wild Turkey Federation 1986). Southern wild turkeys now number more than 1 million.

In Mississippi, for example, the wild turkey numbered an estimated 3,500 in 1941. It now numbers about 350,000. The Mississippi harvest was 253 in 1942, 4,129 in 1967, and about 58,000 in 1988 (Commer 1986, Steffen 1987). A similar, but slightly earlier, restoration occurred in Alabama (Davis and Widder 1985). Restoration continues in eastern Texas (Campo and Dickson 1989).

PINE-OAK FORESTS

The southern pine-oak forests, from New Jersey in the Northeast, extend southwesterly and westerly in a band about 1,036 to 1,295 kilometers (644 to 805 miles) wide into eastern Oklahoma and Texas, excluding most of peninsular Florida and including the bottomland hardwood region along the Mississippi River northerly into southern Indiana.

The 12-state southeastern U.S. area does not coincide exactly with the southeastern pine-oak forest type, but data from the area are useful for determining general land-use patterns of the region. Forests dominate the South. They occupy slightly more than half of the land area (USDA Forest Service 1988): more than twice the area of cropland and pasture combined. About a third of the forest area is occupied by pine types, with a third of this area (roughly 10 percent of the forest area) being planted pine. Some 17 percent of the southeastern area is occupied by bottomland hardwood forests.

Restoration has been very successful in the South. Where once there were only a few thousand turkeys, now there are about a million. *Photo by H. Williamson, U.S. Forest Service.*

Upland pine-oak ecosystems extend from New Jersey in the Northeast into eastern Oklahoma and Texas in the Southwest. *Photo by U.S. Forest Service.*

About 90 percent of the area's forestland is privately owned, and slightly less than 25 percent of the forestland is owned by forest industry. About 10 percent of forestland is public, and more than half of that is national forest. Timber is the most important agriculture crop of the southeastern area, having a value of twice that of soybeans or cotton.

Upland Pine-Oak Ecosystems

The southern upland pine-oak forest type includes 3 pine forest ecosystems from Kuchler's potential natural vegetation delineation (oak-pine, loblolly-shortleaf pine, and longleaf-slash pine) (Garrison et al. 1977). These forests extend from coastal New Jersey in the Northeast, south and westward through the Piedmont and Coastal Plain, into eastern Oklahoma and eastern Texas. Climate of the pine-oak area is generally mild. Mean annual temperature ranges from 15 to 20 degrees Celsius (60 to 68 degrees Fahrenheit) with about 200 to 280 frost-free days. Mean precipitation for the area ranges from 102 to 152 centimeters (40 to 60 inches) annually (Garrison et al. 1977).

Oak-pine ecosystem. In the northern part of the southwestern portion of this area (from Georgia westward) is the oak-pine ecosystem, which occurs from the southernmost ridges and valleys of the Appalachians below 600 meters (2,000 feet), west across the Coastal Plains into northeastern Texas and north into the Ouachita provinces. Soils of this forest type are usually medium to coarse in texture, well drained, and often shallow and droughty. They were derived largely from sandstones and sometimes from shales and granites (White 1980). In 1977, about 60 percent of the oak-pine ecosystem was in crops, and less than 10 percent in pasture (Garrison et al. 1977).

More than half of the forests of the area are composed of hardwoods, usually upland oaks. But pines, mostly shortleaf, are common. This forest type is considered transitional between shortleaf pine types and the later successional upland oaks. On the higher, drier sites, the hardwood components tend to be upland oaks: post, southern red, scarlet, and blackjack. On the moist, more fertile sites, white, southern red, and black oaks are common associates (White 1980). Other associates include sweet gum, hickories, yellow poplar, black gum, winged elm, and red maple. Common understory vegetation includes sourwood, mountain laurel, flowering dogwood, redbud, persimmon, blueberries, huckleberries, and viburnums. Grape, greenbrier, Virginia creeper, trumpet vine, and honeysuckle are common woody vines (White 1980).

Loblolly-shortleaf pine ecosystem. The loblolly-shortleaf pine ecosystem, the most extensive of the southern forest types, occurs south and east of the oak-pine ecosystem. It extends from New Jersey on the eastern coast, south and west through the Piedmont and Gulf Coastal Plain into southern Arkansas, southeastern Oklahoma, and southeastern Texas. The loblolly-shortleaf pine type occurs from sea level to 760 meters (2,500 feet), from ridgetops to small creek bottoms (Mann 1980). Soils, coarse to medium in texture, were derived largely from sandstone and shales. Some 60 to 70 percent of the system is in forest, mostly small woodlots, but there are extensive forests. About 20 percent of the area is in cropland, and a smaller portion is pasture (Garrison et al. 1977).

This forest system is dominated by loblolly, shortleaf, and other pines, and associated hardwoods. Loblolly pine usually dominates on wetter sites and shortleaf on dry, thin soils. This forest type encroaches into original longleaf sites if fire is excluded. Without disturbance, this forest type will eventually revert to more tolerant upland hardwoods.

Common overstory associates are oaks, hickories, sweet gum, black gum, red maple, and winged elm (Garrison et al. 1977). Common understory shrubs include flowering dogwood, viburnums, haws, blueberries,

American beauty berry, yaupon, and several woody vines. The main grasses are bluestems, panicums, and longleaf uniola (Garrison et al. 1977).

Longleaf-slash pine ecosystem. South of the loblolly-shortleaf pine ecosystem is the longleaf-slash pine ecosystem of the southern Gulf Coastal Plain. This ecosystem extends from South Carolina west through Georgia, northern Florida, southern portions of Alabama, Mississippi, and Louisiana, and southeastern Texas. Soils are medium to coarse in texture, acidic, and low in organic matter and nutrients. They were derived mainly from Coastal Plain sediments, from mostly sandy materials, as well as heavy clay and gravel (Garrison et al. 1977).

About half of the area is forested, and the trend is toward more forest and improved pasture and less cropland. Forests are dominated by longleaf and slash pine, singly or in combination. Common overstory associates include other pines, oaks, and sweet gum. Longleaf dominates when periodic burning is done, and hardwoods encroach when fire is excluded. Gallberry, saw palmetto, wax myrtle, and sumac are prominent shrubs. East of the Apalachicola River, wire grasses are common understory plants; bluestems predominate westerly (Garrison et al. 1977).

Oak-Gum-Cypress Ecosystems

A major ecosystem of the South included with the pine-oak forests is oak-gum-cypress, or bottomland hardwood forests. They are mesic (moderately moist) to hydric. These forests covered about 11 million hectares (27 million acres) in 1977, mostly in the southeastern United States from Virginia to eastern Texas and up the Mississippi River to Indiana (USDA Forest Service 1982). These floodplain hardwood forests extend along small streams to major rivers throughout the southeastern region. Climate is similar to that of the 3 major pine ecosystems. Of the total bottomland area, about 10 percent remains in forest. The rest is evenly divided between pasture and crops—mainly cotton, soybeans, and corn (Garrison et al. 1977).

Forest communities are closely associated with sites that are determined mainly by soils, elevation, and degree of flooding. Most oak-gum-cypress forests grow on first bottoms and terraces (Putnam 1951). First bottoms were formed by the present drainage system. They often flood and are composed mostly of clay and fine, sandy loam soils. Terraces were formed by earlier drainage systems, are inundated only at high flood stage, and have mostly silt soils with varying mixtures of sand and clay.

Within the first bottoms and terraces are ridges, flats, sloughs, and swamps (Putnam 1951). New land, or front, is found only in first bottoms along active or recent

Oak-gum-cypress ecosystems extend along small streams to large rivers throughout the region. *Photo by U.S. Forest Service.*

channels. Ridges are banks or fronts of former streams. Flats are between ridges and have little topographical relief. Sloughs are shallow depressions, usually with seasonal water. Swamps are depressions that normally are wet except during drought.

There are 8 general forest types within the oak-gum-cypress complex (Putnam 1951). (1) The sweet gum-water oak type is widely distributed. It is found on terrace flats and in first bottoms, except in sloughs, swamps, and fronts. (2) The white oak-red oak-other hardwoods type, also widely distributed, is found mainly on first bottom and terrace ridges. (3) Hackberry-elm-ash is a successional type following cottonwood, normally occurring on low ridges, flats, and sloughs in first bottoms and on terrace flats and sloughs. (4) Overcup oak-bitter pecan is characteristic of low, poorly drained clay flats, sloughs, and backwater basins. (5) The cottonwood type normally pioneers fronts of major streams. (6) Willow and associates also invade fronts in sloughs and low flats. (7) Riverfront hardwoods are transitional between cottonwood or willow and the sweet gum-water oak type. They occur on all front lands except deep sloughs and swamps. (8) The cypress-tupelo gum type is widely distributed on low and poorly drained flats, deep sloughs, and swamps.

The white-tailed deer is another popular game animal in the South. *Photo by U.S. Forest Service.*

Wildlife of Pine-Oak Forests

The semitropical climate and diverse vegetative systems of the southern pine-oak forests support abundant and diverse wildlife communities. Of 8 general regions of the United States, the Southeast and south-central regions each have more than 1,000 vertebrate species, the highest of all regions (USDA Forest Service 1981). These 2 southern regions supported mean species figures of 94 amphibian, 422 avian, 44 fish, 135 mammalian, and 125 reptilian species.

The southern upland pine-oak forests are productive wildlife habitat. In stands with vegetative diversity, there are generally dense and diverse communities (Dickson and Sequelquist 1979). Small mammals are abundant, especially in young, brushy stands (Atkison and Johnson 1979). Southern pine-oak supports high densities of white-tailed deer, a prime game species throughout the region. Also in this forest are other mammals such as

swamp and cottontail rabbits, the opossum, striped skunk, raccoon, bobcat, and gray fox. Gray and fox squirrels are found in stands with older hardwoods. The endangered red-cockaded woodpecker inhabits the area's old pine stands that have limited hardwoods.

Floodplain bottomland hardwood forests are productive habitats for game and nongame animals. Vegetative productivity and diversity, and hard mast production from pecan, beech, and especially oaks, are high. Gray and fox squirrels thrive in these hardwood forests. Harvest records from the South show bottomlands consistently produced more deer than did other habitat types (Stransky and Halls 1968). Reptile and amphibian populations are high in these mesic to aquatic sites, and the hardwood bottoms have abundant breeding birds and very abundant wintering birds (Dickson 1978).

The abundant wildlife of southern forests attracts numerous wildlife users. In 1980 there were some 6.7 million hunters in the South. Some 65 percent of them hunted big game, 74 percent hunted small game, and 37 percent hunted migratory birds (USDA, Fish and Wildlife Service, and USDC Bureau of Census 1982). There was a higher proportion of hunters in the southern population (12 percent) than in the United States as a whole (10.3 percent).

CHANGES TO THE FORESTS

Originally, nearly all of the 12-state southeastern area was forested. Early settlers cleared timberland for crops and pasture. From the late 1800s to the early 1920s, extensive old-growth timber was logged (USDA Forest Service 1988). By the 1920s, programs for forest protection and regeneration were under way. Those practices and abandonment of cropland and pasture increased the timber area. In the Great Depression years of the 1930s and afterward, more cropland and pasture reverted to forest. By 1952, nearly 60 percent of the total land area in the Southeast was classified as timberland (78 million hectares, 193 million acres).

In the early 1960s, timber area increased to 80 million hectares (197 million acres). Then the expansion stopped and was reversed by conversion to crops and by urban encroachment. This slow decline of the timber area has continued through the surveys of 1985 (74 million hectares, 182 million acres) (USDA Forest Service 1988). Special programs to keep or add to forestland, such as the Conservation Reserve Program (USDA), have somewhat slowed this forest decline.

Upland Pine-Oak Ecosystems

Data from the southeastern area (USDA Forest Service 1988:114) for pine types reflect recent changes. The area in mixed pine-hardwood stands has changed little. From 1952 to 1970, acreage increased from 11 million hectares (27.1 million acres) to 11.8 million hectares (29.2 million acres), and since then has declined slightly to almost 10.9 million hectares (26.9 million acres) in 1985.

Significant losses have occurred in total area of natural pine, from 29.1 million hectares (72 million acres) in 1952 to 16.6 million hectares (41 million acres) in 1985. Much of the natural pine was on abandoned fields and pastures. After pine harvest, these stands have reverted to pine-hardwood or hardwood, have been converted to pine plantations, or have been lost to cropland, home sites, and roads.

Conversely, the area in pine plantations has increased. In 1952, only 0.7 million hectares (1.8 million acres) were in short-rotation pine plantations. By 1985, this area had increased to 8.5 million hectares (20.9 mil-

Area in pine plantations has increased from 0.7 million hectares (1.8 million acres) in 1952 to about 8.5 million hectares (20.9 million acres) in 1985. *Photo by J. McConnell, USDA Soil Conservation Service.*

lion acres) because natural pine stands were cut and regenerated, and cropland and pasture were abandoned and planted to pine.

Oak-Gum-Cypress Ecosystems

Water, soils, and vegetation are closely interdependent in the oak-gum-cypress ecosystem. Floodwaters deposit coarse sands on channel banks. Farther away from stream channels, fine clays settle out of floodwater. These soil deposits alter sites and consequently their vegetation. As soil deposits build over the long term, streams and rivers alter courses, thereby affecting sites and vegetation.

The oak-gum-cypress complex has been substantially influenced by past tree harvest. Composition of present stands often reflects past decisions about which species and individual trees to cut and which to leave (Putnam et al. 1960). Most harvest-regeneration methods in practice today involve clearcuts, which favor commercially valuable, mostly shade-intolerant species such as sweet gum, eastern cottonwood, sycamore, yellow poplar, and oaks.

Area occupied by the oak-gum-cypress complex has declined, but it varies by region. In the mid-South area from Alabama and Tennessee to eastern Texas and Oklahoma, 1.6 million hectares (3.9 million acres) of bottomland hardwoods were converted to other uses from 1962 to 1985. About 6.7 million hectares (16.5 million acres) of this forest remain (Birdsey and McWilliams 1986).

The loss has been mainly through the demise of bottomland hardwood forests of the Mississippi River Delta, mostly converted to soybean fields, with some land to cotton fields and pasture. There was an estimated total of 10 million hectares (25 million acres) in the entire Mississippi system originally (Dunaway 1980). In the 1930s, Forest Service surveys showed 4.8 million hectares (11.8 million acres) remained forested in the primary delta states: Louisiana, Mississippi, and Arkansas (Sternitzke 1976).

By the late 1960s and early 1970s, delta hardwood area in these states had dropped to 2.9 million hectares

Top: Most of the once extensive bottomland hardwoods of the Mississippi Delta have been converted to agricultural crops and pastures. Bottom: Key bottomland habitat throughout the South has been converted to reservoirs.

Photo by J. Dickson, U.S. Forest Service.

Photo by L. Fox, USDA Soil Conservation Service.

(7.2 million acres) (Sternitzke 1976). But since the heavy losses in the 1960s, bottomland habitat loss has been less (Murphy 1975, 1978, Birdsey and McWilliams 1986). Most of the land suitable for agriculture has already been converted. Only marginal sites remain. Also, recent crop prices have not inspired new agricultural ventures. In fact, some land has been planted back to bottomland hardwoods, much of it through the Conservation Reserve Program.

In many places, forest area on bottomland sites has been lost to reservoirs. In eastern Texas, for example, Toledo Bend and Sam Rayburn reservoirs occupy more than 100,000 hectares (250,000 acres) that formerly were primarily covered by bottomland hardwoods (Dickson 1978). Considerable other bottomland hardwood habitat has been lost to stream channelization, such as the Tennessee-Tombigbee Waterway Project in Mississippi, and to the clearing of associated mature vegetation.

Apparently bottomland occupied by hardwoods in the Southeast (Florida, Georgia, South Carolina, North Carolina, and Virginia) has not been subjected to such losses. The occupied area has remained relatively stable over the past 4 decades (Langdon et al. 1981).

HABITAT RELATIONSHIPS

Early biologists described optimum wild turkey habitat as a combination and variety of coniferous and hardwood forest stands (many of them mature stands with numerous oaks), interspersed with grassy openings and open understories that were well watered and remote from human disturbance (Mosby and Handley 1943, Wheeler 1948, Holbrook 1973). What was considered ideal turkey range was mainly influenced by observing that wild turkeys survived man's indiscriminate hunting only in large, inaccessible river swamps or in remote forests. Turkeys in other areas had been continually pursued and had been eliminated. The most important factor affecting turkey populations was protection from man, not some combination of habitats (Stoddard 1963, Dickson et al. 1978). We now see that turkeys are more habitat adaptable and flexible than was originally thought. Some factors that contributed to this view are (1) restoration of wild turkeys; (2) changing attitudes of people toward wild turkeys; and (3) better protection. Stoddard (1963) observed that the wild turkey was originally more an inhabitant of the well-drained upland forests and prairie edges than of the river swamps. Turkeys are now common to abundant in habitats once thought marginal (Little 1980, Hurst 1981).

Biologists recognized early the importance of openings to wild turkey populations. Openings produce green forage, seeds, soft mast, numerous insects, and planted

Habitat diversity is important for meeting the year-round needs of wild turkeys. Openings interspersed with mature forest stands constitute ideal habitat. *Photo by H. Williamson, U.S. Forest Service.*

turkey foods. Openings are used for courtship. Stoddard (1963), based on his experience in southern Georgia, recommended a third of turkey range may be in fields and pastures. Mosby and Handley (1943) thought at least 10 percent of total area should be in well-scattered openings in Virginia, and Wheeler (1948) stressed distribution of openings for production of grass and insects in Alabama. In Tennessee, turkeys used fields of 4 to 8 hectares (10 to 20 acres) extensively (Lewis 1964).

Early conclusions about the importance of openings to turkey habitat have been substantiated by recent studies.

In Alabama, telemetry studies confirmed that turkeys selected openings. Investigators recommended spring and summer habitat should include 12 to 25 percent in well-dispersed openings that produce grass, forbs, and insects (Speake et al. 1975). In south Alabama there were more than 12 turkeys per square kilometer (31 per square mile) in an area with 24 percent openings. But in northwest Alabama, in an area with only 10 percent in poorly distributed openings, turkey density was only about 1 per square kilometer (3 per square mile).

In Missouri, turkey densities in the heavily forested southern range were 0.4 to 5.8 per square kilometer (1 to 15 per square mile), but in northern Missouri, with abundant farm openings, populations exceed 10 per square kilometer (25 per square mile) (National Wild Turkey Federation 1986).

In Iowa, turkey densities averaged 8 to 12 per square kilometer (21 to 31 per square mile) in an area with 7 percent in forest and the rest in diversified agriculture (Little 1980). Both northern Missouri and Iowa previously had been considered marginal turkey range. Also, very large home ranges, suggesting poor habitat, have been reported for turkeys in nearly totally forested areas (Everett et al. 1979, Exum et al. 1987, Kelley et al. 1988, Smith and Lambert 1988).

Modeling Relationships

Flather et al. (1989) constructed a multiresource, multivariate wild turkey habitat model to assess potential impacts on wild turkey populations from land-use shifts and forest management. The approach was to use discriminant function analysis to establish the empirical relationships between land use and abundance classes of wild turkeys on a county-by-county basis for 6 main physiographic regions of the South. USDA Forest Service data were used for area estimates of forest cover types (natural pine, planted pine, oak-pine, upland hardwood, and lowland hardwood) and forest age class. USDA Soil

Openings are important to wild turkeys for a variety of reasons. Turkeys feed on various grasses, forbs, and insects in openings. *Photo by U.S. Forest Service.*

Conservation Service data were used for estimates of all other land types (e.g., crop, pasture, range, and urban land). Abundance data in 3 density categories for wild turkeys came through the Southeastern Cooperative Wildlife Disease Study (University of Georgia) from state wildlife agencies.

Results from the study: (1) turkey densities decreased with increased area in cropland and human-related land use; and (2) turkey densities increased with the area of natural forest types, especially upland and lowland hardwood and old age classes of hardwood.

Songer (1987) used modeling to delineate quality brood habitat and developed methods to estimate habitat spatial characteristics, including juxtaposition, interspersion, and edge. Also, he found significant differences in gobbler use of habitats associated with interspersion. But gobbler use increased when juxtaposition or edge increased (Songer et al. 1988).

Nesting

Turkey hens nest in a variety of habitat types, such as wood's edge, old fields, rights-of-way, and young pine plantations. But nest sites have dense, herbaceous cover and some shrub cover at ground level. There is some form of structure around the nest, and overhead cover frequently is woody brush or vines, or both. The nest site is frequently near some form of opening such as a road or trail.

In Virginia after a pulpwood operation, hen turkeys nested near openings in the forest, in abandoned fields, around old house sites, in thickets, and in treetops (Mosby and Handley 1943). In a more recent study, 3 nests each occurred in large hardwood stands, hardwood leave strips, and thinned 30-to-50-year-old pine stands, and another nest was in a young pine plantation (Holbrook et al. 1987).

Nest sites usually have dense vegetation with some shrub cover, as well as some form of adjacent structure, such as brush or a tree. *Photo by L. Williams.*

On a coastal island off Georgia (Hon et al. 1978), 14 of 23 nests were on similar sites in a pine-saw palmetto-oak scrub community. Four nests were in pond pine-saw palmetto, 4 were in oak-pine forests, and 3 were in old fields. Overhead cover by saw palmetto and other species at the nest site ranged from 50 to 90 percent. In south Georgia, Stoddard (1963) observed that nesting hens preferred brushy clumps in open woodlots—spots that had escaped fire for 2 to 5 years.

On the Francis Marion National Forest, South Carolina, Still and Baumann (1989, 1990) found that nesting wild turkey hens (sample of 37) preferred regeneration stands less than 11 years old and mixed pine-hardwood stands. The hens avoided pure pine and pure hardwood stands.

Substantial nesting habitat data have been produced from studies in various regions of Alabama. Wheeler (1948) described nests in Alabama as being in more open woodland (pine) near openings. Nests were in patches of comparatively heavy ground cover that had escaped burning for 2 or 3 years. Shrubs and hardwood sprouts concealed the eggs. In the Alabama Piedmont, Hillestad (1973) reported that 7 of 8 radio-equipped hens selected

similar nest habitat—ungrazed, recently cutover upland pine and sweet gum forest. Of 40 nests on 4 areas in Alabama and 1 in Kentucky, 23 were in mostly small openings (old fields or cutover areas) with mixed herbaceous vegetation, pine reproduction areas, and abandoned house sites. Three were in bottomland hardwood forests, and the remaining nests were in upland hardwood, pine-hardwood, or pine stands. Most of the nests (75 percent) were either in openings or very near openings, and they were in old field successional stages or the equivalent (Speake et al. 1975).

Of 48 nests in extreme south-central Alabama, 34 (71 percent) were in slash pine plantations, 6 (13 percent) were in cutover tracts, 5 (10 percent) were in bottomland hardwoods, and 3 (6 percent) were in agricultural fields. The pine plantations used were from 6 months to 44 years old. Nests were about equally divided among plantations less than 8 years old (11), 8 to 12 years old (12), and more than 12 years old (11). Most nests were near roads or lanes. Hens preferred sites that had not been recently burned. Discriminant function analysis correctly identified vegetative conditions at nest sites (87 percent) and those at random sites (66 percent) (Exum et al. 1987).

Everett et al. (1981) found 54 nests, of which 20 were in powerline rights-of-way (ROW). Few hens used ROW the first nesting season after winter mowing. But many hens chose the ROW habitat the second and third nesting season after mowing. Rights-of-way provided mixed-herbaceous, low-brushy nesting habitat in a region of extensive mature hardwood forest in northwest Alabama. In this same area, Everett et al. (1985) found 21 of 67 nests on ROW, which accounted for less than 1 percent of the total area. Only 20 nests occurred in upland hardwood forests, which accounted for 71 percent of the total area. Many nests were near edges (roads, fields, and ROW). Nests also were found in pine plantations and creek bottom hardwood forests. The investigators concluded that the vegetative structure that best hid the nest was mixed-herbaceous, low-brushy cover, such as early plant successional stages.

Several studies from pine stands in Mississippi described nest sites. Phalen et al. (1986) and Seiss (1989) reported that 18 of 38 hens nested in unthinned, mature loblolly pine stands, which accounted for about 50 percent of the area. This habitat type was used according to availability. Young (2-to-4-year-old) loblolly pine plantations, which accounted for only 12.5 percent of the available habitat, contained 14 nests and were preferred nest habitat. Plantations less than 2 and more than 4 years old were avoided (Seiss et al. 1990). In a large block dominated by loblolly pine plantations, Smith (1990) reported that all (16) and Burk (1989) reported that 24 of 25 radio-tagged hens nested in plantations 15 to 20 years old that

Two-year-old pine plantations usually have a vegetative density suitable for nesting. *Photo by H. Williamson, U.S. Forest Service.*

had been control burned and commercially thinned. In another area, 4 nests were destroyed in a ryegrass field when the field was cut in mid-May (D. Cotton personal communication: 1988).

Nesting habitat was similar in the southwestern part of the range of the eastern wild turkey. In Tangipahoa Parish, Louisiana, 7 nests were in old pine stands, agricultural areas, unimproved pasture (old field), and pine plantations 4 and 5 years old (Smith and Teitelbaum 1986).

In the east Texas piney woods, turkey hens chose nest sites in pine stands with low timber stocking, low tree midstory density, scattered shrub cover, and abundant herbaceous ground cover (Campo et al. 1989). Previous logging activities enhanced appropriate nest sites.

We do not believe that nesting habitat is a limiting factor for the wild turkey. But more information is needed on nest predation rates in different microhabitats. Kennamer et al. (1981) reported higher predation rates on artificial turkey nests in mature pine stands than in pine plantations. All 30 nests in the mature pine stand were hit by predators. Sparse vegetative cover near the ground was thought to render the artificial nests vulnerable to predators.

By contrast, Seiss (1989) found that although hens preferred to nest in pine plantations, success rates were significantly lower for hens that nested in plantations than for those that nested in mature pine forests.

Turkeys nest in a variety of habitats. Yet the vegetative conditions were similar at ground level: a moderately dense herbaceous (forb and grass) layer with some vine and brush components. This early plant successional stage can be maintained by late-winter burning at intervals of 2 or 3 years. Mowing or bush-hogging can be used also. Forests should be commercially thinned to promote growth of vegetation on the floor. Managers should delay all springtime field activities until after the peak hatching period (mid-May to mid-June). To avoid forcing hens to renest, all mowing or bush-hogging should be delayed until mid-July.

Brood

Young turkeys grow fast and have a high protein requirement, which they satisfy by consuming mostly arthropods, plus some seeds and fruits. Grass-forb vegetation produces an abundance of insects and spiders, and young poults regularly forage in these habitats. The principal features of habitat suitability are (1) vegetative conditions; (2) density; and (3) structure at ground level.

In their first 2 weeks, posthatch poults usually forage in vegetation dense enough to afford protection from numerous predators. Field and forest edges or old fields are excellent brood habitat during this vulnerable period. After the first 2 weeks they more often use open pastures and fields. Openings and fields continue to be used into late summer as juvenile turkeys consume more grass seeds and fruits (Blackburn et al. 1975).

Mosby and Handley (1943) reported that a hen and her 16 poults, within less than 2 days, moved 0.4 kilometers (0.25 miles) from the nest to a field, and remained there 2 to 3 weeks. Wheeler (1948) noted that broods were usually in the woodland where protective vegetation was readily available. When the poults were about 2 weeks old, large numbers were seen in fields or other forest clearings. Broods were observed almost entirely in and around fields where native grasses dominated the ground cover and insects abounded. After the poults were about 6 weeks old, they used all parts of the field, not just the edges.

Telemetry studies have allowed researchers to gather detailed data on brood habitat use, brood movements,

Young broods feed on arthropods and plant material in moderately dense vegetation. Insects and other invertebrates satisfy the protein requirements of the rapidly growing poults. *Photo by P. Pelham.*

Eastern wild turkey poults grow rapidly and have a high-protein diet that includes a variety of arthropods. Grasshoppers are a consistent summer food of young and adult turkeys. *Photo by H. Williamson, U.S. Forest Service.*

and poult survival rates (Zeedyk and Dickson 1985). Hillestad and Speake (1970) and Hillestad (1973) found that after hatching, hens with broods moved immediately into a nearby lightly grazed old field in Alabama that had been abandoned from cultivation 2 years previously. Daily movements of the hens with broods covered 12 to 30 hectares (30 to 75 acres), and most of the day was spent in or along field (permanent pasture) edges. Hens and broods were constantly associated with the woodland-pasture ecotone. Older broods quickly used fields that had been mowed.

Speake et al. (1975) gathered brood habitat information on 10 broods from 85 radio-equipped hens in 4 areas in Alabama. Many types of openings (permanent pastures, mowed hayfields, grainfields, and old fields) were used by hens with broods. Brood range averaged 100 hectares (247 acres). Also in Alabama, Blackburn et al. (1975) and Hamrick and Davis (1971) found that juvenile turkeys had eaten mostly grass seeds and blackberries, foods found in openings or fields.

On a Georgia island, Hon et al. (1978) found 10 broods utilized low areas within oak-pine and pine forest types. Hens with broods particularly used edges of grass ponds and openings along ditches in the forest. The investigators also noted a strong selection of areas that had been burned the previous spring. Broods, after remaining in heavily forested areas for varying periods of time, moved to an association of old fields, Bahia grass fields, grassy depressions, and regenerated pine and oak areas. Most broods remained around this field complex for weeks, gradually extending their movements to other field-woods areas.

Dense, middle-aged pine stands produce little food for turkeys. *Photo by H. Williamson, U.S. Forest Service.*

Thinned and burned pine plantation provides shrubs and forbs used by hens with their broods. *Photo by J. Dickson, U.S. Forest Service.*

Everett et al. (1980) found that poult survival was directly related to the type of brood habitat selected by hens. Hens that selected small food plots (dried ryegrass) and adjacent mature hardwood forest as brood range raised only 8 of 86 (9 percent) of their poults to age 14 days. Hens that selected grazed pastures and adjacent wood's edge raised 40 of 116 (36 percent) of their poults to at least 14 days.

Everett et al. (1985) reported that in northwest Alabama, the brood habitats preferred by 23 hens whose broods survived to 14 days of age were improved pastures, cutover hardwoods, wildlife openings, and rights-of-way. Grazed pastures along creek bottoms were the most preferred brood-rearing habitat. Creek bottom hardwoods and pine woods 18 to 22 years old were used but were not preferred. Upland hardwoods were avoided. Hens with broods moved away from nest sites on the most direct route to pastures, openings, or fields.

In managed pine forests of east Texas, hens with broods selected areas of low timber stocking, low density of midstory trees, and abundant herbaceous ground cover that had been burned (Campo et al. 1989). Brood ranges were much greater in large areas of pine plantations than in forest, field, and pasture areas.

In central Mississippi, on the heavily forested Bienville National Forest, Phalen et al. (1986) and Seiss (1989) found that preferred habitat for 16 broods, age 1 to 14 days, was mature bottomland hardwood forest. This forest type had sparse shrubs and understory, and moderate herbaceous ground cover (grasses, sedges, forbs, and vines). Williams et al. (1973) reported similar

brood habitat conditions in cypress woods of Florida. Hens with broods avoided mature pine stands and pine or hardwood regeneration stands.

Several investigations focused on brood use of pine plantations. Exum et al. (1987) determined that hens with broods less than 9 weeks old used almost exclusively burned slash pine plantations more than 10 years old. But hens avoided plantations not burned for more than 2 years and bottomland hardwood stands along creeks. Smith (1988, 1990) and Burk (1989) found that brood habitat for a total of 14 broods was midrotation-aged (14-to-20-year) plantations that had been commercially thinned and control burned.

In northeast Alabama, where upland hardwood forests dominated, radio monitoring of 21 broods showed that poult survival was higher in taller, denser herbaceous vegetation that probably allowed hens with broods to escape detection by predators. Old fields provided better cover than grazed pastures for young poults. Pastures were good brood habitat for poults more than 2 weeks of age (Metzler and Speake 1985).

Very different macrohabitat types (e.g., pine plantations, bottomland hardwood forests, and fields) are used as brood habitat. As with nest habitat, the common feature is a moderately dense herbaceous layer, with brushy cover nearby. Brood habitat during the first 2 posthatch weeks (e.g., old fields) is usually denser than habitat used by older poults (e.g., grazed pasture).

To avoid long movements by hens with newly hatched broods, nest habitat should be interspersed with or near brood habitat. Brood habitat can be hayfields,

A variety of soft mast is consumed by turkeys as it becomes available from summer to fall. Blackberry fruit is a summer favorite of adult and young turkeys. *Photo by U.S. Forest Service.*

pastures, old fields, burned pine plantations, or other areas that provide a moderately dense grass-forb-dominated plant community, with some woody brush or vines for brood-holding or protective cover. Fields and forests can be manipulated by fire, mowing, shredding, or grazing to maintain the herbaceous, insect-producing layer in conjunction with brushy cover (Hurst and Owen 1980).

The thinning and burning of mature pine stands and young pine plantations will improve brood habitat condi-

tions by enhancing the herbaceous layer. Hurst (1978) reported that poults that fed in recently burned pine-hardwood stands ate significantly more total-animal food than poults that fed on unburned stands 3 and 4 years old. However, plant foods, mostly fruits and seeds, were more abundant on unburned stands. A patchy burn pattern, with burned areas next to unburned areas, would provide the best habitat.

Fall and Winter

During the fall, juvenile and adult turkeys continue their use of pastures, fields, and woods. As the season progresses, they shift their ranges in response to availability of major foods (mast) such as grape and dogwood fruits and oak acorns. Barwick and Speake (1973) and Speake et al. (1975) noted a shift by gobblers in Alabama from fall range (open fields and pastures) to winter range (forested areas) and thought that food availability was the important factor. Gobblers used mixed, uneven-aged stands of pine and hardwood in the winter.

Winter habitat for wild turkeys traditionally has been linked to mast, particularly acorns. Everett et al. (1979) reported that winter habitat in northwest Alabama was mature hardwood forest. Later, Everett et al. (1985) in the same study area reported that winter habitat preferences in 56 hen and 32 gobbler ranges were creek bottom hardwoods and wildlife openings. Upland hardwood forests were used less than expected, but about half of all turkey locations occurred in this type. Kennamer

Soft mast such as flowering dogwood and American beautyberry are excellent fall turkey foods. *Photos by U.S. Forest Service.*

Bottomland hardwood stands are important fall and winter habitat. *Photo by J. Neal, U.S. Fish and Wildlife Service.*

Acorns are a consistent diet item, providing turkeys with carbohydrate energy. Top: Nuttal oak—a red oak of the alluvial bottoms. Middle: Water oak—a red oak of the bottoms. Bottom: Southern red oak—a red oak of the uplands.

et al. (1980b), in an area dominated by pine plantations, reported that turkeys used pine plantations least and natural hardwood stands most in winter. Kennamer et al. (1981) thought that winter habitat was extremely important in maintaining a year-round population of wild turkeys in habitat dominated by short-rotation pine plantations. Smith and Teitelbaum (1986) found that hens used pine plantations 11 to 15 years old and hardwood forests significantly more than expected during winter. Exum et al. (1987) demonstrated that hens and gobblers during fall and winter used bottomland hardwoods frequently and burned pine plantations older than 14 years more than expected, based on availability.

In Louisiana, plantations older than 21 years and improved pastures were used less than expected. In Arkansas, adult male and female turkeys used natural pine forests more than other forest types in the fall and winter (Wigley et al. 1985, 1986b). In South Carolina, the bald cypress-water tupelo forest type and its associated ecotone was the most preferred habitat for gobblers and hens (Still and Baumann 1989). Loblolly pine stands were avoided, longleaf was randomly selected, and slash was preferred.

Turkey use of fields associated with forests continues during winter, especially when foods there are abundant. Acorn crops frequently are light or fail (Dickson 1990). When this happens, turkeys use fields or other stands frequently. Both hens and gobblers used fields and their vicinities during the late-winter and spring months in Tennessee (Lewis 1964). In east Texas, eastern wild turkeys preferred pine-hardwood stands and openings over other types (Hopkins 1981). Smith (1988) reported that turkeys used soybean fields and associated bottomland hardwoods near large blocks of pine plantations when there was a large acorn crop, but many turkeys remained in the pine plantations during a year when there was no acorn crop.

During spring, gobblers display in openings where visual cues can be seen by hens. *Photo by G. Wunz, Pennsylvania Game Commission.*

Spring

As winter flocks break up in late winter and early spring, a variety of habitat is used by hens and gobblers. But openings, important for gobbler displays and close to nesting sites, are used frequently and consistently. The breakup of winter gobbler flocks occurred in March in eastern Alabama, and the gobblers established gobbling and strutting areas in and around permanent pastures. In summer, gobblers spent most of their time feeding in pastures and loafing around edges of pastures (Barwick and Speake 1973). In another Alabama study, non-nesting hens used upland and bottomland forests, upland hardwood-pine, and improved pastures (Hillestad 1973). On 5 study areas in Alabama, 86 percent of hen spring-summer ranges contained openings. On an area in Kentucky, ranges of all hens contained openings. On study areas where openings were not adequate, hens moved longer distances in the spring to areas with more openings (Speake et al. 1975).

In northwest Alabama, at the intersection of the Coastal Plain and Appalachian Plateau, spring habitat preferences for 77 hens and 36 gobblers were noted. Hens preferred pine plantations, wildlife openings, rights-of-way (ROW), creek bottom hardwoods, and pastures. All hen locations in plantations and ROW were for nesting hens. Gobblers preferred creek bottom hardwoods, wildlife openings, and improved pastures. Both sexes exhibited less-than-expected use of the major habitat type, upland hardwoods. In the summer, hens and gobblers used all 10 habitat types present, but they preferred wildlife openings, creek bottom hardwoods, pastures, and ROW. Grazed pastures and adjacent creek bottom hardwoods were very important to turkeys (Everett et al. 1985).

A variety of other stands, such as mature pine and pine-hardwood and some pine plantations, are used in association with openings during the spring. In the Ouachita Mountain region of Arkansas, habitat utilization by 21 turkeys varied by stand characteristics, by season of use, and by turkey sex and age (Wigley et al. 1985, 1986a). Gobbler range in the pinelands of Georgia and Florida was open parklike (prairie-type) forest, maintained by late-winter burns at intervals of 2 or 3 years. Spot burning rather than large-block burning was recommended (Stoddard 1963). In the Piedmont of South Carolina, 8 gobblers used pasture, pine-hardwood, pine, and hardwood stands (Fleming and Webb 1974).

In Tangipahoa Parish, Louisiana, hens frequently used midrotation pine plantations and concentrated their activities around small dairy farm pastures (Smith and Teitelbaum 1986). In west-central Alabama in an area dominated by pine plantations, 32 turkeys used pine plantations during spring, but not in proportion to availability (Kennamer et al. 1980b). In southern Alabama, hens and gobblers used burned pine plantations older than 10 years more than expected, based on availability during spring and summer (Exum et al. 1987).

In the central Piedmont of Virginia, Holbrook et al. (1985, 1987) found that 21 hens and 8 gobblers used habitat of pine plantations, hardwood leave strips, mature pine, mature hardwood, and maintained fields according to availability for the prenesting period or summer.

In bottomland hardwood forests of the Atchafalaya River basin in Louisiana, Hyde and Newsom (1973) observed marked turkeys predominantly in openings, pipeline rights-of-way, roadways, and fields and in hardwood and swamp bottoms. Kimmel and Zwank (1985) related habitat use by 14 hens to flooding in the bottomland hardwood forests and agricultural fields along the Mississippi River. At lower levels, wheat fields were preferred. But when these fields became flooded, uncultivated fields were preferred. Thinned riverfront hardwood forests had the greatest use (Zwank et al. 1988). Palmer (1990) found

In the South, turkeys often roost over water, such as on this cypress roost. *Photo by J. Dickson, U.S. Forest Service.*

that hens preferred mature bottomland hardwood forests during all seasons except for a brief period during spring, when hens were incubating in mature pine forests or young (2-to-6-year-old) pine plantations.

Roosts

Wild turkeys roost in a variety of habitats, often in conifers and often over water if they have the choice (Wheeler 1948, Schroger 1966). On upland sites, turkeys frequently roost on slopes close to but slightly off knolls or ridgetops. Roost sites are often sheltered from weather (Mosby and Handley 1943), and roost trees can afford protection. Wheeler (1948) reported that magnolias and bushy-topped pines were used extensively in cold, windy weather. In Virginia, roost trees were characterized as having a diameter at breast height of 25 to 50 centimeters (10 to 20 inches) with a clean bole for the first 6.1 to 9.1 meters (20 to 30 feet). Branches with a diameter of 5 to 10

centimeters (2 to 4 inches) seemed to be used more often (Mosby and Handley 1943).

In the piney woods of Louisiana, Smith and Teitelbaum (1986) noted that pine plantations 11 to 20 years old were the forest type most often used for roosting, and mixed hardwood-pine stands also were frequently used. In an area with extensive slash pine plantations, Exum et al. (1987) reported that of 122 roost observations, 64 occurred in pine plantations more than 14 years old. Broods frequently roosted in pine plantations in the spring and summer. Forty-four observations of roosting turkeys were made in bottomland hardwoods, mostly in the fall-winter period. In South Carolina, Fleming and Webb (1974) reported that 54 percent of the roost observations (gobblers) were in pine-hardwood habitats. Loblolly pine was the species most often used as a roost tree. Turkeys roosted in hardwoods on only 2 occasions. In pine stands with streamside zones in Mississippi, turkeys roosted in these stands proportional to availability (Smith et al. 1990).

Flooded riverfront hardwood forests were preferred roosting sites in the flooded bottomland hardwood forest adjacent to the Mississippi River (Kimmel and Zwank 1985, Zwank et al. 1988), and the bald cypress-water tupelo type was frequently used for roosting in South Carolina (Still and Baumann 1989).

Roads

Roads are an important part of turkey habitat and can be positive or negative for turkey populations. Roads, by facilitating disturbance and access for poaching, can be detrimental. In West Virginia, turkey populations seemed higher in areas with less than 9.6 kilometers (6 miles) of public roads per 4,050 hectares (10,000 acres). Bailey et al. (1981) concluded that roads themselves do not adversely affect turkeys but that the associated human use is adverse. Turkey hens avoided nesting near open roads in South Carolina (Still and Baumann 1990). Wright and Speake (1975) found that wild turkeys did not frequent a heavily used off-road vehicle area and that foot trail traffic also adversely affected an area's use by turkeys. In a heavily roaded area in Virginia (13.7 kilometers [8.5 miles] of roads per 1,000 hectares [2,470 acres]), turkeys found dead during hunting season died closer to roads than turkeys found dead at other times of the year. Roads were thought to be important factors in the number of turkeys killed and the proportion lost as cripples (Holbrook and Vaughan 1985).

By contrast, roads with controlled access and proper management can be positive for turkeys. Roads can provide access for management activities such as maintaining food plots or trapping. Roads are frequently used by turkeys for travel and can also be excellent feeding and brood habitat if they are in appropriate native herbaceous vegetation or seeded to grasses or legumes. Frequently, natural foods along roads provide more forage, fruit, and insects than do forested areas (Bailey and Rinell 1968). In Mississippi, turkey use of intensively managed loblolly pine plantations was found to be positively correlated to presence of spur roads (Smith 1988), and gated or locked roads have proven to be a very important management tool on the Bienville National Forest.

Water

Biologists generally have considered water an important component of eastern wild turkey habitat. Turkeys require water to live. Oak-pine range is generally well watered, but no relationship has been documented between turkey populations and distribution or availability of water. Turkeys are highly mobile and can get free water and water from succulent vegetative parts, fruits (Hurst 1981), or insects. Brood range was thought to require water such as ponds, but Exum et al. (1985) documented that hens with poults in dry slash pine plantations in southern Alabama seldom crossed available water or approached within 100 meters (109 yards) of it. Broods often remained on upland sites for weeks, apparently without using permanent water supplies. Poults and juveniles were eating berries with a high water content. But free water sources may be important during droughts or in very arid range.

THE FUTURE

Land Use

Technical experts attempted to project and assess future trends in forestland from a regional analysis of historical relationships among major land uses and key variables (USDA Forest Service 1988:114). Projections showed a slow decline in forestland area from 74 million hectares (182 million acres) in 1985 to 70 million hectares (174 million acres) in 2030. Projected net area changes largely reflect the direct conversion of forestland to urban and developed uses, and other land converted to cropland to replace cropland lost to urbanization and development. Cropland is expected to remain relatively constant while urban and related uses rise from 21 million hectares (51 million acres) to 26 million hectares (65 mil-

Roads closed to the public are a key to maintaining high turkey densities. Several recent studies have documented the severity of the illegal kill. *Photo by H. Williamson, U.S. Forest Service.*

Turkey habitat will be lost to urban development and related uses. *Photo by National Wild Turkey Federation.*

lion acres). Pasture and range area is projected to decline by 2.8 million hectares (7 million acres) because of declining demand for red meat. Cropland area could be considerably higher than projections if international grain demand increases, or cropland could be lower than projections if conversion to pines is more than anticipated.

Projected changes in area of forest types are consistent with recent historical trends discussed earlier (USDA Forest Service 1987). The area in pine plantations is projected to more than double by 2030, increasing by about 11 million hectares (28 million acres). But natural pine area is expected to decline by about almost half (7 million hectares, 18 million acres). Mixed pine-hardwood stands are expected to dwindle by 2.4 million hectares (6 million acres), or 22 percent. Natural pine and pine-hardwood stands are expected to revert to hardwoods, be planted to plantations after harvest, or be lost to other land uses.

Area in bottomland hardwoods is projected to decrease by some 1.6 million hectares (4 million acres). Conversion to cropland has decreased substantially, and some agriculture land has been reforested, much of it under special programs such as the Conservation Reserve Program.

Turkeys

In the South, we have traced the precolonial abundance of wild turkeys, demise and extirpation throughout much of the region, and recent restoration success and thriving populations. We are now enjoying the "good old days." Huntable populations are at high densities and are in areas not occupied in recent history. Most older turkey hunters in the South today were not taught turkey hunting by their fathers; their fathers did not have that opportunity. What does the future hold for the wild turkey? We hope we have learned some lessons and are committed to ensuring a bright future for turkeys and turkey hunters.

Projected land uses will affect how turkey populations fare in the South. Flather et al. (1989) concluded that an increased area in human-related land use and a decrease of upland hardwood and oak-pine types will likely result in a slight decline in turkey density until about the year 2000. Then, according to the same experts, the population should recover to about 1985 numbers because of increased acres in older hardwood stands. But recent increased demand for hardwood pulp may diminish this projection. This modeling approach is on a county basis, too large an area to evaluate land-use changes on a smaller scale. And this approach assumes populations in all stocked habitat are at carrying capacity.

Interviews with wild turkey biologists representing 8 southeastern states reflected concern about land-use changes. Turkey habitat will be lost to industrialization and urbanization. Dwindling of older forests will diminish suitability of wild turkey habitat. Land-use patterns that feature single crops over vast expanses are negative for turkeys. Much of the bottomland hardwoods have been converted to soybeans, cotton, rice, and pasture in large blocks. The hope is that remaining bottomland forests will be saved. Some of these areas recently have been reforested.

There is concern about the conversion of land to pine plantations. The area in such plantations is projected to double by 2030 (U.S. Forest Service 1987). To accommodate turkeys in pine plantations, special concessions will have to be implemented, such as streamside zones (Burk et al. 1990), other land uses, thinning, and burning (Smith et al. 1990).

Human activities other than land use will affect the wild turkey's future. There will be more human access and disturbance during nesting season, and poaching will affect turkey populations. Poaching can be a major factor in how populations perform (Dickson et al. 1978), and recent studies have documented substantial illegal kills (Holbrook and Vaughan 1985, Kimmel and Kurzejeski 1985). If turkeys are to flourish, increased education and ethical behavior will be important.

Another situation that should help protect turkeys is land leasing by hunting clubs, which is widespread in the South. This system usually limits public access to turkey range and often transforms game from a short-term exploitable resource on open land to a long-term protected resource.

Another threat to the wild turkey's well-being is the release of pen-raised turkeys into the wild. These birds can be vectors of parasites and diseases such as histomoniasis (Schorr 1988), and they pose a potential genetic pollution threat. Only the trapping and relocation of *wild* turkeys has proved successful.

Overall, we are optimistic about a bright future for the wild turkey in the South. The species is much more adaptable and hardy than earlier thought. We are encouraged because the wild turkey can live in a variety of habitat types and is far more tolerant of man's activities than first thought. The turkey is doing well in mixed forest and field situations. We can have turkeys if we can control man, regulate his activities, plan for the future, and implement plans.

Management Recommendations

The wild turkey has made a remarkable comeback. Limiting factors and threats to population expansion are varied. Much can be done to help the wild turkey. The program of trapping and transplanting wild turkeys has proved successful beyond biologists' imaginations. Suitable areas without turkey populations should continue to be stocked with wild turkeys. Every effort should be made to prohibit the release of pen-raised turkeys for restoration.

The illegal harvest must be curtailed. Poachers steal game from legitimate hunters and can reduce populations. Legal fall or spring hunting of gobblers in a sporting manner usually does not negatively affect turkey populations.

Streamside zones of mature hardwoods are used during all seasons by turkeys. These zones are a key to maintaining viable turkey populations in habitat that has substantial pine plantations. *Photo by U.S. Forest Service.*

Prescribed fire is useful in setting back plant succession in upland pine stands. A 3-to-5-year rotation is recommended. *Photo by U.S. Forest Service.*

Food plots can attract and hold turkeys and probably increase a habitat's carrying capacity somewhat. Top: Chufa is a nut sedge that grows well in sandy loam soil. Middle: Clover is good winter and spring food that contains abundant protein and vitamin A. Bottom: Cereal grains can attract turkeys in summer and fall.

Much can be done by sportsmen. Education and political action can be accomplished through direct peer contact, through organizations such as the National Wild Turkey Federation, and by getting actively involved in the political process.

For information on habitat management, refer to the section "Habitat Relationships" in this chapter, or write the National Wild Turkey Federation for the publication entitled *Game on Your Land*. Turkeys still do well in what traditionally was described as optimum habitat, but the species is more tolerant and adaptable than originally thought.

We believe it has been demonstrated that wild turkeys can be maintained in areas with pine plantations *if* practices to accommodate turkeys are implemented. Plantations in the right condition can provide adequate nesting and brood range, but some habitat diversity needs to be provided for other seasons. Plantations need

Table 1. Some important food crops that can be planted for wild turkeys.[a]

Crop[b]	Planting date	Planting rate kilograms per hectare (pounds per acre)	Soil type	Soil pH	Type of seeding	Period used	Parts used
ladino clover	fall	2.25–4.5 (2–4)	fertile clay, silt loams	6.0–6.5	broadcast	late winter–spring	vegetative, seed
white clover	fall	2.25–4.5 (2–4)	widely adapted	6.5–7.5	broadcast	late winter–spring	vegetative, seed
crimson clover	fall	22 (20)	widely adapted	6.5–7.5	broadcast	late winter–spring	vegetative, seed
corn	March–April	9 (8)	well-drained, high organic	5.5–6.5	drill in rows	fall–winter	seed
oats	September–November	10 bushels per hectare (4 per acre)	well-drained sandy and clay loams	5.5–6.0	drill or broadcast	winter–spring	vegetative, seed
winter wheat	October–November	7 bushels per hectare (3 per acre)	widely adapted	6.0–6.5	drill or broadcast	winter–early summer	vegetative, seed
soybeans	May–July 15	95 (85)	fertile well-drained	5.5–6.5	drill or broadcast	fall–winter	seed
grain sorghum	July 15–30	7–9 (6–8)	well-drained, high organic matter	5.5–6.0	drill in rows	fall–winter	seed
peanuts	April	34–45 (30–40)	well-drained sandy loam	6.0–6.5	drill in rows	fall	seed
Bahia grass	early spring	22 (20)	most soil types	5.5–6.0	broadcast	summer–early fall	vegetative, seed
ryegrass	September–October	45 (40)	widely adapted	5.5–6.5	broadcast	winter–spring	vegetative, seed
cowpeas	May–June	5–7 pecks per hectare (2–3 pecks per acre)	well-drained	6.5–7.5	broadcast	late summer–early fall	vegetative, seed
chufa	May–July	34–45 (30–40)	sandy loams	5.5–6.5	broadcast	fall–winter	seed

[a] Table reprinted from "Game on You: Land-managing the Eastern Wild Turkey in South Carolina," South Carolina Wildlife and Marine Resources Department (Bevill 1978).
[b] Check County Agent's Office for best variety for your area and soil type.

to be kept relatively small (40 hectares, 100 acres), and the interval for cutting adjacent stands must be at least 5 years.

At least 15 percent of turkey range should be kept in mature hardwoods in areas such as streamside zones or pine-hardwood corridors. Turkeys use pine plantations the first couple of years after planting. Then plantations can get too dense for use until the canopy's closure shades out understory vegetation.

Habitat suitability of midrotation pines depends on cover density and abundance of food plants. Knee-high herbaceous cover is important for early brood survival. Pine plantations should be thinned frequently and burned on a rotation of 3 to 5 years after plantations are about 10 years old to allow sunlight through the pine canopy and to allow grass, forbs, and shrubs to grow and bear fruit. Fire should be excluded from mature hardwood areas and other key mast production areas. Asso-

ciated cattle operations or small fields in row crops can provide supplemental food.

Predators kill turkeys, but turkeys have evolved with predation. Predators are what made the turkey wild. Many wild turkey populations thrive in areas with apparent high predator densities. We are not opposed to trapping furbearers and free-ranging dogs, but this protection is usually not warranted where turkey densities are adequate for reproduction.

Food plots of chufas, clover, or small grain can provide supplemental food and can attract turkeys. Food plots can be positive for turkeys if they don't distract managers from other long-term habitat maintenance. Specific recommendations are detailed in Table 1. Care must be taken not to spread diseases such as histomoniasis at sites such as food plots that turkeys use repeatedly. Beware of making predation and poaching easier by concentrating turkeys at food plots.

Chapter 18

EASTERN TURKEY IN MIDWESTERN OAK-HICKORY FORESTS

John B. Lewis
Supervisor, Wildlife Research Section (Retired)
Missouri Department of Conservation
Columbia, Missouri

AREA DEFINED

If you were to draw a line around the outer limits of the Midwest oak-hickory forest, you'd include parts of 9 states (Arkansas, Illinois, Iowa, Kansas, Minnesota, Missouri, Nebraska, Oklahoma, and Wisconsin) (Figure 1). Within the forest's perimeter is a combined land area of 814,445 square kilometers (314,472 square miles), of which 19.4 percent — 158,358 square kilometers (61,142 square miles) — is actually forested.

Although oak-hickory communities occur throughout the eastern deciduous forests, they are best developed and most continuous in the Interior Highland — the Ozark and Ouachita mountains of Missouri, Arkansas, and Oklahoma (Braun 1964). This region also is the western limit of the deciduous forests, where continuous forests are gradually replaced by oak-savannas and ultimately the tall grass prairies of southwestern Missouri, eastern Kansas, and northeastern Oklahoma.

(Eastern Texas contains large areas of oak-hickory and oak-savannas. That region is considered a forest-prairie transition zone by Braun (1964) and will not be discussed in this chapter.)

Within the 9-state area are 4 national forests — 2 that occupy parts of both Arkansas and Oklahoma, another in Missouri, and one in Illinois, with a combined area of 17,010 square kilometers (6,568 square miles) — plus several thousand hectares of other public forest.

The Ozarks, known also as the Interior Highlands or Ozark Plateau, includes southern Missouri and northern Arkansas and extends into extreme southern Kansas and northeastern Oklahoma. This is one of the oldest geological regions in the world, having been a continuous land area since the close of the Paleozoic Era. The area was uplifted twice — the second time toward the close of the Tertiary Period — after which peneplaination occurred, giving the landscape a level appearance. The same process took place later in the Ouachita Mountains (Fenneman 1938).

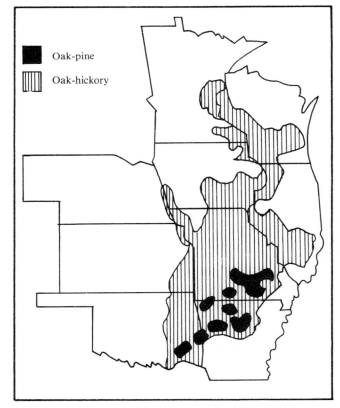

Figure 1. Midwestern oak-hickory and oak-pine forests.

According to Braun (1964), the dominant forests of the Ozark and Ouachita mountains are principally oaks, although shortleaf pine may be codominant with oak or found in pure stands. The pure stands occur more in the Ouachita Mountains than in the Ozarks. The region as a whole is primarily an oak-hickory forest. In the Missouri portion of the Ozarks, elevations vary from 300 to 460 meters (1,000 to 1,500 feet). A few elevations in the St. Francois Mountains reach 518 meters (1,700 feet). The Boston Mountains on the southern edge of the region in Arkansas have elevations up to 730 meters (2,400 feet). The term "mountains" is used most often in the Arkansas portion, where the name Ozarks also originated (Sauer 1920).

Limestone and dolomite are the principal rocks of the region, but a small igneous outcrop occurs in southeast Missouri. The soils are low in fertility and have a high chert content, which gives a droughty character to much of the region. Parent materials on the surface produce soils with a hardpan about 50 centimeters (20 inches) below the surface. This hardpan interferes with water movement and limits root penetration (Winters 1957).

The post oak-blackjack oak community is commonly found on the steep south- and west-facing slopes and on the dry, sandy ridges. Either species may dominate locally or in combination with shortleaf pine to form an oak-pine community. Black oak is frequently mixed with the post oak-blackjack oak type, suggesting that it is replaced by the black oak-hickory forest type. The post-blackjack-oak community is more widespread on the western margins, where the forest-prairie transition zone meets the oak-hickory forest.

White oak is most abundant on north slopes, but it also is found on the ridges and plateaus, often in association with black oak and shortleaf pine. Hickories, winged elm, and persimmon are also found in this association. Common understory trees and shrubs are dogwood, redbud, hop hornbeam, and serviceberry. Sugar maple and red oak grow in association with white oak on moister slopes (Braun 1964).

Forest cover types are so intermingled in the Ozark Region that it is not possible to classify turkey range on this basis. The daily range of a single flock may include practically all of the forest types found within an area of 5 to 8 square kilometers (2 to 3 square miles).

The Ozark Plateau ends in Arkansas, with the Boston Mountains forming the southern edge. Oak-hickory is still the major forest type, but pine and pine-oak communities are more common than in Missouri. Southern red oak and chinquapin are found on ridges and upper slopes, as are the more abundant post oak, blackjack oak, black oak, and white oak. Remnants of the mixed mesophytic forests are found in the Boston Mountains

and are quite similar to the mixed mesophytic forest of the Appalachian Plateau (Braun 1964). Beech is a co-dominant species on some of the more protected slopes and in some deeper valleys.

In the eastern Ouachita Mountains, the principal rock formations are shale, sandstone, quartzite, and chert. In the western portion, sandstone and shale dominate. Upland soils throughout the region have a low fertility.

In the Ouachita Mountains, the vegetation is essentially the same as in the Ozarks. But pine is more abundant and is usually classed as oak-pine type. On the poorer or drier rocky or sandy soils, nearly pure stands of pine occur, especially on south and west aspects. Better soils support pine mixed with oaks and hickories. On these sites, hardwoods eventually will replace pine as the dominant overstory species. Even though the Ouachita Mountains have been mapped as an oak-pine type, today it is probably closer to pine-oak.

To the western and southern edge of the Interior Highlands is a region occupied by oak-hickory forest, oak-hickory savanna, and prairie (Braun 1964). West of the Ozark Plateau, in eastern Kansas and western Missouri, prairie vegetation dominates the uplands and timber is restricted to the rougher topography associated with major streams and their tributaries (Braun 1964).

The climate in the Midwest oak-hickory region is characterized by warm summers (with occasional periods of extreme heat) and winters that are brisk but not severe, except at the region's northern edge. Frost-free dates for the Interior Highlands usually occur from April through mid-October, giving the region a growing season of 120 to 170 days. An occasional late frost affects mast production in the Ozarks. When this happens, only the trees on the highest ridges normally escape damage.

Precipitation ranges from 75 to 130 centimeters (30 to 50 inches) annually, with higher amounts falling on the eastern and southern edges of the region. Total precipitation is more than adequate for optimum plant growth, but the seasonal distribution often creates periods of temporary drought during the summer that may limit turkey distribution on drier upland sites. Excessive rainfall during the nesting and early brood-rearing season may also adversely affect production.

WILD TURKEY POPULATIONS

Historical Abundance and Distribution

Early writings contain numerous accounts of abundant wild turkeys throughout the Midwest oak-hickory region. One example of how many wild turkeys were present when the region was first settled can be found in

Typical midwestern wild turkey oak-hickory habitat.

Bennitt and Nagel (1937). They quoted a statement from the history of Montgomery County, Missouri, in about 1830, referring to the wild turkey as "so numerous and so easily obtained as scarcely to be worthy of consideration." Schorger (1966) and Aldrich (1967a) list numerous accounts of turkey abundance during the early settlement period, leaving little doubt that wild turkey populations in the Midwest oak-hickory region were high.

Although early reports suggest there were lots of wild turkeys, limited data exist on population densities. Leopold (1931) estimated that Missouri's turkey range originally supported 1.9 turkeys per square kilometer (5 per square mile). Based on this estimate, Bennitt and Nagel (1937) calculated the presettlement turkey population in Missouri to be 250,000. They felt, however, that this figure was probably low. Schorger (1966) believed that the original density of 3.9 turkeys per square kilometer (10 per square mile) was a safe assumption for those states that contained good habitat. He commented that in states having large areas of prairie, turkey densities were probably nearer 1.9 birds per square kilometer (5 per square mile). Perhaps the only value to be gained in trying to reconstruct presettlement population densities is to compare them with present population densities as a way of evaluating present habitat quality.

The original limits of the eastern wild turkey's range in the Midwest oak-hickory region are not well defined. Leopold (1931) quoting Hatch says, "Thirty-three years ago (about 1865?) the turkey was . . . not a rare bird in northwest Iowa and southwest Minnesota . . . seen as late as 1871 in Minnesota. Now totally disappeared." Aldrich (1967a) indicated that the only basis for including Minnesota within the former range was a specimen in the University of Kansas collection labeled only "Minnesota."

Aldrich also listed an account from Roberts (1932) and Swanson (1940) that places some doubt about the presence of turkeys in Minnesota. Leopold (1931) commented that the northern limits of the wild turkey range probably were not very stable and that they fluctuated, depending on weather and food supplies. Little (1980) reported that the eastern wild turkey was originally found throughout Iowa. This was also the same for Missouri (Dalke et al. 1946) and Arkansas (Holder 1951). The western and southern extension of the eastern wild turkey's range beyond the heart (Ozarks and Ouachitas) of the oak-hickory region followed the timbered river bottoms that stretched a considerable distance into the Great Plains. Historical accounts in Schorger (1966) report a population for eastern wild turkeys in north-central Kansas at the junction of the North and South forks of the Solomon River. This area is about 322 kilometers (200 miles) west of the Missouri-Kansas border. Masters

and Thackston (1985) indicated that the eastern wild turkey was found throughout much of Oklahoma, except for the southwest corner and the panhandle counties.

By the early 1900s, eastern wild turkey numbers had been drastically reduced over most of the Midwest oak-hickory region. A series of events between 1880 and 1920 nearly eliminated turkeys from the region. Loss of habitat from intensive logging, followed by fire and open range grazing, left large areas unsuitable for turkeys. Unrestricted hunting further reduced the turkey population. The eastern wild turkey disappeared from the western two-thirds of Oklahoma by 1925 (Masters and Thackston 1985). By 1933, turkeys disappeared from the northeast corner of the state. By 1941, only isolated populations remained in the Ouachita Mountains in 6 southeastern Oklahoma counties.

Capel (1973) reported that the eastern wild turkey was never abundant in Kansas and was eliminated from the state by 1900. The last turkey sighted in southwestern Minnesota was in 1871 (Leopold 1931), and turkeys were gone from Wisconsin 10 years later (Hartman 1959). Turkeys disappeared from southern Iowa in 1910 (Little 1980), and at about the same time in northern Missouri (Leopold 1931). Turkeys were never completely eliminated in southern Missouri. Isolated flocks survived in more heavily timbered parts of the Ozarks. Surveys conducted during the 1940s in Arkansas showed turkeys still in 47 counties (Holder 1951). Wild turkey populations in the Midwest oak-hickory region reached an all-time low during the late 1940s with only 4 states in the region maintaining populations (Mosby 1949). Occupied range in 1949 had declined to 40,467 square kilometers (15,625 square miles), or about 5 percent of the original range. None of the states in the Midwest oak-hickory region had hunting seasons on wild turkeys in 1949 (Mosby 1949).

Present Abundance and Distribution

Today wild turkeys are well established throughout the Midwest oak-hickory region. Turkeys now occupy 151,843 square kilometers (58,627 square miles), an increase of more than 200 percent since the early 1950s. Factors that have contributed to the successful restoration include (1) improved capture techniques; (2) improved habitat conditions; (3) better law enforcement; and (4) public support for conservation programs. These factors, plus the wild turkey's ability to adapt to habitat conditions previously thought unsuited, made possible the turkey's comeback in the Midwest oak-hickory region.

All states in the Midwest oak-hickory region now have spring hunting seasons, and fall hunting is allowed

A mixture of oak species (water oak shown here) is a prime source of mast in these oak-hickory forests. *Photo by L. Williams.*

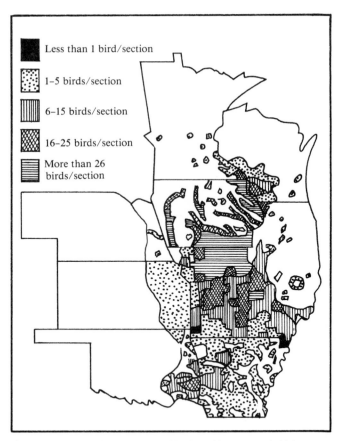

Less than 1 bird/section

1–5 birds/section

6–15 birds/section

16–25 birds/section

More than 26 birds/section

Figure 2. Eastern wild turkey densities in midwestern oak-hickory region (Kennamer 1986).

in several. Wild turkey densities vary from less than 0.4 birds per square kilometer to better than 10 birds per square kilometer (1 to 26 birds per square mile) (Figure 2). Densities in the heavily forested region range from 2 to 6 birds per square kilometer (5 to 16 per square mile). In some localized areas within the mixed timber-agriculture portion of the region (Figure 3) turkey numbers have been estimated to exceed 8 per square kilometer (20 per square mile) (Hanson 1984, Lewis and Kurzejeski 1984). The variation in turkey density may result from differences in food availability during winter. In the agricultural regions, waste grain provides a reliable food source (Lewis and Kurzejeski 1984). In heavily forested parts of the region, variable mast crops are the major source of winter foods.

Restoration efforts continue in many midwestern states and have been completed in Missouri and Iowa. Illinois is still involved in expanding the wild turkey's range; since 1970, nearly 800 turkeys have been trapped and transplanted to 59 locations, all of which have been successful (Garver 1987). Arkansas has essentially completed its restoration program, except for a few supplemental releases (M. Widner, Arkansas Game and Fish,

personal communication: 1991). In Wisconsin and Minnesota, restoration activities are likely to continue well into the 1990s. Restoration activity in most states in the Midwest should be completed by the mid-1990s.

If we accept the assumption that turkey harvest data can be used as an index to population density, then turkey numbers should continue to increase in the future. Using spring harvest data from Missouri (L.D. Vangilder, Missouri Department of Conservation, unpublished data), the length of time needed for turkey populations to stabilize after reintroduction can be estimated. In the heavily timbered traditional turkey range in southern Missouri, the harvest continued to increase for 20 years after the opening of hunting in 1960 (Figure 4). Although the harvest increased during this period, so did the number of hunters and the length of the season, factors that affect the harvest. In north-central Missouri, which lies in the mixed timber-agriculture region of the Midwest, harvest seemed to stabilize 15 years after the spring season opened (Figure 4). While many factors may affect the rate of growth and expansion of reintro-

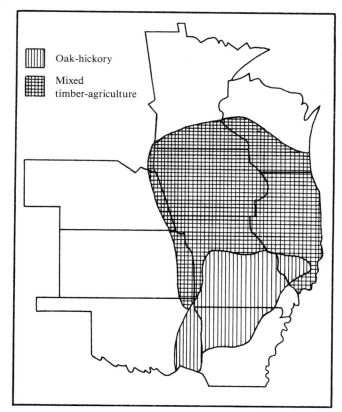

Figure 3. Separation between oak-hickory forest and mixed timber-agricultural regions in the Midwest.

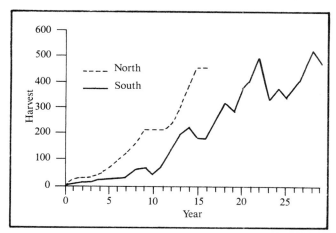

Figure 4. Time difference between northern and southern Missouri wild turkey populations in reaching stability.

duced turkey populations, it appears that populations may increase for at least 20 years after reintroduction. It is quite possible that populations may peak before hunting pressure adequately reflects turkey densities.

Many restoration programs in the Midwest are relatively new, so the potential exists during the next decade and beyond for continued increases in wild turkey numbers and in occupied range. The most significant factor affecting the ability of these newly established populations to reach their potential is the maintenance and enhancement of existing habitats.

HABITAT CHANGES

The Louisiana Purchase in 1803 opened the Midwest oak-hickory region to settlement, and habitat conditions have been changing ever since. Early explorers reported that the forests of the region were rather open and composed of mature trees with heavy stands of native grasses present in the understory (Martin 1955). Habitat conditions prior to settlement probably were stable except where fire temporarily may have improved habitat.

In 1796, the human population of the upper Louisiana territory (Native Americans excluded) north of the present Missouri and Arkansas state line was 3,582 (Viles 1911 in McKinley 1960). By 1810, there were almost 20,000 settlers in Missouri. And by 1850, the population had increased to almost 700,000 (Lively and Bright 1948). Populations increased rapidly between 1850 and 1880, with the rural population in Missouri peaking in 1900 (Lively and Bright 1948). Population growth across the region may not have been comparable to Missouri's, but rural populations probably peaked around the turn of the century or shortly after. During this period (1900 to 1920) more people were living off the land than at any other time.

As the region was settled, timber was cleared to make way for agriculture. During the early settlement period (1800 to 1850) the amount of land cleared probably had little impact on wild turkey habitat conditions. Clearings generally were small and may have enhanced habitat conditions by adding a measure of diversity. After the Civil War, commercial timber cutting began. Most virgin pine in Missouri and Arkansas was cut between 1880 and 1920 (Anonymous 1975). Some cutting of hardwood for charcoal and railroad ties began before the Civil War, but most hardwood forests were left uncut until most of the pine had been removed. Cutover lands were usually abandoned by the large timber companies and were sold for taxes.

The early settlers used fire to improve forage conditions for their livestock. "Burning the woods" was a springtime ritual across much of the Midwest oak-hickory region. No records are available on how extensive these springtime fires were. Old settlers, however, would tell of days when the air was darkened with smoke for weeks at a time (Anonymous 1975). In Missouri, it was estimated that forest fires burned over every acre, on land that eventually was controlled by the national forest, at least once every 3 years. In Missouri, the U.S. Forest Service initiated a fire protection program in 1936. Before that, an average of 113,400 hectares (280,000 acres) of public land was burned annually (Anonymous 1975). Ten years later, the amount had been reduced to about 3,240 hectares (8,000 acres). However, the damage of 100-plus years of burning had taken its toll. The current distribution of age classes on the national forest lands in the region shows, in part, the effects of past abuses to the habitat. Almost 70 percent of the timber on the Mark Twain National Forest in Missouri falls into the 40- to 79-year age class, and 82 percent of timber on the Ozark National Forest in Arkansas is in the 50- to 70-year age class.

Turning livestock out to graze on unfenced lands has been practiced since the earliest settlers arrived. Initially the entire region was just one big open range. By the turn of the century, however, such grazing had been limited to the more heavily forested parts of the region. By 1935, open range in Missouri was restricted to the Ozarks, although there were still 3,165,322 hectares (7,815,612 acres) open to grazing (Anonymous 1975). Open range in Missouri was closed in 1965. Nevertheless, the damage to vegetation and to habitat caused from soil loss may last for a long time, and the land may never recover completely.

Habitat for wild turkeys in the Midwest oak-hickory region began to improve on public lands after initiation of fire protection and timber management programs. Dates for implementing these programs varied somewhat across the region, but most of the states had programs in place by the late 1930s. Major habitat improvements occurred after the adoption of even-aged silviculture as a timber management system. Even-aged management made it possible to develop better timber and wildlife management coordination through programs like the featured species and habitat diversity concepts.

While habitat conditions for wild turkeys have improved on public lands, the same has not been true on private land. The 9 states in the Midwest oak-hickory region have lost almost 809,389 hectares (2 million acres) of commercial timberland since the mid-1950s. Two states, Missouri and Arkansas, had a combined loss of 1,214,083 hectares (3 million acres). But 4 states had a net gain of 930,080 hectares (2,300,000 acres) of commercial timberland. Iowa lost more than 327,755 hectares (800,000 acres) of commercial forestland between 1954 and 1974 through conversion to pasture and other agriculture lands. Missouri converted 526,103 hectares (1,300,000 acres) of commercial forest to wooded and improved pasture between 1959 and 1972. Higher cattle

prices during the late 1960s and early 1970s provided the incentive to convert low-income timbered areas into pasture for beef production. Conversion of timberland to agricultural uses is continuing across the Midwest oak-hickory region, although at a much slower rate now than in the mid-1960s.

The conversion of almost 1.2 million hectares (3 million acres) of commercial timberland in Missouri and Arkansas was initially viewed as a serious loss of wild turkey habitat. There's no doubt that in some areas habitat loss was complete. However, the continued increase of turkey populations and harvests in the affected areas raises some speculation about the overall effects of the timber loss. In some areas where conversion was not total, habitat diversity might have been improved.

Impoundments on many of the major streams have resulted in the loss of wild turkey habitat throughout the region. The loss of these riparian habitats in Missouri equals the size of a small county (101,174 hectares, 250,000 acres) at conservation-pool level and a large county (195,467 hectares, 483,000 acres) at the flood-pool level. Not only is permanently flooded land lost, but also the areas bordering most of these reservoirs are affected by an increase in disturbances such as roads, cabins, and all the activities connected with water recreation. The dam building seems to have subsided for the immediate future, primarily because most of the major streams have already been dammed. This slackening may not hold true, because the U.S. Army Corps of Engineers has plans for dams on many of the smaller streams.

A current item of concern is what the Conservation Reserve Program (CRP) will do to wild turkey habitat in northern Missouri and southern Iowa. These 2 states enrolled 1,133,147 hectares (2,797,894 acres) in CRP. Additional land will be enrolled in future signups. The key to wild turkey abundance in this part of the Midwest oak-hickory region is the intensity of agriculture. The conversion of cropland to pasture may not be in the best interest of wild turkeys if most of the croplands are removed from fairly large areas. The CRP is a 10-year program that began in 1986. After contracts expire, some CRP lands may go back to crops. Some may eventually revert to timber. The majority of these lands, however, are likely to remain in grass. The large-scale conversion of cropland to grass may have a negative effect locally on habitat conditions for wild turkeys.

Habitat is dynamic, probably more so today than during the presettlement period. The major forces that could affect wild turkey habitat (fire, unregulated grazing, conversion of timberland to other uses, and poor timber management practices) seem to be under control or at least declining. New programs like CRP may have a short-term impact, but they probably will not seriously threaten habitat conditions across the region. Wild tur-

HABITAT RELATIONSHIPS

In the Midwest, a mixture of woodlots and small agricultural fields constitutes excellent habitat.

keys are now firmly established throughout the variety of habitats in the region. They are much more adaptable at surviving in habitats previously thought unsuited. So, unless a major catastrophe occurs, wild turkeys will be around for a long time in the Midwest oak-hickory region.

Investigations of home range and habitat use of the eastern wild turkey have been conducted over a wide diversity of the species' range (Lewis 1963, Ellis and Lewis 1967, Hillestad 1973, Porter et al. 1980, Crim 1981). Findings of these and other studies are highly variable, partly because of both geographic variation and differences in experimental design. Brown (1980), in reviewing studies of turkey home range and habitat use, questioned the appropriateness of using home range comparisons for developing management strategies. Despite these inherent variations, findings from a northern Missouri study (Kurzejeski and Lewis 1990) support the contention of many authors that wild turkey home range and habitat use are most often affected by available food resources (Mosby and Handley 1943, Wheeler 1948, Porter et al. 1983).

Seasonal home ranges seem to be directly related to food availability, with winter food exerting the greatest impact on movements and habitat use patterns throughout the Midwest oak-hickory range. Extensive use of crop fields as winter food sources has been well documented within the Midwest oak-hickory region (Little 1980, Crim 1981, Porter et al. 1983, Lewis and Kurzejeski 1984). Porter et al. (1983) described snow depth as a factor limiting turkeys' ability to move to available food sources in southern Minnesota. High interspersion of crop fields may be critical to turkey survival in the northern portion of the Midwest oak-hickory region, but it does not appear to be limiting farther south.

In north-central Missouri, estimates of spring home range for wild turkey hens were compiled from 529 locations of 34 hens. The mean home range was 100.4 hectares (248 acres), and there was no difference observed between years (Kurzejeski and Lewis 1990). Movements associated with spring breakup were similar to those in southern Missouri. Extensive use of crop fields occurred in the winter of 1981. This change required increased movement that year to spring range: 3.1 kilometers (1.9 miles). In 1982, when birds were wintering much closer to preferred nesting locations, the average spring movement was only 1.3 kilometers (0.8 miles). Overall, most spring movements were less than 1.5 kilometers (0.9 miles) from winter range, although rare movements were up to 11.5 kilometers (7.1 miles). Winter-to-spring dispersal movements usually were completed within a day, but some hens took several days to make the move.

Crop fields not bordered by mature timber stands were seldom used and never exhibited consistent use in northern Missouri (Kurzejeski and Lewis 1990). Both Porter et al. (1980) and Crim (1981) alluded to the importance of timber and crop field associations as wintering areas. Timbered borders of fields were used during the winter extensively for loafing and roosting. Management of harvested crop fields was the only other major factor affecting use after harvest. Fields that were fall plowed were never used. Chisel-plowed and moderately grazed fields, however, were used by turkeys if located next to timber.

Although crop fields undoubtedly are important in the mixed timber-agriculture areas within the Midwest oak-hickory region, turkeys seem to prefer acorns (Korschgen 1967). Even though turkeys prefer acorns, crop fields provide an essential and abundant backup food resource in the northern part of the region. This dependable food supply may be responsible for the higher populations of turkeys in the northern mixed timber-agriculture lands. The lack of cropland, combined with variation in annual mast production, may limit turkey densities in the more heavily forested parts of the Midwest oak-hickory region.

Wild turkeys in the mixed timber-agricultural region of the Midwest reach population densities reported to exceed 30 birds per square kilometer (75 per square mile) of timber (Hanson 1984, Lewis and Kurzejeski 1984). That wild turkeys are now thriving in areas previously thought not suitable demonstrates their adaptability. Dickson et al. (1978) reported there was not a prescribed set of optimum habitat conditions for all populations of turkeys. Basically, wild turkeys are habitat generalists. They adapt to a variety of environmental conditions (Dickson et al. 1978).

Winter

Food availability and food location dictate the movements of wild turkeys during winter, especially in the northern part of the Midwest oak-hickory region. Recent studies in Missouri, Iowa, and Minnesota leave little doubt that winter food supply is critical to the survival of turkeys in these areas. Farther south in the Missouri Ozarks, Dalke et al. (1946) noted that in late winter when natural food supplies became scarce, turkeys would move to different wintering areas and use open fields along the larger streams.

A study in south-central Missouri (Ellis and Lewis 1967) supported the earlier observations made by Dalke et al. (1946) that wild turkey movements in winter are dominated by food. More than half of all turkey observations from December 1, 1965, through March 31, 1966, were made in a 12.1-hectare (30-acre) bottomland cornfield and 2 adjacent wooded ridges.

Data from a wild turkey telemetry study in north-central Missouri showed that during the winter (January 1 to March 14) of 1981, hens spent more than a third of their time in bottomland crop fields, and just less than

half (45.3 percent) of the locations were in forested areas (Kurzejeski and Lewis 1990). In the fall of 1982, exceptional mast production resulted in a change in the use of winter habitat on the area. Crop fields accounted for only 5.6 percent of the radio locations, while timbered areas contained 60 percent of the locations. Old fields and pastures made up the rest. Mast production in 1983 was marginal, and turkeys again made extensive use of crop fields.

During the winters of 1977–78 and 1978–79, Crim (1981) found that adult gobblers in south-central Iowa differed from other age and sex classes in their patterns of habitat use. Adult males were found most often in oak-hickory poletimber, which made up 64 percent of the timbered area. Use of this habitat was more than its availability suggested. Although limited data did not allow for detailed analyses of preferences in roosting sites, adult males used the oak-hickory poletimber the most. Some roosted in oak-hickory sawtimber and lowland hardwoods. But none were found in pine plantations. Adult gobblers did use cornfields, but not as much as did other age and sex groups. Weather seemed to have little effect on gobblers, and no differences in habitat use were detected during the 3-month winter period or between years.

Crim (1981) found adult females and juveniles of both sexes most frequently in oak-hickory poletimber. Cornfield use increased after crop harvest, and it remained fairly constant through the winter and into March, when use of grassland increased. During cold weather, adult hens and juveniles utilized conifers during daytime and for roosting. Birds would loaf in conifers during the day, making a trip to the cornfield to feed, then returning to the conifers to roost.

Crim (1981) found no difference between winter home range estimates for different age and sex groups of turkeys in south-central Iowa during October to March, 1977–78 and 1978–79. Home ranges were smallest each year during February, averaging 57 hectares (141 acres) in 1978 and 55 hectares (136 acres) in 1979. The January-through-March mean home range for 1978 was 141 hectares (348 acres) and for 1979, 152 hectares (375 acres). Winter home ranges for wild turkeys in Iowa were comparable to those for hens in northern Missouri, 141 hectares (348 acres) in 1981 and 86 hectares (212 acres) in 1982 (Kurzejeski and Lewis 1990), as well as in Minnesota, where Porter et al. (1980) indicated that winter home ranges averaged about 100 hectares (247 acres).

Porter et al. (1980), studying the effects of food plots on 2 separate wild turkey populations in southeastern Minnesota, showed that small cornfields were beneficial, especially during winters with deep snow. During the winter of 1977–78, snow depth restricted turkey movements. Birds in the area without cornfields suffered

Left: In the wild turkey's northern range, turkeys can feed in shallow or packed snow. *Photo by W. Porter.* Right: But persistent deep, dry snow can cover food and cause problems. *Photo by National Wild Turkey Federation.*

60 percent mortality. Birds with access to cornfields had less than 15 percent mortality.

In Iowa, Crim (1981) sampled food availability and found that in October there was as much food left in the cornfields after harvest as was available in the upland timber. In Minnesota, Porter et al. (1980) detected that in at least 80 percent of the cornfields, 10 percent of the corn present on November 1 remained in the fields throughout the winter. Apparently crop fields play a major role in maintaining wild turkey populations in the northern part of the Midwest oak-hickory range. However, data from northern Missouri (Kurzejeski and Lewis 1990) indicate that turkeys prefer to remain in wooded

Fields with waste grain help turkey flocks winter in good condition. *Photo by D. Reid.*

Corn is an important agriculture commodity of the region and a supplemental food for wild turkeys. *Photo by L. Williams.*

areas when mast is plentiful and that row crops serve as a backup food source during low mast years.

Winter habitat needs appear to exert the greatest influence on wild turkey movements in the Midwest oak-hickory region. There is, however, no conclusive evidence to show that winter foods act in a limiting capacity.

If population density can serve as an indicator of habitat quality, then the data from Missouri, Iowa, and Minnesota support a 50:50 mix of mast-producing timber and open lands as the ideal turkey habitat (Little 1980). High interspersion of crop fields may not be essential, but crop fields not bordered by mature timber were seldom used in north-central Missouri.

Spring

With the onset of warmer weather, winter flocks begin to break up. The timing of this spring dispersal will vary from year to year and is influenced by weather. In some years, a warming period may occur in January to late February and trigger adult gobblers to move in

search of hens. Winter flocks in south-central Missouri usually begin to disintegrate toward the end of March, but a late spring may delay this activity for 2 to 3 weeks or more (Ellis and Lewis 1967).

Breeding activity influences turkey movements during spring and usually results in the redistribution of flocks over their entire range. On the study area in Lake Spring, Missouri, linear movements concurrent with spring dispersal were greater than at any other season (Ellis and Lewis 1967).

Spring movements differ between age and sex classes. Nonbreeding juvenile males usually are not influenced by mating activity, and their movements depend largely on environmental factors. Juvenile hens lacking previous nesting experience are searching for nest sites and usually move more than any other age or sex class. Adult hens often return to previously used nesting habitat, which may or may not be near where they wintered. Adult males show no such attachment to a specific site but usually remain within their normal year-round range (Ellis and Lewis 1967).

In north-central Missouri, 34 hens were monitored between March 15 and May 31 in 1981, 1982, and 1983 (Lewis and Kurzejeski 1984). Habitat use was determined from 529 telemetry locations, and significant habitat preferences were observed. Timbered pasture (grassland with scattered overstory trees) was significantly preferred over other cover types. But the actual importance of timbered pasture was questionable because of the small percentage of this cover type within the spring home range. Timbered pasture was used during the spring for courtship and mating, and to some

Wherever the wild turkey occurs, brood habitat is essential for year-round habitat suitability. *Photo by M. Alarzani.*

Openings in forest habitat are important for the wild turkey's year-round needs. *Photo by D. Baumann.*

extent for feeding. It is, however, thought to be not a critical habitat component if other open lands are present.

Cropland received considerable use in the spring, ranking second in preference (Kurzejeski and Lewis 1990). Semiopen woodland was third in preference, followed by semiopen grassland. Forest and pasture were the least used habitats during spring.

Although timbered pasture was the preferred habitat type during the spring in north-central Missouri, hens did not select it for nesting (Kurzejeski and Lewis 1990). Data on 40 nest sites provided an insight on nest site selection. One nest was in a winter wheat field, and 4 nests were in lightly grazed pastures. Slightly more than half of the nests were in timber and semiopen woodlands. Twelve hens placed their nests in semiopen grassland.

The presence of dense vegetation was the predominant characteristic at most nest sites. Only 2 nests were located in mature timber without a dense understory. Many hens nested in habitat edges. The mean distance from all nest sites to edge (change in cover type) was 38.7 ± 3.4 meters, (127 ± 11 feet). Data were not adequate to test difference in nest success as it related to cover type.

Reporting on nest habitat selection in Minnesota, Lazarus and Porter (1985) determined nesting habitat was characterized by a moderate-to-dense understory with a diversity of woody and herbaceous species. Vegetation was similar both at the immediate nest site and in a 0.5-hectare (1.2-acre) area around the nest. Apparently nest site selection, whether in Minnesota, Missouri, or other parts of the country, is determined primarily according to concealment cover at the site and in the immediately surrounding area.

Summer and Fall

No significant habitat preferences were exhibited by 23 radioed hens during the summer (June 1 to August 31) in north-central Missouri (Kurzejeski and Lewis 1990). However, seasonal use of pasture was greatest in the summer, including about 19 percent of the home range and 18 percent of all locations. Hens with broods were more prevalent in pastures (34 percent) than hens without broods (13 percent). Brood flocks were observed less in forested habitat (57 percent) than hens without broods (67 percent). Brood home range contained less forest cover and more open land than any other seasonal home range. Open areas presumably received more use during summer because they provide a variety of foods, especially insects.

The mean distance for all brood locations from habitat edge (change in cover type) was 43.5 meters

Grapes and dogwood are important fall foods for wild turkey flocks in the deciduous forests. *Photos by H. Williamson, U.S. Forest Service.*

(142.7 feet) compared with 66.6 meters (218.5 feet) for broodless hens. This difference supports the conclusion that broods during the summer were associated more often with open lands and habitat edge than were broodless hens.

Composition of home ranges in fall (September 1 to November 30) for 23 hens in north-central Missouri did not change from summer. As was observed during all seasons, forest cover made up the greatest percentage of available and used habitats. More than 75 percent of locations were in forest or semiopen woodland. Use of pasture during fall was second only to use during summer, with 13 percent of locations occurring in this cover type. Insect availability was probably responsible for use of pastures during this period.

MANAGEMENT

Population Management

The harvest of wild turkeys by hunters provides information valuable in management of the species. Harvest data give managers an insight to annual population fluctuations and the amount of occupied habitat. Harvest figures provide for references between population densities and habitat quality. Although harvest figures are not always directly related to population densities or habitat quality, there is sufficient evidence to suggest a very close relationship (Conner 1988). Van Horne (1983), however, warns against assuming simple density-habitat quality relationships without supporting data on population density. In many instances, harvest data are the only available source of population information on which to base decisions on habitat management programs. Examples of perceived differences in the habitat quality within the Midwest oak-hickory region based on harvest data are shown in Table 1.

Turkey harvest data in Missouri are analyzed by county and then by the proportion of that county occupied by commercial timber (Table 2). Realizing that timber constitutes only one habitat component, managers may evaluate the relative contribution of other habitat components (percent of open land, percent of open land in crops, and so on).

Band recovery data from spring hunting in Missouri (Lewis 1980) suggests differential harvest vulnerability between subadult and adult gobblers. Adult gobblers normally are more vulnerable than subadults during spring hunting because adults are sexually mature. The ratio of subadults to adults in Missouri's spring harvests is correlated positively with production from the previous years. The lengthening of spring seasons in Missouri was accompanied by an increase in the percent of subadults in the harvest and in hunter success. The longer seasons and increased hunting pressure probably accounted for the higher harvest of subadults.

Continued high harvest of subadults for several years may ultimately reduce the carryover of gobblers in the population to the following year. If this happens, the spring harvest of gobblers will depend to a large degree on subadults from the previous year's production. Knowledge about the subadult-adult gobbler harvest ratios is important from a management standpoint if for no other reason than being able to make intelligent predictions about how many turkeys will be available for next year's harvest.

Habitat Management — Historical Perspective

Some of the very earliest habitat management efforts for wild turkeys in the Midwest oak-hickory region were initiated by A. Starker Leopold (1943b) on state and federal refuges in the Missouri Ozarks. He proposed that refuges be closed to hunting and that grazing be restricted. Fire-control measures were implemented, and timber was to be handled under a balanced program of "good silviculture" and "good game management." He also suggested having 15 to 25 percent of the total area in open lands and that it be well distributed. Maintenance of supplemental food supplies (food plots) and construction of numerous ponds to provide for permanent water over the entire area were parts of his management program.

Results of this early management effort for wild turkeys on Caney Mountain Refuge were very successful. In 1939, before the management program was implemented, there were 10 turkeys on or in the immediate vicinity of

Table 1. Eastern wild turkey estimated populations, occupied range, and 1991 spring harvest in the Midwest oak-hickory region.

State	Population estimate	Square kilometers of occupied range (square miles)	Spring 1991 harvest	Harvest per square kilometer (square mile)
Arkansas	60,000	37,205 (14,365)[a]	6,020	0.16 (0.42)
Illinois	30,000	10,686 (4,126)	3,475	0.33 (0.84)
Iowa	80,000	5,600 (2,162)	7,838	1.40 (3.62)
Kansas	20,000	3,134 (1,210)	2,200[b]	0.70 (1.82)
Minnesota	10,000	11,137 (4,300)	1,724	0.15 (0.40)
Missouri	320,000	55,895 (21,581)	32,170	0.58 (1.49)
Nebraska	200	52 (20)	15[b]	0.29 (0.75)
Oklahoma	20,000	16,835 (6,500)	1,892[b]	0.11 (0.29)
Wisconsin	80,000	11,300 (4,363)	6,862	0.61 (1.57)
Total	620,200	151,843 (58,627)	62,196	0.41 (1.06)

[a] Includes only the Ozarks and Ouachita portion of Arkansas.
[b] Harvest of eastern only.

Table 2. Missouri's 1990 spring turkey harvest relative to percentage of commercial timberland by county.

Percent of county in timber	Number of counties	Square kilometers of occupied range (square miles)	Spring 1990 harvest	Harvest per square kilometer (square mile)
40–80	38	38,650 (14,923)	14,582	0.38 (0.98)
15–39	31	12,002 (4,634)	8,518	0.71 (1.84)
5–14	45	5,242 (2,024)	6,958	1.32 (3.44)
Total	114	55,894 (21,581)	30,058	0.54 (1.39)

the 2,225-hectare (5,500-acre) refuge. In just 4 years, the turkey population increased to 88 birds on the refuge and from 58 to 248 in a zone of 310 square kilometers (120 square miles) outside the refuge.

The direct habitat management practices employed by Leopold have been the stock-in-trade of wildlife managers for years. The practice he recommended that was different was managing the woodlands under a balanced program of silviculture and game management.

The silvicultural system used on U.S. Forest Service and state lands from 1934 to 1962 was group selection based on harvest cuts at 10-year intervals. Group selection cutting affords some measure of wildlife habitat benefits, but it is difficult to regulate and administer on large areas through time (Roach 1974). The timber management objective during this period was to increase pine on all suitable sites. The management emphasis on pine—or the lack of effort to coordinate wildlife habitat

The midwestern region has some of the highest turkey densities and high-quality spring hunting. When the redbud blooms, it's time to get ready to hunt. *Photo by G. Smith.*

needs into the silviculture program—may have been what Leopold objected to as incompatible with good game management.

In 1962, even-aged silviculture was introduced into the Midwest oak-hickory region. Early applications of this new system created some concerns for wildlife managers and timber managers. Problems with even-aged management arose from earlier mismanagement on much of the forested lands. Age class distribution was out of balance. Initial inventories determined that large acreages should be regenerated, a strategy that would have adversely affected wildlife and timber supplies in both the short and long term.

In an effort to overcome some problems posed by applying even-aged silviculture, a "Wildlife Habitat Management Guide to the National Forest in Missouri" was developed in 1970 (Evans 1974). This wildlife habitat management program was based on a concept of diversity to provide a broad range of habitat needs.

Elements of the habitat guide were designed to provide a sustained mast component through time. The guide required that 40 percent of the timber in each compartment of 404 hectares (1,000 acres) be appropriate tree species and size classes capable of providing mast production. Forage was identified as another element needed to provide habitat diversity. Forage was to be supplied temporarily from regeneration and would amount to 10 or 12 percent of a compartment. Permanent forage (open and semiopen habitats) was to be maintained or developed on 10 percent of the compartment.

Old growth was the last element needed to round out the concept of habitat diversity. The guide recommended that 10 percent of each compartment be maintained as old growth and that old growth be represented on all sites and for all vegetative types. The habitat diversity concept received national recognition as a reasonable alternative to the unbalanced management programs on the national forests in the early 1970s.

At about the same time, the featured species approach to habitat management was being implemented on U.S. Forest Service lands in the Southeast. In the featured species concept, a single wildlife species is selected to receive the major emphasis on a unit of land. Habitat needs of that species are then used to guide timber management activities toward achieving proper habitat conditions (Holbrook 1974, Zeedyk and Hazel 1974). The featured species concept and the habitat diversity concept are similar to a certain degree. The featured species plan could include the management for more than a single species on a single tract, and this tactic would result in a certain measure of habitat diversity.

One problem with the habitat diversity concept, as pointed out by Van Horn (1983), is that habitat diversity is not necessarily directly correlated to maximum species diversity. In effect, both the habitat diversity and the featured species concepts were management systems that probably benefited the generalist species more than any species with specialized habitat needs. Even though these earlier concepts were beset with problems, they did accomplish one thing: They demonstrated that a better system was needed for evaluating timber and wildlife management.

Habitat Management—Present Emphasis

The U.S. Forest Service oversees the management of 17,011 square kilometers (6,568 square miles) within the Midwest oak-hickory region (Table 3). As the largest land management agency in the region, the Forest Service has played a dominant role in developing and implementing coordinated timber and wildlife management programs.

Before 1990, management practices on Forest Service lands were established by the National Forest Management Act (NFMA) of 1976. Changes in management emphasis as a result of NFMA have been explained by several authors (Nelson et al. 1983, Salwasser et al. 1983, Verner 1983, Conner 1988). In 1990, the U.S. Forest Service adopted "New Perspectives" as a plan for managing the National Forest System. This new approach was implemented primarily as a result of popular demand for less emphasis on timber production and more on resource values and uses. There will be less emphasis on even-aged timber management under the New Perspective program. Timber will continue to be grown and harvested, but the program will employ a wider range of silviculture systems than those of the past. What this may mean to the future of the wild turkey resource on Forest Service lands in the Midwest oak-hickory region is anybody's guess.

Forest Service regulations under the NFMA required that fish and wildlife habitats be managed to maintain viable populations of all existing native vertebrate species and to maintain and improve habitat of management indicator species (MIS). The criteria for the selection of MIS include federal and state endangered and threatened plant and animal species, species with special habitat needs that may be affected by future management, and species that are commonly hunted, fished, or trapped.

Another important directive in the NFMA is that MIS population trends will be monitored on how they are affected by habitat changes created by management. Salwasser et al. (1983) points out that monitoring wildlife and fish is a crucial part of natural resource management and that if a monitoring program focuses on just habitat or a species, it is likely to miss the underlying cause-and-effect relationship.

One of the more difficult requirements in the NFMA regulations deals with maintaining viable populations

Table 3. Area of commercial timberland by state and ownership class.

State	All ownership	National forest	Other public	Forest industry	Farmer	Other private
Arkansas[1]	36,024[a]	9,200	1,401	3,539	7,302	14,582
	(13,909)	(3,552)	(541)	(1,367)	(2,819)	(5,630)
Illinois[2]	16,306	914	658	53	7,397	7,285
	(6,296)	(353)	(254)	(20)	(2,856)	(2,813)
Iowa[3]	5,903	—	451	67	3,994	1,391
	(2,279)	—	(174)	(26)	(1,542)	(537)
Kansas[4]	4,147	—	168	—	2,520	1,459
	(1,601)	—	(65)	—	(973)	(563)
Minnesota[5]	7,894	—	1,311	2	4,619	1,963
	(3,048)	—	(506)	(1)	(1,783)	(758)
Missouri[6]	50,704	5,915	1,158	1,566	24,834	17,229
	(19,577)	(2,284)	(447)	(605)	(9,589)	(6,652)
Nebraska[7]	1,127	—	23	—	832	273
	(435)	—	(9)	—	(321)	(105)
Oklahoma[8]	19,210	982	1,386	4,256	5,243	7,345
	(7,417)	(379)	(535)	(1,643)	(2,024)	(2,836)
Wisconsin[9]	7,770	—	306	—	5,082	2,382
	(3,000)	—	(118)	—	(1,962)	(920)
Total	149,086	17,011	6,862	9,483	61,821	53,908
	(57,562)	(6,568)	(2,649)	(3,662)	(23,869)	(20,814)

[a] Square kilometers (square miles).
[1] Hines 1988.
[2] Hahn 1985.
[3] Spencer and Jakes 1980.
[4] Spencer et al. 1984.
[5] Vasilevsky and Hackett 1980.
[6] Spencer and Essex 1976.
[7] Raile 1986.
[8] Hines and Bertelson 1987.
[9] Raile 1985.

(Lacava and Hughes 1984, Reed et al. 1986). Resource managers are legally required to maintain minimum viable populations (MVP) for all species. But the forest planning regulations do not provide clear guidelines to how this might be done.

Conner (1988) noted some problems with the MVP approach. He suggested that incorporating MVP as management constraints might result in holding wildlife populations at a level close to extirpation or extinction.

MVP objectives for wild turkeys have been established under the current resource management plans on national forestlands within the Midwest oak-hickory region. Although the term "MVP" has been used, a more realistic term is "minimum acceptable populations" (MAP). In Missouri's Mark Twain National Forest, the MAP for wild turkeys was set at 8 to 15 per 404 hectares (1,000 acres). Pattern Recognition (PATREC) models have been developed for the wild turkey in Missouri and are being used on the Mark Twain National Forest (Kurzejeski and Lewis 1985). The wild turkey PATREC model was constructed using the best estimate of those habitat parameters (standards and guides) needed for maintaining both low and high population densities. Variations in land capability and management emphasis are responsi-

ble for the differences in MAP of turkeys in the Mark Twain Forest.

Approximately 35 percent (206,556 hectares, 509,987 acres) of the Forest Service lands in Missouri is to be managed with wildlife receiving the major emphasis.

On the Shawnee National Forest in Illinois, MAP objectives were set at 4 to 15 wild turkeys per 259 hectares (640 acres). There are 103,286 hectares (255,029 acres) of forestland in the Shawnee National Forest. Of this, only 58.3 percent (60,215 hectares, 148,679 acres) has been classified as suitable for timber management. Habitat suitability models will be used to monitor the effects of management activities on wild turkeys. The present standards, however, are general and will make it difficult to monitor the future effects of timber management—or the lack of it—on wild turkey densities and habitat.

Wild turkeys on the Ozark and Ouachita national forests in Arkansas and Oklahoma will be managed under the featured species concept. The old land and resource management plans indicated that turkeys would be featured on 427,824 hectares (1,056,400 acres) on these national forests. Minimum population objectives (MPO) have been established at 10 turkeys per 259 hectares (640 acres), in accord with the U.S. Forest Service's Region 8 guidelines.

The previous Ozark and Ouachita National Forest Management plans were vague on the coordination between timber and wildlife management activities. A more comprehensive explanation should have been provided about the effects of timber management, or lack of it, on wild turkeys and their habitats. The lack of detailed information would have made it difficult to monitor population response to habitat changes.

Since passage of the NFMA of 1976, wildlife management on national forests in the Midwest oak-hickory region has been improved. Many positive changes have been made, including (1) maintenance of viable populations of all existing native vertebrate species; (2) maintenance and improvement of habitat conditions for MIS; and (3) monitoring of MIS population trends compared with habitat changes as a result of management. These were steps in the right direction, but continued efforts are needed to make wildlife management work.

Basic management for any species depends on the land and its capability. Before any land-use decision can be formulated, units of land must be classified according to their capability. Habitats generally are too diverse to be treated with a blanket set of standards and guides, which appears to be the approach on the Ozark and Ouachita national forests in Arkansas and Oklahoma and the Shawnee in Illinois.

Habitat Management — Industrial Forests

In the Midwest oak-hickory region, industrial timber companies own 9,483 square kilometers (3,662 square miles) — about 6.4 percent — of the commercial timberland (Table 3). Most of these lands are in the Ozarks and Ouachitas in Missouri, Arkansas, and Oklahoma. The following description of industrial forest management is from Bob McAnally (Arkansas Game and Fish personal communication: 1988).

"Industrial forest management in the mountain regions of Arkansas generally favors those wildlife species associated with early stages of plant succession. Wild turkey population densities are generally lower on industrial lands than on national forests and other public lands. The few exceptions are industrial lands that have yet to be cut, lands that have received relatively light management, and lands belonging to some of the smaller companies that manage for hardwood and pine sawtimber products.

"Most larger industrial landowners manage on a relatively short rotation based on a growth-economic curve. Most of these lands are managed for pine monoculture, but no hardwood control measures are 100 percent effective. So some residual hardwoods persist in most stands. These trees usually are of low quality, and their mast production is low. Management varies by company, depending on the type of product produced, as well as the type of processing mills and their proximity.

"Most stand sizes are relatively large, and there seems to be little consideration for wildlife when regenerating adjacent stands. It is common to see adjacent stands regenerated within a relatively short time. Most of the larger companies practice even-aged management: utilizing clear-cutting, mechanical site preparation, and direct planting of pine seedlings. Seed tree and shelterwood treatments, as well as selective cutting, are used less frequently, particularly by large companies.

"Industrial managers seem more responsive to public concerns than ever before. With the increased emphasis on leasing for hunting clubs, it is likely that wildlife habitat quality will receive more emphasis in the future.

"Road density on industrial lands generally is higher than that on public lands. Road construction standards and road density vary from area to area and from company to company. Most industrial landowners make little effort to control access. Heavy cattle grazing occurs on a high percentage of industrial forests, negatively affecting habitat for many wildlife species. Most of this grazing is by trespass and is probably tolerated by companies for fear of being burned out. A large percentage of these lands was grazed before companies bought them."

According to McAnally, the future for wild turkeys on industrial lands may be brighter than it seems. "Much industrial land in Arkansas is in pine regeneration 10 to 15 years old and is too thickly vegetated to support turkey populations of moderate-to-high density. As these stands age and are managed, they will provide better habitat for turkeys. Controlled burning and thinning of these stands will further enhance the habitat quality for turkeys.

"Between 1976 and 1986, industrial forest ownership of timberland in southeast Oklahoma increased by 6 percent, making up a total of 30 percent of commercial forest in that region (Birdsey and Bertelson 1987). During this period, land devoted to loblolly and shortleaf pine plantations also increased. Although Birdsey and Bertelson (1987) reported that harvests exceeded growth for softwoods and hardwoods on industrial forest ownership, the volume of softwood and hardwood sawtimber increased slightly during this period. However, habitat quality for wild turkeys on industrial forest may have declined in southeast Oklahoma, partly because of an increase in pine plantations.

"Missouri is the only other state in the Midwest oak-hickory region with a significant amount of forest industry ownership. About 3 percent of the state's timberland is owned and managed by forest industry. The Pioneer Forest owns about 40 percent of the forest industry lands in Missouri. These lands have been managed primarily by selective cutting, although in some instances even-aged management has been used. The Pioneer Forest may be unique in that timber products are not its only objective. The owner has a keen interest in wildlife, and this is reflected in how these lands are managed."

Habitat Management — Other Public

The category "other public" is a combination of federally, state-, county-, and municipally owned lands. These lands account for about 5 percent of the commercial timberland in the Midwest oak-hickory region (Table 3). Lands in this category include state forests, state wildlife management areas, state parks, county and municipal parks, U.S. Fish and Wildlife Service refuges, and areas controlled by the U.S. Army Corps of Engineers around impoundments.

Just how much habitat these lands provide for wild turkeys varies considerably. State forests and wildlife management areas provide the most. This habitat differs, however, from state to state and by area type. The level of timber and wildlife coordination on most state forests and wildlife management areas does not match the level on national forest lands. Although timber and wildlife management is generally restricted on state parks, these areas do provide some benefits for wildlife.

The Missouri Department of Conservation manages about 88,000 hectares (217,000 acres) licensed from the Corps of Engineers, U.S. Fish and Wildlife Service, and other organizations. Corps lands are prone to unpredictable flooding, usually restricting forest management options. These factors limit the amount of management the Missouri Department of Conservation is willing to undertake. And since licenses to manage the land could be revoked, management of these lands receives a relatively low priority. The same probably holds true in other states in the Midwest oak-hickory region.

Habitat Management — Private Nonindustrial Lands

On privately owned timberland in the Midwest oak-hickory region, little management for wildlife or timber takes place. Private nonindustrial owners control 78 percent of the timberland in the region (Table 3). These lands, in combination with cropland, can support high turkey densities. The category "private" includes lands owned by farmers, estates, private individuals, and corporations. It also includes Native American lands. Farmers own 41 percent of the timberland in the Midwest oak-hickory region. Farmer-owned timberland can be characterized as small holdings — less than 40 hectares (100 acres). Most of these lands were originally in timber

and have been logged once or twice. Residual stands vary from pole- to small sawlog in size, and they occur on poorer land associated with the rougher topography along drainage systems. In the past, these areas were grazed and often still are. They provided the landowner with fence posts and firewood and some rough lumber for building materials. Overall, privately owned timberland is quite variable in quality for wildlife habitat and timber products.

These small tracts of privately owned timberland were once viewed as unsuitable for wild turkeys. But opinions have changed with the successful reestablishment of wild turkeys into woodlot habitats throughout much of the Midwest oak-hickory region. Wild turkey densities associated with the small timbered tracts in northern Missouri and southern Iowa are some of the highest in the country. But suitable habitat for wild turkeys takes more than just timber. It takes the right mix of timber and agriculture (Little 1980).

Recent indications are that conditions on private timberland may be improving. The Forest Incentive Act, which was passed in 1973, made money available to private land owners for timber-stand improvement and tree plantings. This program is administered by the Agricultural Stabilization and Conservation Service, but the responsibility for determining what work will be done lies with foresters in the various state conservation agencies. How much has been accomplished isn't known, but this program seems to be gaining momentum.

Privately owned timberland in Missouri may be classified as Forest Cropland under the provisions of a State Forestry Law enacted in 1946. To qualify, land must (1) be at least 8 hectares (20 acres); and (2) support a growth of timber. Taxes on these lands are reduced as an incentive for landowners to raise trees as a permanent crop. Payments are made to counties to make up for lost tax revenues at the rate of 50¢ per acre for each acre of Forest Cropland. In 1984, there were 123,104 hectares (303,961 acres) of privately owned Forest Cropland in Missouri (MDC Annual Report 1984–85). Although Forest Croplands are but a small percent of total private forestland, they show a commitment by owners to manage these lands for 25 years.

Privately owned timberland has been very important in the successful reestablishment of wild turkeys in the Midwest oak-hickory region. Although the quality of the timber may not equal that on public lands, turkey restoration in the mixed timber-agricultural portions of the area would not have occurred without it.

Management Recommendations

Management recommendations for wild turkeys in the Midwest oak-hickory region fall into 2 basic categories: (1) those for the heavily forested southern part; and (2) those for the mixed timber-agriculture part in the north. Within these 2 major habitat types are wide variations in habitat conditions. It's not possible to provide a simple recipe to cover all situations. Yet some general guidelines are offered that may be useful in planning habitat improvements on smaller management units.

Oak mast is a major food for wild turkeys, especially in the more heavily forested southern part of the Midwest oak-hickory region. To ensure that adequate mast supplies are available will require maintaining 40 percent to 60 percent of the management area in oak-hickory and oak-pine stands that are 50 or more years old. Regulating timber harvests to achieve a balance in the age size class distribution within a management unit could meet this objective. At least 50 percent of the saw-log component within any management unit should be maintained so that the crown closure is approximately 70 percent. This pattern will allow for grasses and forbs to develop in the understory.

Wildlife openings should be maintained in a grass- or wheat-legume mixture and renovated every 3 years. In areas where timber makes up more than 95 percent of the management unit, wildlife openings are very important and should be at least 1 percent of the total management unit. In areas of low site index, the development of savannas would improve overall habitat diversity by providing nesting and brood-rearing habitats. Rock outcrop and glades can provide insect foraging areas and can be maintained by periodic controlled burning.

Because most of the public ownership is in the heavily forested southern part of the region, implementing these recommendations should be relatively simple if they are included in a coordinated timber and wildlife management plan. Some of these recommendations have been implemented through the National Wild Turkey Federation Superfund and the U.S. Forest Service's challenge cost-sharing program. The hope is that these and other efforts will continue and expand.

Habitat management for wild turkeys in the mixed timber-agriculture part of the Midwest oak-hickory region has been mainly by accident rather than by design. Wild turkey habitats in this part of the region have been influenced by past land-use practices, which will continue to dictate what happens. Nevertheless, some recommendations for landowners who enjoy turkeys and turkey hunting are relatively easy to follow and will improve habitat. Wild turkey populations throughout the mixed timber-agriculture part of the region reach their highest densities in areas that have a 50:50 mix of mast-producing woodlands and open lands (Kurzejeski and Lewis 1990).

Row crops (corn, soybeans, milo) should make up at least 15 percent of the open lands within any manage-

ment unit. At least 30 percent of the crop fields should be bordered by mature timber at least 8 hectares (20 acres) in size. The open lands in crop fields that are not tilled or grazed after harvest should total 20 percent to 40 percent. The remainder of the open lands (pastures, hay, and old fields) should be maintained in varying stages of succession to provide for nesting and brood-rearing habitats. Timbered corridors connecting bottomland crop fields to wooded uplands should be maintained wherever possible.

Wild turkey populations will respond to improved habitat conditions, but the work spent on habitat improvements may be in vain without good controls over hunting. Harvest strategies should be based on population density estimates that reflect habitat capability and management intensity.

FUTURE PROSPECTS

The future looks very promising for wild turkeys in the Midwest oak-hickory region. Restoration efforts have been completed in Missouri and Iowa and will be by the mid-1990s in the remaining states.

Population densities will probably continue to increase, particularly in states still involved in restoration. The key to continued success of wild turkeys in the Midwest oak-hickory region is the maintenance and enhancement of existing habitats on private lands. Factors that influence habitat quality on private land are difficult to predict and could change almost overnight. Federal farm programs have affected — and probably will continue to affect — the major land-use decisions on private land in the region. The 1985 Farm Bill, which included the Conservation Reserve Program, might have a negative impact on wild turkey densities in the mixed timber-agriculture areas. Conversion of cropland to grass may drop the percentage of cropland below what is needed to maintain the high densities of turkeys now found in northern Missouri and southern Iowa.

Hunting opportunities for wild turkeys within the Midwest oak-hickory region may be reduced in the future because of an increase in private hunting leases. Hunting leases currently cover a very small percentage of private land in the region, but the trend is growing. Positive and negative effects can be associated with leasing. Positive affects may result from leasing because landowners may do a better job of habitat management for the compensation they receive. A negative aspect of leasing could be that as more land is leased, less will be available for hunters who are unwilling or cannot afford to pay.

Turkey hunting continues to grow in popularity across the Midwest oak-hickory region, and probably will do so for several years, especially in states with expanding turkey populations. The possibility exists for turkey-hunting opportunity and quality to be depressed if more land is committed to leasing. Leasing could concentrate an increasing number of hunters on public lands, thereby lowering the quality of hunting on these areas. Another problem connected with leasing might be underutilization of the resource by having relatively few hunters control most of the land. Although lease hunting is not yet a problem in this region, it might become a problem if the trend continues.

Prospects for the future welfare of wild turkeys on public lands in the Midwest oak-hickory region are very promising. Even though public land makes up only a small percentage of the region, turkey densities overall are higher there than on adjacent private forestland because of past and present management programs. Recent changes in U.S. Forest Service regulations require that wildlife habitats be managed to (1) maintain viable populations of all species; and (2) maintain and improve habitats for management indicator species. Wild turkeys have been designated as a MIS on most of the national forest lands in the Midwest oak-hickory region, assuring that any population change caused by management will be closely monitored. Although the future welfare of wild turkeys on public land seems secure, changes in management emphasis could reduce densities, especially if large areas fall into a category of limited management or no management.

Wild turkey restoration efforts in the Midwest will be completed by the mid-1990s.

Chapter 19

RIO GRANDE TURKEY

Samuel L. Beasom
Director
Caesar Kleberg Wildlife
Research Institute
Kingsville, Texas

Don Wilson
Upland Game Program Leader
Texas Parks and Wildlife Department
Austin, Texas

The Rio Grande turkey is similar in size and general appearance to the other subspecies of wild turkey. But the Rio Grande can be distinguished by the coloration of the tips of the tail feathers and the upper tail coverts (feathers of the lower back, covering the base of the tail feathers). In the Rio Grande, these feather tips are buff or tan, contrasting with the dark brown tips of the easterly subspecies and the white tips of the westerly subspecies. The Rio Grande is a highly gregarious, nomadic bird that often shows strong fidelity to traditional winter roost sites and often moves long distances from there to nest.

HISTORY AND RESTORATION

The turkey population in Kansas, Oklahoma, and Texas, before settlement by Europeans, was an estimated 3 million birds of the eastern and Rio Grande subspecies

The Rio Grande Turkey is adapted to arid habitat and is intermediate in appearance between the eastern and western subspecies. *Photo by Texas Parks and Wildlife Department.*

(Schorger 1966:59–60). Assuming that the 2 subspecies were of similar densities within their original distribution, about 1.8 to 2 million of the total were Rio Grandes. No estimates are available concerning the original population of Rio Grande birds in Mexico.

Throughout their range, turkeys apparently were dramatically affected by the processes of human civilization. Indiscriminate hunting during the late 1800s and habitat destruction from then through the early 1900s exacted a heavy toll on wild turkey populations in the United States (Gore 1969) and Mexico (Leopold 1948). By about 1928 to 1940, only about 100,000 Rio Grande turkeys remained in Texas, and the subspecies apparently was extirpated from Kansas and Oklahoma (Anonymous 1929, Schorger 1966:455).

Three steps were taken to restore Rio Grande turkeys to their native ranges: (1) legislation (the first enacted in 1881); (2) establishment of informal refuge areas, where hunting was voluntarily curtailed by landowners; and (3) restocking with wild-trapped birds (Gore 1969). Of these measures, restocking seemed the most successful.

Nobody knows when turkeys first were trapped and transplanted in Texas, but the tactic is believed to have begun before 1920. F.M. Cowsert, an employee of the Texas Game, Fish and Oyster Commission, reported trapping and transplanting turkeys from Sutton County in 1924 (Glazner 1963). The first recorded turkey stocking occurred in 1930, when 353 turkeys were trapped, but there is no record of how many areas were stocked. From 1930 through 1991, 22,968 turkeys have been stocked on 750 sites in Texas, and 5,735 were shipped to other states and countries (Table 1).

Oklahoma began its formal restoration program in 1948, when 21 turkeys were released in Harper County. About a year earlier, turkeys began to appear naturally in the 12 westernmost counties along the Canadian and Washita rivers. Presumably these birds drifted into Okla-

homa from transplants of Rio Grande turkeys in nearby places in the Texas Panhandle (Ellis 1948, Walker 1949a). To date, about 18,000 Rio Grande turkeys have been stocked in Oklahoma, and the subspecies has been restored to its original range in the state (J. Herd personal communication: 1989).

Restoration of the Rio Grande turkey in Kansas began in the late 1950s through natural movement of birds from Oklahoma (Schorger 1966:445). These efforts became formal in 1959 with the transplant of 43 birds from other locations in Kansas and 26 from Oklahoma. From 1964 to 1989, about 3,050 Rio Grande turkeys were transplanted in and north of their original range (P. Van Well personal communication: 1989).

Little information is available on restoration efforts in Mexico although we know that a few large landowners have implemented voluntary protection and transplant programs (J. Carrera personal communication: 1988).

GEOLOGY, CLIMATE, AND FOREST TYPES

Geology

The geology of Rio Grande turkey range is varied and includes outcrops of the oldest (over 1.1 billion years) known rocks as well as sands deposited continuously along the Texas and Mexico coast (M.W. McBride, General Geology of the Range of the Rio Grande Turkey, unpublished report, 6 pp.). The topography varies from flat coastal plains to canyons developed by streams breaching the resistant Cap Rock of the High Plains.

The rocks of the Balcones Fault Zone of Texas, southward and eastward in Texas and Mexico to the Gulf shores, include chalky limestone and shales of the Upper Cretaceous and Tertiary and Quaternary detrital sandstones and shales. The marine sediments of Late Cretaceous age represent the last—and one of the most extensive—of marine transgressions in the area. The Cenozoic deposits of the Tertiary and Quaternary periods are primarily records of streams that drained the highlands to the north, east, and west, depositing their silt and sands along the edges of an ever-retreating Gulf of Mexico. Although these rocks record occasional marine incursions, no other was as extensive or lengthy as those during the Cretaceous.

Soils developed on Cretaceous rocks are more alkaline than those developed on the Tertiary-Quaternary classics, and may have originally supported slightly different vegetation. But both areas are now dominated by row crop production (McMahan et al. 1984). The Late Cretaceous rocks constitute the Blackland Prairie (Gould 1975), and the Tertiary-Quaternary rocks belong to the

Table 1. Rio Grande turkeys transplanted in Texas, 1930–91, as compiled from records in the Texas Parks and Wildlife Department.

Date	Restoration areas	Turkeys released
1930–39	132	3,356
1940–49	109	4,022
1950–59	108	2,961
1960–69	39	1,149
1970–79	60	1,415
1980–89	262	8,933
1990–91	40	1,132
Total	750	22,968[a]

[a] An additional 5,735 birds were captured and shipped to other states and foreign countries.

Post Oak Savanna, Gulf Prairies and Marshes, and South Texas Plains.

The Gulf Coastal Plain of northeast Mexico is a direct continuation of that of Texas (Humphrey 1956). Tertiary rocks of the Mexican Coastal Plain, however, are finer-grained than rocks in Texas, indicating a source predominantly of limestones and shales for the eastward-draining streams. The Coastal Plain is narrower in Mexico than in Texas because the steeper coastward dips reflect the proximity of the mountains to the west.

The Hill Country is a region with no strict geographic definition but is usually used by geologists to include the area along the dissected eastern edge of the Edwards Plateau (west and north of the Balcones Fault System) plus the outcrop area of Precambrian and Paleozoic rocks in central Texas (M.W. McBride, General Geology of the Range of the Rio Grande Turkey, unpublished report, 6 pp.). Precambrian rocks that outcrop in Llano and adjacent counties are metaigneous, metasedimentary, and large exposures of unmetamorphosed igneous rocks such as granites. These are surrounded by outcrops of Paleozoic limestones and clastics. This Precambrian-Paleozoic complex has undergone extensive structural deformation. To the east, south, and west, however, it is overlain by a thick section of Cretaceous rocks that record little or no deformation.

The dense, resistant Lower Cretaceous Edwards Limestone that now crops out extensively west of the Hill Country probably also covered this entire area at one time. It has, however, been removed by erosion over most of the area east and south of the Precambrian outcrop. Here most of the surface rocks are pre-Edwards Cretaceous. The Edwards is confined to isolated exposures along stream divides and in the downthrown fault blocks of the Balcones Fault Zone. Most of the Cretaceous rocks—both Edwards and pre-Edwards—are marine-shelf and near-shore limestones that contain numerous fossils (including scallops, clams, and snails), as well as massive reefs formed by now extinct rudistids (relatives of oysters). Tracks formed when dinosaurs roamed vegetated tidal marshes are visible in several areas of the Hill Country.

West of the Precambrian-Paleozoic complex in Texas—and extending south into Mexico—is a broad outcrop of Lower Cretaceous limestones. Rocks within this outcrop band are sometimes referred to as Edwards and associated limestones. They are largely dense and relatively pure limestones that were deposited in a broad, marine-shelf environment. The depth of the water over the shelf was not uniform, varying from very near sea level to a deeper basin in southwest Texas and extending into Mexico. The Mexican extension of this area is both structurally and stratigraphically more complex than the Texas area (Humphrey 1956).

The northern end of the Edwards Plateau is a geological transition between the plateau and the High Plains (Gould 1969). In this transition area, the Edwards Limestone is covered by surface deposits of Pleistocene cover sand with numerous isolated playa deposits.

The eastern edge of the High Plains of Texas and Oklahoma is geologically characterized by a narrow outcrop band of red and reddish brown Triassic-Permian sandstones, siltstones, shales, and evaporites, generally referred to as "redbeds." The readily eroded redbeds are exposed in deep canyons and draws where streams have stripped away the overlying Quaternary caprock characteristic of the High Plains.

Climate

The climate in the Rio Grande turkey's range varies from tropical in Mexico to continental in Kansas. The temperatures recorded throughout the Rio Grande's range show a much wider variation than the rainfall, which is from 38 to 90 centimeters (15 to 35 inches). Temperatures have ranged from −35 degrees Celsius (−32 degrees Fahrenheit) in Garden City, Kansas, to 48 degrees Celsius (120 degrees Fahrenheit) in Altus, Oklahoma. The mean January temperature varies from 19 degrees Celsius (66 degrees Fahrenheit) in Tampico, Mexico, to −4 degrees Celsius (25 degrees Fahrenheit) in Amarillo, Texas. The mean July temperature varies from 30 degrees Celsius (86 degrees Fahrenheit) in Del Rio, Texas, to 23 degrees Celsius (74 degrees Fahrenheit) in Clayton, New Mexico. The growing season varies from 365 days in Tampico, Mexico, to 174 days in Garden City, Kansas. The date of the last frost ranges from rare in Tampico, Mexico, to April 25 in Clayton, New Mexico, and Garden City, Kansas (Table 2).

Forest and Range Types

The range of the Rio Grande turkey described in 1967 (Glazener 1967:453) was very similar to its original state (Schorger 1966:43, 49). It extended from northern Veracruz and southern San Luis Potosi to Nuevo Leon, Tamaulipas, and parts of Coahuila in Mexico to eastern New Mexico, western Oklahoma, and southern Kansas in the United States (Figure 1). South to north, the range extended at least 1,930 kilometers (1,200 miles) from latitude 20° to latitude 37° 30′, but nowhere was it more than about 650 kilometers (400 miles) wide—longitude 96° 30′ to longitude 104°.

The Rio Grande turkey occupies plains grasslands, shinnery, prairie, oak-hickory, oak-pine, piñon-juniper,

Table 2. Temperature (degrees Celsius) data points within the range of the Rio Grande turkey (Glazener 1967).

State	Station	Average January	Average July	Average frost date Last	Average frost date First	Growing season days
Tamaulipas	Tampico	19	28	Rare and irregular		365
Nuevo Leon	Linares	15	27	Feb 10	Dec 2	295
Texas	Brownsville	16	29	Jan 30	Dec 26	330
	Corpus Christi	14	28	Jan 26	Dec 27	335
	Del Rio	11	30	Feb 22	Nov 29	280
	San Angelo	8	29	Mar 25	Nov 9	229
	Amarillo	−4	25	Apr 11	Nov 2	205
New Mexico	Tucumcari	3	26	Apr 16	Oct 27	194
	Clayton	1	23	Apr 25	Oct 21	179
Oklahoma	Altus	5	29	Mar 28	Nov 9	226
	Woodward	2	28	Apr 12	Oct 27	198
	Boise City	1	25	Apr 20	Oct 25	184
Kansas	Pratt	1	27	Apr 17	Oct 23	189
	Garden City	−1	26	Apr 25	Oct 26	174

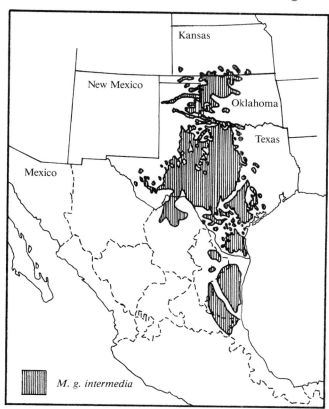

M. g. intermedia

Figure 1. Currently occupied range, within the original distribution, of the Rio Grande turkey (modified from Glazener 1967).

Texas savanna, and southwestern shrubsteppe forest and range types of Garrison et al. (1977). These types, in the descriptions that follow, will be related geographically to the ecoregions of Gould (1975).

Plains grasslands. The plains grasslands occur in the High Plains and Rolling Plains ecoregions of Texas and in western Oklahoma and southern Kansas, all of which are part of the Great Plains area of the United States. The area is approximately 50 percent each of rangeland and cultivated crops. The primary use of the rangelands is grazing by cattle. Turkey habitat is principally limited to rangeland and its border zone along cultivated land. Predominant woody vegetation on upland areas is honey mesquite, lotebush, redberry juniper, narrow-leaved yucca, and skunkbush. In drainages, eastern cottonwood, plains cottonwood, American sycamore, salt cedar, and sugar hackberry predominate. Important grasses are little bluestem, buffalo grass, grama, sandbur, sand dropseed, and three-awn. Common forbs are bladderpod, scarlet globe mallow, and wild buckwheat.

Shinnery. Turkey range in this forest and range type occurs in upland sandy sites along the Canadian River in Oklahoma and Texas and the Cap Rock Escarpment between the High Plains and Rolling Plains ecoregions of Texas. The primary land use is cattle grazing. The most abundant woody plants in this area are honey mesquite, sand shinnery oak, narrow-leaved yucca, and sand sagebrush. Among grasses, little bluestem, side oats grama, three-awn, and sandbur prevail. Important forbs include common sunflower, pepperweed, and goatweed.

Prairie. This type occurs in disjunct locations in the Cross Timbers and Prairies, Blackland Prairie, and Gulf Prairies and Marshes ecoregions of Texas and in northwestern Oklahoma and southern Kansas. Most suit-

able soils are under cultivation, but many cattle ranches remain. Prairie is marginal as turkey habitat except where it has been invaded by woody vegetation. Woody invaders include honey mesquite, post oak, blackjack oak, Hercules'-club, elm, huisache, and live oak. Big bluestem, little bluestem, yellow Indian grass, and Scribner's dicanthelium are common grasses. Common forbs are western ragweed, pepperweed, and rose-ring gaillardia.

Oak-hickory. This type occurs in the Post Oak Savanna, Blackland Prairie, and Cross Timbers and Prairies ecoregions of Texas. Most suitable soils are under cultivation. But extensive wooded areas occur in the east, and extensive woodland-savanna areas occur in the west. The principal use of rangeland-woodland areas is grazing by domestic livestock, predominantly cattle. As the name implies, woody vegetation is dominated by a complex of oaks and hickories, but other common species are American and cedar elm, dogwood, southern wax myrtle, American sycamore, honey mesquite, and yaupon. Common herbaceous species are little and silver bluestem, tall dropseed, Canada wild rye, Texas winter grass, tick clover, beggar-ticks, and Texas croton.

Oak-pine. Rio Grande turkeys occupy this forest type only in the Lost Pines area in Bastrop County in the Post Oak Savanna ecoregion of Texas and in central Coahuila and Nuevo Leon, Mexico. The principal land use is cattle ranching. Woody vegetation typical of the area in Texas is loblolly pine, eastern red cedar, post and blackjack oak, American elm, dogwood, and yaupon. Typical herbaceous vegetation of the area in Texas is silver bluestem, tall dropseed, smut grass, Canada wild rye, Texas croton, rose-ring gaillardia, and Texas paintbrush. In the Mexican range, woody vegetation in this forest and range type includes a complex of oaks (principally Emory, gray, and wavy-leaved). Mexican piñon, limber pine, Texas persimmon, guajillo, and yucca. Characteristic herbaceous species include side oats grama, tobosa, buffalo grass, muhly, plains blackfoot, zexmenia, and verbena.

Piñon-juniper. This forest and range type overlaps Rio Grande turkey range in the southern Post Oak Savanna, eastern and southern Edwards Plateau, and one location in Brewster County in the Trans Pecos Mountains and Basins ecoregions of Texas. The principal land use is ranching: cattle, sheep, and goats. The area has a complex of junipers (principally ashe and redberry), live oak, honey mesquite, pecan, American sycamore, cottonwood, and cedar elm. Common herbaceous species include silver and little bluestem, side oats grama, bush muhly, three-awn, Maximilian sunflower, bluebonnet, and zexmenia.

Texas savanna. This forest and range type occurs in the South Texas Plains and Edwards Plateau ecoregions. The land area is used principally for sheep, goat, and cattle ranching. Honey mesquite is, by far, the most abundant woody plant. But live oak, blackbrush, guajillo, ceniza, granjeno, Texas persimmon, and whitebrush are common to locally abundant. Herbaceous vegetation typical of the area is little bluestem, three-awn, buffalo grass, hooded windmill grass, thin paspalum, western ragweed, plains blackfoot, dozedaisy, ragweed parthenium, and slender vervain.

Southwestern shrubsteppe. This forest and range type occurs in the Trans Pecos and the southwestern extremity of the Edwards Plateau ecoregions of southwest Texas. It also occurs in northern and eastern Coahuila, Mexico. The principal land use is cattle ranching. Turkey range in this type, west of the Pecos River in Texas and in Coahuila, is typified by a woody vegetation cover of tarbush, creosote bush, hackberry, Emory oak, western soapberry, Texas black walnut, redberry and ashe juniper, guayacan, and honey mesquite. East of the Pecos River in Texas, the prominent features in turkey range are live oak, pecan, redberry and ashe juniper, and honey mesquite. Typical herbaceous plants are tobosa grass, black and side oats grama, bush muhly, curly mesquite, two-leaved senna, one-seed croton, western ragweed, verbena, and ragweed parthenium.

Since 1967, the Rio Grande turkey's range has expanded to include most of Oklahoma west of Highway 69 and western Kansas to the Nebraska border. In addition, these birds have been transplanted into Africa, California, Colorado, Cuba, Hawaii, Idaho, Iowa, central New Mexico, North and South Dakota, Oregon, Utah, Washington, and Wyoming. The long-term prospects of the birds in these new locations are unclear. Some apparently have become established, some have not, some have not existed long enough to determine, and some apparently are hybridizing with other existing or introduced subspecies. Therefore, this chapter will focus on the Rio Grande turkey in its original range.

HABITAT RELATIONSHIPS

Roosts

Winter roost characteristics. When selecting winter roost sites, Rio Grande turkeys apparently choose the tallest available trees without regard for species. Across the range of the Rio Grande subspecies, the birds use a wide variety of tree species. The most common ones, however, seem to be live oak, hackberry, pecan, cedar elm, cottonwood, and willow. There seems to be no preference between live and dead trees, but most species used are deciduous. The average height of roost trees in Texas and Oklahoma is about 12 to 13 meters (40 to 43 feet), with a range of about 8 to 14 meters (26 to 47 feet) (Crockett 1973, Haucke 1975). Roost trees have large crowns with spreading, horizontal branches about 2.5 to 5 centimeters (1 to 2 inches) in diameter.

Winter roost sites are usually by a stream or in a deep valley (Thomas et al. 1966, Cook 1973). Crockett (1965) suggested that permanent water was important in site selection. But data from Haucke (1975) and Crockett (1973) indicate that tree height was more important. The water correlation is probably spurious because trees along watercourses tend to be taller. Furthermore, some winter roost sites are great distances from watercourses, valleys, or both.

There is an approximately 3,885-square-kilometer (1,500-square-mile) intrusion of coastal sands in Kenedy and Brooks counties in south Texas, which has no natural drainages or natural permanent water. The area has a dense population of wild turkeys—up to 25 per square kilometer (65 per square mile)—that exhibits a strong winter roost concentration and seasonal shift phenomenon (Beasom 1970). The roosts are made up almost entirely of an overstory of live oaks in groves of several hundred to several thousand trees. Haucke (1975) re-

Typical mesquite summer roost tree for hens with young poults, Live Oak County, Texas. *Photo by S. Beasom.*

ported the average distance to permanent water in this area (available at windmills) was about 900 meters (984 yards).

Summer roost characteristics. Some Rio Grande turkeys, particularly gobblers, use winter roosts throughout the year. In contrast, nesting hens and hens with preflight poults roost on the ground, where they are particularly vulnerable to predation. Cook (1972) described nesting cover and the severity of nest predation, but no data are available on the relationship between cover and predation. Considering the uniformly high rate of early deaths (68 to 74 percent) for eastern turkeys while ground roosting (Glidden and Austin 1975, Everett et al. 1980, Speake 1980, Speake et al. 1986), we can infer that losses to Rio Grande turkeys are similar.

No information is available on early aboveground roosting habits of Rio Grande turkeys. In south Texas, Rio Grandes began roosting in trees at about 2 weeks old (S.L. Beasom personal observations). Trees selected were invariably mesquites, and perches were horizontal limbs about 2 to 3 meters (6 to 9 feet) above ground. The birds rarely used the same tree more than 1 to 3 nights. By 4 weeks of age, poults are strong flyers, and they begin to roost in taller trees—usually hackberries in south Texas. One hen with 9 poults 4 weeks old was observed ascending to a power line support to roost. The support was about 15 meters (50 feet) high, and on this occasion only the hen and 5 poults were successful in reaching the perch. The 4 other poults roosted together in a nearby mesquite. For about 30 days thereafter, the entire group roosted together on the power line support.

Man-made roosts. Where suitable roost trees are scarce or absent, Rio Grande turkeys will readily roost on man-made structures. This phenomenon has been re-

ported in at least 3 locations in south Texas (Haucke 1975). On the Santa Gertrudis Division of the King Ranch in Kleberg County, turkeys commonly roost on power lines and their supports and occasionally use windmill towers and oil storage tanks. On the Laureles Division of the King Ranch in Nueces County, the birds commonly roost on windmill towers, corrals, and little-used camp houses. On both areas, trees taller than about 6 meters (20 feet) are rare. Matagorda Island has no trees, and turkeys use artificial roost structures, power lines, and wooden observation towers.

In a relatively treeless expanse of west Texas, Kothmann (1971) and Kothmann and Litton (1975) reported extensive roosting on power lines, power line supports, windmill towers, and oil tanks. In fact, the birds often roost at such high densities on power lines in the region that they become a nuisance to utility companies. Schorger (1966:168) reported that Rio Grandes in Oklahoma frequently roost on power lines.

Food Habits

Male and female Rio Grande turkeys, regardless of age, have similar diets. So reports on their food habits generally focus on aggregate consumption. Beasom and Pattee (1978), however, found a significantly higher intake of snails and snail shells by laying hens than by prelaying or postlaying hens or gobblers.

Although it is popularly believed that young poults eat proportionally more insects than do other turkeys, the only available evidence (S.L. Beasom personal files) is not supportive. Examination of the crop contents of 18

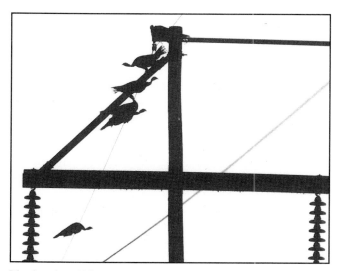

Rio Grande gobblers preparing to roost on power line and support, Kleberg County, Texas. *Photo by H. Lieck.*

poults (4 to 12 weeks old) and 51 hens collected May through July 1968 and 1970 to 1972 from 2 areas on the King Ranch in Kleberg and Kenedy counties, south Texas, revealed no significant difference in the relative amounts of insects (hens 24.5 percent, poults 28.9 percent) versus vegetation (hens 75.5 percent, poults 71.1 percent). It is significant that this period included years of above-average rainfall (1968 and 1972) and below-average rainfall (1970–71). Obviously, this evaluation does not provide insight into diet during the first month of life of the poults. Such data remain unavailable.

Since the Rio Grande turkey lives across such a divergent area, available data on diets are evaluated regionally in this chapter. In addition, seasons differ markedly. So, when data permit, regional evaluations are by season. Some reports are almost anecdotal, but they are nonetheless important to an overall understanding of the bird's diet.

South Texas. In this region, grass and flat sedge seeds generally predominate in the spring and summer diets (Table 3). Fruits and seeds of woody plants begin to appear in diets in appreciable amounts in summer and continue in importance through fall. Forb seeds generally are eaten all year, but their greatest contribution to the diet is in fall and winter. Green vegetation (foliage of forbs and grasses) also is eaten in all seasons, but its primary importance seems to be during winter and spring, when fruits and seeds are scarcest. Animal matter (principally insects) is universally important to turkeys in this region in all seasons. During egg laying, hens seem to seek out snails to fulfill an increased demand for calcium in the shell-formation process. Beasom and Pattee (1978) found that laying hens consumed about 9 times more snails than either prelaying or postlaying hens.

The most important species of grasses and grasslike plants for turkeys seem to be those with clustered seed heads or large seeds that the bird can strip to quickly collect large quantities. These include paspalums, bristle grasses, windmill grasses, signal grasses, panic grasses, and flat sedges.

Among mast-producing species, live oak is widely regarded for its importance to turkeys. In south Texas, however, mast production is erratic and its distribution is limited. Sugar hackberry and honey mesquite have a wider distribution and more regular mast crops. Locally important mast producers are lime prickly ash, prickly pear, granjeno, anaqua, bumelia, persimmon, mustang grape, and bluewood.

Forbs and half-shrubs important as mast producers are lantana, ground-cherry, croton, milk pea, wild tobacco, false dandelion, indigo bush, and euphorbias.

Edwards Plateau and Rolling Plains, Texas. In the western Edwards Plateau and eastern Rolling Plains vegetation area (Gould 1975), more overlap exists in the

Table 3. Rankings of the foods of highest use by Rio Grande turkeys in south Texas, as calculated from seasonal food habit studies of Beck and Beck (1955), A; Pattee (1977), B; Beasom (personal files), C; and Glazener (1945), D. (Ties were assigned equal ranks.)

Food item	Spring[a]		Summer		Fall		Winter	
	A	B	A	C	A	D	A	B
green matter	5	5	2		2		1	1
paspalum	2	2		5	9	5		
animal matter	1	1	5	2	5	2	5	6
signal grass	3	6	4	4				
bristle grass	4		12	1	15		4	
lantana	6	11		14		5	9	
windmill grass	7	12	12	3			6	7
wild tobacco	7	13					8	3
panic grass	8	7	8	6				
flat sedge	12	4	10	7			7	
croton			6	10	4	1		8
oak acorns		9	11		1	3		13
honey mesquite	5		3		10			
false dandelion							3	4
euphorb	10	10						5
ground-cherry	11	3				6		11
milk pea		8				4		2
prickly pear			12		6		2	
hackberry	13		1		7			
grape			7	14				
lime prickly ash			8		13			
groundsel	9						10	
crabgrass				11	3			
granjeno				8				
condalia					11			
palafoxia			9		12			
coreopsis							5	
beggar-tick							10	
polytaenia								12
pinnate tansy mustard								10
smallflower corydalis								9
Texas virgin's bower				9				
yellow wood sorrel				13				
buffel grass				12				
Texas grass					8			
dropseed		14						
leatherweed					14			
sida								14
stiffstem flax				15				

[a] Spring = March–May, summer = June–August, fall = September–November, and winter = December–February.

Rio Grande's seasonal use of major plant groups (Table 4). Again, grasses, such as Texas cup grass and panicums, make up a substantial part of spring and summer diets. Other items continue important through fall (bristle grasses and white tridens) and winter (rescue grass and little barley).

Similarly, some woody plants (honey mesquite and pecan) provide substantial food to the turkeys in summer and fall. Other woody plants are eaten heavily through winter (tasajillo and bumelia) and spring (skunkbush and prickly pear).

Seeds, fruits, or tubers of some forbs (silverleaf nightshade, ground-cherry, wild onion, milk vetch, and

Croton (goatweed) is an important turkey food throughout the Rio Grande's range. *Photo by H. Lieck.*

Table 4. Rankings of the foods of highest use by Rio Grande turkeys in the Rolling Plains and Edwards Plateau of Texas as calculated from studies by Quinton et al. (1980), A and Litton (1977), B. (Ties were assigned equal ranks.)

Food item	Spring[a] A	Spring B	Summer A	Summer B	Fall A	Fall B	Winter A	Winter B
animal matter	1	1	1	1	4	1		5
bristle grass	2		5	8	6	9		
Texas cup grass	3		9					
bumelia	4		5	5	7	4		6
skunkbush	4		6					
prickly pear	5		2	4	5			
white tridens	6	3	4	6	2	5		
tasajillo			3			3		10
wild onion			10		3	8		11
rescue grass		2		3		2		1
ground-cherry		7		9		10		
filaree						7		4
silverleaf nightshade	6		6					
honey mesquite			8			11		
pecan			10		1			
sand dropseed			10			10		
lotebush	4							
bladderpod								3
panic grass	13			2				
little barley	9			10				
hackberry	10					6		
milk vetch	8					8		2
croton				7				
littleleaf sumac			7					
squirreltail grass	7							
grama	6							
plantago								7
juniper							8	
walnut			10					
pigeonberry						12		
wild mercury			10					
ephedra								9
gaura		5						
agarita		6						
green matter		11						
catnip noseburn		12						
tobosa grass								12
evening primrose								13
broomweed						12		

[a] Spring = March–May, summer = June–August, fall = September–November, and winter = December–February.

filaree) are eaten heavily by turkeys in spring, summer, or fall. The bulk of the winter diet consists of green vegetation from rescue grass, milk vetch, bladderpod, and filaree.

Reports from the central Edwards Plateau vegetational area (Gould 1975), often referred to as the heart of the Rio Grande turkey range (Walker 1954), list major foods as follows:

(1) Acorns, sumac berries, cedar elm seeds, animal matter, and greens (Walker 1941);

(2) Grasses for year-round food, and trees and woody plants as the principal source of food from November to February (Blakey 1944b);

(3) Acorns, sumac and juniper berries; seeds of elm, hackberry, and grasses (Taylor 1951);

(4) Seeds of panic grass, grama, dropseed, and paspalum; fruits of southern dewberry, grape, prickly pear, and tasajillo; acorn, elm, hackberry, and pecan mast; sumac and juniper berries; greens of winter grasses and forbs (Walker 1951).

Nutritional considerations. An evaluation of the relative importance of any food item, although important in general terms, should be based on more than traditional tabulations of volume or weight. Items that make up a large proportion of the biomass in the diet but are relatively low in nutritional value may be overemphasized. And foods that are relatively low in biomass but highly nutritious may be underemphasized. For example, Pattee and Beasom (1981) found that vegetation made up about 50 percent of the diet of Rio Grande turkey hens in late April but contributed only 20 percent of the crude protein intake, 5 percent of the crude calcium intake, and 18 percent of the crude phosphorus intake.

A food may be relatively high in one nutrient but low in others. In March, hoary milk pea made up 27 percent of the total protein, 7 percent of the total calcium, and 21 percent of total phosphorus; Pennsylvania pellitory comprised 4 percent of total protein, 20 percent of total calcium, and 8 percent of the total phosphorus (Pattee 1977, Pattee and Beasom 1981). Other foods may be important sources of all 3 nutrients. In February, pepperweed made up 21 to 26 percent of the total intake of protein, calcium, and phosphorus; in March, wild tobacco made up 17 to 23 percent of the total intake of these nutrients.

Animal matter (insects and snails) collectively provides much higher amounts of protein, calcium, and phosphorus than do plants. But there are dramatic variations. For example, in April, insects make up 39 to 68 percent of the total intake of protein and 32 to 62 percent of the total intake of phosphorus but less than 1 percent of the calcium. In contrast, snails made up 58 to 94 percent of the calcium but only 3 to 12 percent of the protein and 4 to 20 percent of the phosphorus.

Pattee (1977) and Pattee and Beasom (1979) suggested that adequate (for reproduction) levels of protein, calcium, phosphorus, and essential amino acids could be acquired from only 2 sources: (1) insects; or (2) prepared foods (poultry laying pellets). Their work demonstrated that in years of below-average rainfall, the use of highly nutritious commercial turkey laying pellets can boost the turkey reproductive rate nearly 300 percent above the rate on unfed areas.

Traditional supplements such as corn and grain sorghum are probably not as effective. They contain no more than half of the protein, calcium, and phosphorus needed for reproductive development of turkeys (National Research Council 1971).

Supplementation with pellets has not been tested in years of above-average rainfall, but previous work (Beasom 1973) suggests that it would be much less effective. In years of favorable weather, the nesting season is naturally early and prolonged, and virtually all hens nest under favorable conditions.

Supplementation is effective when it results in (1) an earlier start of nesting (presumably leaving more time for possible renesting); (2) a greater proportion of hens nesting; and (3) a longer nesting season (presumably because of a greater tendency to renest). Such supplemental feeding apparently does not affect clutch size or poult survival.

The work of Beasom and Pattee (1980) showed a strong degree of predictability on whether a year would result in high or low turkey productivity (presumably because of nutritional relationships). Apparently climatic conditions in late summer and early fall have more impact on the turkey reproductive success of the following spring than do conditions during that spring. The investigators determined that 97.3 percent of the variabil-

ity in annual rate of turkey productivity on the Santa Gertrudis Division of the King Ranch was explainable by a model composed of (1) soil moisture storage the previous August; (2) combined total precipitation for the previous September and October; and (3) total precipitation for the current March. Similarly, 98.3 percent of the variability in annual rate of turkey productivity on the Encino Division of the King Ranch—about 22 kilometers (13.8 miles) farther south and on a different soil type—was explainable by a model composed of (1) combined total precipitation the previous August and September; (2) soil moisture storage in the previous September; and (3) soil moisture storage in the current May. So in south Texas, at least, a manager can plan a supplemental feeding program to enhance turkey reproductive success only if necessary and well in advance. For example, if August-to-October rainfall is well below average, managers there should plan to supplement between February and mid-May.

Water Relationships

The dependence of the Rio Grande wild turkey on surface water has been pointed out in many early historical accounts (Glazener 1967:483). Whether because of the water or the taller roost trees only along streams and river bottoms, turkeys were generally found there. Lea (1957:302) stated that in the early days of the Santa Gertrudis Division of the King Ranch in south Texas (ca. 1850), turkeys were found in numbers only along the wooded banks of Santa Gertrudis Creek. Some authors have reported that the bird's important winter roost sites are strategically near to or over water (Thomas et al. 1966, Cook 1973, Crockett 1973).

It is popularly believed that on the semiarid ranges inhabited by Rio Grande turkeys, the birds must drink every day (Walker 1951, 1954; Schorger 1966:177). This belief, however, has not been proved scientifically.

Nest-Site Selection

Rio Grande turkeys apparently select nest sites that have good concealing cover and are relatively near water. Glazener (1959) suggested that a drastic reduction in ground cover discourages turkey nesting. In the Edwards Plateau, where grazing pressure is often high, there is a disproportionate selection of roadside rights-of-way for nesting (Walker 1949a) because of more adequate cover. Cook (1972) found 87 percent of nests in cover taller than 45.7 centimeters (18 inches). Nests are primarily within 0.4 kilometers (0.25 miles) of permanent water in herbaceous cover or in woody cover that has a screening of

Nest site of Rio Grande hen in seacoast bluestem base cover in lightly grazed rangeland, Live Oak County, Texas. *Photo by S. Beasom.*

herbaceous vegetation or vines (Cook 1972, Ransom et al. 1987). Commonly associated cover plants include little bluestem, Canada wild rye, Texas winter grass, Johnsongrass, sunflower, Texas virgin's bower, buffalo gourd, granjeno, agarita, persimmon, and spiny aster.

Such nest sites probably are selected over less concealed ones because of improved survival and more favorable climatic conditions (Beasom 1970). Geiger (1950:230–240) reported that vegetation cover resulted in (1) reduced temperature extremes; (2) higher relative humidity; and (3) reduced wind movement at the ground surface.

Francis (1968) suggested for ring-necked pheasants that nesting success was negatively affected by high potential evapotranspiration (a function of temperature) and high temperature of eggs from direct exposure to the sun or from high air temperature. Both factors were affected by the amount of herbaceous ground cover. In south Texas, Beasom (1973:134) noted a similar relationship between wild turkey productivity and herbaceous cover. Although no cause-and-effect relationship was established, he found a direct correlation among years and

study areas between the amount of vegetative cover and turkey reproductive success. In years of above-average rainfall, in which the cover index was high, reproductive success was about 500 to 700 percent greater than in dry years, in which the index was low.

Seasonal Habitat Use

Winter. In most places within their range, Rio Grande turkeys exhibit a winter flocking behavior (Thomas et al. 1966, 1973). Although usually segregated by sex and age classes, the birds concentrate at winter roost sites and tend to be relatively sedentary, rarely traveling more than 1.6 to 3.2 kilometers (1 to 2 miles) from it (Watts 1969, Thomas et al. 1973). Because these roosts tend to be in riparian (waterside) habitats, most of the birds' winter activities occur there and on associated slopes and nearby uplands. In the Edwards Plateau, turkeys spend much of their time—especially in late winter—in juniper brakes in draws and on associated slopes. The dense juniper apparently provides excellent thermal

Traditional riparian winter roost site in the Rio Grande Plains, Texas. *Photo by D. Wilson.*

Ideal habitat is a combination of wooded riparian zones, upland savanna, and small agricultural fields. *Photo by J. Dickson.*

Shelterbelts in agricultural areas are used extensively by turkeys during winter and enhance an area's habitat suitability. *Photo by J. Dickson, U.S. Forest Service.*

cover, and the rather stable berry crop provides a consistent food from about December to March (Walker 1951).

At one location in the Coastal Plains of south Texas, more than 60 percent of all winter turkey observations were in a riparian-woodland plant community, whereas riparian-savanna accounted for less than 5 percent (Baker 1979, Baker et al. 1980). Turkeys used riparian woodland—which had a woody plant density more than 150 times greater than on the riparian savanna—for roosting, loafing, and feeding. Mesquite-bristle grass, huisache-bunchgrass, and live oak-chaparral received approximately equal use, principally for feeding.

Spring. Most Rio Grande wild turkeys continue to use winter roost sites during early spring, but their attachment to a specific site gradually wanes. During March and April, many of the turkeys disperse from winter concentration sites to nesting areas. For mating activities, the birds begin to use areas that are more open (nonwooded). These places may be roads, pipeline and power line rights-of-way, mowed areas, disturbed sites, or areas with naturally short herbaceous vegetation. Baker (1978) recorded about 80 percent of hen and gobbler observations in mowed pastures—in which the herbaceous vegetation was about 10 to 20 centimeters (4 to 8 inches) tall—during this season. Large clearings are used more in this season than in any other.

Hens may disperse to distances of 40 kilometers (25 miles) or more, but gobblers do not move so far (Glazener 1967:470). In the Edwards Plateau, spring movement tends to be from riparian to upland habitats (Thomas et al. 1966, 1973). Distances moved may be as far as 41.6 kilometers (26 miles), with an average of 17.4 kilometers (10.9 miles). In Jim Hogg County in southern Texas, single hens were observed in very open mesquite prairie 24 to 32 kilometers (15 to 20 miles) west of the nearest live oak winter ranges. Gobblers, however, were never sighted there (G. Fuller personal communication: 1988). Watts (1968, 1969) and Baker (1979) reported that only hens dispersed from the Welder Wildlife Refuge in southern Texas. Watts further suggested that about half of the hens migrated and half were residents, spreading out over the refuge to nest. Hens that remained were observed primarily in habitats that afforded the best nesting cover (live oak-chaparral and mesquite-bristle grass). Gobblers tended to use open areas as the center of their activities throughout the spring. The disproportionate movements of hens suggests that (1) they require only a single insemination to fertilize their eggs; or (2) they travel long distances to be inseminated; or (3) their dispersal takes them to the vicinity of males from other winter roost sites.

Summer. In south Texas, turkey gobblers continue to use open areas for strutting in early summer but usually only for brief periods after leaving roosts and before returning to them. The gobblers spend most of the daylight hours feeding in open or wooded areas that contain good seed-producing grasses such as paspalums, bristle grasses, and signal grasses. During midday, they loaf in the shade of trees. Baker (1979) and Baker et al. (1980) reported that gobblers loafed primarily in riparian woodland habitat that had a dense overstory of hackberry trees and a relatively open understory. Gobblers also use groves of live oak with similar structure and even small (2 to 3 trees) groups of mesquites that have large canopies.

Hens with poults spend most of their time in areas that have abundant food-producing herbaceous vegetation. Bunchgrass seems to be preferred, especially by hens with poults less than 2 weeks old. These preflight poults hide in dense herbage when disturbed, and the hen temporarily leaves. Young poults probably would be especially vulnerable to predation without such cover. As poults age, the hen-poult groups begin to use areas with less dense herbaceous cover. They may travel into more-open feeding areas. Rarely, however, do they venture more than their flight distance from woody escape cover. In the High Plains of Texas, DeArment (1959) noted a propensity of hen-poult groups to use hay meadows, but the same groups also used mixed grass-shrub habitats.

During the early morning when vegetation is wet from dew, all sex and age classes—but especially hens and poults—frequent areas of sparse vegetation or bare ground. Roads or mowed rights-of-way seem particularly suited for these visits because the birds can feed along the edges while remaining relatively dry. In the Coastal Plains of south Texas, turkeys did not use a dense, brushy pasture until it was partially cleared with only live oaks and scattered, tall mesquites being retained. After clearing, hen-poult (8 to 12 weeks old) groups and loosely associated groups of hens and gobblers fed in this area daily throughout the summer (Baker 1979, Baker et al. 1980).

Fall. In fall, as mast ripens, turkeys increase use of wooded habitats. Turkeys on the Welder Refuge spent

Riparian habitat along the Devil's River, Val Verde County, Texas. *Photo by S. Beasom.*

Habitat of the Rio Grande turkey in Coahuila, Mexico. *Photo by J. Dickson.*

Mesquites and associated understory are used as loafing cover by Rio Grande turkeys in summer and early fall, Brooks County, Texas. *Photo by S. Beasom.*

most of the fall in riparian woodland habitat, where they fed extensively on hackberry mast (Baker 1979). Also during this period, dispersed birds of all sex and age classes began to form combined flocks and expand their movements. During late fall, there is a gradual return to winter concentration sites (Baker 1979), with gobblers tending to return earlier than hens or hen-poult groups.

HISTORICAL HABITAT IMPACTS AND ALTERATION

Brush

The first historical accounts of habitat within the original range of the Rio Grande turkey suggest the entire area was a virtually treeless prairie or savanna (Bonnell 1840, Bartlett 1854, McClintock 1930, Inglis 1964). Woody vegetation apparently occurred in noticeable densities only along watercourses (in prairie areas), in scattered groves of trees distributed at long intervals (in savannas), or in broken topography where it might receive the benefit of extra moisture or protection from fire.

Treeless prairie or vast spaces between wooded areas are of questionable value as turkey habitat. It is doubtful that turkeys would venture far from protective woody cover into such areas. The birds are ill-adapted for prairie life. They lack concealing coloration, and their large size could make it difficult for them to hide in grass from predators. In addition, for only short intervals can they run fast enough to elude coyotes or gray wolves (Schorger 1966:187). Their capacity for sustained flight is limited. Schorger (1966:54, 185, 387–388) cited numerous examples of humans, either on foot or on horseback, running down and capturing turkeys tired from flight. Other predators surely would be more efficient than humans in such capture attempts.

So it is not surprising that turkeys apparently occurred only in association with wooded areas of pristine prairie lands (Lea 1957:302, Gore 1973). Turkeys depend totally on trees for roosting and for escape from ground-dwelling predators. In summarizing the logbooks of 30 early travelers across southern Texas (late 17th century to early 20th century) Inglis (1964:90) said: "As expected, no turkeys were seen in locations where there were clear-cut comments about the complete or nearly complete lack of woody cover. However, birds were recorded in localities where there were mottes of brush in relatively open country and where conditions were classified as having 'moderate' amounts of brush based on the available descriptions. Even in these cases, it seems apparent that those birds observed were associated with river or creek bottoms."

In the High Plains of Texas and in western Oklahoma, turkeys apparently used prairie areas more than did birds farther south. Schorger (1966:55) reported observers seeing flocks of thousands of birds returning from the prairies to roosting areas on the Canadian River. It is likely that the birds here and elsewhere ranged onto prairie areas at least seasonally to forage. But since the farthest a turkey can fly in a single flight is about 1.6 kilometers (1 mile) (Schorger 1966:185), it is doubtful the birds would often venture much farther than that from protective woody cover.

Brush encroachment. The original range of the Rio Grande turkey experienced a dramatic increase in density of woody cover between the late 1600s and the late 1800s. Some naturalists thought woody species invaded the prairies from a distant source—that is, brought in by livestock (Price and Gunter 1942). More likely the woody species were always present and were held down by an external factor such as fire (Tharp 1926, Bogusch 1952, Johnston 1963). An evaluation of reports of the travels of Fernando del Bosque in 1675, Alonso de Leon in 1689 and 1690, and Teran de los Rios in 1691 (see Inglis 1964) confirm this belief. All the travelers reported seeing at least widely scattered, short brush throughout, and trees along watercourses, during their journeys.

An evaluation of the reports of the early explorers suggests extensive brush establishment and expansion from the early 1700s to the late 1800s (see Inglis 1964). This phenomenon seemed relatively slow until about the mid-1800s, when the rate apparently increased dramatically. Significantly, it was in the mid-1800s that the commercial livestock industry began in Texas. The only previous notable concentrations of livestock were at 3 locations: (1) the Spanish mission near San Antonio; (2) the Spanish mission near Goliad; and (3) along the lower Rio Grande (Lehmann 1969:9–17). Bray (1901) related the brush expansion to overgrazing, which reduced herbaceous material that can carry a fire. Historically, fires did less permanent damage to grass than to brush. The growth zone of grasses is at or below ground level, so it is relatively protected from the heat. In contrast, the growth zone for brush tends to be at the tips of branches, where fire's maximum temperatures usually occur. So brush tends to be killed by fire.

Brush expansion evidently was beneficial to turkeys in the Edwards Plateau. Walker (1949a:17) reported, "The history of the turkey population in Mason County indicated that turkeys were not abundant in early times when the hardwood vegetation was confined chiefly to stream courses. As the hardwoods encroached on the grasslands, following heavy livestock grazing and cessation of firing of the prairies by Indians, turkeys apparently increased." Ramsey (1958:16) chronicled a similar

Juniper encroachment has been extensive in the Edwards Plateau, Rolling Plains, and High Plains of Texas, as shown by this example from Sutton County. *Photo by S. Beasom.*

sentiment: "The tall grasses began to disappear and were replaced by the shorter grasses—cedar [juniper], shinoak, liveoak, persimmon, postoak, blackjack [oak], and other species. This change in vegetation actually improved turkey habitat, everything else being equal, since most of the encroaching species provided either food, roosting sites, cover, or all three for wild turkeys." Another report suggested that turkeys were confined to stream courses before live oak and juniper invaded the divide areas between watersheds of the Edwards Plateau (Anonymous 1945:19).

Brush control. By the early 1900s, brush expansion had advanced to the point that stockmen recognized it as an impediment to cattle production. It competed with grass. In Sutton County, Texas, Wiedenfeld and McAndrew (1968) noted that because of the brush, stocking rates had decreased from 125 to 50 animal units per 259 hectares (1 square mile [section]) between 1898 and 1948. In another report from central Texas, stocking decreased from 300 head per 259 hectares (square mile) in 1867 to not more than 50 by 1898 (Taylor 1951).

By the 1930s and 1940s, large-scale efforts to eliminate brush had begun. Initially, grubbing by hand, oiling with kerosene or diesel, bulldozing, and chaining received the most attention (Walker 1949a). These efforts evolved into a wide array of mechanical and chemical control methodologies over the next 30 or so years. By 1964, Smith and Rechenthin (1964:13) estimated that 12.1 to 14.2 million hectares (30 to 35 million acres) of brush had been treated in Texas. Between 1956 and 1977, about 0.6 million hectares (1.5 million acres) of rangeland were treated annually in the state by mechanical and chemical methods (Scifres et al. 1979).

Regardless of the control technique applied, most brush tends to regenerate. The regeneration may take

from about 3 to 30 years depending on the technique used and on climatic conditions immediately before and after treatment. In part because of the apparent invincibility of the brush and because of economic reality, a new philosophy of brush control emerged in the late 1970s. The early eradication philosophy gave way to brush management (Scifres 1979). The new rationale was to manage woody vegetation on rangeland so as to attain the maximum long-term benefit from all resources. This attitude—that brush should not be controlled just for the sake of control—indicates that some woody plant cover is not only tolerable in livestock production but also desirable.

Improved pastures. Brush-control practices commonly are followed by pasture reseeding. The reseedings frequently are with introduced species, and almost invariably they involve a single species. The most frequent used species are coastal bermuda, Klein grass, love grasses, buffel grass, Kleberg bluestem, and various Old World bluestems. How reseeding affects turkeys is unknown. If it is directly beneficial, it would be through providing nesting cover. The plant species typically used are not good food producers for wild turkeys. Turkeys may, however, be indirectly benefited by reseeding. Livestock tend to concentrate on improved pastures, thereby reducing grazing pressure on food-producing native plants.

Monocultures of introduced grasses are of marginal benefit to Rio Grande turkeys. *Photo by H. Lieck.*

Severe grazing (left) depletes nesting and brood cover, Wise County, Texas. *Photo by D. Huckabee, USDA Soil Conservation Service.*

Throughout the range of the Rio Grande turkey in Texas, a total of about 4.8 percent of the land area is currently in improved pastures (Anonymous 1981). These pastures typically return to native brush or native herbaceous species unless maintained by periodic brush control and fertilizer applications.

Relationships with Livestock

Grazing by domestic livestock can harm wild turkeys in several ways: (1) trampling of eggs; (2) causing nest abandonment; (3) increasing nest depredation; (4) altering nest microclimate; (5) influencing nest-site selection; (6) altering food availability; and (7) altering movement patterns. Overgrazing has been a major cause of habitat loss to Rio Grande turkeys in Mexico (Leopold 1948) and Texas (Gore 1973).

Trampling. Merrill (1975) theorized that the heavy concentration of livestock during grazing periods of rest-rotation systems greatly increased the probability of nest destruction by trampling. Bryant et al. (1981) were the

first to test this theory. Based on a hypothetical step density of cattle, they calculated a relative danger from trampling loss for turkey nests in pastures subject to 5 systems: (1) continuous; (2) 4-pasture deferred rotation; (3) high-intensity, low-frequency; (4) short duration; and (5) Savory grazing. They concluded that the relative danger of nest loss to trampling was similar under all systems examined, partly because cattle travel more in larger than in smaller pastures (Malechek and Smith 1976).

This hypothetical assessment was then partially tested in 2 field investigations. Koerth et al. (1983) found similar rates of trampling loss by cattle for simulated ground nests placed in (1) a continuously grazed pasture at 8.0 hectares (19.6 acres) per steer; and (2) a short-duration-grazed pasture at 5.3 hectares (13 acres) per steer.

Bareiss et al. (1986) found similar rates of loss for artificial nests of turkeys under 2 different continuously grazed (7.3 and 2.8 hectares [17.9 and 6.9 acres] per animal unit) and short-duration-grazed (4.5 and 2.8 hectares [11 and 6.9 acres] per animal unit) pastures. But under a maximum stock density of 0.4 hectares (1 acre) per animal unit (in the smaller grazing units of the pasture) a nest was trampled in one area, and the investigators speculated (p. 260) that this might serve as a hypothesis, "i.e., trampling losses may not be a management concern unless paddock density exceeds 0.4 ha[1 acre]/ AU."

Nest depredation. The extent that depredations are influenced by livestock grazing is widely reported in the literature. Blakey (1944a), Anonymous (1945), Walker (1949a), and Thomas and Green (1957) felt that heavy grazing predisposes turkey nests to depredation because of lack of cover. Taylor (1943) reported that conservative grazing would help provide improved nesting cover. If, however, only isolated locations of favorable cover (protected from grazing) are available for nesting, high predation rates can occur (Blakey 1944b, Ransom et al. 1987).

Baker (1979) found that different grazing systems had differing effects on the rate of depredation on simulated turkey nests. Multiple comparison tests showed that 4-pasture deferred-rotation and high-intensity, low-frequency treatments had similar nest survival rates and that survival on both was higher than on continuously grazed treatments.

Nest-site selection. Nest-site selection by turkeys seems to be inversely related to grazing pressure. Rio Grande hens usually select lightly grazed or ungrazed areas for nesting (Walker 1948). Merrill (1975) reported 58 percent of 70 nests in areas under complete rest from grazing, 17 percent in 4-pasture deferred-rotation pastures, and 25 percent in pastures under light, continuous grazing. Ransom et al. (1987) found all of 8 nests in areas excluded from grazing.

Herbaceous cover may, however, become too dense or too tall for appropriate nesting sites. In the second year after constructing an 11.2-hectare (27.7-acre) grazing exclosure where turkeys had not previously nested, Merrill (1975) found 4 nests—an incredible density of 1 nest per 2.8 hectares (7 acres). After the fifth year, however, turkeys no longer nested in the exclosure.

Although many other factors could be involved, a similar situation has occurred at 2 other locations. During a series of years (1968 to 1975) with above-average rainfall and light or no grazing, the standing crop of herbaceous vegetation increased dramatically and wild turkey populations declined from abundant to rare on the Rob and Bessie Welder Wildlife Refuge (W.C. Glazener personal communication: 1984) and on the Aransas National Wildlife Refuge (the late E.F. Johnson personal communication: 1984). On the Welder Refuge in 1968, Watts (1969) estimated 175 turkey hens were resident nesters, whereas by 1972, Smith (1977) accounted for only 6.

Area of use and foods. Very little information has been gathered on why wild turkeys use specific areas. Korschgen (1967) and Brown (1980) suggested that the area over which a turkey ranges will vary with food supplies. Certainly livestock grazing intensity affects turkey food availability, and Blakey (1944b) reported how heavy grazing (by goats and cattle) can result in progressive elimination of important mast-producing species such as sumacs, poison ivy, elbowbush, Texas persimmon, wild plum, honeysuckle, greenbrier, grape, catclaw acacia, Texas buckeye, Hercules'-club, wafer ash, dogwood, and hog plum. Schulz and Guthery (1987) found that short-duration grazing at 4.5 and 8.4 hectares (11 and 20.8 acres) per animal unit and continuous grazing at 7.3 hectares (18 acres) per animal unit had no differential effect on wild turkey home range. They concluded that the food supply for turkeys must have been similar under the 2 grazing regimes.

During 4 winter censuses in the Edwards Plateau, Walker (1948, 1949b) observed triple the number of turkeys in lightly grazed areas as in overgrazed areas. Yet it is apparent that some grazing is better for the birds than complete deferment. As suggested by Whisenhunt (1950), some sandy rangeland sites in south Texas produce abundant annual foods for turkeys though subjected to heavy seasonal (periodic) grazing.

Water Development

Water development for livestock probably has had a positive influence on the Rio Grande turkey throughout its range. To be sure, not all water development involves permanent supplies. But even those that are not permanent should facilitate the bird's exploitation of range resources. In the Edwards Plateau, Ramsey (1958) felt that the development of windmills and stock tanks enabled the birds to nest over a wider range. And a further testament: "It has been clearly demonstrated that water developments have helped to maintain the spread of the wild turkey population. . . . Wild turkeys were seldom seen on the higher elevations or 'divide country' before windmills and other watering devices were installed for livestock" (Anonymous 1945:29).

Glazener (1967:483) reported that creation of 9 ponds on the Welder Wildlife Refuge had a marked effect on distribution of turkeys, particularly nesting hens. A classic example of the same situation exists on the Norias Division of the King Ranch in Kenedy County, south Texas (Anonymous 1945:29, Schorger 1966:417). The area is part of the region McClintock (1930) referred to in 1846 as the "Wild Horse Desert" because it was devoid of surface water. He and another traveler (Bartlett 1854:520) gave accounts of wildlife seen, such as wild

Photo by S. Beasom.   *Photo by H. Hauke.*

The advent of windmills to provide a dependable water source in livestock tanks has been a positive factor for Rio Grande turkeys.

horses, deer, and pronghorns, but made no mention of wild turkeys. The area was acquired as ranchland in the 1860s. By the early 1900s permanent water—in troughs at windmills—was available within no more than about 3.2 kilometers (2 miles) in any direction. Lehmann (1957) reported that turkeys were rare on the area in 1912, but increases were "quite apparent" by 1920. By 1945, the turkey density had increased to about 8 birds per 12 square kilometers (21 per square mile).

Inundation by Lake Corpus Christi usurped this traditional winter roost site for Rio Grande turkeys. *Photo by H. Lieck.*

In contrast, reservoir development to create new water supplies and electrical power for the increasing human population has doubtless harmed turkeys. When new reservoirs fill, they inundate actual or potential roost sites and rich bottomland feeding sites (Gore 1973). When the Lake Mathis Reservoir filled, it inundated a traditional winter roost site of large live oak trees on the Twin Oaks Ranch in Live Oak County, Texas (L. Cartwright personal communication: 1988). Although there had been some variation from year to year, this roost historically had harbored about 300 turkeys. After the inundation, turkeys shifted to large willows along nearby creeks. But no permanent (traditional) sites have been established, and far fewer birds are involved.

Proliferation of such reservoirs has been staggering. In 1920, for example, Texas had about 500,000 acre-feet of reservoirs. By 1980, there were more than 53 million acre-feet of reservoirs in Texas (Figure 2) (Anonymous 1988). Although many of these reservoirs are in eastern Texas, outside the range of the Rio Grande turkey, the general pattern of reservoir increase holds true within the bird's range.

Farming

Row crop agriculture has had a substantial impact on the Rio Grande turkey, beginning in the latter 1800s and on into the early 1900s. Williams and Crump (1980:2) characterized this situation on much of the bird's range: ". . . cattle ranching dates to the 1870's, small areas of land were cultivated in the 1890's, and in

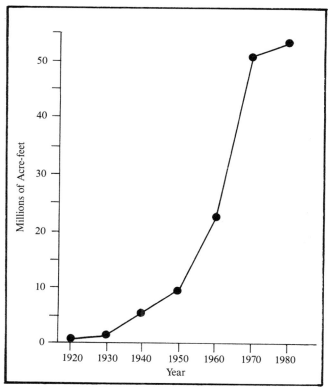

Figure 2. Proliferation of reservoir development in Texas, showing acrefeet of storage capacity (Anonymous 1988).

Rural homesites along riparian areas usurp important winter habitat. *Photo by J. Dickson, U.S. Forest Service.*

the early 1900's large areas of native grassland were converted to crops." About 26 percent of the original range of the Rio Grande turkey in Texas has been cleared for farming (calculated from Anonymous 1981). Because of the large scale of most farming activities, turkeys benefit little from them. Leopold (1948, 1959:270–272) reported that the Rio Grande birds were largely eliminated from their native range in Mexico by large-scale clearing of alluvial bottoms for farming. Where farmed areas are adjacent to woodland tracts, however, turkeys use—and doubtless derive some benefit from—small grains and clovers.

Human Encroachment

About 3.2 percent of the land area within the range of the Rio Grande turkey in Texas is occupied by towns, unincorporated communities, farm and ranch headquarters, industrial developments, mineral or oil excavation sites, roadways, or other developments associated with man's habitation (Anonymous 1981). Although data are unavailable, the remainder of the range in the other states occupied by these birds has been similarly affected.

Such developments doubtless have affected turkeys more than the involved area would suggest. For example, towns and rural homesites frequently are associated with riparian communities, which are often focal points for turkey activities. When the site (San Pedro Springs) of the present-day city of San Antonio, Texas, was discovered in 1709, it was described as ". . . a luxuriant growth of trees, high walnuts [pecans], poplars [cottonwoods],

Farmed areas adjacent to hedgerows or other woodland tracts provide usable turkey habitat. *Photo by S. Beasom.*

Highway 90, crossing Turkey Creek in Kinney County, has doubtless contributed to the abandonment by Rio Grande turkeys of an elm tree roost site at the crossing. *Photo by S. Beasom.*

Table 5. Species of roost trees, and locations in which used, for Rio Grande turkeys (Walker 1941; Crockett 1965, 1973; Glazener 1967; Haucke 1975).

Species	Location[a]
American elm	EP, WOK, CT
bald cypress	EP
black walnut	WOK
black willow	STX, EP, RP, WOK
blackjack oak	EP, CT
bur oak	WOK
cedar elm	STX, EP, CT
eastern cottonwood	CT, STX, EP, RP, HP, WOK
Emory oak	TP
honey mesquite	STX
juniper	EP, TP
live oak	STX, EP
netleaf hackberry	STX, EP, WOK
pecan	EP, RP, WOK, CT
plains cottonwood	HP, WOK, ENM
post oak	EP, CT
sugar hackberry	STX, EO, WOK, CT
sycamore	STX, EP, RP, HP, WOK, CT
Texas oak	EP
Texas walnut	EP, TP
western soapberry	STX, EP, TP, RP, HP, WOK

[a] CT = Cross Timbers, Texas; STX = south Texas; EP = Edwards Plateau, Texas; RP = Rolling Plains, Texas; HP = High Plains, Texas; TP = Trans Pecos, Texas; WOK = western Oklahoma; and ENM = eastern New Mexico.

elms and mulberries watered by a copious spring . . . . The river, which is formed by this spring, could supply not only a village but a city" (Inglis 1964:20). Since turkeys were common to the area then (Buckley 1911), and they are known to frequently roost in tall pecans, cottonwoods, and elms, it is likely that establishment and growth of the city resulted in a loss of important turkey habitat.

Roadway development probably also has hindered Rio Grande turkeys. Texas alone has 438,370 kilometers (273,981 miles) of developed roadways (Anonymous 1988), approximately half within the range of the Rio Grande turkey. This incredible network results in a myriad of stream crossings, many of which are in sight of trees that would otherwise be suitable roosting sites. Because turkeys lose their affinity for roosts that are frequently disturbed by humans, such trees are effectively lost as roosts.

MANAGEMENT RECOMMENDATIONS

Woody Cover

Woody plants are crucial to Rio Grande turkeys. The birds eat mast from at least 30 species, and they use at least 21 species for roosting (Table 5). They use wide-crown, high-canopy species for loafing cover and shade. Shrubs, half-shrubs, and some trees are used as nesting cover. Virtually all woody species are used, as appropriate, for escape cover.

Ironically, however, the primary land use within the range of the Rio Grande turkey is ranching. As the historical accounts mentioned, ranchers have selectively or—in most cases—indiscriminantly removed woody plants from rangeland to increase grass production for livestock. The degree of clearing recommended for livestock production is often not the most advantageous for turkeys. Walker (1951) reported several examples of extensive block clearing in the Edwards Plateau that eliminated cover and many important winter turkey foods. He further stated that turkeys may use some parts of the cleared areas as summer range, "but generally speaking, large blocks of cleared land are poor turkey habitat" (p. 15). Turkeys disappeared from one ranch in the Edwards Plateau where the rancher carefully protected all roost sites but cleared surrounding trees and shrubs (Glazener 1967:481).

Even though Rio Grande turkeys must have some woody cover, they do not thrive in dense, brushy areas or areas with extensive closed-canopy forests. Baker and Passmore (1979) reported that turkeys extensively used a partially brush-cleared area for which no pretreatment use was recorded. The grasses and forbs that increase after clearing portions of such areas increase the diversity and availability of foods for turkeys as well as livestock.

Low, thorny brush, such as prickly pear and agarita, can enhance nesting cover of Rio Grande turkeys. *Photo by S. Beasom.*

How much brush to leave untreated has received little study, but Walker and Springs (1952) and Litton (1977) suggested that 50 percent or more should be left to maintain turkey populations. Lehmann (1960) reported that up to 80 percent could be removed without detriment to wild turkeys on the King Ranch in south Texas. This report, however, must be interpreted with caution. This area had far less human disturbance than did most Rio Grande turkey ranges. Since these birds are strongly affected by human disturbance (Gore 1973), a ceiling of 50 percent on clearing seems more appropriate to the welfare of turkeys.

Given that turkeys and livestock can benefit from some brush treatments, the following guidelines are offered:

(1) Do not remove mast-producing food plants unless they are in extensive stands where some thinning would benefit other food-producing plants;
(2) Do not remove known roost trees;
(3) Do not use a root plow unless preparing a food plot, because its use results in a dramatic reduction in diversity of posttreatment regrowth (Fulbright and Beasom 1987);
(4) Create no opening greater than 0.8 kilometers (0.5 miles) across;
(5) Leave scattered trees and small stands on about half the treated area and blocks of brush with scattered openings on the remainder;
(6) If treated areas are to be reseeded, sow species that will provide both food and cover for turkeys as well as forage for livestock. A mixture of grasses and forbs is preferred. Recommended grasses are plains bristle grass, any of the panicums or paspalums, and sorghum almum. Recommended forbs are bush sunflower, milk pea, vetch, clover, Maximilian sunflower, Engelmann daisy, and Illinois or velvet bundle flower.

Grazing

Because Rio Grande wild turkeys are a product of rangelands, it is prudent to strive for a grazing management system that is mutually compatible with turkeys and livestock. It is human nature to try to select one best system. No *one* system, however, is likely to be best in all situations. Net economic returns from cattle grazed continuously are hard to beat with any system of deferment (Launchbaugh et al. 1978), but continuous grazing often results in range degradation (Merrill and Young 1954). The only continuous-grazing system that seems compatible with turkeys is light grazing, which is difficult to justify because of its low per-unit-area livestock production (Kothmann 1975).

High-intensity, low-frequency grazing seems good for turkey feeding areas but not nesting (Merrill 1975). This system, however, frequently results in low weaning weights of cattle and decreased calf crops, so it has thus become unpopular among producers (Bryant et al. 1981).

Although much remains to be learned, short-duration grazing also probably results in conditions adequate for turkey food production but not good for nesting. Bareiss et al. (1986) reported that short-duration grazing resulted in similar food production and nesting cover to areas grazed continuously. This finding is of questionable value to the birds, however, because earlier studies have not ranked continuously grazed areas highly in either food production or nesting cover for turkeys. Heitschmidt et al. (1987) also concluded that vegetation responded similarly in short-duration and continuously grazed areas.

Some investigators argue that rapid-rotation systems are most effective in grazing management where the rotation is not systematic. (A. Savory personal communication: 1981, C.A. Ball personal communication: 1988). It is conceivable that nonsystematic rotation also would benefit turkeys. Such an approach would result in a variety of vegetation effects and so an increased diversity for wildlife. In nonsystematic rotation, livestock would be rotated at differing rates. Some pastures may even be skipped periodically to enhance structural (physical) differences between pastures.

The 4-pasture deferred-rotation system (3 equal herds rotated through 4 equal pastures at 4-month intervals) seems well suited to livestock production and apparently also to turkey food production (Bryant et al. 1981). But the system is less suited for turkey nesting. Merrill (1975) recorded turkey nest densities nearly 4 times greater in areas excluded from grazing than in areas under this system. Although the 4-pasture deferred-rotation comes close, no one system exclusively results in high-quality range for domestic livestock and Rio Grande turkeys.

All things considered, it seems that herd stocking rate is at least as important as the grazing system, if not more so (Bryant et al. 1981). Therefore, we offer the following generic guidelines to favor turkey management under any grazing system:

(1) Provide grazing exclosures within any existing grazing system. Blakey (1944b) recommended that 40 to 200 hectares (100 to 500 acres) be excluded from grazing within each 1,200 to 2,000 hectares (3,000 to 5,000 acres) of rangeland for 24 months. An exclosure probably should be grazed every 4 to 5 years in drier locations of Rio Grande turkey range and every 2 to 3 years in the moister areas. The grazing should be restricted to July and August to permit regrowth prior to the following nesting season and to give the birds ample time for nesting.

The desirable vegetation height of exclosures is about 46 to 61 centimeters (18 to 24 inches). In addition, there should be adequate interspaces to permit movement of day-old poults to feeding habitats.

(2) Roadside or railroad rights-of-way or other fenced-out areas may provide an alternative to pasture exclosures in some locations, but they should not be depended upon entirely. Ring-necked pheasant populations have been increased 200 to 300 percent in parts of Illinois from roadside cover management (Warner and Joselyn 1986, Warner et al. 1987). Predation, however, can become a problem. The problem of nest depredation can become serious with all techniques that encourage turkey nesting in limited habitats. Ample evidence shows that predators are attracted to such sites. In Oregon, Haensley et al. (1987) observed depredation rates of ring-necked pheasant nests 4 times greater than elsewhere in strip-type habitats. Best (1986:308) referred to these areas as ecological traps, ". . . man-made areas that, on the basis of physical and/or vegetational characteristics, appear to be suitable habitats for nesting but which, by virtue of some confounding factor(s) (for example, brood parasitism, predation, human disturbance), result in population sinks." Of course, the more limited the nesting habitats are, the greater the problem likely will be. Some sort of predator control immediately before and during nesting would likely result in more turkeys under such circumstances. In south Texas, net turkey productivity has been increased about 100 percent by intensive predator control during February to June (Beasom 1973, 1974a).

Mowing of fenced-out areas should be delayed until July to minimize disturbance to nesting birds. The areas should then remain unmowed until the following July.

(3) Another technique to enhance nesting cover, where limited, is to plant or protect low, thorny brush such as agarita, lotebush, prickly pear, and tasajillo. These plants provide protection from grazing and permit nest-concealing herbaceous vegetation

to develop (Stoddard 1931, Walker 1949a, Moore 1972).

(4) Assuming that ungrazed areas are available, provide moderate grazing intensities on the remaining area to stimulate production and availability of food plants. Research has demonstrated that relatively heavy grazing pressure disproportionately favors turkey food plants such as one-seed croton and little barley (Correll and Johnston 1970), some panic grasses (Stubbendieck et al. 1982), and western ragweed and paspalum (Baker 1988).

Provision of Water

Water is important to Rio Grande turkeys. It is a focal point for their activities, and its availability apparently affects habitat use. Therefore, we suggest the following guidelines:

(1) Where possible, provide water in ground-level ponds or catchments (Lehmann 1957), as opposed to standard livestock water troughs. Ground-level waterings can be easily provided at windmills or other permanent water sources by attaching a drip-pipeline that extends out about 10 to 20 meters (33 to 66 feet), preferably creating a basin near some escape cover. If troughs must be used, assure that they remain full at all times—particularly during spring and summer, when poults are small. Low water levels in troughs become death traps to poults. They must perch on the edge and stretch downward to drink.

(2) Fence small, ground-level waterings to exclude livestock. Continued trampling will eliminate protective cover and can destroy the basins. Do not use net wiring unless crawls are created under it. Turkeys prefer to go under or through fences. Barbed wire fences with only 2 or 3 strands are preferred. The bottom wire should be about 46 centimeters (18 inches) above the ground, and it should be smooth (barbless).

(3) Where rotational grazing systems are used, maintain the water in deferred pastures.

Water supplied artificially is helping maintain the Rio Grande turkey in arid areas and during arid times. *Photo by J. Dickson.*

This shallow, concrete livestock trough in Terrell County, Texas, provides an excellent source of permanent water for Rio Grande turkeys. *Photo by S. Beasom.*

Turkey feeders are used extensively by Rio Grande turkeys. *Photo by W. Whitehead.*

(4) Where short-duration grazing is used, maintain fenced outwaters at least 0.4 kilometers (0.25 miles) from the main livestock watering facility. Prasad and Guthery (1986) found that turkeys rarely use water troughs at the centers of short-duration-grazed pastures.

(5) Where adequate subsurface moisture is unavailable and ground-level catchments provide the only source of water for livestock, fence part (preferably half) of it to prevent or defer grazing so that ground cover will be maintained.

(6) In arid areas where adequate water is unavailable or undependable, independent watering devices (gallinaceous guzzlers) can be constructed. These guzzlers are fashioned in a wide range of styles, but all have a rainfall-collecting surface and a storage tank.

Diet Supplementation

Some authors maintain that the provision of artificial feedstuff (corn, sorghum, wheat, or oats) for turkeys is detrimental because it reduces wildness and increases the likelihood of disease transmission (Walker 1949a, Glazener 1967:484). Others suggest that the practice will reduce the bird's natural dispersal tendencies (Taylor 1943; Jackson 1945; Walker 1949a; Taylor 1951; Thomas et al. 1966, 1973). There has been disagreement on whether supplementation will (Ramsey and Taylor 1942, Walker 1949a) or will not (Thomas et al. 1966,

1973) result in net population gains. Cox (1948) reported that turkey use of supplemental feed is affected by range condition. Under excellent conditions, wild turkeys may not use supplements. During droughts, they tend to use supplements a great deal. Reportedly, however, they have abandoned supplemented ranges (Walker 1951) under these conditions, presumably for lack of adequate cover. Regardless of potential problems, supplementation is extensively applied in Rio Grande turkey range with no obvious biological problems.

Where natural food supplies for Rio Grande turkeys are limited, either seasonally or yearlong, local populations likely could be stabilized or increased by a well-planned, biologically appropriate supplemental feeding program. Using the best information available, such a program would annually be as follows:

(1) July to January—Provide high-energy foods, such as grain sorghum or corn. These can be grown and left standing in food plots or provided at feed stations. Food plots have the advantage of also supplying some insects to the bird's diet but are subject to poor performance if rainfall is low or use by feral hogs and deer is heavy. Feeding stations sup-

plied with commercial grain provide a much more dependable—albeit perhaps more expensive—food supply. These stations can have grain broadcast on the ground or in feeders that usually are fenced or elevated to prevent loss of feed to, or damage by, other animals. Although amounts consumed can vary markedly, depending upon the supply of natural foods, 114 to 227 grams (0.25 to 0.50 pounds) per bird each day should be planned.

(2) February to April—If fall rainfall is well below average, provide poultry laying ration (at least 16 to 18 percent protein) or its equivalent, using the same guidelines as in No. 1. A small amount of whole-kernel corn can be included with the ration initially to facilitate the turkeys' consumption of the prepared ration. But the corn should be discontinued after a few days. Gallinaceous birds tend to eat to fulfill their energy requirements (Mellen et al. 1954), so the high-energy corn would deter the intake of an adequate amount of the high-protein laying ration.

Where calcium is deficient, supplementation of a calcium-rich substance, such as grit from oyster shells, could be beneficial. To help the birds find this grit, it should be placed on the ground near water sources or at established feed stations. Begin this supplementation in mid-March with 2,270 to 4,540 grams (5 to 10 pounds) at each site, replenishing as necessary through June.

(3) May to June—Provide a combination of grains and prepared ration. Food plots planted with grains can fulfill both needs if they attract insects. As previously indicated, however, plantings are subject to climatic vagaries. If a prepared ration is used, it should contain at least 20 percent protein (because of the needs of growing chicks).

Other considerations are the size of area to be supplemented and selectivity and economic efficiency of the feeding program. Rio Grande turkeys tend to be nomadic, often traveling extensively and occupying up to about 6,500 to 7,700 hectares (16,000 to 19,000 acres) annually (Traweek et al. 1983). On smaller areas, turkeys will visit surrounding properties, thus decreasing the efficiency of a feeding program. An alternative is a cooperative effort between adjoining neighbors.

FUTURE

The human population in the range of the Rio Grande turkey will continue to grow. Between 1930 and 1980, the number of people in Texas increased from 5.8 million to 14.2 million. The projection is 28 million to

Historic trends in diminishing size of land ownerships will hurt Rio Grande turkeys because of increased human activity. *Photo by S. Beasom.*

34 million by 2030 (Anonymous 1983). Most of the growth will be in urban situations, but this growth will substantially affect turkeys. Urban sprawl will continue to eat away at the quantity of turkey habitat, and the increased demand on natural resources will affect the quality of turkey habitat.

For the near future, at least on larger landholdings, there will probably be a trend toward more conservative land-use practices that consider the needs of wildlife as another renewable crop. As ownerships are split through inheritance, however, size of landholdings will decline. In addition, the trend by urbanites to buy rural lots or ranchettes will further diminish tract size, and potential impacts on turkeys will increase. As a general rule, management must intensify on smaller ownerships, to meet economic or recreational demands. Turkeys, because of their nomadic tendencies, will therefore be thrust into more human contact and less-suitable habitat. Where this sequence occurs, the birds will almost invariably disappear.

Brush encroachment on rangeland will continue. Some brushy areas will get minimum management, a condition that will generally favor turkeys. On other rangelands, however, the tendency to maximize livestock production will prevail. On these areas, large-scale brush removal and establishment of improved or tame grass pastures will be detrimental to turkeys.

Water development for human consumption will increase commensurate with continued population expansion. This development will result in continued inundation of turkey habitat and an associated reduction in local wild turkey populations.

Former turkey roost usurped by Interstate 37, Live Oak County, Texas. *Photo by S. Beasom.*

Roadway development has been and will continue to be a negative influence in turkey habitats. New road construction and widening or straightening of existing roads exact a cost in actual or potential roost trees where roads breach riparian corridors. Roost trees made visible from a well-traveled roadway, even if not destroyed, will be abandoned. Such a situation probably forces the birds to roost in less-desirable locations.

Expansion of farmed lands will continue, again to keep pace with an expanding human population. This trend will entail a conversion of some lands now classified as improved pastures, as well as a reclamation of some of the better soils now classified as brush-covered rangeland.

All of these factors will negatively affect Rio Grande turkeys. The total population will be reduced by an amount proportional to the amount of land taken out of rangeland and converted to some other highest and best use. This situation will result in an increased demand for the remaining turkey resource. So landholdings that continue to favor wild turkey production—whether because of an absence of arable land or otherwise—should realize an increased value of trespass rights to pursue the Rio Grande turkey for sport hunting.

Chapter 20

MERRIAM'S TURKEY

Harley G. Shaw
Research Biologist
Arizona Game and Fish Department
Phoenix, Arizona

Cheryl Mollohan
School of Forestry
Northern Arizona University
Flagstaff, Arizona

The Merriam's turkey is the race of the mountains in the southwestern United States. Its range, at the time of exploration by white settlers, included the ponderosa pine forests of Colorado, New Mexico, and northern Arizona (Ligon 1946). The range may have extended slightly into Oklahoma along the Cimarron River and at least into the Guadalupe (and possibly the Franklin) Mountains of Texas (Schorger 1966).

Within this historic range, the Merriam's subspecies was relatively isolated from other races of turkeys. It barely, and perhaps not at all, abutted the Rio Grande turkey to the east and the Gould's turkey to the south. This isolation, along with a lack of paleontological or archaeological evidence of modern wild turkeys in the Southwest before about A.D. 500, has led several workers to postulate that the Merriam's race is actually derived from birds imported by early Pueblo cultures (Mc-

Cusick 1986, Rea 1980, Hargrave 1970, Breitburg 1988). These writers suggest that the Merriam's subspecies was derived from the eastern turkey or, possibly, the Gould's.

An alternate hypothesis, fostered by D.E. Brown (personal communication: 1989), suggests that the Merriam's subspecies was derived from Gould's or Rio Grande turkey stock that shifted northward concurrently with postglacial movement of Rocky Mountain and Madrean forests during the recent Holocene epoch. Continued shift of vegetation communities, according to this hypothesis, subsequently eliminated forest corridors between Gould's range and isolated current Merriam's range as Chihuahuan and Sonoran desert vegetations encroached. Whatever the true origin of Merriam's, current evidence supports the hypothesis that it was a relative newcomer when Europeans found it in what we now consider historic range.

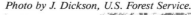
Photo by M. Tarby. *Photo by J. Dickson, U.S. Forest Service.*

The Merriam's turkey is a light-colored bird of the western coniferous mountains.

GENERAL HABITAT

Climate

Merriam's turkeys endure drastic climatic extremes. Temperatures range from −37 degrees to 38 degrees Celsius (−35 degrees to 100 degrees Fahrenheit). Heavy snows and fast-moving storms are characteristic of the areas used by these turkeys for winter range. Severe weather is often interspersed with periods of clear, warm weather, even in midwinter. Deep snows seldom remain on the ground for long, but they may influence seasonal movement of turkeys. Merriam's turkeys are known to move long distances (64 kilometers, or 40 miles) between summer and winter ranges (Phillips 1982).

In Merriam's habitat, annual precipitation averages more than 37.5 centimeters (15 inches) and can get as high as 60 centimeters (23 inches). Distribution of precipitation through the year varies greatly within the Merriam's range. Historic range of the subspecies in Arizona occurs where winter precipitation makes up 50 to 65 percent of annual precipitation, with the rest falling as summer thunderstorms. Spring months are usually dry, with green-up depending on accumulated winter moisture.

Habitats in southeastern Colorado have total annual precipitations of 50 to 55 centimeters (19.5 to 21.5 inches) (Hoffman 1973). Much of the precipitation (65 to 74 percent) falls during late spring and summer, with the rest spread between September and April. Sixty-six percent of the precipitation—58.4 centimeters (23 inches) a year—in the Sacramento Mountains of New Mexico resulted from summer thunderstorms, the balance falling in midwinter (Goerndt 1983).

Within transplanted populations, Mackey (1982) noted that precipitation in south-central Washington was 61 centimeters (24 inches) a year, with most of the precipitation falling in winter. In western South Dakota and northern Nebraska, where high densities of Merriam's

Merriam's turkey wintering area in Black Hills, South Dakota, is nonhistoric Merriam's turkey range. *Photo by H. Shaw.*

turkeys exist in transplanted populations, much of the precipitation falls between February and June. A successful transplant on the North Kaibab National Forest in Arizona succeeded where winter precipitation constitutes better than 65 percent of the yearly total. This area, however, is known for drastic fluctuations in turkey numbers because of periodic heavy winter mortality on a limited winter range.

Physiography

Much of the Merriam's range lies in relatively steep terrain of western mountains. Historical habitat in Arizona included the Mogollon, Defiance, and South Kaibab parts of the Colorado Plateau Province. These areas have large expanses of flat terrain that is dissected by large, steep-walled canyons.

The Merriam's subspecies is believed to have also existed in the larger mountains of the Basin and Range Province of southeastern Arizona and south-central New Mexico. But turkey populations in some of these ranges were eliminated before their taxonomic status was determined.

A recent determination of the single early specimen from the Chiricahua Mountains of southeastern Arizona (cf. Schorger 1966:48) identifies this bird as a member of the Gould's subspecies (Rea personal communication). Subsequent transplants of Merriam's into these areas have eliminated any chance that pure historic stock will be found. So the true taxonomic status of turkeys of southern Arizona and New Mexico may never be determined. Arizona north of the Gila River, northern New Mexico, and Colorado seem solidly within historical Merriam's range.

Broken, mountainous terrain constitutes turkey habitat in Colorado. Native ranges in southern New Mexico have steep mountains rising from Chihuahuan desert or grassland habitats, topped by conifer forests.

Transplanted Merriam's turkeys have adapted to a wide variety of terrains. Mackey (1982) describes south-central Washington terrain as flat expanses broken by canyons. Transplanted populations in Nebraska, South Dakota, and Wyoming live in mountain conifer forests similar to historic habitats and along riparian stream bottoms that extend far out into relatively flat grassland or sagebrush.

Because habitat areas available for the Merriam's are extensive and have not yet been broken up by agriculture or human developments, the question of minimum area of habitat required by this subspecies has not been addressed. The Sacramento Mountains in New Mexico, with greater than 2,500 square kilometers (1,000 square miles) of potential turkey habitat, support a permanent, historical turkey population. Populations of Merriam's turkeys have been reestablished on mountain islands in southern Arizona, but these populations are barely viable. These mountain ranges, with the exception of the Chiricahua Mountains, each contain less than 650 square kilometers (250 square miles) of potential Merriam's habitat.

Perhaps populations transplanted into nonhistoric range, if they have adequate food, yield a better view of habitat area limitations that Merriam's will tolerate. A transplanted population has thrived on the Kaibab Plateau—with greater than 1,500 square kilometers (600 square miles) of habitat—north of the Grand Canyon in Arizona for more than 30 years. But transplants into smaller expanses of habitat (500 square kilometers, or 200 square miles) in the northwest corner of the state (Mount Dellenbaugh, Blackrock Mountain) have met with only limited success or have failed. A transplant of turkeys onto Mount Trumbull, however, with less than 520 square kilometers (200 square miles) of habitat, was successful. A population of 100 to 200 turkeys has resided within this area for approximately 30 years.

Populations in the isolated riparian communities in Nebraska, South Dakota, and Wyoming have succeeded

Cottonwood-bur oak mix in riparian bottom, Niobrara River vicinity, Nebraska. Surrounding ridges are covered with ponderosa pine in this nonhistoric Merriam's turkey habitat. *Photo by H. Shaw.*

Flock of Merriam's turkeys in open stand of bur oak near Niobrara River, Nebraska. *Photo by P. Woodruff.*

where available habitat area is considerably smaller than any of the aforementioned areas, but where food resources are rich. These food resources often include access to grainfields or barnyards where livestock are fed in the winter.

Within their native range, Merriam's turkeys occur at elevations ranging from 1,067 meters (3,500 feet) to above 3,048 meters (10,000 feet). At lower elevations, they historically occurred along riparian deciduous habitats extending into desert, sagebrush, or prairie habitats (Davis 1982).

Although geological strata, soils, vegetation, and distribution of turkeys are undoubtedly related, virtually no research has assessed the influence of these physical factors on turkey distribution. Any substrate that supports suitable vegetation is apparently acceptable to the turkeys. Turkey range in Arizona, for example, occurs on a variety of subhumid soils with substrata ranging from

Precambrian igneous and sedimentary rocks to Upper Tertiary and Quaternary volcanic substrate (Hendricks 1985). Middle Tertiary volcanic and sedimentary rocks constitute portions of Arizona turkey range (winter and summer) toward the eastern Mogollon rim. The Sacramento Mountains' turkey populations in New Mexico live on soils derived from underlying limestone bedrock or colluvial and alluvial sediments from such rock. A large proportion of turkey range in Arizona and New Mexico is on sedimentary or metamorphic substrata, but the significance of this variety is unclear.

Vegetation

The historic distribution of Merriam's turkey closely coincides with the distribution of ponderosa pine, but other vegetation types provide important habitat components (Jantzen and MacDonald 1967). These include the mixed conifer and aspen subclimax communities within the Rocky Mountain Conifer Forest and portions of the Great Basin Conifer Woodland, where it adjoins Rocky Mountain Conifer Forest vegetation types (Brown 1982). The mixed conifer parts of the Rocky Mountain Conifer Forest are typically summer range; the Great Basin Woodland is winter range; the ponderosa pine type is used throughout the year.

Associated species in the ponderosa pine include Gambel oak; one-seed, alligator, Rocky Mountain, and Utah juniper; Colorado piñon pine; and several species of evergreen oaks, including some shrub species. The major associated species of the mixed conifer type are Douglas fir, ponderosa pine, white fir, limber pine, Engle-

mann spruce, and corkbark fir. Minor species are aspen and blue spruce. Aspen often grows in large, pure stands and may be classed as a distinct type. Such pure stands do not constitute turkey habitat.

The Great Basin Conifer Woodland, or piñon-juniper vegetation, contains Colorado piñon pine and a variety of juniper species. It frequently grades into a stand of nearly pure juniper at lower elevations. Its use by turkeys depends on the presence of ponderosa pine or deciduous riparian stringers along canyons to provide suitable roosting sites.

Gambel oak is intermixed with the ponderosa or piñon-juniper types and is an important producer of mast through much of the Merriam's range. Colorado piñon is an important periodic producer of mast on win-

Meadow surrounded by ponderosa pine and Gambel oak, Spanish Peaks Wildlife Area near Trinidad, Colorado. This habitat is managed specifically for Merriam's turkey by state of Colorado. *Photo by H. Shaw.*

ter range. The various species of juniper are relatively consistent seed producers and provide mast when pine seeds or acorns are absent.

HABITAT COMPONENTS

Several new studies of Merriam's turkey habitat have occurred since the reviews of Jantzen and MacDonald (1967) and Schorger (1966). Until the advent of radio-telemetry equipment, little effort had been made to classify habitat by type of use, except for some quantitative evaluation of roosts (Hoffman 1968, Boeker and Scott 1969). Earlier studies assessed general habitat use based upon sightings of birds, probably resulting in a bias that favored habitats where birds were most visible (Jonas 1966, Shaw and Smith 1977).

Like many other animal species, Merriam's turkeys use different habitats depending upon time of year and sex and age of birds (Table 1). Much of the recent information on Merriam's turkey, based upon telemetry studies, has been gathered outside the historical range of the subspecies (Bryant and Nish 1975, Mackey 1982, Lutz and Crawford 1987b, Wertz and Flake 1988, Rumble and Anderson 1989). Work within historical range has been completed in New Mexico (Schemnitz et al. 1985, Jones 1981, Goerndt 1983, Lockwood 1987) and in Arizona (Mollohan and Patton 1991, Wakeling 1991). Field studies from both historical and newly established areas, along with a recent survey of expert opinion conducted by Mollohan (1988), are summarized in Tables 2 through 4. Habitat parameters and citations in the discussion to follow refer to these tables. The survey of expert opinion was assembled by Mollohan from responses of 16 individuals considered knowledgeable about turkey habitat in Arizona and New Mexico on roosting, nesting, and

brood range needs. It does not necessarily represent results of formal research. Rather, it provides an overview of concepts currently being applied in Merriam's turkey management, for comparison with current and future research findings.

Spring Habitat

Spring habitat used by turkeys involves leaving winter concentration areas and dispersing throughout available habitat for breeding and nesting. Relatively long movements may occur between winter and summer ranges. After the breeding season, gobblers and nonnesting hens sort into single-sex groups. Little is known about habitat requirements of birds in these categories. Increased food supplies in the form of grasses, forbs, and insects allow birds to move over a wide range of habitats.

Migration corridors. Phillips (1982) has called attention to the importance of maintaining migration corridors for Merriam's turkeys, but little information is available on this subject. Movements from winter range generally begin in late March or early April, depending on severity of weather, and they probably occur only through acceptable forest habitats. Interruption of contiguous forest habitats by large clearcut areas (or perhaps freeways) could isolate areas of habitat. Summer home developments and extensive road systems could also modify movements of some turkeys populations between summer and winter ranges.

Breeding-strutting grounds. No detailed studies have been done on specific habitat needs of Merriam's gobblers for strutting grounds. Hoffman (1986) found gobblers in Colorado moving an average of 3.7 kilometers (2.3 miles) from winter to breeding ranges. Once on the breeding grounds, gobblers were extremely mobile,

Table 1. Phenology of turkey behavior patterns and related habitats.

| Season | Hens | | Gobblers | |
	Behavior	Habitat	Behavior	Habitat
spring	migration, dispersal, breeding, roosting, feeding, escape, laying, incubating.	migration corridors, breeding sites, nest sites, roosts, escape cover, shelter.	migration, dispersal, strutting, breeding, feeding, loafing, roosting.	migration corridors, strutting sites, breeding sites, roosts, escape cover, loafing sites, shelter.
summer	brooding, roosting, feeding, loafing, escape.	brood roosts, escape cover, shelter, feeding areas, loafing cover.	feeding, loafing, roosting, escape.	feeding, loafing, roosts, escape cover, shelter.
fall	feeding, loafing, roosting, escape, migration.	roosts, escape cover, loafing sites, feeding areas, shelter. migration corridors	[same as for hens]	[same as for hens]
winter	aggregation on winter range, feeding, loafing, escape.	feeding sites, escape cover, shelter, winter roosts.	aggregation, feeding sites, loafing, escape, shelter.	feeding sites, escape cover, shelter.

Table 2. Merriam's turkey nesting habitat characteristics.

Habitat variable	Component characteristic and source
Slope	46 percent; most nests on steep slope (Schemnitz et al. 1985; Leidlich et al. 1990). 2–60 percent; average 36 percent (Mackey 1982). Average 53 percent (Mollohan and Patton 1991). Average 53 percent. Strong selection for canyons (Wakeling 1991).
Aspect	All nests (sample of 13) on east-facing slopes (Petersen and Richardson 1975). 58 percent on mesic exposure (Goerndt 1983). No strong selection for aspect (Mollohan and Patton 1991).
Location	83 percent (sample of 6) in slash; 17 percent in clumps of oak sprouts (Phillips 1982). 75 percent at base of tree; 75 percent partially covered by dead limbs or vegetation (Mackey 1982). 53 percent at base of trees or stumps; 29 percent in brushy cover; 18 percent in slash piles (Goerndt 1983). 60 percent of initial nests in rock slides or outcrops; 100 percent of renests in slash or shrubs (Rumble and Anderson 1989). 50 percent at base of trees on uphill side (Crites 1988). Selected ponderosa pine habitat; avoided open grasslands and rock outcrops. Riparian areas, shrub hillsides, crop meadows, and feedlot corrals used in proportion to availability (Hengel and Anderson 1990). Clumpy, uneven-aged mixed conifer forest (Wakeling 1991).
Basal area, square meters per hectare (square feet per acre)	2.3–77.6 (10–340), average 26 (114) (Schemnitz et al. 1985). Average 36.1 (157) (Hengel and Anderson 1990). 22 (96) (Wakeling 1991).
Understory vegetation (percentage of cover)	36 (Mackey 1982). 70–93 ground level; 58–84 elbow height (Crites 1988). 75.1 (Hengel and Anderson 1990).
Shrub density, plants per hectare (plants per acre)	1,150 (466) used versus 398 (161) available (Lutz and Crawford 1987). 17,480 (7,077) (Mollohan and Patton 1991). 14,719 (5,959) (Wakeling 1991).
Tree density, trees per hectare (acre)	546 (218) (Hengel and Anderson 1990).
Horizontal cover	25 meters (82 feet) average unobstructed view at 1 meter (3.3 feet) height (Mackey 1982). Coverboard intercept 90–100 percent 0.3 meters (1 foot) above ground at 9 meters (30 feet) (Schemnitz et al. 1985). Visibility (average contacts with vegetation on 10-meter [33-foot] transect at 0.5-meter [1.7-foot] level) was 3.8 versus 0.5 on random. At 1-meter level (3.3 feet), both used and random were 0.5 (Lutz and Crawford 1987). Average distance to cover 2.2 meters (7.3 feet) (Hengel and Anderson 1990). Average distance a turkey decoy was covered was 13.3 meters (44 feet) (Mollohan and Patton 1991). Average distance a human was covered was 24 meters (79 feet). Turkey decoy covered at 15 meters (49 feet) (Wakeling 1991).
Slash	30–40 metric tons per hectare (13–18 tons per acre). Nests located in recently thinned stands in or adjacent to accumulation of slash (Lutz and Crawford 1987). Slash index 12.7. Height 38 centimeters (15 inches) (Mollohan and Patton 1991).
Distance to water, meters (feet)	27–1,930 (90–6,333) (Goerndt 1983). 46–2,032 (150–6,667); average 533 (1,750) (Lockwood 1987). 305–1,609 (1,000–5,280) (Mollohan 1988).

covering home ranges averaging 1,541 hectares (3,806 acres), with activity centers averaging 415 hectares (1,025 acres). Distances between consecutive roosts at this time averaged 2,036 meters (1.3 miles).

Home ranges of all males studied overlapped. Hens moved an average of 9.6 kilometers (6.0 miles) from wintering to breeding areas, and breeding season occupied home ranges that were smaller (653 hectares, or 1,613 acres). Average movements between roosting sites for

hens during the breeding season were 1.4 kilometers (0.9 miles).

Nest sites. A generalized image of a suitable nest site is emerging from a variety of studies from different areas (Table 2). Nests usually are at sites that offer complete protection from one side (either dense vegetation or terrain), dense cover on the remaining sides between 0 and 0.5 meters (0 to 1.5 feet), and unrestricted visibility on 3 sides in the 0.5-to-0.9-meter (1.5-to-3-foot) vegeta-

Table 3. Roost-site characteristics for Merriam's turkey.

Variable	Winter	Summer	Reference
Size of site, hectares (acres)	0.2–1.8 (0.5–4.5) 0.1–1.6 (0.25–4.0) 0.1 (0.25) —	0.1–0.3 (0.25–0.75) 0.1–0.2 (0.25–0.5) 0.5 (1.2) 0.4–0.6 (1.0–1.5)	Hoffman 1968 Phillips 1980 Goerndt 1983 Mollohan and Patton 1991
Aspect	East–northeast dominant No preference Northeast No preference	— No preference Random No preference	Boeker and Scott 1969 Phillips 1980 Jones 1981 Mollohan and Patton 1991
Slope, percentage	Average 37 8–35 Average 51 38	Average 37 5–40 51 —	Hoffman 1968 Mackey 1984 Hengel and Anderson 1990 Mollohan and Patton 1991
Trees per site	4–44 1–37, average 13 10–150, average 27 Average 8 3–150 6–7 —	3–11, average 6 Often single 4–20, average 8 Average 2 1–27 1.5–2 1–18, average 5	Hoffman 1968 Boeker and Scott 1969 Phillips 1980 Goerndt 1983 Mollohan 1988 Hengel and Anderson 1990 Mollohan and Patton 1991
Tree height, meters (feet)	— 15–30 (50–100); average 24 (80) 9 (30) minimum; average 16 (52.5) 11 (35) minimum; average 23 (75) More than 15 (50)	12–30 (40–100); average 21 (68) — 12 (39) minimum; average 21 (68) — —	Hoffman 1968 Boeker and Scott 1969 Jones 1981 Goerndt 1983 Mollohan 1988
Distance to first branch, meters (feet)	Average 8 (27.5) — 3.5–4.5 (12–15) —	3–15 (10–50); average 6.6 (21.5) 4–17 (12–55); average 11 (35) 3.5–4.5 (12–15) Average 9.5 (31)	Boeker and Scott 1969 Mackey 1984 Hengel and Anderson 1990 Mollohan and Patton 1991
Canopy cover, percent	Average 66 73 73.5 60 —	— — — — 15–88; average 53	Jones 1981 Goerndt 1983 Mackey 1984 Mollohan 1988 Mollohan and Patton 1991
Tree dbh, centimeters (inches)	Average 53 (21) — 18–107 (7–42); average 46 (18) 31–76 (12–30); average 49 (19) 49 (19) 25 (10)	32–90 (13–36); average 57 (23) 46–97 (18–38); average 72 (29) — 25–61 (10–24) 51 (20) — 10–61 (4–24); average 25 (10)	Hoffman 1968 Boeker and Scott 1969 Goerndt 1983 Mollohan 1988 Hengel and Anderson 1990 Rumble 1990 Mollohan and Patton 1991
Basal area, square meters per hectare (square feet per acre)	More than 21 (90) Average 40 (174) Average 22 (94) More than 18 (80) 49.2 (214) —	21 (90) — — 18 (80) 46.2 (201) 13–52 (57–228); average 32 (140)	Boeker and Scott 1969 Jones 1981 Phillips 1982 Mollohan 1988 Hengel and Anderson 1990 Mollohan and Patton 1991

tion layer. Relatively solid cover is normal at about 2.4 to 3.7 meters (8 to 12 feet) above the nest, with a forest canopy overhead.

A high percentage of nests are on slopes steeper than 30 percent, and the protected side may be the base of a large tree, a rock ledge or overhang, a talus slope, or a dense stand of low vegetation (such as an oak thicket).

The low vegetation on the more open side may consist of shrubby or herbaceous live vegetation or slash. Overstory protection in the 2.4-to-3.7-meter (8-to-12-foot) level may be conifer or deciduous live vegetation.

Lockwood (1987) has noted the propensity of hens to return to the same general area to nest. He also noted a tendency for nests to be near water. Other sources,

Black sagebrush meadow surrounded by ponderosa pine-piñon-juniper mix, Defiance Plateau, Navajo Reservation, Arizona. Edges of this meadow are used by broods. It is historic Merriam's turkey range. *Photo by H. Shaw.*

however, suggest that a wide range of distances from water is possible (Table 2).

Lockwood (1987) found 4 vegetative types (ponderosa pine, spruce-fir, aspen-fir, and oak) used more than their availability would suggest. Ponderosa pine and spruce-fir habitats were the most important types used in the Sacramento Mountains in New Mexico. Lockwood noted, however, that a mixed conifer microhabitat was present at 84 percent of the nest sites, regardless of the broader vegetation class involved. He also noted that oak was present at 60 percent of the sites. Wakeling (1991) found a selection of mixed conifer sites in Arizona. Hens avoided ponderosa pine.

Lockwood (1987) considered brood lanes (used mainly for feeding by broods immediately after hatching) an important associate of nest sites. He described brood lanes as having little or no canopy cover and a dense ground cover at the 0-to-0.5-meter (0-to-1.5-foot) level. These lanes tended to be 20 to 50 meters (66 to 164 feet) wide and were adjacent to the nest site. Slash was a major component of brood lanes. Orientation was normally with the long axis up and down the slope. Such lanes existed at 92 percent of the nests inspected in New Mexico, but they have not been reported by other authors.

Summer Habitat

Hens with newly hatched broods seek areas where insects are abundant. As summer progresses, hens with broods aggregate. Feeding gradually shifts to vegetable

Table 4. Characteristics of brood habitat for Merriam's turkey.

Variable	Characteristics and source
Location	Oak and pine habitat used more than expected. Fir and nonforested areas over 1 hectare (2.4 acres) more than expected (Mackey 1982). Logged mixed conifer, aspen glens, and meadows more than expected. Higher insect biomasses occurred in headers and moist canyons than in open riparian forested areas (Goerndt 1983). Kentucky bluegrass meadows (Rumble 1990). Riparian, wet meadow, and forest meadow vegetation types. Avoided open grasslands and ponderosa pine forests (Hengel and Anderson 1990). Small openings in ponderosa pine or mixed conifer habitats (Mollohan and Patton 1991).
Aspect	Random (Goerndt 1983). Not significant (Green 1990).
Slope	15.6 percent used versus 23.7 percent on control plots. Slopes over 50 percent used less than available. Slopes between 10 and 19 percent used more than available (Mackey 1982). 11.5 to 17.9 percent (Rumble 1990). No difference from random plots (Mollohan and Patton 1991).
Canopy cover	51–60 percent used more than available. More than 60 percent not used (Mackey 1982). 11–41 percent (Rumble 1990). 46 percent (Mollohan and Patton 1991). 48.5 percent (Goerndt 1983). No difference from random (Green 1990).
Ground cover	33.5 percent used versus 47.9 percent for control plots (Mackey 1982). 42 percent used versus 30.5 percent for random (Green 1990). 44–86 percent used versus 34 percent for random (Rumble 1990). 66 percent (Mollohan and Patton 1991).
Ground cover height	41–61 centimeters (16–24 inches) used more than available. 61–81 centimeters (24–32 inches) used less than available (Mackey 1982). 34–43 centimeters (13–17 inches) used versus 34 (13) random (Rumble 1990). 25 centimeters (10 inches) (Mollohan and Patton 1991).
Number of forb species	11 used versus 8 for random sites (Green 1990). 9 (Mollohan and Patton 1991).
Characteristics of openings	0.5 hectare (1.2 acres) (Goerndt 1983). 0.16–1.6 hectares (0.4–4.0 acres) (Mollohan 1988). Large meadows. 36 hectares (90 acres) used compared with 16 hectares (40 acres) average. More than 0.2 hectare (0.5 acre) Openings at 96 percent of feeding sites (Mollohan and Patton 1991). Nonforested areas greater than 1 hectare (2.5 acres) (Mackey 1982).
Slash	Use positively correlated to slash density (Green 1990). 10.4 volume index; 29.7 centimeters (11.4 inches) average diameter (Mollohan and Patton 1991).

matter, including green forage. Late-summer habitat often reflects the increasing role of mast and seed heads in the diet as green forage declines.

Gobbler groups and flocks of hens without poults continue to stay separated from hens with broods. Gobblers and poultless hens apparently select habitats distinctly different from those used by hens with poults at this time (Shaw and Smith 1977), but no habitat studies have focused on these social groups.

Brood range. Interpretation of brood range studies is complicated by failure of observers to differentiate between immediate posthatching brood habitat and habitat of older broods. The previously mentioned brood lanes observed by Lockwood (1987) were used immedi-

ately after hatching by hens with very young poults. Lockwood also noted a general selection for spruce-fir habitats by hens with broods.

Most investigators have said that hens with broods use small forest openings with good escape cover and overstory nearby (Table 4). Mackey (1982) in Washington noted use of sites with somewhat less herbaceous ground cover than found on randomly selected sites. Green (1988) found broods selecting sites with more ground cover than occurred on randomly selected sites. Green worked with direct sightings; Mackey was working with radio-marked birds. So Green's data may have reflected the most open feeding sites for broods, while Mackey's data represent a conglomerate of forms of habitat use.

Heavily logged stand of ponderosa pine on Defiance Plateau, Navajo Reservation, Arizona. *Photo by H. Shaw.*

Gambel oak-ponderosa pine riparian stringer with piñon-juniper on ridges, Defiance Plateau, Navajo Reservation, Arizona. *Photo by H. Shaw.*

More-recent studies of radio-marked turkeys have disclosed a relatively wide range of acceptable opening sizes. Mollohan and Patton (1991) noted strong selection for small openings in the forest in Arizona. Rumble (1990) in South Dakota and Hazel (1989) in Wyoming have noted use of relatively large openings. This disparity in acceptable opening size may be related to height of herbage in the openings.

Mackey (1982) noted use of sites with ground cover that was slightly shorter than cover found on control sites. His ground cover height (45 centimeters, or 17.6 inches) for brood sites was, however, higher than ground cover that might be expected on sites in much of the native range of Merriam's turkey. In his study area, grasses at times were actually taller than adult turkeys, creating dense cover at levels normally occurring in the shrub vegetational layer in other areas. Dense shrubbery more than 61 centimeters (24 inches) high is normally considered unacceptable as turkey habitat.

Distance to water for broods did not seem a major factor in moist habitats of Arizona's White Mountains

Wet meadow in ponderosa pine forest showing signs of past erosion and subsequent recovery as a result of improved grazing practices. These meadows provide feeding areas for broods of Merriam's turkey. Potholes in drainage are one of the few limited water sources in much of Merriam's range. *Photo by R. Smith, Arizona Game and Fish Department.*

Ponderosa pine forest with mixture of alligator juniper. This area is in lower-elevation summer range and upper reaches of winter range for Merriam's turkey in Arizona. *Photo by R. Smith, Arizona Game and Fish Department.*

(Green 1988) and New Mexico's Sacramento Mountains (Schemnitz et al. 1985). Shaw and Smith (1977), however, found a strong association of brood groups with earthen-dam stock tanks on the xeric south rim of the Grand Canyon. The possible inference is that water availability may be a major factor in distribution of turkey populations in drier habitats.

Although documentation of historical populations is difficult, the increase in turkeys on the south rim of the Grand Canyon during the past 50 years seems directly related to increased development of free water. Free water was virtually lacking on this area before man-made water developments.

Roosts. Summer roosts have received less attention than winter roosts. Turkeys are less inclined to return regularly to summer roosts than they are to winter roosts. In summer, turkeys are more inclined to roost where night finds them. Slightly larger trees seemed to be used in summer than in winter (Table 3), and sites with fewer trees were used in summer. Basal area (square feet of tree trunk per acre, measured at breast height) for summer and winter roost sites was similar, as was distance to the first branch. Phillips (1982) and Schemnitz et al. (1985) reported no selection for aspect (direction a site faces) at summer roost sites. Roost sites must not be isolated from contiguous feeding and loafing habitats (Boeker and Scott 1969, Hengel and Anderson 1990).

Hengel and Anderson in Wyoming have recorded characteristics of ground roost sites used by hens with young poults. Shrub hillsides were preferred over other habitats for ground roosts. Ponderosa pine forest, deciduous tree habitats, forest meadows, and feedlot corrals

Mixture of ponderosa pine, juniper species, and piñon pine. Another example of lower-elevation summer or upper winter range for Merriam's turkey in Arizona. *Photo by R. Smith, Arizona Game and Fish Department.*

Mixed conifer vegetation is good Arizona summer range for Merriam's. *Photo by R. Smith, Arizona Game and Fish Department.*

Water sources are limited in much of Merriam's range. Improper logging around stock tanks or springs can remove cover that is badly needed by birds approaching water during dry spells. *Photo by R. Smith, Arizona Game and Fish Department.*

were used in proportion to their availability. Avoided were riparian areas, meadows, and grasslands.

Vegetation height at ground roost sites averaged 36.7 centimeters (15 inches). Tree densities were low: basal area of 1.4 square meters per hectare (6 square feet per acre). Ground and shrub-layer vegetation averaged less than 50 percent.

Feeding-loafing-escape. Feeding habitat meshes with loafing habitat in a mix of thickets and small openings that provide herbaceous understory. This juxtaposition of feeding, loafing, and escape habitats is only now being clearly understood and described. Mollohan and Patton (1991) have noted use of downed snags under the forest canopy for loafing sites. These are normally adjacent to small openings that have good forbs and grass cover. Rumble (1990) has noted use of low rock outcrops on ridgetops for loafing. These, too, were below relatively dense forest overstory.

Fall and Winter Habitat

Use of fall habitats reflects a shift in food habits to more mast and grass seed heads and fewer insects and forbs. As food becomes scarce, birds may be forced to feed in areas of less adequate cover, and they may be-

A temporary water source with improved cover and food sources nearby. *Photo by R. Smith, Arizona Game and Fish Department.*

A winter roost site in Arizona. *Photo by B. Wakeling.*

come more vulnerable to predation (Ron Day, Arizona Game and Fish Department, personal communication: 1989). As aggregates of birds grow larger, use of roost sites shifts toward winter patterns.

Roosts.   Characteristics of fall and winter roosts are available from investigations in Arizona, Colorado, New Mexico, and Washington, and they also are provided for Arizona and New Mexico by a survey of expert opinion (Table 3). For most of the characteristics, minimum figures are of greatest significance. Results suggest that winter roost sites should not be less than 0.1 hectares (0.25 acres), and sites of about half a hectare (1.25 acres) or more are preferred. Although single-tree winter roosts were recorded by some workers, the larger numbers in winter turkey flocks normally require sites with multiple trees, at least 10 trees preferred.

Roost sites were composed of moderately dense stands of suitable trees, with canopy cover of 60 to 75 percent and basal areas exceeding 18 square meters per hectare (80 square feet per acre). Stands where Douglas fir and white fir were the major roost trees had higher basal areas and larger diameters than sites with ponderosa pine. In these habitats, basal areas of more than 23 square meters per hectare (100 square feet per acre) and reaching 40 square meters per hectare (174 square feet per acre) were recorded. Scott and Boeker (1975) documented abandonment of a site after it had been reduced to 16.8 square meters per hectare (73.6 square feet per acre).

Steepness of slope for winter roosts was not a critical factor, although exposure to early morning sun seemed important. Most workers reported roost-site selection on northeast slopes, but Phillips (1982) found no preference for slope direction in central Arizona. He noted that logging had removed a high percentage of available roosts in his area and that turkeys had little choice of sites.

Mackey (1982) suggested that thermal cover may be a factor in aspect selection. It may be that denser, more properly shaped trees grow on certain aspects. Or, possibly, greater protection from prevailing winds occurs on these aspects. In New Mexico, 54 percent of the roosts were on the upper third of the slope to ridgetops; 27 percent were on the middle third; and 19 percent were on the lower third (Lockwood 1987).

The need for openings uphill from roosts (for easy flights in) was reported by some early workers (Hoffman 1968) but was discounted by later observers (Table 3). Turkeys can enter roosts from directly below the tree. A wide range of distances to openings has been reported by various observers (46 to 396 meters, or 150 to 1,300 feet).

One of the more interesting characteristics noted for winter roosts was nearness to water (actually closer than for summer roosts). This finding may reflect the better dispersion of water during the winter on relatively dry Merriam's ranges. It is certainly difficult to explain on the basis of water requirements of the birds at this time of year.

Winter roosts must be adjacent to adequate winter feeding and loafing habitat. Scott and Boeker (1975) noted the turkeys stopped using a traditional winter roost when the site was isolated from habitat suitable for other requirements. Of special interest is the apparent tendency to select Douglas fir and white fir over ponderosa pine for roosts. This was true on winter range in New Mexico (Schemnitz et al. 1985) and in Washington (Mackey 1984). Mackey suggested that this selection was because of better thermal cover and better perches provided by Douglas fir. Schemnitz et al. (1985) noted that dominant or codominant Douglas fir and white fir were selected, ponderosa pine and southwestern white pine were used occasionally, but Gambel oak and aspen were never used. On most Arizona winter ranges and many summer ranges, these preferred conifer species are absent, so ponderosa pine is the tree of choice. Mackey found few roosts in selectively logged areas, but Schemnitz et al. (1985) reported that 50 percent of their roost sites had been selectively logged.

Mackey found no statistically significant differences in tree size and canopy structure between Merriam's roost sites and control sites. Percent of canopy cover was higher in roost areas than on control plots, and canopy height was greater in roost areas. Lowest live-limb heights were greater in roost areas, and basal area was higher.

Minimum tree height for roosts was 9 to 11 meters (30 to 35 feet). Trees well over 15 meters (50 feet) were preferred. This tendency undoubtedly reflects other tree characteristics that are needed to make a roost tree, in-cluding the trunk diameter (18 centimeters or 7 inches) and distance to first branch (8 to 11 meters or 26 to 35 feet). In the arid Southwest, trees of 15 meters (50 feet) or more are required to produce the appropriate shape, including the well-spaced horizontal branches needed for a roost tree.

Feeding-loafing-escape. Virtually no information has been published on structural and spatial characteristics of the Merriam's winter feeding and loafing habitat. Rumble (1990) noted that winter range in the Black Hills of South Dakota has dense canopy cover and little or no understory vegetation. Habitats selected by turkeys reflected winter diet (food availability). In this area, ponderosa pine seeds were the major winter food. Seed production was related to basal area, and wintering areas averaged 26.5 square meters per hectare (115 square feet per acre). Turkeys used more-open forest stands only when pine seed crops failed and the birds were forced to seek other foods. At such times, birds sought out kinnikinnick seeds, seeds of forbs and grasses, and vegetation from forbs and grasses. Domestic grains in feedlots were also used.

Wakeling (1991) found that mortality was greater at feeding sites than at other sites. Turkeys at loafing and roost sites were less vulnerable to mortality.

A pure stand of piñon-juniper vegetation. Turkeys use this vegetation type extensively for winter habitat and occasionally for summer brood range. Proximity to larger conifers such as ponderosa pine is essential for roosts. *Photo by R. Smith, Arizona Game and Fish Department.*

Gambel oak is a key mast producer throughout Merriam's turkey summer and winter range. *Photo by R. Smith, Arizona Game and Fish Department.*

The limited information available concentrates on winter food habits. Results from these studies suggest that Merriam's turkeys depend on winter food sources that fluctuate widely. Scott and Boeker (1975) reported heavy use of acorns and piñon pine nuts on the White Mountain Apache Indian Reservation in Arizona, but they considered both of these foods unreliable annual food sources. Juniper was the most consistent mast producer on the area, accounting for 40 percent of the annual diet during a year of drought and mast crop failure.

Schemnitz et al. (1985) reported that watercress was an important food for turkeys in New Mexico. They emphasized the importance of available springs and seeps with open water and aquatic vegetation during periods of deep snow when other foods are unavailable.

Little has been reported on the relationship between snow depth and use of winter range. Hoffman (1973) reported that turkeys in Colorado were forced to concentrate in areas of supplemental feeding or move to elevations lower than prime winter range to avoid deep snows during an unusually hard winter coupled with a failure of mast crops. Sutcliffe (1982) reported a preference for south-facing slopes, probably because of shallower snow depths and the sun's warmth. He also suggested that turkeys are restricted in their movements in the snow and tend to follow the snow line back to higher elevations.

Merriam's turkeys compete for winter foods with a variety of other wildlife species and domestic livestock. Mast crops are used by elk, mule deer, black bears, coyotes, foxes, band-tailed pigeons, and a variety of other species over most of the Merriam's range. Increasing elk herds in much of the turkey range may compete directly for grass seed heads on winter range.

Most winter range of the Merriam's is on federal (primarily U.S. Forest Service) land, which is often grazed by cattle and sheep. During years of other food failures, fall and winter grazing of winter range could deplete turkey foods.

RESEARCH NEEDS

Concern in the West over the effects of logging and grazing on public lands, combined with access to good radio-tracking equipment, has led to emphasizing research on turkey movements and structural habitat requirements. Biologists are developing insights into how much structural habitat modification turkeys will tolerate. And biologists are converting this knowledge to guidelines for protecting key habitats, particularly for nesting and roosting. Because such widely dispersed habitats are involved, results are often variable. To prevent inappropriate application of results from specific localities to turkey habitat at large, we need continued

replication of habitat selection studies throughout the range of the Merriam's turkey.

Because roosts are so conspicuous, they have received considerable study, even before we had radio-tracking equipment. Data on roost sites and roost trees have been incorporated into forest management strategies in many areas. On southwestern forests, for instance, marking and saving of potential roost sites is standard management practice.

Studies are needed, however, on (1) the actual use of these sites by turkeys after timber harvest is completed; and (2) the relations of roost use to the timber-harvest practices surrounding the roost sites. Also needed are studies to differentiate more clearly the characteristics of seasonal roosts. Summer and winter roosts have not always been adequately differentiated in previous studies. Special roost requirements — such as those for young broods, laying hens, and breeding gobblers — have received little attention.

Studies that delineate habitat requirements of Merriam's turkeys according to the behavior involved are fairly recent developments. Research on feeding, loafing, and escape habitat for various sex and age classes of turkeys require prolonged observations that are difficult

Merriam's nest in northern Arizona. This is a typical nest micro site. *Photo by J. Dickson, U.S. Forest Service.*

to accomplish in the field, even with radio-marked birds. Such data accumulate slowly and must be gathered during all seasons. Continuous monitoring is needed to allow even temporary habitats, such as spring and fall migration corridors, to be determined.

Researchers must find ways to convert their detailed measurements of habitat site characteristics to generalizations about landscapes that provide good habitat. While nest sites, for example, have traits that are easily described and relatively consistent, these sites are not easy to locate without the aid of radio-marked turkeys. Nest-site components are subtle, and they involve a variety of habitat elements. Their distribution relative to breeding habitats and brood range may be a factor in overall reproductive success. For wildlife managers working without the benefit of telemetry, the ability to recognize vegetative communities that provide suitable nesting sites is more important than the ability to identify individual sites. The same applies for other forms of habitat use.

The recent focus on structural habitat in many studies of Merriam's turkey has, perhaps, usurped research on important basic information needed in turkey management. Data on good food habits for all seasons of the year have not been gathered in any part of the Merriam's range, and factors affecting food availability and nutritional status of the birds are poorly understood.

We need to better understand how habitat and food interactions affect vulnerability of turkeys to predation and severe climate. Lack of nutritious food near suitable cover, for example, may be a major factor in increasing winter losses of turkeys to predators. If death rates are higher in particular habitat complexes, and if man-caused factors create these complexes, then they can be modified through improved management.

Uniform measurements of habitat characteristics and standard methods of analyzing habitat data are badly needed. Such standardization would facilitate comparison of study results between areas, and it would allow managers to better understand the habitat extremes that turkeys will tolerate. It would also make easier (1) the job of incorporating habitat study findings into the plans of agencies that manage habitat; and (2) the merging of turkey habitat management with other land uses.

For Merriam's, we have little information on the overall effects of timber harvest, grazing, or recreational uses of land on turkey habitat and turkey populations. Quantitative information is needed for effective management. We know little about competition between turkeys and livestock or wild ungulates.

The success of many transplants of Merriam's turkeys outside historical range and into nontraditional habitats demonstrates that the subspecies can adapt to a variety of climatic regimes and structural habitat complexes. This record suggests that food availability may be an overriding factor in determining turkey densities in many areas.

Studies in New Mexico and Arizona have disclosed that southwestern turkey populations tend to have low productivity, apparently because of yearling hens failing to nest (Lockwood 1987, Shaw et al. unpublished data). Merriam's yearlings in the Black Hills of South Dakota are known to nest (Rumble and Anderson 1989), and high rates of nesting by yearling Rio Grande turkey hens have been found in northeastern Colorado (Schmutz 1989).

Yearling nesting may be related to a climatic gradient. Perhaps higher productivity occurs in areas where adequate precipitation falls in late winter or early spring, providing reliable feed for hens and good insect crops for poults. Spring and early summer are periods of drought in Arizona and New Mexico.

These constraints on productivity may be preventing southwestern turkeys from reaching the carrying capacity of the available structural habitat. Better understanding of this phenomenon might lead to (1) range management practices, such as fencing key meadow edges for turkeys; or (2) supplementary feeding programs during periods of stress in order to increase turkey numbers.

Understanding the factors that affect turkey productivity may require comparison of nutritional and habitat conditions over the entire range of the subspecies. We badly need studies of factors affecting production of key mast-producing plant species. Data on food habits must be compared with habitat needs and population before we can completely understand the factors controlling the subspecies. Coordination among biologists working throughout the range of the Merriam's turkey is essential.

THE FUTURE

In general, the future of the Merriam's turkey seems bright. Much of its habitat lies on public lands, and wildlife biologists are taking stronger roles in managing resources on these lands. Merriam's turkey habitat is abundant. Because of the many successful transplants outside of historic range, more wild turkeys probably now exist in the western United States than at any past time. Increasing information from field research is providing better guidelines for protection of existing habitat.

Harvest strategies for most states are sound. Changes will be needed, but danger of overharvest of turkey populations is nonexistent. With such good harvest strategies in place, the greatest threats to turkey populations now lie in excessive modification of their habitats through logging, grazing, and fuelwood cutting.

These land uses, however, are not necessarily destructive. History shows they can exist concurrently with wildlife. Logging, properly done, can enhance turkey habitat. Likewise, fuelwood cutting can be designed to increase production of grass seed heads on winter range. Whether grazing can provide similar benefits is uncertain, but we undoubtedly can learn to protect key habitats for turkeys without eliminating livestock.

As the human populations of the western states shift from rural to urban concentrations, the value of wildlife as a nonconsumptive—as well as consumptive—resource will increase. This is especially true on public lands near large urban areas where viewing of wildlife such as the Merriam's turkey already provides considerable recreation. Developing guidelines that not only mesh management of habitat with other resource uses but also recognize the needs of all groups interested in wildlife is the greatest challenge facing biologists concerned with Merriam's turkey research and management.

Merriam's turkey habitat is abundant and made up mostly of public lands.

Chapter 21

GOULD'S TURKEY

Sanford D. Schemnitz
Professor, Wildlife Science
New Mexico State University
Las Cruces, New Mexico

William D. Zeedyk
Director, Wildlife and Fisheries
Southwestern Region
USDA Forest Service
Albuquerque, New Mexico

Gould's turkey *(Meleagris gallopavo mexicana)* was first described by Gould (1856) based on a type specimen from Bolanos, Jalisco, in Mexico, and later described in more detail by Elliot (Nelson 1900). Nelson (1900) verified subspecies differences between *M. g. gallopavo* and *M. g. mexicana*. Aldrich (1967b) and Schorger (1966) described the taxonomy and distribution of *M. g. mexicana*. Leopold provided early information on this subspecies in Mexico (1948, 1959), and there have been at least 2 popular articles based on hunting trips (Harbour 1985, Bland 1986).

Rea (1980) reviewed the status of late Pleistocene and Holocene turkeys in the Southwest. Unfortunately, only 2 fossil records exist for Mexico from cave sites in Sonora, southeast of Cananea. Both specimens were identified as *M. gallopavo*, with no subspecies differentiation. Rea hypothesized that *M. g. merriami* escaped from captivity, possibly originating from *mexicana*, and became feral with the breakdown of native southwestern culture.

Gould's turkey somewhat resembles Merriam's. But Gould's has a distinctive white tip on the tail feathers and tail coverts as compared with a light buff tone in Merriam's. The lower back and rump in Gould's have a greenish iridescence. In adult males, spurs are poorly developed or sometimes lacking. Gould's turkeys are larger and have longer legs, larger feet, and longer central tail feathers than other subspecies. Vocalizations of Gould's turkeys seem similar to those of other species except that the alarm "putt" is higher pitched, resembling a "pitt, pitt." The gobble of the Gould's male is distinguished by a lower tonal frequency than the gobble of either the Merriam's or the Rio Grande (Dahlquist et al. 1990).

Gould's turkey is the largest of the 5 subspecies (see chapter 3, Systematics and Population Genetics). Adult gobblers collected in northwestern Chihuahua during summer averaged 7.1 kilograms (15.7 pounds). Gobblers harvested during spring in Chihuahua and males captured in the winter in the Peloncillo Mountains in New Mexico were much heavier, averaging about 10 kilograms (22.0 pounds) (Table 1).

New information comes from recent studies in New Mexico. Bohl and Gordon (1958) authenticated the first New Mexican specimen of Gould's turkey in the Peloncillo Mountains since the collection by Mearns (1907) along the U.S.-Mexico border in the San Luis Mountains in 1892. Detailed reports on distribution, ecology, habitat, status, and various details of life history have been published by Schemnitz and Zeedyk (1982), Potter (1984), Potter et al. (1985), Schemnitz et al. (1985b), Schemnitz and Willging (1986), Willging (1987), Schemnitz and Pinto (1987), Figert (1989), and Schemnitz et al. (1990).

DISTRIBUTION

Past distribution of Gould's turkey in Mexico as documented by Leopold (1948, 1959) was from northern Chihuahua and Sonora south to southwestern Michoacan and Rio Balsas valley in northern Guerrero. Leopold (1948:395) wrote, "Turkeys have been locally exterminated or severely thinned out in many localities, but scattered breeding stocks remain on most of the ancestral range." Historic distribution of Gould's turkey in the United States extended into southwestern New Mexico. Schorger (1966) mentioned that turkeys inhabited the Hatchet Mountains (east of the Animas Mountains) in New Mexico, but we have been unable to substantiate Schorger's report.

It is not clear from historical records whether *M. g.*

Table 1. Weights of Gould's turkeys.

| Age | Sex | Number | Weight in kilograms (pounds) | | Location and time of year |
			Mean	Range	
adult	male	5	7.1 (15.7)	6.8 (15.1)–7.5 (16.6)	Northwestern Chihuahua, summer[a]
adult	male	13	10.0 (22.0)	7.9 (17.5)–12.5 (27.5)	Southwest of Nueva Casas Grandes, Chihuahua, spring[b]
adult	male	3	9.8 (21.7)	9.5 (21.0)–10.0 (22.0)	Peloncillo Mountains, New Mexico, winter[c]
yearling	male	3	5.6 (12.3)	5.4 (12.0)–5.9 (13.0)	Peloncillo Mountains, New Mexico, winter
yearling	male	3	5.2 (11.4)	4.1 (9.0)–6.2 (13.7)	Northwestern Chihuahua, summer
adult	female	2	4.3 (9.6)	4.4 (9.4)–4.4 (9.7)	Northwestern Chihuahua, summer
adult	female	7	5.4 (11.9)	5.0 (11.0)–5.9 (13.0)	Peloncillo Mountains, New Mexico, winter
adult	female	1	5.9 (13.0)		Southwest of Nueva Casas Grandes, Chihuahua, spring
yearling	female	4	3.5 (7.7)	2.7 (6.0)–4.3 (9.5)	Northwestern Chihuahua, summer
yearling	female	1	4.1 (9.0)		Peloncillo Mountains, New Mexico, winter

[a] Schorger (1966).
[b] Schemnitz (unpubl. 1987, 1988).
[c] Figert (1989).

mexicana occurred in Arizona. One specimen collected in the Chiricahua Mountains in 1881 was identified as *M. g. merriami* by A.S. Leopold. This identification, however, could have been in error.

The Sierra Madre Occidental Mountains are the center of the remaining Gould's turkey range, extending south from the U.S.-Mexico border and straddling the states of Chihuahua, Sonora, Sinaloa, and Durango. Separated populations occur farther south in Valparaiso Mountains in Zacatecas, in Nayarit and the Huicholes Mountains of Jalisco (A. LaFón personal communication: 1990). Leopold (1948) noted the extirpation of Gould's turkeys at San Luis Springs, Chihuahua, near the U.S.-Mexico border. Leopold's map of turkey range

The Gould's turkey is a large, light-colored bird of the western Sierra Madres. *Photo by R. Aaltonen.*

showed an absence of turkeys adjacent to the U.S. border south of Hidalgo County, New Mexico, in the San Luis Mountains. But Schemnitz saw flocks of 15 and 32 adult and immature Gould's turkeys in this area in August 1985.

In the United States today, Gould's turkeys live in the Animas and San Luis mountains of New Mexico, and in the Peloncillo Mountains of New Mexico and Arizona. Since recent studies began in 1982, the Gould's turkey has been gradually spreading northward and westward while increasing in numbers in the Peloncillo Mountains. The turkeys also may be increasing in the Animas and San Luis mountains, especially in the Deer Creek area of the Gray Ranch. The Peloncillo Mountains population reaches into extreme southeastern Arizona, and both the Peloncillo and San Luis populations possibly range into contiguous habitat in Mexico.

Gould's turkeys, wild-trapped in Mexico, were released in 1983 at Fort Huachuca in southeastern Arizona near Sierra Vista, where a few survive.

Currently, the Chiricahua Mountains of Arizona are occupied by a low-density population of *M. g. merriami*, or perhaps even *M. g. merriami-mexicana* hybrids, originating from introductions of Merriam's in the 1930s and 1950s by the Arizona Game and Fish Department. Potentially suitable habitat for Gould's—Madrean Evergreen Woodland—extends westward in Arizona along the international boundary as far west as Tumacacori Mountains, south of Tucson, and includes the Galiuro, Huachuca, Patagonia, and perhaps Chiricahua mountains. This habitat is contiguous with occupied Gould's habitat, but it is separated from historical Merriam's habitat by a desert barrier inhospitable to Merriam's.

Ten observations of turkeys were made in southeastern Cochise County, Arizona, 1.5 to 3 kilometers (1 to 2 miles) west of the New Mexico border between 1980 and 1987. Photographs of 3 adult male turkeys were taken in April 1985 near San Bernardino Wildlife National Refuge, east of Douglas, Arizona, and 24 kilometers (15 miles) west of the nearest occupied Gould's turkey habitat in New Mexico. The identity of these turkeys is uncertain. One bird showed a large white patch on the wing and perhaps was a domestic–Gould's hybrid. This sighting was within 24 kilometers (15 miles) of a known free-ranging hybrid population in Guadalupe Canyon, Hidalgo County, New Mexico.

HABITAT

Physiography

The Peloncillo, Animas, and San Luis mountains in the United States and the Sierra Madre Occidental

Mountains of Mexico are oriented north-south. The mountains in the United States vary in altitude from about 1,400 to 2,000 meters (4,500 to 6,500 feet), with elevations up to 3,000 meters (9,840 feet) in Mexico. Turkey habitat in Chihuahua and Sonora is rough and dissected with steep and rocky canyons. Occupied range of Gould's turkeys in New Mexico is separated from historic Merriam's habitat to the north by a broad, seemingly impassible desert barrier about 93 kilometers (58 miles) wide. It has no cover, water, or roost trees.

Climate

The occupied New Mexico habitat has a continental climate, characterized by wide daily and annual temperature fluctuations and distinct seasons. Summers are hot, winters mild. The freeze-free period averages 185 days. Respective low and high mean temperatures were 14 degrees Celsius (57 degrees Fahrenheit) and 33 degrees Celsius (91 degrees Fahrenheit) in the summer, and −5 degrees Celsius (23 degrees Fahrenheit) and 13 degrees Celsius (55 degrees Fahrenheit) in the winter (Cox 1973). Record extremes are −23 degrees Celsius (−9 degrees Fahrenheit) and 44 degrees Celsius (111 degrees Fahrenheit). Winter temperatures rarely drop below −18 degrees Celsius (0 degrees Fahrenheit) and usually rise above 0 degrees Celsius (32 degrees Fahrenheit) during the day.

Average annual precipitation for this area is 45 centimeters (18 inches), more than half of which falls from July through September. A lesser peak occurs during the winter in the form of rain and snow. Mean annual snowfall is about 25.4 centimeters (10 inches), and average annual evapotranspiration (total water loss from soil and plants) is 234 centimeters (92 inches). The climate in Mexico is similar, but winter temperatures are colder and more snow falls in higher mountainous elevations.

Vegetation

The vegetation of the New Mexico habitat has been broadly classified as a Madrean Evergreen Woodland (Brown 1982). Eight habitat types with distinct vegetative characteristics have been delineated in the Peloncillo Mountains of New Mexico, based on the work of Moir (1979), Willging (1987), and USDA Forest Service (1987). The main habitat type, border piñon-Toumey oak-bull muhly, a savanna type, covered 33 percent of the area (Table 2). Three additional types, Emory oak-bear grass-side oats grama, an oak savanna; blue grama-side oats grama, a grama steppe; and Toumey oak-manzanita, a chaparral type, totaled 52 percent of the study area.

The habitat used by radio-marked hens based on

490 telemetry observations by York (1991) documented a habitat preference for the piñon pine, piñon-ricegrass habitat, and 3 riparian habitats: Emory oak-canyon grape, Arizona white oak-bull muhly, and Chihuahua pine-silverleaf oak.

In Mexico, much of the occupied habitat is in the temperate pine-oak upland forest (Leopold 1959). Riparian habitats in the canyon bottoms provide the primary source of water, food, brood habitat, escape cover, and roost trees.

POPULATIONS

Population density information for Gould's turkey has been scant. Leopold (1948) cited densities of 16 turkeys per square kilometer (43 per square mile) in oak woodland in Mexico. He mentioned a population of 4 birds per square kilometer (11 per square mile) in pine-oak-juniper woodland in northern Chihuahua in 1937 that increased to 12 birds per square kilometer (32 per square mile) by 1948.

During the winter of 1986–87, a similar area in Chihuahua, 64 kilometers (40 miles) southwest of Nueva Casas Grande, had an estimated population of 15 turkeys per square kilometer (39 per square mile). Fifteen adult gobblers, estimated to be half the adult gobbler population, were harvested from 324 hectares (800 acres) during April and early May 1987. This breeding concentration may not have been representative of average densities over a broad area.

The population trend in New Mexico's Peloncillo Mountains has been upward. Potter (1984) found only 16 turkeys, 0.3 turkeys per square kilometer (0.9 per square mile) in occupied habitat of approximately 3,600 hectares (8,892 acres). By 1986, the population estimate was 45 turkeys, 0.7 birds per square kilometer (1.7 per square mile) (Willging 1987). And by autumn 1988, the population had grown to an estimated 75 turkeys in 13,000 hectares (0.5 per square kilometer, 1.5 per square mile). Two years of drought conditions and low production contributed to a decline in population to an estimated 50 birds in 1990. An estimate was given of less than 50 Gould's turkeys in Arizona (National Wild Turkey Federation 1986).

LIFE HISTORY

Gobbling

Most gobbling occurs during April and May. In Chihuahua, the gobbling period was from April 10 to May 20 (Leopold 1959), with prime gobbling throughout May (Bland 1986). This was later than in New Mexico, where peak gobbling activity was in late April. Over an 8-year period, the earliest date of gobbling in New Mexico was April 4, and the latest gobbling was heard on June 12. Later gobbling by Gould's turkeys than by other subspecies could indicate a later reproductive period timed to coincide with plant green-up, which normally begins about the last week of June in Gould's habitat.

Nesting

Leopold (1959) mentioned an average clutch size of 11 (range 8 to 18) in Mexico, and nests within 183 meters (200 yards) of water. In 1988, a nest of a radio-tagged Gould's hen with 9 eggs was located, the first to be reported and described in the scientific literature (Schemnitz et al. 1990). The nest was in the Emory oak-bear grass-side oats grama habitat type, oak-juniper subtype (U.S. Forest Service 1987). The nest was under an Arizona white oak at the base of a Schott yucca. Shrub growth in the vicinity of the nest was dense (35 percent ground cover). Crown canopy (97 percent) and vertical vegetation density were greater at the nest than away. The nest was 3.2 kilometers (2.0 miles) from the hen's point of capture the previous winter and was 200 meters (650 feet) from water. Seven eggs hatched on June 22, 1988, and 3 poults survived to maturity. Between the ages of 2 and 3 weeks, 4 poults died from unknown causes.

This hen and 2-week-old brood moved 1.6 kilometers (1 mile) from the site to a riparian habitat of predominately large Emory oak. Another group of hens (with 8 poults) moved 1.6 kilometers (1 mile) in 2 days when the poults were 1 week old. High initial poult mortality and the mobility of hens with young broods are similar to characteristics of Merriam's turkeys in New Mexico (Schemnitz et al. 1985). Estimated hatching dates from back dating 6 broods in 4 years of study were from June 2 to June 28.

Table 2. Habitat types of Peloncillo Mountains study area, Coronado National Forest.

Habitat type	Area		Percentage of total
	Hectares	Acres	
border piñon–Toumey oak–bull muhly	6,805	16,814	33.0
Emory oak–bear grass–side oats grama	6,580	16,260	32.0
side oats grama–blue grama	3,263	8,064	16.0
border piñon–piñon rice grass	2,474	5,372	11.0
Toumey oak–Manzanita	712	1,760	3.5
Arizona white oak–bull muhly	522	1,290	2.6
Chihuahua pine–silverleaf oak	223	550	1.1
Emory oak–canyon grape	157	388	0.8
	20,436	50,498	100.0

A known brood-rearing area in Blair Canyon. *Photo by D. York.*

Brood Habitat

One area, Blair Well Canyon, Peloncillo Mountains, has been a consistent place for sighting broods each summer since 1982. The brood area is an open, wide-bottomed valley within 1.5 kilometers (0.9 miles) of permanent water. The vegetation type is oak savanna with large Emory and Arizona white oak trees widely spaced or clumped in groves, and with an understory of grama grasses and rice grass. Average tree height is about 9 to 10 meters (30 to 33 feet). Vegetation on the side slopes is denser, with bear grass as a major shrub component. Gray and Emory oak and alligator juniper are the domi-

nant trees. Average shrub height is 5 meters (16 feet). The hens and broods used the open bottomlands and savannas for feeding and the side slopes for cover. Bear grass was important for cover. On several occasions, hen and poults were seen to run uphill among the bear grass clumps, quickly disappearing from view. Young poults, from 1 to 4 weeks old, hid in the accumulation of dead leaves at the base of bear grass clumps. Other brood-rearing areas such as Deer Flats and Cloverdale riparian areas were similar to Blair Well.

Movements

Gould's turkeys seem to range widely and be highly mobile, although little specific information on movements is available, because of a paucity of radio-marked birds. Investigators in the United States were frustrated and perplexed by the frequent disappearance and then reappearance of known birds. Potter (1984) speculated that birds might be moving south into Mexico. In contrast, however, during the 5-day period September 16 to 21, 1988, 2 radioed hens and 3 poults moved 11.2 kilometers (7 miles) northward in 6 days and joined a flock of 15 other hens and poults. A late fall-early winter flock of the same 20 turkeys moved a distance of 2.4 to 3.2 kilometers (1.5 to 2.0 miles) per day during their feeding activities in October and November 1988. The total area used was 11.6 to 13.0 square kilometers (4.5 to 5.0 square miles). Subsequently, some of these birds returned to range that had been used early the previous spring (D. York personal communication: 1990). During the deer-

Juniper tree *(Juniperus deppeana)* with berries is a reliable mast producer heavily used by Gould's turkey in Peloncillo Mountains. *Photo by D. York.*

This bear grass *(Nolina microcarpa)* slope is excellent escape cover and feeding area for Gould's turkeys. *Photo by D. York.*

A typical Chihuahua pine *(Pinus leiophylla)* roost tree at Blair Well, Peloncillo Mountains, New Mexico. *Photo by D. York.*

Clanton Tank roost site is a consistently used roost site. It is composed of large Chihuahua pines *(Pinus leiophylla)* in the 55-centimeter (22-inch) dbh range and with an average height of 16.8 meters (55 feet). *Photo by D. York.*

hunting season, turkeys avoided the only well-traveled road through the center of the main Peloncillo Mountain winter range. York (1991) found the yearly home range of 8 radioed hen turkeys to average 4,385 hectares (10,835 acres) during a drought period in 1989 and subsequent mast crop failures in 1990.

Roosts

Roost trees are an essential component of Gould's turkey habitat. Roost sites consist of 1 to 28 dominant and codominant trees. Turkey roost sites in northern Chihuahua are similar to those in the Peloncillo Mountains.

In the United States, the preferred tree species is Chihuahua pine, the only tall pine in occupied range (Table 3). The Apache pine and the Chihuahua pine are widely used in Mexico. Turkeys also sometimes roost in cottonwood, Emory oak, Arizona walnut, and Arizona sycamore. The absence of roost trees probably limits occupancy of otherwise suitable Gould's turkey habitats in southwestern New Mexico. Possibly because of a shortage of available roost sites, Gould's turkeys roost frequently in the same trees.

Foods

Leopold (1959) described foods of Gould's turkey in Mexico as many and varied, with oak acorns the most important food. Other mast foods mentioned included juniper, pine, manzanita, cherry, and madrone. Grass

Table 3. Summary of roost tree measurements at 31 Gould's turkey roost sites, Peloncillo Mountains, 1988.

Species of trees	Number of sites	Average number of trees utilized in roost	Average diameter dbh in centimeters (inches)	Average height in meters (feet)	Average age (years)	Average basal area in square meters per hectare (square feet per acre)
Chihuahua pine	26	5.6	53.1 (20.9)	16.4 (53.8)	84.8	12.6 (54.9)
Emory oak	4	2.4	65.8 (25.9)	20.0 (65.6)	137.8	12.4 (54.0)
Mixed species	1	a	61.9 (24.4)	12.2 (40.0)	109.4	12.5 (54.4)

[a] One roost site included 5 species of trees (4 Arizona sycamore, 2 Fremont cottonwood, 2 Emory oak, 1 Arizona walnut, 1 Arizona white oak).

Emory oaks *(Quercus emoryi)* on Pendleton Ranch are used as roost trees. *Photo by D. York.*

Pointleaf manzanita *(Arctostaphylos pungens)* berries are produced regularly and are a sought-after food of the Gould's turkey in the Peloncillo Mountains. *Photo by D. York.*

The "Quem-Nomi-Bocu" *(Quercus emoryi, Nolina microcarpa, Bouteloua curtipendula)* habitat type makes up 32 percent of the study area in the Peloncillo Mountains. The only scientifically recorded Gould's turkey nest occurred in this habitat type. *Photo by D. York.*

seeds, grass leaves, and insects—especially grasshoppers—were favorite foods.

A microhistological fecal analysis was used to determine Gould's food habits by season during 1983 in New Mexico (Potter 1984). During the spring months (April to June), juniper berries were the most important food, but the newly emerging mustard forbs also were heavily utilized.

Grass became increasingly important during summer (July to September), especially the seed of barnyard grass, which was common around some of the stock watering ponds. The fruits of manzanita and juniper continued to be a major component in the summer, and insects reached a high of 13 percent composition.

In the fall (October to December), grass was the principal food, with the seed of piñon rice grass accounting for almost half of the grass component. Forbs reached their lowest point in the fall, but the fruits of manzanita, onion, skunkbush, juniper, and canyon grape were heavily utilized.

The most varied diet occurred in winter (January to March), but the bulk of the winter diet was juniper berries and manzanita and onion seeds. In the year of

study, however, no oak acorns and little pine seed were produced. They probably would have been preferred.

Diets noted in visual observations of feeding turkeys agreed with the fecal analysis with one exception. On several occasions in June, turkeys were observed feeding on aquatic vegetation including water starwort, waterwort, duckweed, pondweed, and green algae at the edge of stock watering ponds. Probably aquatic invertebrates also were taken. Heavy use of riparian forbs and grasses was noted at a fenced spring (seep) in November.

Gould's turkeys use these oak trees at Deer Flats for loafing sites. *Photo by D. York.*

Rock cement dam built to improve water supply by New Mexico Chapter, National Wild Turkey Federation in Blair Canyon, Peloncillo Mountains, southwestern New Mexico. *Photo by D. York.*

A 7-year (1985–91) food-habits analysis by York (1991) was consistent with that of Potter (1984). On a seasonal basis, the same species of fruits, grasses, and forbs were used in similar proportions during both studies (Figure 1).

Water

Water is a key component in arid regions and a limiting factor of wild turkey habitat. The Peloncillo Mountains contain no natural lakes or perennial streams, and very few natural springs. Livestock grazing, however, is the primary land use, so numerous stock pond and watering facilities have been installed. There are about 40 dirt or concrete stock tanks on the Coronado National Forest, with permanent water averaging about 3.2 kilometers (2 miles) or less from any point. But water is not equally distributed throughout the turkey range. Some range is used only when water is seasonally present in intermittent streams, potholes, and tinahuas. Substantial range expansions and denser populations may be possible with additional water development.

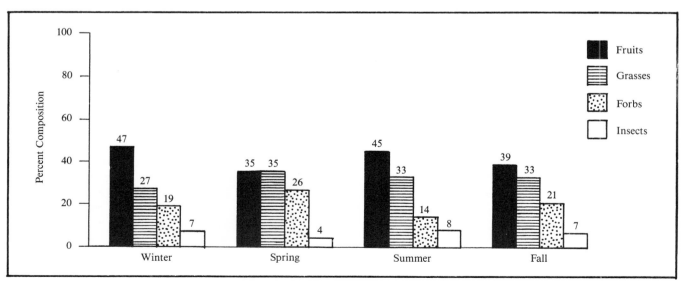

Figure 1. Percent composition of grasses, forbs, fruits, and insects found in Gould's turkey fecal samples during the 4 seasons (York 1991).

LIMITING FACTORS

Predation

Although various predators inhabit the Gould's range, few instances of predation have been recorded. Two hundred thirty-nine coyote droppings and 83 great horned owl pellets have been analyzed, but no turkey remains have been found in these samples. Direct evidence was found of mountain lion predation on 2 radio-collared hens and 2 gobblers. It may be more limiting than previously thought. Two radio-collared adult hens were taken by bobcats during the spring of 1990 (York 1991). A dense and widespread population of feral hogs occupies the entire New Mexico habitat and constitutes a potential source of nest predation, though no such losses have been observed.

Poaching

During our studies, extending from 1982 to 1989 in New Mexico, we found little evidence of poaching. Two piles of feathers provided circumstantial evidence of poaching, and a definite instance of poaching was observed by a graduate student who found fresh feathers at a camp in Skeleton Canyon.

One of these instances occurred during deer-hunting season. So notices have been posted at key sites, and hunters are contacted directly to increase their awareness of the protected status of Gould's turkey. Also, the presence of research personnel likely acts as a deterrent to poaching. Although the Peloncillo population frequents private ranchlands near human habitations, the local ranchers and their employees tend to be protective of the turkeys.

In Mexico, experienced hunters and guides believe that poaching of turkeys for food is common. Bland (1986:192) commented, "Too often the local hunters roost-shoot the birds, causing them to move. This roost/site information seems to be passed down from one generation of hunters to another, and if it wasn't for a lack of guns and shells there wouldn't be any turkeys." Turkeys and other wildlife in the vicinity of ejidos (communes) have drastically declined while turkey populations on larger private ranches have been maintained.

Disease and Parasites

Very little is known about disease and parasites in Gould's turkeys. Blood and cloacal swab samples were taken from Gould's turkeys from Chihuahua transplanted to Fort Huachuca, Arizona, and tested for *Mycoplasma gallisepticum*, avian influenza, and salmonellosis. No evidence of infection was found (Breland 1987). Schemnitz examined 5 adult males from northern Chihuahua in May 1987 and 1988 and found heavy infestations of *Raillietina*, a tapeworm.

Hybridization

The southwestern New Mexico Gould's turkey population has faced the threat of contamination from a rancher's flock of about 20 domestic–Gould's turkeys, which may interact with wild turkeys. Fortunately, the ranch owner agreed to reduce and eventually eliminate the hybrid flock. About 10 birds remained during winter 1990–91. Hybridization may be a problem in parts of Mexico, although most wild turkey range in Mexico is in mountainous terrain on large ranches, where domestic poultry is not raised.

MANAGEMENT

Land Ownership

Much of today's occupied Gould's turkey habitat in the United States is in public ownership, managed by the U.S. Forest Service. A lesser amount is managed by the Bureau of Land Management. Another large block of 125,457 hectares (310,000 acres), the Gray Ranch in the Animas Mountains, was bought by the Nature Conservancy. With purchase of the Gray Ranch, protection of the main Gould's turkey range in New Mexico from adverse

Turkey trap in Chihuahua, Mexico. The burgeoning human population puts intense pressure on wildlife populations for sustenance. *Photo by J. Dickson.*

Bear grass slopes in the "Quem-Nomi-Bocu" habitat type. Good brood area can be found along the Swahili Trail in the Peloncillo Mountains. *Photo by D. York.*

Bundles of bear grass, which is good brood habitat, harvested by Mexicans near Blair Well. It's one of the many uses of public lands that could conflict with turkeys and other wildlife. *Photo by D. York.*

Land Use

The bear grass subtype is a key summer brood habitat. Extensive cutting of bear grass for commercial use could pose a potential threat to turkey brood habitat. Bear grass cutting is permitted by the Forest Service but is limited to small, scattered areas. As a result of early studies by Potter and Schemnitz, the Forest Service limits bear grass cutting to protect escape cover for turkey broods.

The cutting of green oak and juniper for fuelwood, particularly in riparian areas, can degrade turkey habitat. Fuelwood cutting on the national forests is controlled by permit and is restricted to dead, fallen trees in an effort to maintain turkey food sources and the microclimate of riparian habitats. But enforcement is difficult because of the remoteness of national forests.

Livestock grazing is an important factor in wild turkey habitat management (Schemnitz et al. 1985). In some grazing allotments, Willging (1987) found disproportionate use by cattle of riparian areas in spring and summer, causing severe overgrazing and habitat degradation. Pastures with deferred summer grazing or seasonal rest were used by breeding turkeys more often than pastures exposed to yearlong grazing. On some allotments of the Coronado National Forest, an increase in turkey populations coincides with above-average precipitation and lower cattle-stocking rates.

Habitat Improvement

Several projects have been implemented in the Peloncillo Mountains to improve water availability and enhance riparian vegetation. These have been joint endeavors between the New Mexico Chapter of the Na-

Select cutting of bear grass in Blair Canyon. *Photo by D. York.*

development or land subdivision is assured, even though previous owners were highly protective of the turkeys.

The Peloncillo turkey flocks frequently use the small tracts of private lands scattered throughout the national forest, since such tracts typically occupy the preferred riparian habitat and contain reliable water sources.

Unfortunately, the long-range outlook in Mexico is not bright. A burgeoning human population will cause turkey habitat to gradually shrink as segments are usurped for agriculture and urban development. Fortunately, much of the current habitat is at higher elevations, remote, steep, rocky, and not especially attractive for human settlement or agriculture.

Ponderosa pine and piñon-juniper Gould's turkey habitat in western Chihuahua, Mexico. *Photo by J. Dickson.*

Oak savanna Gould's turkey habitat in western Chihuahua, Mexico. Riparian zones are critical habitat, especially for roosting. *Photo by J. Dickson.*

tional Wild Turkey Federation (which provided labor) and the USDA Forest Service (which furnished materials and supplies through the Challenge Cost Share Program). Future habitat enhancement projects are planned primarily to encourage range expansion and improve habitat quality.

RECOVERY

Several agencies, including the U.S. Army, Fort Huachuca, and the Arizona Game and Fish Department have been working to import Gould's turkeys from Mexico. Efforts are in progress to facilitate transplants of turkeys from Mexico to Arizona and possibly other states. Lengthy quarantine requirements, imposed by federal regulations and designed to protect domestic poultry, have been a deterrent to release efforts.

Confining the birds to isolation pens in compliance with quarantine regulations has resulted in high mortality in a restoration effort at Fort Huachuca, Arizona (Breland 1987). Wild birds do not adjust well to the stress of confinement.

A small number of Gould's turkeys from the Mexico transplant exist on Fort Huachuca from releases of 9 turkeys in 1983 and 12 in 1987. Turkeys, presumably from this transplant, have been seen by personnel of the Bureau of Land Management 16 kilometers (10 miles) to the east along the San Pedro River.

Restoration efforts and increases in populations in New Mexico (Schemnitz and Pinto 1987, Willging 1987) bring hope for expansion to all suitable range and the eventual removal of Gould's turkey from New Mexico's list of endangered species. Conceivably, there could be limited hunting at some future time.

Chapter 22

WILD TURKEYS OUTSIDE THEIR HISTORIC RANGE

Gerald A. Wunz
Wildlife Research Biologist
Pennsylvania Game Commission
Milroy, Pennsylvania

According to Aldrich (1967a), there is no definite evidence that wild turkeys ever lived much beyond the area they occupied at the beginning of European colonization of North America. The borders of the wild turkey's historic range extended from southern Maine westward to south-central South Dakota, then southwest to Arizona and south to include all but the southeastern and southernmost parts of Mexico (Leopold 1948, Aldrich and Duvall 1955, Schorger 1966).

Today, nearly 250,000 turkeys are living on about 210,000 square kilometers (81,000 square miles) of habitats that are outside the borders of this ancestral range. Some 215,000 of these birds inhabit this new range in the contiguous United States. The remainder live in Hawaii, a few islands in the South Pacific, southern Canada, and central Europe.

The introduction of turkeys outside their native range had already started before European explorers set eyes on this grand bird. Turkeys, presumably those domesticated by the Aztecs in Mexico, had been distributed among Native American inhabitants as far south as Costa Rica by the time of the Cortez expedition in 1519. But it was the Spanish explorers who recognized the commercial value of such a large bird as a domestic species. The Spaniards had the means—their sailing ships—to spread it far and wide.

Later, the appreciation of wild turkeys as supreme game birds would also result in numerous attempts to introduce wild turkeys in various places throughout the world, as well as in North America. On the magnitude of this endeavor, Lindzey (1967a:259) wrote: "It would require much patient investigation for very little return to even begin tracing the history of existing populations or introductions of wild turkeys outside of the United States." Fortunately, Schorger (1966) and others had already paved the way for the following updated attempt at such an investigation.

CENTRAL AND SOUTH AMERICA AND THE WEST INDIES

Native Americans spread domestic turkeys throughout much of Central America. Wright (1914) reported that after the subjugation of Mexico by Cortez in 1521, the conquistadors transported domestic turkeys to Panama and to islands of the Caribbean. Other references imply that turkeys may have been taken to some of the Greater Antilles by previous expeditions, arriving in Cuba perhaps as early as 1511. Eventually, turkeys were found on all islands of the Antilles, where they thrived as domestic birds.

Dates on the arrival of turkeys in South America are uncertain, but turkeys were unknown there before the Spaniards introduced them. Turkeys reportedly arrived in Peru from Nicaragua, presumably soon after the Spanish discovery of this bird as a domestic species in Central America. By 1587, domestic turkeys were reported on Puna Island in the Gulf of Guayaquil, Ecuador, and by 1646 in Chile. The only references found that indicated feral populations ever existed in South America were those referring to the origin of some turkeys released in the Hawaiian Islands as being from free-ranging, Chilean domestic stock (Long 1981, Lever 1987).

In the Bermudas, imported turkeys increased rapidly. By 1624, many of them had become feral because they were too numerous for the early colonists there to care for. Domestic turkeys imported by Jesuits to Hispaniola Island (Haiti and the Dominican Republic) were reported to have become feral. Baron de Wimpffen had noticed them during his visits there in the late 1700s (Wetmore and Swales 1931). Turkeys of unspecified origin were introduced on Adros Island, largest of the Bahamas, in 1954 (Bond 1979). In 1952 and 1953, 78 wild-trapped Rio Grandes from Texas were transplanted to Cuba and to the Dominican Republic. Lack of further information suggests viable populations did not develop from introductions on these islands or other areas in this region.

EUROPE

Early in the 16th century, turkeys were introduced into Europe through Spain as domesticated stock that had originated in Mexico. Turkeys were firmly established on Spanish poultry farms by 1530 and in much of Europe by 1860. The color of these imported turkeys, reportedly ranging from white to black, and their plump bodies fit the descriptions of present-day domestic turkeys (Schorger 1966).

When wild turkeys were first transplanted from their native range in North America is uncertain. There are reports that such birds were shipped from Virginia to England as early as 1742, and some indications suggest shipments may have occurred earlier. But the dates these birds actually arrived are usually lacking (Schorger 1966). In 1825, Lafayette brought wild turkeys home from Maryland. These, however, were imported to improve the domestic breed in France (Levasseur 1829) rather than to establish wild populations.

British Isles

The first documented use of turkeys as game birds outside their native range seems to have been during the 18th century when King George II kept a flock of 3,000 at Richmond Park near Surrey, England. They were hunted with dogs and shot from trees in which they had taken refuge (Schorger 1966). This concentration of turkeys was an irresistible temptation to local poachers.

The ensuing problems for the royal gamekeepers caused the next king, George III, to eliminate the turkey population (Lever 1987). A reference (Pennants 1781) to turkeys living at Richmond and other parks in England as "off-color" compared with wild turkeys cast doubt on the purity of the stock to Schorger (1966) and caused Lever (1987) to refer to them as "semi-feral." Also Darwin (1868) reported that turkeys believed to be of wild stock that were imported from the United States and kept in parks in England differed from each other in body shape, plumage color, and barred wing patterns.

Perhaps the first reference to actual transplants of wild-trapped stock is that of Gilmour (1876), who received 3 wild turkeys reportedly caught near the southern end of Lake Huron in Ontario, Canada, and released in Argyllshire, Scotland. Because of initial success (17 poults produced), more trapped wild turkeys were imported in succeeding years. By 1892, the flock had increased to about 200 birds, but later the population died out.

During the 1870s, Canadian turkeys released in Invernesshire bred successfully for a number of years. The fact Lever (1987) also referred to these populations as "semi-feral" suggests these Canadian turkeys had been pen-reared, even if they may have been of wild origin.

In the 1890s, turkeys of unspecified sources were released in Gloucestershire and in the 1920s near Suffolk, England (Lever 1987). Before World War II, semiferal turkeys that were bred on the grounds of a zoo and a park in Bedfordshire, England, died out in the early 1940s, supposedly from lack of supplemental winter feeding. Fitter (1959) reported turkeys were established in the late 1950s in the wild on the Hinsel estate in Berwickshire. These birds lasted at least until 1966 (H. Spittler and U. Palmer personal communication: 1988). R. Prytherch (personal communication: 1979) said a small population of "so-called wild turkeys" existed at that time in East Anglia. The lack of more recent reports suggests that most of these populations no longer exist, and any that do could probably not be considered truly wild.

In Ireland in 1982, "wild" turkey eggs (type or origin unknown) were imported from the United States to County Limerick. Poults that hatched were distributed among landowners in the counties of Cork, Donegal, Sligo, and Clare. In 1985, eggs and birds were widely distributed to several other counties (Lever 1987). There have been no recent reports on the results of these attempts.

Mainland Europe

There seems to be no information of feral domestic or wild populations of turkeys ever existing in southern Europe. H. Spittler and U. Palmer (personal communication: 1988), however, could account for 31 areas in which turkeys were liberated to start populations in Germany, Austria, Hungary, Czechoslovakia, Sweden, and East Prussia (now part of Poland) from 1875 to World War II. Most of these efforts were immediate failures or short-lived successes. At least 4 attempts, all failures, were made to establish turkeys in France (Etchecopar 1955).

Most of the stock involved in these releases was of unspecified sources, but some references mention turkeys coming from "America, Mexico, or domestic crosses." Regardless of origin, undoubtedly all of these turkeys were pen-raised before they were released. Such was the background of turkeys from eggs imported into Austria that were hatched and released near Grafenegg in 1880. They turned out to be perhaps the longest-lasting feral population of turkeys in Europe.

Subsequently, birds or eggs from Grafenegg were transplanted to other areas in Austria, Germany, Hungary, and Czechoslovakia. Although most of these releases failed, populations persisted on some large estates until World War I and the decline of the feudal system (Alberti 1922). The Grafenegg population persisted until 1945 (Spittler 1977).

The information gathered by H. Spittler and U. Palmer (personal communication: 1988), indicating the small turkey populations started in East Prussia and Pomerania (now in Poland) soon failed, seems to conflict with information from Aliev and Khanmamedov (1966), who referred to the turkey as an excellent game bird that has bred successfully for a long time in the Baltic Sea region of Poland and Latvia. Aliev and Khanmamedov also report "interesting experiments" on breeding were made in the Transcaucasia region of the southern portions of the old U.S.S.R. between the Black and Caspian seas. But they did not elaborate on these turkeys or the recent status of any populations that may remain in Poland or the Baltic nations (Long 1981). Small populations were started in Vostergotland and Vanern in Sweden in the 1930s, both of which vanished soon after 1940.

After World War II, pen-raised "wild" turkeys from private and state game farms in the United States had become readily available for stocking. This availability seemed to renew interest among Europeans, mostly in West Germany and Czechoslovakia, in establishing turkeys as a game bird.

During the 1960s, birds from this source were imported into Poland and raised on farms for several years before being released into the wild. There are no recent reports on their status. In the early 1970s, turkeys hatched from eggs from Poland and released in Hungary were tame and soon vanished (F. Nemes personal communication: 1989). Eight eastern wild turkeys sent to Yugoslavia in the late 1970s failed, probably because of their low numbers (J. Dickson personal communication: 1990).

In Austria from 1971 to 1980, birds hatched from eggs imported from a game farm in Pennsylvania were released east of Vienna by Oberforster Hans Gruber. Temporary populations developed on 3 areas. One of these (at Drosendorf on Thaya) migrated across the river to Czechoslovakia, where it still exists (U. Palmer personal communication: 1988).

Czechoslovakia. M. Vach (personal communication: 1990) lists 24 attempts between 1781 and 1954 to introduce turkeys into the area of Czechoslovakia. The birds, imported from England, Germany, and Austria, were pen-raised and of varying ancestry. Most releases were made in central Bohemia Province of western Czechoslovakia. One release persisted as a small population that was hunted. A preserved specimen of these turkeys, shot in 1943, was reported to resemble a Rio Grande turkey. No turkey populations survived both World Wars, and none of the 5 releases made during the 1950s lasted more than 3 or 4 years.

Since 1980, game-farm eastern poults and Merriam's turkey eggs were imported from America. A resulting population, estimated at 1,380 birds that are hunted in spring and fall, "has been annually supported by the release of captive bred chicks." These turkeys inhabit about 800 square kilometers (310 square miles) of oak, pine, and spruce forests in central Bohemia.

A small population of Merriam's-origin birds lives in "largely pine forests with some oaks." Small flocks are reportedly living at 11 other sites in Bohemia. Poaching and low production (1.6 to 2.7 poults per hen) seem to limit populations (M. Vach personal communication: 1990). Photographs of birds from the largest population, which show them ranging close to buildings, indicate plumage of eastern wild turkey heritage. The birds exhibit behavior of turkeys with a game-farm origin.

West Germany. In Germany, both before and after World War II, more efforts were made to establish turkeys as a game bird than elsewhere in Europe. In 1957 and 1958, some 300 eggs from private and state game farms in Pennsylvania were sent to northern Germany and Bavaria, but their eventual disposition was not known (Kaufman 1962). Hellwig (1972) and Behrendt (1978) reported turkeys were released near Kassel, in the Mosel River Valley, in the Pfalz, and near Offenburg. There were no further reports that any of these 4 releases succeeded.

Ten game-farm turkeys and 200 eggs from the Pennsylvania Game Commission farm were sent to the Nordrhein-Westfalen Wildlife Research Institute near Bonn, West Germany, in 1957 and 1958 (Kauffman 1962). Beginning in 1958, progeny of these birds were released in 4 major forest areas in the west-central state of Nordrhein-Westfalen. Turkeys failed to establish in 2 areas, but they reproduced and persisted in the others. Later these 2 populations decreased despite infusions of more turkeys that were raised in pens at the Institute. Spittler (1977) reported only 10 to 20 birds remained in the forest near Krefeld and 40 near Bonn. He concluded

Shipping wild turkeys to Germany for restoration. *Photo by G. Wunz, Pennsylvania Game Commission.*

that periodic releases of artificially raised turkeys were necessary to maintain the population. The total population estimate in 1988 was 80 to 90 birds.

Since 1971, Dr. Gunter Kuckulies (personal communication: 1983) has attempted to naturalize Rio

Grande turkeys raised from eggs (5 shipments of 80 eggs each) imported from a Texas game farm. Some reproduced after being released near Lüneburg in the northeast section of West Germany, but the turkeys remained relatively tame. In 1976, the population was 38. By 1983, it was down to 11. The lack of recent reports suggests this population has disappeared.

The failures of turkeys from pen-raised origin to establish expanding populations in Germany caused Dr. Walter Wirth of Oberneisen to request advice of wild turkey specialists in the United States. After a survey of habitat suitability (Wunz and Wunz 1976) and negotiations through a complex maze of international regulations and decorum (Palmer 1978), 15 wild-trapped turkeys donated by Vermont were shipped air freight and released in the Northwest Taunus Forest of central West Germany in 1978.

The rolling terrain of this plateau area, dissected by stream courses, resembles turkey habitats in much of the northeastern United States. Forests cover 40 to 45 percent of this area, ranging from wooded fragments of 100 hectares (250 acres) to forest blocks of 4,000 hectares (10,000 acres) that are interspersed with villages and farmland, mostly in the valleys.

Forests are nearly 50 percent hardwoods, mainly red beech and oaks and less-common associates of ash,

German habitat: hardwoods and conifer plantation in Tannus Forest. *Photo by I. Wirth.*

cherry, and maple. The remainder are conifer plantations of Norway spruce, Scotch pine, larch, and Douglas fir that are usually in small blocks interspersed within the hardwood stands. Common understory or woods border species are hornbeam, mountain ash, dogwood, elderberry, buckthorns, hawthorns, blackthorn, dog rose, and blackberries.

The turkeys released into this habitat reproduced and expanded their range, in typical fashion expected of wild-trapped turkeys. By 1985, they occupied an area of nearly 800 square kilometers (310 square miles). The total population was estimated at about 500 turkeys, 300 of which could be accounted for (Wunz et al. 1985). By 1987, the population was maintaining a fair density in the area of the original release site. But the outlying populations had decreased, and some had disappeared. The main population continued to decrease in 1988 and 1989 (W. Wirth personal communication: 1989). Other than greatly increased human disturbance during this period, resulting from log salvage operations after a severe windthrow of trees in the forests of this area, any reason for these declining populations is unknown.

Hunting of these birds has been restricted to spring only and to a small area. Perhaps because of a conservative attitude and the inexperience of hunters in adapting to proper spring hunting methods, few birds have been taken. H. Spittler (personal communication: 1976) reported that turkeys of game-farm origin were being hunted near Bonn by stalking much in the traditional manner of hunting the Auerhahn or capercaillie. Apparently these turkeys would allow hunters to approach within gun range.

RUSSIA, MIDDLE EAST, AND ASIA

Although no records of arrival dates for turkeys in Russia have been uncovered, travelers in southern Russia at the turn of the 18th and 19th centuries noted turkeys in the Crimea and near the Black Sea. Schorger (1966) speculated these may have been wandering or feral populations.

Turkeys were seen as early as 1607 in Persia (Iran), reportedly brought there by Armenian traders. A wildlife status survey during the late 1960s in Iran (J. Hassinger personal communication: 1989) found no evidence of free-ranging turkey populations, not even in the oak forests of northern Iran near the Transcaucasian region of the former U.S.S.R., where Aliev and Khanmamedov (1966) had reported turkeys earlier.

A similar survey in Afghanistan in 1965 revealed no evidence of turkeys, even in what appeared to be acceptable habitat in the monsoonal areas near the eastern border with Kashmir and West Pakistan (J. Hassinger

personal communication: 1989). Domestic turkeys were known in India by at least the start of the 17th century, but none were reported as becoming feral. Early introductions into the Philippine Islands did not thrive, supposedly because of the humid tropical climate. Although later introductions had established turkeys as a domestic species, there are no references to feral populations.

AFRICA

Domestic turkeys had been brought to Africa's west coast by 1682. There are no indications that feral populations ever existed on this continent. On the island of St. Helena, in the South Atlantic, nearly 1,600 kilometers (1,000 miles) west of the southwest coast of Africa, turkeys were introduced by Portuguese mariners early in the 16th century. Visitors in 1588 and 1606 reported feral populations (Schorger 1966), but there are no further reports of turkeys on this island that was the site of Napoleon's exile from 1815 to 1821.

In 1984, 27 Rio Grande birds trapped in Texas were transferred near the equator to Gabon on the west coast of Africa. There have been no reports on their status (D. Wilson personal communication: 1989).

POLYNESIA AND THE SOUTH PACIFIC

Hawaii

The Hawaiian Islands were formed by volcanos rising from the depths of the Pacific Ocean. Despite their great geographic isolation from any other major landform, plants, birds, insects, and other invertebrates found their way there and evolved into large numbers of species endemic only to this archipelago (Holing 1989). To these were added even larger numbers of exotic plants and animals, some brought by the early Polynesian immigrants. Far more were introduced during Caucasian settlement and exploitation of the islands.

This plethora of native and exotic species can exist because of the great variety of natural communities—ranging from arid shrub and grasslands to rain forests and alpine meadows—that resulted from the tropical location, northeast prevailing trade winds, and rugged, mountainous landscapes. The State Division of Forestry and Wildlife lists 7 game mammals (3 of which are feral domestic animals) and 17 upland game birds, including the wild turkey.

The history of importing turkeys as game birds to Hawaii may have started as early as 1788. But feral turkeys that existed until the 1940s were reputedly descen-

Hawaii wild turkey habitat on Molokai. This is typical habitat of Kiawe roost trees. *Photos by D. Gonzales, Hawaii Chapter National Wild Turkey Federation.*

dants of free-ranging domestic stock imported from Chile in 1815 (Long 1981, Lever 1987). Since then, many wild turkeys of game-farm origin were released on most of the major islands. Lewin (1971) recorded that game-farm turkeys, mostly of eastern turkey origin, were released in 1959 and 1960. In 1961, wild-trapped Rio Grande birds from Texas were transplanted to the Puu Waawaa Ranch on the island of Hawaii.

Today's high-density turkey populations—estimates ranging from 6,000 to 16,000—on the Hawaiian Islands are credited to about 400 wild-trapped Rio Grande turkeys imported from southern Texas from 1961 to 1963. The birds were released on 6 of the major islands: Hawaii, Maui, Molokai, Lanai, Oahu, and Kauai. The attempts failed on Oahu and Kauai, where environmental factors—namely, wetter climates and possibly poaching—may have been against establishment of this subspecies (Gonzalez 1982).

These turkeys have done best on Hawaii, Molokai, and Lanai, particularly in the dry habitats on the lee sides of mountains, where annual rainfall is less than 50 centimeters (20 inches), away from the moisture laden northeasterly trade winds. These turkeys favor habitats of open forests and brushlands, interspersed with grasslands that are reminiscent of the Rio Grande turkey's native range. The difference is the rough terrain of the islands.

On the big island of Hawaii, turkeys range from sea level up to nearly 3,000 meters (10,000 feet) in the open,

parklike forests and savannas on the lee slopes of Mauna Kea and Mauna Loa (D. Gonzalez personal communication: 1989). The upper, moist slopes are forested with large koa trees, with a mixture of ohia trees increasing down the slope to the drier, parklike forest association of the smaller mamani and naio trees. Near midelevation (1,000 meters, 3,000 feet) are savannas of widely spaced small trees of ohia and lama and exotic pampas grass and kikuyu grass. Below 600 meters (2,000 feet) the habitat is dominated by introduced kiawe (mesquite) trees interspersed with the larger, rare native wiliwili trees and understories of exotic lantana shrubs and prickly pear cactus (Lewin 1971, Burger 1981).

The turkeys on Molokai inhabit the dry west and southwest half of the island, ranging down to the rugged coastal terrain of shrub lands primarily of kiawe trees, lantana shrubs, and grasses. Turkeys on Lanai and Maui occupy habitats similar to those on Molokai (D. Gonzalez and P. Bromley personal communication: 1989).

Kramer et al. (1985) generically list the major food items of turkeys in the Hawaiian Islands as seeds, berries, plant tops, insects, and snails. Only kiawe tree beans are listed specifically. Gonzalez (1982) has observed wild turkeys feeding on insects, occasionally on small lizards, but mainly on berries and seed heads of grasses and forbs.

The reproductive chronology is what would be expected for turkeys living near the latitude of the Tropic of Cancer: mating starting in March, nesting in April, and broods appearing in late April and May. The average brood size of 4 to 6 reported by Gonzalez (1982) is surprisingly small, since raptors are limited to a small native hawk, the io, found only on the island of Hawaii, and a single native owl, the pueo, neither of which is considered a threat to turkeys. There are no native ground predators. Gonzalez (1982) lists feral dogs and cats, wild pigs, mongooses, and man (all exotic species) as the main predators of turkeys. Poaching, predation, and summer droughts are believed to affect turkey populations.

On the 4 islands that have turkey populations, only fall hunting is permitted. It is limited to weekends and state holidays from early November until late January. At check stations operated only the first 2 weeks of the 1984 season on public hunting areas, 62 turkeys were reported (Walker 1986). Considering that public areas make up only 10 percent of the area occupied by turkeys and open to hunting, a recent estimate by Gonzalez (personal communication: 1989) of nearly 1,000 turkeys harvested seems plausible.

Turkey populations of the islands inhabit 520 square kilometers (200 square miles) of range, which is only 3 percent of the total Hawaiian land area of 16,640 square kilometers (6,425 square miles). The Rio Grande turkeys are not expected to spread much farther beyond the limited dry climate zones to which they presently seem confined. There may be some potential for the eastern or Florida subspecies in areas that receive 75 to 150 centimeters (30 to 60 inches) of rain, especially where such forests are interspersed with pastures.

Increasing public anxiety over the effects of exotic species upon Hawaii's unique endemic biota, however, may hamper even experimental introductions or transfers of wild-trapped Rio Grandes to other islands of the state. This concern, plus the continued problem of habitat loss because of a resident human population that has doubled in the past 40 years to 1 million, plus massive real estate and tourist developments, is a combination that does not bode well for the wild turkey in paradise.

Australia

In 1928, an attempt was made to establish wild turkeys on Rottnest Island in Western Australia with birds of unspecified origin from the South Perth Zoo (Lever 1987). These birds soon vanished. But others—liberated on Prime Seal Island, a small island of the Fernaux Group in Bass Strait between the mainland and Tasmania—established a population (Tarr 1950). R. Schodde (personal communication: 1988) indicated that the stock released was pen-reared but possibly of eastern turkey origin, and that the population was thriving on this 15-square-kilometer (6-square-mile) island at least until

1952. Since then, there have been no official reports that turkeys still exist on Prime Seal Island.

B. Penfold (personal communication: 1988) has no knowledge of turkeys on this island but says turkeys are found on Flinders Island, also of the Fernaux Group in Bass Strait, and that "hundreds" are harvested annually during his organized goose hunts on the island. K. Rayner (personal communication: 1989) of Tasmania elaborates that shortly after settlement of Flinders Island early in the 1800s as a base for sealers and whalers, domestic turkeys and pigs were liberated as food sources. The turkeys maintain very high densities on this 1,000-square-kilometer (390-square-mile) island in the edges of temperate rain forests and in small pockets of cover in open pastures and fertile farmland. They have adapted to this moist, southern hemispheric environment by nesting in October and November and breeding very successfully, particularly since there are no predators. Photos show that colors of the heads, legs, and plumage of the adult males are similar to Bronze domestics, but the birds are slimmer in body. They are hunted with shotguns, and 15 to 20 birds are usually taken in a half-day hunt. As a result, the birds are wary of man, but "they are not cunning like the hunting stories attribute wild turkeys in America to be."

New Zealand

The turkeys in New Zealand originated from domestic turkeys that had strayed from farmsteads. Thomson (1922) reported these feral turkeys were common around Hawkes Bay in the North Island in 1892 and had moved inland by 1922. In the absence of predators of consequence, they have become locally abundant on both the North and South islands (Falla et al. 1967).

These birds commonly occupy sheep pastures that are interspersed with scattered trees and resemble savan-

Typical habitat with Monterey pine near Taupo, North Island, New Zealand. *Photo by S. Schemnitz.*

nas. Apparently these turkeys seldom roost in trees, preferring to use fence posts and farm gates. Although Oliver (1955) suggested these feral birds originated from Gould's turkeys, it is likely they are descendants of Mexican domestics. These birds have retained the physical traits of short legs and stocky bodies and the relatively tame behavioral traits of domestic turkeys (Howard and Schemnitz 1988).

Fiji

According to Wood and Wetmore (1926), turkeys of unspecified origin may have been introduced to the Fijian Archipelago (located approximately 2,200 kilometers [1,400 miles] east by northeast of Australia). If so, the lack of further reports suggests they failed to become established.

New Caledonia

Situated about 1,100 kilometers (700 miles) east by northeast of Australia, the island of New Caledonia is a French protectorate of nearly 19,900 square kilometers (7,700 square miles). No records could be found of turkeys ever being released or existing on this island until Speegle (1984) reported shooting turkeys there in 1984. He describes the island as rugged terrain with coniferous and deciduous forests covering most of the mountains, and he implies much of the land is devoted to cattle ranching.

His Australian guide, B. Penfold (personal communication: 1989), indicated turkeys occupy nearly all of the island, mostly the dry western side, but he knew nothing of their origin. (Color photos of turkeys that accompanied the article suggest they may be Rio Grande or hybrids—*Editor's note*.) They appear similar to the domestic-origin birds on Flinders Island. Since a query to authorities on the island was not answered, the pedigree of these birds remains a mystery.

NORTH AMERICA

Northeastern United States

All of today's wild turkey populations in the northeastern states are descendants of the remnant Appalachian population that at its lowest point lived only as far north as central Pennsylvania. By the early 1950s, these birds had spread north into western New York state. Beginning in 1969 and 1970, when 31 turkeys were trapped and transferred to Vermont (W. Drake personal communication: 1988), the birds were subsequently leapfrogged to all the remaining northeastern states, which now have restored populations. All of these states had previous histories of failures to establish turkeys using game-farm stock.

Maine, New Hampshire, and Vermont. Among the northeastern states bordering on ancestral turkey range, only Maine does not yet have turkeys living north of this historic line. Restoration efforts using wild-trapped birds, started in 1977, have established turkeys to the edge of former range in Maine's central coastal area. It is not expected that their range can be extended very far inland and northward from the relatively moderate climate of this coastal area to the less-hospitable coniferous forest zones, where even the small amounts of existing farmland are decreasing (Bozenhard 1988).

In these northern states, farmland (mostly dairy) seems the critical factor for the survival of turkeys living beyond their historic range. In addition to remnants of crops grown, the spreading of cow manure (containing undigested grain and other nutrients) serves as a reliable source of winter food for turkeys in this area. But perhaps as important is that open fields allow wind and sun to pack and reduce deep snow while also providing edges and reverting pastures for shrubs that yield winter foods, such as roses and barberries (Wallin personal communication: 1980, Walski 1984, Wunz 1987d).

This reliance of turkeys on dairy farms is most apparent in the contrast between results of turkey restoration efforts in New Hampshire and Vermont. Historically, turkeys were found only in the southern parts of both states. In New Hampshire, where restoration efforts began in 1975, the turkey population remains below 2,500 birds, with a spring hunting harvest of more than 100 birds. There have been no fall hunting seasons. Although turkeys are established at places in New Hampshire's Connecticut River Valley nearly 80 kilometers (50 miles) north of ancestral range, these northern populations are scattered, are of low density, and seem to be expanding slowly, if at all, in number and range. Probably fewer than 400 wild turkeys, on 1,000 square kilometers (380 square miles), are now living north of their former range limits (T. Walski personal communication: 1989).

By contrast, Vermont's turkey population now numbers 15,000 and occupies nearly all of the state except the northeast quarter, which adjoins and is similar in habitat to New Hampshire. From northwest Vermont, bordering Lake Champlain, wild turkeys have moved into the farmlands of Quebec, more than 160 kilometers (100 miles) north of ancestral range in southern Vermont. Some 8,000 to 10,000 birds occupy this area of about 10,000 square kilometers (3,850 square miles) of new range, where hunters take about 600 to 800 wild turkeys during spring and 800 to 1,000 in the fall (S. Darling personal communication: 1988).

Stocked turkeys in northerly latitudes become established where forests are interspersed with agriculture land. *Photo by W. Porter.*

Although most of the land in both states was once cleared and farmed, New Hampshire today has only 3 percent still in farmland. It competes with Maine for the distinction of being the most forested state. Farming continues on 15 percent of Vermont land, endowed in places with more tillable soils than New Hampshire. Therein seems to be the reason for this striking difference in turkey carrying capacity between the habitats of these 2 northern states.

New York. In northern New York state during the early 1980s, wild-trapped turkeys were established north of historic range on the eastern Lake Ontario Plain, the St. Lawrence Valley, and the Champlain Valley, which surround the uplands of Tug Hill and the Adirondack Mountains. Some of these birds have crossed the border into Quebec, nearly 240 kilometers (150 miles) north of ancestral range in New York.

Wild turkeys from the New York releases have increased to 2,300 birds occupying an area of 11,100 square kilometers (4,270 square miles) in this new range. The spring harvest has reached 100 birds and is increasing.

About half of the total area occupied is forest and brush. The brush is from farm abandonments in these marginal agricultural areas. The forests are mostly northern hardwoods similar to the extended turkey ranges in northern New England. The future for turkeys in this part of New York, as in New England, will depend on how fast and how widely farming decreases (D. Austin personal communication: 1988).

Great Lakes States

Michigan. Turkeys were found originally in the southern half of Michigan's Lower Peninsula, south of a line extending from the "thumb area" on Lake Huron southwest to Ottawa County on Lake Michigan. Some evidence indicates wild turkeys may have occurred 80 kilometers (50 miles) or so farther north in Oscoda County in the northeastern part of the Lower Peninsula (Rusz 1986). All of the turkeys now living north of ancestral range in the Lower Peninsula originated from stocking of game-farm birds that began in the 1950s. Some of these birds were trapped in the 1960s and 1970s and transferred to the Upper Peninsula's southernmost county, Menominee (Bronner 1982).

Although these birds of game-farm origin continue to exhibit less than wild behavior and have been relatively slow to increase in numbers and expand in range (Rusz 1986), recent counts indicate nearly 46,000 birds occupy about 31,000 square kilometers (12,000 square miles) of woods. In places, this extended range reaches 190 kilometers (120 miles) north of historic range in the Lower Peninsula. In the Upper Peninsula, the extended range is 130 kilometers (80 miles) above Wisconsin's historic range on the west shore of Lake Michigan. Fall hunting seasons, which were stopped in 1969 because of adverse effects on the turkey population, reopened on a large scale in this northern range in 1989. More than 6,000 birds were taken during the 1989 spring season (J. Urbain personal communication: 1989).

Habitats are usually a mosaic of second-growth oaks or northern hardwoods, conifer swamps, and pine plantations interspersed with farmland (Bronner 1982, Kulowiec and Haufler 1985). During winter, these turkeys commonly assemble in large flocks, sometimes numbering in the hundreds, at farmsteads to feed on grain provided for livestock, or for the turkeys.

Wisconsin. The northern extent of ancestral range in Wisconsin has been a line from Green Bay on Lake Michigan southwestward to the Mississippi River, south of LaCross, near the border of Iowa and Minnesota. Since 1976, when wild-trapped turkeys were first imported from Missouri (followed by an intensive in-state trap-and-transfer effort), the population has increased dramatically to nearly 50,000 birds. The occupied range

In Minnesota wild turkey broods use agriculture fields and develop rapidly. *Photo by W. Porter.*

of 31,000 square kilometers (12,000 square miles), a third of which is forest, is largely confined to the southwest quarter of the state (E. Frank personal communication: 1989).

About half of the turkey population and occupied range are north of former range limits. In some counties bordering the Mississippi, turkeys live 160 kilometers (100 miles) farther north than ever before. Nearly half of the 4,400-bird spring harvest in 1988 was taken on this new range. The forests are primarily oak-hickory wooded ridges and hills in farming areas.

Farms, especially dairy, are considered the most important component of turkey habitat there. Apparently turkeys in Wisconsin feed as commonly in manure spread on fields as do turkeys in the northeastern states. There is potential for extending turkey range even farther north in Wisconsin, but the risk of frequent winter kills may make such an expansion impractical (E. Frank personal communication: 1989).

Minnesota. Historic records indicate that turkeys barely entered southern Minnesota. Now turkeys are found 190 kilometers (120 miles) farther north, even above St. Paul. During the 1960s, an attempt to establish turkeys with a Merriam's-eastern game-farm hybrid population at first looked very successful. But later it failed. Twenty-nine wild-trapped turkeys from Missouri, stocked in 1973, were largely responsible for the present population of more than 8,000 turkeys and a spring harvest of 700 (G. Nelson personal communication: 1988).

Most of the state's occupied turkey range of 4,000 square kilometers (1,540 square miles) of woodland is in the Coulee Country bordering the Mississippi River from north of the Minnesota River to the Iowa border. This hilly area of river breaks has oak forests interspersed with farms, mostly dairy. Similar habitat has turkeys in places on the Minnesota River between Minneapolis and Mankato and upstream, and near the St. Croix River north of St. Paul.

There seem to be opportunities to extend turkey range farther west and northwest along wooded riparian corridors in the prairies. But turkeys stocked in the forests of the northeast section, where there is little or no agriculture, will face the same risks previously mentioned for Wisconsin (G. Nelson personal communication: 1988).

Upper Midwest

Nebraska. Although wooded stream corridors extend farther west and north, the eastern turkey's original range did not extend beyond southeast South Dakota or into northwestern Nebraska. But wild turkeys live today in Pine Ridge and the upper North Platte River of north-

Good Merriam's turkey habitat in the Black Hills. *Photo by M. Rumble.*

Meadow in mixed conifer stand in Black Hills, South Dakota. *Photo by H. Shaw.*

western Nebraska. They originated from 28 Merriam's turkeys trapped and transplanted from the Black Hills of Wyoming and South Dakota in 1959. These birds increased to the present population of better than 5,000,

occupying 2,200 square kilometers (850 square miles) of habitat. Harvests have been 1,500 in spring season and about the same in the fall (K. Menzel personal communication: 1988). Large numbers of Rio Grande turkeys from Texas were imported, but they have failed to establish a viable population anywhere in Nebraska.

The deciduous stream-course habitats usually include box elder, cottonwood, green ash, chokecherry, snowberry, and prairie rose. The Pine Ridge, a long, narrow escarpment, is more typical Merriam's habitat of open stands of ponderosa pine with mid- and short-grass understories (Suetsuga 1976). Also, some turkeys live in unusual habitats on the prairie. These are semiwild hybrids, appearing to have resulted from crosses of Merriam's, eastern, and domestic turkeys, that use planted shelterbelts for cover and then forage in surrounding crop fields and grassland pastures. Shelterbelts smaller than 4 hectares (10 acres) may be used if they have large trees, such as cottonwoods, for roosting. Other than adaptations such as this, essentially all of the conventional turkey habitats in northwest Nebraska have been occupied (K. Menzel personal communication: 1989).

South Dakota. Only the extirpated eastern wild turkey, which historically lived in the Missouri River breaks and along its tributaries southeast of Pierre, was native to South Dakota. The isolated Black Hills never

Aspen stand with reseeded log road in a mixed conifer stand of the Black Hills, South Dakota. *Photo by H. Shaw.*

had wild turkeys until 29 wild-trapped Merriam's birds from New Mexico and Colorado were released there from 1948 to 1951 (Peterson and Richardson 1975). Birds from this rapidly expanding population were then transplanted into the smaller units of habitat and riparian corridors across the state.

They have increased to 49,000 and occupy a total of 19,000 square kilometers (7,300 square miles). About 3,000 birds are taken in the spring season and the same number in fall. Although 150 Rio Grande turkeys from Texas and Oklahoma were stocked, their numbers linger at only 100 birds (L. Rice personal communication: 1988).

Turkey densities in the Black Hills, which is typical Merriam's habitat of ponderosa pine forest, vary from 1 to 5 per square kilometer (3 to 13 per square mile). Wild turkeys living in the prairie area in riparian corridors of cottonwood and ash, and in fragmented woodlands made up of these trees plus bur oak and hickory, reach high densities—12 or more per square kilometer (30 per square mile)—typical for such habitats in farm or grassland areas. Essentially all of the best habitats in South Dakota are occupied by turkeys (L. Rice personal communication: 1988).

North Dakota. Turkeys were not native anywhere in North Dakota. Attempts to establish wild populations started in 1951 with the release of pen-raised birds. All told, nearly 2,000 of these birds, reportedly of eastern turkey origin from game farms in Pennsylvania and Maryland, were stocked. In 1953, 8 wild-trapped Merriam's turkeys from New Mexico were released. In 1955, 53 wild Rio Grande birds from Texas were imported.

Prime Merriam's habitat in south-central South Dakota. *Photo by L. Flake.*

Wintering flocks often feed on agricultural crops, such as these Merriam's on a silage pile. *Photo by M. Rumble.*

Nest (top) and brood habitat in South Dakota. *Photos by M. Rumble.*

Most of the Rio Grandes became hybridized with easterns, either intentionally or accidentally (Jacobsen 1963).

The Rio Grandes, or their crosses with eastern turkeys, number only 500 birds. The Merriam's turkeys maintain a population of 1,500 birds in scattered patches of ponderosa pine forests, limited to a 600-square-kilometer (230-square-mile) area in southwest North Dakota. The eastern birds of game-farm origin, numbering 10,000, occupy nearly 2,000 square kilometers (800 square miles) of hardwood draws, woodlots, and wooded stream bottoms, mainly along the Missouri River. These birds commonly visit cattle feedlots for winter foods. A total annual harvest of about 2,000 birds is taken in spring and fall seasons. Turkeys are still expanding into habitats, such as grasslands, formerly thought unacceptable for turkeys (L. Tripp personal communication: 1988).

Rocky Mountains and Great Basin

Montana. The first wild turkeys to grace the vacant habitats of Montana were those transplanted from Colorado and Wyoming beginning in 1954. Only Merriam's turkeys have been legal to import, and they have done well enough in various parts of the state to reach an estimated 10,000 to 15,000 birds living on a total range of more than 26,000 square kilometers (10,000 square miles). Hunters take about 500 wild turkeys in spring and 1,200 in fall.

The habitats are riparian corridors of hardwoods and some extensive ponderosa pine forests with open understories or shrub communities of chokecherry, snowberry, and Oregon grape. The largest occupied range is in Custer National Forest of southeastern Montana. There may be additional room for turkeys in Montana, but the best habitats are occupied (Jonas 1966, S. Knapp personal communication: 1988).

Idaho. Wild turkey introductions in Idaho began in 1962 when wild-trapped Merriam's turkeys from Colorado were released in the lower Salmon River drainage in the west-central part of the state (Shorger 1966). Subsequent releases were made in the western side of Idaho from the southern part up into the northern panhandle in open ponderosa pine forest habitats. By 1979, these turkeys had increased to 2,500 and had occupied 3,600 square kilometers (1,400 square miles) of the estimated total potential range of 6,200 square kilometers (2,400 square miles) (Bailey 1980). Ten years later, the population was an estimated 3,000 to 4,000 Merriam's turkeys living on about 5,200 square kilometers (2,000 square miles).

In 1981 and 1982, large numbers of Rio Grande birds were imported from Texas, Oklahoma, Kansas, and California and released in mostly riparian hardwood habitats along the Snake River across southern Idaho. The populations that initially did well have since decreased to an estimated 1,000 to 2,000 birds living on less than 1,300 square kilometers (500 square miles) of range. One population on the Utah border has occupied an upland area of single-leaf piñon and juniper.

In 1984, 16 wild-trapped turkeys from Pennsylvania were stocked in the lower Clearwater River area, where previous releases of Merriam's turkeys had not done well, probably because of a wetter climate there. The annual rainfall of 75 to 100 centimeters (30 to 40 inches) has nurtured a unique habitat for this area: It contains such species as western red cedar and western hemlock, in addition to grand fir and Douglas fir. The remoteness of the area and the shyness of these eastern turkeys make the population difficult to monitor. They are estimated to number somewhere between 50 and 150 (G. Will personal communication: 1989).

Transplanted Merriam's occupy foothills in north-central Wyoming. The Tongue River is in the background. *Photo by G. Wunz, Pennsylvania Game Commission.*

Wyoming. The Laramie Peak area of southeastern Wyoming may have been the first place (at least the first outside of ancestral range) to have wild-trapped turkeys released in an interstate transfer. Merriam's turkeys from New Mexico were transplanted there in 1935. The population promptly increased, as we have since come to expect of wild stock. Some of their progeny, plus birds from New Mexico, were transplanted to Wyoming's part of the Black Hills in the 1950s. Turkeys were subsequently leapfrogged to habitats in northeast and eastern Wyoming (Schorger 1966).

The present population may be nearly 20,000 birds that occupy 6,500 square kilometers (2,500 square miles) of mostly ponderosa pine forests and riparian hardwoods. Turkeys on the eastern slopes of the Big Horn Mountains of north-central Wyoming live in slightly different habitats: ponderosa and lodgepole pine with hawthorn thickets on the lower slopes connected to riparian bottoms of cottonwood. The severe winters at higher elevations of the central, western, and southern parts of the state will probably limit further expansion of turkeys into forests and riparian areas there that otherwise may have supported turkeys. Hunters take about 700 turkeys in spring and 1,100 in fall (H. Harja personal communication: 1989).

Colorado. Historically, Merriam's turkeys ranged from Denver south along the eastern slope of the Rocky and Sangre de Cristo Mountains, in the mesas and canyons of southeast Colorado, and on the south and west slopes and adjoining plateaus of the San Juan Mountains in southwestern Colorado. They avoided the high moun-

Riparian habitats are very important for wild turkeys. Often they are essential for suitable habitat. Clockwise from top left: Northeastern Wyoming; Powder River, Wyoming; Platt River, Nebraska; Prairie woodland habitat.

tains and plateaus in the interior (Ligon 1946). All introductions of Merriam's turkeys beyond historic range, beginning in the 1950s, have been north of Highway I-70 between Denver and Grand Junction. Scattered populations that may total 1,500 birds now live along the Front Range north to Wyoming and in northwest Colorado near Rifle. About 100 birds in total are taken during spring and fall hunting seasons.

These introduced birds occupy about 500 square kilometers (200 square miles) of typical Merriam's habitat of ponderosa pine and aspen with scattered openings of grass. Characteristic shrub communities of oak, however, are replaced by mountain mahogany, skunkbush, chokecherry, wild plum, and hawthorn where turkeys now inhabit the Front Range north of Denver. There is apparently no need for further transplants. Existing populations should be able to expand into any suitable habitat that remains unoccupied (R. Hoffman personal communication: 1988).

Possibly the Rio Grandes that have been established in eastern Colorado, especially those along the North Platte River, were beyond ancestral range limits for that subspecies. Ligon (1946) suggests that if this area was occupied, it was probably by eastern turkeys. Rio Grandes transplanted from Texas, Oklahoma, and Kansas in the early 1980s have increased to about 700 birds and occupy 150 square kilometers (60 square miles) of riparian corridors on the South Platte, Republican, and Arkansas rivers. About 100 square kilometers (40 square miles) remain to be inhabited by this subspecies (R. Hoffman personal communication: 1988).

New Mexico. The whole state was within historical range, which was occupied mainly by Merriam's turkeys. Small populations of Gould's turkeys were found in the southwest corner. Rio Grande birds may have lived along the Canadian River corridor in northeast New Mexico (Ligon 1946). In 1974, 19 Rio Grande birds from Texas were released on the Bosque Del Apache National Wild-

North Kaibab hunter with turkey. *Photo by G. Wunz, Pennsylvania Game Commission.*

life Refuge, which is at least 320 kilometers (200 miles) west of the "historic" Rio Grande turkey range. They have increased to about 300 birds that occupy 259 square kilometers (100 square miles) of cottonwood and tamarisk bosque along the Rio Grande River. A small release of birds from Texas, made during the 1970s in southeastern New Mexico, increased to about 50 birds that range in riparian habitats of a Pecos River tributary (D. Sutcliffe personal communication: 1990).

Arizona. Merriam's turkeys were native to every substantial pine-forested upland of the state except the Kaibab Plateau in northern Arizona. A few small mountain ranges in southeastern Arizona had Gould's turkeys (Ligon 1946). The Grand Canyon of the Colorado had been an effective natural barrier until 126 wild-trapped Merriam's birds were successfully transplanted to 2 places on the Kaibab from 1940 to 1963. The result has been a combined population of 3,000 birds ranging over about 2,900 square kilometers (1,100 square miles).

These turkeys have been hunted in the fall since 1955, and in the spring since 1964. About 50 are taken in spring and 140 in the fall (R. Engel-Wilson personal communication: 1988).

Kaibab forests are ponderosa pine and mixed conifers interspersed with meadows. Deep snows commonly force turkeys to move down from the elevation of 2,450 to 2,750 meters (8,000 to 9,000 feet) on the plateau to spend the winter in piñon, juniper, and Gambel oak habitats at slightly lower altitudes. Because there are no good winter habitats at lower elevations to which turkeys could move to escape deep snow, some die during severe winters. Fortunately, the population usually recovers in a year or so (F. Phillips personal communication: 1985).

There is little, if any, unoccupied Arizona habitat for the Merriam's turkey. Merriam's birds transplanted into southeastern Arizona mountain ranges (formerly inhabited by Gould's turkeys) have languished or failed. Restoration attempts with Gould's birds from Mexico are in progress there.

In 1961 and 1962, Rio Grande turkeys from Texas were stocked at 2 sites, but they failed to establish lasting populations. Nonetheless, the presence of apparently suitable riparian habitats in southeastern Arizona holds some promise for introductions of the Rio Grande subspecies (R. Engel-Wilson personal communication: 1988).

Utah. Attempts to introduce wild turkeys into Utah started in 1925 when game-farm eastern toms and domestic hens were liberated on Antelope Island in Great Salt Lake. They persisted under rigid protection until the 1950s. Meantime, at least 3 unsuccessful attempts were made with pen-raised eastern birds.

From 1952 to 1957, 89 wild-trapped Merriam's turkeys were transplanted from Colorado and Arizona to 5 areas in Utah. In 4 of these areas, the birds succeeded. Turkeys from these flocks were subsequently trapped and transferred within the state. The result has been 6 areas in southern Utah where Merriam's turkeys are established. The lone release made in northern Utah failed.

Utah's total wild turkey population is estimated at less than 1,000, living on about 5,200 square kilometers (2,000 square miles) of isolated mountain ranges or plateaus at 1,500 to 2,700 meters (5,000 to 9,000 feet) of elevation in ponderosa pine, piñon pine, aspen, Gambel oak forest with many openings and wet meadows. About 40 Merriam's turkeys are taken during the spring season. (D. Bunnell personal communication: 1978, J. Roberson personal communication: 1988).

In 1984, 92 wild-trapped Rio Grande turkeys from Texas were imported and released in stream bottom riparian habitats of cottonwood and oak in central Utah. They have succeeded to the point that a spring hunt may be opened, but there are no good estimates of their numbers. Potential range is estimated at 5,000 square kilometers (2,000 square miles) for Rio Grandes and 10,000 square kilometers (4,000 square miles) for Merriam's (J. Roberson personal communication: 1988). The riparian habitats of cottonwood and Russian olive of northeastern Utah seem particularly suitable for Rio Grandes.

Nevada. Wild turkeys were first introduced into Nevada in 1960 and 1962 when 44 Merriam's birds from Arizona were released in the Spring Mountains near Las Vegas and on the eastern slope of the Sierra Nevada Range near Lake Tahoe. These birds flourished for some time, but those in the Spring Mountain habitat of piñon pine and juniper eventually disappeared. Although the ponderosa and mixed conifer forest of the Tahoe area is more typically Merriam's habitat, a rarity in Nevada, the turkey population lingers at less than 100.

From 1987 to 1989, 256 Rio Grande turkeys trapped in Texas were stocked in the Spring Mountains and in riparian corridors in 3 valleys east and south of Carson City. Preliminary results have been promising enough to consider additional experimental introductions of Rio Grandes in other riparian and piñon-juniper habitats in Nevada (S. Stiver personal communication: 1989).

Pacific Coast

The varied climates in West Coast states that result from interactions between ocean and mountains have produced a variety of habitat niches, ranging from desert to temperate rain forest, that may be suited to 3 or perhaps 4 subspecies of wild turkeys. Rio Grande and Merriam's have adapted to the drier montane habitats. In the coastal redwood and Douglas fir areas north of San Francisco, where annual rainfall is 90 to 255 centimeters (35 to 100 inches) and Merriam's, Rio Grandes, and hybrids have not done well, quite possibly eastern turkeys could adapt to this unique habitat and establish populations.

California. California has a long history of attempts to introduce turkeys, beginning with Mexican turkeys released on Santa Cruz Island in 1877. About 1,200 Mexican turkeys, mostly of game-farm ancestry, were released between 1888 and 1918 (Schorger 1966). From about 1928 until 1951, 3,350 game-farm hybrid turkeys were stocked in 23 counties. They became established in only 3 counties, from which they were trapped and transferred to 30 release sites in various parts of the state.

The first wild-trapped Rio Grande turkeys in California were 62 birds from Texas, stocked east of San Diego in 1959. By 1975, Rio Grandes had been released in 33 areas, some three-quarters of which were successful establishments. Wild-trapped Merriam's turkeys from Arizona, Colorado, and Wyoming started populations in

Oak-savanna habitats in the coastal mountains of California. *Photos by G. Wunz, Pennsylvania Game Commission.*

4 of 5 attempted sites (Harper and Smith 1973, Graves 1975).

The sum of all the turkey populations in California now exceeds 100,000, occupying nearly 41,000 square kilometers (15,000 square miles). About 10 percent of the range is occupied by Merriam's, but nearly all California turkey populations are believed to be hybridized to varying degrees. About 23,000 square kilometers (9,000 square miles) of potential range is yet to be occupied. Hunts have been allowed in fall (since 1968) and spring (since 1970), with an annual take of nearly 10,000 (J. Massie personal communication: 1988).

Most turkey populations in California are associated with oak and grass savannas. Because 9 different species of oaks grow here, nearly all habitats have 1 or more species in combination with ponderosa pine, digger pine, other hardwoods, and grassland at elevations from 150 to 900 meters (500 to 3,000 feet). Wild oats, a common component of these grasslands, was the food most used year-round by turkeys. Some scattered turkey populations occur at higher elevations in the mountainous areas of northeastern counties, where habitats are composed of pine, oak, juniper, and wet meadows (Harper and Smith 1973, Anonymous 1980).

Oregon. Attempts to introduce turkeys in Oregon started in the late 1800s, presumably with pen-raised stock. From 1926 to 1933, 1,500 game-farm birds of eastern and Merriam's ancestry were released at numerous sites, none of which succeeded. In 1961, 60 wild-trapped Merriam's turkeys from Colorado, Arizona, and New Mexico were released at several sites in north-central and northeastern Oregon, but only those on the eastern slope of the Cascade Mountains near the Columbia River have maintained significant populations.

Since 1975, more than 1,000 wild Rio Grandes from California, Kansas, and Texas were imported and released in southwestern Oregon and in most of the sites where Merriam's turkeys had failed or lingered as low populations (K. Durbin personal communication: 1989).

Better than 16,000 square kilometers (6,200 square miles) of range are occupied by an estimated 6,000 to 10,000 birds. Hunters took 563 during the 1988 spring season. The populations that seem to be doing best are

Ponderosa pine turkey habitat in northeastern Oregon. *Photo by G. Wunz, Pennsylvania Game Commission.*

the Rio Grandes and hybrids inhabiting the inland counties of southwestern Oregon, where oaks, ponderosa pine, and buckbrush ceanothus are prominent species (K. Durbin personal communication: 1989).

The Merriam's birds on the east slope of the Cascades occupied their typical niche of open ponderosa pine forests, with local associates of Douglas fir, snowberry, and Oregon white oak — the only oak indigenous to the Pacific Northwest. In addition to the east slope, there appears to be considerable Merriam's habitat in the Blue Mountains of northeast Oregon, even though oak would be a rare or absent component. Of the total unoccupied range in Oregon, estimated at about 100,000 square kilometers (38,600 square miles), there may be considerable potential for eastern turkeys in the wetter climate areas of the Willamette Valley and coastal counties west of the Cascade Mountain Range.

Washington. Wild turkeys were introduced into Washington in 1960 and 1961 when 54 Merriam's birds from Arizona, New Mexico, and Wyoming were released at 4 sites east of the Cascade Range. One of 2 releases that succeeded was in south-central Washington in pine-fir-oak habitat like that previously mentioned across the Columbia River in Oregon. The other site in the Columbia River basin and Selkirk Mountains in the northeast corner of the state was similar, but without oak, and both were interspersed with pasture and grainfields. Fall seasons were started in 1966, and spring hunts have been scheduled since 1970. Recent annual harvests have been about 65 birds. By the late 1970s, these populations had declined and remained at low levels. The combined populations are estimated at greater than 2,000 Merriam's birds (Mackey and Jonas 1982, D. Blatt personal communication: 1988).

The problem of decreased and stagnated turkey populations seems common in most western states with isolated turkey populations that arose from a single release of only a small number of birds from a common genetic source. In hopes that increased genetic variability may be a practical solution, an additional 160 wild-trapped Merriam's birds from South Dakota were released in 1988.

From 1984 to 1988, 313 Rio Grande turkeys trapped in Oklahoma and Texas were released at 14 sites in the more arid habitats of eastern Washington, mostly in canyons and riparian zones at lower elevations. During the first spring hunting allowed on these birds in 1988, 21 were taken from an estimated total of 800 to 1,000 birds (D. Blatt personal communication: 1989).

Perhaps the most unusual introduction has been the 55 eastern turkeys transplanted from Pennsylvania during 1987 to 1989 into southwestern Washington, where annual rainfall averages more than 130 centimeters (50 inches). The habitats of the release sites are forested with

60 to 75 percent Douglas fir and 25 to 40 percent deciduous species, mainly big-leaf maple, red alder, and black cottonwood. The deciduous species are most prominent in the valleys that are also interspersed with small dairy farms and horse pastures.

To compensate for the shortage of mast trees, understories and openings have a large variety of food-producing shrubs such as salal, tall Oregon grape, blackberries, snowberry, blueberries, and Scotch broom, in addition to green grasses and forbs that continue to provide forage during the region's mild winters. The dense vegetation and the wariness of these birds have hindered counting of their numbers, believed to be well in excess of 100 birds. Broods have been raised each summer, even during the first year when only a lone male, a juvenile, was available to service the 17 hens released (D. Blatt personal communication: 1989).

Canada

Ontario. Wild turkeys in Canada occurred naturally only in southern Ontario. According to Edminster (1954) and Mosby (1959), the northern extremity of turkey range was a line extending from the mouth of the Niagara River at the west end of Lake Ontario westward to the southeast shore of Lake Huron. Archaeological evidence reported by Alison (1976) showed that turkeys could have occurred nearly 160 kilometers (100 miles) farther north in Ontario.

Dobell and Reid (1988) suggested that turkeys at one time or another may have occupied all of Ontario south of the edge of the Canadian Shield, an extensive Precambrian granite peneplain (land worn down by erosion) extending from the southeast end of Georgian Bay eastward to the vicinity of the northeast corner of Lake Ontario. This area of about 85,000 square kilometers (32,700 square miles) would more than double the range formerly known to have been occupied by turkeys.

Unfortunately for the original wild turkeys in Ontario, they occupied the region of mildest climate and most tillable and fertile soils in eastern Canada, a combination highly attractive to human settlers. Consequently, turkeys and much of their habitat had vanished by 1904. Clarke (1948) gave little hope that wild turkeys could ever be restored to the fragmented habitats that remained. At least 10 attempts from 1948 to 1975 to establish populations with game-farm stock failed.

Wild turkey restoration in Grand River Valley, Ontario. *Photo by Ontario Ministry of Natural Resources.*

Woodlots and agriculture fields in combination support wild turkey populations in Ontario. *Photo by D. Reid.*

Beginning in 1984, a total of 276 wild-trapped turkeys from Missouri, Iowa, Michigan, New York, Vermont, and New Jersey were released at 7 sites, 4 of which are north of the area definitely known as turkey range at the time of settlement by Europeans. Turkeys appear to be established on all sites, except one that was recently stocked. The population in 1988 was estimated at 4,800 turkeys (half of which were north of the former range line). They occupy about 2,900 square kilometers (1,100 square miles).

One of these successful sites on the northeast shore of Lake Ontario is 120 kilometers (75 miles) east of any archaeological evidence of turkeys and is considered at the "edge of historical range" (J. Harkes and D. Simkin personal communication: 1989). Within-province trap and transfer and the first spring hunting season were started in 1987. From 4 areas open to hunting in 1989, 121 birds were taken.

Of the total area south of the Canadian Shield, nearly a third (85,000 square kilometers, 33,000 square miles) is still covered with a mixed forest of mainly hardwoods, including American beech, northern red oak, white ash, American elm, and maples. Understories or shrub communities have beaked hazelnut, red osier dogwood, and viburnums that are characteristic of the Great Lakes-St. Lawrence forest zones. Most of the forests are fragmented into woodlots in agricultural land; the larger blocks are often wooded wetlands.

Further expansion of turkeys north onto the less-fertile Canadian Shield is questionable where forests become more coniferous and winters are more severe. A habitat survey of the Blind River area on the northwest shore of Lake Huron showed marginal possibilities of establishing turkeys there in the vicinity of dairy and beef farms (D. Reid personal communication: 1989).

Quebec and the Maritime Provinces. Carrigan (1986) documented 29 sightings of turkeys during a 1-year period south and southwest of Montreal and within 16 kilometers (10 miles) of the New York state border. Additional sightings have been made near the Vermont border, indicating these birds were migrants from established populations in these states. The birds live in a dairy-farming area. Although extensive agricultural habitats extend northeastward in the St. Lawrence Valley, the potential for turkeys is questionable farther north in Quebec, where winters are harsh.

Any potential for introducing turkeys to New Brunswick would probably be limited to the south coastal area on the Bay of Fundy and on the isthmus with Nova Scotia. The climate, moderated by the surrounding sea, and the agricultural habitats may make Prince Edward Island and Nova Scotia hospitable for wild turkeys. A habitat suitability survey by Walski (1988) of Nova Scotia's Annapolis Valley, which parallels the Bay of Fundy, concluded that turkeys should do well in this and other agricultural habitats of the province. In addition to grain and hayfields, he found in adjacent shrub communities and forests such turkey-food-producing species as American beech, white ash, northern red oak, American mountain ash, apple, sumac, rose, dwarf juniper, and sensitive fern. Also, manure spread on fields would provide a reliable food source for turkeys during the winter.

The failures of game-farm turkeys released previously by sportsmen in Nova Scotia have prompted efforts by the Digby Fish and Game Association to get wild-trapped birds for future stocking. Pen-raised birds released on Prince Edward Island in 1960 disappeared. Attempts in 1987 and 1988 were made with similar stock on New Brunswick's Grand Manan Island in the Bay of Fundy.

Manitoba. From 1958 to 1962, 124 pen-raised turkeys were imported into Manitoba by sportsmen from a hatchery in Mandan, North Dakota (Anonymous 1968). The origin of these birds, presumably of eastern extraction, was from eggs bought from game farms in Pennsylvania and Maryland (Jacobsen 1963). Some of these birds survived and established populations that have been trapped and transplanted by local sportsmen's groups, with approval of the provincial wildlife agency, from the initial release sites to new areas, all south and west of Winnipeg (C. Hummelt personal communication: 1989). The birds were trapped by herding them into wire pens or baiting them into farm buildings (Anonymous 1968).

There is a possibility that some turkeys in the Pembina Hills and Red River escarpment areas could have migrated from a population previously established in North Dakota. The turkey population found in the Turtle Mountain Provincial Park on the international border, where no turkeys have been stocked on the Manitoba side, probably originated from North Dakota, with which it shares this 1,300-square-kilometer (500-square-mile) upland.

Occupied habitats vary from the heavily forested Turtle Mountains clad in aspen, white birch, highbush cranberry, and beaked hazelnut, to aspen parklands in the sandhill country and to the riparian habitats of cottonwood, green ash, chokecherry, buffalo berry, and snowberry that are typical of the northern plains (L. Bidlake personal communication: 1989). Surveys by

the province's wildlife agency during the late 1970s indicated a population of about 350 turkeys, which later increased to 1,500.

Although these birds are relatively tame and still frequent farmsteads in winter, over time they have become somewhat wilder. The scattered populations occupy a total of up to 2,200 square kilometers (850 square miles). They have been hunted during the spring since the mid-1970s. In 1989, 248 were taken in the southern quarter of the province, which was open to turkey hunting (L. Bidlake and C. Hummelt personal communication: 1989).

Saskatchewan and Alberta. A semiwild flock of 100 to 200 birds of game-farm origin stocked by a sportsmen's club also exists in southeastern Saskatchewan in the Pipestem Creek drainage (D. Hjertaas personal communication: 1989). These turkeys occupy similar habitat and have behavior traits similar to the Manitoba birds. They also share the distinction of living farther north than any other free-ranging turkey population in North America and are 640 kilometers (400 miles) beyond the ancestral range limits in South Dakota.

In 1962, the Alberta Fish and Wildlife Division released 21 wild-trapped Merriam's turkeys from South Dakota in the Cypress Hills Provincial Park. This forested upland area of 1,000 square kilometers (390 square miles), surrounded by extensive grassland prairies, straddles the border with Saskatchewan about 65 kilometers (40 miles) north of the Montana border. The birds reproduced well during the first year and soon established a population that has persisted at about 400 birds. The habitat is composed of forests of lodgepole pine, white spruce, and aspen, interspersed with grassy meadows and shrub communities of hawthorn, saskatoon serviceberry, chokecherry, buffalo berry, silverberry, red osier dogwood, snowberry, and rose (D. Hjertaas and L. Dube personal communication: 1989).

In 1972 and 1973, 12 Merriam's birds from the Cypress Hills and 13 from Nebraska were transplanted in the Porcupine Hills, which parallel the Rocky Mountains in southwest Alberta. These turkeys established a population of 300 on this range of more than 1,100 square kilometers (420 square miles) that vegetationally resembles the Cypress Hills. Then in 1988, local sportsmen's groups trapped and transferred 49 of these birds to 2 sites in the foothills of the Rocky Mountains in similar habitats west and southwest of the Porcupine Hills.

Production has been good, and large flocks have been seen. Occasionally, wild turkeys range north into south-central Alberta from the Sweetgrass Hills of Montana. At this writing, there are no turkey hunting seasons in either province, but Alberta is considering a spring hunt that, initially at least, would be limited to the Porcupine Hills (L. Dube personal communication: 1989).

British Columbia. Game-farm turkeys were stocked on the Gulf Islands, in the Strait of Juan de Fuca at the southeast end of Vancouver Island, at various times from 1910 to 1962. None of these efforts resulted in lasting populations (Lever 1987, W. Monroe personal communication: 1989). A sportsmen's group also released turkeys, probably of similar origin, near Armstrong in the Okanogan Valley of south-central British Columbia 160 kilometers (100 miles) north of the international border. These apparently suffered the same fate.

A wild population of Merriam's turkeys, however, has existed in British Columbia since the 1960s, when birds from a transplanted population in northeastern Washington state appeared across the border to maintain a toehold in a small habitat near the Columbia River. In the mid-1970s, Merriam's turkeys from a transplanted population in the northern panhandle of Idaho moved north to eventually occupy about 260 square kilometers (100 square miles) of range on the border and extending 80 kilometers (50 miles) north on the east shore of Kootenay Lake. The birds are still expanding their range, and estimates of their numbers range from 700 to 1,500 (W. Warkentin personal communication: 1989).

Merriam's turkeys from northwestern Montana also have crossed into the southeast corner of British Columbia and may soon join those recently trapped from the Kootenay Lake area and transferred east of Cranbrook to the foothills of the Rocky Mountains. These 2 populations now occupy more than 375 square kilometers (150 square miles). The habitat in these areas is mixed conifer and deciduous forests of lodgepole pine, Douglas fir, white birch, and aspen and shrub communities of serviceberry, red osier dogwood, snowberry, and kinnikinnick on the edges of interspersed hayfields, pastures, and orchards. There is more forest and less agricultural land in the Cranbrook area (W. Warkentin personal communication: 1989).

British Columbia's first turkey hunt was in the spring of 1989. There was a surprisingly large demand for the 30 permits issued by drawing, and 11 gobblers were taken. In addition to this latent interest in turkey hunting, there may be considerable potential for expanding turkey populations and range, particularly in the Okanogan Valley. The dry and relatively mild winter climate of this area should be hospitable to Merriam's turkeys, and perhaps to Rio Grandes.

A test of their adaptability to this area may result from the 1989 releases of wild-trapped turkeys at the south end of this valley in Washington state. Merriam's stock from South Dakota was released within 3 kilometers (2 miles) of the border and Rio Grandes from Texas within 11 kilometers (7 miles) of the border (D. Blatt personal communication: 1989). There may also be a place for eastern turkeys in the wetter climate areas of the lower Frazer River Valley and possibly in the farming area on the southeastern shore of Vancouver Island.

THE FUTURE FOR WILD TURKEY INTRODUCTIONS

Although the best of the habitats outside of native range in the United States already have turkeys established, 185,000 square kilometers (71,000 square miles) still remain to be occupied. Turkeys in this new range constitute only 8 percent of the total wild turkey population and contribute 10 percent to the total harvest. Nonetheless, they have been especially important in spreading opportunities to enjoy wild turkeys far and wide.

Canada's wild turkey population, though still relatively small, tripled in 5 years. It may have the potential to occupy an additional 100,000 square kilometers (38,000 square miles).

That wild turkeys have accepted various habitats both in North America and abroad—even some of those habitats in ancestral range that have been drastically altered by man's activities—attests to the bird's adaptability and tenacity. No doubt this versatile species would be far more widespread by now if wild-trapped turkeys had always been transplanted instead of making many attempts with pen-raised stock or birds of domestic backgrounds and if the habitat requirements of the various subspecies had been known and considered before introductions were attempted.

Now that wild-trapped Rio Grandes, Merriam's, and eastern turkeys are readily available, there is no reason to either: (1) attempt introductions with game-farm stock; or (2) mismatch the subspecies of released turkeys with an obviously unacceptable environment. For example, before the successful introductions of turkeys in West Germany, a detailed habitat survey had revealed sufficient similarities to the climate of the northeast United States (including vegetation and other environmental factors) to strongly suggest wild-trapped eastern turkeys would succeed (Wunz and Wunz 1976). The same general criteria were used in the following appraisal of potential habitats elsewhere in the world.

Potential Habitats

Rio Grande turkeys. Of all the wild turkey subspecies, Rio Grandes seem to have more opportunities for being established outside their ancestral range than any other. This is because of their affinity for semiarid habitats and Mediterranean-like climates, an environment that is probably more common worldwide than any other within the broad climatic tolerance limits for all races of wild turkeys. There may be as much as 4 million square kilometers (1.5 million square miles) of this range acceptable to Rio Grandes in the Mediterranean basin; in the acacia savannas of south and east Africa; in the dry woodlands and savannas of acacia and mesquite in the Middle East, northeast India, Pacific coastal drylands, and pampas of South America; and in Australia, as described in McKell et al. (1972).

Considering political and social environments as well as vegetation and climate, the regions in which Rio Grandes probably have their best chance of becoming established are the remnant xerophytic (limited water) forests of oaks and pine in some of the countries that rim the Mediterranean and especially in the dry forests and savannas of eucalyptus and acacia that make up 2 million square kilometers (770,000 square miles) in sparsely human populated areas of Australia.

Despite their potential abroad, Rio Grandes seem to have difficulty establishing viable populations in suitable-looking habitats in the Great Plains farther north than their ancestral range limits in Kansas. Instead, Merriam's turkeys—commonly associated with coniferous mountain environments—have occupied some of these habitats of riparian hardwoods in the northern grasslands.

Oddly enough, Rio Grandes apparently are acclimated at more northern latitudes in eastern Oregon and Washington, where they occupy their characteristic habitats, as well as some that are more typical of Merriam's habitat. Although winter temperatures in the northwestern states sometimes are low, it appears that prolonged periods of cold weather common to the northern plains still serve as a barrier to the northward spread of this subspecies there, as has been true throughout history.

Eastern turkeys. Potential habitat for eastern turkeys in the Pacific Northwest states, New Zealand, Australia, and mostly in Europe could total nearly 1 million square kilometers (385,000 square miles). The likelihood that eastern turkeys might be introduced into these exotic habitats should be enhanced by the traditions of sport hunting and conservation ethics that have been in place in many of the countries that would be involved.

Eastern turkeys already have demonstrated their adaptability to the mixed deciduous and coniferous forests of Europe. And the existence of feral populations of domestic turkeys in temperate zone islands of the South Pacific suggests that the suitable-appearing forests and landscapes of New Zealand, Tasmania, and southeastern Australia should also be hospitable for them.

The largest remaining region of potential turkey habitat in North America is the Pacific coastal area stretching 1,200 kilometers (700 miles) from northern California to southern British Columbia. Encouraging preliminary results from wild-trapped eastern turkeys released in southwestern Washington indicate that this moist coniferous forest region has been sufficiently altered by logging and agriculture to have become acceptable habitat.

Merriam's turkeys. More than any other subspecies, Merriam's turkeys have been spread far and wide in North America, but apparently not abroad. Their successful introductions to pine-clad uplands throughout the West and Northwest suggests they may also succeed in similar montane environments in Europe, Asia, and northwest Africa. Most of these habitats would be restricted to certain elevations and would be relatively small and fragmented, as they are in North America. But considering that Merriam's turkeys have occupied habitats that structurally, at least, look more suitable for Rio Grandes in the northern Great Plains, there may be some possibilities for Merriam's birds also in the semiarid grasslands of the colder parts of the world.

Florida turkeys. There seems to be no record of Florida turkeys transplanted outside the United States. Possibly this subspecies could adapt to some of the Caribbean Islands and to subtropical forests elsewhere in the world. The present economic and political instability where most of these habitats occur, however, would preclude considering introductions other than in certain ecosystems in Hawaii and the eastern coastal areas of Australia.

Gould's turkeys. Early references to introduction attempts with turkeys from Mexico were not clear about which subspecies were involved or whether the birds were of trapped, pen-raised, or domestic stock. In any event, there are no recent reports of transplants of Gould's turkeys outside their ancestral range. Probably there are potential habitats for this bird, which appears to prefer a more southerly montane environment or the transition between Rio Grande and Merriam's habitat. Until the habitat limits of this race are better defined and a good source of trapping stock is made available, Gould's turkeys are not likely to be transplanted much beyond their ancestral range, which extends north to southwest New Mexico and southeast Arizona.

Problems with Introductions

Some introduced wild turkey populations that increased rapidly at first have since declined and linger at low density levels. This problem seems most prevalent in insular populations, particularly those of Merriam's turkeys that resulted from a small number of birds released on isolated mountain ranges or uplands in the western United States. The pattern seems to fit the current theory that a deficiency in genetic variability was responsible.

The turkey population in West Germany, which originated from a flock of hens and a nearby flock of toms trapped in Vermont, could be similarly affected. Until more is known about this phenomenon, a practical precaution may be to use wild-trapped birds from different sources, but of the same subspecies and within a climatic zone similar to where the birds will be released. It also seems wise to avoid the intentional mixing of the various subspecies until the long-term results in existing hybrid populations are determined.

Another concern is the turkeys living at latitudes considerably north of their ancestral range limits in North America: by more than 160 kilometers (100 miles) in the east and 640 kilometers (400 miles) in the west. These populations could become a nemesis for state and provincial agencies responsible for their welfare.

Some of these transplants or natural invasions have succeeded during a long series of mild winters. Throughout history, turkeys probably have advanced northward during a period of temperate winters only to suffer the consequences when harsh winters returned. The survival of turkey populations at these latitudes has been dependent mainly on farms to supplement natural foods and provide openings in forests where sun and wind can reduce depth and duration of snow cover. Trying to have turkeys even farther north, however, may require artificial feeding or habitat developments that may be expensive.

The future for establishing wild turkeys is particularly dismal in some of the developing countries, where much of this potential range is and where human populations are increasing at geometric rates. Without question, the deforestation and intrusions into habitats that can result from human population growth, both here and abroad, are the greatest threats turkeys will eventually face. Attempts to establish turkeys in places where deforestation and intrusions already are problems, or where wild turkeys would not be appreciated aesthetically or for sport, would be foolish and probably futile.

Perhaps a more immediate threat to proposed transplants is the growing concern over exotic species, which could lead to constraints against these introductions. Quarantines may be already in effect that require confining imports in close quarters for several weeks before release, an ordeal that wild turkeys would have difficulty tolerating.

Even though wild turkeys usually have filled a vacant habitat niche wherever they have been introduced and no significant environmental problem has been attributed to them, the bad examples already set by some exotics seem to have resulted in some stereotyping of all non-natives as undesirable. Rowley (1975:243) typified this concern: "At times the pressure from sportsmen to introduce exotic game birds is very strong, but such introductions are simply not worth the gamble. Few would gain anything, and who would wish a second 'rabbit' on Australia?" Although this viewpoint may seem unreasonable to the wild turkey's staunch supporters, it may have a positive consequence: The intense ecological surveys that would be needed to allay these environmental concerns could also result in a better match between introduced birds and potential habitat. In any event, the former laissez-faire trial and error method of introducing foreign species seems to be coming to an end.

While keeping these problems in mind, we should recognize that opportunities have never been better to significantly spread wild turkeys around the world into promising habitats. These areas may total 2 or 3 times the 1.6 million square kilometers (0.6 million square miles) now occupied by wild turkeys in the United States.

Paramount to this potential is the greatly increased availability of wild-trapped stock of the 3 major subspecies—made possible by the highly successful restoration of this magnificent game bird to much of its original range.

JOHN SIDELINGER

That the wild turkey has accepted various habitats both in North America and abroad attests to the bird's tenacity and adaptability.

IV

The Wild Turkey's Value and Future

Chapter 23

RECREATIONAL USE

Rob Keck
Executive Vice President
National Wild Turkey Federation
Edgefield, South Carolina

Jay Langston
Assistant Director of Publications
National Wild Turkey Federation
Edgefield, South Carolina

In the spring of 1991, more than 200,000 wild turkey gobblers were bagged by approximately 2 million recreational hunters. They hunted in every state but Alaska. That harvest was roughly 7 times the estimated population of eastern wild turkeys 40 years earlier.

With the explosion of wild turkey numbers over the past quarter century, recreational opportunities have increased dramatically. In the mid-1960s, fewer than 20 states had spring gobbler seasons, yet in 1991 sportsmen in all 48 contiguous states plus Hawaii hunted spring gobblers, a goal never before achieved. Wild turkeys increased by more than 1 million between 1985 and 1990, and the 1989 edition of Kim Long's *American Forecaster* called turkey hunting the "in thing" for the last decade of the 20th century (Long 1988).

The economic impact of our largest native game bird has been dramatic. The direct and indirect economic benefits derived annually from wild turkey hunting are in excess of $500 million (Baumann et al. 1989).

The wild turkey is far more than an economic boon to many local economies and numerous industries. The bird's recognition as prime table fare and as the ultimate sport of fair chase has elevated the wild turkey above all other game species in the satisfaction and enjoyment derived from the total hunting experience it offers.

The Native Americans so revered the strutting of the wild turkey that they imitated it in their native dance. Today's turkey hunter has also become so enamored with the quality, challenge, and beauty of this bird that mere participation in the sport is considered a most desirable experience. The intangible benefits of this expanded hunting resource has caused sportsmen to invest far more back into the resource than they've taken from it. Turkey hunting has become one of today's most heralded and exciting recreational pursuits.

The aim of this chapter is to acquaint you with the values, hunting techniques, processing, and photographing of the wild turkey. In these ways, you can appreciate the quality of this magnificent bird to its fullest.

TURKEY HUNTERS

With restoration came the revival of the sport of wild turkey hunting, beginning in the late 1950s and early 1960s. Individuals, sportsmen's clubs, and state and federal agencies began a concerted effort to revive the wild turkey from its near extinction of the early 1900s.

As the sport has grown, wild turkey hunters in America have gone through some major developments in their participation. Turkey hunters were a group of complete rank amateurs when the sport was first introduced. Today's turkey hunters include a variety of beginners, many advanced hunters, and even a small but growing group of highly sophisticated experts.

Experience Levels

Beginning turkey hunters can be broken down into 3 groups: (1) inexperienced beginners; (2) experienced beginners; and (3) "uneducated" beginners. Yet all these beginners mainly want to know, "Where can I find turkeys, and how can I kill one?"

An inexperienced beginner is someone who has never or seldom hunted turkeys. An experienced beginner is someone who has gone on fewer than 2 dozen turkey hunts.

Then there is the uneducated person — just getting into the sport. Turkey hunting may be his first hunting experience of any kind. He will have a hard time understanding the concepts behind wild turkey hunting because he will be consumed with just the act of hunting itself.

A variation at the entry level is the person who has had experience hunting other game and is well versed in principles of hunting. Such a hunter seems to readily understand the concepts behind turkey hunting.

Advanced wild turkey hunters include those who have developed some expertise. Technically speaking, they are not experts, but they can be considered accomplished hunters. This group is the upper echelon of wild turkey hunters. They hunt every possible morning of the season and eat, sleep, and drink turkey most of the year. They are capable of taking their limit most seasons, and their high degree of success brings them local notoriety. Another group of advanced hunters have hunted only about 5 years, but they have taken an impressive number of turkeys by hunting hard and often.

The real experts at hunting the wild turkey are quite accomplished hunters and woodsmen. They hunt wild turkeys with a high degree of success. Some of these experts hunt continuously, pursuing the various subspecies and taking advantage of seasons as they occur around the nation. They attend numerous calling contests and give lectures and seminars as they tour the country. Some of these experts market audiocassettes, videos, and record albums, and a few even manufacture turkey calls. Some of these experts are successful guides who operate their own hunting camps and schools. Some experts are relatively unknown but possess the skill, experience, and proficiency of the others.

Who Is the Turkey Hunter?

Who is the turkey hunter? Demographics from a 1988 survey of National Wild Turkey Federation (NWTF) members revealed that the stereotype of the hunter as poor and uneducated is wrong. The typical turkey hunter makes more money than the average citizen, has taken at least some college courses, and is a middle-aged (35 to 44 years) white male who lives in a small city or town (population under 10,000) or in a rural area (Smith 1988).

There is substantial crossover by hunters of other game species into turkey hunting. With spring hunting available in 49 states (and no conflict with other seasons, as in the fall), recruitment from other hunting disciplines is high. The NWTF survey showed 94 percent of its members hunted deer, 79 percent hunted squirrel, and almost 68 percent hunted waterfowl. These dedicated hunters averaged 35 days afield hunting, and a third spent more than 50 days afield.

Hunters wishing to extend their turkey hunting travel outside their home states to take advantage of staggered spring hunting seasons. Nearly half the Federation respondents crossed state lines to hunt annually.

Turkey hunters also fish. In fact, almost 90 percent of the respondents fished an average of 21 days annually.

When asked about their preference for fall or spring turkey hunting, 48 percent said they hunted turkeys in both seasons; 50 percent said they hunted turkeys primarily in the spring. Only 2.5 percent of the respondents hunted turkeys primarily in the fall (Smith 1988).

Much has happened on the turkey-hunting scene in recent years. One of the most evident developments is the great transformation of the turkey hunter from novice to advanced to expert levels of accomplishment. In most of the original wild turkey range, generations had come and gone without the opportunity to turkey hunt. The mechanics of the sport were lost. And don't forget: In many parts of the country, sport hunting for turkey never did exist. Subsistence and market hunting were the norm in those places.

Only after reintroduction of the wild turkey into and beyond its ancestral range did the opportunity to hunt wild turkeys become available for so many. Commercial interests as well as influences from conservation groups like the National Wild Turkey Federation contributed to an evolution and proliferation of related turkey-hunting equipment. People wanted to hunt turkeys and read about it, and they spent more money on it than ever before.

As recently as the mid-1970s, it was difficult to find good camouflage turkey-hunting clothing. Mouth calls weren't found in every sporting goods store. Turkey-hunting stories didn't appear with great frequency in major outdoor publications. Books, videos, and audiocassettes on the mechanics of turkey hunting were scarce or nonexistent. Special turkey shotguns and sophisticated turkey loads were practically unheard of. Turkey-hunting schools, seminars, and contests were just beginning. Good turkey art and photography were in short supply. Professional turkey-hunting guides were found in only a few places. A code of ethics and responsibilities for turkey hunters had not developed.

Now, however, the sport of turkey hunting has arrived.

Turkey hunters don't mind spending money for their sport. They want to look good, sound authentic, shoot well, and show they're real turkey hunters.

In 1988 and 1989, there were 7,738 hunters from Missouri, Arizona, Minnesota, Pennsylvania, South Carolina, and West Virginia who were surveyed on their spending related to resident turkey hunting (Baumann et al. 1990). They spent an average of $54.52 a year for clothing, calls, ammunition, and guns. According to another survey taken from 1987 through 1989 by all states having turkey hunting, there were 1,766,026 licensed turkey hunters. Using figures from the 2 surveys, we can estimate some $96.3 million spent in connection with resident turkey hunting in an average year (Baumann et al. 1990).

The average amount spent by hunters in the 6-state survey for transportation, lodging, food, land, taxidermy, and other items averaged $83.39. Figuring the same number mentioned for all states having turkey hunting, we can estimate $147.3 million spent in these categories in an average year (Baumann et al. 1990).

Turkey hunters spend even more when they travel out of state. Missouri, Arizona, South Carolina, and West Virginia had 681 respondents who were surveyed about their expenditures for clothing, calls, ammunition, guns, transportation, lodging, food, land leasing, taxidermy, and other items. This group spent $205,462 for an average of $302 each (Baumann et al. 1990). A survey of NWTF members in 1988 revealed that 47.2 percent traveled out of state to turkey hunt. Considering the Federation's approximately 60,000 members in 1990, we show $8.5 million ($302 × 0.472 × 60,000) per year spent by members in out-of-state turkey hunting. The national total of nonresident turkey-hunting expenditures, including non-Federation members, would be much higher.

HUNTING TECHNIQUES

Sport Hunting

The turkey hunter who measures the success of the season by harvest alone has missed the value of an experience found in few other shooting sports. The shooter must find and live those values to achieve the status of responsible hunter, rather than that of slob. The future of turkey hunting hinges on the spirit of fair chase—the way these birds are hunted, and how every turkey hunter would want to be treated by his fellow sportsmen.

It is ironic that the bird that under fair-chase conditions is the most challenging of North American game can sometimes be killed easily by unscrupulous hunters. The wariest of turkeys can be assassinated on its roost, shot at long range in open fields, and butchered over bait. In many states, some of these acts have not been declared illegal. But even where there is no law against roost shooting or sniping at long range with varmint rifles, the acts are not sport hunting and should be condemned.

The turkey hunter with a measure of integrity will take his birds honorably. Opportunities that provide no challenge should be passed up. The attraction of hunting the wild turkey is in meeting the challenge of predicting the bird's behavior or in fooling him. Satisfaction should be derived from the ways in which these challenges are attempted. Taking the bird should be rewarding only when it is the culminating step in meeting significant challenges. Killing alone is meaningless and obscene. Unfortunately, public acknowledgment of the hunter's accomplishments (and the prestige he derives from them) is generally allocated exclusively on the basis of bagging turkeys, not on an appraisal of the challenges met. The turkey taken in fair chase looks no different from the one shot over bait.

Take pride in adhering to a fair-chase philosophy. Allow it to become a dominant aspect of your enjoyment. This philosophy does not stop at refusing to undertake the unethical. It can be developed so that even ethical, yet essentially meaningless, kills are passed up. For instance, there is nothing unethical about shooting a bird that flushes at your feet as you search for the flock in the fall. But what satisfaction is derived from killing the bird? This is no accomplishment for an experienced hunter. It's not that the shot is too easy. In fact, the bird you call to your blind may present an easier chance. The called bird is an opportunity created by your effort and skill, but the flushing bird is a result of chance. Strive to make the birds you successfully harvest an accomplishment you can learn from.

Don't misunderstand the difficulties in following the fair-chase philosophy. After a week of hard hunting in the fall, when all your friends are bringing turkeys home, the temptation is great to put any turkey on the table. Those of us who have ever succumbed to that temptation have failed to recognize that the real accomplishment is not in killing but in killing under the conditions we set. A great warmth and sense of accomplishment comes from doing it the right way, particularly after passing up opportunities that present no significant challenge (Fears 1981).

Spring Gobbler Hunting

"Fall hunting is fun. It is as gay and bright and frothy as light summer literature. It smells good, and it looks good and it feels good, but like making love to chorus girls—there ain't no depth to it.

"Fall hunting is maneuvers.

"Spring hunting is war."

Tom Kelley (1973), in the classic work *Tenth Legion*, succinctly captured the impact of the spring hunt in this statement. War it is.

Turkey hunters spend a lifetime pursuing this noble bird and never seem to learn all that they feel should be known about the wild turkey. The wild turkey's innate wariness and sharp senses make him a deceptive quarry, and the hunter's strategy and tactics are responses to the gobbler's reproductive urges.

The skillful hunter who uses all of his woods savvy (including understanding of the bird, calling, technical execution, and excellent shooting skills) can be successful consistently. The essential elements of the successful hunt include (1) finding hunting areas, preseason scouting and learning the birds' location and movements, choosing proper dress and equipment, being in good physical condition, selecting the best calling positions; (2) planning and performing highly specialized strategies and calling maneuvers; (3) understanding turkey sounds and knowing how to imitate them on a variety of calling devices; (4) judging distances of birds both for setup and for shooting; and (5) executing the shot. The turkey hunter soon discovers there are few constants in the sport, and the words "always" and "never" disappear from his vocabulary.

Spring turkey hunting is a game of sounds. To become a successful turkey hunter, you must be a good listener. Essential to understanding the wild turkey and its environment is the ability to identify turkey sounds and the multitude of other sounds in the woods. All too often, the unfolding scenario of turkey activity is obscured by terrain or vegetation. After finding an area used by turkeys, it's important to listen from a high point for gobbling. You should listen from the moment the first gray light brightens the eastern sky all day until dark.

Male turkeys can and will gobble at any time of day. Peak periods occur during the first morning hour, the last hour in the evening, and at any time a gobbler is without the company of a hen. Gobbling attracts hens. The hunter, by imitating the call of a hen, attracts gobblers when they are without hens. This strategy involves a reversal of how the scenario usually unfolds in the world of the wild turkey. Normally hens go to toms. In turkey hunting, the hunter—imitating a hen—is trying to attract the tom. With this ploy, the hunter becomes the hunted.

If you hear no gobbling, it is often productive to imitate the staccato notes of a barred owl, the raucous call of a crow, or the scream of a hawk. Such sudden, shocking sounds often make gobblers gobble when they have been quiet. Making hen calls as locaters is a last resort with sometimes silent toms or fast-approaching vocal ones that give the hunter no warning or chance to set up.

Intimate knowledge of the territory the gobbler is using is critical to hunter success. Knowing the terrain and its features and the bird's preferred roosting and strutting areas is more important than perfect calling. Barriers such as creeks, ditches, thickets, roads, fences, or broad, open fields can make a tom hang up out of gun range. Knowing the topography of the land will help you choose a good calling position.

The thrill of spring gobbler hunting is calling the bird into close gun range and carefully choosing the shot. Positioning, combined with calling, helps achieve that end.

Calling devices number literally in the hundreds, but all can be classified in either of 2 categories—friction or air. Friction callers include boxes, slates, and push pins of many shapes, sizes, and combinations of materials. Air callers include the natural human voice, leaves, tubes, bellows, and wing bone and diaphragm types. All have the capability of calling turkeys. The smart hunter masters several different calling devices so that when the gobbler doesn't respond to one, he can draw another from his arsenal to achieve success. Often combinations of calling devices used simultaneously or in sequence are effective in creating multiple hen voices, thus improving your odds.

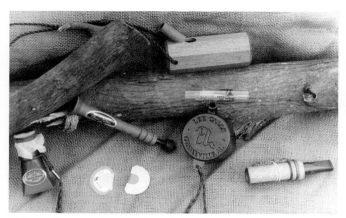
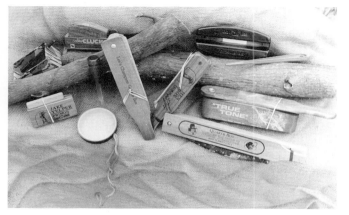

Turkey calls operate by air (left) or friction (right). *Photos by J. Phillips.*

Turkeys can be called consistently with 2 basic sounds from the turkey vocabulary—a simple yelp and a cluck. Combinations and variations of these basic calls—delivered in different rhythms and pitches—can be used to effectively call turkeys. Cackling, cutting, lost calling, purring, and gobbling are but a few other of the more than 2 dozen turkey vocalizations hunters imitate to call wild turkeys.

The key here is to experiment and not be timid. Find something the gobbler likes and keep giving it to him. Any of these calls used properly will bring the old boy in when he is receptive.

A dominant gobbler will often come to hen calls. But when he's occupied with hens, he may respond better to the challenging calls of another gobbler. Subdominant toms often steer clear of challenges and might respond better to gobbler clucks or the lost call of another turkey. If a gobbler does not respond to your calling one day, you can often turn the tables by exploring the possibilities of why not and continuing to experiment.

The serious turkey hunter gains experience and confidence by watching and listening to wild turkeys. Also, cassette tapes, video recordings, calling seminars, contests, and even domestic turkeys can provide the aspiring caller with turkey music to listen to and imitate.

Approaching a roosting gobbler is risky business. The hunter gets as close as possible without exposing himself to the roosted turkey. Under some conditions, that distance might be 200 meters (219 yards) or just 75 meters (82 yards), depending on the terrain and vegetation. Once you're in position, the temptation is to call and make the turkey gobble. To hear gobbling is a major enjoyment of turkey hunting. Resisting the temptation is tough. But the rule of thumb is to call sparingly while the bird is still in the tree and call only until you feel the tom has heard you. Ideally, the gobbler should interrupt your call with his gobble. When he does, lay the call down, unless there happens to be calling competition from some nearby roosting hens. Then match that calling note for note and add a little.

When the gobbler's pink feet touch the ground, your calling should intensify and become excited and aggressive. Then time the calls to the tom's gobbling. If he gobbles frequently, call frequently. If gobbling is sporadic (less than half a dozen gobbles in 10 minutes), back off the calling and deliver the call only once or twice. Sometimes empty time between calls or playing hard to get works well on stubborn toms. In this situation, your ears and eyes are so important. Be alert. Listen for steps or drumming. Sometimes you hear nothing, and then—like a ghost—there he stands. Also, he may move off and gobble 300 meters (328 yards) away, forcing you to change locations.

Ideally, select a calling site that does not allow you to see farther than your effective shooting range. Select open woods and areas such as logging roads or log landings. The best calling location is one that allows the tom and the hunter good visibility, but preferably for not more than about 45 meters (50 yards).

Shotguns are the overwhelming preference of spring gobbler hunters nationwide (Smith 1988). In fact, 37 states out of 49 allow shotguns only in the spring. That's the way it should be.

The game of spring gobbler hunting forces the hunter to exercise restraint. Shots at more than 32 meters (35 yards) are risky, although with modern loads and extra-full chokes in souped-up turkey guns, hunters can sometimes take turkeys as far away as 55 meters (60 yards). At such marginal distances, however, many gobblers are crippled and lost.

The hunter must decide the parameters of the game he plays. Your choice of shotgun and load should consistently pattern and should kill effectively at your chosen distance. Otherwise you should never squeeze the trigger. This knowledge is possessed by too few turkey hunters. If there is a flaw in the turkey hunter's preparation and expertise, it likely is here.

Far too many hunters think powerful equipment makes bagging any tom possible at 55 meters (60 yards). The mistake is in trying to let equipment compensate for lack of knowledge about that equipment, and the wild turkey suffers.

Turkey hunters must learn to judge distance. Without this skill, the gun and load make little difference. The hunter will not bag turkeys consistently.

The hunter must also learn the point of aim and point of impact for each turkey gun he owns. When shooting a turkey, shotguns are aimed like rifles, and many don't shoot where they are aimed. Most shoot high, some right, some left. Sighting devices can be valued pieces of equipment.

Finding the right load to match the gun can be time-consuming and expensive. But it's necessary if the turkey hunter expects to go to the woods with the necessary confidence in his shooting equipment. Choices of No. 4, 5, 6, and 7½ shot in varied load weights with varied powder charges will yield great variations in pattern density and point of impact. A hunter who shoots successfully with a 12-gauge 3-inch magnum with an extra-full choke and 2 ounces of buffered No. 6 shot won't necessarily have a superior pattern with a 12-gauge 3-inch magnum with a regular full choke and $1^7/8$ ounces of buffered No. 6 shot. Every combination is different.

The turkey hunter must find his answers by going to the range, shooting his gun on a bench rest, and testing all feasible combinations at different distances on a 76-centimeter (30-inch) circle target. That's the only way to develop the confidence necessary to squeeze the trigger on a gobbling longbeard. There are few worse feelings than to squeeze the trigger and watch that old boy glide off down the ridge. Avoid shots at running or flying gobblers unless the bird has been already hit.

The satisfaction derived from a perfectly executed shot lasts long after the smoke clears. We, as hunters, have an absolute obligation to be responsible. We can accept no less.

Effective shooting is dependent on using a shotgun and shell capable of delivering enough shot to a turkey's head and neck to assure a quick kill. *Photos by T. Fegely.*

Fall Hunting

Fall turkey hunting offers varied opportunities not found during the spring. The air is crisp, the foliage brilliant, and turkeys are flocked together. Family groups of old hens and their broods of the year are usually independent of single adult toms or of small gangs of gobblers.

Fall flocks can be found scratching through hardwood and mature pine stands in search of fresh-fallen mast. Or they might be spotted in fields as they prey on insects and devour weed seeds. It is the time of year a turkey hunter can hear all sorts of turkey music and lots of it.

For several reasons, the novice hunter will find this season provides a much greater chance to bag a bird than does spring. For one, there are more turkeys available than in the spring. Another is that both hens and gobblers usually are legal birds. Juvenile birds of either sex are somewhat more predictable and may rally to the call easier than longbearded spring toms.

Fall hunting might be better described as fall flock finding, which is the most difficult step to successful fall turkey hunting. Finding fall birds can require much time and leg work. Once a flock is located, the fall hunter deliberately scatters them, chooses a calling position close to the break point, and uses kee-kees or lost calls of a jake, and the assembly clucks of the dominant hen to bring back the scattered birds.

Consistently, the chances for locating a flock increase when you find food concentrations used by turkeys and locate fresh sign. Plate-sized scratchings in the leaf litter on the forest floor can show direction of travel and how long since birds fed in that area. Droppings, tracks, and molted feathers can indicate sex and age of the birds.

Fall flocks, such as this group of jakes, are usually segregated according to age and sex. *Photo by L. Rue III.*

When you find a flock, maneuver as close to it as possible. Then run directly at the birds, making a great deal of noise to scatter them. Soon the gregarious instincts of turkeys will trigger their effort to regroup. Age of the birds, time of day, weather conditions, and how often they've been hunted will affect how quickly they reassemble. Young birds scattered early in the day may begin calling and getting back together within minutes after the break. Yet the same birds scattered late in the day may wait until the next morning. Old gobblers might regroup whenever they think about it—in 2 hours or 2 days.

At the break point, you should select a tree, preferably wider than your shoulders, or construct a rough blind. Even without calling but just patiently waiting there, you should hear and see turkeys regroup. The whistling kee-kee can bring young birds on the run, but a few choice yelps or clucks can do the job. With your call, try to imitate the sounds of the responding birds. If you hear a long series of yelps, chances are you're listening to the old hen. Don't try to compete with her calling, but rather chase her from the scene. If you don't, all the young turkeys will go to her, not to you.

The real beauty in this fall situation is that probably more than 1 turkey will answer your call and work toward your position at the same time. This response offers you the opportunity to be selective. In the event you miss a bird, you can stay put and still call additional birds to your location.

The fall hunter, no less than the spring hunter, should persevere at his blind. Allow extra time, and wait. Patience is a key element to the successful fall hunter. When you're in good turkey woods, patience is measured in hours, not minutes.

Turkey Calling Contests

With the return of the wild turkey to huntable numbers and the desire of hunters to perfect their calling skills, calling contests have developed. The growth of turkey calling contests has paralleled the opening of turkey seasons around the country. It was only natural that interest was and is very high where turkey calling is new and many turkey hunters are still at the novice level. Turkey calling contest mania hit fever pitch during the mid-1970s and continued through the following decade. Tape recorders—and more recently video recorders—were used by competitors and audience to record the calls. They aimed to either imitate the champion or copy a particular style of calling for use in the field.

Just where the first contest originated is of some debate. Was it Alabama, Arkansas, or Pennsylvania? Each lays claim. But what is of unquestioned significance is that calling competitions have become focal

Competitive calling contests bring the best turkey callers together to match skills. *Photo by J. Langston.*

points of county fairs, outdoor shows, chapters of the National Wild Turkey Federation, or separate competitions. Such contests probably have generated more attention in the media than has any other aspect of turkey hunting. They've at least highlighted the term "wild turkey" for the general public.

Callers are judged most often by a panel of 3 to 7 qualified judges. The competitors are evaluated on 5 or 6 basic calls of the wild turkey and scored most often on a scale of 1 to 20 (perfect). In competitions with 5 or 7 judges, the high score and low score are not counted in the total. Champion callers compete as much for prestige as for the trophies, hunting equipment, or cash that may be awarded. Such bragging rights by champions have spawned numerous call-manufacturing companies that today produce some of the finest calling instruments available to turkey hunters.

Hundreds of local, regional, state, open, and national competitions are available to the competitive caller today. The most prestigious of all turkey calling events is the NWTF's Grand National Calling Championship held in conjunction with the NWTF National Convention. This event pits champions of state and open competitions against one another. Additionally, the Grand National Junior competition and the Grand National Owl Hooting Championships are held along with this event.

Safety

No aspect of the wonderful sport of turkey hunting has eroded the quality of the sport more than turkey-hunting accidents. Almost everyone who has hunted turkeys for a length of time has had a brush with potential danger.

In 1989, 24 states had no hunting accidents, yet Pennsylvania had 7. Seven out of 350,000 hunters is one accident per 50,000 participants. Far less than skiing, swimming, or boating. But how many are too many? The future of sport hunting depends on our cleaning up our ranks.

Turkey hunting, by its close-range, camouflaged nature, is a potentially dangerous sport. Camouflaged hunters blend into the surroundings. Yet the movement of a bare hand when calling, the reaching for a handkerchief, turning a head, or some other movement may seem to be a turkey and can trigger an error in judgment from a nearby hunter (Charles Farmer, NWTF Wild Turkey Hunter Safety Slide Module). Movement plus sounds of a wild turkey and contrasting color are common factors of turkey-hunting accidents, causing serious, sometimes fatal mistakes.

Statistics from Pennsylvania show that it is more likely for an experienced hunter to be involved in a turkey-hunting accident than a novice. The average offender has 15 years of turkey-hunting experience, hardly a novice (M. Schmidt personal communication: 1988). Why is the experienced hunter, the very one who says he couldn't commit the offense, the one most frequently involved in an accident?

The reasoning is this: The more experienced the hunter is, the more convinced he can become because of the proven "connect-the-dot theory." The more experience — or more "dots" he connects — the more convinced the hunter becomes. Finally he has connected enough dots in his mind to be convinced beyond a shadow of a doubt that he is looking at a turkey. In reality, connecting the last dot (squeezing the trigger on a gobbler) was in error. It was not a gobbler.

How many times have you driven down a highway and noticed a dead skunk lying in the road? You know it is a dead skunk because you've seen them there before, and maybe you caught them in your fox traps nearby in the past. You know it's a skunk by its shape and color. In fact, as you get closer, you identify its white stripe. You see the shape of its tail and head because you know what they look like at close range. As you get up to the object, you realize it's a blown-out whitewall tire. All of us who have hunted have conceived similar misinterpretations before, like the charred-stump "bear" or the "antlers" on the doe. The analogy to turkey hunting is strong.

Other elements can contribute to the accident problem: illegal hunting, competitive hunting, peer pressure, crowded conditions, imperfect eyesight, and limited visibility.

Though the accident problem is complex and has no simple answers, the NWTF is committed to bringing about solutions. Here are some of the steps in the right direction: (1) identifying the problem; (2) discussing the problem; (3) developing visual aids such as the "Turkey Hunting Safety and Ethics" module, a movie, and printed materials on defensive turkey hunting; and (4) working with the target group of experienced turkey hunters. There is a strong commitment to reduce turkey-hunting accidents through partnerships with state wildlife resource agencies, chapters of the NWTF, and, of course, turkey hunters themselves.

Defensive Turkey Hunting

Turkey hunting is a secretive, camouflage sport that requires patience and presents some unique safety problems. So the National Wild Turkey Federation has developed 10 commandments of defensive turkey hunting for the hunter who wants to become safer, protect himself and fellow hunters, and make a great sport better.

(1) Never stalk a turkey thinking you are going to slip within gun range. The chances of getting close enough for a shot are slim, but the chances of becoming involved in an accident are increased.

(2) Eliminate the colors red, white, and blue from your turkey-hunting outfit. Red is the color most hunters count on to differentiate a gobbler's head from the hen's blue-colored head. White can look like the snowball-colored top of a gobbler's head. Leave those white T-shirts and socks at home. Not only will these colors put you in danger, but they can be seen by turkeys as well.

(3) Never move, wave, or make turkey sounds to alert another hunter of your presence. A quick movement may draw fire. Yell in a loud voice and remain hidden, or at least whistle clearly like a human.

(4) Never attempt to approach closer than 69 meters (75 yards) to a roosting turkey. The wild turkey's eyesight and hearing are much too sharp to let you get any closer.

(5) Be particularly careful when using the gobbler call. The sound and motion may attract other hunters.

(6) When selecting your calling position, don't try to hide so well that you cannot see what's happening. Remember, eliminating movement is your key to success, not total concealment.

(7) If possible, select a calling position that provides a background as wide as your shoulders, and one that will completely protect you from the top of your head down. Small trees won't hide slight movements of your hands or shoulders, which might look like a turkey to another hunter who might be stalking your sweet calls. Position yourself so you can see 180 degrees in front of you.

(8) Camouflage conceals you. It does not make you invisible. When turkey hunting, think and act defensively. Avoid all unnecessary movement. Remember, you are visible to both turkeys and hunters when you move even slightly. Sitting perfectly still will help you kill more turkeys than all the camo you can wear.

(9) Never shoot at a sound or movement. Be 100 percent certain of your target before you pull the trigger.

(10) When turkey hunting, assume that every sound you hear is made by another hunter. Once you pull the trigger, you can never call that shot back.

Turkey hunting is a lot like fishing for lunker bass. If your gobbler gets away, he'll be there another day. Anytime you begin to place more emphasis on the kill than on the experience, you are headed toward doing something foolish. Squeezing that trigger should never overshadow knowing exactly what is out in front of your barrel.

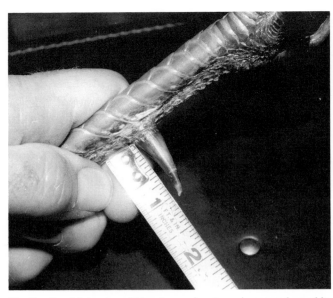

Hunting for old, trophy gobblers is popular. A scoring procedure adds weight, beard length, and total spur length for a composite score. *Photo by H. Williamson, U.S. Forest Service.*

Trophies and Trophy Scoring

What constitutes a trophy? The word means different things to different people at different times. All too often in our modern competitive society we judge success in terms of the fastest, the most, the biggest, or the longest. In the sport of turkey hunting, a trophy may not be measured in inches or pounds. Beard length, spur length, and body weight are generally incidental to the quality of the hunt. A boy's first hen in the fall or a hard-won jake in the spring may constitute a trophy. It is important for us to focus on the trophy experience. For the future of our sport, we must emphasize the trophy by the quality of the experience.

Many times a gang of jakes, who gobble at every hen call but have no intention of coming in, can cause frustration. After you walk miles, reposition many times, and switch to lost calls or gobbler calls, the birds finally come to the gun. Such a trophy is short on spur and beard and light on the scale, but hunting these birds is exciting and thrilling because of the challenges. Any one of their number is a hard-earned trophy that will provide memories to last a lifetime.

The National Wild Turkey Federation maintains a record of harvested turkeys entered by turkey hunters nationwide. The Federation acknowledges all legally harvested turkeys of either sex. No prizes or awards are presented for the biggest ones.

All these turkeys must be weighed—to the nearest ounce—on scales inspected and certified accurate for trade by the state department of agriculture, or on an accurate scale by a licensed guide or outfitter, or on the official scales of a governmental wildlife agency. Beard and spur length measurements must be made with a measuring device that is accurate to $1/16$ inch. In order to standardize measurement, all measurements are to be recorded in $1/16$-inch increments.

To ascertain your bird's total score, use this formula: weight (pounds and ounces) plus 10 times spur length (right and left) plus 2 times beard length. Each beard must be measured from the center point of the protrusion from the skin to the end of the longest bristle. Spurs must be measured along the outside center, from the point at which the spur protrudes from the scaled leg skin to the tip of the spur. All measurements and weights must be converted to decimals for use in this formula.

An example of how this formula works is to score Thomas Moravec's current world record "typical" gobbler. Moravec's tom weighed 25 pounds 3 ounces, had spurs measuring 2 inches and $2^2/16$ inches long, with a beard $10^{10}/16$ inches long. Convert all weights and measurements to decimals.

Next, multiply the total of both spur lengths $(2 + 2.125)$ by 10 and you get 41.25 points. Now multiply the beard's length (10.625) by 2, yielding 21.25 points. Add these 2 figures to the weight (25.1875 pounds) and you get a grand total of 87.6875 points:

$$
\begin{array}{ll}
25.1875 & \text{pounds} \\
41.25 & \text{points} \\
\underline{21.25} & \text{points} \\
87.6875 & \text{points}
\end{array}
$$

All measurements must be verified by a current member of the NWTF or another licensed hunter from that state. Hunters must enter each turkey on an official entry application form, including certification that the turkey was taken by legal means, in the spirit of fair chase, and that the bird was not released for commercial hunting or confined within any artificial barrier. All entries must be signed, witnessed, and mailed to

National Wild Turkey Records
P.O. Box 530
Edgefield, SC 29824-0530

PROCESSING THE KILL

A wild turkey's role as a valuable resource does not end at the climax of a successful hunt. Turkeys provide beautiful trophies and terrific table fare with little expense (National Rifle Association 1988).

Care should be exercised in protecting a trophy for the taxidermist or for the camera. Avoid damage to or loss of feathers. Use a damp cloth to wipe all blood and other residue from the feathers.

It is not necessary to remove the entrails unless the bird cannot be kept cool and out of direct sunlight for several hours. Refrigerated, the entire bird can be kept half a day if necessary, until it is either frozen whole for the taxidermist or butchered for the table.

To remove the entrails, cut from the tail to the tip of the breastbone, cut around the anus, and make a lateral cut 10 centimeters (4 inches) wide through the soft flap of skin. Insert your hand, and pull out the viscera, trying not to tear them. The gizzard, liver, and heart can be kept for gravy or for the cat. Before cooking the gizzard, don't forget to slice it to remove its pouch of grit.

Newspaper, paper towels, or a cloth can be used to wipe out the body cavity, and a damp cloth should be used immediately to absorb blood and any other fluids from the feathers.

The wild turkey makes an excellent trophy to display, whether you prefer a full body mount prepared by a professional taxidermist or a do-it-yourself cape.

Full or partial body mounts can be created in virtually any pose a turkey can assume. Modern freeze-drying techniques of wild turkey heads have added very positively to the overall look of wild turkey trophies. Some taxidermists have become specialists in this art form. Full body mounts start at about $300 and can reach double that for certain poses. The satisfaction you get from a well-done mount lasts a lifetime. In fact, when considering the economics of a full body mount, remember this old saying: The bitterness of poor quality remains long after the sweetness of low price is forgotten.

The do-it-yourselfer can fashion a simple trophy by cutting off the tail, spreading the fan in a semicircle, then pinning it to a piece of cardboard. Dust all fleshy areas with a thick layer of borax, and let the tail dry several weeks.

Another attractive presentation is the cape of the bird, which is prepared as follows:

(1) To begin, hang your tom by the head.
(2) With a sharp knife, cut the skin where the feathers on the neck meet the skin of the head. Continuing down the back and toward the tail, remove

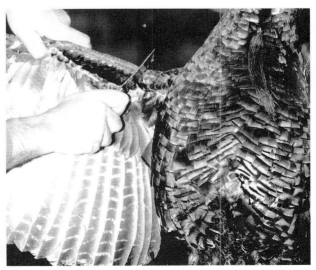

A preferred method of skinning and dressing a turkey yields both an attractive wall mount of the cape and fan and skinless breast fillets and legs. The first step is to hang the bird by the head and cut off the wings at the first joint (continued on page 398). *Photos by J. Langston.*

The beard is then removed by pulling gently and cutting the loose skin at the base. *Photo by J. Langston.*

Remove the lower legs by cutting around the joint where the feathers meet the scaly part of the leg. *Photo by J. Langston.*

Begin removing the cape by inserting a knife into the neck skin where the feathers start on the back of a gobbler's neck. Continue the cut down the neck and back following the subtle division seen between the back and breast feathers. *Photo by J. Langston.*

Continue the cuts down to the base of the tail feathers and sever the fan by cutting the fatty tissue known as the "pope's nose." *Photo by J. Langston.*

the skin in an approximately 2-inch-wide strip. You will notice that the feathers are attached to the skin in rows and the narrow strip of skin actually holds a much wider angular blanket of feathers.

(3) Remove the skin to and including the "pope's nose."
(4) With a knife and a spoon, remove fat and flesh.
(5) Cover the wet skin with a thin layer of borax.
(6) Place the borax-covered skin on a large piece of flat corrugated cardboard, skin side *toward* the cardboard.
(7) With straight pins, pin the head end to the cardboard.

The cape and fan can then be put aside until the job of butchering is completed. *Photo by J. Langston.*

The remainder of the turkey's skin is removed by pulling and trimming with a knife where needed. *Photo by J. Langston.*

The skin is removed from the legs by rolling it down as far as possible, and then it is severed with a circular cut of the knife (continued on page 400). *Photo by J. Langston.*

(8) Fan the tail, spreading it to the desired width, and pin each feather in place.

(9) With the blade of a knife, lay each feather back in its natural place.

(10) Let the skin dry 3 to 4 weeks.

(11) Remove the pins, shake the borax loose, and hang the skin.

(12) You may wish to mount the cape on a piece of wood cut to fit the cape, which gives the mount a finished look.

Skinning versus Plucking

The traditional view has been that no turkey is fit for the table without its skin fully intact. After the hunt, each turkey was laboriously plucked, though the lengthy chore was not enjoyable after a short night, rocky ridges, and the stretched nerves of hunting.

The choice of skinning or plucking depends largely on your method of cooking. For the types of cooking that tend to dry out the flesh of the bird, the moisture-sealing skin should be left on. Plucking rather than skinning also helps when you aim to freeze the bird. You'll reduce the risk of freezer burn.

Other treatments of the skinless bird make it moist and tender. My choice of preparation—deep frying and grilling—doesn't require the skin to be intact.

When you've had a little practice, the entire skinning operation takes less than 3 minutes per bird. This method of preparation also removes much of the cholesterol and fat that tend to concentrate in the skin.

The breast sponge is then cut away and discarded. *Photo by J. Langston.*

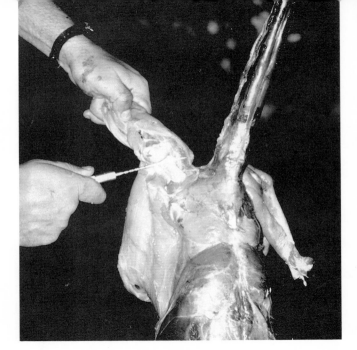

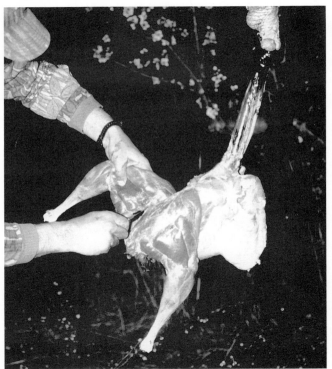

The upper wings and legs are removed. *Photos by J. Langston.*

After hanging the bird by the head, remove the appendages. Beginning with the legs, apply pressure to the front of one leg, thus straining the joint. Sever the skin and tendons to the knuckle. Repeat the procedure on the other leg.

Extend one wing parallel to the ground. At the second joint, slice perpendicular through the feathers, skin, and joint. Twist off the outer wing. Do likewise to the other wing. At this point, the beard can be sliced from the chest.

Work your thumb between the skin and flesh. As the gap enlarges, insert one hand around the wing stub and the other around the skin. Pull in opposite directions until the wing stub is skinless. Repeat on the other side. Slice the skin around the neck at the base of the caruncles and strip away the skin. Work the skin down and away from the carcass. On the lower back, use a knife to separate the tight-clinging skin from the meat. Cut off the "pope's nose." Pull the skin from the drumsticks. Your knife will ease the skin over the end of the bone. The skinning job is complete. Now the entrails can be removed (about as described earlier) while the bird is still hanging. Then sever the head from the neck.

If you intend to either bake or smoke the bird, then plucking is prudent, leaving the skin intact. Two methods are commonly used to pluck a wild turkey: wet or dry.

If a source of nearly boiling water is available, wet plucking is the most effective. Simply dunk the bird headfirst into a large caldron of hot water, submerging it to where the feathers end on the thighs. Swish the bird only 10 seconds in the bath. Any longer will begin to

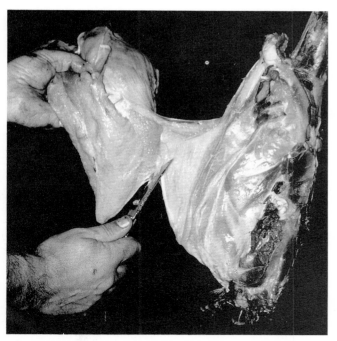

The breast fillets are removed by inserting the knife blade along the ribs and cutting toward the keel bone, being careful to keep the breast half in one large piece. *Photo by J. Langston.*

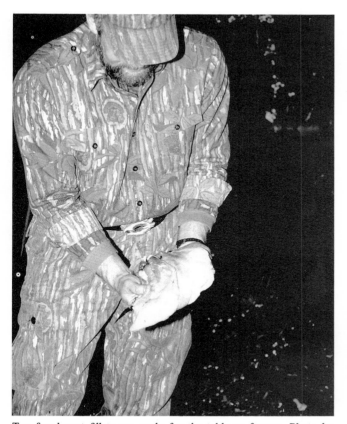

Two fine breast fillets are ready for the table or freezer. *Photo by J. Langston.*

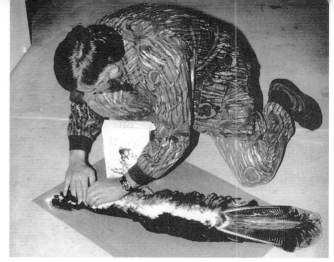

The butchering process completed, now it is time to prepare the cape for an attractive wall mount. The first step is to sprinkle a liberal amount of borax onto the fleshy side of the skin, working it in with the fingers. *Photo by J. Langston.*

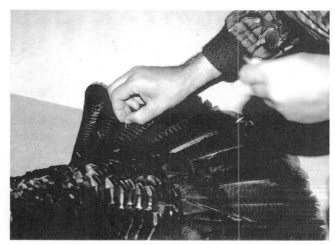

Two paneling nails are used to fasten the neck skin to a piece of large cardboard. Other nails are then used to hold the spread fan in place for drying. *Photo by J. Langston.*

Feathers are easily smoothed and put back in place by using a flat knife blade (continued on page 402). *Photo by J. Langston.*

The finished cape should dry for 2 to 3 weeks and then be hung for display. *Photo by J. Langston.*

cook the bird. Next, hang the bird head-up, and begin pulling feathers. Work until all are removed. The larger wing feathers will be difficult to pull. You may need to use pliers.

If you lack a source of hot water, dry plucking is the alternative. Hang the bird head-up, sever the outer wing bones at the joint with a knife, pull the larger feathers with a pair of pliers, and pluck the rest by hand. Next, remove the entrails and wash the body cavity with water.

The last step when using either process is to remove the small, hairlike feathers, or down. This is best done with a flame from either a small propane torch or a torch made from tightly rolled newspaper. The bird's skin should be dry before this singeing. Lightly run the flame over the bird, being careful not to burn the skin.

Other Trophies

It's darn near a sin to waste any part of the turkey. In fact, not many parts can't be put to some good use. The wing bones can be transformed into turkey calls; the primary wing feathers into arrow fletchings; the secondary wing, tail, and body feathers into fishing flies. Among the numerous other articles that can be fashioned from feathers, spurs, beards, and bones are Christmas

wreaths, dry flower arrangements, pins, earrings, necklaces, bolos, blankets, and hats. Also, a neatly trimmed turkey feather in a personal note card gives a touch of class to any communication.

PHOTOGRAPHY

Photography is another way to interact with and enjoy the wild turkey. Many factors contribute to wildlife photography's status as one of the fastest-growing nonconsumptive outdoor activities. Among these factors are today's portable video cameras and highly automated 35mm single-lens reflex cameras, higher game and nongame populations, and the ability of people to travel to where wild animals roam. The science and art of high-quality photography and videography also play major roles in sharing the outdoors experience and in recording events or wildlife in scientific research. To effectively photograph animals in an outdoors setting and correctly capture the creatures' movements and color, the delicate relationship among lighting conditions, aperture, shutter speed, and film speed must be properly balanced.

Wildlife photography has grown tremendously in recent years. A recent national survey revealed that more than 29.4 million people traveled away from home to observe, photograph, or feed wildlife, specifically spending 80.4 million days photographing wildlife (U.S. Fish and Wildlife Service 1988a).

The primary and secondary nonconsumptive wildlife users spent nearly $14.3 billion in 1985, of which $9.8 billion was spent on equipment. There was $715.4 million spent on cameras, lenses, and other photographic equipment. An additional $810.1 million was spent on film to photograph wildlife. Wildlife photography, of which wild turkey photography is a part, is definitely a large and growing activity (U.S. Fish and Wildlife Service 1988a).

Photographing the wild turkey has special rewards. It allows the photographer to study the species in detail, and it affords a year-round opportunity to pursue these magnificent creatures. Besides the exercise you gain by traveling through the habitat of these birds, you get the souvenir of recorded images to retell your experiences. The pursuit of wild turkeys with a camera to capture properly exposed, sharply focused photographs is in many respects more difficult than bagging a bird. The acquisition of useful, pleasing, artistic, and educational wild turkey photographs can require a large commitment of time, effort, planning, and expense.

Wild turkey photography and wildlife photography in general are tools vital to the public's education about our natural resources. Conservation ideals and key wildlife management principles can be expressed to the public by properly composed, eye-appealing still photography, videography, and cinematography.

Equipment

The major costs incurred when selecting equipment for still photography are for camera bodies and lenses. Low-quality equipment will compromise the quality of the finished product. Money invested in high-quality equipment will pay dividends in superior results, justifying the added cost.

Bodies and lenses. The 35mm single-lens reflex (SLR) camera is the most popular choice of wildlife photographers today. Camera bodies in this design range in price from $200 to $3,000. A large selection of lenses and other equipment make 35mm SLR the choice for most wildlife photographers because of its versatility in field situations.

Today's auto-exposure and auto-focus cameras offer much convenience, but at a price. That price is justified oftentimes when a photographer has limited time to react. A word of caution: While photographing wild turkeys at close range, turn off the auto-focus mode. The whirring sound produced by the camera's lens motor will often send the wary birds into the next county, spoiling a long-awaited opportunity. The advantages of a totally manual camera are that it is more rugged and will still function when batteries lose power.

A camera with the capacity to change focusing screens offers the photographer a choice to match personal requirements. The split-image screens found in most 35mm SLR cameras have the tendency to darken when you use a lens aperture smaller than f4.

The debates between advocates of fixed-focal-length and zoom lens systems are often long and heated. Both systems have their merits and disadvantages. Prices range from approximately $100 for an average quality 50mm, f2.8 manual fixed-focal-length lens to $10,000 for some high-powered, auto-focus zoom lenses.

The advantages of zoom lenses are many. The most pronounced is versatility in the field. Because of your ability to cover a greater range of shooting distances, you will miss fewer shots. The ability to crop and compose photographs more precisely also is a plus. And fewer lenses to carry in the field and keep track of is a boon to photographers who must walk long distances or change positions frequently.

What are the disadvantages of using zoom lenses in the field? They are more sensitive to adverse handling. They're bulkier and heavier. They tend to have smaller maximum apertures than fixed-focal-length lenses that correspond to the lower power settings. The average cost of zoom lenses is higher than for comparable fixed lenses, but this difference can be rationalized if a zoom lens is replacing several fixed-focus lenses. Less-expensive zoom lenses at maximum apertures tend to produce poorer quality than comparable fixed-focus lenses.

The advantages and disadvantages of fixed-focal-length lenses to shoot wildlife are myriad. They are lighter and more compact than zoom lenses. Sharper images at maximum aperture are the rule. And they are more rugged. But having to buy at least twice as many lenses to shoot the same situations will reduce mobility and comfort and add to costs of acquiring and maintaining equipment.

Zoom lenses needed to photograph wild turkeys and other wildlife fill the gap between 35mm and 400mm. In special situations, the largest sizes are needed—up to 600mm. To span this gap, a 35mm-135mm zoom, plus a 200mm-400mm zoom, as offered by a major camera equipment manufacturer, will cover practically every situation. Another option would be to choose 3 zooms: a 35mm-70mm, an 80mm-200mm, and the 200mm-400mm. Another photo equipment manufacturer offers 28mm-80mm, 70mm-200mm, and 250mm-600mm auto-focus zoom lenses. There are several other options in zoom lens packages.

The well-equipped user of fixed-focal-length lenses will need a 35mm, 50mm, 90mm or 100mm, 135mm, 180mm or 200 mm, 250mm or 300mm, 400mm, and a 500mm or 600mm lens to shoot various situations. The shorter-length lenses in a particular range (such as 90mm instead of 100mm) often offer lower maximum apertures. Such a lens could mean losing photo opportunities in low light.

Mirror lenses are another option for the wildlife photographer. They range from 300mm to 1,000mm and tend to be fragile. They also tend to produce a "vignetting," or halo, effect, which is unnatural in wildlife photography.

Tele-extenders transform shorter lenses into longer telephotos and are easily adaptable to most manufacturer's lenses. They provide more magnification but reduce available light through the lens. In some situations, though, they may prove beneficial (Chambers and Rue 1984).

Film. When photographing wild turkeys, your choice of film—either black and white or color—is a matter of preference. Most professional wildlife photographers, aiming for marketability to print media, shoot color-slide film. Black-and-white prints are also desired by some publishers. So photographers sometimes carry 2 camera bodies, one loaded with color-slide film and the other with black-and-white print film. This tactic allows a photographer to tailor photos to a specific assignment or artistic taste. Some professional wildlife photographers rely solely on color-slide film, making any required black-and-white prints from these. Print quality suffers slightly.

Two major brands of color positive (slide) film are regarded seriously by wildlife photographers: (1) Kodak's Kodachrome and Ektachrome; and (2) Fuji's Fujichrome. They have been proven to yield quality images.

Kodachrome 25 (ASA 25) is the granddaddy of color positive transparency film. It has the smallest grain, thus producing the sharpest reproduction when enlarged several hundred percent. Kodachrome 64 (ASA 64) is the most popular wildlife photographer's film, also having a fine grain. It yields very sharp images when enlarged to magazine page size.

Setting up a lab to develop Kodachrome is quite costly, so most photographers rely on Qualex photo processing labs to do the work. On the other hand, Ektachrome and Fujichrome films are E-6 process films and can be handled by local labs. Because of variation in processing quality, choice of labs is critical. When you find a good processor, stick with it.

Fujichrome offers a wide ASA range in commercial color film, with speeds ranging from ASA 50 to ASA 400. When photographing wild turkeys in a low-light setting, Fujichrome is a film to be relied upon.

The debate still persists over the choice of Kodachrome or Fujichrome for taking publication-quality photography. Fuji films have progressed in quality until the difference is a matter of personal preference.

The choice between shooting color positive (slide) film or color negative (print) film is normally dictated by cost. It is less expensive to shoot transparencies and have color prints reproduced from the best slides. Also, if the photographer wishes to sell his work to a publisher, he will fare better by shooting transparency film.

The option of shooting black-and-white film is one often taken by the wildlife photographer. The normal range of film speed for black-and-white photography lies between ASA 64 and ASA 400. Kodak's Plus-X (ASA 125) is the optimum black-and-white film for the wildlife photographer. Its fine grain yields sharp images. If a faster black-and-white film is desired for low-light situations, Kodak's Tri-X (ASA 400) will produce a grainier print, but still up to publication standards.

The most economical way to buy film is in large quantities from mail-order houses. To take advantage of this method, proper film storage is critical. Film should be stored unopened, away from heat and light. A refrigerator is best for short-term storage and a freezer for long-term storage. When time comes to use film, set it out for several hours to warm to room temperature to prevent condensation.

The use of filters is usually minimal for wildlife photographers, but may be appropriate in some situations. Polarizing or UV filters will deepen the color of blue sky and will reduce reflections in color photography. It will also reduce reflections when used with black-and-white film. Colored filters can be used to achieve special effects or highlight certain shades and colors.

Once quality images are in hand, the prudent photographer uses a system of storage that will protect slides and photographs. Polypropylene organizers, such as Clear-File, or 20th Century Plastics EZ2C arrival photo pages are safe choices. Polyvinylchloride, or PVC, storage sheets should not be used, due to their chemical makeup, which will attack prints, negatives, and transparencies.

Other equipment. Photographing wild turkeys with heavy, high-powered lenses will require the use of a tripod to hold the camera and lens. If a tripod is not used, camera shake will often blur the photographs, making them useless for publication. A well-built tripod can be bought at anywhere from $100 to $500.

The shiny surfaces of all photo equipment, including tripods, should be camouflaged. Wrapping the upper section of a tripod's legs with foam, then masking it with camouflage tape will serve double duty: (1) hide the tripod; and (2) reduce the chance for making game-scaring noises.

Total camouflage is as critical for the wildlife photographer as for the hunter. This would include clothing, equipment, and the use of blinds. Blinds can be constructed of either man-made materials or naturally occurring foliage. A combination of the 2 is also advised.

VIDEO PRODUCTION

More sportsmen than ever before are taking video cameras into the field to record their hunts and outdoor adventures. Besides having the basic hunting skills to get the game within camera range, you need some additional know-how to improve your home movies. This section will specifically address videotaping turkeys.

The first priority is access to game. If you get serious about shooting game with a camera instead of a gun, you will soon find that many true sanctuaries will become available. Landowners who may resist hunters will often grant permission to those wishing to videotape or photograph game. Keep in mind that landowner respect is paramount to being invited back. Always offer the landowner a chance to view the footage, and offer to make him a copy.

Once you gain access to prime videotaping locations, a few equipment modifications are in order. When dealing with turkeys, camouflage is paramount. Turkeys

Videotaping turkeys and other wildlife has become popular in recent years. *Photo by R. Strickland.*

ment for the wild turkey videographer. A good remote microphone can run anywhere from $30 to $1,000. Select one that is omnidirectional (will pick up sound from all directions). It should also have at least a 6-meter (20-foot) cord. The microphone should have its own internal battery. When buying a microphone, be sure to take the camera along and make sure the fittings are compatible. Buy extra batteries. You'll need replacements often.

After locating a place to test your new video equipment, do a rack focus. This is accomplished by zooming out and focusing on the farthest object seen. Zoom back, keeping the focus setting locked in place. This tactic will keep everything farther than approximately 3 meters (10 feet) in focus and will reduce movement later. Always operate the camera in the manual (not automatic) focus setting. Otherwise the lens will focus on twigs, limbs, or other objects near your subject.

When videotaping with another hunter, plan signals to prepare the cameraman for coming action. Make sure the hunter signals if he or she is going to call, and record this. One of the biggest faults with amateur videography is that there is not enough footage of scenes before the hunt. Calling, setting up, walking through the woods—all these scenes will make your video better.

Once the turkey is in view, frame him up and stay with a medium shot. Try to get the subject in the middle of the viewfinder, but not too close. The background should still play a prominent part. Keep this picture in the viewfinder, a technique that looks much better than zooming in and out repeatedly. I always look through the viewfinder with one eye, keeping the other open to check where the turkey or other subject may be going. This habit may help if you need to move. You may spot a big tree or some other large object. When the subject walks behind it, move the camera.

When you're videotaping a hunt, the gunshot can be a problem. The natural reaction is to flinch at the gun blast. To avoid this, the cameraman should relax his hands and head. Slowly move the hands away from the camera, if possible. After the shot, hands and face can be moved back into position close to the camera. The key to a smooth video at the gun blast is to have the hunter signal the cameraman when the shot will be fired. And always use a tripod.

After a successful shot, get a posthunt interview with the hunter. If you're using a tripod, set up the camera and have the cameraman get in the picture with the shooter. Before doing this, always make sure the turkey is completely still and clean. Nonhunters may view the tape, and some are not favorably impressed by a bloody turkey.

One last very important point: When you're in the field videotaping and concentrating on the viewfinder, it's easy to lose touch with the hunt. A hunting accident is

will have many chances to see a cameraman who's panning a camera around. Cameras and other equipment should preferably be covered with camouflage tape. If you're hesitant about camouflage tape on your video camera, get a camouflage T-shirt or other camouflage material and make a removable cover. Make sure this material covers everything except the lens and the color sensor. (The color sensor is always in the front of the camera and looks like a small piece of clear—or almost clear—plastic or dull glass.)

The next key ingredient is a quality tripod. This piece of gear is bulky and will slow travel down a bit. But a tripod will improve the quality of your work 100 percent. Use camouflage tape or paint to cover your tripod.

When you're buying a tripod to hold a video camera steady, the head is the most critical feature to evaluate. A fluid-head mount is the most desired. It allows smooth camera panning when you videotape moving subjects.

A remote microphone is another vital piece of equip-

possible, so use utmost caution when filming (Strickland 1991).

Composition for Posthunt Photography

The developments of compact, automatic-focusing, point-and-shoot 35mm cameras and portable home video cameras have enabled today's turkey hunter to easily record a hunt. And modern equipment gives hunters with limited technical photographic knowledge the ability to photograph a trophy or picturesque scenery and thereby share their hunts.

This section will address the components of quality postkill wild turkey photography.

Without question, the most photographed element of the turkey hunt is of the bird once it is in hand. Hunters who have invested time, money, and energy into having a successful hunt almost certainly will photograph the hard-won trophy. Many hunters, though, never take advantage of the beauty and color surrounding

Placing the subject of the photograph in the lower, right-hand corner is one way to use the "rule of thirds" to give a sense of movement and perspective. *Photo by J. Langston.*

them, such as the dogwoods of spring or the blazing leaves of fall.

The staff of the National Wild Turkey Federation annually sees hundreds of photographs of dead turkeys. Some of these photos are submitted by proud hunters for possible publication in *Turkey Call* magazine, some accompany Wild Turkey Records applications, and others are just trophy photos. Unfortunately, most of these photos are below publication quality and far from aesthetically pleasing. The poor results are not usually because of poor exposure but rather because the bird was in shabby shape when photographed.

To get good photographs, you must exercise all possible care to keep the bird neat and in good physical condition. Avoid pulling out or crushing feathers, and keep them from getting wet or covered with blood. Clean all parts of the bird that will show in the camera's viewfinder.

Immediately after shooting a turkey, the hunter must move quickly and carefully to secure his quarry. Resist the temptation to pick up or bluntly dispatch a flopping bird. More feathers are lost at this point than at any other.

If the bird becomes wet, possibly from rolling into a creek or in dew-soaked grass, avoid stroking or pulling feathers. They will come out rather easily. Hang the bird from a limb to allow it to air dry, and later fluff the plumage until it returns to near-normal condition. Some photographers have used a hair dryer to dry feathers, returning them to their original appearance.

How the bird is carried from the woods also is important in keeping it in good condition for photography. Probably the best way to transport it is to grab the bird by the legs and sling it over your shoulder, with the breast of the bird resting on your back.

A bird as regal as the wild turkey deserves respect in its handling and photographic presentation. With a good-looking subject in hand, you should search for a pleasing background to stage the photo. Look for large or unusually shaped tree trunks, unusual rock formations, or weathered stumps or deadfalls to add ruggedness to the background. Blossoms such as wild azaleas, redbuds, or dogwoods add color to photographic backdrops. Old barns, grist mills, or backwoods hunting camps will add a nostalgic touch to photos.

Spreading the turkey's wings, fanning the tail, and showing the beauty of the plumage can enhance the overall effect. And don't forget to include your hunting partners in a few of the shots.

Shadows are often a problem when photographing during the middle of the day. Waiting to start the photo session until late afternoon or early the next morning gives you softer lighting. The camera's flash also is an option. "Fill flash" is a technique used by professional photographers to reduce shadows in bright light.

Choosing a picturesque setting for a posthunt photograph adds a lot to amateur photography. *Photo by T. Humphrey.*

Eliminate nonessential subjects from the photo. Never hang birds from children's swing sets or pose with toys or near garbage cans. Photographs with alcohol or tobacco products in view detract from the beauty of the hunt and reduce chances for publication.

Framing and positioning hunter and trophy is a major aspect of good photography. Adhering to the "rule of thirds" is critical to properly composing photos. Simply put, this rule says the key part of the scene—such as the hunter's face or his bird—should be on an imaginary line a third of the distance from top or bottom of the frame and a third of the distance from either side of the scene in the viewfinder. This alignment will give the photo a professional touch (Chambers and Rue 1984).

Remember to shoot plenty of film. Professional photographers often shoot hundreds of frames of a single subject in different positions to assure they get the best possible photo. When shooting a single-lens reflex 35mm camera, bracket exposures to be sure of getting the proper exposure. (To bracket a photo, shoot it at its metered setting or f-stop, then shoot the same photo 1 and then 2 f-stops below and above the metered setting.) Re-peat this same procedure when using fill flash, to achieve a different effect. Pick the most pleasing result to make into enlarged prints or to submit for publication. Failing to photograph a beautiful setting with a properly handled trophy is missing a once-in-a-lifetime opportunity. So shoot plenty of film.

CONCLUSION

In 1991, there were about 4 million turkeys, 1 million more than existed 5 years earlier. This is a far cry from fewer than 20,000 at the turn of this century. The wild turkey resource we enjoy today didn't happen by accident. To bring the wild turkey back from the brink of extinction required several decades of wildlife management, trial and error, and hard work. By the end of this century, wildlife agencies in cooperation with the National Wild Turkey Federation propose to stock wild-trapped birds into 50 million acres of remaining wild turkey habitat.

But conservationists will need to overcome future obstacles in order to achieve this goal and the continued management of wild turkeys. There is a growing movement of antimanagement of natural resources that could appeal to many urban nonhunters. Also, suitable habitat will decrease because of land-use pressures from a burgeoning human population.

To continue the successful management of wild turkeys, we must become more involved in the legislative decisions that affect natural resources and their wise use. At the same time, we must educate the nonhunting public on the principles of conservation and modern wildlife management. Accomplishing these monumental tasks will require substantial effort and money.

Pittman-Robertson funds, funds from state and federal wildlife resource agencies, corporate donations, individual and NWTF chapter contributions, and dollars generated through the NWTF Wild Turkey Super Fund will float the program. For example, total net dollars generated through Wild Turkey Super Fund in the next decade for on-the-ground wild turkey projects will exceed $50 million.

Sportsmen (conservationists) have an obligation to discuss questions and challenge activities that threaten the wild turkey resource and the user. Developing a posture on these issues is sometimes difficult and occasionally lonesome. But the dividends start to come in on the late summer day when you glimpse an old hen with her brood chasing grasshoppers through the clover you planted on that old log landing. The satisfaction you derive in putting far more back into the resource than you've taken away is your reward. The person who has made the significant contribution to the wild turkey is you, the turkey hunter.

Chapter 24

THE FUTURE

James G. Dickson
Research Wildlife Biologist
USDA Forest Service, Southern Forest Experiment Station
Wildlife Habitat Laboratory, Nacogdoches, Texas

With the wild turkey, we've come a long way in a short time. In the 1940s, there were only tens of thousands of wild turkeys nationwide. Now we have some 4 million wild turkeys. They thrive in areas more northerly and westerly than their original distribution. There are wild turkey populations in every state but Alaska, and even on several other continents. A nucleus of hundreds of thousands of new, devoted wild turkey hunters

has developed. Restoration has been immensely successful. We trapped and transplanted *wild* turkeys, our eastern forests matured, and we protected turkey flocks while developing sport hunting.

What does the future hold, and where do we go from here? To protect the wild turkey resource that we consider precious, we cannot be complacent with past successes. We need to be active and productive to maintain what we've accomplished and to be more successful in protecting and managing habitat, building and managing wild turkey populations, and promoting sport hunting.

As the nation's population grows, there will be increasing demands on our land base to produce food and fiber for a burgeoning human population, to satisfy demands for other recreation, and to preserve forests without management alternatives. Wild turkeys, their habitat, and turkey enthusiasts must compete with human demands for a myriad of land uses that may or may not be compatible with wild turkey needs.

What does the future hold for this great game bird? *Photo by G. Griffen.*

Some potential habitat, such as this wheat monoculture, is unsuitable because of land-use patterns. *Photo by J. Dickson, U.S. Forest Service.*

Urban encroachment will eliminate some wild turkey habitat. *Photo by J. Langston, National Wild Turkey Federation.*

Protection will be a prime factor in flock success or failure. *Photo by H. Williamson, U.S. Forest Service.*

Changes in land use will occur on a broad scale, and generally they will be somewhat negative for wild turkeys.

In about the past 30 years, forest- and rangeland have declined by about 5 percent. In recent years, significant declines have occurred in areas of southern pines, bottomland hardwoods, and aspen-birch and elm-ash-cottonwood associations. Western conifer stands have decreased in age with cutting, but eastern hardwoods have matured. Nationwide, the area of forestland probably will continue to decline slightly through conversion to urban and crop uses (Flather and Hoekstra 1989). We will need to protect and manage suitable wild turkey habitat to ensure continued success.

RESEARCH NEEDS

To manage wild turkeys more effectively, we need solid, quantitative information from research in a variety of areas. Cause-and-effect relationships can be determined in laboratory research where conditions are controlled. But the inherent wildness of wild turkeys that intrigues us makes them difficult to study. In natural systems, not all of the many interacting variables can be identified, and certainly they are difficult to assess and measure.

Most previous wild turkey research has involved short terms, small samples, and often a case history approach. Solid, broad-scale, long-term studies with large samples are needed in order to correctly define long-term relationships. Also, we need to conduct studies in controlled situations where treatments can be applied and compared with controls. Studies are needed where all variables are identified and defined. And to facilitate comparison of results, we need to apply standard, easily duplicated research techniques across broad areas.

New technology has brought us a long way in understanding the wild turkey. Small and efficient transmitters, computers, multivariate statistics, and Geographic Information Systems (GIS) have helped us gather and analyze more information (Zeedyk and Dickson 1985). These and other technological developments should become even more useful in generating and analyzing information in the future to develop more effective management.

We still don't have broad-scale, consistent means for monitoring populations. This shortcoming limits our ability to set optimum harvest regulations. Generally, we do not have good data on effects of legal or illegal harvest on wild turkey populations. Overall, our questionnaires,

New technology will help analyze data and make management decisions easier. *Photo by W. Porter.*

Standardized research techniques would facilitate comparison of results. *Photo by U.S. Forest Service.*

surveys, and check stations inadequately assess harvest in specific or broad areas.

How can we maximize recreational opportunity? Several states have a substantial fall harvest. But at what level can we harvest turkeys in the fall and still provide quality hunting in the spring? We are just beginning to have enough data to manage populations.

We now understand basic elements of wild turkey biology, but we need more specific ecological information for effective management. More than half of wild turkey nests are unsuccessful in producing even a single poult. We do not think nesting sites are limiting, but can habitat be manipulated to ensure more successful nests?

We know predators take many turkeys (especially young poults and some nesting hens), but we don't know (1) the relationships of wild turkey densities to predator densities; (2) how predators find nests and turkeys; or (3) ultimately, what long-term effects predators have on wild turkey populations. Hens with young poults forage in dense herbaceous vegetation near tree cover. What are optimum conditions to ensure adequate poult nutrition and survival from predation?

Information is needed to define relationships of turkey populations with their environment. What are the roles of wild turkeys in forest systems, and what are their relationships with other organisms? Are there substantial competitors in the short or long term? During the period of low wild turkey populations in the early 1900s, remnant flocks generally were limited to inaccessible areas of mature hardwoods. Since then, we have determined that mature hardwoods are still important for quality habitat, but today's flocks are far more tolerant of other habitats

Predators kill turkeys, but we don't know what long-term influence predators have on wild turkey populations. *Photo by L. Rue III.*

We need sound data that relate food production, quality, and consumption with wild turkey physiology and productivity. *Photo by D. Baumann.*

than previously imagined. Human accessibility had a greater effect on those low populations than did big trees. Now we find turkeys in a variety of habitats previously regarded marginal. For example, wild turkeys are thriving in the agriculture-dominated landscape of northern Missouri and Iowa.

But what is minimal habitat? How much area in unsuitable-aged pine plantations can flocks tolerate, and how much area in mature stands is needed for turkeys in the South? What about road densities, logging, or grazing effects in the West? What forest management and silvicultural system—in which physiographic regions and in which forest types—favor the wild turkey over the long term? We have developed models to quantify habitat. When will we have sufficient, valid, quantitative data and models good enough to predict wild turkey populations from habitat measurements? The more verified, quantitative information we have, the better we can manage forest systems for wild turkeys—and for a variety of other wildlife.

We have identified wild turkey foods in different regions, at different life stages, and in different seasons, and we have some data on nutrition, survival, and productivity. But we need sound data that relates food pro-

duction, quality, and consumption to wild turkey physiology and productivity. Do we need to—and are we able to—manipulate habitat to compensate for temporary shortfalls in major foods such as oak mast? Can oak stands be managed to produce acorns more consistently? Could early acorn monitoring each season tell us when winter food plots will be needed?

Fruit of the flowering dogwood is a key fall food. Dogwood anthracnose is a fungus disease that is killing dogwoods in the Northeast. What effects will this or other diseases and insects have on future habitat suitability? In arid western range, habitat conditions are often extremely variable and productivity is sometimes very low. Can we promote nesting of juvenile Merriam's or Rio Grande hens in drought years by providing water or foods? Can supplemental foods maintain annual productivity in northerly range where snow covering of ground food seriously affects wild turkey physiological condition and winter survival? What about the disadvantages of supplemental foods? Is wildness sacrificed? Are barnyard birds what we really want? Are parasites and diseases transmitted at feeding sites where turkeys are concentrated?

Objective genetic information could be useful in refining restoration and management. We still rely on subspecies defined by taxonomic rules based on morphological data. Can we identify and measure wild turkey enzymes precisely enough to determine genetic relationships objectively? We suspect genetic pollution of wild populations from releases of pen-raised turkeys, but we have few data and an incomplete understanding of this phenomenon.

What role have diseases played in wild turkey populations? We know wild turkeys have been exposed to

Much about wild turkey social phenomena remains unexplained. *Photo by G. Wunz, Pennsylvania Game Commission.*

many pathogens and sometimes carry a host of different antibodies, but we don't know the short- and long-term relationships between wild turkey populations and diseases. We know some turkeys die from histomoniasis and avian pox, and we know *Mycoplasma* can be devastating in poultry houses, but we don't know how many turkeys in the wild die from diseases. Nor do we know what effects various diseases have on predation, productivity, or populations.

Our information on wild turkey behavior and social phenomena remains based mostly on old studies of other bird species and general turkey field observations. Every hunter knows what a beard is, but its function remains a mystery. How a gobbler drums is still debated and perhaps always will be. Is it always the dominant gobbler

There will also be protests against land management decisions. *Photo by R. Conner, U.S. Forest Service.*

that mates? Why do several gobblers display together, and why don't gobblers maintain discrete territories? Finding these and other answers surely would be intriguing.

MANAGEMENT

The wild turkey would benefit from more effective management programs. We live in a political world, and the wild turkey and turkey hunters need political support. But biological information should be the foundation on which wild turkey management is built.

We have restored the wild turkey to most of the suitable habitat in North America, and populations have thrived and expanded. Are these populations in the exponential growth phase of the sigmoid growth curve? Can we expect population declines that normally occur in new populations after the growth phase ends? Will environmental constraints such as diseases and predators, or productivity-depressing mechanisms in populations depress future turkey numbers? Will we have to maintain some level of restocking to maintain population viability?

What are the prospects for introducing wild turkeys into temperate zones worldwide? This has been tried, and future prospects look promising. Should this tactic be attempted everywhere feasible, or could wild turkeys become pests anywhere?

We need to be more effective in managing public and private land for the wild turkey. The wild turkey should be an integral part of land management planning and practices, not just a by-product.

THE HUMAN FACTOR

We are just beginning to understand and integrate the human factor into wild turkey management. Several recent studies have detailed the characteristics of turkey hunters (Healy and Healy 1990). We need to define the turkey enthusiast better, as well as his economic contributions.

The human population's distribution, relationships with the land, and attitudes are changing in America, and we will have to deal with these changes. Our population is becoming more urban, and antihunting sentiment is growing. Only about 10 percent of the U.S. populace hunts. Most older turkey hunters relate to rural America, but we are really an urban society. For example, Texas has a rural cowboy image, but in fact is demographically urban. Almost half of the state's 16 million residents live in 2 metropolitan areas, removed from turkey range. And this general pattern is widespread across the nation.

We will need to educate an increasingly urban population. *Photo by Ontario Ministry of Natural Resources.*

How important is it to have the opportunity to hear an old longbeard challenge the spring dawn? *Photo by M. Biggs.*

With the return of the wild turkey, we have a new generation of turkey hunters. But a growing human population increasingly will not understand natural resource management. *Photo by National Wild Turkey Federation.*

How successful we are in promoting the wild turkey and its recreational use will depend, to a great degree, on how well we deliver our messages and influence other people. For example, we will need to convince the nature enthusiast that turkey hunters have the wild turkey's best interest at heart. Our image will be important in generat-

ing support for our activities. We need to make every effort to develop and promote ethics and good sportsmanship in wild turkey hunting and to help hunters develop beyond the sack-'em-up mentality. Just getting a turkey is *not* what turkey hunting is about. A hunter doesn't have to shoot every turkey called up, and he or she can have a great year with little impact on the wild turkey resource. We will need to be eloquent spokesmen to explain how we can love turkeys, do anything for them, yet kill one; that the kill is part of the hunt, but we don't hunt just to kill.

The value we place on wild turkeys is beyond definition. How important is it to have the opportunity to challenge a longbeard every spring? How would you feel if you thought you would never hear a gobbler again? Is that important?

We need to educate our youth that not every species is endangered and that wildlife goals can be accomplished through management of land and species.

Many of the challenges to resource management come from a public largely ignorant of natural processes. We need cooperative, concerted efforts to educate the public about natural phenomena such as plant succession, population dynamics, and predator-prey relationships. We need to educate a new generation of young turkey enthusiasts into the thrill of calling a gobbler and an understanding and appreciation of things wild. And to be successful, we must compete with video games. Take a kid to the woods and call up a turkey. You'll enjoy it more than by yourself.

We need to make every effort to protect wild turkey flocks from the unscrupulous who would kill turkeys

Photo by J. Dickson.

Photo by G. Smith.

Call up a turkey for a kid. You'll sow seeds for the future.

Turkey hunting can be a dangerous sport. Camouflaged hunters must use extreme caution. *Photo by K. Kieser.*

illegally. The jerk who illegally kills a turkey taints us all. Turkeys can be vulnerable in some places and at some times. Studies in Florida, Missouri, and Virginia have substantiated significant illegal kills in wild turkey flocks. Education, peer pressure, and stiff penalties all can be effective.

Also, we need to enhance and direct education toward safety in turkey hunting. The turkey hunter is particularly vulnerable when dressed like a bush and sounding like a turkey. Today's shotgun loads are deadly on turkeys and people alike, if hunters are not careful! We need turkey hunters and license sales to support management programs, but we need to ensure that everyone is a safe hunter.

COOPERATION

To maximize our influence and to be effective in achieving our goals, we need to establish and maintain firm ties among conservation organizations. The wild turkey conservation organization—the National Wild Turkey Federation—can extend its influence by cooperating with other advocate groups, such as the Rocky Mountain Elk Foundation, that have similar goals. NWTF will have to work closely with land management organizations such as the U.S. Forest Service, with hunter advocates such as the National Shooting Sports Foundation, and with political advocates such as the Wildlife Management Institute to promote programs

Photo by H. Williamson, U.S. Forest Service.

Photo by D. Bounds, U.S. Forest Service.

Cooperation will be a key to providing for the future of the wild turkey and recreational use.

over a broad base. Making Tracks is a cooperative effort between the U.S. Forest Service and the National Wild Turkey Federation to benefit the wild turkey on public land. It is successful and should be continued and expanded.

May we be wise enough to leave something better than we found it, and to leave a legacy for our children. *Photo by P. Pelham.*

NWTF should develop rapport with conservation organizations that do not oppose hunting, such as the National Audubon Society. Without liaison and dialogue, some conservation organizations could migrate toward antihunting sentiment, a serious threat to the wild turkey and its recreational use.

But overall, I am optimistic about the future of the wild turkey. Restoration will continue in the remaining unstocked habitat. And in some areas where releases have failed, we will try again. Habitat will continue to dwindle, but improved management can be more effective in maintaining viable wild turkey populations. May we never lose the excitement and the thrill of hearing an old longbeard drum as he stalks the hen of his dreams. And may we be wise enough to leave something better than we found it. May we leave a legacy for our children.

Appendix A
Scientific Names of Plants Cited in Text

Acacia: *Acacia* spp.
Acacia, catclaw: *Acacia greggii*
Agarita: *Berberis trifoliolata*
Alder, red: *Alnus rubra*
Alfalfa: *Medicago sativa*
Anaqua: *Ehretia anacua*
Apple: *Malus pumila*
Arrowhead: *Sagittaria* sp.
Arrowroot: *Sagittaria lancifolia*
Ash: *Fraxinus* spp.
Ash, green: *Fraxinus caroliniana*
Ash, European: *Fraxinus excelsior*
Ash, white: *Fraxinus americana*
Aspen: *Populus tremuloides*
Aster, spiny: *Aster spinosus*
Bahia grass: *Paspalum notatum*
Bald cypress: *Taxodium distichum*
Barberry: *Berberis* spp.
Barberries: *Berberis thunbergii, Berberis vulgaris*
Barberry, Japanese: *Berberis thunbergii*
Barley, little: *Hordeum pusillum*
Barynard grass, common: *Echinochloa crusgalli*
Basswood: *Tilia americana*
Bay, loblolly: *Gordonia lasianthus*
Bear grass: *Nolina microcarpa*
Beauty berry, American: *Callicarpa americana*
Beauty bush, American: *Callicarpa americana*
Beech, American: *Fagus grandifolia*
Beech, red: *Fagus sylvatica*
Beggar-tick: *Bidens* spp.
Bent grass: *Agrostis* spp.
Bermuda grass, coastal: *Cynodon* sp.
Birch, sweet: *Betula lenta*
Birch, white: *Betula papyrifera*
Birch, yellow: *Betula alleghaniensis*
Blackberry: *Rubus* spp.
Blackbrush: *Acacia rigidula*
Blackfoot, plains: *Melampodium leucanthum*
Black gum: *Nyssa sylvatica*
Blackhaw, rusty: *Virburnum rufidulum*
Blackthorn: *Prunus spinosa*

Bladderpod: *Lesquerella* spp.
Blueberry: *Vaccinium* spp.
Bluebonnet: *Lupinus* spp.
Bluegrass: *Poa* spp.
Bluegrass, Kentucky: *Poa pratensis*
Bluestem: *Andropogon* spp.
Bluestem, big: *Andropogon gerardi*
Bluestem, Kleberg: *Dichanthium annulatum*
Bluestem, little: *Andropogon scoparius*
Bleustem, old world: *Bothriochloa* spp.
Bluestem, silver: *Bothriochloa saccharoides*
Bluewood: *Condalia obovata*
Box elder: *Acer negundo*
Bristle grass: *Setaria* spp.
Bristle grass, plains: *Setaria macrostachya*
Broom, Scotch: *Cytisus scoparius*
Broomweed: *Xanthocephalum* spp.
Buckeye: *Aesculus* spp.
Buckeye, Texas: *Aesculus glabra*
Buckthorns, European: *Rhamnus cathartica, Rhamnus frangula*
Buckwheat, wild: *Eriogonum* spp.
Buffalo berry: *Shepherdia argentea*
Buffalo gourd: *Cucurbita foetidissima*
Buffel grass: *Cenchrus ciliaris*
Bumelia: *Bumelia* spp.
Bundle flower, Illinois: *Desmanthus illinoensis*
Bundle flower, velvet: *Desmanthus velutinus*
Bushsunflower: *Simsia calva*
Carpet grass: *Axonopus affinis*
Ceanothus, buckbrush: *Ceanothus cuneatus*
Ceniza: *Leucophyllum frutescens*
Cherry: *Prunus* spp.
Cherry, black: *Prunus serotina*
Cherry, European: *Prunus avium*
Chestnut, American: *Castanea dentata*
Chinquapin: *Castanea pumila*
Chokecherry: *Prunus virginiana*
Chufa: *Cyperus esculentus*
Clover: *Trifolium* spp.
Clover, red: *Trifolium pratense*

Clover, tick: *Desmodium* spp.
Clover, white: *Trifolium repens*
Club moss: *Lycopodium* sp.
Condalia: *Condalia* spp.
Coreopsis: *Coreopsis* spp.
Corn: *Zea mays*
Corydalis, smallflower: *Corydalis micrantha*
Cotton: *Gossypium* spp.
Cottonwood: *Populus* spp.
Cottonwood, black: *Populus trichocarpa*
Cottonwood, eastern: *Populus deltoides*
Cottonwood, plains: *Populus sargentii*
Crab apple: *Malus* spp.
Crab apple, Asian: *Malus* sp.
Crabgrass: *Digitaria* spp.
Cranberry, highbush: *Viburnum opulus*
Creosote bush: *Larrea tridentata*
Croton: *Croton* spp.
Croton, one-seed: *Croton monanthogynus*
Croton, Texas: *Croton texensis*
Cucumber tree: *Magnolia acuminata*
Cup grass, Texas: *Eriochloa sericea*
Curly mesquite: *Hilaria belangeri*
Currant: *Ribes* sp.
Dandelion: *Taraxacum* sp.
Dewberry: *Rubus* sp.
Dewberry, southern: *Rubus trivialis*
Dichanthelium, Scribner's: *Dichanthelium oligosanthes*
Dock: *Rumex* sp.
Dogwood: *Cornus* spp.
Dogwood, European: *Cornus mas*
Dogwood, flowering: *Cornus florida*
Dogwood, red osier: *Cornus stolonifera*
Douglas fir: *Pseudotsuga menziesii*
Dozedaisy: *Aphanostephus* spp.
Dropseed: *Sporobolus* spp.
Dropseed, sand: *Sporobolus cryptandrus*
Dropseed, tall: *Sporobolus asper*
Duckweed: *Lemna* sp.
Elbowbush: *Forestiera pubescens*
Elderberry, European: *Sambucus racemosa*
Elm: *Ulmus* spp.
Elm, American: *Ulmus americana*
Elm, cedar: *Ulmus crassifolia*
Elm, winged: *Ulmus alata*
Engleman daisy: *Engelmannia pinnatifida*
Ephedra: *Ephedra* spp.
Euphorbia: *Euphorbia* spp.
Evening primrose: *Oenothera* spp.
False dandelion: *Pyrrhopappus* spp.
Fern, sensitive: *Onoclea sensibilis*
Fescue: *Festuca* sp.
Fescue, red: *Festuca rubra*
Fescue, tall: *Festuca arundinacea*

Filaree: *Erodium* spp.
Filaree, California: *Erodium cicutarium*
Fir, corkbark: *Abies lasiocarpa*
Fir, grand: *Abies grandis*
Fir, white: *Abies concolor*
Flatpea: *Lathyrus sylvestris*
Flat sedge: *Cyperus* spp.
Flax, stiffstem: *Linum rigidum*
Gaillardia, rose-ring: *Gaillardia pulchella*
Gallberry: *Ilex* sp.
Gallberry: *Ilex glabra*
Gaura: *Gaura* spp.
Goatweed: *Croton* sp.
Grama: *Bouteloua* spp.
Grama, black: *Bouteloua eriopoda*
Grama, blue: *Bouteloua gracilis*
Grama, side oats: *Bouteloua curtipendula*
Granjeno: *Celtis pallida*
Grape: *Vitis* spp.
Grape, canyon: *Vitis arizonica*
Grape, mustang: *Vitis mustangensis*
Greenbrier: *Smilax* spp.
Ground-cherry: *Physalis viscosa*
Groundsel: *Senecio* spp.
Guajillo: *Acacia berlandieri*
Hackberry: *Celtis* spp.
Hackberry, netleaf: *Celtis reticulata*
Hackberry, sugar: *Celtis laevigata*
Haws: *Crataegus* spp.
Hawthorn: *Crataegus* spp.
Hawthorn, Washington: *Crataegus phaenopyrum*
Hawthorns, European: *Crataegus monogyna, Crataegus oxycantha*
Hazelnut, beaked: *Corylus cornuta*
Heather: *Calluna vulgaris*
Hemlock: *Tsuga canadensis*
Hemlock, western: *Tsuga heterophylla*
Hemp: *Cannabis* spp.
Hercules'-club: *Zanthoxylum clava-herculis*
Hickory: *Carya* spp.
Hickory, pignut: *Carya glabra*
Holly: *Ilex* spp.
Holly, American: *Ilex opaca*
Holly, yaupon: *Ilex vomitoria*
Honeysuckle: *Lonicera* spp.
Hop hornbeam: *Ostrya virginiana*
Hornbeam, American: *Carpinus caroliniana*
Hornbeam, European: *Carpinus betulus*
Huckleberry: *Gaylussacia* spp.
Huckleberry: *Vaccinium* spp.
Huisache: *Acacia farnesiana*
Huisache: *Acacia tortuosa*
Indian grass, yellow: *Sorghastrum nutans*
Indigobush: *Amorpha fruticosa*

Ironwood: *Bumelia* sp.
Johnsongrass: *Sorghum halepense*
Juniper: *Juniperus* spp.
Juniper, alligator: *Juniperus deppeana*
Juniper, ashe: *Juniperus ashei*
Juniper, dwarf: *Juniperus communis*
Juniper, one-seed: *Juniperus monosperma*
Juniper, redberry: *Juniperus pinchoti*
Juniper, Rocky Mountain: *Juniperus scopulorum*
Juniper, Utah: *Juniperus osteosperma*
Kiawe (mesquite): *Prosopis chilensis*
Kikuyu grass: *Pennisetum clandestinum*
Kinnikinnick: *Arctostaphylos uva-ursi*
Klein grass: *Panicum coloratum*
Koa: *Acacia koa*
Lama: *Diosyras ferrea*
Lantana: *Lantana* spp.
Lantana: *Lantana camara*
Larch, European: *Larix decidua*
Leatherweed: *Jatropha dioica*
Lespedeza, Korean: *Lespedeza stipulacea*
Lotebush: *Condalia obtusifolia*
Love grass: *Eragrostis* spp.
Madrone: *Arbutus* sp.
Magnolia, cucumber tree: *Magnolia acuminata*
Magnolia, southern: *Magnolia grandiflora*
Magnolia, sweet bay: *Magnolia virginiana*
Maiden-cane: *Panicum hemitomon*
Mamani: *Sophora chrysophylla*
Manzanita: *Arctostaphylos pungens*
Maple: *Acer* spp.
Maple, big-leaf: *Acer macrophyllum*
Maple, European: *Acer pseudoplatanus*
Maple, red: *Acer rubrum*
Maple, striped: *Acer pensylvanicum*
Maple, sugar: *Acer saccharum*
Mercury, wild: *Argythamnia* spp.
Mesquite: *Prosopis* spp.
Mesquite, honey: *Prosopis glandulosa*
Milk pea: *Galactia* spp.
Milk pea, hoary: *Galactia canescens*
Milk vetch: *Astragalus* spp.
Moss: *Lycopodium* spp.
Mountain ash, American: *Sorbus americana*
Mountain ash, European: *Sorbus aucuparia*
Mountain laurel: *Kalmia latifolia*
Mountain mahogany: *Cercocarpus montanus*
Muhly: *Muhlenbergia* spp.
Muhly, bull: *Muhlenbergia emersleyi*
Muhly, bush: *Muhlenbergia porteri*
Mulberry: *Morus rubra*
Mulberry, red: *Morus rubra*
Naio: *Myoporum sandwichense*
Nightshade: *Solanum* spp.

Nightshade, silverleaf: *Solanum elaeagnifolium*
Noseburn: *Tragia* sp.
Noseburn, catnip: *Tragia nepetaefolia*
Nut-rushes: *Scleria* spp.
Oak: *Quercus* spp.
Oak, Arizona white: *Quercus arizoniea*
Oak, black: *Quercus velutina*
Oak, blackjack: *Quercus marilandica*
Oak, bluejack: *Quercus incana*
Oak, bur: *Quercus macrocarpa*
Oak, Chapman: *Quercus chapmanii*
Oak, chestnut: *Quercus prinus*
Oak, Emory: *Quercus emoryi*
Oaks, European: *Quercus robur, Quercus petraea*
Oak, Gambel: *Quercus gambelii*
Oak, garry: *Quercus garryana*
Oak, gray: *Quercus grisea*
Oak, laurel: *Quercus laurifolia*
Oak, live: *Quercus virginiana*
Oak, myrtle: *Quercus myrtifolia*
Oak, northern red: *Quercus rubra*
Oak, Oregon white: *Quercus garryana*
Oak, overcup: *Quercus lyrata*
Oak, post: *Quercus stellata*
Oak, runner: *Quercus pumila*
Oak, sand live: *Quercus virginiana* var. *geminata*
Oak, sand shinnery: *Quercus havardii*
Oak, scarlet: *Quercus coccinea*
Oak, scrub: *Quercus ilicifolia*
Oak, shin: *Quercus pungens* var. *vaseyana*
Oak, silverleaf: *Quercus hypoleucoides*
Oak, southern red: *Quercus falcata*
Oak, swamp chestnut: *Quercus michauxii*
Oak, Texas: *Quercus shumardii* var. *texana*
Oak, Toumey: *Quercus toumeyi*
Oak, turkey: *Quercus laevis*
Oak, water: *Quercus nigra*
Oak, wavyleaf: *Quercus undulata*
Oak, white: *Quercus alba*
Oats, wild: *Avena barbata, Avena fatua*
Oats, wild: *Avena* spp.
Ohia: *Metrosideras collina*
Olive, autumn: *Elaeagnus umbellata*
Olive, Russian: *Elaeagnus angustifolia*
Onion: *Allium* sp.
Onion, wild: *Allium* spp.
Orchard grass: *Dactylis glomerata*
Oregon grape: *Berberis repens*
Oregon grape, tall: *Berberis aquifolium*
Paintbrush, Texas: *Castilleja indivisa*
Palafoxia: *Palafoxia* spp.
Palm, cabbage: *Sabal palmetto*
Palmetto, saw: *Serenoa repens*
Pampas grass: *Cortaderia selloana*

Panic grass: *Panicum* spp.
Parthenium, ragweed: *Parthenium hysterophorus*
Paspalum: *Paspalum* spp.
Paspalum, thin: *Paspalum setaceum*
Pawpaw: *Asimina* sp.
Pecan: *Carya illinoensis*
Pecan, bitter: *Carya aquatica*
Pellitory, Pennsylvania: *Parietaria pennsylvanica*
Pennywort: *Hydrocotyle* spp.
Pepperweed: *Lepidium* spp.
Persimmon: *Diospyros* spp.
Persimmon, Texas: *Diospyros texana*
Pickerelweed: *Pontederia cordata*
Pigeonberry: *Rivina humilis*
Pine: *Pinus* spp.
Pine, Apache: *Pinus engelmannii*
Pine, Chihuahua: *Pinus leiophylla*
Pine, Colorado piñon: *Pinus edulis*
Pine, digger: *Pinus sabiniana*
Pine, limber: *Pinus flexilis*
Pine, loblolly: *Pinus taeda*
Pine, lodgepole: *Pinus contorta*
Pine, longleaf: *Pinus palustris*
Pine, Mexican piñon: *Pinus cembroides*
Pine, piñon: *Pinus edulis*
Pine, pond: *Pinus serotina*
Pine, ponderosa: *Pinus ponderosa*
Pine, Scotch: *Pinus sylvestris*
Pine, shortleaf: *Pinus echinata*
Pine, silverleaf piñon: *Pinus monophylla*
Pine, slash: *Pinus elliottii*
Pine, white: *Pinus strobus*
Piñon, Mexican: *Pinus cembroides*
Piñon, border: *Pinus discolor*
Plantago: *Plantago* spp.
Plum, hog: *Prunus rivularis*
Plum, wild: *Prunus* spp.
Plum, wild: *Prunus americana*
Poison ivy: *Toxicodendron radicans*
Polecatbush: *Rhus* sp.
Polytaenia: *Polytaenia* spp.
Pondweed: *Potamogeton* sp.
Prickly ash, lime: *Zanthoxylum fagara*
Prickly pear cactus: *Opuntia* spp.
Pumpkin: *Cucurbita* spp.
Ragweed, western: *Ambrosia psilostachya*
Raspberry: *Rubus* spp.
Redbay: *Persea borbonia*
Redbud: *Cercis canadensis*
Red cedar, eastern: *Juniperus virginiana*
Red cedar, western (arborvitae): *Thuja plicata*
Redwood, coastal: *Sequoia sempervirens*
Rescue grass: *Bromus* spp.
Rescue grass: *Bromus unioloides*

Rhododendron: *Rhododendron* spp.
Rice grass, piñon: *Piptochaetium fimbriatum*
Rose: *Rosa* spp.
Rose, dog: *Rosa canina*
Rose, multiflora: *Rosa multiflora*
Rye, Canada wild: *Elymus canadensis*
Ryegrass: *Lolium multiflorum*
Sagebrush, sand: *Artemesia filifolia*
Salal: *Gaultheria shallon*
Salt cedar: *Tamarix gallica*
Sandbur: *Cenchrus* spp.
Saw grass: *Cladium jamaicensis*
Sedge: *Carex* spp.
Senna, two-leaved: *Cassia roemeriana*
Serviceberry: *Amelanchier* spp.
Serviceberry, Saskatoon: *Amelanchier alnifolia*
Sida: *Sida* spp.
Signal grass: *Brachiaria* spp.
Silverberry: *Elaeagnus commutata*
Skunkbush: *Rhus aromatica*
Smut grass: *Sporobolus indicus*
Snowberry: *Symphoricarpos albus*
Snowberry: *Symphoricarpos occidentalis*
Soapberry, western: *Sapindus drummondii*
Sorghum: *Sorghum* spp.
Sorghum almum: *Sorghum almum*
Sorrel, wood: *Oxalis* sp.
Sorrel, yellow wood: *Oxalis stricta*
Sourwood: *Oxydendrum arboreum*
Spicebush: *Lindera benzoin*
Spring beauty: *Claytonia* sp.
Spruce, blue: *Picea pungens*
Spruce, Englemann: *Picea engelmannii*
Spruce, Norway: *Picea abies*
Spruce, white: *Picea glauca*
Squirreltail grass: *Hordeum jubatum*
Staggerbush: *Lyonia lucida*
Staggerbush, rusty: *Lyonia ferruginea*
Star grass: *Hypoxis* spp.
Star grass: *Hypoxis leptocarpa*
Starwort, water: *Callitriche* sp.
Sumac: *Rhus* spp.
Sumac, littleleaf: *Rhus microphylla*
Sumac, skunkbush: *Rhus aromatica*
Sunflower: *Helianthus* spp.
Sunflower, common: *Helianthus annuus*
Sunflower, Maximilian: *Helianthus maximilianii*
Sweet gum: *Liquidambar styraciflua*
Sycamore: *Platanus occidentalis*
Sycamore, American: *Platanus occidentalis*
Sycamore, Arizona: *Platanus wrightii*
Tansy mustard, pinnate: *Descurainia pinnata*
Tarbush: *Flourensia cernua*
Tesajillo: *Opuntia leptocaulis*

Texas grass: *Vaseyochloa multinervosa*
Three-awn: *Aristida* spp.
Tobacco, wild: *Nicotiana repanda*
Tobosa grass: *Hilaria mutica*
Toothwort: *Dentaria* sp.
Trefoil, bird's-foot: *Lotus corniculatus*
Tridens: *Tridens* sp.
Tridens, white: *Tridens albescens*
Trumpet vine: *Campsis radicans*
Tupelo, water: *Nyssa aquatica*
Uniola, longleaf: *Chasmanthium sessiliflorum*
Verbena: *Verbena* spp.
Vervain, slender: *Verbena halei*
Vetch: *Vicia* spp.
Viburnum: *Viburnum* spp.
Viburnum, mapleleaf: *Viburnum acerifolium*
Violet, dogtooth: *Erythronium* sp.
Virginia creeper: *Parthenocissus quinquefolia*
Virgin's bower, Texas: *Clematis drummondii*
Wafer ash: *Ptelea trifoliata*
Walnut: *Juglans* spp.
Walnut, black: *Juglans nigra*

Walnut, Texas black: *Juglans microcarpa*
Watercress: *Nasturtium* sp.
Waterwort: *Elatine* sp.
Wax myrtle: *Myrica cerifera*
Wax myrtle, southern: *Myrica cerifera*
Wheat: *Triticum aestivum*
Whitebrush: *Aloysia lycioides*
Wiliwili: *Erythrina sandwichensis*
Willow: *Salix* spp.
Willow, black: *Salix nigra*
Windmill grass: *Chloris* spp.
Windmill grass, hooded: *Chloris cucullata*
Winter grass, Texas: *Stipa leucotricha*
Wire grass: *Aristida stricta*
Witch hazel: *Hamamelis virginiana*
Yaupon: *Ilex vomitoria*
Yellow poplar: *Liriodendron tulipifera*
Yucca: *Yucca* spp.
Yucca, narrow-leaved: *Yucca angustifolia*
Yucca, Schott: *Yucca schottii*
Zexmenia: *Zexmenia* spp.

Appendix B
Scientific Names of Animals Cited in Text

Antelope, pronghorn: *Antilocapra americana*
Armadillo: *Dasypus novemcinctus*
Anole, green: *Anolis carolinensis*
Badger: *Taxidea taxus*
Bat, Hawaiian: *Lasiurus cinereus semotus*
Bear, black: *Ursus americanus*
Bear, grizzly: *Ursus arctos*
Bison: *Bison bison*
Blackbird, red-winged: *Agelaius phoeniceus*
Bobcat: *Felis rufus*
Capercaillie: *Tetrao urogallus*
Cat, domestic: *Felis domesticus*
Chaffinch: *Fringilla coelebs*
Coachwhip, eastern: *Masticophis flagellum flagellum*
Cock, domestic: *Gallus* spp.
Cougar (mountain lion): *Felis concolor*
Coyote: *Canis latrans*
Crow, common: *Corvus brachyrhynchos*
Deer: *Odocoileus* spp.
Deer, mule: *Odocoileus hemionus*
Deer, white-tailed: *Odocoileus virginianus*
Dog, domestic: *Canis familiaris*
Dove, mourning: *Zenaida macroura*
Eagle, golden: *Aquila chrysaetos*
Eagle, imperial: *Aquila heliaca*
Elk: *Cervus elaphus*
Fisher: *Martes pennanti*
Fowl, jungle: *Gallus gallus*
Fox, gray: *Urocyon cinereoargenteus*
Fox, red: *Vulpes vulpes*
Goose, Canada: *Branta canadensis*
Goshawk: *Accipiter gentilis*
Groundhog: *Marmota monax*
Grouse, red: *Lagopus lagopus scoticus*
Grouse, ruffed: *Bonasa umbellus*
Guineafowl: *Numida meleagris*
Hare, snowshoe: *Lepus americanus*
Hawk, broad-winged: *Buteo platypterus*
Hawk, Hawaiian: *Buteo solitarius*
Hawk, red-shouldered: *Buteo lineatus*

Hawk, red-tailed: *Buteo jamaicensis*
Hog, feral: *Sus scrofa*
Horse, wild: *Equus caballus*
Jackrabbit, black-tailed: *Lepus californicus*
Junco, dark-eyed: *Junco hymemalis*
Lynx: *Felis lynx*
Magpie: *Pica* spp.
Mongoose: *Herpestris auropuntatus*
Opossum: *Didelphis virginiana*
Owl, barred: *Strix varia*
Owl, great horned: *Bubo virginianus*
Owl, Hawaiian: *Asio flammeus sandwichensis*
Owl, screech: *Otus asio*
Owl, short-eared: *Asio flammeus*
Peafowl: *Pavo cristatus*
Pheasant, ring-necked: *Phasianus colchicus*
Pig, domestic: *Sus scrofa*
Pigeon, band-tailed: *Columba fasciata*
Pigeon, domestic: *Columba livia*
Prairie chicken, lesser: *Tympanuchus pallidicintus*
Pronghorn: *Antilocapra americana*
Ptarmigan, willow: *Lagopus lagopus*
Quail, northern bobwhite: *Colinus virginianus*
Quail, coturnix: *Coturnix coturnix*
Quail, Gambel's: *Callipepla gambelii*
Rabbit, cottontail: *Sylvilagus floridanus*
Rabbit, swamp: *Sylvilagus aquaticus*
Raccoon: *Procyon lotor*
Rat, Polynesian: *Ratus exulans hawaiiensis*
Raven, common: *Corvus corax*
Ringtail: *Bassariscus astutus*
Robin, European: *Erithacus rubecula*
Seal, Hawaiian: *Monachus schavinslandi*
Skunk, hognose: *Conepatus mesoleucus*
Skunk, spotted: *Spilogale putorius*
Skunk, striped: *Mephitis mephitis*
Snail: *Carinifex* sp.
Snail: *Physa* sp.
Snake, gray rat: *Elaphe obsoleta spiloides*
Snake, king: *Lampropeltis* spp.

Snake, pine: *Pituophis melanoleucus*
Squirrel, fox: *Sciurus niger*
Squirrel, gray: *Sciurus carolinensis*
Squirrel, rock: *Spermophilus variegatus*
Turkey, eastern: *Meleagris gallopavo silvestris*
Turkey, Florida: *Meleagris gallopavo osceola*
Turkey, Gould's: *Meleagris gallopavo mexicana*
Turkey, Merriam's: *Meleagris gallopavo merriami*

Turkey, Mexican/domestic: *Meleagris gallopavo gallopavo*
Turkey, ocellated: *Meleagris ocellata*
Turkey, Rio Grande: *Meleagris gallopavo intermedia*
Turkey, wild: *Meleagris gallopavo*
Woodpecker, red-cockaded: *Picoides borealis*
Wolf, gray: *Canis lupus*
Wolf, red: *Canis rufus*

References Cited

Adair, J. 1775. The history of the American Indians. London: E. and C. Dilly. 464 pp.

Adrian, W.J. 1984. Investigation of disease as a limiting factor in wild turkey populations. Ph.D. Thesis. Colorado State University, Fort Collins. 63 pp.

Akey, B.L. 1981. Mortality in Florida wild turkey poults *(Meleagris gallopavo osceola)*. M.S. Thesis. University of Florida, Gainesville. 78 pp.

Akey, B.L., J.K. Nayar, and D.J. Forrester. 1981. Avian pox in Florida wild turkeys: *Culex nigripalpus* and *Wyeomyia vanduzeei* as experimental vectors. J. Wildl. Dis. 17(4):597–599.

Alberti, D.E. 1922. Das Trutwild (The wild turkey). Pages 587–596 *in* Die Hohe Jagd. Fifth ed. Berlin: Paul Parey-Verlag. 750 pp.

Aldrich, J.W. 1967a. Historical background. Pages 3–16 *in* O.H. Hewitt, ed., The wild turkey and its management. Washington, DC: The Wildlife Society. 589 pp.

———. 1967b. Taxonomy, distribution and present status. Pages 17–44 *in* O.H. Hewitt, ed., The wild turkey and its management. Washington, DC: The Wildlife Society. 589 pp.

Aldrich, J.W., and A.J. Duvall. 1955. Distribution of American gallinaceous game birds. U.S. Dept. Interior, Fish and Wildl. Serv. Circ. 34. 30 pp.

Alexander, M.L. 1921. Wild life resources of Louisiana, their nature, value, and protection. New Orleans: Louisiana Wild Life and Fisheries Commission. Bull. No. 10. 164 pp.

Aliev, F.F., and A.I. Khanmamedov. 1966. Results and prospects of the acclimatization of birds in Transcaucasia. Pages 33–34 *in* A.I. Yanushevich, ed., Proc. conf. on acclimatization of animals in the USSR, Frunze, 1963. Jersualem: Israel Program for Scientific Translations. 250 pp.

Alison, R.M. 1976. The history of the wild turkey in Ontario. The Can. Field Nat. 90(4):481–485.

Allendorf, F.W., and R.F. Leary. 1986. Heterozygosity and fitness in natural populations of animals. Pages 57–76 *in* M.E. Soulé, ed., Conservation biology: the science of scarcity and diversity. Sunderland, MA: Sinauer Associates Inc. 584 pp.

Altman, P.L., and D.S. Dittmer. 1962. Growth including reproduction and morphological development. Washington, DC: Federation of American Societies for Experimental Biology. 608 pp.

Alverson, D.R., and R. Noblet. 1977. Spring relapse of *Leucocytozoon smithi* (Sporozoa: Leucocytozoidae) in turkeys. J. Med. Entomol. 14(1):132–133.

American Ornithologists' Union. 1983. Check-list of North American birds, 6th edition. American Ornithologists' Union. Lawrence, KS: Allen Press Inc. 877 pp.

American Poultry Association. 1985. The American standard of perfection. Troy, NY: American Poultry Association Inc. 336 pp.

Amrine, J.W., and D.F. Hindal. 1988. Rose rosette: a fatal disease of multiflora rose. West Virginia University Agric. and For. Exp. Sta. Circ. 147. 4 pp.

Amundson, T.E. 1985. Health management in wild turkey restoration programs. Proc. National Wild Turkey Symp. 5:285–294.

Anderson, D.R., and K.P. Burnham. 1976. Population ecology of the mallard: VI. The effect of exploitation on survival. U.S. Dept. Interior, Fish and Wildl. Serv. Resour. Publ. 128. 66 pp.

Anderson, D.R., and K.P. Burnham. 1981. Bobwhite population responses to exploitation: two problems. J. Wildl. Manage. 45(4):1052–1054.

Anderson, D.R., K.P. Burnham, and G.C. White. 1985. Problems in estimating age-specific survival rates from recovery data of birds ringed as young. J. Animal Ecol. 54(1):89–98.

Anderson, D.R., A.P. Wywialowski, and K.P. Burnham. 1981. Tests of the assumptions underlying life table methods for estimating parameters from cohort data. Ecology 62(4):1121–1124.

Anderson, R.J., and D.E. Samuel. 1980. Evaluation of reclaimed surface mines as wild turkey brood range. Proc. National Wild Turkey Symp. 4:186–202.

Anonymous. 1929. Review of Texas wildlife and conservation. Austin: Texas Game, Fish and Oyster Commission. 129 pp.

Anonymous. 1968. The history of Manitoba's wild gobblers unlimited. Wild Turkey Newsletter. 6 pp.

Anonymous. 1975. Plan for managing the National Forests in Missouri: Mark Twain and Clark. USDA Forest Service, Eastern Region. 117 pp.

Anonymous. 1980. Hunting wild turkeys in California. Sacramento: California Dept. Fish and Game Pamphlet. 4 pp.

Anonymous. 1981. Soil and water conservation: the Texas approach: a long range plan. Temple: Texas State Soil and Water Conserv. Board. 288 pp.

Anonymous. 1983. Water for Texas—planning for the future. Austin: Texas Dept. Water Resources. 2 Vol. Draft.

Anonymous. 1986. Beech scale nectria. Pennsylvania Bureau of Forestry Pathology Leaflet 14. 3 pp.

Anonymous. 1988. Texas almanac and state industrial guide. Dallas, TX: The Dallas Morning News. 640 pp.

Ashcraft, D.W. 1930. The correlative activities of the alimentary canal of the fowl. Am. J. Physiol. 93(1):105–110.

Atkinson, C.T. 1988. Epizootiology of *Haemoproteus meleagridis* (Protozoa: Haemosporina) in Florida: potential vectors and prevalence in naturally infected *Culicoides* (Diptera: Ceratopogonidae). J. Med. Entomol. 25(1):39–44.

Atkinson, C.T., and D.J. Forrester. 1987. Myopathy associated with megaloschizonts of *Haemoproteus meleagridis* in a wild turkey from Florida. J. Wildl. Dis. 23(3):495–498.

Atkinson, C.T., D.J. Forrester, and E.C. Greiner. 1988a. Pathogenicity of *Haemoproteus meleagridis* (Haemosporina: Haemoproteidae) in experimentally infected domestic turkeys. J. Parasitol. 74(2):228–239.

Atkinson, C.T., D.J. Forrester, and E.C. Greiner. 1988b. Epizootiology of *Haemoproteus meleagridis* (Protozoa: Haemosporina) in Florida: seasonal transmission and vector abundance. J. Med. Entomol. 25(1):45–51.

Atkinson, C.T., E.C. Greiner, and D.J. Forrester. 1983. Experimental vectors of *Haemoproteus meleagridis* Levine from wild turkeys in Florida. J. Wildl. Dis. 19(4):366–368.

Atkinson, C.T., E.C. Greiner, and D.J. Forrester. 1986. Pre-erythrocytic development and associated host responses to *Haemoproteus meleagridis* (Haemosporina: Haemoproteidae) in experimentally infected domestic turkeys. J. Protozool. 33(3):375–381.

Audubon, J.J. 1840–1844. The birds of America. Dover edition, 1967.

423

Vol. 5. New York: Dover Publications, Inc. 346 pp.

Austin, D.E., and L.W. DeGraff. 1975. Winter survival of wild turkeys in the southern Adirondacks. Proc. National Wild Turkey Symp. 3:55–60.

Backs, S.E., R.P. Bouta, and R.M. Platte. 1985. Use of landowner and resident observations to evaluate wild turkey releases. Proc. National Wild Turkey Symp. 5:259–268.

Backs, S.E., and C.H. Eisfelder. 1990. Criteria and guidelines for wild turkey release priorities in Indiana. Proc. National Wild Turkey Symp. 6:134–143.

Bailey, F.M. 1928. Birds of New Mexico. Sante Fe: New Mexico Dept. Game and Fish. 233 pp.

Bailey, J.A. 1984. Principles of wildlife management. New York: John Wiley and Sons. 373 pp.

Bailey, R.W. 1955. Two records of turkey brood survival after death of the hen. J. Wildl. Manage. 19(3):408–409.

———. 1956. Sex determination of adult wild turkeys by means of dropping configuration. J. Wildl. Manage. 20(2):220.

———. 1959. Preliminary report on wild turkey banding studies as applicable to management in West Virginia. Proc. National Wild Turkey Symp. 1:146–158.

———. 1964. Wild turkey: population trends, productivity and harvest. Ann. P-R Proj. Rep. Charleston: West Virginia Conservation Commission. 14 pp. mimeo.

———. 1967. Behavior. Pages 93–111 in O.H. Hewitt, ed., The wild turkey and its management. Washington, DC: The Wildlife Society. 589 pp.

———. 1973. Restoring wild-trapped turkeys to nonprimary range in West Virginia. Pages 181–185 in G.C. Sanderson and H.C. Shultz, eds., Wild turkey management: current problems and programs. Columbia: The Missouri Chapter of the Wildlife Society and University of Missouri Press. 355 pp.

———. 1980. The wild turkey status and outlook in 1980. Proc. National Wild Turkey Symp. 4:1–8.

———. 1983. 50 years of turkey hunting. Delmont, PA: Penn's Wood Products Inc. 132 pp.

Bailey, R.W., J.R. Davis, J.E. Frampton, J.V. Gwynn, and J. Shugars. 1981. Habitat requirements of the wild turkey in the Southeast Piedmont. Pages 14–23 in P.T. Bromley and R.L. Carlton, eds., Proc. symposium: Habitat requirements and habitat management for the wild turkey in the southeast. Elliston: Virginia Wild Turkey Foundation. 180 pp.

Bailey, R.W., and D.J. Putnam. 1979. The 1979 turkey restoration survey. Turkey Call 6(3):28–30.

Bailey, R.W., and K.T. Rinell. 1965. Wild turkey population trends, productivity and harvest. Charleston: West Virginia Conservation Commission. Fed. Aid Wildl. Restor. Proj. W-39-R-7. 15 pp. mimeo.

Bailey, R.W., and K.T. Rinell. 1967a. Events in the turkey year. Pages 73–91 in O.H. Hewitt, ed., The wild turkey and its management. Washington, DC: The Wildlife Society. 589 pp.

Bailey, R.W., and K.T. Rinell. 1967b. Management of the eastern turkey in the northern hardwoods. Pages 261–302 in O.H. Hewitt, ed., The wild turkey and its management. Washington, DC: The Wildlife Society. 589 pp.

Bailey, R.W., and K.T. Rinell. 1968. History and management of the wild turkey in West Virginia. Charleston: West Virginia Dept. Natural Resour. Div. Game and Fish. Bull. 6. 59 pp.

Bailey, R.W., H.G. Uhlig, and G. Breiding. 1951. Wild turkey management in West Virginia. Charleston: Conservation Commission of West Virginia. Bull. No. 2. 49 pp.

Bailey, W., D. Dennett, Jr., H. Gore, J. Pack, R. Simpson, and G. Wright. 1980. Basic considerations and general recommendations for trapping the wild turkey. Proc. National Wild Turkey Symp. 4:10–23.

Baker, B.W. 1978. Ecological factors affecting wild turkey nest predation on south Texas rangelands. Proc. Ann. Conf. Southeast.

Assoc. Fish and Wildl. Agencies 32:126–136.

———. 1979. Habitat use, productivity and nest predation of Rio Grande turkeys. Ph.D. Thesis. Texas A&M University, College Station. 46 pp.

Baker, B.W., S.L. Beasom, and N.J. Silvy. 1980. Turkey productivity and habitat use on south Texas rangelands. Proc. National Wild Turkey Symp. 4:145–158.

Baker, B.W., and M.F. Passmore. 1979. Limiting factors of Rio Grande turkeys in south Texas: a review. Welder Wildl. Found. Symp. 1:215–222.

Baker, D.L. 1988. Responses of bobwhites, eastern meadowlarks, mourning doves, and their habitat to two intensities of continuous grazing. M.S. Thesis. Texas A&I University, Kingsville. 47 pp.

Baldwin, W.P. 1947. Trapping wild turkeys in South Carolina. J. Wildl. Manage. 11(1):24–36.

Balser, D.S., H.H. Dill, and H.K. Nelson. 1968. Effect of predator reduction on waterfowl nesting success. J. Wildl. Manage. 32(4):669–682.

Barber, H.L. 1984. Eastern mixed forest. Pages 345–354 in L.K. Halls, ed., White-tailed deer: ecology and management. Harrisburg, PA: Stackpole Books. 870 pp.

Bareiss, L.J., P. Schulz, and F.S. Guthery. 1986. Effects of short-duration and continuous grazing on bobwhite and wild turkey nesting. J. Range Manage. 39(3):259–260.

Barkalow, F.S., Jr. 1942. Inventory of wildlife resources. Pages 59–60 in Annual report of 1939–40. Montgomery: Alabama Dept. Conservation. 92 pp.

Barrett, M.W. 1981. Environmental characteristics and functional significance of pronghorn fawn bedding sites in Alberta. J. Wildl. Manage. 45(1):120–131.

Barrowclough, G.F. 1980. Genetic and phenotypic differentiation in a wood warbler (genus Dendroica) hybrid zone. Auk 97(4):655–668.

Bartholomew, G.A., and R.E. MacMillen. 1961. Water economy of the California quail and its use of sea water. Auk 78(4):505–514.

Bartlett, J.R. 1854. Personal narrative of explorations and incidents in Texas, New Mexico, California, Sonora, and Chihuahua. Vol. II. Chicago: Rio Grande Press Inc. 624 pp.

Bartush, W.S., M.S. Sasser, and D.L. Francis. 1985. A standardized turkey brood survey method for northwest Florida. Proc. National Wild Turkey Symp. 5:173–181.

Barwick, L.H., D.H. Austin, and L.E. Williams, Jr. 1970. Roosting of young turkey broods during summer in Florida. Proc. Ann. Conf. Southeast. Assoc. Game and Fish Comm. 24:231–243.

Barwick, L.H., W.M. Hetrick, and L.E. Williams, Jr. 1973. Foods of young Florida wild turkeys. Proc. Ann. Conf. Southeast. Assoc. Game and Fish Comm. 27:92–102.

Barwick, L.H., and D.W. Speake. 1973. Seasonal movements and activities of wild turkey gobblers in Alabama. Pages 125–133 in G.C. Sanderson and H.C. Schultz, eds., Wild turkey management: current problems and programs. Columbia: The Missouri Chapter of The Wildlife Society and University of Missouri Press. 355 pp.

Baskett, T.S., D.A. Darrow, D.L. Hallett, M.J. Armbruster, J.A. Ellis, B.F. Sparrowe, and P.A. Korte. 1980. A handbook for terrestrial habitat evaluation in central Missouri. U.S. Dept. Interior, Fish and Wildl. Serv. Resour. Publ. 133. 155 pp.

Basore, N.S., L.B. Best, and J.B. Wooley, Jr. 1986. Bird nesting in Iowa no-tillage and tilled cropland. J. Wildl. Manage. 50(1):19–28.

Bassett, D., M. Larson, and W. Moir. 1987. Forest and woodland habitat types (plant associations) of Arizona south of the Mogollon Rim and southwestern New Mexico. Second ed. Albuquerque, NM: USDA Forest Service, Southwestern Region.

Baumann, D.P., Jr., L.D. Vangilder, C.I. Taylor, R. Engel-Wilson, R.O. Kimmel, and G.A. Wunz. 1991. Expenditures for wild turkey hunting. Proc. National Wild Turkey Symp. 6:157–166.

Bayer, M., and W.F. Porter. 1988. Evaluation of a guild approach to habitat assessment for forest-dwelling birds. Environ. Manage. 12(6):797–801.

Beasom, S.L. 1970. Turkey productivity in two vegetative communities in south Texas. J. Wildl. Manage. 34(1):166–175.

———. 1973. Ecological factors affecting wild turkey reproductive success in south Texas. Ph.D. Thesis. Texas A&M University, College Station. 215 pp.

———. 1974a. Intensive short-term predator removal as a game management tool. Trans. N. Am. Wildl. and Nat. Resour. Conf. 39:230–240.

———. 1974b. Relationships between predator removal and white-tailed deer net productivity. J. Wildl. Manage. 38(4):854–859.

Beasom, S.L., and O.H. Pattee. 1978. Utilization of snails by Rio Grande turkey hens. J. Wildl. Manage. 42(4):916–919.

Beasom, S.L., and O.H. Pattee. 1980. The effect of selected climatic variables on wild turkey productivity. Proc. National Wild Turkey Symp. 4:127–135.

Beasom, S.L., and C.J. Scifres. 1977. Population reactions of selected game species to aerial herbicide applications in south Texas. J. Range Manage. 30(2):138–142.

Beattie, J., and D.H. Shrimpton. 1958. Surgical and chemical techniques for in vivo studies of the metabolism of the intestinal microflora of domestic fowls. Quart. J. Exp. Physiol. 43(4):399–407.

Beck, D.E. 1977. Twelve-year acorn yield in southern Appalachian oaks. USDA Forest Service Res. Note SE-244. 8 pp.

———. 1986. Thinning Appalachian pole and small sawtimber stands. Pages 85–98 in H.C. Smith and M.C. Eye, eds., Proc.: Guidelines for managing immature Appalachian hardwood stands. Morgantown: West Virginia University Books. 283 pp.

Beck, D.E., and R.F. Harlow. 1981. Understory forage production following thinning in southern Appalachian cove hardwoods. Proc. Ann. Conf. Southeast. Assoc. Fish and Wildl. Agencies 35:185–196.

Beck, J.R., and D.O. Beck. 1955. A method for nutritional evaluation of wildlife foods. J. Wildl. Manage. 19(2):198–205.

Behrendt, R. 1978. Truthuhner eroberten den Shutterwald (Wild turkeys conquered the Schutter Forest). Munchen: Der Deutsche Jager. BLV Publ. Soc. 38–43 pp.

Bell, D.J., W.M. McIndoe, and D. Gross. 1959. Tissue components of the domestic fowl. 3. The non-protein nitrogen of plasma and erythrocytes. Biochem. J. 71(2):355–364.

Bell, D.J., and P.D. Sturkie. 1965. Chemical constituents of blood. Pages 32–84 in P.D. Sturkie, ed., Avian physiology, Second ed. Ithaca, NY: Comstock Publishing Associates. 766 pp.

Bellantoni, N.F. 1983. The wild turkey in prehistoric Connecticut: an ethnohistorical and archaeological review. Storrs: University of Connecticut. 10 pp. mimeo.

Bendell, J.F. 1955. Disease as a control of a population of blue grouse, *Dendragapus obscurus fuliginosus* (Ridgway). Can. J. Zool. 33(3):195–223.

Bendire, C. 1892. Life histories of North American birds. Smithsonian Contributions to Knowledge 28. Washington, DC: Smithsonian Institution. 446 pp.

Bennitt, R., and W.O. Nagel. 1937. A survey of the resident game and furbearers of Missouri. University of Missouri Studies 12(2):3–215.

Bent, A.C. 1932. Life histories of North American gallinaceous birds. New York: Dover Publications Inc. 490 pp.

Berger, A.J. 1981. Hawaiian birdlife. Second ed. Honolulu: University Press of Hawaii. 260 pp.

Bergerud, A.T. 1971. The population dynamics of Newfoundland caribou. Wildl. Monograph 25:1–55.

Berry, J.K. 1986. Geographic information systems: learning computer-assisted map analysis. J. Forestry 84(10):39–43.

Berryman, J.H. 1972. The principles of predator control. J. Wildl. Manage. 36(2):395–400.

Best, L.B. 1986. Conservation tillage: ecological traps for nesting birds? Wildl. Soc. Bull. 14(3):308–317.

Bevill, W.V., Jr. 1973. Some factors influencing gobbling activity among wild turkeys. Proc. Ann. Conf. Southeast. Assoc. Game and Fish Comm. 27:62–73.

———. 1975. Setting spring gobbler hunting seasons by timing peak gobbling. Proc. National Wild Turkey Symp. 3:198–204.

———. 1978. Game on your land—managing the eastern wild turkey in South Carolina. Columbia: South Carolina Wildlife and Marine Resources Dept. 42 pp.

Biellier, H.V., and C.W. Turner. 1955. The thyroxine secretion rate of growing turkey poults. Poultry Sci. 34(5):1158–1162.

Bigland, C.H. 1964. Blood clotting time of five avian species. Poultry Sci. 43(4):1035–1039.

Billingsley, B.B., Jr., and D.H. Arner. 1970. The nutritive value and digestibility of some winter foods of the eastern wild turkey. J. Wildl. Manage. 34(1):176–182.

Birdsey, R.A., and D.F. Bertelson. 1987. Forest statistics for southeast Oklahoma counties—1986. USDA Forest Service Resour. Bull. SO-119. 30 pp.

Bishopp, F.C., and H.L. Trembley. 1945. Distribution and hosts of certain North American ticks. J. Parasitol. 31(1):1–54.

Bissonnette, T.H. 1936. Sexual photoperiodicity. J. Heredity 27(5):171–180.

———. 1937. Photoperiodicity in birds. Wilson Bull. 49(4):241–270.

Bissonnette, T.H., and M.H. Chapnick. 1930. Studies on the sexual cycle in birds. II. The normal progressive changes in the testis from November to May in the European starling *(Sturnis vulgaris)*, an introduced non-migratory bird. Am. J. Anat. 45(2):307–343.

Blackburn, W.E., J.P. Kirk, and J.E. Kennamer. 1975. Availability and utilization of summer foods by eastern wild turkey broods in Lee County, Alabama. Proc. National Wild Turkey Symp. 3:86–96.

Blakey, H.L. 1937. The wild turkey on the Missouri Ozark Range. Preliminary Report. USDA Bur. Biol. Surv. Leaflet BS-77. 32 pp. mimeo.

———. 1944a. Wild turkey vs. range management. Texas Game and Fish 2(10):6–7, 14–15.

———. 1944b. Welfare of the wild turkey closely associated with range management. College Station, TX: Agric. Exp. Sta. Prog. Rep. 894. 3 pp.

Bland, D. 1986. Gould's turkey—king of the mountain. Pages 190–204 in Turkey hunters digest. Northbrook, IL: DBI Book Inc. 256 pp.

Blankenship, L.H., and L.W. Varner. 1977. Factors affecting hematological values of white-tailed deer in south Texas. Proc. Ann. Conf. Southeast. Assoc. Fish and Wildl. Agencies 31:107–115.

Boeker, E.L., and V.E. Scott. 1969. Roost tree characteristics for Merriam's turkey. J. Wildl. Manage. 33(1):121–124.

Bogusch, E.R. 1952. Brush invasion in the Rio Grande Plain of Texas. Texas J. Sci. 4(1):85–91.

Bohl, W.H., and S.P. Gordon. 1958. A range extension of *Meleagris gallopavo mexicana* into southwestern New Mexico. Condor 60(5):338–339.

Bolden, S.L., G.R. McDaniel, and L.M. Krista. 1980. Occurrences of aortic atherosclerosis in the Alabama wild turkey. Alabama Acad. Sci. J. 51(3):182–183.

Bond, J. 1979. Birds of the West Indies. Fourth Am. ed., The International Series. Houghton-Mifflin. 256 pp.

Bones, J.T. 1978. The forest resources of West Virginia. USDA Forest Service Resour. Bull. NE-56. 105 pp.

Bonnell, G.W. 1840. Topographical description of Texas. Austin: Clark, Wing, and Brown. 150 pp.

Boyd, C.E., and R.D. Oglesby. 1975. Status of wild turkey restoration in east Texas. Proc. National Wild Turkey Symp. 3:14–21.

Bozenhard, P. 1988. Maine state report. Northeast Wild Turkey Tech. Committee Newsl. 25:17–18.

Braun, E.L. 1964. Deciduous forest of eastern North America. New York and London: Hafner Publishing Co. 596 pp.

Bray, W.L. 1901. The ecological relations of the vegetation of western Texas. Bot. Gazette 32(4):262–291.

Breitburg, E. 1988. Prehistoric new world turkey domestication: origins, development, and consequences. Ph.D. Thesis. Southern Illinois University, Carbondale. 166 pp.

Breland, W.R. 1988. Reintroduction of the Gould's turkey in southeastern Arizona. Proc. Western Wild Turkey Workshop 4:12–26.

Bridges, J.M., and R.D. Andrews. 1977. Agricultural pesticides in wild turkeys in southern Illinois. Trans. Illinois State Acad. Sci. 69(4):473–478.

Brittas, R. 1988. Nutrition and reproduction of the willow grouse *Lagopus lagopus* in central Sweden. Ornis Scand. 19(1):49–57.

Brommer, W.N. 1982. Summary of the wild turkey management workshop. Michigan Wildlife Division, Dept. Natural Resources. Mt. Pleasant: Central Michigan University. 16 pp.

Brooks, R.T., T.S. Frieswyk, and A.M. Malley. 1987. Forest wildlife habitat statistics for New Hampshire. USDA Forest Service Resour. Bull. NE-97. 107 pp.

Brown, C. 1988. 1988 NWTF wild turkey records listing. Turkey Call 15(2):10–25.

Brown, D.E., ed. 1982a. Biotic communities of the American Southwest—United States and Mexico. Desert Plants 4(1–4):1–342.

———. 1982b. Madrean evergreen woodland. Desert Plants 4(1):59–65.

Brown, E.K. 1980. Home range and movements of wild turkeys—a review. Proc. National Wild Turkey Symp. 4:251–261.

Brown, E.K., and D.L. Gilbert. 1980. Movements and mortality of pen raised wild turkeys released on a hunting preserve. Proc. National Wild Turkey Symp. 4:280–292.

Brown, K.I. 1961. The validity of using plasma corticosterone as a measure of stress in the turkey. Proc. Soc. Exp. Biol. and Med. 107(3):538–542.

Brownie, C., D.R. Anderson, K.P. Burnham, and D.S. Robson. 1978. Statistical inference from band recovery data—a handbook. U.S. Dept. Interior, Fish and Wildl. Serv. Resour. Publ. 131. 212 pp.

Brownie, C., D.R. Anderson, K.P. Burnham, and D.S. Robson. 1985. Statistical inference from band recovery data—a handbook. Washington, DC: U.S. Dept. Interior, Fish and Wildlife Serv. Res. Publ. 156. 305 pp.

Brownie, C., J.E. Hines, and J.D. Nichols. 1986. Constant-parameter capture-recapture models. Biometrics 42(3):561–574.

Brownie, C., and K.H. Pollock. 1985. Analysis of multiple capture-recapture data using band-recovery methods. Biometrics 41(2):411–420.

Bryant, F.C., F.S. Guthery, and W.M. Webb. 1981. Grazing management in Texas and its impact on selected wildlife. Pages 94–112 *in* Wildlife-livestock relationships symposium. Moscow: University of Idaho. 614 pp.

Bryant, F.C., and D. Nish. 1975. Habitat use by Merriam's turkey in southwestern Utah. Proc. National Wild Turkey Symp. 3:6–13.

Buckelew, F.M. 1925. The life of F.M. Buckelew: the Indian captive. Bandera, TX: Hunter's Printing House. 187 pp.

Buckley, E.C. 1911. The Aguayo expedition into Texas and Louisiana, 1719–1722. Quart. Texas State Hist. Assoc. 15(1):1–65.

Buckner, J.L., and J.L. Landers. 1979. Fire and disking effects on herbaceous food plants and seed supplies. J. Wildl. Manage. 43(3):807–811.

Burk, J.D. 1989. Use of streamside management zones within mid-rotation-aged loblolly pine plantations by wild turkeys. M.S. Thesis. Mississippi State University, Mississippi State. 73 pp.

Burk, J.D., G.A. Hurst, D.R. Smith, B.D. Leopold, and J.G. Dickson. 1990. Wild turkey use of streamside management zones in loblolly pine plantations. Proc. National Wild Turkey Symp. 6:84–89.

Burke, N.S., M.E. Lisano, and J.E. Kennamer. 1977. Variations in plasma thyroxine (T_4) and triiodothyronine (T_3) in eastern wild turkeys. J. Wildl. Manage. 41(4):650–656.

Burnham, K.P., and D.R. Anderson. 1979. The composite dynamic method as evidence for age-specific waterfowl mortality. J. Wildl. Manage. 43(2):356–366.

Burnham, K.P., and D.R. Anderson. 1984. Tests of compensatory vs. additive hypotheses of mortality in mallards. Ecology 65(1):105–112.

Burnham, K.P., D.R. Anderson, G.C. White, C. Brownie, and K.H. Pollock. 1987. Design and analysis methods for fish survival experiments based on release-recapture. American Fisheries Society Monograph 5. 437 pp.

Burnham, K.P., G.C. White, and D.R. Anderson. 1984. Estimating the effect of hunting on annual survival rates of adult mallards. J. Wildl. Manage. 48(2):350–361.

Burrough, P.A. 1986. Principles of geographical information systems for land resources assessment. Oxford, UK: Clarendon Press. Monograph on Soil and Response Surveys No. 12. 193 pp.

Burroughs, R.D., ed. 1961. The natural history of the Lewis and Clark expedition. East Lansing: Michigan State University Press. 340 pp.

Burrows, W.H., and S.J. Marsden. 1938. Artificial breeding of turkeys. Poultry Sci. 17(5):408–411.

Burrows, W.T., and I.L. Kosin. 1953. The effects of ambient temperature on production and fertilizing capacity of turkey spermatozoa. Physiol. Zool. 26(2):131–146.

Busch, R.H., and L.E. Williams, Jr. 1970. A Marek's disease-like condition in Florida turkeys. Avian Dis. 14(3):550–554.

Butts, G.L. 1977. Aerial pursuit of red-tailed hawks *(Accipitridae)* by turkey *(Meleagrididae)* hens. Southwest. Nat. 22(3):404–405.

Byrd, M.A. 1959. Observations on *Leucocytozoon* in pen-raised and free-ranging wild turkeys. J. Wildl. Manage. 23(2):145–156.

Cain, S.A. (chairman) 1972. Predator control—1971. Report to the Council on Environmental Quality and the Department of Interior by the Advisory Committee on Predator Control. Washington, DC. 207 pp.

Calder, W.A., III, and J.R. King. 1974. Thermal and caloric relations of birds. Pages 259–413 *in* D.S. Farner and J.R. King, eds., Avian biology. Vol. 4. New York: Academic Press. 504 pp.

Campbell, J.G. 1957a. Studies on the influence of sex hormones on the avian liver. I. Sexual differences in avian liver clearance curves. J. Endocrinol. 15(3):339–345.

———. 1957b. Studies on the influences of sex hormones on the avian liver. II. Acute liver damage in the male fowl and the protective effect of oestrogen, as determined by a liver function test. J. Endocrinol. 15(3):346–350.

Campbell, R.W. 1979. Gypsy moth: forest influence. USDA Forest Service Agric. Inf. Bull. 423. 44 pp.

Campo, J.J., and J.G. Dickson. 1989. Eastern wild turkey management in Texas. Austin: Texas Parks and Wildlife Dept. 4 pp. mimeo.

Campo, J.J., C.R. Hopkins, and W.G. Swank. 1984. Mortality and reproduction of stocked eastern turkeys in east Texas. Proc. Ann. Conf. Southeast. Assoc. Fish and Wildl. Agencies 38:78–86.

Campo, J.J., W.G. Swank, and C.R. Hopkins. 1989. Brood habitat use by eastern wild turkeys in eastern Texas. J. Wildl. Manage. 53(2):479–482.

Capel, S.W. 1973. Introduction of Rio Grande turkeys into Kansas. Pages 11–17 *in* G.C. Sanderson and H.C. Shultz, eds., Wild turkey management: current problems and programs. Columbia: The Missouri Chapter of The Wildlife Society and University of Missouri Press. 355 pp.

Capen, D.E. 1981. The use of multivariate statistics in studies of wildlife habitat. USDA Forest Service. Gen. Tech. Rep. RM-87. 249 pp.

Carrigan, G. 1986. Sightings of wild turkeys, District St. Bernard De LaColle–Huntingdon (S.W. Quebec). Northeast Wild Turkey Tech. Committee Newsl. 23:56.

Carriker, M.A., Jr. 1956. Report on a collection of Mallophaga, largely Mexican (Part II). Florida Entomol. 39(3):119–132.

Cartwright, M.E., and R.A. Smith. 1990. Attitudes, opinions, and characteristics of a select group of Arkansas spring turkey hunters. Proc. National Wild Turkey Symp. 6:177–187.

Carvell, K.L. 1980. The impact of silvicultural practices on the density, height and composition of the understory—with special reference to wildlife habitat. West Virginia For. Notes 8:17–19.

Castetter, E.F., and M.E. Opler. 1936. Ethnobiological studies in the

American southwest. III. University of New Mexico Biol. Series 4(5):25–26.

Castle, M.D., and B.M. Christensen. 1984. Blood and gastrointestinal parasites of eastern wild turkeys from Kentucky and Tennessee. J. Wildl. Dis. 20(3):190–196.

Castle, M.D., and B.M. Christensen. 1985. Isolation and identification of *Aegyptianella pullorum* (Rickettsiales, Anaplasmataceae) in wild turkeys from North America. Avian Dis. 29(2):437–445.

Castle, M.D., B.M. Christensen, and T.E. Rocke. 1988. Hematozoan parasites of Rio Grande wild turkeys from southern Texas. J. Wildl. Dis. 24(1):88–96.

Caswell, F.D., G.S. Hochbaum, and R.K. Brace. 1985. The effect of restrictive regional hunting regulations on survival rates and local harvests of southern Manitoba mallards. Trans. N. Am. Wildl. and Nat. Resour. Conf. 50:549–556.

Caughley, G. 1974. Interpretation of age ratios. J. Wildl. Manage. 38(3):557–562.

———. 1977. An analysis of vertebrate populations. London: John Wiley and Sons. 234 pp.

———. 1979. What is this thing called carrying capacity? Pages 2–8 *in* M.S. Boyce and L.D. Hayden-Wing, eds., North American elk: ecology, behavior and management. Laramie: University of Wyoming Press. 294 pp.

Chalmers, G.A., and M.W. Barrett. 1982. Capture myopathy. Pages 84–94 *in* G.L. Hoff and J.W. Davis, eds., Noninfectious diseases of wildlife. Ames: Iowa State University Press. 174 pp.

Chesness, R.A., M.M. Nelson, and W.H. Longley. 1968. The effect of predator removal on pheasant reproductive success. J. Wildl. Manage. 32(4):683–697.

Christensen, B.M., H.J. Barnes, and W.A. Rowley. 1983. Vertebrate host specificity and experimental vectors of *Plasmodium (Novyella) kempi* sp. n. from the eastern wild turkey in Iowa. J. Wildl. Dis. 19(3):204–213.

Christensen, V.L., C.R. Parkhurst, and F.W. Edens. 1982. Conductance and qualities of wild and domestic turkey eggs. Poultry Sci. 61(8):1753–1758.

Clark, L.G. 1985. Adjustment by transplanted wild turkeys to an Ohio farmland area. Proc. National Wild Turkey Symp. 5:33–47.

Clarke, C.H.E. 1948. The wild turkey in Ontario. Sylva 4(6):4–12.

Clawson, S.G. 1958. A wild turkey population on an area treated with heptachlor and dieldrin. Alabama Birdlife 6(3–4):4–8.

Clay, T. 1938. A revision of the genera and species of Mallophaga occurring on gallinaceous hosts. Part I. *Lipeurus* and related genera. Proc. Zool. Soc. London, Series B 108:109–204.

Clutton-Brock, T.H., F.E. Guinness, and S.D. Albon. 1982. Red deer: behavior and ecology of sexes. Chicago: The University of Chicago Press. 378 pp.

Cobb, S. 1960. Observations on the comparative anatomy of the avian brain. Perspectives in Biol. and Med. 3(3):383–408.

Cochran, W.W., and R.D. Lord, Jr. 1963. A radio-tracking system for wild animals. J. Wildl. Manage. 27(1):9–24

Colwell, W.M., C.F. Simpson, L.E. Williams, Jr., and D.J. Forrester. 1973. Isolation of a herpesvirus from wild turkeys in Florida. Avian Dis. 17(1):1–11.

Commer, M., Jr. 1986. The history of Mississippi's wildlife monarch, the wild turkey. Mississippi State: Mississippi Chapter, National Wild Turkey Federation. 9 pp.

Connell, J.H. 1970. A predator-prey system in the marine intertidal shores. Ecol. Monographs 40:49–78.

———. 1972. Community interactions on marine rocky intertidal shores. Ann. Rev. Ecol. Sys. 3:169–192.

Conner, R.N. 1988. Wildlife populations: minimally viable or ecologically functional? Wildl. Soc. Bull. 16(1):80–84.

Connolly, G.E. 1978. Predators and predator control. Pages 369–394 *in* J. Schmidt and D. Gilbert, eds., Big game of North America. Harrisburg, PA: Stackpole Books. 494 pp.

Connolly, G.E., and W. Longhurst. 1975. The effects of control on coyote populations. University of California, Davis, Div. Agric.

Sci. Bull. 1872. 37 pp.

Conroy, M.J., and R.T. Eberhardt. 1983. Variation in survival and recovery rates of ring-necked ducks. J. Wildl. Manage. 47(1):127–137.

Considine, T.J., Jr., and T.S. Frieswyk. 1980. Forest statistics for New York. USDA Forest Service Resour. Bull. NE-71. 118 pp.

Considine, T.J., Jr., and D.S. Powell. 1980. Forest statistics for Pennsylvania—1978. USDA Forest Service Resour. Bull. NE-65. 88 pp.

Cook, R.L. 1972. A study of nesting turkeys in the Edwards Plateau of Texas. Proc. Ann. Conf. Southeast. Assoc. Game and Fish Comm. 26:236–244.

———. 1973. A census technique for the Rio Grande turkey. Pages 279–283 *in* G.C. Sanderson and H.C. Schultz, eds., Wild turkey management: current problems and programs. Columbia: The Missouri Chapter of The Wildlife Society and University of Missouri Press. 355 pp.

Cook, R.L., and H.G. Gore. 1978. Learn about turkey. Austin: Texas Parks and Wildl. Dept. Leaflet 9000–53. 7 pp.

Cook, R.S., D.O. Trainer, and W.C. Glazener. 1966. *Haemoproteus* in wild turkeys from the coastal bend of south Texas. J. Protozool. 13(4):588–590.

Cooley, R.A., and G.M. Kohls. 1944. The genus *Amblyomma* (Ixodidae) in the United States. J. Parasitol. 30(2):77–111.

Correll, D.S., and M.C. Johnston. 1970. Manual of the vascular plants of Texas. Renner: Texas Research Foundation. 1881 pp.

Covert, C.L., and E.D. Michael. 1975. Habitat utilization by wild turkey on Coopers Rock State Forest in West Virginia. Trans. Northeast. Section, The Wildlife Society 32:62–79.

Cox, D.N. 1973. Soil survey of Hidalgo County, New Mexico. Washington, DC: USDA Soil Conserv. Serv. 90 pp.

Cox, M.L. 1948. Investigation of Rio Grande turkey in lower south Texas. U.S. Dept. Interior, Fish and Wildlife Serv., Pittman-Robertson Quart. 8(1):98–99.

Cracraft, J. 1968. First record of the turkey *Meleagris gallopavo* from the Pleistocene of Mexico. Condor 70(3):274.

Cram, E.B. 1928. Nematodes of pathological significance found in some economically important birds in North America. USDA Tech. Bull. 49. 10 pp.

Crawford, J.A., and R.S. Lutz. 1984. Final report on Merriam's wild turkey habitat use and movements. Portland: Oregon Dept. of Fish and Wildlife. Proj. P-R-W-79-R-2. 39 pp. mimeo.

Crim, G.B. 1981. Eastern wild turkey winter habitat in south-central Iowa. M.S. Thesis. Iowa State University, Ames. 33 pp.

Crites, M.J. 1988. Ecology of the Merriam's turkey in north-central Arizona. M.S. Thesis. University of Arizona, Tucson. 59 pp.

Crockett, B.C. 1965. Quantitative evaluation of winter roosting sites of the Rio Grande turkey in north central Oklahoma. M.S. Thesis. Oklahoma State University, Stillwater. 45 pp.

———. 1973. Quantitative evaluation of winter roost sites of the Rio Grande turkey in north-central Oklahoma. Pages 211–218 *in* G.C. Sanderson and H.C. Schultz, eds., Wild turkey management: current problems and programs. Columbia: The Missouri Chapter of The Wildlife Society and University of Missouri Press. 355 pp.

Crow, T.R. 1988. Reproductive mode and mechanisms for self-replacement of northern red oak *(Quercus rubra)*—a review. For. Sci. 34(1):19–40.

Curio, E. 1976. The ethology of predation. New York: Springer-Verlag. 249 pp.

Dahlquist, F.C., S.D. Schemnitz, and B.K. Flachs. 1990. Distinguishing individual male wild turkeys by discrimination of vocalizations. Proc. National Wild Turkey Symp. 6:149–156.

Dale, M.E., and D.E. Hilt. 1986. Thinning pole and small sawtimber mixed oak stands. Pages 99–133 *in* H.C. Smith and M.C. Eye, eds., Proc: Guidelines for managing immature Appalachian hardwood stands. Morgantown: West Virginia University Books. 283 pp.

Dalke, P.D., W.K. Clark, Jr., and L.J. Korschgen. 1942. Food habit trends of the wild turkey in Missouri as determined by dropping analysis. J. Wildl. Manage. 6(3):237–243.

Dalke, P.D., A.S. Leopold, and D.L. Spencer. 1946. The ecology and management of the wild turkey in Missouri. Jefferson City: Missouri Conservation Commission Tech. Bull. 1. 86 pp.

Darwin, C. 1868. The variation of animals and plants under domestication. Vol. 1. New York: Orange Judd Co. 486 pp.

Davidson, V.E., and K.E. Graetz. 1957. Managing habitat for white-tailed deer and wild turkeys. Trans. N. Am. Wildl. and Nat. Resour. Conf. 22:412–424.

Davidson, W.R. 1987. Disease monitoring in wild turkey restoration programs. Proc. Ann. Conf. Western Assoc. Fish and Wildl. Agencies 67:113–118.

Davidson, W.R., and V.F. Nettles. 1988. Field manual of wildlife diseases in the southeastern United States. Athens: Southeastern Cooperative Wildlife Disease Study, College of Veterinary Medicine, The University of Georgia. 309 pp.

Davidson, W.R., V.F. Nettles, C.E. Couvillion, and E.W. Howerth. 1985. Diseases diagnosed in wild turkeys *(Meleagris gallopavo)* of the southeastern United States. J. Wildl. Dis. 21(4):386–390.

Davidson, W.R., V.F. Nettles, C.E. Couvillion, and H.W. Yoder, Jr. 1982. Infectious sinusitis in wild turkeys. Avian Dis. 26(2):402–405.

Davidson, W.R., E.B. Shotts, J. Teska, and D.W. Moreland. 1989. Feather damage due to mycotic infections in wild turkeys. J. Wildl. Dis. 25(4):534–539.

Davidson, W.R., H.W. Yoder, M. Brugh, and V.F. Nettles. 1988. Serological monitoring of eastern wild turkeys for antibodies to *Mycoplasma* spp. and avian influenza viruses. J. Wildl. Dis. 24(2):348–351.

Davis, H.E. 1949. The American wild turkey. Georgetown, SC: Small-Arms Technical Publishing Co. 328 pp.

Davis, J.H. 1980. General map of ecological communities of Florida. Fort Worth, TX: U.S. Dept. Agric. 1 p.

Davis, J.R. 1959. A preliminary report on nest predation as a limiting factor in wild turkey populations. Proc. National Wild Turkey Symp. 1:138–145.

———. 1966. Internal and external parasites and diseases of wild turkeys. Page 28B in Annual progress report. Montgomery: Alabama Dept. Conservation.

———. 1971. Spring weather and wild turkeys. Alabama Conserv. 41(1):6–7.

———. 1973. Movements of wild turkeys in southwestern Alabama. Pages 135–139 in G.C. Sanderson and H.C. Shultz, eds., Wild turkey management: current problems and programs. Columbia: The Missouri Chapter of The Wildlife Society and University of Missouri Press. 355 pp.

———. 1976. Management for Alabama wild turkeys. Montgomery: Alabama Game and Fish Commission, Alabama Dept. Conservation and Natural Resources. Special Rep. No. 5. 130 pp.

Davis, J.R., and E.J. Widder. 1985. History of wild turkey restocking in Alabama. Montgomery: Alabama Dept. Conservation and Natural Resources. Special Rep. 9. 29 pp.

Davis, P.G. 1982. Man and wildlife in Arizona: the American exploration period 1824–1865. Phoenix: Arizona Game and Fish Department. 232 pp.

Dawson, W.R., R.L. Marsh, W.A. Buttemer, and C. Carey. 1983. Seasonal and geographic variation of cold resistance in house finches *Carpodacus mexicanus*. Physiol. Zool. 56(3):353–369.

Dawson, W.R., R.L. Marsh, and M.E. Yacoe. 1983. Metabolic adjustments of small passerine birds for migration and cold. Am. J. Physiol. 245(6):R755–R767.

DeArment, R.D. 1959. Turkey hen-poult ratios as an index to reproductive trends. Proc. National Wild Turkey Symp. 1:27–31.

———. 1975. Either sex turkey harvest in the Texas panhandle. Proc. National Wild Turkey Symp. 3:189–190.

Decker, S.R. 1988. Nutritive quality and metabolizable energy of eight wild turkey foods in New Hampshire. M.S. Thesis. University of New Hampshire, Durham. 37 pp.

DeGraff, L.W., and D.E. Austin. 1975. Turkey harvest management in New York. Proc. National Wild Turkey Symp. 3:191–197.

Dellinger, G.P. 1973. Habitat management for turkeys in the oak-hickory forests of Missouri. Pages 235–244 in G.C. Sanderson and H.C. Schultz, eds., Wild turkey management: current problems and programs. Columbia: The Missouri Chapter of The Wildlife Society and University of Missouri Press. 355 pp.

Dennis, D.F., and T.W. Birch. 1981. Forest statistics for Ohio—1979. USDA Forest Service Resour. Bull. NE-68. 79 pp.

De Selm, H.R., E.E.C. Clebsch, G.M. Nichols and E. Thor. 1973. Response of herbs, shrubs and tree sprouts in prescribed-burn hardwoods in Tennessee. Tall Timbers Fire Ecol. Conf. 13:331–344.

Devine, H.A., and R.C. Field. 1986. Geographic information systems: the gist of GIS. J. Forestry 84(8):17–22.

DeYoung, C.A., and J.C. Priebe. 1987. Comparison of inventory methods for wild turkeys in south Texas. Proc. Ann. Conf. Southeast. Assoc. Fish and Wildl. Agencies 41:294–298.

Dickneite, D.F. 1973. Restoration of the eastern wild turkey in Missouri. Pages 19–24 in G.C. Sanderson and H.C. Shultz, eds., Wild turkey management: current problems and programs. Columbia: The Missouri Chapter of The Wildlife Society and University of Missouri Press. 355 pp.

Dickson, D.R., and T.M. Bowers. 1976. Forest statistics for Connecticut. USDA Forest Service Resour. Bull. NE-44. 40 pp.

Dickson, J.G. 1978. Forest bird communities of the bottomland hardwoods. Pages 66–73 in R.M. DeGraaf, tech. coord., Proc. of the workshop management of southern forests for nongame birds. USDA Forest Service Gen. Tech. Rep. SE-14. 176 pp.

———. 1982. Impact of forestry practices on wildlife in southern pine forests. Pages 224–230 in Increasing forest productivity. Proc. of the 1981 Convention of the Society of American Foresters. SAF Publ. 82-01. 369 pp.

———. 1990. Oak and flowering dogwood production for eastern wild turkeys. Proc. National Wild Turkey Symp. 6:90–95.

Dickson, J.G., C.D. Adams, and S.H. Hanley. 1978. Response of turkey populations to habitat variables in Louisiana. Wildl. Soc. Bull. 6(3):163–166.

Dickson, J.G., and C.A. Segelquist. 1979. Breeding bird populations in pine and pine-hardwood forests in east Texas. J. Wildl. Manage. 43(2):549–555.

Dill, H.H., and W.H. Thornsberry. 1950. A cannon-projected net trap for capturing waterfowl. J. Wildl. Manage. 14(2):132–137.

Dixon, E.S., 1853. A treatise on the management of ornamental and domestic poultry. Third ed. Philadelphia: E.H.Butler. 480 pp.

Dobell, J., and D. Reid. 1988. Province of Ontario report. Northeast Wild Turkey Tech. Comm. Newsl. 25:44–49.

Dodge, E.S. 1945. Notes from the six nations on the hunting and trapping of wild turkeys and passenger pigeons. J. Washington Acad. Sci. 35(11):342–343.

Domermuth, C.H., D.J. Forrester, D.O. Trainer, and W.J. Bigler. 1977. Serologic examination of wild birds for hemorrhagic enteritis of turkey and marble spleen disease of pheasants. J. Wildl. Dis. 13(4):405–408.

Domm, L.V., and E. Taber. 1946. Endocrine factors controlling erythrocyte concentration in the blood of the domestic fowl. Physiol. Zool. 19(3):258–281.

Donahue, M.A., M.E. Lisano, and J.E. Kennamer. 1982. Effects of alpha-chloralose drugging on blood constituents in the eastern wild turkey. J. Wildl. Manage. 46(2):468–474.

Donohoe, R.W. 1985. Distribution and population status of midwestern wild turkeys, spring 1983. Proc. National Wild Turkey Symp. 5:303–307.

———. 1990. The wild turkey: past, present and future in Ohio. Columbus: Ohio Dept. of Natural Resources, Division of Wildlife. Ohio Fish and Wildl. Rep. 11. 47 pp.

Donohoe, R.W., and C.E. McKibben. 1973. Status of the wild turkey in

Ohio. Pages 25–33 *in* G.C. Sanderson and H.C. Shultz, eds., Wild turkey management: current problems and programs. Columbia: The Missouri Chapter of The Wildlife Society and University of Missouri Press. 355 pp.

Donohoe, R.W., C.E. McKibben, and C.B. Lowry. 1968. Turkey nesting behavior. Wilson Bull. 80(1):103–104.

Donovan, M.L. 1985. A turkey habitat suitability model utilizing the Michigan resource information system (MIRIS). M.S. Thesis. The University of Michigan, Ann Arbor. 36 pp.

Donovan, M.L., D.L. Rabe, and C.E. Olson, Jr. 1987. Use of geographic information systems to develop habitat suitability models. Wildl. Soc. Bull. 15(4):574–579.

Dooling, R.J. 1982. Auditory perception in birds. Pages 95–130 *in* D.E. Kroodsma and E.H. Miller, eds., Acoustic communication in birds. Vol. 1. New York: Academic Press. 371 pp.

Doran, D.J. 1978. The life cycle of *Eimeria dispersa* Tyzzer 1929 from the turkey in gallinaceous birds. J. Parasitol. 64(5):882–885.

Doster, G.L. 1974. Aspirated corn kernels cause death of cannon-netted wild turkeys. J. Wildl. Manage. 38(3):578.

Drake, W. 1987. The effect of removing poor acorn producing oaks on acorn production of remaining oaks. Harrisburg: Pennsylvania Game Commission. Final Rep. Proj. No. 06105. 11 pp. mimeo.

Dreis, R.E., C.F. Smith, and L.E. Myers. 1973. Wisconsin's wild turkey restoration experiment. Pages 45–48 *in* G.C. Sanderson and H.C. Shultz, eds., Wild turkey management: current problems and programs. Columbia: The Missouri Chapter of The Wildlife Society and University of Missouri Press. 355 pp.

Duebbert, H.F., and H.A. Kantrud. 1974. Upland duck nesting related to land use and predator reduction. J. Wildl. Manage. 38(2):257–265.

Dukes, H.H. 1947. The physiology of domestic animals. Sixth ed. Ithaca, NY: Comstock Publishing Co. 817 pp.

Eaton, S.W., F.M. Evans, J.W. Glidden, and B.D. Penrod. 1976. Annual range of wild turkeys in southwestern New York. New York Fish and Game J. 23(1):20–33.

Eaton, S.W., T.L. Moore, and E.N. Saylor. 1970. A ten year study of the food habits of a northern population of wild turkeys. Sci. Studies 26:43–64.

Eberhardt, L.L. 1987. Population projections from simple models. J. Appl. Ecol. 24(1):103–118.

Edminster, F.C. 1954. American game birds of field and forest: their habits, ecology, and management. New York: Charles Scribner's Sons. 490 pp.

Ellis, J.A., J.N. Burroughs, M.J. Armbruster, D.L. Hallett, P.A. Korte, and T.S. Baskett. 1979. Appraising four field methods of terrestrial habitat evaluation. Trans. N. Am. Wildl. and Nat. Resour. Conf. 44:369–379.

Ellis, J.E. 1966. Home range and movements of the eastern wild turkey. M.S. Thesis. University of Missouri, Columbia. 100 pp.

Ellis, J.E., and J.B. Lewis. 1967. Mobility and annual range of wild turkeys in Missouri. J. Wildl. Manage. 31(3):568–581.

Ellis, R.J. 1948. Welfare status and outlook for the wild turkey in western Oklahoma. Oklahoma Coop. Wildl. Res. Unit, Quart. Prog. Rep. 2(1):15–16.

Elton, C.S., and M. Nicholson. 1942. The ten-year cycle in numbers of the lynx in Canada. J. Animal Ecol. 11(2):215–244.

Emerson, K.C. 1951. A list of Mallophaga from gallinaceous birds of North America. J. Wildl. Manage. 15(1):193–195.

Eng, R.L. 1959. Status of turkey in Montana. Proc. National Wild Turkey Symp. 1:19.

Eriksen, R.E., J.V. Gwynn, and K.H. Pollock. 1985. Influence of blaze orange on spring wild turkey hunter success. Wildl. Soc. Bull. 13(4):518–521.

Errington, P.L. 1943. An analysis of mink predation upon muskrats in north-central United States. Iowa Agric. Exp. Sta., Res. Bull. 320:797–924.

———. 1946. Predation and vertebrate populations. Quart. Rev. Biol.

21:144–177, 221–245.

Etchecopar, R.D. 1955. L'acclimatation des oiseaux en France au cours des 100 dernieres annees (The acclimatization of birds in France during the past 100 years). La Terre et la Vie Ser. 2,9:42–53.

Evans, P.G.H. 1987. Electrophoretic variability of gene products. Pages 105–162 *in* F. Cooke and P.A. Buckley, eds., Avian genetics: a population and ecological approach. Orlando, FL: Academic Press. 488 pp.

Evans, R.D. 1974. Wildlife habitat management program: a concept of diversity for the public forests of Missouri. Pages 73–83 *in* Timber-wildlife management symp. Missouri Academy of Science. Occasional Paper 3.

Eve, J.H., F.E. Kellogg, and R.W. Bailey. 1972. Blood parasites in wild turkeys of eastern West Virginia. J. Wildl. Manage. 36(2):624–627.

Eve, J.H., F.E. Kellogg, and F.A. Hayes. 1972. Blood parasitism of wild turkeys in the southeastern United States. J. Am. Vet. Med. Assoc. 161(6):638–640.

Everett, D.D., Jr. 1982. Factors limiting populations of wild turkeys on state wildlife management areas in north Alabama. Ph.D. Thesis. Auburn University, Auburn, AL. 135 pp.

Everett, D.D., D.W. Speake, and W.K. Maddox, 1979. Wild turkey ranges in Alabama mountain habitat. Proc. Ann. Conf. Southeast. Assoc. Fish and Wildl. Agencies 33:233–238.

Everett, D.D., D.W. Speake, and W.K. Maddox. 1980. Natality and mortality of a north Alabama wild turkey population. Proc. National Wild Turkey Symp. 4:117–126.

Everett, D.D., Jr., D.W. Speake, and W.K. Maddox. 1981. Use of rights-of-way by nesting wild turkeys in North Alabama. Proc. symposium: Environmental concerns in rights-of-way management 2:64-1-64-6.

Everett, D.D., Jr., D.W. Speake, and W.K. Maddox. 1985. Habitat use by wild turkeys in northwest Alabama. Proc. Ann. Conf. Southeast. Assoc. Fish and Wildl. Agencies 39:479–488.

Everett, D.D., D.W. Speake, W.K. Maddox, D.R. Hillestad, and D.N. Nelson. 1978. Impact of managed public hunting on wild turkeys in Alabama. Proc. Ann. Conf. Southeast. Assoc. Fish and Wildl. Agencies 32:116–125.

Exum, J.H. 1985. Ecology of the eastern wild turkey on an even-aged pine forest in southern Alabama. Ph.D. Thesis. Auburn University, Auburn, AL. 109 pp.

Exum, J.H., J.A. McGlincy, D.W. Speake, J.L. Buckner, and F.M. Stanley. 1985. Evidence against dependence upon surface water by turkey hens and poults in southern Alabama. Proc. National Wild Turkey Symp. 5:83–89.

Exum, J.H., J.A. McGlincy, D.W. Speake, J.L. Buckner, and F.M. Stanley. 1987. Ecology of the eastern wild turkey in an intensively managed pine forest in southern Alabama. Tallahassee, FL: Tall Timbers Research Station Bull. 23. 70 pp.

Falla, R.A., R.B. Sibson, and E.G. Turbott. 1967. A field guide to the birds of New Zealand and outlying islands. Boston: Houghton Mifflin Co. 254 pp.

Farner, D.S. 1942. The hydrogen ion concentration in avian digestive tracts. Poultry Sci. 21(5):445–450.

Fears, J.W. 1981. The wild turkey book. Clinton, NJ: Amwell Press. 274 pp.

Fenneman, N.M. 1938. Physiography of eastern United States. New York: McGraw-Hill. 714 pp.

Ffolliott, P.F., R.E. Thill, W.P. Clary, and F.R. Larson. 1977. Animal use of ponderosa pine forest openings. J. Wildl. Manage. 41(4):782–784.

Figert, D.E. 1989. Status, reproduction, and habitat use of Gould's turkey in the Peloncillo Mountains of New Mexico. M.S. Thesis. New Mexico State University, Las Cruces. 102 pp.

Filson, J. 1754. The discovery, settlement, and present state of Kentucke. Wilmington, DE: James Adams. 118 pp.

Fitter, R.S.R. 1959. The ark in our midst. London: Collins. 320 pp.

Flather, C.H., T.W. Hoekstra, D.E. Chalk, N.D. Cost, and V.A.

Rudis. 1989. Recent historical and projected regional trends of white-tailed deer and wild turkey in the southern United States. USDA Forest Service Gen. Tech. Rep. RM-172. 22 pp.

Fleming, W.J., and D.W. Speake. 1976. Losses of the eastern wild turkey from a stable Alabama population. Proc. Ann. Conf. Southeast. Assoc. Game and Fish Comm. 30:377–385.

Fleming, W.H., and L.G. Webb. 1974. Home range, dispersal and habitat utilization of eastern wild turkey gobblers during the breeding season. Proc. Ann. Conf. Southeast. Assoc. Game and Fish Comm. 28:623–632.

Fluke, W.G. 1940. Propagating wild turkeys in the wild. Pennsylvania Game News 11(1):4, 32.

Folk, R.H., III, and R.L. Marchinton. 1980. Effects of intensive deer hunting on behavior of wild turkeys. J. Wildl. Manage. 44(4):922–927.

Foote, L.E. 1959. Summarization of the first national wild turkey symposium. Proc. National Wild Turkey Symp. 1:192–198.

Forbes, S.E., L.M. Lang, S.A. Liscinsky, and H.A. Roberts. 1971. The white-tailed deer in Pennsylvania. Harrisburg: Pennsylvania Game Commission. Res. Bull. 170. 41 pp.

Forrester, D.J., L.T. Hon, L.E. Williams, Jr., and D.H. Austin. 1974. Blood protozoa of wild turkeys in Florida. J. Protozool. 21(4):494–497.

Forrester, D.J., P.P. Humphrey, S.R. Telford, Jr., and L.E. Williams, Jr. 1980. Effects of blood-induced infections of *Plasmodium hermani* on domestic and wild turkey poults. J. Wildl. Dis. 16(2):237–244.

Forrester, D.J., J.K. Nayar, and G.W. Foster. 1980. *Culex nigripalpus*: a natural vector of wild turkey malaria *(Plasmodium hermani)* in Florida. J. Wildl. Dis. 16(3):391–394.

Forrester, D.J., J.K. Nayar, and M.D. Young. 1987. Natural infection of *Plasmodium hermani* in the northern bobwhite, *Colinus virginianus*, in Florida. J. Parasitol. 73(4):865–866.

Forsythe, S. 1978. Habitat evaluation for white-tailed deer prior to a whole tree utilization clearcut in the southcentral ridge and valley province of Virginia. M.S. Thesis. Virginia Polytechnic Institute and State University, Blacksburg. 101 pp.

Fowler, C.W., and T.D. Smith, eds. 1981. Dynamics of large mammal populations. New York: John Wiley & Sons. 477 pp.

Francis, W.J. 1968. Temperature and humidity conditions in potential pheasant nesting habitat. J. Wildl. Manage. 32(1):36–46.

Franciscan Fathers. 1910. An ethnologic dictionary of the Navajo language. Saint Michaels, AZ: Franciscan Fathers. 536 pp.

Frankel, O.H., and M.E. Soulé. 1981. Conservation and evolution. Cambridge, England: Cambridge University Press. 327 pp.

Fretwell, S.D. 1975. The impact of Robert MacArthur on ecology. Ann. Rev. Ecol. and Syst. 6:1–13.

Frieswyk, T.S., and A.M. Malley. 1985a. Forest statistics for Vermont – 1973 and 1983. USDA Forest Service Resour. Bull. NE-87. 102 pp.

Frieswyk, T.S., and A.M. Malley. 1985b. Forest statistics for New Hampshire – 1973 and 1985. USDA Forest Service Resour. Bull. NE-88. 100 pp.

Fulbright, T.E., and S.L. Beasom. 1987. Long-term effects of mechanical treatments on white-tailed deer browse. Wildl. Soc. Bull. 15(4):560–564.

Gansner, D.A., and O.W. Herrick. 1987. Impact of gypsy moth on the timber resource. Pages 11–20 *in* S. Fosbroke and R.R. Hicks, Jr., eds. Coping with the gypsy moth in the new frontier: a workshop for forest managers. Morgantown: West Virginia University Books. 153 pp.

Gardiner, J.L., and E.E. Wehr. 1949. Some parasites of the wild turkey *Meleagris gallopavo silvestris* in Maryland. Proc. Helminthol. Soc. Wash. 16(1):16–19.

Gardner, D.T., and D.H. Arner. 1968. Food supplements and wild turkey reproduction. Trans. N. Am. Wildl. and Nat. Resour. Conf. 33:250–258.

Gardner, D.T., D.W. Speake, and W.J. Fleming. 1972. The effects of a spring "gobblers-only" hunting season on wild turkey reproduction and population size. Proc. Ann. Conf. Southeast. Assoc. Game and Fish Comm. 26:244–252.

Garrison, G.A., A.J. Bjugstad, D.A. Duncan, M.E. Lewis, and D.R. Smith. 1977. Vegetation and environmental features of forest and range ecosystems. U.S. Dept. Agric., Agric. Handbook 475. 68 pp.

Garver, J.K. 1987. The wild turkey in Illinois. Springfield: Illinois Dept. Conservation, Division of Wildlife Resources. 28 pp.

Gehrken, G.A. 1975. Travel corridor technique of wild turkey management. Proc. National Wild Turkey Symp. 3:113–117.

Geiger, R. 1950. The climate near the ground. Cambridge, MA: Harvard University Press. 482 pp.

Gerstell, R. 1942. The place of winter feeding in practical wildlife management. Harrisburg: Pennsylvania Game Commission. Res. Bull. 3. 121 pp.

Gerstell, R., and W.H. Long. 1939. Physiological variations in wild turkeys and their significance in management. Harrisburg: Pennsylvania Game Commission. Res. Bull. 2. 60 pp.

Gilbert, A.B. 1963. The effect of oestrogen and thryroxine on the blood volume of the domestic cock. J. Endocrinol. 26(1):41–47.

———. 1971a. The ovary. Pages 1163–1208 *in* D.J. Bell and B.M. Freeman, eds., Physiology and biochemistry of the domestic fowl. London: Academic Press. 1488 pp.

———. 1971b. The female reproductive effort. Pages 1153–1162 *in* D.J. Bell and B.M. Freeman, eds., Physiology and biochemistry of the domestic fowl. London: Academic Press. 1488 pp.

Gilmour, J. 1876. On the introduction of the wild turkey *(Meleagris gallopavo)* in Argyllshire. Glasgow: Proc. Nat. Hist. Soc. 2:11–16.

Gilpin, D.D. 1959. Recent results of wild turkey restocking efforts in West Virginia. Proc. National Wild Turkey Symp. 1:87–91.

Glazener, W.C. 1945. Management of turkeys in lower south Texas. U.S. Dept. Interior, Fish and Wildl. Serv., Pittman-Robertson Quart. 5(4):158–160.

———. 1959. Wild turkey research needs. Proc. National Wild Turkey Symp. 1:177–182.

———. 1963. Wild turkey restoration in progress in Texas. Texas Game and Fish 21(1):8–10, 27.

———. 1967. Management of the Rio Grande turkey. Pages 453–492 *in* O.H. Hewitt, ed., The wild turkey and its management. Washington, DC: The Wildlife Society. 589 pp.

Glazener, W.C., R.S. Cook, and D.O. Trainer. 1967. A serologic study of diseases in the Rio Grande turkey. J. Wildl. Manage. 31(1):34–39.

Glidden, J.W. 1977a. Analysis of various wild turkey nesting characteristics. Albany: New York Dept. of Environmental Conservation. Fed. Aid Wildl. Restor. Proj. W-48-R-24. 5 pp. mimeo.

———. 1977b. Net productivity of a wild turkey population in southwestern New York. Trans. Northeast. Fish and Wildl. Conf. 34:13–21.

———. 1980. An examination of fall wild turkey hunting statistics from different ecological areas of southwestern New York. Proc. National Wild Turkey Symp. 4:76–85.

Glidden, J.W., and D.E. Austin. 1975. Natality and mortality of wild turkey poults in southwestern New York. Proc. National Wild Turkey Symp. 3:48–54.

Glover, F.A. 1948. Winter activities of wild turkey in West Virginia. J. Wildl. Manage. 12(4):416–427.

Glover, F.A., and R.W. Bailey. 1949. Wild turkey foods in West Virginia. J. Wildl. Manage. 13(3):255–265.

Gluesing, E.A., and D.M. Field. 1982. Forest-wildlife relationships: an assessment of the biological state-of-the-art. Mississippi State: Mississippi Agric. and For. Exp. Sta. Unpubl. Rep. 135 pp.

Gluesing, E.A., and D.M. Field. 1986. Limitations of existing food-habit studies in modeling wildlife-habitat relationships. Pages 251–253 *in* J.Verner, M.L. Morrison, and C.J. Ralph, eds., Wildlife 2000: modeling habitat relationships of terrestrial vertebrates.

Madison: University of Wisconsin Press. 470 pp.

Goerndt, D.L. 1983. Merriam's turkey habitat in relation to grazing and timber management of a mixed conifer forest in southcentral New Mexico. M.S. Thesis. New Mexico State University, Las Cruces. 96 pp.

Goerndt, D.L., S.D. Schemnitz, and W.D. Zeedyk. 1985. Managing common watercress and spring/seeps for Merriam's turkey in New Mexico. Wildl. Soc. Bull. 13(3):297–301.

Gonzalez, D. 1982. Hawaiian gobbler. Turkey Call 9(6):10–13.

Good, H.G., and L.C. Webb. 1940. Spring foods of the wild turkey in Alabama. Alabama Game and Fish News 12(3):3–4, 13.

Goodrum, P.D., D.W. Lay, E.G. Marsh, A.J. Nicholson, F.S. Henika, et al. 1945. Principal game birds and mammals of Texas: their distribution and management. Austin: Texas Game, Fish and Oyster Commission. 149 pp.

Gore, H.G. 1969. Exploitation and restoration of turkey in Texas. Proc. Ann. Conf. Southeast. Assoc. Game and Fish Comm. 23:37–45.

———. 1973. Land-use practices and Rio Grande turkeys in Texas. Pages 253–262 in G.C. Sanderson and H.C. Schultz, eds., Wild turkey management: current problems and programs. Columbia: The Missouri Chapter of The Wildlife Society and University of Missouri Press. 355 pp.

Gottschalk, K.W. 1986. Changes in herbaceous ground cover and woody regeneration in fenced and unfenced oak-hickory forest stands following gypsy moth defoliation and timber harvesting. Page 162 in International congress of ecology. 71st Annual Meeting, Ecological Society of America. Syracuse: State University of New York and Syracuse University. 377 pp.

———. 1987. Prevention: the silvicultural alternative. Pages 92–104 in S. Fosbroke and R.R. Hicks, Jr., eds., Coping with the gypsy moth in the new frontier: a workshop for forest managers. Morgantown: West Virginia University Books. 153 pp.

Gould, F.W. 1962. Texas plants—a checklist and ecological summary. Texas Agric. Exp. Sta. Misc. Publ. 585. 112 pp.

Gould, J. 1856. On a new turkey, *Meleagris mexicana*. Proc. Zool. Soc. London 24:61–63.

Grant, H.G., K.D. Ley, and C.F. Simpson. 1975. Isolation and characterization of a herpesvirus from wild turkeys *(Meleagris gallopavo osceola)* in Florida. J. Wildl. Dis. 11(4):562–565.

Grant, W.L., ed. 1907. Voyages of Samuel de Champlain: 1604–1618. New York: Barnes & Noble Inc. 374 pp.

Graves, W.C. 1975. Wild turkey management in California. Proc. National Wild Turkey Symp. 3:1–5.

Gray, B.T. 1986. Bioenergetics of the wild turkey in Michigan. M.S. Thesis. Michigan State University, East Lansing. 57 pp.

Gray, B.T., and H.H. Prince. 1988. Basal metabolism and energetic cost of thermoregulation in wild turkeys. J. Wildl. Manage. 52(1):133–137.

Green, H.E. 1982. Reproductive behavior of female wild turkeys in northern lower Michigan. J. Wildl. Manage. 46(4):1065–1071.

Green, H.P. 1990. Long term population trends and habitat use by Merriam's turkey *(Meleagris gallopavo merriami)* on summer range in the White Mountains, Arizona. M.S. Thesis. Northern Arizona University, Flagstaff. 50 pp.

Greenwood, R.J., and A.B. Sargeant. 1973. Influence of radio packs on captive mallards and blue-winged teal. J. Wildl. Manage. 37(1):3–9.

Greiner, E.C., and D.J. Forrester. 1979. Prevalence of sporozoites of *Leucocytozoon smithi* in Florida blackflies. J. Parasitol. 65(2):324–326.

Grenon, A.G. 1986. Habitat use by wild turkeys reintroduced in southeastern Michigan. M.S. Thesis. The University of Michigan, Ann Arbor. 48 pp.

Gribben, K.J. 1986. Population estimates for the wild turkey in east-central Mississippi. M.S. Thesis. Mississippi State University, Mississippi State. 95 pp.

Grier, J.W. 1984. Biology of animal behavior. St. Louis, MO: Times Mirror/Mosby College Publishing. 693 pp.

Grigg, G.W. 1957. The structure of stored sperm in the hen and the nature of the release mechanism. Poultry Sci. 36(2):450–451.

Guthery, F.S., and S.L. Beasom. 1977. Responses of game and non-game wildlife to predator control in south Texas. J. Range Manage. 30(6): 404–409.

Gutierrez, R.J., R.M. Zink, and S.Y. Yang. 1983. Genic variation, systematic, and biogeographic relationships of some galliform birds. Auk 100(1):33–47.

Gyllensten, U., C. Reuterwall, and N. Ryman. 1979. Genetic variability in Scandinavian populations of willow grouse *(Lagopus lagopus* L.) and rock ptarmigan *(Lagopus mutus* L.). Hereditas 91(2):301.

Haensly, T.F., J.A. Crawford, and S.M. Meyers. 1987. Relationships of habitat structure to nest success of ring-necked pheasants. J. Wildl. Manage. 51(2):421–425.

Hahn, J.T. 1987. Illinois forest statistics, 1985. USDA Forest Service Resour. Bull. NC-103. 101 pp.

Hakluyt, R. 1889. A discourse of western planting: 1584. Hakluyt's Voyage 13(2):175–282.

Hale, E.B., and M.W. Schein. 1962. The behaviour of turkeys. Pages 531–564 in E.S.E. Hafez, ed., The behaviour of domestic animals. London: Bailliere, Tindall, and Cox. 619 pp.

Halls, L.K., ed. 1975. Proc. third national wild turkey symposium. Austin: Texas Parks and Wildl. Dept. 227 pp.

Hammond, J.C. 1944. Lack of water as a cause of loose, slimy gizzard linings accompanying early mortality in poults. Poultry Sci. 23(6):477–480.

Hamrick, W.J., and J.R. Davis. 1971. Summer food items of juvenile wild turkeys. Proc. Ann. Conf. Southeast. Assoc. Game and Fish Comm. 25:85–89.

Hamrum, C.L. 1953. Experiments on the senses of taste and smell in the bob-white quail *(Colinus virginianus virginianus)*. Am. Midl. Nat. 49(3):872–877.

Hanson, G.A. 1984. Ecology of the wild turkey in a farmland environment. Des Moines: Iowa Conservation Commission. Ann. Rep. P-R Proj. W-115-R, Study 6, Job 1. 12 pp. mimeo.

Harbour, D. 1983. Advanced wild turkey hunting and world records. Piscataway, NJ: Winchester Press. 284 pp.

———. 1985. In search of the Gould's. Turkey Call 12(5):10–15.

Hardy, F.C. 1959. Results of stocking wild-trapped and game farm turkeys in Kentucky. Proc. National Wild Turkey Symp. 1:61–65.

Hargrave, L.L. 1970. Feathers from a sand dune cave: a basketmaker cave near Navajo Mountain, Utah. Flagstaff: Museum of Arizona Tech. Series No. 9:1–53.

Harlow, W.M., and E.S. Harrar. 1958. Textbook of dendrology. Fourth ed. New York: McGraw-Hill Book Co. Inc. 561 pp.

Harper, H.T., and W.A. Smith. 1973. California's turkey stocking program. Pages 55–63 in G.C. Sanderson and H.C. Schultz, eds., Wild turkey management: current problems and programs. Columbia: The Missouri Chapter of The Wildlife Society and University of Missouri Press. 355 pp.

Hartman, F.E., and G.A. Wunz. 1974. Did hurricane Agnes hurt our wildlife supply? Pennsylvania Game News. 45(3):44–46.

Hartman, G.F. 1959. Wisconsin's wild turkey project. Proc. National Wild Turkey Symp. 1:22–24.

Hatkin, J.M., W.E. Phillips, Jr., and G.A. Hurst. 1986. Isolation of *Listeria monocytogenes* from an eastern wild turkey. J. Wildl. Dis. 22(1):110–112.

Haucke, H.H. 1975. Winter roost characteristics of the Rio Grande turkey in south Texas. Proc. National Wild Turkey Symp. 3:164–169.

Haucke, H.H., and E.D. Ables. 1972. Characteristics of wild turkey roosts on King Ranch. Texas J. Sci. 23(4):599–600.

Hawkins, R.E., L.D. Martoglio, and G.G. Montgomery. 1968. Cannon-netting deer. J. Wildl. Manage. 32(1):191–195.

Hayden, A.H. 1969. Opportunist—yes, picky—no! Pennsylvania Game News 40(7):25–29.

———. 1979a. Home range and habitat preference of wild turkey broods in northern Pennsylvania. Trans. Northeast. Section, The Wildlife Society 36:76–87.

———. 1979b. Wild turkey food habits and nutritional studies. Harrisburg: Pennsylvania Game Commission. Ann. Rep. 10 pp. mimeo.

———. 1980. Dispersal and movements of wild turkeys in northern Pennsylvania. Trans. Northeast. Section, The Wildlife Society 37:258–265.

———. 1982. Wild turkey habitat preferences. Harrisburg: Pennsylvania Game Commission. Final Rep. Proj. 04030, Job 6. 15 pp. mimeo.

———. 1985. Summer baiting as an indicator of wild turkey population trends and harvest. Proc. National Wild Turkey Symp. 5:245–252.

Hayden, A.H., and E. Nelson. 1963. The effects of starvation and limited rations on reproduction of game-farm wild turkeys. Trans. Northeast. Section, The Wildlife Society 20:1–11.

Hayden, A.H., and G.A. Wunz. 1975. Wild turkey population characteristics in northern Pennsylvania. Proc. National Wild Turkey Symp. 3:131–140.

Hazlewood, R.L. 1965. Carbohydrate metabolism. Pages 313–371 *in* P.D. Sturkie, ed., Avian physiology. Second ed. Ithaca, NY: Comstock Publishing Associates. 766 pp.

Healy, W.M. 1977. Wild turkey winter habitat in West Virginia cherry-maple forests. Trans. Northeast. Section, The Wildlife Society 34:7–12.

———. 1978. Feeding activity of wild turkey poults in relation to ground vegetation and insect abundance. Ph.D. Thesis. West Virginia University, Morgantown. 116 pp.

———. 1981. Habitat requirements of wild turkeys in the southeastern mountains. Pages 24–34 *in* P.T. Bromley and R.L. Carlton, eds., Proc. symposium: Habitat requirements and habitat management for the wild turkey in the southeast. Ellison: Virginia Wild Turkey Foundation. 180 pp.

———. 1985. Turkey poult feeding activity, invertebrate abundance, and vegetation structure. J. Wildl. Manage. 49(2):466–472.

———. 1990. Symposium summary: looking toward 2000. Proc. National Wild Turkey Symp. 6:224–228.

Healy, W.M., and G.B. Healy, eds. 1990. Proc. sixth national wild turkey symposium. Edgefield, SC: National Wild Turkey Federation. 228 pp.

Healy, W.M., R.O. Kimmel, and E.J. Goetz. 1975. Behavior of human imprinted and hen-reared wild turkey poults. Proc. National Wild Turkey Symp. 3:97–107.

Healy, W.M., and E.S. Nenno. 1978. Turkey broods and hairy snoods. Turkey Call 5(3):12–17.

Healy, W.M., and E.S. Nenno. 1980. Growth parameters and sex and age criteria for juvenile eastern wild turkeys. Proc. National Wild Turkey Symp. 4:168–185.

Healy, W.M., and E.S. Nenno. 1983. Minimum maintenance versus intensive management of clearings for wild turkeys. Wildl. Soc. Bull. 11(2):113–120.

Healy, W.M., and E.S. Nenno. 1985. Effect of weather on wild turkey poult survival. Proc. National Wild Turkey Symp. 5:91–101.

Healy, W.M., and J.C. Pack. 1983. Managing seeps for wild turkeys in northern hardwood forest types in West Virginia. Trans. Northeast. Section, The Wildlife Society 40:19–30.

Hecklau, J.D., W.F. Porter, and W.M. Shields. 1982. Feasibility of transplanting wild turkeys into areas of restricted forest cover and high human density. Trans. Northeast. Section, The Wildlife Society 39:96–104.

Heisey, D.M., and T.K. Fuller. 1985. Evaluation of survival and cause-specific mortality rates using telemetry data. J. Wildl. Manage. 40(3):668–674.

Heitschmidt, R.K., S.L. Dowhower, and J.W. Walker. 1987. 14 vs. 42 paddock rotational grazing: aboveground biomass dynamics, forage production, and harvest efficiency. J. Range Manage. 40(3):216–223.

Hellwig, W. 1972. Das wilde Truthuhn in unseren Revieren (the wild turkey in our hunting grounds). Munchen: Die Pirsch, BLV Publ. Soc. 5:103–104.

Helm-Bychowski, K.M., and A.C. Wilson. 1986. Rates of nuclear DNA evolution in pheasant-like birds: Evidence from restriction maps. Proc. National Acad. Sci. 83(3):688–692.

Hendricks, D.M. 1985. Arizona soils. Tucson: University of Arizona, College of Agriculture. 244 pp.

Hengel, D.A., and S.H. Anderson. 1990. Habitat use, diet, and reproduction of Merriam's turkeys near Laramie Peak, Wyoming. Laramie: Wyoming Coop. Fish and Wildl. Res. Unit., University Wyoming. Final Rep. 220 pp.

Henry, V.G. 1969. Predation on dummy nests of ground nesting birds in the southern Appalachians. J. Wildl. Manage. 33(1):169–172.

Hensler, G.L., and J.D. Nichols. 1981. The Mayfield method of estimating nesting success: a model, estimators and simulation results. Wilson Bull. 93(1):42–53.

Hensley, T.S., and J.R. Cain. 1979. Prevalence of certain antibodies to selected disease-causing agents in wild turkeys in Texas. Avian Dis. 23(1):62–69.

Hess, E.H. 1972. "Imprinting" in a natural laboratory. Sci. Am. 227(2):24–31.

Hestbeck, J.B., and R.A. Malecki. 1989. Estimated survival rates of Canada geese within the Atlantic Flyway. J. Wildl. Manage. 53(1):91–96.

Hewitt, O.H., ed. 1967. The wild turkey and its management. Washington, DC: The Wildlife Society. 589 pp.

Hibben, C.R., and M.L. Daughtrey. 1988. Dogwood anthracnose in northeastern United States. Plant Dis. 72(3):199–203.

Hightower, B.G., V.W. Lehman, and R.B. Eads. 1953. Ectoparasites from mammals and birds on a quail preserve. J. Mammal. 34(2):268–271.

Hillerman, J.P., F.H. Kratzer, and W.O. Wilson. 1953. Food passage through chickens and turkeys and some regulating factors. Poultry Sci. 32(2):332–335.

Hillestad, H.O. 1973. Movements, behavior, and nesting ecology of the wild turkey in eastern Alabama. Pages 109–123 *in* G.C. Sanderson and H.C. Schultz, eds., Wild turkey management: current problems and programs. Columbia: The Missouri Chapter of The Wildlife Society and University of Missouri Press. 355 pp.

Hillestad, H.O., and D.W. Speake. 1970. Activities of wild turkey hens and poults as influenced by habitat. Proc. Ann. Conf. Southeast. Assoc. Game and Fish Comm. 24:244–251.

Hinde, R.A. 1970. Animal behaviour: a synthesis of ethology and comparative psychology. Second ed. New York: McGraw-Hill Book Co. 876 pp.

Hines, F.D. 1988. Forest statistics for Arkansas' Ouachitas Counties. USDA Forest Service Gen. Tech. Rep. SO-137. 28 pp.

Hines, F.D., and D.F. Bertelson. 1987. Forest statistics for east Oklahoma counties, 1986. USDA Forest Service Resour. Bull. SO-121. 57 pp.

Hoffman, D.M. 1962. The wild turkey in eastern Colorado. Denver: Colorado Game and Fish Department Tech. Bull. 12. 47 pp.

———. 1968. Roosting sites and habits of Merriam's turkeys in Colorado. J. Wildl. Manage. 32(4):859–866.

———. 1973. Some effects of weather and timber management on Merriam's turkeys in Colorado. Pages 263–271 *in* G.C. Sanderson and H.C. Schultz, eds., Wild turkey management: current problems and programs. Columbia: The Missouri Chapter of The Wildlife Society and University of Missouri Press. 355 pp.

Hoffman, R.W. 1986. Chronology of breeding and nesting activities of wild turkeys in relation to timing of spring hunting seasons. Denver: Colorado Division of Wildlife. Fed. Aid Rep. Proj. 01-03-045 (W-37-R). 34 pp. mimeo.

———. 1990. Chronology of gobbling and nesting activities of Merriam's wild turkeys. Proc. National Wild Turkey Symp. 6:25–31.

Hohn, O. 1961. Endocrine glands, thymus and pineal body. Pages 97–115 *in* A.J. Marshall, ed., Biology and comparative physiology of birds. Academic Press. New York: 468 pp.

Holbrook, H.L. 1952. The Francis Marion turkey project. Proc. Ann. Conf. Southeast. Assoc. Game and Fish Comm. 6:567–574.

———. 1957. The Francis Marion turkey project: a progress report. Proc. Ann. Conf. Southeast. Assoc. Game and Fish Comm. 11:355–363.

———. 1973. Management of wild turkey habitat in southern forest types. Pages 245–252 *in* G.C. Sanderson and H.C. Schultz, eds., Wild turkey management: current problems and programs. Columbia: The Missouri Chapter of The Wildlife Society and University of Missouri Press. 355 pp.

———. 1974. A system for wildlife habitat management on southern national forests. Wildl. Soc. Bull. 2(3):119–123.

———. 1975. Featured species concept—its application to wild turkey management on southern national forests. Proc. National Wild Turkey Symp. 3:118–121.

Holbrook, H.L., and J.C. Lewis. 1967. Management of the eastern turkey in the southern Appalachian and Cumberland Plateau Region. Pages 343–370 *in* O.H. Hewitt, ed., The wild turkey and its management. Washington, DC: The Wildlife Society. 589 pp.

Holbrook, H.T., and M.R. Vaughan. 1985. Influence of roads on turkey mortality. J. Wildl. Manage. 49(3):611–614.

Holbrook, H.T., M.R. Vaughan, and P.T. Bromley. 1985. Wild turkey management on domesticated pine forests. Proc. National Wild Turkey Symp. 5:253–258.

Holbrook, H.T., M.R. Vaughan, and P.T. Bromley. 1987. Wild turkey habitat preferences and recruitment in intensively managed Piedmont forests. J. Wildl. Manage. 51(1):182–187.

Holder, T.H., coord. 1951. A survey of Arkansas game. Little Rock: Arkansas Game and Fish Commission. Fed. Aid Publ. Proj. 11-R. 155 pp.

Holing, D. 1987. Hawaii: the eden of endemism. Nat. Conservancy News 37(1):7–13.

Holling, C.S. 1959. The components of predation as revealed by a study of small mammal predation of the European pine sawfly. Can. Entomol. 91(5):293–320.

Hon, L.T., D.J. Forrester, and L.E. Williams, Jr. 1975. Helminths of wild turkeys in Florida. Proc. Helminthol. Soc. Wash. 42(2):119–127.

Hon, L.T., D.J. Forrester, and L.E. Williams, Jr. 1978. Helminth acquisition by wild turkeys *(Meleagris gallopavo osceola)* in Florida. Proc. Helminthol. Soc. Wash. 45(2):211–218.

Hon, T., D.P. Belcher, B. Mullis, and J.R. Monroe. 1978. Nesting, brood range and reproductive success of an insular turkey population. Proc. Ann. Conf. Southeast. Assoc. Fish and Wildl. Agencies 32:137–149.

Hooper, R.M. 1969. Prescribed burning for laurel and rhododendron control in the southern Appalachians. USDA Forest Service Res. Note SE-116. 6 pp.

Hopkins, C.R. 1981. Dispersal, reproduction, mortality, and habitat utilization of restocked eastern turkeys in east Texas. Ph.D. Thesis. Texas A&M University, College Station. 117 pp.

Hopkins, C.R., D.H. Arner, J.E. Kennamer, and R.D. Clanton. 1980. Movements of turkeys in a high density population in the Mississippi Delta. Proc. National Wild Turkey Symp. 4:272–279.

Hornocker, M.G. 1970. An analysis of mountain lion predation upon mule deer and elk in the Idaho Primitive Area. Wildl. Mono. 21:1–39.

———. 1972. Predator ecology and management—what now? J. Wildl. Manage. 36(2):401–404.

Hough, A.F. 1936. A climax forest community on East Tionesta Creek in northwestern Pennsylvania. Ecology 17(1):9–28.

———. 1965. A twenty-year record of understory vegetational change in a virgin Pennsylvania forest. Ecology 46(3):370–373.

Hough, A.F., and R.D. Forbes. 1943. The ecology and silvics of forests in the high plateaus of Pennsylvania. Ecol. Monographs 13(3):299–320.

Hough, W. 1914. Culture of the ancient Pueblos of the upper Gila river region, New Mexico and Arizona. U.S. National Mus. Bull. 87.

139 pp.

Howard, R., and S.D. Schemnitz. 1988. Kiwi capers—a wild turkey hunt in New Zealand. Turkey Call 15(1):18–21.

Howell, S.F. 1939. The determination of the urea in chicken blood. J. Biol. Chem. 128(2):573–578.

Howerth, E.W. 1985. Salmonellosis in a wild turkey. J. Wildl. Dis. 21(4):433–434.

Howerth, E.W., and N. Rodenroth. 1985. Fatal systemic toxoplasmosis in a wild turkey. J. Wildl. Dis. 21(4):446–449.

Hudson, G.E., P.J. Lanzillotti, and G.D. Edwards. 1959. Muscles of the pelvic limb in galliform birds. Am. Mid. Nat. 61(1):1–67.

Huffaker, C.B. 1958. Experimental studies on predation. II. Dispersion factors and predator-prey oscillations. Hilgardia 27:343–383.

Huffaker, C.B., and C.E. Kennett. 1956. Experimental studies on predation: predation and cyclamen mite population on strawberries in California. Hilgardia 26:191–222.

Huggins, E.J., and C.F. Dauman. 1961. *Mediorhynchus grandis* (Acanthocephala: Gigantorhynchidae) in a wild turkey of South Dakota. J. Parasitol. 47(4,2):30–31.

Humphrey, W.E. 1956. Tectonic framework of northeast Mexico. Trans. Gulf Coast Assoc. Geol. Soc. 6:25–35.

Hurst, G.A. 1978. Effects of controlled burning on wild turkey poult food habits. Proc. Ann. Conf. Southeast. Assoc. Fish and Wildl. Agencies 32:30–37.

———. 1980. Histomoniasis in wild turkeys in Mississipi. J. Wildl. Dis. 16(3):357–358.

———. 1981. Habitat requirements of the wild turkey on the southeast Coastal Plain. Pages 2–13 *in* P.T. Bromley and R.L. Carlton, eds., Proc. symposium: Habitat requirements and habitat management for the wild turkey in the southeast. Elliston: Virginia Wild Turkey Foundation. 180 pp.

———. 1988. Population estimates for the wild turkey on Tallahala Wildlife Management Area. Jackson: Mississippi Dept. Conservation Completion Rep. P-R Proj. W-48, Study 21. 46 pp.

Hurst, G.A., and C.N. Owen. 1980. Effects of mowing on arthropod density and biomass as related to wild turkey brood habitat. Proc. National Wild Turkey Symp. 4:225–232.

Hurst, G.A., and W.E. Poe. 1985. Amino acid levels and patterns in wild turkey poults and their food items in Mississippi. Proc. National Wild Turkey Symp. 5:133–143.

Hurst, G.A., and W.E. Poe. 1989a. Poult food habits studied. Turkitat 7(2):4.

Hurst, G.A. and W.E. Poe. 1989b. Fire and wild turkey food. Turkey Call 16(5):40–41.

Hurst, G.A., and W.E. Poe. 1989c. Food habits of wild turkey poults on a 2 year old loblolly pine plantation. Unpubl. Rep. Columbus, MS: Weyerhaeuser Co.

Hurst, G.A., and B.D. Stringer, Jr. 1975. Food habits of wild turkey poults in Mississippi. Proc. National Wild Turkey Symp. 3:76–85.

Hurt, J.J., R.A. Lock, and K. Menzel. 1973. Movement of Merriam's turkey in the pine ridge of Nebraska. Pages 101–107 *in* G.C. Sanderson and H.C. Schultz, eds., Wild turkey management: current problems and programs. Columbia: The Missouri Chapter of The Wildlife Society and University of Missouri Press. 355 pp.

Hyde, K.M., and J.D. Newsom. 1973. A study of a wild turkey population in the Atchafalaya River basin of Louisiana. Proc. Ann. Conf. Southeast. Assoc. Game and Fish Comm. 27:103–113.

Ignatoski, F.J. 1973. Status of wild turkeys in Michigan. Pages 49–53 *in* G.C. Sanderson and H.C. Schultz, eds., Wild turkey management: current problems and programs. Columbia: The Missouri Chapter of The Wildlife Society and University of Missouri Press. 355 pp.

Inglis, J.M. 1964. A history of vegetation on the Rio Grande Plain. Austin: Texas Parks and Wildl. Dep. Bull. No. 45. 122 pp.

Jackson, A.S. 1945. Brazos Clear Fork wildlife development. U.S. Dept. Interior, Fish and Wildl. Serv., Pittman-Robertson Quart.

5(4):157–158.

Jackson, D. 1988. The wild turkey in Iowa, 1988. Ann. Midwest Deer and Turkey Study Group 13:162–166.

Jacobsen, T.E. 1963. The history and status of the wild turkey in North Dakota, 1951–1963. Bismark: North Dakota State Game and Fish Dept. Proj. W-67-R-2, P-R Rep. 38 pp.

Jacobson, H.A., and G.A. Hurst. 1979. Prevalence of parasitism by *Amblyomma americanum* on wild turkey poults as influenced by prescribed burning. J. Wildl. Dis. 15(1):43–47.

Jahn, L.R. 1973. Summary: needs and opportunities for managing turkey populations. Pages 317–324 *in* G.C. Sanderson and H.C. Schultz, eds., Wild turkey management: current problems and programs. Columbia: The Missouri Chapter of The Wildlife Society and University of Missouri Press. 355 pp.

James, D., L.G. Fooks, and J.R. Preston. 1983. Success of wild-trapped compared to captivity-raised birds in restoring wild turkey populations to northwestern Arkansas. Proc. Arkansas Acad. Sci. 37:38–41.

James, F.C. 1970. Geographic size variation in birds and its relationship to climate. Ecology 51(3):365–390.

———. 1983. Environmental component of morphological differentiation in birds. Science 221(4606):184–186.

Jameson, J.F., ed. 1909. Narratives of New Netherland 1609–1664. New York: Barnes and Noble Inc. 478 pp.

Jansen, V. 1959. Summary of 1958 Michigan turkey populations. Proc. National Wild Turkey Symp. 1:19.

Jantzen, R.A. 1959. Research needs for Merriam's turkey in Arizona. Proc. National Wild Turkey Symp. 1:183–191.

Jantzen, R.A., and D. McDonald. 1967. Merriam's turkey management. Pages 493-534 *in* O.H. Hewitt, ed., The wild turkey and its management. Washington DC: The Wildlife Society. 589 pp.

Jenkins, D., A. Watson, and G.R. Miller. 1963. Population studies on red grouse, *Lagopus lagopus scoticus* (Lath.) in north-east Scotland. J. Anim. Ecol. 32(3):317–376.

Jensen, L.S., H.C. Saxena, and J. McGinnis. 1963. Nutritional investigations with turkey hens. 4. Quantitative requirements for calcium. Poultry Sci. 42(3):604–607.

Jensen, L.S., R.K. Wagstaff, J. McGinnis, and F. Parks. 1964. Further studies on high calcium diets for turkey hens. Poultry Sci. 43(6):1577–1581.

Jessup, D.A., A.J. DaMassa, R. Lewis, and K.R. Jones. 1983. *Mycoplasma gallisepticum* infection in wild-type turkeys living in close contact with domestic fowl. J. Am. Vet. Med. Assoc. 183(11):1245–1247.

Johnson, A.S. 1970. Biology of the raccoon in Alabama. Auburn Exp. Sta. Bull. 402. 148 pp.

Johnson, B.C. 1959. History of turkey restoration in Mississippi and its effect on present management. Proc. National Wild Turkey Symp. 1:65–69.

Johnson, E.P., and C.J. Lange. 1939. Blood alterations in typhlohepatitis of turkeys, with notes on the disease. J. Parasitol. 25(2):157–167.

Johnson, E.P., G.W. Underhill, J.A. Cox, and W.L. Threlkeld. 1938. A blood protozoan of turkeys transmitted by *Simulium nigroparvum* (Twinn). Am. J. Hygiene 27(3):649–665.

Johnson, F.A., J.E. Hines, F. Montalbano III, and J.D. Nichols. 1986. Effects of liberalized harvest regulations on wood ducks in the Atlantic Flyway. Wildl. Soc. Bull. 14(4):383–388.

Johnson, P.S., C.D. Dale, and K.R. Davidson. 1986. Planting northern red oak in the Missouri Ozarks: a prescription. Northern J. Appl. Forestry 3(1):66–68.

Johnson, R.N. 1971. Comparative survival of radio-marked and non-radio-marked pen-reared juvenile cock pheasants released into the wild. St. Paul: Minnesota Dept. Natural Resources. Quart. Prog. Rep. 31(1):23–32.

Johnston, M.C. 1963. Past and present grasslands of southern Texas and northeastern Mexico. Ecology 44(3):456–466.

Jolles, J., I.M. Ibrahimi, E.M. Prager, F. Schoentgen, P. Jolles, and A.C. Wilson. 1979. Amino acid sequence of pheasant lysozyme. Evolutionary change affecting processing of prelysozyme. Biochemistry 18(13):2744–2752.

Jonas, R.J. 1966. Merriam's turkey in southeastern Montana. Helena: Montana Fish and Game Dept. Tech. Bull. 3. 36 pp.

———. 1968. Adverse weather affects Merriam's turkey reproduction in Montana. J. Wildl. Manage. 32(4):987–989.

Jones, K.H. 1981. Effects of grazing and timber management on Merriam's turkey habitat in mixed conifer vegetation of southcentral New Mexico. M.S. Thesis. New Mexico State University, Las Cruces. 62 pp.

Judd, S.D. 1905. The grouse and wild turkeys of the United States, and their economic value. U.S. Dept. Agric., Biol. Surv. Bull. 24. 55 pp.

Juhn, M., and P.C. Harris. 1958. Molt of capon feathering with prolactin. Proc. Soc. Exp. Biol. and Med. 98(3):669–672.

Jungherr, E. 1948. Avian monocytosis. Pages 623–636 *in* H.E. Biester and L.H. Schwarte, eds., Diseases of poultry. Second ed. Ames: Iowa State College Press. 1176 pp.

Kalmbacher, R.S. 1976. Management factors affecting establishment and productivity of birdsfoot trefoil-tall fescue in woodland clearings. Ph.D. Thesis. Pennsylvania State University, University Park. 71 pp.

Kaplan, E.L., and P. Meier. 1958. Nonparametric estimation from incomplete observations. J. Am. Stat. Assoc. 53(282):457–481.

Kare, M.R. 1965. The special senses. Pages 406–446 *in* P.D. Sturkie, ed., Avian physiology. Second ed. Ithaca, NY: Comstock Publishing Associates. 766 pp.

Kare, M.R., and J. Beily. 1948. The toxicity of sodium chloride and its relation to water intake in baby chicks. Poultry Sci. 27(6):751–758.

Kare, M.R., and W. Medway. 1959. Discrimination between carbohydrates by the fowl. Poultry Sci. 38(5):1119–1127.

Kauffman, H.H. 1962. Pennsylvania wild turkeys in Germany. Pennsylvania Game News 33(5):27–29.

Kaupp, B.F. 1923. The respirations of fowls. Vet. Med. 18(1):36–40.

Keler, St. von. 1958. The genera *Oxylipeurus* Mjoberg and *Splendoroffula* Clay and Meinertzhagen (Mallophaga). Deutsche Entomologische Zeitschrift n. s. 5(3/4):299–362.

Kelley, R.L., G.A. Hurst, and D.E. Steffen. 1988. Home ranges of wild turkey gobblers in central Mississippi. Proc. Ann. Conf. Southeast. Assoc. Fish and Wildl. Agencies 42:470–475.

Kellogg, F.E., T.H. Eleazer, and T.R. Colvin. 1978. Transmission of blackhead from junglefowl to turkey. Proc. Ann. Conf. Southeast. Assoc. Fish and Wildl. Agencies 32:378–379.

Kellogg, F.E., A.K. Prestwood, R.R. Gerrish, and G.L. Doster. 1969. Wild turkey ectoparasites collected in the southeastern United States. J. Med. Entomol. 6(3):329–330.

Kellogg, F.E., and W.M. Reid. 1970. Bobwhites as possible reservoir hosts for blackhead in wild turkeys. J. Wildl. Manage. 34(1):155–159.

Kelly, G. 1975. Indexes for aging eastern wild turkeys. Proc. National Wild Turkey Symp. 3:205–209.

Kelly, T. 1973. Tenth legion. Monroe, LA: Spur Enterprises. 119 pp.

Kendeigh, S.C. 1934. The role of environment in the life of birds. Ecol. Monographs 4(3):299–417.

Kennamer, J.E. 1970. A study of reproduction and movement of the eastern wild turkey in the Delta area of Mississippi. Ph.D. Thesis. Mississippi State University, Mississippi State. 49 pp.

———., ed. 1986a. Guide to the American wild turkey. Edgefield, SC: National Wild Turkey Federation. 189 pp.

———. 1986b. Meat specialist reveals preliminary tests data. Turkitat 4(1):4.

———. 1988a. Eggs begin the new generation. Turkey Call 15(2):26–27.

———. 1988b. Pen-raised turkeys a threat to wild populations. Turkey Call 15(5):22–23.

Kennamer, J.E., and D.H. Arner. 1967. Winter food available to the wild turkey in a hardwood forest. Proc. Ann. Conf. Southeast.

Assoc. Game and Fish Comm. 21:123–129.

Kennamer, J.E., D.H. Arner, C.R. Hopkins, and R.C. Clanton. 1975. Productivity of the eastern wild turkey in the Mississippi Delta. Proc. National Wild Turkey Symp. 3:41–47.

Kennamer, J.E., J.R. Gwaltney, and K.R.Sims. 1980a. Food habits of the eastern wild turkey on an area intensively managed for pine in Alabama. Proc. National Wild Turkey Symp. 4:246–250.

Kennamer, J.E., J.R. Gwaltney, and K.R. Sims. 1980b. Habitat preferences of eastern wild turkeys on an area intensively managed for pine in Alabama. Proc. National Wild Turkey Symp. 4:240–245.

Kennamer, J.E., J.R. Gwaltney, K.R. Sims, and A. Hosey, Jr. 1981. Effects of forest management on wild turkeys in the coastal plain regions. Pages 131–136 *in* P.T. Bromley and R.L. Carlton, eds., Proc. symposium: Habitat requirements and habitat management for the wild turkey in the southeast. Elliston: Virginia Wild Turkey Foundation. 180 pp.

Kennamer, J.E., and M.C. Kennamer, eds. 1985. Proc. fifth national wild turkey symposium. Edgefield, SC: National Wild Turkey Federation. 332 pp.

Kennamer, J.E., and M.C. Kennamer. 1990. Current status and distribution of the wild turkey, 1989. Proc. National Wild Turkey Symp. 6:1–12.

Kennamer, J.E., and W.H. Lunceford, Jr. 1973. Armadillos tested as potential egg predators of wild turkeys in the Mississippi Delta. Pages 175–177 *in* G.C. Sanderson and H.C. Schultz, eds., Wild turkey management: current problems and programs. Columbia: The Missouri Chapter of The Wildlife Society and University of Missouri Press. 355 pp.

Kennamer, M.C., R.E. Brenneman, and J.E. Kennamer. 1992. Guide to the American wild turkey. Part 1: Status—numbers, distribution, seasons, harvest, and regulations. Edgefield, SC: National Wild Turkey Federation. 149 pp.

Keith, L.B. 1963. Wildlife's ten-year cycle. Madison: University Wisconsin Press. 201 pp.

Kilpatrick, H.J., T.P. Husband, and C.A. Pringle. 1988. Winter roost site characteristics of eastern wild turkeys. J. Wildl. Manage. 52(3):461–463.

Kimmel, F.G., and P.J. Zwank. 1985. Habitat selection and nesting responses to spring flooding by eastern wild turkey hens in Louisiana. Proc. National Wild Turkey Symp. 5:155–171.

Kimmel, V.L. 1983. Response of the eastern wild turkey to a tape-recorded chick call. M.S. Thesis. Pennsylvania State University, University Park. 70 pp.

Kimmel, V.L., and E.W. Kurzejeski. 1985. Illegal hen kill—a major turkey mortality factor. Proc. National Wild Turkey Symp. 5:55–67.

Kimmel, V.L., and W.M. Tzilkowski. 1986. Eastern wild turkey response to a tape-recorded chick call. Wildl. Soc. Bull. 14(1):55–58.

Kimura, M. 1983. The neutral theory of molecular evolution. Cambridge, England: Cambridge University Press. 367 pp.

Kingsley, N.P. 1975. The forest-land owners of New Jersey. USDA Forest Service Resour. Bull. NE-39. 24 pp.

Kingsley, N.P., and D.S. Powell. 1978. The forest resources of Kentucky. USDA Forest Service Resour. Bull. NE-54. 97 pp.

Kingston, N. 1984. Trematodes. Pages 668–690 *in* M.S. Hofstad et al., eds., Diseases of poultry. Eighth ed. Ames: Iowa State University Press. 831 pp.

Kirkham, K.B., and K.L. Carvell. 1980. Effect of improvement cutting and thinnings on the understories of mixed oak and cove hardwood stands. Morgantown: West Virginia University Agric. and For. Exp. Sta. Bull. 673. 17 pp.

Kirkpatrick, R.D., M.R. Roy, G.A. Wise, and L.L. Hardman. 1972. Contents of southern Indiana wild turkey droppings. Proc. Indiana Acad. Sci. 81:165–168.

Kirkpatrick, R.L. 1980. Physiological indices in wildlife management. Pages 99–112 *in* S.D. Schemnitz, ed., Wildlife management techniques manual, Fourth ed. Washington, DC: The Wildlife Society. 686 pp.

Kirschner, N., G.H. Pritham, G.O. Bressler, and S. Gordeuk, Jr. 1951. Composition of normal turkey blood. Poult. Sci. 30(6):875–879.

Kleinholz, L.H., and H. Rahn. 1940. The distribution of intermedin: a new biological method of assay and results of tests under normal and experimental conditions. Anat. Rec. 76(2):157–172.

Kneeling, H.C. 1910. The Indians: my experiences with the Cheyenne Indians. Kansas State Hist. Soc. Colls. 11:306–315.

Knoder, C.E. 1959a. Morphological indicators of heritable wildness in turkeys and their relation to survival. Proc. National Wild Turkey Symp. 1:116–137.

———. 1959b. An aging technique for juvenal wild turkeys based on the rate of primary feather molt and growth. Proc. National Wild Turkey Symp. 1:159–176.

Knowlton, F. 1972. Preliminary interpretations of coyote population mechanics with some management implications. J. Wildl. Manage. 36(2):369–382.

Koeln, G.T. 1980. A computer technique for analyzing radio-telemetry data. Proc. National Wild Turkey Symp. 4:262–271.

Koerth, B.H., W.M. Webb, F.C. Bryant, and F.S. Guthery. 1983. Cattle trampling of simulated ground nests under short duration and continuous grazing. J. Range Manage. 36(3):385–386.

Korschgen, L.J. 1967. Feeding habits and food. Pages 137–198 *in* O.H. Hewitt, ed., The wild turkey and its management. Washington, DC: The Wildlife Society. 589 pp.

———. 1973. April foods of wild turkeys in Missouri. Pages 143–150 *in* G.C. Sanderson and H.C. Schultz, eds., Wild turkey management: current problems and programs. Columbia: The Missouri Chapter of The Wildlife Society and University of Missouri Press. 355 pp.

Kothmann, H.G. 1971. High-rise roosts. Texas Parks and Wildl. 29(6):26–29.

Kothmann, H.G., and G.W. Litton. 1975. Utilization of man-made roosts by turkey in west Texas. Proc. National Wild Turkey Symp. 3:159–163.

Kothmann, M.M. 1975. Vegetation and livestock responses to grazing management on the Texas Experimental Ranch. Texas Agric. Exp. Sta. Prog. Rep. 3310. 4 pp.

Kozicky, E.L. 1942. Pennsylvania wild turkey food habits based on droppings analysis. Pa. Game News 13(8):10–11, 28–29, 31.

———. 1948. Life history and management of the wild turkey *(Meleagris gallopavo silvestris)* in Pennsylvania. Ph.D. Thesis. Pennsylvania State College, University Park. 258 pp.

Kramer, R.J., R.L. Walker, T. Telfer, and T. Sutterfield. 1985. Hunting in Hawaii. Honolulu: Division Forestry and Wildlife. 28 pp.

Krementz, D.G., M.J. Conroy, J.E. Hines, and H.F. Percival. 1988. The effects of hunting on survival rates of American black ducks. J. Wildl. Manage. 52(2):214–226.

Krementz, D.G., J.D. Nichols, and J.E. Hines. 1989. Postfledging survival of European starlings. Ecology 70(3):646–655.

Kubisiak, J., N. Paisley, and B. Wright. 1991. Wisconsin 1991 wild turkey studies report: research update. Proc. Midwest Deer and Wild Turkey Study Group. Des Moines: Iowa Dept. Nat. Resour. 174 pp.

Kulowiec, T.G. 1986. Habitat utilization, movements, and population characteristics of resident northern Michigan turkeys. M.S. Thesis. Michigan State University, East Lansing. 124 pp.

Kulowiec, T.G., and J.B. Haufler. 1985. Winter and dispersal movements of wild turkeys in Michigan's northern lower peninsula. Proc. National Wild Turkey Symp. 5:145–153.

Kurzejeski, E.W., and J.B. Lewis. 1985. Application of PATREC modeling to wild turkey management in Missouri. Proc. National Wild Turkey Symp. 5:269–283.

Kurzejeski, E.W., and J.B. Lewis. 1990. Home ranges, movements, and habitat use of wild turkey hens in northern Missouri. Proc. National Wild Turkey Symp. 6:67–71.

Kurzejeski, E.W., L.D. Vangilder, and J.B. Lewis. 1987. Survival of wild turkey hens in north Missouri. J. Wildl. Manage. 51(1):188–193.

LaCava, J., and J. Hughes. 1984. Determining minimum viable population levels. Wildl. Soc. Bull. 12(4):370–376.

Lambert, E.P. 1986. Home range, movements, and habitat use of the eastern wild turkey in commercially managed pine forests of southeast Louisiana. M.S. Thesis. Southeastern Louisiana University, Hammond. 75 pp.

Lambert, E.P., W.P. Smith, and R.D. Teitelbaum. 1990. Wild turkey use of dairy farm-timberland habitats in southeastern Louisiana. Proc. National Wild Turkey Symp. 6:51–60.

Lancaster, J.E., and J. Fabricant. 1988. The history of avian medicine in the United States. IX. Events in the history of avian mycoplasmosis 1905–70. Avian Dis. 32(4):607–623.

Lancia, R.A., and W.D. Klimstra. 1978. Contents of wild turkey droppings collected in winter on Crab Orchard National Wildlife Refuge. Trans. Illinois Acad. Sci. 71(4):422–426.

Lang, L., S. Liscinsky, and P. Donahue. 1982. Cutting intensity in a pole stage northern hardwood stand. Harrisburg: Pennsylvania Game Commission. Final Rep. Proj. 04050. 14 pp. mimeo.

Latham, R.M. 1947. Differential ability of male and female game birds to withstand starvation and climatic extremes. J. Wildl. Manage. 11(2):139–149.

———. 1956. Complete book of the wild turkey. Harrisburg, PA: The Stackpole Co. 265 pp.

———. 1958. Factors affecting distribution and abundance of wild turkeys in Pennsylvania. Ph.D. Thesis. Pennsylvania State University, University Park. 154 pp.

———. 1959. Some considerations concerning the emergency winter feeding of wild turkeys in northern states. Trans. N. Am. Wildl. and Nat. Resour. Conf. 24:414–421.

———. 1967. Turkey hunting. Pages 535–548 in O.H. Hewitt, ed., The wild turkey and its management. Washington, DC: The Wildlife Society. 589 pp.

Launchbaugh, J.L., C.E. Owensby, F.L. Schwartz, and L.R. Corah. 1978. Grazing management to meet nutritional and functional needs of livestock. Int. Rangeland Congr. 1:541–546.

Lavine, S.A., and V. Scuro. 1984. Wonders of turkeys. New York: Dodd, Mead & Co. 62 pp.

Lawson, J. 1709. A new voyage to Carolina. London: John Lawson. 258 pp.

Lay, D.W. 1959. Brief summary of turkey range management. Proc. National Wild Turkey Symp. 1:97–100.

Laymon, S.A., and R.H. Barrett. 1986. Developing and testing habitat-capability models: pitfalls and recommendations. Pages 87–91 in J. Verner, M.L. Morrison, and C.J. Ralph, eds., Wildlife 2000: modeling habitat relationships of terrestrial vertebrates. Madison: University of Wisconsin Press. 470 pp.

Lazarus, J.E., and W.F. Porter. 1985. Nest habitat selection by wild turkeys in Minnesota. Proc. National Wild Turkey Symp. 5:67–81.

Lea, T. 1957. The King Ranch. 2 vols. New York: Little, Brown and Co. 838 pp.

Lee, L. 1959. The present status of the wild turkey in New Mexico. Proc. National Wild Turkey Symp. 1:11–18.

Legion, J.S. 1946. History and management of Merriam's wild turkey. Santa Fe: New Mexico Game and Fish Commission. 84 pp.

Lehmann, V.W. 1957. Conservation and management of game. Pages 761–766 in T. Lea, The King Ranch. Vol. 2. New York: Little, Brown and Co. 838 pp.

———. 1960. Problems of maintaining game on ranges subjected to brush control. Proc. World Forestry Congr. 3:1807–1809.

———. 1969. Forgotten legions—sheep in the Rio Grande Plain of Texas. El Paso: Texas Western Press. 226 pp.

Leidlich, D.W., D.R. Lockwood, S.D. Schemnitz, D.H. Sutcliffe, and W. Haussamen. 1991. Merriam's wild turkey nesting ecology in the Sacramento Mountains, south-central New Mexico. Las Cruces: New Mexico Agric. Exp. Sta. Res. Bull. 757. 38 pp.

Leighton, A.T., Jr., and R.N. Shoffner. 1961. Effect of light regime and age on reproduction of turkeys. 2. Restricted vs. unrestricted light. Poultry Sci. 40(4):871–884.

Leopold, A.S. 1931. Report on a game survey of the north central states. Sporting Arms and Ammunition Manufacturers' Institute. 299 pp.

———. 1933. Game management. New York: Charles Scribner's Sons. 481 pp.

———. 1943a. The molts of young wild and domestic turkeys. Condor 45(4):133–145.

———. 1943b. Wild turkey management in Missouri. Jefferson City: Missouri Dept. Conservation. Final Rep. P-R Proj. 1-5-R. 51 pp. mimeo.

———. 1944. The nature of heritable wildness in turkeys. Condor 46(4):133–197.

———. 1948. The wild turkeys of Mexico. Trans. N. Am. Wildl. Conf. 13:393–401.

———. 1950. Vegetation zones of Mexico. Ecology 31(4):507–518.

———. 1953. Intestinal morphology of gallinaceous birds in relation to food habits. J. Wildl. Manage. 17(2):197–203.

———. 1959. Wildlife of Mexico. The game birds and mammals. Berkeley: University of California Press. 568 pp.

———. 1964. Predator and rodent control in the United States. Trans. N. Am. Wildl. and Nat. Resour. Conf. 29:27–49.

Leopold, B.D. 1989. Mississippi's mammal predators: conflict or challenge. Pages 5–6 in Predators: they're part of the picture. Mississippi Wildl. Fed. Conserv. Yearbook.

Levasseur, A. 1829. Lafayette in America in 1824–1825. Vol. II. Philadelphia: Carey and Lea. 265 pp.

Lever, C. 1987. Naturalized birds of the world. Harlow, Essex, England: Longman Scientific & Technical. 615 pp.

Lewin, V. 1971. Exotic game birds of the Puu Waawaa Ranch, Hawaii. J. Wildl. Manage. 35(1):141–155.

Lewis, J.B. 1959. Wild turkey restoration in Missouri—attempts and methods. Proc. National Wild Turkey Symp. 1:70–74.

———. 1961. Wild turkeys in Missouri, 1940–1960. Trans. N. Am. Wildl. and Nat. Resour. Conf. 26:505–513.

———. 1967. Management of the eastern turkey in the Ozarks and bottomland hardwoods. Pages 371–408 in O.H. Hewitt, ed., The wild turkey and its management. Washington, DC: The Wildlife Society. 589 pp.

———. 1975. Evaluation of spring turkey seasons in Missouri. Proc. National Wild Turkey Symp. 3:176–183.

———. 1980. Fifteen years of wild turkey trapping, banding, and recovery data in Missouri. Proc. National Wild Turkey Symp. 4:24–31.

———. 1987. Success story: wild turkey. Pages 31–43 in H. Kallman, et al., eds. Restoring America's wildlife 1937–1987. Washington, DC: U.S. Dept. Interior, Fish and Wildl. Serv. 394 pp.

Lewis, J.B., and R.P. Breitenbach. 1966. Breeding potential of subadult wild turkey gobblers. J. Wildl. Manage. 30(3):618–622.

Lewis, J.B., and G. Kelly. 1973. Mortality associated with the spring hunting of gobblers. Pages 295–299 in G.C. Sanderson and H.C. Schultz, eds., Wild turkey management: current problems and programs. Columbia: The Missouri Chapter of The Wildlife Society and University of Missouri Press. 355 pp.

Lewis, J.B., and E.W. Kurzejeski. 1984. Wild turkey productivity and poult mortality in north central Missouri. Jefferson City: Missouri Dept. Conservation. Final Rep. P-R Proj. W-13-R-38. 41 pp. mimeo.

Lewis, J.B., D.A. Murphy, and J. Ehrenreich. 1964. Effects of burning dates on vegetative production on Ozark forests. Proc. Ann. Conf. Southeast. Assoc. Game and Fish Comm. 18:63–72.

Lewis, J.C. 1962. Wild turkeys in Allegan County, Michigan. M.S. Thesis. Michigan State University, East Lansing. 35 pp.

———. 1963. Observations on the winter range of wild turkeys in Michigan. J. Wildl. Manage. 27(1):98–102.

———. 1964. Populations of wild turkeys in relation to fields. Proc. Ann. Conf. Southeast. Assoc. Game and Fish Comm. 18:49–56.

———. 1967. Physical characteristics and physiology. Pages 45–72 in O.H. Hewitt, ed., The wild turkey and its management. Washington, DC: The Wildlife Society. 589 pp.

———. 1973. The world of the wild turkey. Philadelphia, PA: J.B. Lippincott Co. 158 pp.

Lewontin, R.C. 1974. The genetic basis of evolutionary change. New York: Columbia University Press. 346 pp.

Ligon, J.S. 1946. History and management of Merriam's wild turkey. Santa Fe: New Mexico Game and Fish Commission, University of New Mexico Publ. Biol. 1. 84 pp.

Lindzey, J.S. 1967a. Highlights of management. Pages 245–260 *in* O.H. Hewitt, ed., The wild turkey and its management. Washington, DC: The Wildlife Society. 589 pp.

———. 1967b. A look to the future. Pages 549–552 *in* O.H. Hewitt, ed., The wild turkey and its management. Washington, DC: The Wildlife Society. 589 pp.

Lindzey, J.S., and D.D. Wanless. 1973. Problems in wild turkey management and research. Pages 229–233 *in* G.C. Sanderson and H.C. Schultz, eds., Wild turkey management: current problems and programs. Columbia: The Missouri Chapter of The Wildlife Society and University of Missouri Press. 355 pp.

Linnaes, C. 1758. Systema natura. Tenth ed. Holimar. 376 pp.

Lisano, M.E., and J.E. Kennamer. 1977a. Seasonal variations in plasma testosterone level in male eastern wild turkeys. J. Wildl. Manage. 41(2):184–188.

Lisano, M.E., and J.E. Kennamer. 1977b. Values for several blood parameters in eastern wild turkeys. Poultry Sci. 56(1):157–166.

Liscinsky, S. 1984. Tree seed production. Pennsylvania Game News 55(8):23–25.

Little, T.W. 1980. Wild turkey restoration in "marginal" Iowa habitat. Proc. National Wild Turkey Symp. 4:45–60.

Little, T.W., J.M. Keinzler, and G.A. Hanson. 1990. Effects of fall either-sex hunting on survival in an Iowa wild turkey population. Proc. National Wild Turkey Symp. 6:119–125.

Little, T.W., and K.L. Varland. 1981. Reproduction and dispersal of transplanted wild turkeys in Iowa. J. Wildl. Manage. 45(2):419–427.

Litton, G.W. 1977. Food habits of the Rio Grande turkey in the Permian Basin of Texas. Austin: Texas Parks and Wildlife Dept. Tech. Series No. 18. 22 pp.

Lively, C.E., and M.L. Bright. 1948. The rural population resources of Missouri. Jefferson City: Missouri Agric. Exp. Sta. Res. Bull. 428. 42 pp.

Lobdell, C.H., K.E. Case, and H.S. Mosby. 1972. Evaluation of harvest strategies for a simulated wild turkey population. J. Wildl. Manage. 36(2):493–497.

Locke, L.N. 1987. Aspergillosis. Pages 145–150 *in* M. Friend, ed., Field guide to wildlife diseases: general field procedures and diseases of migratory birds. U.S. Dept. Interior, Fish and Wild. Serv. Resour. Publ. 167. 225 pp.

Lockwood, D.R. 1987. Final report on wild turkey investigations. Santa Fe: New Mexico Game and Fish Dept. P-R Proj. W-104-R-27, WP 1, J1. 19 pp. mimeo.

Lockwood, D.R., and D.H. Sutcliffe. 1985. Distribution, mortality, and reproduction of Merriam's turkey in New Mexico. Proc. National Wild Turkey Symp. 5:309–316.

Loftis, D.L. 1988. Regenerating oaks on high quality sites, an update. Pages 199–209 *in* H.C. Smith, A.W. Perkey, and W.E. Kidd, Jr., eds., Proceedings: Guidelines for regenerating Appalachian hardwood stands. Morgantown: West Virginia University Books. 293 pp.

Logan, T.H. 1973. Seasonal behavior of Rio Grande wild turkeys in western Oklahoma. Proc. Ann. Conf. Southeast. Assoc. Game and Fish Comm. 27:74–91.

Long, J.L. 1981. Introduced birds of the world. New York: Universe Books. 528 pp.

Long, K. 1988. American forester. Philadelphia: Running Press. 192 pp.

Loomis, E.C. 1984. External parasites. Pages 586–613 *in* M.S. Hofstad et al., eds., Diseases of poultry. Eighth ed. Ames: Iowa State

University Press. 831 pp.

Lorenz, K.Z. 1937. The companion in the bird's world. Auk 54(3):245–273.

Lotka, A.J. 1925. Elements of physical biology. Baltimore: Williams and Wilkins. 460 pp.

———. 1956. Elements of mathematical biology. New York: Dover. 465 pp.

Lucas, A.M., and P.R. Stettenheim. 1972. Avian anatomy: integument. Parts I & II. U.S. Dept. Agric., Agric. Handbook 362. Michigan State University, East Lansing. 750 pp.

Luckett, L.M. 1980. Management of the wild turkey on national forest lands in North Carolina. Proc. National Wild Turkey Symp. 4:159–167.

Lull, H.W. 1968. A forest atlas of the northeast. USDA Forest Service Northeast. Forest Exp. Sta. 46 pp.

Lund, E.E., and A.M. Chute. 1971a. Histomoniasis in the chukar partridge. J. Wildl. Manage. 35(2):307–315.

Lund, E.E., and A.M. Chute. 1971b. Bobwhite, *Colinus virginianus*, as host for *Heterakis* and *Histomonas*. J. Wildl. Dis. 7(1):70–75.

Lund, E.E., and A.M. Chute. 1972a. Reciprocal responses of eight species of galliform birds and three parasites: *Heterakis gallinarum*, *Histomonas meleagridis*, and *Parahistomonas wenrichi*. J. Parasitol. 58(5):940–945.

Lund, E.E., and A.M. Chute. 1972b. *Heterakis* and *Histomonas* infections in young peafowl, compared to such infections in pheasants, chickens, and turkeys. J. Wildl. Dis. 8(4):352–358.

Lund, E.E., and A.M. Chute. 1972c. The ring-necked pheasant *(Phasianus colchicus torquatus)* as a host for *Heterakis gallinarum* and *Histomonas meleagridis*. Am. Midl. Nat. 87(1):1–7.

Lund, E.E., and A.M. Chute, 1972d. Potential of young and mature guinea fowl in contaminating soil with *Histomonas*-bearing heterakid eggs. Avian Dis. 16(5):1079–1086.

Lund, E.E., and A.M. Chute. 1974. The reproductive potential of *Heterakis gallinarum* in various species of galliform birds: implications for survival of *H. gallinarum* and *Histomonas meleagridis* to recent times. Int. J. Parasitol. 4(5):455–461.

Lund, E.E., A.M. Chute, and G.C. Wilkins. 1975. The wild turkey as a host for *Heterakis gallinarum* and *Histomonas meleagridis*. J. Wildl. Dis. 11(3):376–381.

Luttrell, M.P. 1989. An investigation on the persistence of *Mycoplasma gallisepticum* in an eastern population of wild turkeys. M.S. Thesis. The University of Georgia, Athens. 60 pp.

Lutz, H.J. 1930. The vegetation of Heart's Content, a virgin forest in northwestern Pennsylvania. Ecology 11(1):1–29.

Lutz, R.S., and J.A. Crawford. 1987a. Seasonal use of roost sites by Merriam's wild turkey hens and hen-poult flocks in Oregon. Northwest Sci. 61(3):174–178.

Lutz, R.S., and J.A. Crawford. 1987b. Reproductive success and nesting habitat of Merriam's wild turkeys in Oregon. J. Wildl. Manage. 51(4):783–787.

Lynch, J.E., and H.F. Stafseth. 1954. Electrophoretic studies on the serum proteins of turkeys. II: The composition of pullorum immune turkey serum. Poultry Sci. 33(1):54–61.

MacDonald, D. 1960–64. Wild turkey-perdator relationships. Santa Fe: New Mexico Dept. of Game and Fish. P-R Proj. W-97-R. mimeo.

MacDonald, D., and R.A. Jantzen. 1967. Management of the Merriam's turkey. Pages 493–534 *in* O.H. Hewitt, ed., The wild turkey and its management. Wash., DC: The Wildlife Society. 589 pp.

Mackey, D.L. 1982. Habitat use by broods of Merriam's turkeys in southcentral Washington. M.S. Thesis. Washington State University, Pullman. 87 pp.

———. 1984. Roosting habitat of Merriam's turkeys in south-central Washington. J. Wildl. Manage. 48(4):1377–1382.

Mackey, D.L., and R.J. Jonas. 1982. Seasonal habitat use and food habits of Merriam's turkeys in southcentral Washington. Proc. Western Wild Turkey Workshop 1:99–110.

Madson, J.B. 1975. The crowd goes turkey hunting. Proc. National Wild Turkey Symp. 3:222–227.

Malechek, J.C., and B.M. Smith. 1976. Behavior of range cows in response to winter weather. J. Range Manage. 29(1):9–12.

Mann, W.F., Jr. 1980. Loblolly pine—shortleaf pine. Page 56 *in* F.H. Eyre, ed., Forest cover types of the United States and Canada. Washington, DC: Society of American Foresters. 148 pp.

Manning, P.J., and C.C. Middleton. 1972. Atherosclerosis in wild turkeys: morphologic features of lesions and lipids in serum and aorta. Am. J. Vet. Res. 33(6):1237–1246.

Markley, M.H. 1967. Limiting factors. Pages 199–244 *in* O.H. Hewitt, ed., The wild turkey and its management. Washington, DC: The Wildlife Society. 589 pp.

Marquis, D.A. 1987. Silvicultural techniques for circumventing deer damage. Pages 125–136 *in* Proc. Deer, forestry and agriculture: interactions and strategies for management. Warren, PA: Society of American Foresters. 183 pp.

———. 1988. Guidelines for regenerating cherry-maple stands. Pages 167–188 *in* H.C. Smith, A.W. Perkey, and W.E. Kidd, Jr., eds., Proc.: Guidelines for regenerating Appalachian hardwood stands. Morgantown: West Virginia University Books. 293 pp.

Marquis, D.A., and R. Brenneman. 1981. The impact of deer on forest vegetation in Pennsylvania. USDA Forest Service Gen. Tech. Rep. NE-65. 7 pp.

Marquis, D.A., R.L. Ernst, and S.L. Stout. 1984. Prescribing silvicultural treatments in hardwood stands of the Alleghenies. USDA Forest Service Gen. Tech. Rep. NE-96. 90 pp.

Marsden, S.J., and C.W. Knox. 1937. The breeding of turkeys. Pages 1350–1366 *in* Yearbook of Agriculture, 1937. Washington, DC: U.S. Dept. Agric. U.S. Government Printing Office. 1497 pp.

Marsden, S.J., and J.H. Martin. 1939. Turkey management. First ed. Danville, IL: The Interstate. 708 pp.

Marsden, S.J., and J.H. Martin. 1945. Turkey management. Third ed. Danville, IL: The Interstate. 758 pp.

Marsden, S.J., and J. H. Martin. 1955. Turkey management. Sixth ed. Danville, IL: The Interstate. 999 pp.

Marsh, R.L., C. Carey, and W.R. Dawson. 1984. Substrate concentrations and turnover of plasma glucose during cold exposure in seasonally acclimatized house finches, *Carpodacus mexicanus*. J. Comp. Physiol. B 154(5):469–476.

Marshall, A.J. 1960. Biology and comparative physiology of birds. Vol. II. New York: Academic Press. 468 pp.

Marshall, F.H.A. 1960. The breeding season. Pages 1–42 *in* A.S. Parkes, ed., Marshall's physiology of reproduction. Vol. 1 (Part 1). Third ed. London: Longmans, Green and Co. Ltd. 688 pp.

Martin, A.C., F.H. May, and T.E. Clarke. 1939. Early winter food preferences of the wild turkey on the George Washington National Forest. Trans. N. Am. Wildl. Conf. 4:570–578.

Martin, D.D., and B.S. McGinnes. 1975. Insect availability and use by turkeys in forest clearings. Proc. National Wild Turkey Symp. 3:70–75.

Martin, D.J. 1984. The influence of selected timber management practices on habitat use by wild turkeys in east Texas. M.S. Thesis. Texas A&M University, College Station. 129 pp.

Martin, R.M., M.E. Lisano, and J.E. Kennamer. 1981. Plasma estrogens, total protein, and cholesterol in the female eastern wild turkey. J. Wildl. Manage. 45(3):798–802.

Martin, S.C. 1955. Range problems in the Missouri Ozarks. USDA Forest Service Central States Forest Exp. Sta. Misc. Release 9. 33 pp.

Masters, R.E., and R.E. Thackston. 1985. Restoration and status of the eastern wild turkey in Oklahoma. Proc. National Wild Turkey Symp. 5:317–326.

Matthews, H., and F.H.A. Marshall. 1960. Cyclical changes in the reproductive organs of the lower vertebrates. Pages 156–225 *in* A.S. Parkes, ed., Marshall's physiology of reproduction, Vol. I (Part 1). Third ed. London: Longmans, Green and Co. Ltd. 688 pp.

Matthiessen, P. 1972. The tree where man was born. In conjunction with E. Porter. The African experience. New York: E.P. Dutton & Co. Inc. 247 pp.

Mautz, W. 1986. Wild turkey energy metabolism and the nutritional value of winter foods. Concord: New Hampshire Fish and Game Dept. Fed. Aid Proj. W-75-R-8. mimeo.

Maxfield, B.G., W.M. Reid, and F.A. Hayes. 1963. Gastrointestinal helminths from turkeys in the southeastern United States. J. Wildl. Manage. 27(2):261–271.

Mayfield, H. 1961. Nesting success calculated from exposure. Wilson Bull. 73(3):255–261.

Mayr, E. 1963. Animal species and evolution. Cambridge, MA: Belknap Press. 797 pp.

———. 1970. Populations, species, and evolution. Cambridge, MA: Belknap Press. 453 pp.

McCabe, K.F., and L.D. Flake, 1985. Brood rearing habitat use by wild turkey hens in southcentral South Dakota. Proc. National Wild Turkey Symp. 5:121–131.

McCabe, R.A., and E.L. Kozicky. 1972. A position on predator management. J. Wildl. Manage. 36(2):382–394.

McCartney, M.G. 1952. Total blood and corpuscular volume in turkey hens. Poultry Sci. 31(1):184–185.

McClintock, W.A. 1931. Journal of a trip through Texas and northern Mexico in 1846–1847. Southwest. Hist. Quart. 34(3):231–256.

McCullough, D.R. 1979. The George Reserve deer herd: population ecology of a K-shaped species. Ann Arbor: University of Michigan Press. 271 pp.

———. 1984. Lessons from the George Reserve, Michigan. Pages 211–242 *in* L.K. Halls, ed., White-tailed deer: ecology and management. Harrisburg, PA: Stackpole Books. 870 pp.

McDougal, L.A., M.R. Vaughan, and P.T. Bromley. 1990. Wild turkey and road relationships on a Virginia national forest. Proc. National Wild Turkey Symp. 6:96–106.

McDowell, R.D. 1956. Productivity of the wild turkey in Virginia. Richmond: Virginia Commission of Game and Inland Fisheries, Tech. Bull. I. 44 pp.

McGinnes, B.W., and T.H. Ripley. 1962. Evaluation of wildlife response to forest wildlife management: a preliminary report. Proc. Society of American Foresters: 167–171.

McGlincey, J.A., J.L. Buckner, J.H. Exum, D.W. Speake, and F.M. Stanley. 1986. Wild turkey ecology and management in even-aged pine forests. Forest Manage. Guidelines No. 13. Bainbridge, GA: International Paper Co. 14 pp.

McIlhenny, E.A. 1914. The wild turkey and its hunting. New York: Doubleday, Page & Co. 245 pp.

McKell, C.M., J.P. Blaisdell, and J.R. Goodin, eds. 1972. Wildland shrubs—their biology and utilization. USDA Forest Service Gen. Tech. Rep. INT-1. 494 pp.

McKenney, T.L. 1846. Memoirs official and personal. Vol. 1. New York: Paine and Burgess. 340 pp.

McKinley, D. 1960. A chronology and bibliography of wildlife in Missouri. The University of Missouri Bull. 61(13). Library Series No. 26. 128 pp.

McKusick, C.R. 1980. Three groups of turkeys from southwestern archaeological sites. Contrib. Sci. Nat. Hist. Mus. Los Angeles Co. 330:225–235.

———. 1986. Southwest Indian turkeys—prehistory and comparative osteology. Globe, AZ: Southwest Bird Laboratory. 56 pp.

McMahan, C.A., R.G. Frye, and K.L. Brown. 1984. The vegetation types of Texas, including cropland. Austin: Texas Parks and Wildlife Dept. Bull. 7000-120. 40 pp.

McMahon, G.L., and R.N. Johnson. 1980. Introduction of the wild turkey into the Carlos Avery Wildlife Management Area. Proc. National Wild Turkey Symp. 4:32–44.

McNab, B.K. 1971. On the ecological significance of Bergmann's rule. Ecology 52(5):845–854.

Mearns, E.W. 1907. Mammals of the Mexican boundary of the United States. U.S. National Mus. Bull. 56. 530 pp.

Mech, L.D. 1970. The wolf: the ecology and behavior of an endangered species. Garden City, NY: Natural History Press. 384 pp.

Mellen, W.J., F.W. Hill, and H.H. Dukes. 1954. Studies of the energy requirements of chickens. 2. Effect of dietary energy level on the basal metabolism of growing chickens. Poultry Sci. 33(4):791–798.

Menzel, K., and J.J. Hurt. 1973. Releases of Merriam's turkeys in nontypical habitat. Pages 187–192 in G.C. Sanderson and H.C. Shultz, eds., Wild turkey management: current problems and programs. Columbia: The Missouri Chapter of The Wildlife Society and University of Missouri Press. 355 pp.

Menzel, K.E. 1975. Population and harvest data for Merriam's turkeys in Nebraska. Proc. National Wild Turkey Symp. 3:184–188.

Merrill, L.B. 1975. Effect of grazing management practices on wild turkey habitat. Proc. National Wild Turkey Symp. 3:108–112.

Merrill, L.B., and V.A. Young. 1954. Results of grazing single classes of livestock in combination with several classes when stocking rates are constant. Texas Agric. Exp. Sta. Prog. Rep. 1726. 7 pp.

Metzler, R., and D.W. Speake. 1985. Wild turkey poult mortality rates and their relationship to brood habitat structure in northeast Alabama. Proc. National Wild Turkey Symp. 5:103–111.

Michael, E.D. 1978. Effects of highway construction on game animals. Proc. Ann. Conf. Southeast. Assoc. Fish and Wildl. Agencies 32:48–52.

Miller, B.K. 1983. Ecology of transplanted eastern wild turkeys in west-central Indiana farming habitat. M.S. Thesis. Purdue University, West Lafayette, IN. 167 pp.

Miller, B.K., P.D. Major, and S.E. Backs. 1985. Movements and productivity of transplanted eastern wild turkeys in west-central Indiana farmland. Proc. National Wild Turkey Symp. 5:233–244.

Miller, B.K., and D.W. May. 1990. Mandatory landowner consent as a method of controlling wild turkey hunter density and hunter success rates. Proc. National Wild Turkey Symp. 6:214–223.

Miller, M.R. 1981. Ecological land classification terrestrial subsystem: a basic inventory system for planning and management on the Mark Twain National Forest. USDA Forest Service, Eastern Region. 56 pp.

Mitton, J.B., and M.C. Grant. 1984. Associations among protein heterozygosity, growth rate, and developmental homeostasis. Ann. Rev. Ecol. Syst. 15:479–499.

Mobley, H.E., R.S. Jackson, W.E. Balmer, W.E. Ruziska, and W.A. Hough. 1978. A guide for prescribed fire in southern forests. USDA Forest Service, Southeastern Area. 40 pp.

Moir, W.H. 1979. Soil-vegetation patterns in the central Peloncillo Mountains, New Mexico. Am. Midl. Nat. 102(2):317–331.

Mollohan, C.M. 1988. Merriam's turkey habitat expert opinion survey—summary. Flagstaff: Northern Arizona University School of Forestry. Unpubl. Rep. 29 pp.

Mollohan, C.M., and D.R. Patton. 1991. Development of a habitat suitability model for Merriam's turkey. Flagstaff: Northern Arizona University and Arizona Game and Fish Dept. Unpubl. Rep. 217 pp.

Montei, A.K. 1973. Rio Grande turkey diets in brushlands of north-central Texas. M.S. Thesis. Texas Tech University, Lubbock. 64 pp.

Mooney, J. 1896. The ghost-dance religion and the Sioux outbreak of 1890. Ann. Rep. Bur. Am. Eth. 14(2):641–1136.

Moore, M.H. 1972. Managing bobwhites in the cutover pinelands of south Florida. National Bobwhite Quail Symp. 1:56–65.

Morrison, D.F. 1976. Multivariate statistical methods. New York: McGraw Hill Book Co. 415 pp.

Mortensen, A., and A.S. Blix. 1986. Seasonal changes in resting metabolic rate and mass-specific conductance in Svalbard ptarmigan, Norwegian rock ptarmigan and Norwegian willow ptarmigan. Ornis Scand. 17(1):8–13.

Morton, T. 1637. New English Canaan: or New Canaan, containing an abstract of New England. Amsterdam: J.F. Stamm. 188 pp.

Mosby, H.S. 1949. The present status and the future outlook of the eastern and Florida wild turkeys. Trans. N. Am. Wildl. Conf.
14:346–358.

———. 1959. General status of the wild turkey and its management in the United States, 1958. Proc. National Wild Turkey Symp. 1:1–11.

———. 1967. Population dynamics. Pages 113–136 in O.H. Hewitt, ed., The wild turkey and its management. Washington, DC: The Wildlife Society. 589 pp.

———. 1973. The changed status of the wild turkey over the past three decades. Pages 71–76 in G.C. Sanderson and H.C. Shultz, eds., Wild turkey management: current problems and programs. Columbia: The Missouri Chapter of The Wildlife Society and University of Missouri Press. 355 pp.

———. 1975. The status of the wild turkey in 1974. Proc. National Wild Turkey Symp. 3:22–26.

Mosby, H.S., and C.O. Handley. 1943. The wild turkey in Virginia: its status, life history and management. Richmond: Virginia Division of Game, Commission of Game and Inland Fisheries. P-R Projects. 281 pp.

Moss, R., A. Watson, and R. Parr. 1975. Maternal nutrition and breeding success in red grouse (Lagopus lagopus scoticus). J. Anim. Ecol. 44(1):233–244.

Mukherjee, T.K., G.W. Friars, and J.D. Summers. 1969. Estimates of changes in plasma cholesterol and protein in relation to certain reproductive traits in female breeder turkeys. Poultry Sci. 48(6): 2081–2086.

Munro, S.S. 1938. The effect of dilution and density on the fertilizing capacity of fowl sperm suspensions. Can. J. Res. Sec. D 16:281.

National Oceanic and Atmospheric Administration. 1978. Climates of the states. Detroit, MI: Gale Research Co. 1185 pp.

National Research Council. 1971. Nutrient requirements of domestic animals. No. 1. Nutrient requirements for poultry. Washington, DC: National Academy of Science. 54 pp.

———. 1977. Nutrient requirements of domestic animals. No. 1. Nutrient requirements of poultry. Washington, DC: National Academy of Science. 62 pp.

National Rifle Association. 1988. Wild turkey hunting. Washington, DC: NRA Hunter Services Division. 182 pp.

National Wild Turkey Federation. 1986. Guide to the American wild turkey. Edgefield, SC: National Wild Turkey Federation. 189 pp.

Nayar, J.K., and D.J. Forrester. 1985. Susceptibiity of Culex nigripalpus to several isolates of Plasmodium hermani from wild turkeys in Florida. J. Am. Mosquito Control Assoc. 1(2):253–255.

Nayar, J.K., M.D. Young, and D.J. Forrester. 1980. Wyeomyia vanduzeei: an experimental host for wild turkey malaria Plasmodium hermani. J. Parasitol. 66(1):166–167.

Nayar, J.K., M.D. Young, and D.J. Forrester. 1981a. Plasmodium hermani: experimental transmission by Culex salinarius and comparison with other susceptible Florida mosquitoes. Exp. Parasitol. 51(3):431–437.

Nayar, J.K., M.D. Young, and D.J. Forrester. 1981b. Culex restuans: an experimental vector for wild turkey malaria, Plasmodium hermani. Mosquito News 41(4):748–750.

Nayar, J.K., M.D. Young, and D.J. Forrester. 1982. Experimental transmission by mosquitoes of Plasmodium hermani between domestic turkeys and pen-reared bobwhites. J. Parasitol. 68(5): 874–876.

Nei, M. 1978. Estimation of average heterozygosity and genetic distance from a small number of individuals. Genetics 89(3):583–590.

Nelson, E.W. 1900. Description of a new subspecies of Meleagris gallopavo and proposed changes in the nomenclature of certain North American birds. Auk 17(2):120–126.

Nelson, R.D., H. Black, Jr., R.E. Radtke, and J. Mumma. 1983. Wildlife and fish management in the Forest Service: a goal oriented approach. Trans. N. Am. Wildl. and Nat. Resour. Conf. 48:87–95.

Nenno, E.S., and W.M. Healy. 1979. Effects of radio packages on behavior of wild turkey hens. J. Wildl. Manage. 43(3):760–765.

Nenno, E.S., and J.S. Lindzey. 1979. Wild turkey poult feeding activity in old field agricultural clearing, and forest communities. Trans. Northeast. Section, The Wildlife Society 36:97–109.

Nettles, V.F. 1976. Organophosphate toxicity in wild turkeys. J. Wildl. Dis. 12(4):560–561.

Nettles, V.F., J.M. Wood, and R.G. Webster. 1985. Wildlife surveillance associated with an outbreak of lethal H5N2 avian influenza in domestic poultry. Avian Dis. 29(3):733–741.

Neu, C.W., C.R. Byers, and J.M. Peek. 1974. A technique for analysis of utilization-availability data. J. Wildl. Manage. 38(3):541–545.

Nevo, E., A. Beiles, and R. Ben-Schlomo. 1984. The evolutionary significance of genetic diversity: ecological, demographic, and life history correlations. Pages 13–213 *in* G.S. Mani, ed., Evolutionary dynamics of genetic diversity. Berlin: Springer-Verlag. 312 pp.

Newcomer, W.S. 1958. Physiologic factors which influence acidophilia induced by stressors in the chicken. Am. J. Physiol. 194(2): 251–254.

Newman, C.C., and E. Griffin. 1950. Deer and turkey habitats and populations of Florida. Tallahassee: Florida Game and Fresh Water Fish Commission Tech. Bull. 1. 30 pp.

Nichols, J.D., M.J. Conroy, D.R. Anderson, and K.P. Burnham. 1984. Compensatory mortality in waterfowl populations: a review of evidence and implications for research and management. Trans. N. Am. Wildl. and Nat. Resour. Conf. 49:535–554.

Nichols, J.D., and G.M. Haramis. 1980. Inferences regarding survival and recovery rates of winter-banded canvasbacks. J. Wildl. Manage. 44(1):164–173.

Nichols, J.D., and J.E. Hines. 1983. The relationship between harvest and survival rates of mallards: a straightforward approach with partitioned data sets. J. Wildl. Manage. 47(2):334–348.

Nixon, C.M., M.W. McClain, and K.R. Russell. 1970. Deer food habits and range characteristics in Ohio. J. Wildl. Manage. 34(4): 870–886.

Noblet, R., T.R. Adkins, and J.B. Kissam. 1972. *Simulium congareenarum* (Diptera: Simuliidae), a new vector of *Leucocytozoon smithi* (Sporozoa: Leucocytozoidae) in domestic turkeys. J. Med. Entomol. 9(6):580.

Noblet, R., and H.S. More, IV. 1975. Prevalence and distribution of *Leucocytozoon smithi* and *Haemoproteus meleagridis* in wild turkeys in South Carolina. J. Wildl. Dis. 11(4):516–518.

Noon, B.R. 1981. Techniques for sampling avian habitats. Pages 42–52 *in* D.E. Capen, ed., The use of multivariate statistics in studies of wildlife habitat. USDA Forest Service Gen. Tech. Rep. RM-87. 249 pp.

Odum, E.P. 1971. Fundamentals of ecology. Third ed. Philadelphia, PA: W.B. Saunders Co. 574 pp.

Oliver, W.R.B. 1955. Birds of New Zealand. Wellington, New Zealand: A.H. and A.W. Reed. 661 pp.

Olsen, M.W. 1960. Nine year summary of parthenogenesis in turkeys. Proc. Soc. Exp. Biol. and Med. 105(2):279–281.

Olsen, M.W., and R.M. Fraps. 1944. Maturation, fertilization, and early cleavage of the egg of the domestic turkey. J. Morphol. 74(2):297–305.

Olsen, M.W., and S.J. Marsden. 1954. Natural parthenogenesis in turkey eggs. Science 120(3118):545–546.

Owen, C.N. 1976. Food habits of wild turkey poults *(Meleagris gallopavo silvestris)* in pine stands and fields and the effects of mowing hayfield edges on arthropod populations. M.S. Thesis. Mississippi State University, Mississippi State. 62 pp.

Pack, J.C. 1986a. Prime wild turkey habitat survey. Pages 1–14 *in* J.W. Glidden, ed., Northeast wild turkey newsletter. Northeast. Section, The Wildlife Society. 51 pp.

———. 1986b. Report on wild turkey hunting regulations, harvest and trends and population levels in West Virginia 1940–1986. Charleston: West Virginia Dept. of Natural Resources. Fed. Aid Wildl. Restor. Prog. Rep. Proj. W-48-R-2. 62 pp. mimeo.

Pack, J.C., R.P. Burkert, W.K. Igo, and D.J. Pybus. 1980. Habitat utilized by wild turkey broods within oak-hickory forests of West Virginia. Proc. National Wild Turkey Symp. 4:213–224.

Pack, J.C., and W.K. Igo. 1981. Wild turkey brood range study. Charleston: West Virginia Dept. of Natural Resources. Fed. Aid. Wildl. Restor. Final Rep. Proj. W-39-R-23. 34 pp. mimeo.

Pack, J.C., W.K. Igo, and C.I. Taylor. 1988. Use of prescribed burning in conjunction with thinnings to increase wild turkey brood range habitat in oak-hickory forests. Trans. Northeast. Section, The Wildlife Society 44:37–44.

Pack, J.C., and C.I. Taylor. 1990. Wild turkey population dynamics study newsletter. 1991(2):1–17.

Page, L.A., and J.E. Grimes. 1984. Avian chlamydiosis (Ornithosis). Pages 283–308 *in* M.S. Hofstad et al., eds., Diseases of poultry. Eighth ed. Ames: Iowa State University Press. 831 pp.

Paine, R.T. 1980. Food webs: linkage, interaction strength, and community infrastructure. J. Animal Ecol. 49(3):667–686.

Palmer, T. 1978. International gobbling. Turkey Call 5(1):13–15.

Palmer, W.E. 1990. Relationships of wild turkey hens to forested habitats in east-central Mississippi. M.S. Thesis. Mississippi State University, Mississippi State. 117 pp.

Palmer, W.E., G.A. Hurst, and J.R. Lint. 1990. Effort, success, and characteristics of spring turkey hunters on Tallahala Wildlife Management Area, Mississippi. Proc. National Wild Turkey Symp. 6:208–213.

Parker, W.A., III. 1967. A quantitative study of available late winter foods of the eastern wild turkey *(Meleagris gallopavo silvestris)* on the longleaf pine region of Mississippi. M.S. Thesis. Mississippi State University, Mississippi State. 24 pp.

Parsons, E.C. 1939. Pueblo Indian religion. Chicago: University of Chicago Press. Vol. 1.

Pattee, O.H. 1977. Effects of nutrition on wild turkey reproduction in south Texas. Ph.D. Thesis. Texas A&M University, College Station. 63 pp.

Pattee, O.H., and S.L. Beasom. 1979. Supplemental feeding to increase wild turkey productivity. J. Wildl. Manage. 43(2):512–516.

Pattee, O.H., and S.L. Beasom. 1981. A partial nutritional analysis of wild turkey hen diets in springtime. Proc. Ann. Conf. Southeast. Assoc. Fish and Wildl. Agencies 35:225–232.

Patterson, T.L. 1927. Gastric movements in the pigeon with economy of animal material. Comparative Studies V. J. Lab. and Clin. Med. 12(9):1003–1008.

Paulsen, T.M., A.L. Moxon, and W.O. Wilson. 1950. Blood composition of broad-breasted bronze breeding turkeys. Poultry Sci. 29(1):15–19.

Peattie, D.C., ed. 1940. Audubon's America: the narratives and experiences of John James Audubon. Boston: Houghton Mifflin Co. 329 pp.

Peckham, M.C. 1984. Vices and miscellaneous diseases and conditions. Pages 741–782 *in* M.S. Hofstad et al., eds., Diseases of poultry. Eighth ed. Ames: Iowa State University Press. 831 pp.

Pennant, T. 1781. An account of the turkey. Philosophical Trans. of the Royal Soc. London 71(1):67–81.

Peters, J.R., and T.M. Bowers. 1977a. Forest statistics for Massachusetts. USDA Forest Service Resour. Bull. NE-48. 43 pp.

Peters, J.R., and T.M. Bowers. 1977b. Forest statistics for Rhode Island. USDA Forest Service Resour. Bull. NE-49. 38 pp.

Petersen, L.E., and A.H. Richardson. 1973. Merriam's wild turkey in the Black Hills of South Dakota. Pages 3–9 *in* G.C. Sanderson and H.C. Schultz, eds., Wild turkey management: current problems and programs. Columbia: The Missouri Chapter of The Wildlife Society and University of Missouri Press. 355 pp.

Petersen, L.E., and A.H. Richardson. 1975. The wild turkey in the Black Hills. Pierre: South Dakota Dept. Game, Fish and Parks Bull. 6. 51 pp.

Petrides, G.A. 1942. Age determination in American gallinaceous birds. Trans. N. Am. Wildl. Conf. 7:308–328.

———. 1945. First winter plumages in the Galliformes. Auk 62(2): 223–227.

Phalen, P.S. 1986. Reproduction, brood habitat use, and movement of wild turkey hens in east-central Mississippi. M.S. Thesis. Mississippi State University, Mississippi State. 63 pp.

Phalen, P.S., G.A. Hurst, and W.J. Hamrick. 1986. Brood habitat use and preference by wild turkeys in central Mississippi. Proc. Ann. Conf. Southeast. Assoc. Fish and Wildl. Agencies 40:397–404.

Pharris, L.D., and R.C. Goetz. 1980. An evaluation of artificial wild turkey nests monitored by automatic camera. Proc. National Wild Turkey Symp. 4:108–116.

Phillips, F.E. 1980. A basic guide to roost site management for Merriam's turkey. Phoenix: Arizona Game and Fish Dept. Wildl. Digest 12. 6 pp.

———. 1982. Wild turkey investigations and management recommendations for the Bill Williams Mountain area. Phoenix: Arizona Game and Fish Dept. Special Rep. 13. 50 pp.

Pick, H.L., Jr., and M.R. Kare. 1962. The effect of artificial cues on the measurement of taste preference in the chicken. J. Comp. and Physiol. Psychol. 55(3):342–345.

Pinkovsky, D.D., D.J. Forrester, and J.F. Butler. 1981. Investigations on black fly vectors (Diptera: Simuliidae) of *Leucocytozoon smithi* (Sporozoa: Leucocytozoidae) in Florida. J. Med. Entomol. 18(2):153–157.

Pohl, H. 1971. Seasonal variation in metabolic functions of bramblings. Ibis 113(2):185–193.

Pollock, K.H., J.E. Hines, and J.D. Nichols. 1985. Goodness-of-fit tests for open capture-recapture models. Biometrics 41(2): 399–410.

Pollock, K.H., C.T. Moore, W.R. Davidson, F.E. Kellogg, and G.L. Doster. 1989. Survival rates of bobwhite quail based on band recovery analysis. J. Wildl. Manage. 53(1):1–6.

Pollock, K.H., J.D. Nichols, C. Brownie, and J.E. Hines. 1990. Statistical inference for capture-recapture experiments. Wildl. Monographs 107:1–97.

Pollock, K.H., S.R. Winterstein, C.M. Bunck, and P.D. Curtis. 1989. Survival analysis in telemetry studies: the staggered entry design. J. Wildl. Manage. 53(1):7–15.

Pollock, K.H., S.R. Winterstein, and M.J. Conroy. 1989. Estimation and analysis of survival distributions for radio-tagged animals. Biometrics 45(1):99–109.

Poole, E.L. 1938. Weights and wing areas in North American birds. Auk 55(3):511–517.

Poole, R.W. 1974. An introduction to quantitative ecology. New York: McGraw Hill Book Co. 532 pp.

Porter, W.F. 1977. Utilization of agricultural habitats by wild turkeys in southeastern Minnesota. Int. Congr. Game Biol. 13:319–323.

———. 1978. Behavior and ecology of the wild turkey *(Meleagris gallopavo)* in southeastern Minnesota. Ph.D. Thesis. The University of Minnesota, Minneapolis. 122 pp.

———. 1980. An evaluation of wild turkey brood habitat in southeastern Minnesota. Proc. National Wild Turkey Symp. 4:203–212.

Porter, W.F., and K.E. Church. 1987. Effects of environmental pattern on habitat preference analysis. J. Wildl. Manage. 51(3):681–685.

Porter, W.F., D.J. Gefell, and H.B. Underwood. 1990. Influence of hunter harvest on the population dynamics of wild turkeys in New York. Proc. National Wild Turkey Symp. 6:188–195.

Porter, W.F., and J.R. Ludwig. 1980. Use of gobbling counts to monitor the distribution and abundance of wild turkeys. Proc. National Wild Turkey Symp. 4:61–68.

Porter, W.F., G.C. Nelson, and K. Mattson. 1983. Effects of winter conditions on reproduction in a northern wild turkey population. J. Wildl. Manage. 47(2):281–290.

Porter, W.F., R.D. Tangen, G.C. Nelson, and D.A. Hamilton. 1980. Effects of corn food plots on wild turkeys in the upper Mississippi Valley. J. Wildl. Manage. 44(2):456–462.

Porter, W.F., H.B. Underwood, and D.J. Gefell. 1990. Application of population modeling techniques to wild turkey management. Proc. National Wild Turkey Symp. 6:107–118.

Portmann, A. 1961. Sensory organs: skins, taste, and olfaction. Pages 37–48 *in* A.J. Marshall, ed., Biology and comparative physiology of birds. Part I. New York: Academic Press. 468 pp.

Potter, T.D. 1984. Status and ecology of Gould's turkey in New Mexico. M.S. Thesis. New Mexico State University, Las Cruces. 104 pp.

Potter, T.D., S.D. Schemnitz, and W.D. Zeedyk. 1985. Status and ecology of Gould's turkey in the Peloncillo Mountains of New Mexico. Proc. National Wild Turkey Symp. 5:1–24.

Powell, D.S., and D.R. Dickam. 1984. Forest statistics for Maine— 1971 and 1982. USDA Forest Service Resour. Bull. NE-81. 194 pp.

Powell, D.S., and N.P. Kingsley. 1980. The forest resources of Maryland. USDA Forest Service Resour. Bull. NE-61. 103 pp.

Powell, J.A. 1965. The Florida wild turkey. Tallahassee: Florida Game and Fresh Water Fish Commission Tech. Bull. 8. 28 pp.

———. 1967. Management of the Florida turkey and eastern turkey in Georgia and Alabama. Pages 409–451 *in* O.H. Hewitt, ed., The wild turkey and its management. Washington, DC: The Wildlife Society. 589 pp.

Powell, J.A., and L.F. Gainey. 1959. The aerial drop method of releasing wild trapped turkeys for restocking purposes. Proc. National Wild Turkey Symp. 1:55–61.

Prasad, N.L.N.S., and F.S. Guthery. 1986. Wildlife use of livestock water under short duration and continuous grazing. Wildl. Soc. Bull. 14(4):450–454.

Preston, J.R. 1959. Turkey restoration efforts in the Ozark region of Arkansas. Proc. National Wild Turkey Symp. 1:43–54.

Prestwood, A.K. 1968. Parasitism among wild turkeys *(Meleagris gallopavo silvestris)* of the Mississippi Delta. Ph.D. Thesis. The University of Georgia, Athens. 67 pp.

Prestwood, A.K., F.E. Kellogg, and G.L. Doster. 1971. Coccidia in eastern wild turkeys of the southeastern United States. J. Parasitol. 57(1):189–190.

Prestwood, A.K., F.E. Kellogg, and G.L. Doster. 1973. Parasitism and disease among southeastern wild turkeys. Pages 159–167 *in* G.C. Sanderson and H.C. Schultz, eds., Wild turkey management: current problems and programs. Columbia: The Missouri Chapter of The Wildlife Society and University of Missouri Press. 355 pp.

Prestwood, A.K., F.E. Kellogg, and G.L. Doster. 1975. Parasitism among wild turkey in the southeast. Proc. National Wild Turkey Symp. 3:27–32.

Price, W.A., and G. Gunter. 1942. Certain recent geological and biological changes in south Texas, with consideration of probable causes. Proc. and Trans. Texas Acad. Sci. 26:138–156.

Prince, H.H., and B.T. Gray. 1986. Bioenergetics of the wild turkey in Michigan. Lansing: Michigan Dept. Natural Resources, Wildlife Division. Final Rep. 57 pp. mimeo.

Prosser, C.L., and F.A. Brown, Jr. 1961. Comparative animal physiology. Second ed. Philadelphia, PA: W.B. Saunders Co. 688 pp.

Pumphrey, R.J. 1961. Sensory organs: vision. Pages 55–68 *in* A.J. Marshall, ed., Biology and comparative physiology of birds. Part I. New York: Academic Press. 468 pp.

Putnam, D.J., E.S. Nenno, and J.S. Lindsey. 1975. Brood range and foods of wild turkey studied. Harrisburg: Pennsylvania Agric. Sta., Science in Agriculture 23(1):4.

Putnam, J.A. 1951. Management of bottomland hardwoods. USDA Forest Service South. For. Exp. Sta. Occas. Pap. 116. 60 pp.

Pybus, D.J. 1977. Understory characteristics and utilization by wild turkey broods in West Virginia. M.S. Thesis. West Virginia University, Morgantown. 106 pp.

Quinton, D.A., and A.K. Montei. 1977. Preliminary study of the diet of Rio Grande turkeys in north-central Texas. Southwest. Nat. 22(4):550–553.

Quinton, D.A., A.K. Montei, and J.T. Flinders. 1980. Brush control and Rio Grande turkeys in north-central Texas. J. Range Manage. 33(2):95–99.

Raile, G.K. 1985. Timber resource of Wisconsin's Southwest Survey Unit, 1983. USDA Forest Service Resour. Bull. NC-87. 88 pp.

———. 1986. Nebraska's second forest inventory. USDA Forest Service Resour. Bull. NC-96. 87 pp.

Ramsey, R.R. 1958. Turkeys for tomorrow. Texas Game and Fish 16(11):16–17, 28.

Ramsey, R.R., and W.P. Taylor. 1942. A winter feeding program for the wild turkey in Texas. Texas Agric. Exp. Sta. Proj. Rep. 808. 3 pp.

Ransom, D., Jr., O.J. Rongstad, and D.H. Rusch. 1987. Nesting ecology of Rio Grande turkeys. J. Wildl. Manage. 51(2):435–439.

Rapoport, S., and G.M. Guest. 1941. Distribution of acid-soluble phosphorus in the blood cells of various vertebrates. J. Biol. Chem. 138(1):269–282.

Raybourne, J.W. 1974. Wild turkey nesting and brooding study. Elkins, WV: Northeast Wild Turkey Committee, 9th Annual Workshop. 8 pp.

Rea, A.M. 1980. Late Pleistocene and Holocene turkeys in the Southwest. Contrib. Sci. Nat. Hist. Mus. Los Angeles Co. 330:209–224.

Reagan, J.M., and K.D. Morgan. 1980. Reproductive potential of Rio Grande turkey hens in the Edwards Plateau of Texas. Proc. National Wild Turkey Symp. 4:136–144.

Reed, J.M., P.D. Doerr, and J.R. Walters. 1986. Determining minimum population sizes for birds and mammals. Wildl. Soc. Bull. 14(3):255–261.

Reid, W.M. 1967. Etiology and dissemination of the blackhead disease syndrome in turkeys and chickens. Exp. Parasitol. 21(2):249–275.

———. 1984. Cestodes. Pages 649–668 in M.S. Hofstad et al., eds., Diseases of poultry. Eighth ed. Ames: Iowa State University Press. 831 pp.

Reid, W.M., P.L. Long, and L.R. McDougald. 1984. Coccidiosis. Pages 717–723 in M.S. Hofstad et al., eds., Diseases of poultry. Eighth ed. Ames: Iowa State University Press. 831 pp.

Rhian, M., W.O. Wilson, and A.L. Moxon. 1944. Composition of blood of normal turkeys. Poultry Sci. 23(3):224–229.

Rice, F.H. 1985. L.E.D. volume unit meter: a practical aid for radio-telemetry research. Proc. National Wild Turkey Symp. 5:327–332.

———. 1986. Response of wild turkeys to surface coal mining in north-central Pennsylvania. M.S. Thesis. Pennsylvania State University, University Park. 218 pp.

Rickard, L.G. 1985. Proventricular lesions associated with natural and experimental infections of *Dispharynx nasuta* (Nematoda: Acuariidae). Can. J. Zool. 63(11):2663–2668.

Ringer, R.K., and K. Rood. 1959. Hemodynamic changes associated with aging in the broad breasted Bronze turkey. Poultry Sci. 38(2):395–397.

Ritchie, W.A. 1944. The pre-Iroquoian occupations of New York state. Roch. Mus. Arts and Sci. Mem. 1:1–416.

Roach, B.A. 1974. Scheduling timber cutting for sustained yield of wood products and wildlife. Pages 33–42 in Timber-wildlife management symposium. Missouri Acad. Sci. Occas. Pap. 3.

Robbins, C.T. 1983. Wildlife feeding and nutrition. New York: Academic Press. 343 pp.

Roberts, H.A. 1956. Investigations of the frequency and kinds of disease and parasites found among wild turkeys in Pennsylvania. Page 7 in Semi-annual progress report. Harrisburg: Pennsylvania Game Commission.

———. 1959. Aspects of harvest and hunting pressure in Pennsylvania wild turkey range. Proc. National Wild Turkey Symp. 1:31–42.

Roberts, T.S. 1932. The birds of Minnesota. Vol. 1. Minneapolis, MN: University Press. 691 pp.

Robinette, J. 1968. Nutrient requirements of turkeys. Animal Nutrition and Health 28:16–19.

Robinson, R.M. 1975. Diseases of Texas wild turkeys. Proc. National Wild Turkey Symp. 3:33–35.

Robinson, W.L., and E.G. Bolen. 1984. Wildlife ecology and management. New York: Macmillan Pub. Co. 478 pp.

Rocke, T.E. 1985. Mycoplasmosis in wild turkeys. Ph.D. Thesis. The University of Wisconsin, Madison. 107 pp.

Rocke, T.E., and T.M. Yuill. 1987. Microbial infections in a declining wild turkey population in Texas. J. Wildl. Manage. 51(4):778–782.

Rogers, F.T. 1916. Contribution to the physiology of the stomach: the hunger mechanism of the pigeon and its relation to the central nervous system. Am. J. Physiol. 41(5):555–570.

Rogers, J.P., J.D. Nichols, F.W. Martin, C.F. Kimball, and R.S. Pospahala. 1979. An examination of harvest and survival rates of ducks in relation to hunting. Trans. N. Am. Wildl. and Nat. Resour. Conf. 44:114–126.

Rogers, J.S. 1972. Measures of genetic similarity and genetic distance. Studies in Genetics, Univ. Texas Publ. 7213:145–153.

Rogers, R.E. 1985. Feeding activity of wild turkey poults in prescribed burned and thinned oak-hickory forests. Trans. Northeast. Section, The Wildlife Society 41:167–177.

Romanoff, A.L., and A.J. Romanoff. 1949. The avian egg. New York: John Wiley & Sons. 918 pp.

Romans, B. 1776. A concise natural history of east and west Florida. A 1967 facsimile reproduction of the 1775 edition. Gainesville: University of Florida Press. 342 pp.

Roseberry, J.L. 1979. Bobwhite population responses to exploitation: real and simulated. J. Wildl. Manage. 43(2):285–305.

———. 1981. Bobwhite population responses: a reply. J. Wildl. Manage. 45(4):1054–1057.

Roseberry, J.L., and W.D. Klimstra. 1984. Population ecology of the bobwhite. Carbondale: Southern Illinois University Press. 259 pp.

Rosenweig, M.L., and R.H. MacArthur. 1963. Graphical representation and stability conditions of predator-prey interactions. Am. Nat. 47:209–223.

Roslien, D.J., and A.O. Haugen. 1970. Some blood parasite and disease antibody findings in wild Rio Grande turkeys stocked in Iowa. Proc. Iowa Acad. Sci. 77:93–96.

Ross, A.S., and G.A. Wunz. 1990. Habitats used by wild turkey hens during the summer in oak forests in Pennsylvania. Proc. National Wild Turkey Symp. 6:39–43.

Ruble, A. de. 1877. Le mariage de Jeanne D'Albert. Paris: A. Labitte. 321 pp.

Ruff, M.D. 1984. Nematodes and acanthocephalans. Pages 614–648 in M.S. Hofstad et al., eds., Diseases of poultry. Eighth ed. Ames: Iowa State University Press. 831 pp.

Rumble, M.A. 1990. The ecology of Merriam's turkey *(Meleagris gallopavo merriami)* in the Black Hills, South Dakota. Ph.D. Thesis. University of Wyoming, Laramie. 166 pp.

Rumble, M.A., and S. Anderson. 1989. Habitat utilization and nesting characteristics of turkeys in ponderosa pine. Proc. 1987 shrub ecology workshop. Laramie: University of Wyoming. 74 pp.

Rundquist, V.M. 1973. Pen-reared wild turkeys as shooting-preserve game. Pages 309–316 in G.C. Sanderson and H.C. Schultz, eds., Wild turkey management: current problems and programs. Columbia: The Missouri Chapter of The Wildlife Society and University of Missouri Press. 355 pp.

Rusch, D.H., E.C. Meslow, P.D. Doerr, and L.B. Keith. 1972. Response of great horned owl populations to changing prey densities. J. Wildl. Manage. 36(2):282–296.

Rush, G. 1973. The hen-brood release as a restoration technique. Pages 193–197 in G.C. Sanderson and H.C. Schultz, eds., Wild turkey management: current problems and programs. Columbia: The Missouri Chapter of The Wildlife Society and University of Missouri Press. 355 pp.

Rusz, P.J. 1987. Implications of continued transplanting of turkeys of game farm origin: the Michigan case. Edgefield, SC: National Wild Turkey Federation. 56 pp.

Ryan, C.A. 1965. Chicken chymotrypsin and turkey trypsin. Part I: Purification. Arch. Biochem. Biophysiol. 110(1):169–174.

Sadler, K.C. 1954. An investigation of methods for trapping and transplanting wild turkeys. Columbia: Missouri Dept. Conservation. P-R Rep. W-13-R-8. 8 pp. mimeo.

Salwasser, H., C.K. Hamilton, W.B. Krohn, J.F. Lipscomb, and C.H. Thomas. 1983. Monitoring wildlife and fish: mandates and their implications. Trans. N. Am. Wildl. and Nat. Resour. Conf.

48:297–307.

Sanders, I.L. 1988. Guidelines for regenerating Appalachian oak stands. Pages 189–198 *in* H.C. Smith, A.W. Perkey, and W.E. Kidd, Jr., eds., Proc.: Guidelines for regenerating Appalachian hardwood stands. Morgantown: West Virginia University Books. 293 pp.

Sanders, I.L., P.S. Johnson, and R. Rogers. 1984. Evaluating oak advance reproduction in the Missouri Ozarks. USDA Forest Service Res. Pap. NC-251. 16 pp.

Sanderson, G.C., ed. 1972. Special section devoted to the symposium on predator ecology and management. J. Wildl. Manage. 36(2): 209–404.

Sanderson, G.C., and H.C. Schultz, eds. 1973. Wild turkey management: current problems and programs. Columbia: The Missouri Chapter of The Wildlife Society and University of Missouri Press. 355 pp.

Sauer, C.O. 1920. The geography of the Ozark Highlands of Missouri. The Geographic Society of Chicago. Chicago: University of Chicago Press. Bull. 7. 245 pp.

Scanlon, P.F., T.G. O'Brien, N.L. Schauer, J.L. Coggin, and D.E. Steffen. 1979. Heavy metal levels in feathers of wild turkeys from Virginia. Bull. Environ. Contamination and Toxicol. 21(4/5): 591–595.

Schamberger, M., and A. Farmer. 1978. The habitat evaluation procedures: their application in project planning and impact evaluation. Trans. N. Am. Wildl. and Nat. Resour. Conf. 43:274–283.

Schamberger, M., and W.B. Krohn. 1982. Status of the habitat evaluation procedures. Trans. N. Am. Wildl. and Nat. Resour. Conf. 47:154–164.

Schemnitz, S.D. 1956. Wild turkey food habits in Florida. J. Wildl. Manage. 20(2):132–137.

Schemnitz, S.D., D.E. Figert, and R.C. Willging. 1990. Ecology and management of Gould's turkey in southwestern New Mexico. Proc. National Wild Turkey Symp. 6:72–83.

Schemnitz, S.D., D.L. Goerndt, and K.H. Jones. 1985. Habitat needs and management of Merriam's turkey in southcentral New Mexico. Proc. National Wild Turkey Symp. 5:199–231.

Schemnitz, S.D., and V. Pinto. 1987. Status of Gould's turkey in New Mexico and Mexico. Proc. Western Wild Turkey Workshop 4:43–44.

Schemnitz, S.D., T.D. Potter, and W.D. Zeedyk. 1985. Status, ecology and management of Gould's turkey. Pages 538–581 *in* Proc. Wildl. Symp. Mexico. Vol. I.

Schemnitz, S.D., and R.C. Willing. 1986. Gould's turkey status report. Proc. Western Wild Turkey Workshop 3:24–25.

Schemnitz, S.D., and W.D. Zeedyk. 1982. Ecology and status of Gould's turkey in New Mexico. Proc. Western Wild Turkey Workshop 1:110–125.

Schleidt, W.M. 1968. Annual cycle of courtship behavior in the male turkey. J. Comp. and Physiol. Psychol. 66(3):743–746.

———. 1970. Precocial sexual behavior in turkeys (*Meleagris gallopavo* L.). Animal Behav. 18(4):760–761.

Schmutz, J.A., and C.E. Braun. 1989. Reproductive performance of Rio Grande wild turkeys. Condor 91(3):675–680.

Schorger, A.W. 1963. The domestic turkey in Mexico and Central America in the sixteenth century. Wisconsin Acad. Sci. 52: 133–152.

———. 1966. The wild turkey: its history and domestication. Norman: University of Oklahoma Press. 625 pp.

———. 1970. A new species of (*Meleagris gallopavo*). Auk 87(1): 168–170.

Schorr, L.F., W.R. Davidson, V.F. Nettles, J.E. Kennamer, P. Villegas, and H.W. Yoder. 1988. A survey of parasites and diseases of pen-raised wild turkeys. Proc. Ann. Conf. Southeast. Assoc. Fish and Wildl. Agencies 42:315–328.

Schroeder, R.L. 1985. Habitat suitability index models: eastern wild turkey. U.S. Dept. Interior, Fish and Wildl. Serv. Biol. Rep. 82. 33 pp.

Schulz, P.A., and F.S. Guthery. 1987. Effects of short duration grazing on wild turkey home ranges. Wildl. Soc. Bull. 15(2):239–241.

Schumacher, R.W. 1977. Movements of eastern wild turkey released in a cottonwood plantation. M.S. Thesis. Mississippi State University, Mississippi State. 98 pp.

Schwartzkopff, J. 1955. On the hearing of birds. Auk 72(4):340–347.

Scifres, C.J. 1979. Brush management: principles and practices for Texas and the southwest. College Station: Texas A&M University Press. 360 pp.

Scifres, C.J., D.L. Drawe, J.L. Mutz, O.E. Bontrager, and J.W. McAtee. 1979. Range improvement practices for the coastal prairie: needs, present applications, and research advances. Proc. Welder Wildl. Found. Symp. 1:15–24.

Scott, H.M., and L.F. Payne. 1937. Light in relation to the experimental modification of the breeding season of turkeys. Poultry Sci. 16(2):90–96.

Scott, H.M., P.J. Serfontein, and D.H. Sieling. 1933. Blood analyses of normal Bronze turkeys. Poultry Sci. 12(1):17–19.

Scott, M.L., M.C. Nesheim, and R.J. Young. 1982. Nutrition of the chicken. Third ed. Ithaca, NY: M.L. Scott and Associates. 562 pp.

Scott, T.G., and C.H. Wasser. 1980. Checklist of North American plants for wildlife biologists. Washington, DC: The Wildlife Society. 58 pp.

Scott, V.E., and E.L. Boeker. 1972. An evaluation of wild turkey call counts in Arizona. J. Wildl. Manage. 36(2):628–630.

Scott, V.E., and E.L. Boeker. 1973. Seasonal food habits of Merriam's turkeys on the Fort Apache Indian Reservation. Pages 151–157 *in* G.C. Sanderson and H.C. Schultz eds., Wild turkey management: current problems and programs. Columbia: The Missouri Chapter of The Wildlife Society and University of Missouri Press. 355 pp.

Scott, V.E., and E.L. Boeker. 1975. Ecology of Merriam's wild turkey on the Fort Apache Indian Reservation. Proc. National Wild Turkey Symp. 3:141–158.

Scott, W.E.D. 1890. Description of a new subspecies of wild turkey. Auk 7(4):376–377.

Seber, G.A.F. 1982. The estimation of animal abundance and related parameters. Second ed. New York: MacMillan Publishing Co., Inc. 654 pp.

———. 1986. A review of estimating animal abundance. Biometrics 42(2):267–292.

Seiss, R.S. 1989. Reproductive parameters and survival rates of wild turkey hens in east-central Mississippi. M.S. Thesis. Mississippi State University, Mississippi State. 99 pp.

Seiss, R.S., P.S. Phalen, and G.A. Hurst. 1990. Wild turkey nesting habitat and success rates. Proc. National Wild Turkey Symp. 6:18–24.

Selye, H. 1976. Stress in health and disease. Boston: Butterworths. 1256 pp.

Sennett, G.B. 1879. Further notes on the ornithology of the lower Rio Grande of Texas from observations made during the spring of 1878. U.S. Geol. and Geog. Surv. Terr. Bull. 5(3):371–440.

Shaffer, C.H., and J.W. Gwynn. 1967. Management of the eastern turkey in oak-pine and pine forests of Virginia and the Southeast. Pages 303–342 *in* O.H. Hewitt, ed., The wild turkey and its management. Washington, DC: The Wildlife Society. 589 pp.

Shaffer, K. 1975. The esthetics of wild turkey hunting. Proc. National Wild Turkey Symp. 3:218–221.

Shaffner, C.S. 1954. Feather papilla stimulation by progesterone. Science 120(3113):345.

———. 1955. Progesterone induced molt. Poultry Sci. 34(4):840–842.

Shapiro, A.B., and A.M. Schechtman. 1949. Effect of adrenal cortical extract on the blood picture and serum proteins of fowl. Proc. Soc. Exp. Bio. and Med. 70(3):440–445.

Shaw, H.G. 1973. The roadside survey for Merriam's turkeys in Arizona. Pages 285–293 *in* G.C. Sanderson and H.C. Schultz, eds., Wild turkey management: current problems and programs. Columbia: The Missouri Chapter of The Wildlife Society and University of Missouri Press. 355 pp.

Shaw, H.G., and R.L. Smith. 1977. Habitat use patterns of Merriam's turkey in Arizona. Phoenix: Arizona Game and Fish Dept. Fed. Aid Rep. Proj. W-78 R, WP 4, J11. 33 pp. mimeo.

Shaw, S.P. 1959. Timber sales and turkey management on eastern national forests. Proc. National Wild Turkey Symp. 1:100–104.

Sherrow, D. 1984. The disappearance of the Connecticut wild turkey. Hartford: Connecticut Dept. Environmental Protection. 28 pp. mimeo.

Short, H.L., R.M. Blair, and C.A. Segelquist. 1974. Fiber composition and forage digestibility by small ruminants. J. Wildl. Manage. 38(2):197–209.

Short, H.L., and E.A. Epps, Jr. 1976. Nutrient quality and digestibility of seeds and fruits from southern forests. J. Wildl. Manage. 40(2):283–289.

Shotts, E.B., W.R. Davidson, and J. Teska. 1987. Mycotic infections of the feathers of wild turkeys. Lincoln, NE: Program Abstracts of the 1987 Wildlife Disease Association Meeting. mimeo.

Shufeldt, R.W. 1914. The turkey prehistoric and the turkey historic. Pages 26–103 *in* E.A. McIlhenny ed., The wild turkey and its hunting. New York: Doubleday, Page & Co. 245 pp.

Shult, M.J. 1973. Turkey biology as related to management. Pages 1–13 *in* Turkey management seminars, Austin: Texas Agric. Extension Service. 27 pp.

Sibley, C.G. 1960. The electrophoretic patterns of avian egg-white proteins as taxonomic characters. Ibis 102(2):215–284.

Sickels, A.C. 1959. Comparative results of stocking game farm and wild trapped turkeys in Ohio. Proc. National Wild Turkey Symp. 1:75–87.

Siivonen, L. 1957. The problem of the short-term fluctuations in numbers of tetraoneds in Europe. Finnish Game Foundation, Papers on Game Res. 19:1–44.

Siller, W.G. 1959. Avian nephritis and visceral gout. Lab. Investig. 8(6):1319–1357.

Simmons, G.F. 1925. Birds of the Austin region. Austin: University of Texas Press. 387 pp.

Sinnott, E.W. 1946. Botany principles and problems. Fourth ed. New York: McGraw-Hill Book Co. 726 pp.

Sisson, D.C., D.W. Speak, J.L. Landers, and J.L. Buckner. 1990. Effects of prescribed burning on wild turkey habitat preference and nest site selection in south Georgia. Proc. National Wild Turkey Symp. 6:44–50.

Sjoberg, A.F. 1953. The culture of the Tonkawa, a Texan Indian tribe. Texas J. Sci. 5:280–304.

Slagle, A.K. 1963. An electronic system for the study of the movements of wild animals. M.A. Thesis. University of Missouri, Columbia. 107 pp.

Smith, D.M. 1975. Behavioral factors influencing variability of roost counts for Rio Grande turkeys. Proc. National Wild Turkey Symp. 3:170–175.

———. 1977. The social organization of Rio Grande turkeys in a declining population. Ph.D. Thesis. Utah State University, Logan. 98 pp.

Smith, D.R., G.A. Hurst, J.D. Burk, B.D. Leopold, and M.A. Melchoirs. 1990. Use of loblolly pine plantations by wild turkey hens in east-central Mississippi. Proc. National Wild Turkey Symp. 6:61–66.

Smith, G. 1988. A profile: members of the National Wild Turkey Federation, Inc. Turkey Call 15(5):8.

Smith, H.E. 1986. The rest of the Ben Franklin story. Turkey Call 13(6):4.

Smith, H.N., and C.A. Rechenthin. 1964. Grassland restoration: the Texas brush problem. Temple, TX: USDA Soil Conserv. Serv. 33 pp.

Smith, R.H. 1962. Turkey population trend techniques. Phoenix: Arizona Game and Fish Department. Job Completion Rep. Fed. Aid Proj. W-78-R-7, Work Plan 1, Job 5. mimeo.

Smith, R.L. 1974. Ecology and field biology. Second ed. New York: Harper & Row. 849 pp.

Smith, W.A., and B. Browning. 1967. Wild turkey food habits in San Luis Obispo County, California. California Fish and Game 53(4):246–253.

Smith, W.P., E.P. Lambert, and R.D. Teitelbaum. 1989. Seasonal movement and home range differences among age and sex groups of eastern wild turkey within southeastern Louisiana. Proc. Int. Biotelem. Conf. 10:151–158.

Smith, W.P., and R.D. Teitelbaum. 1986. Habitat use by eastern wild turkey hens in southeastern Louisiana. Proc. Ann. Conf. Southeast. Assoc. Fish and Wildl. Agencies 40:405–415.

Smyth, J.R., Jr., and T.W. Fox. 1951. The thyroxine secretion rate of turkey poults. Poultry Sci. 30(4):607–614.

Snedecor, J.G., H. Mathews, and W.B. MacGrath, Jr. 1956. The blood sugar response of turkey poults to insulin. Poultry Sci. 35(2):355–360.

Snoeyenbos, G.H. 1984. Pullorum disease. Pages 66–78 *in* M.S. Hofstad et al., eds., Diseases of poultry. Eighth ed. Ames: Iowa State University Press. 831 pp.

Snyder, R.L. 1953. Ability of spring released wild turkeys to survive and adapt to a natural environment. Pages 23–24 *in* Quarterly progress report. Harrisburg: Pennsylvania Game Commission.

Sokal, R.R., and F.J. Rohlf. 1981. Biometry. Second ed. San Francisco, CA: W.H. Freeman and Co. 859 pp.

Solomon, M.E. 1949. The natural control of animal populations. J. Animal Ecol. 18(1):1–35.

Songer, E.F. 1987. Habitat quality modeling of wild turkey broods for the eastern wild turkey in east-central Mississippi. M.S. Thesis. Mississippi State University, Mississippi State. 57 pp.

Songer, E.F., R.L. Kelley, and G.A. Hurst. 1989. Testing wild turkey use of habitats ranked by spatial estimators. Int. Biotelem. Conf. 10:244–253.

Southeastern Section of the Wildlife Society. 1959. Proc. First National Wild Turkey Symposium. Southeastern Section, The Wildlife Society. 200 pp.

Speake, D.W. 1980. Predation on wild turkeys in Alabama. Proc. National Wild Turkey Symp. 4:86–101.

Speake, D.W., L.H. Barwick, H.O. Hillestad, and W. Stickney. 1969. Some characteristics of an expanding turkey population. Proc. Ann. Conf. Southeast. Assoc. Game and Fish Comm. 23:46–58.

Speake, D.W., T.E. Lynch, W.J. Fleming, G.A. Wright, and W.J. Hamrick. 1975. Habitat use and seasonal movements of wild turkeys in the Southeast. Proc. National Wild Turkey Symp. 3:122–130.

Speake, D.W., and R. Metzler. 1985. Wild turkey population ecology on the Appalachian Plateau Region of northeastern Alabama. Montgomery: Alabama Dept. of Conservation. P-R Project W-44-6. 42 pp. mimeo.

Speake, D.W., R. Metzler, and J. McGlincy. 1985. Mortality of wild turkey poults in northern Alabama. J. Wildl. Manage. 49(2):472–474.

Speckmann, E.W., and R.K. Ringer. 1962. The influence of reserpine on plasma cholesterol, hemodynamics and arteriosclerotic lesions in the broad breasted bronze turkey. Poultry Sci. 41(1):40–45.

Speckmann, E.W., R.K. Ringer, and L.F. Wolterink. 1961. The cardiac output of the broad breasted bronze turkey. Poultry Sci. 40(5):1460.

Speegle, R.E. 1984. Rusa deer hunt nets more than expected. Turkey Call 11(6):46.

Spencer, J.S., Jr., and B.L. Essex. 1976. Timber in Missouri, 1972. USDA Forest Service Resour. Bull. NC-30. 108 pp.

Spencer, J.S., Jr., and P.J. Jakes. 1980. Iowa's forest resources, 1974. USDA Forest Service Resour. Bull. NC-52. 90 pp.

Spencer, J.S., J.K. Strickler, and W.J. Moyer. 1984. Kansas forest inventory, 1981. USDA Forest Service Resour. Bull. NC-83. 134 pp.

Spicer, R.L. 1959. Wild turkey in New Mexico: an evaluation of habitat development. Albuquerque: New Mexico Dept. Game and Fish Bull. 10, 64 pp.

Spittler, H. 1977. On the acclimatization of the wild turkey *(Meleagris gallopavo)* in North Rhine–Westphalia. Int. Congr. Game Biol. 13:313–318.

Spraker, T.R., W.J. Adrian, and W.R. Lance. 1987. Capture myopathy in wild turkeys *(Meleagris gallopavo)* following trapping, handling and transportation in Colorado. J. Wildl. Dis. 23(3):447–453.

Stabler, R.M., N.J. Kitzmiller, and C.E. Braun. 1974. Hematozoa from Colorado birds. IV. Galliformes. J. Parasitol. 60(3):536–537.

Stangel, P.W., P.L. Leber, and J.I. Smith. 1992. Systematics and population genetics. *In* J.G. Dickson, ed., The wild turkey: biology and management. Harrisburg, PA: Stackpole Books.

Steadman, D.W. 1980. A review of the osteology and paleontology of turkeys (Aves: Meleagridinae). Contrib. Sci. Nat. Hist. Mus. Los Angeles Co. 330:131–207.

Steblein, P.F., and W.F. Porter. 1989. Application of geographic information systems to wildlife management. Forest Resources Issues Conf. Pennsylvania State University, University Park. Unpubl. Rep.

Steffen, D.E. 1987. Mississippi mail survey of game harvest and hunter effort for 1986–87. Jackson: Mississippi Dept. Wildlife Conservation. 49 pp.

Steffen, D.E., C.E. Couvillion, and G.A. Hurst. 1990. Age determination of eastern wild turkey gobblers. Wildl. Soc. Bull. 18(2):119–124.

Stephen, A.M. 1936. Hopi journal of Alexander M. Stephen. New York: Columbia University Contr. Anth. 23.

Still, H.R., Jr., and D.P. Baumann, Jr. 1989. Wild turkey activities in relation to timber types on the Francis Marion National Forest. Pages 137–141 *in* T.A. Waldrop, ed., Pine hardwood mixtures: management and ecology of the type. USDA Forest Service Gen. Tech. Rep. SE-58.

Still, H.R., Jr., and D.P. Baumann, Jr. 1990. Wild turkey nesting ecology on the Francis Marion National Forest. Proc. National Wild Turkey Symp. 6:13–17.

Stiven, A.E. 1961. Food energy available for and required by the blue grouse chick. Ecology 42(3):547–553.

Stoddard, H.L. 1931. The bobwhite quail—its habits, preservation and increase. New York: Charles Scribner's Sons. 559 pp.

———. 1936. Management of wild turkey. Proc. N. Am. Wildl. Conf. 1:352–356.

———. 1963. Maintenance and increase of the eastern wild turkey on private lands of the coastal plain of the deep southeast. Tallahassee, FL: Tall Timbers Res. Sta. Bull. 3. 49 pp.

Stone, W.B., and S.A. Butkas. 1978a. Lead poisoning in a wild turkey. New York Fish and Game J. 25(2):169.

Stone, W.B., and S.A. Butkas. 1978b. Notes on winter mortality in wild turkeys. New York Fish and Game J. 25(2):183–184.

Stone, W.B., L.W. DeGraff, S.W. Eaton, and B.L. Weber. 1972. Blood parasites of wild turkeys in New York. New York Fish and Game J. 19(2):116–122.

Strachey, W. 1849. The historie of travaile into Virginia Britannia (1612). Hakluyt. Soc. 6. 221 pp.

Stransky, J.J., and L.K. Halls. 1967. Woodland management trends that affect game in coastal plain forest types. Proc. Annu. Conf. Southeast. Assoc. Game and Fish Comm. 21:104–108.

Stransky, J.J., and L.K. Halls. 1978. Forage yield increased by clearcutting and site preparation. Proc. Annu. Conf. Southeast. Assoc. Fish and Wildl. Agencies 32:38–41.

Stringer, B.D., Jr. 1977. Food habits and behavior of wild turkey poults in east central Mississippi. M.S. Thesis. Mississippi State University, Mississippi State. 31 pp.

Stromborg, K.L., C.E. Grue, J.D. Nichols, G.R. Hepp, J.E. Hines, and H.C. Bourne. 1988. Postfledging survival of European starlings exposed as nestlings to an organophosphorus insecticide. Ecology 69(3):590–601.

Strong, R.M. 1911. On the olfactory organs and the sense of smell in birds. J. Morphol. 22(3):619–661.

Stubbendieck, J., S.L. Hatch, and K.J. Kjar. 1982. North American range plants. Second ed. Lincoln: University of Nebraska Press.

464 pp.

Sturkie, P.D. 1955. Effects of gonadal hormones on blood sugar of the chicken. Endocrinology 56(5):575–578.

———. 1965. Avian physiology. Second ed. Ithaca, NY: Comstock Publishing Associates. 766 pp.

Sturkie, P.D., and R.K. Ringer. 1955. Effects of suppression of pituitary gonadotrophins on blood pressure in the fowl. Am. J. Physiol. 180(1):53–56.

Suchy, W.J., W.R. Clark, and T.W. Little. 1983. Influence of simulated harvest on Iowa wild turkey populations. Proc. Iowa Acad. Sci. 90:98–102.

Suchy, W.J., G.A. Hanson, and T.W. Little. 1990. Evaluation of a population model as a management tool in Iowa. Proc. National Wild Turkey Symp. 6:196–204.

Suetsuga, H. 1976. The wild turkey in Nebraska. Lincoln: Nebraska Game and Parks Commission. 14 pp.

Sutcliffe, D. 1982. Winter habitat preferences and requirements. Proc. Western Wild Turkey Workshop 1:39–44.

Swank, W.G., D.J. Martin, J.J. Campo, and C.R. Hopkins. 1985. Mortality and survival of wild trapped eastern wild turkeys in Texas. Proc. National Wild Turkey Symp. 5:113–120.

Swanson, E.B. 1940. Use and conservation of Minnesota game: 1850–1900. Ph.D. Thesis. University of Minnesota, Minneapolis. 249 pp.

Sweeney, J.M., ed. 1980. Proc. Fourth National Wild Turkey Symp. Edgefield, SC: National Wild Turkey Federation. 292 pp.

Tabatabai, F.R., and M.L. Kennedy. 1984. Spring food habits of the eastern wild turkey in southwestern Tennessee. J. Tennessee Acad. Sci. 59(4):74–76.

Tarr, H.E. 1950. The distribution of foreign birds in Australia. Emu 49:189–198.

Taylor, R.J. 1984. Predation. Population and Community Biology Series. London: Chapman and Hall Ltd. 166 pp.

Taylor, W.P. 1943. The wild turkey in Texas. Proc. and Trans. Texas Acad. Sci. 27:231–232.

———. 1949. Notes on the Rio Grande wild turkey in central Texas. Proc. Oklahoma Acad. Sci. 30:110–114.

Telford, S.R., Jr., and D.J. Forrester. 1975. *Plasmodium Huffia hermani* sp. n. from wild turkeys *(Meleagris gallopavo)* in Florida. J. Protozool. 22(3):324–328.

Tharp, B.C. 1926. Structure of Texas vegetation east of the 98th meridian. Austin: University of Texas Bull. 2606. 100 pp.

———. 1939. The vegetation of Texas. Texas Acad. Sci. Publ. Nat. Hist. Ser. 2. 74 pp.

Thomas, G.E. 1989. Nesting ecology and survival of hen and poult eastern wild turkeys in southern New Hampshire. M.S. Thesis. University of New Hampshire, Durham. 67 pp.

Thomas, J.W. 1964. Diagnosed diseases and parasitism in Rio Grande wild turkeys. Wilson Bull. 76(3):292.

Thomas, J.W., R.G. Anderson, C. Maser, and E.L. Bull. 1979. Snags. Pages 60–77 *in* J.W. Thomas, ed., Wildlife habitats in managed forests: the Blue Mountains of Oregon and Washington. USDA Forest Service Agric. Handbook 553. 512 pp.

Thomas, J.W., and H. Green. 1957. Something to gobble about. Texas Game and Fish 15(11):9–11, 24.

Thomas, J.W., C.V. Hoozer, and R.G. Marburger, 1964. Wild turkey behavior affected by the presence of golden eagles. Wilson Bull. 76(4):384–385.

Thomas, J.W., C.V. Hoozer, and R.G. Marburger. 1966. Wintering concentrations and seasonal shifts in range of the Rio Grande turkey. J. Wildl. Manage. 30(1):34–49.

Thomas, J.W., R.G. Marburger, and C.V. Hoozer. 1973. Rio Grande turkey migrations as related to harvest regulation in Texas. Pages 301–308 *in* G.C. Sanderson and H.C. Schultz, eds., Wild turkey management: current problems and programs. Columbia: The Missouri Chapter of The Wildlife Society and University of Missouri Press. 355 pp.

Thomas, J.W., J.C. Pack, J.D. Gill, and R.W. Bailey. 1973. Even-age management, turkeys, and turkey hunters—a new study. Pages 273–276 in G.C. Sanderson and H.C. Schultz, eds., Wild turkey management: current problems and programs. Columbia: The Missouri Chapter of The Wildlife Society and University of Missouri Press. 355 pp.

Thomson, G.M. 1922. The naturalization of plants and animals in New Zealand. London: Cambridge University Press. 607 pp.

Tilghman, N.G. 1989. Impacts of white-tailed deer on forest regeneration in northwestern Pennsylvania. J. Wildl. Manage. 53(3): 524–532.

Trainer, D.O. 1973. Some diseases of wild turkeys from Texas and Wisconsin. Pages 169–173 in G.C. Sanderson and H.C. Schultz, eds., Wild turkey management: current problems and programs. Columbia: The Missouri Chapter of The Wildlife Society and University of Missouri Press. 355 pp.

Trainer, D.O., and W.C. Glazener. 1975. Wild turkeys as monitors of infectious diseases. Proc. National Wild Turkey Symp. 3:36–40.

Trainer, D.O., W.C. Glazener, R.P. Hanson, and B.D. Nassif. 1968. Infectious disease exposure in a wild turkey population. Avian Dis. 12(1):208–214.

Trautman, C.C., L.F. Fredrickson, and A.V. Carter. 1974. Relationships of red foxes and other predators to populations of ring-necked pheasants and other prey, South Dakota. Trans. N. Am. Wildl. and Nat. Resour. Conf. 39:241–252.

Traweek, M.S., B.D. Davis, B.E. Del Monte, and C. Van Hoozer. 1983. Turkey winter range requirements. Austin: Texas Parks and Wildlife Dept. Final Rep., P-R Proj. W-108-R-6. 39 pp. mimeo.

Tregle, J.G., Jr., ed. 1975. The history of Louisiana. Baton Rouge: Louisiana State University Press.

Trent, T.T., and O.J. Rongstad. 1974. Home range and survival of cottontail rabbits in southwestern Wisconsin. J. Wildl. Manage. 38(3):459–472

Trost, R.E. 1987. Mallard survival and harvest rates: a reexamination of relationships. Trans. N. Am. Wildl. and Nat. Resour. Conf. 52:264–284.

Tubbs, C.H., R.M. DeGraaf, M. Yamasaki, and W.M. Healy. 1987. Guide to wildlife tree management in New England northern hardwoods. USDA Forest Service Gen. Tech. Rep. NE-118. 30 pp.

Tuleja, T. 1987. The turkey. Pages 15–40 in A.K. Gillespie and J. Mechling, eds., American wildlife in symbol and story. Knoxville: University Tennessee Press. 251 pp.

Turner, C.D. 1966. General endochrinology. (4th ed.) Philadelphia: W.B. Saunders Co. 579 pp.

Tzilkowski, W.M. 1971. Winter roost sites of wild turkeys in southwest Pennsylvania. Trans. Northeast. Section, The Wildlife Society 28: 167–178.

Uhlig, H.G., and H.L. Wilson. 1952. A method of evaluating an annual mast index. J. Wildl. Manage. 16(3):338–343.

U.S. Department of Agriculture. 1988. The South's fourth forest: alternatives for the future. USDA Forest Service Resour. Rep. 24. 512 pp.

U.S. Fish and Wildlife Service. 1972. 1970 national survey of fishing, hunting, and wildlife associated recreation. Washington, DC: U.S. Fish and Wildl. Serv. 107 pp.

———. 1977. 1975 national survey of fishing, hunting, and wildlife associated recreation. Washington, DC: U.S. Fish and Wildl. Serv. 91 pp.

———. 1981. Standards for the development of habitat suitability index models. U.S. Dept. Interior, Fish and Wildl. Serv., Division of Ecological Services. Ecological Services Manual 103. 68 pp.

———. 1988a. 1985 national survey of fishing, hunting, and wildlife associated recreation. U.S. Dept. Interior, Fish and Wildl. Serv. 167 pp.

———. 1988b. Supplemental environmental impact statement: issuance of annual regulations permitting the sport hunting of migratory birds. Washington, DC: U.S. Dept. Interior, Fish and Wildl.

Serv. 340 pp.

U.S. Forest Service. 1984. America's renewable resources: a supplement to the 1979 assessment of the forest and range land situation in the United States. USDA Forest Service FS-386. 84 pp.

Van der Donck, A. 1841. A description of Netherlands (1656). New York Hist. Soc. Coll. 2(1):125–242.

Van Doren, M., ed. 1928. The travels of William Bartram. New York: Dover Publications. 414 pp.

Van Horn, B. 1983. Density as a misleading indicator of habitat quality. J. Wildl. Manage. 47(4):893–901.

Van Norman, T.J. 1989. Factors affecting wild turkey distribution and numbers. M.S. Thesis. Texas A&M University, College Station. 121 pp.

Van Tienhoven, A., and R.G.D. Steel. 1957. The effect of different diluents and dilution rates on fertilizing capacity of turkey semen. Poultry Sci. 36(3):473–479.

Vander Haegen, W.M. 1987. Population dynamics and habitat preference of wild turkeys in western Massachusetts. M.S. Thesis. University of Massachusetts, Amherst. 67 pp.

Vander Haegen, W.M., W.E. Dodge, and M.W. Sayre. 1988. Factors affecting productivity in a northern wild turkey population. J. Wildl. Manage. 52(1):127–133.

Vander Haegen, W.M., M.W. Sayre, and W.E. Dodge. 1989. Winter use of agricultural habitats by wild turkeys in Massachusetts. J. Wildl. Manage. 53(1):30–33.

Vangilder, L.D., and T.G. Kulowiec. 1988. Documentation for Missouri Department of Conservation turkey population model. Columbia: Missouri Dept. of Conservation. 19 pp. mimeo.

Vangilder, L.D., E.W. Kurzejeski, V.L. Kimmel-Truitt, and J.B. Lewis. 1987. Reproductive parameters of wild turkey hens in north Missouri. J. Wildl. Manage. 51(3):535–540.

Vangilder, L.D. and S.L. Sheriff. 1990. Survival estimation when fates of some animals are unknown. Trans. Missouri Acad. of Sci. 24:56–68.

Vangilder, L.D., S.L. Sheriff, and G.S. Olson. 1990. Characteristics, attitudes and preferences of Missouri's spring turkey hunters. Proc. National Wild Turkey Symp. 6:167–176.

Vasilevsky, A., and R.L. Hackett. 1980. Timber resource of Minnesota's central hardwood unit, 1977. USDA Forest Service Resour. Bull. NC-46. 65 pp.

Verner, J. 1983. An integrated system for monitoring wildlife on the Sierra National Forest. Trans. N. Am. Wildl. and Nat. Resour. Conf. 48:355–366.

Victor, B.J., and A.R. Tipton. 1981. Effects of forest conversion on the feeding ecology of wild turkey poults. Trans. Northeast. Section, The Wildlife Society 38:105.

Vieillot, L.P. 1817. Dindon: in nouveau dictionnaire d'histoire naturelle, nouv. ed. 9:444–470.

Vince, M.A. 1964. Synchronization of hatching in American bobwhite quail (Colinus virginianus). Nature 203(4950):1192–1193.

Vogel, J.A., and P.D. Sturkie. 1963. Cardiovascular responses of the chicken to seasonal and induced temperature changes. Science 140(3574):1404–1406.

Vohs, P.A., Jr., and L.R. Carr. 1969. Genetic and population studies of transferrin polymorphisms in ring-necked pheasants. Condor 71(4):413–417.

Volterra, V. 1928. Variations and fluctuations of the number of individuals in animal species living together. J. du Vonseil international pour l'Exploration de la Mer. 3:3–51.

Wagner, F.H., and L.C. Stoddart. 1972. Influence of coyote predation on black-tailed jackrabbit populations in Utah. J. Wildl. Manage. 36(2):329–342.

Wakeling, B.F. 1991. Population and nesting characteristics of Merriam's turkey along the Mogollon Rim, Arizona. Phoenix: Arizona Game and Fish Dept., Fed. Aid Proj. W-78-R. Tech. Rep. 7. 110 pp.

Walker, E.A. 1941. The wild turkey and its management in the Edwards Plateau. Pages 21–22 *in* Texas Game, Fish and Oyster Commission Quart. Prog. Oct.–Dec.

———. 1948. Rio Grande turkey in the Edwards Plateau of Texas. Austin: Texas Game, Fish and Oyster Commission. Final Rep., P-R Proj. 22-R. 20 pp. mimeo.

———. 1949a. Factors influencing wild turkey. Austin: Texas Game, Fish and Oyster Commission. Fed. Aid Rep. Ser. 4. 28 pp.

———. 1949b. The status of the wild turkey west of the Mississippi River. Trans. N. Am. Wildl. Conf. 14:336–345.

———. 1949c. A study of factors influencing wild turkey populations in the central mineral region of Texas. Austin: Texas Game, Fish and Oyster Commission. Final Rep. Fed. Aid Proj. 33-R. Ser. 4. 28 pp. mimeo.

———. 1951. Land use and wild turkeys. Texas Game and Fish 9(11):12–16.

———. 1954. Distribution and management of the wild turkey in Texas. Texas Game and Fish 12(8):12–14, 22, 26–27.

Walker, E.A., and A.J. Springs. 1952. Factors concerned with the success and failure of turkey transplants in Texas. Austin: Texas Game, Fish and Oyster Commission, Completion Rep., P-R Proj. W-44-R-2. 21 pp. mimeo.

Walker, R.L. 1986. Hawaiian data. Pages 46 and 63 *in* J.E. Kennamer, ed., Guide to the American wild turkey. Edgefield, SC: National Wild Turkey Federation. 189 pp.

Walls, D.T. 1964. Wild turkey brood range requirements and contributions of spring seeps to the winter range, Cameron County, Pennsylvania. Trans. Northeast. Section, The Wildlife Society 21:1–19.

Walsh, S.J. 1985. Geographic information systems for natural resource management. J. Soil and Water Conserv. 40(2):202–205.

Walski, T.W. 1987. Summary of wild turkey restoration and turkey management plan for New Hampshire. Concord: New Hampshire Fish and Game Dept. 55 pp.

———. 1984. Farmland plays major role in turkey population. Page 10 *in* Northeastern agricultural newsletter. Concord: New Hampshire Dept. Agriculture. Sept.

———. 1988. Evaluation of potential wild turkey habitat (Annapolis Valley of Nova Scotia). Concord: New Hampshire Fish and Game Dept. Unpubl. Rep. 10 pp. mimeo.

———. 1989. Results of wild turkey radio telemetry study. Concord: New Hampshire Fish and Game Dept. Unpubl. Rep. 4 pp.

Warner, R.E., and G.B. Joselyn, 1986. Responses of Illinois ringnecked pheasant populations to block roadside management. J. Wildl. Manage. 50(4):525–532.

Warner, R.E., G.B. Joselyn, and S.L. Etter. 1987. Factors affecting roadside nesting by pheasants in Illinois. Wildl. Soc. Bull. 15(2): 221–228.

Warnick, R.E., and J.O. Anderson. 1973. Essential amino acid levels for starting turkey poults. Poultry Sci. 52(2):445–452.

Watson, A., R. Moss, P. Rothery, and R. Parr. 1984. Demographic causes and predictive models of population fluctuations in red grouse. J. Anim. Ecol. 53(2):639–662.

Watts, C.R., 1968. Rio Grande turkeys in the mating season. Trans. N. Am. Wildl. and Nat. Resour. Conf. 33:205–210.

———. 1969. The social organization of wild turkeys on the Welder Wildlife Refuge, Texas. Ph.D. Thesis. Utah State University, Logan. 60 pp.

Watts, C.R., and A.W. Stokes. 1971. The social order of turkeys. Sci. Am. 224(6):112–118.

Weaver, J.K., and H.S. Mosby. 1979. Influence of hunting regulations on Virginia wild turkey populations. J. Wildl. Manage. 43(1): 128–135.

Webb, L.G. 1941. Spring and winter foods of the wild turkey in Alabama. M.S. Thesis. Auburn University, Auburn, AL. 50 pp.

Webb, W.S. 1946. Indian Knoll sites OH 2, Ohio County, Kentucky. Anth. Arch. Rep. 3(1):111–340.

Wedel, W.R. 1943. Archaeological investigations in Platte and Clay counties, Missouri. U.S. National Mus. Bull. 183. 284 pp.

Weinrich, J., E.E. Langenau, Jr., and T. Reis. 1985. Relationship between winter census and spring harvest of wild turkeys in northern lower Michigan. Proc. National Wild Turkey Symp. 5:295–301.

Weiss, H.S., and M. Sheahan. 1958. The influence of maturity and sex on the blood pressure of the turkey. Am. J. Vet. Res. 19(70): 209–211.

Welsh, R.J., and R.O. Kimmel. 1990. Turkey sightings by hunters of antlerless deer as an index to wild turkey abundance in Minnesota. Proc. National Wild Turkey Symp. 6:126–133.

Welty, J.C. 1982. The life of birds. Third ed. Philadelphia, PA: Saunders College Publishing. 754 pp.

Wentz, W.W., and F.C. Hardy. 1959. Turkey management as a factor in the multiple use management of the Cumberland National Forest. Proc. National Wild Turkey Symp. 1:104–115.

Wertz, T.L., and L.D. Flake. 1988. Wild turkey nesting ecology in south central South Dakota. Prairie Nat. 20(1):29–37.

West Virginia Department of Natural Resources. 1974. Wild turkey management plan. Pages 2–8 *in* West Virginia Wildlife Resources Plan.

Wetmore, A., and B.H. Swales. 1931. The birds of Haiti and the Dominican Republic. U.S. National Mus. Bull. 155. 483 pp.

Whatley, H.E., M.E. Lisano, and J.E. Kennamer. 1977. Plasma corticosterone level as an indicator of stress in the eastern wild turkey. J. Wildl. Manage. 41(2):189–193.

Wheeler, R.J., Jr. 1948. The wild turkey in Alabama. Montgomery: Alabama Dept. of Conservation Bull. 12. 92 pp.

Whisenhunt, M. 1950. Deer and turkey populations on the Norias division of the King Ranch. Austin: Texas Game, Fish and Oyster Commission. Proj. Rep., P-R Proj. W-28-D-4. 8 pp. mimeo.

White, F.H., D.J. Forrester, and L.E. Williams, Jr. 1981. Isolations of *Salmonella* from wild turkeys in Florida. J. Wildl. Dis. 17(3): 327–330.

White, F.M. 1980. Shortleaf pine-oak. Page 60 *in* F.H. Eyre, ed., Forest cover types of the United States and Canada. Society of American Foresters. 148 pp.

Whitmore, R.C. 1981. Applied aspects of choosing variables in studies of bird habitats. Pages 38–41 *in* D.E. Capen, ed., The use of multivariate statistics in studies of wildlife habitat. USDA Forest Service Gen. Tech. Rep. RM-87. 249 pp.

Wiedenfeld, C.C., and J.D. McAndrew. 1968. Soil survey of Sutton County, Texas. USDA Soil Conserv. Serv. 33 pp.

Wigal, D.D. 1973. Status of the introduced Rio Grande turkey in northeastern Iowa. Pages 35–43 *in* G.C. Sanderson and H.C. Shultz, eds., Wild turkey management: current problems and programs. Columbia: The Missouri Chapter of The Wildlife Society and University of Missouri Press. 355 pp.

Wigal, D.D., and A.O. Haugen. 1968. Survival reproductive success and spread of introduced Rio Grande turkeys in northeast Iowa. Proc. Iowa Acad. Sci. 75:130–141.

Wigley, T.B., and M.A. Melchiors. 1986. State wildlife management programs for private lands in the southeast. Proc. Southeast. Assoc. Fish and Wildl. Agencies 40:313–319.

Wigley, T.B., J.M. Sweeney, M.E. Garner, and M.A. Melchiors. 1985. Forest habitat use by wild turkeys in the Ouachita Mountains. Proc. National Wild Turkey Symp. 5:183–197.

Wigley, T.B., J.M. Sweeney, M.E. Garner, and M.A. Melchiors, 1986a. Effects of forest characteristics on wild turkey habitat use in the Ouachita Mountains. Fayetteville: Arkansas Agric. Exp. Sta. Bull. 887. 24 pp.

Wigley, T.B., J.M. Sweeney, M.E. Garner, and M.A. Melchiors. 1986b. Wild turkey home ranges in the Ouachita Mountains. J. Wildl. Manage. 50(4):540–544.

Willging, R.C. 1987. Status, distribution, and habitat use of Gould's turkey in the Peloncillo Mountains, New Mexico. M.S. Thesis. New Mexico State University, Las Cruces. 95 pp.

Williams, G.L., K.R. Russell, and W.K. Seitz. 1978. Pattern recognition as a tool in the ecological analysis of habitat. Pages 521–531 *in* A. Marmelstein, ed., Classification, inventory, and analysis of fish and wildlife habitat. U.S. Dept. Interior, Fish and Wildl. Serv., Office of Biological Services. FWS/OBS-78/76.

Williams, J.C., and J.O. Crump. 1980. Soil survey of Donley County, Texas. USDA Soil Conserv. Serv. 127 pp.

Williams, L.E., Jr. 1959. Analysis of wild turkey field sign: an approach to census. M.S. Thesis. Auburn University, Auburn, AL. 74 pp.

———. 1961. Notes on wing molt in the yearling wild turkey. J. Wildl. Manage. 25(4):439–440.

———. 1966. Capturing wild turkeys with alpha-chloralose. J. Wildl. Manage. 30(1):50–56.

———. 1973. Movements, nesting ecology, and brood studies. Page 77 *in* G.C. Sanderson and H.C. Schultz, eds. Wild turkey management: current problems and programs. Columbia: The Missouri Chapter of The Wildlife Society and University of Missouri Press. 355 pp.

———. 1974. Flight attainment in wild turkeys. J. Wildl. Manage. 38(1):151–152.

———. 1981. The Book of the wild turkey. Tulsa, OK: Winchester Press. 181 pp.

———. 1984. The voice and vocabulary of the wild turkey. Gainesville, FL: Real Turkeys. 85 pp.

Williams, L.E., Jr., and D.H. Austin. 1988. Studies of the wild turkey in Florida. Gainesville: Florida Game and Freshwater Fish Commission. Tech. Bull. 10. 232 pp.

Williams, L.E., Jr., D.H. Austin, and N.F. Eichholz. 1976. The breeding potential of the wild turkey hen. Proc. Ann. Conf. Southeast. Assoc. Fish and Wildl. Agencies 30:371–376.

Williams, L.E., Jr., D.H. Austin, and T.E. Peoples. 1974. Movement of wild turkey hens in relation to their nests. Proc. Ann. Conf. Southeast. Assoc. Game and Fish Comm. 28:602–622.

Williams, L.E., Jr., D.H. Austin, and T.E. Peoples. 1978. Turkey harvest patterns on a heavily hunted area. Proc. Ann. Conf. Southeast. Assoc. Fish and Wildl. Agencies 32:303–308.

Williams, L.E., Jr., D.H. Austin, and T.E. Peoples. 1980. Turkey nesting success on a Florida study area. Proc. National Wild Turkey Symp. 4:102–107.

Williams, L.E., Jr., D.H. Austin, T.E. Peoples, and R.W. Phillips. 1971. Laying data and nesting behavior of wild turkeys. Proc. Ann. Conf. Southeast. Assoc. Game and Fish Comm. 25:90–106.

Willaims, L.E., Jr., D.H. Austin, T.E. Peoples, and R.E. Phillips. 1973a. Observations on movement, behavior, and development of turkey broods. Pages 79–99 *in* G.C. Sanderson and H.C. Schultz, eds., Wild turkey management: current problems and programs. Columbia: The Missouri Chapter of The Wildlife Society and University of Missouri Press. 355 pp.

Williams, L.E., Jr., D.H. Austin, T.E. Peoples, and R.E. Phillips. 1973b. Capturing turkeys with oral drugs. Pages 219–227 *in* G.C. Sanderson and H.C. Schultz, eds., Wild turkey management: current problems and programs. Columbia: The Missouri Chapter of The Wildlife Society and University of Missouri Press. 355 pp.

Williams, R. 1643. A key into the language of America: or an help to the language of the natives in that part of America called New England. *In* The complete writings of Roger Williams. Vol. 1. 1963. 197 pp.

Williamson, J.F., and G.T. Koeln. 1980. A computerized wild turkey habitat evaluation system. Proc. National Wild Turkey Symp. 4:233–239.

Winchester, C.F. 1939. Influence of thyroid on egg production. Endocrinology 24(5):697–701.

Winchester, C.F., and G.K. Davis. 1952. Influence of thyroxine on growth of chickens. Poultry Sci. 31(1):31–34.

Winget, C.M., G.C. Ashton, and A.J. Cawley. 1962. Changes in gastrointestinal pH associated with fasting in the laying hen. Poultry Sci. 41(4):1115–1120.

Winters, E. 1957. The east-central upland soils. Pages 553–577 *in* A. Stefferud, ed., The yearbook of agriculture, 1957. Washington, DC: U.S. Dept. Agric., U.S. Government Printing Office. 784 pp.

Wise, G.D. 1973. Restoration of the wild turkey in Indiana. Pages 65–69 *in* G.C. Sanderson and H.C. Schultz, eds., Wild turkey management: current problems and programs. Columbia: The Missouri Chapter of The Wildlife Society and University of Missouri Press. 355 pp.

Witter, D.J., S.L. Sheriff, J.B. Lewis, and F.E. Eyman. 1982. Hunter orange for spring turkey hunting: hunter perceptions and opinions. Proc. Ann. Conf. Southeast. Assoc. Fish and Wildl. Agencies 36:791–799.

Wolf, W.W., Jr. 1988. Sheltered cutting to regenerate oaks—the Gladfelter experience. Pages 210–218 *in* H.C. Smith, A.W. Perkey, and W.E. Kidd, Jr., eds. Proc.: Guidelines for regenerating Appalachian hardwood stands. Morgantown: West Virginia University Books. 293 pp.

Wolgast, L.J. 1973. Genetic and ecological factors influencing acorn yields in scrub oak. Trans. Northeast. Section, The Wildlife Society 30:231–255.

Wolterink, L.F., J.A. Davidson, and E.P. Reineke. 1947. Hemoglobin levels in the blood of Beltsville small white poults. Poult. Sci. 26(5):559.

Wood, C.A., and A. Wetmore. 1926. A collection of birds from the Fiji Islands. Part III. Field observations. Ibis, series 12, 2(1):91–136.

Wright, A.H. 1914. Early records of the wild turkey. Auk 31: 334–358, 463–473; 32:61–81, 207–224, 348–366.

Wright, E.J. 1986. Interactive effects of turkeypox and malaria *(Plasmodium hermani)* on turkey poults. M.S. Thesis. University of Florida, Gainesville. 78 pp.

Wright, G.A. 1975. Compatibility of the eastern wild turkey with recreational and land management activities at Land Between the Lakes, Kentucky. M.S. Thesis. Auburn University, Auburn, AL. 75 pp.

Wright, G.A., and D.W. Speake. 1975. Compatibility of the eastern wild turkey with recreational activities at Land Between the Lakes, Kentucky. Proc. Ann. Conf. Southeast. Assoc. Game and Fish Comm. 29:578–584.

Wright, S. 1978. Evolution and the genetics of populations, Vol. 4. Variability within and among populations. Chicago: Univ. of Chicago Press. 580 pp.

Wunz, G.A. 1971. Tolerances of wild turkeys to human disturbance and limited range. Proc. Ann. Conf. Northeast. Assoc. Game and Fish Comm. 28:46–57.

———. 1973. Evaluation of game farm and wild-trapped turkeys in Pennsylvania. Pages 199–209 *in* G.C. Sanderson and H.C. Schultz, eds., Wild turkey management: current problems and programs. Columbia: The Missouri Chapter of The Wildlife Society and University of Missouri Press. 355 pp.

———. 1978a. Analyses of Pennsylvania's wild turkey productivity. Harrisburg: Pennsylvania Game Commission. P-R Proj. W-46-R-25. Final Rep. 7 pp. mimeo.

———. 1978b. Forest clearing evaluation. Harrisburg: Pennsylvania Game Commission. Final Rep. Job III-1. 7 pp. mimeo.

———. 1978c. The wild turkey: our all American bird. Pennsylvania Game News 49(4):7–18.

———. 1979. Wild turkey study. Harrisburg: Pennsylvania Game Commission. P-R Proj. W-46-R-25. Final Rep. 7 pp. mimeo.

———. 1981. Evaluation of supplemental winter feeding of wild turkeys. Harrisburg: Pennsylvania Game Commission. P-R Proj. 04030. Final Rep. 3 pp. mimeo.

———. 1982. Importance of ecological data in the management of wild turkeys. Proc. Western Wild Turkey Workshop 1:126–132.

———. 1983. Seeding trees and shrubs for turkeys. Turkitat 1(2):3.

———. 1984. Establishment, maintenance and wildlife preferences of herbaceous plant species planted in forest clearings. Trans. Northeast. Section, The Wildlife Society 41:130–141.

———. 1985. Wild turkey establishment and survival in small range units in farmland and suburban environments. Proc. National Wild Turkey Symp. 5:49–53.

———. 1986a. 1985—Pennsylvania's year of the turkey. Turkey Call

13(4):38–39.

———. 1986b. Where do we go from here? Turkey Call 13(5):26–29.

———. 1987a. Creating long-lasting forest clearings in Pennsylvania. Trans. Northeast. Section, The Wildlife Society 44:61–71.

———. 1987b. Rocket-net innovations for capturing wild turkeys. Turkitat 6(2):2–4.

———. 1987c. Wildlife habitat management in overbrowsed forests. Pages 99–106 *in* Deer, forestry, and agriculture interactions and strategies for management. Society of American Foresters. 183 pp.

———. 1987d. Winter, the quiet killer. Turkey Call 14(1):32–35.

———. 1989a. Establishment and management of wild turkey food and cover plantations. Harrisburg: Pennsylvania Game Commission. Final Rep. Proj. 06277. 14 pp. mimeo.

———. 1989b. Timber management and its effects on wild turkeys. Pages 110–120 *in* J.F. Finley and M.C. Brittingham, eds., Timber management and its effects on wildlife. University Park: Pennsylvania State University. 296 pp.

———. 1989c. Wild turkey tolerance of human disturbance and hunting. Harrisburg: Pennsylvania Game Commission. Ann. Rep. Proj. 06274. 3 pp.

———. 1990. Relationship of wild turkey populations to clearings created for brood habitat in oak forests in Pennsylvania. Proc. National Wild Turkey Symp. 6:32–38.

Wunz, G.A., and A.H. Hayden. 1967. The wild turkey in Pennsylvania. Pennsylvania Game News 38(11):7–13.

Wunz, G.A., and A.H. Hayden. 1975. Winter mortality and supplemental feeding of turkeys in Pennsylvania. Proc. National Wild Turkey Symp. 3:61–69.

Wunz, G.A., A.H. Hayden, and R.R. Potts, III. 1983. Spring seep ecology and management. Trans. Northeast. Section, The Wildlife Society 40:19–30.

Wunz, G.A., and L.M. Lang. 1981. Broadcast seeding clear-cuttings to increase shrubs and tree variety for wildlife. Trans. Northeast. Section, The Wildlife Society 38:23–28.

Wunz, G.A., and A.S. Ross. 1990. Wild turkey production, fall and spring harvest interactions and responses to harvest management in Pennsylvania. Proc. National Wild Turkey Symp. 6:205–207.

Wunz, G.A., and S.L. Sheriff. 1990. Survival estimation when fates of some animals are unknown. Trans. Missouri Acad. Sci. 24:57–68.

Wunz, G.A., and W.K. Shope. 1980. Turkey brood survey in Pennsylvania as it relates to harvest. Proc. National Wild Turkey Symp. 4:69–75.

Wunz, G.A., J.A. Wallin, and W. Wirth. 1985. Game farm and wild turkey introductions to West Germany. Proc. National Wild Turkey Symp. 5:25–31.

Wunz, G.A., and E.P. Wunz. 1976. Wild turkey habitat evaluation and establishment recommendations for Germany. Oberneisen, West Germany: Unpubl. Rep. 5 pp.

Wynn, T.S., and G.A. Hurst. 1990. Telemetry data management: a GIS-based approach. Proc. National Wild Turkey Symp. 6:144–148.

Yoder, H.S., Jr. 1980. Mycoplasmosis. Pages 40–42 *in* S.B. Hitchner, C.H. Domermuth, G. Purchase, and J.E. Williams, eds., Isolation and identification of avian pathogens. Second ed. College Station, TX: The American Association of Avian Pathologists. 155 pp.

York, D.L. 1991. Habitat use, diet, movements, and home range of Gould's turkey in the Peloncillo Mountains, New Mexico. M.S. Thesis. New Mexico State University, Las Cruces. 104 pp.

Young, M.D., E.C. Greiner, and D.J. Forrester. 1979. Unusual mixed haemosporidan infections in turkey blood cells. J. Parasitol. 65(6):978–979.

Young, M.D., J.K. Nayer, and D.J. Forrester. 1977. Mosquito transmission of wild turkey malaria, *Plasmodium hermani*. J. Wildl. Dis. 13(2):168–169.

Zar, J.H. 1974. Biostatistical analysis. Englewood Cliffs, NJ: Prentice-Hall Inc. 620 pp.

Zeedyk, W.D. 1969. Wildlife habitat under even-aged forest management. USDA Forest Service, Southern Region, Atlanta. 9 pp. mimeo.

———. 1982. Summer requirements of Merriam's wild turkey in Arizona and New Mexico. Proc. Western Wild Turkey Workshop 1:39–44.

Zeedyk, W.D., and J.G. Dickson. 1985. Fifth national wild turkey symposium summary. Proc. National Wild Turkey Symp. 5:333–339.

Zeedyk, W.D., and R.B. Hazel. 1974. The southeastern featured species plan. Pages 58–62 *in* Timber-wildlife management symposium. Missouri Acad. Sci. Occasional Pap. 3.

Zimmer, J.T. 1924. The wild turkey. Chicago: Field Mus. Nat. Hist. Zool. Leaflet 6.

Zink, R.M., and J.V. Remsen, Jr. 1986. Evolutionary processes and patterns of geographic variation in birds. Pages 1–69 *in* R.F. Johnston, ed., Current ornithology. Vol. 4. New York: Plenum Press.

Zinn, G., and K.D. Jones. 1987. Forests and the West Virginia economy. Summary of findings, conclusions, and recommendations. Morgantown: West Virginia Agric. and For. Exp. Sta. Bull. 691. 26 pp.

Zwank, P.J., T.H. White, Jr., and F.G. Kimmel, 1988. Female turkey habitat use in Mississippi river batture. J. Wildl. Manage. 52(2):253–260.

The Authors

DR. SAMUEL L. BEASOM (Rio Grande Turkey) has been director of the Caesar Kleberg Wildlife Research Institute at Texas A&I University for approximately 10 years. During the 10 years prior to this position, he served as a teacher-researcher at Texas A&M University, a population analyst for the New Mexico Department of Fish and Game, and a research wildlife biologist for the U.S. Forest Service. His research focuses on predator-prey interactions, population management, improving censusing techniques, and habitat management for game animals. He and his graduate students have studied and published extensively on the Rio Grande turkey and have developed key practices to improve management of this subspecies, which inhabits a more arid climate than the other subspecies of this grand game bird.

DR. LYTLE H. BLANKENSHIP (Physiology), retired professor of wildlife science, Texas A&M University, received a B.S. from Texas A&M University, an M.S. from the University of Minnesota, and a Ph.D. from Michigan State University. He has worked with the Michigan and Minnesota Departments of Conservation; the U.S. Fish and Wildlife Service; the Department of Wildlife and Fisheries Sciences, Texas A&M (Kenya); and the Texas Agricultural Experiment Station. He also has consulted for the World Bank, Organization of American States, U.S. Fish and Wildlife Service, and Exxon, among others. He has assisted more than 15 graduate students in degree programs and has authored more than 40 technical papers. Blankenship served on the Wildlife Society Council for 10 years, including 6 as southwest section representative and 2 as president.

RON E. BRENNEMAN (History) is a native of Pennsylvania. He received a B.S. in biology in 1973 and an M.S. in wildlife ecology in 1975 from Pennsylvania State University. He is a certified wildlife biologist and has authored or coauthored more than 25 technical publications. From 1975 to 1978, he was with the Clemson University, Baruch Forest Science Institute, in Georgetown, South Carolina. From 1978 to 1989, he was a forest ecologist with International Paper Company in Pennsylvania and New York. His work has included research and management of many species, including wild turkeys, white-tailed deer, feral hogs, red-cockaded woodpeckers, and snowshoe hares, as well as their relationships to forest management. Since 1989, Brenneman has been with the National Wild Turkey Federation, Edgefield, South Carolina, where he is assistant director of research and management.

DR. WILLIAM R. DAVIDSON (Population Influences: Diseases and Parasites), associate professor, is costaffed between the Warnell School of Forest Resources and the Southeastern Cooperative Wildlife Disease Study, College of Veterinary Medicine at the University of Georgia. He holds a B.S. in wildlife management and an M.S. and a Ph.D. in veterinary parasitology, and he is a certified wildlife biologist. Davidson has more than 17 years experience in his area of specialization: wildlife diseases. He is author of more than 75 scientific publications, including studies on diseases and parasites of wild turkeys, and he has edited or authored 2 books on wildlife diseases.

DR. JAMES G. DICKSON (Introduction, Physical Characteristics, Eastern Turkey in Southern Pine-Oak Forests, The Future) is a research wildlife biologist and former project leader of the Wildlife Habitat Research Laboratory of the U.S. Forest Service, Southern Forest Experiment Station, Nacogdoches, Texas. His research has provided significant new information for managing southern forests for wildlife. Dickson is also a director, chairman of the Directors' Research and Management Committee, and former secretary of the National Wild Turkey Federation. He holds a B.S., an M.S., and a Ph.D. from 3 universities and has taught at 2 other universities. He has authored more than 60 scientific and popular publications and has made more than 150 wildlife presentations to various professional and sporting organizations, many concerning wild turkey biology and hunting.

DR. WILLIAM M. HEALY (Behavior, Population Influences: Environment) is a certified wildlife biologist who received his training in forestry and wildlife management from Pennsylvania State University and West Virginia University. He works as a research wildlife biologist for the U.S. Forest Service, Northeastern Forest Experiment Station, in Amherst, Massachusetts. He has been studying wildlife-habitat relationships in eastern forests for about 25 years and has worked with everything from mice to white-tailed deer. Healy studied turkeys in the mountains of West Virginia to determine their winter and brood habitat requirements. The studies involved raising poults from abandoned nests and playing the role of the hen. In 1992, the National Wild Turkey Federation awarded Healy the Henry S. Mosby Award for outstanding research.

DR. GEORGE A. HURST (Foods and Feeding, Eastern Turkey in Southern Pine-Oak Forests) received B.S. and M.S. degrees from North Carolina State University and a Ph.D. from Mississippi State University. He is professor of wildlife management in the Department of Wildlife and Fisheries at Mississippi State University. Since 1971, he has conducted research on relationships of forest management, particularly loblolly pine plantation management, to wildlife habitat and populations. His research on wild turkeys began in 1972 and pertained to poult food habits, behavior, and brood habitat management. Since 1983, he has been coproject leader of the Mississippi Cooperative Wild Turkey Research Project, a multi-objective project studying many phases of wild turkey ecology, including population estimates, dynamics, habitat use, movements, and hunter effort and success. Hurst is a recipient of the National Wild Turkey Federation's Henry S. Mosby Award.

ROB KECK (Recreational Use) is the executive vice president of the National Wild Turkey Federation, headquartered in Edgefield, South Carolina. He has authored chapters and illustrated for numerous wildlife publications, has appeared on national television, and served as talent, writer, and technical expert on 4 award-winning videos produced by 3M Company. He has taken the coveted U.S. Open and World Turkey Calling Championships and was elected to the Pennsylvania Turkey Hunters' Hall of Fame. He is a past national director of the National Trappers Association, served 10 years on the National Rifle Association's Hunting and Wildlife Conservation Committee, and is a member of the American Society of Association Executives and the Outdoor Writers Association. A native of Pennsylvania, Keck received a B.A. from Millersville State College and did graduate work at Pennsylvania State University.

DR. JAMES EARL KENNAMER (History) is a certified wildlife biologist. A native of Alabama, he received a B.S. degree in game management from Auburn University in 1964, and an M.S. in 1967 and a Ph.D. in 1970 from Mississippi State University. His research was on the wild turkey. He taught and conducted research at Auburn University from 1970 until 1980. Since 1980, he has served as director of research and management for the National Wild Turkey Federation, Edgefield, South Carolina, and has worked with private industry and both state and federal agencies. He has authored or co-authored 32 scientific publications, as well as chapters in 3 books, and served as editor for the *Fifth National Wild Turkey Symposium Proceedings*. Kennamer is a member of the Outdoor Writers Association of America and of Alpha Zeta, Sigma XI, and Gamma Sigma Delta honorary fraternities.

MARY C. KENNAMER (History) is a native of Jackson, Mississippi, and received a B.S. in 1968 from what was then Mississippi State College for Women, with a major in journalism and an art minor. She has held positions with daily newspapers and university libraries. In 1980, she began working for *Turkey Call* magazine when she and her husband joined the staff of the National Wild Turkey Federation. She has also served as editor of *Pinfeathers* and *Turkitat* newsletters, and now works as research and management information specialist, which involves compiling and maintaining information, maintaining the research library holdings and a computer database, tracking NWTF grant-in-aid projects, public relations and information, and writing and editing.

ERIC W. KURZEJESKI (Population Management) is a wildlife research biologist with the Missouri Department of Conservation, Fish and Wildlife Research Center, in Columbia. Eric received degrees in wildlife from the University of Missouri–Columbia: a B.S. in 1977 and an M.S. in 1979. He began his career as a research biologist in 1980, as project coordinator of a long-term wild turkey population dynamics study in northern Missouri. He worked exclusively on this project, which involved trapping and radio marking of more than 400 turkeys, until 1985. His current research interests include population dynamics of Galliformes; population survey and census techniques; impacts of forest management on habitats and populations; and effects of federal farm programs on wildlife habitat conditions and populations of northern bobwhites.

JAY LANGSTON (Recreational Use) is the assistant director of publications for the National Wild Turkey Federation, where he has served since 1990 as the editor of *The Caller* and assistant editor of *Turkey Call*. Langston began his outdoor writing career with the *Mid-South Hunting & Fishing News*. After receiving a B.A. in journalism from Memphis State University in 1988, he was promoted to associate editor. He later became the editor of Game & Fish Publications' *Arkansas Sportsman*,

Louisiana Game & Fish, and *Mississippi Game & Fish* magazines. Langston also is an award-winning outdoor writer and photographer.

DR. PAUL L. LEBERG (Systematics and Population Genetics) has a B.S. in wildlife and biology from the University of Wisconsin–Stevens Point, an M.S. in biology from Memphis State University, and a Ph.D. from the University of Georgia. He conducted postdoctoral research in population ecology and genetics at Rutgers University. He is currently an assistant professor of biology at the University of Southwestern Louisiana, where he teaches ornithology, mammalogy, and wildlife biology. Leberg studies wild turkeys to gain a better understanding of how introduction programs have affected the genetic structure of wildlife populations. His other research interests include viability, demographics, genetics, and management of vertebrate populations.

DR. BRUCE D. LEOPOLD (Population Influences: Predators) received a B.S. in forest science from Pennsylvania State University and an M.S. in forestry from Mississippi State University. He then studied desert mule deer in Texas, leading to a doctorate in wildlife ecology at the University of Arizona in 1984. He remained in Arizona, where he served as a lecturer-research associate, assisting in studies concerning desert mule deer and desert bighorn sheep. He then joined the U.S. Bureau of Reclamation as a field biologist until 1987, when he joined the Wildlife and Fisheries Department at Mississippi State University. Leopold has performed research on wild turkeys, red-cockaded woodpeckers, green-tree reservoirs, wood ducks, white-tailed deer, black bears, and bobcats (captive and field studies).

JOHN B. LEWIS (Eastern Turkey in Midwestern Oak-Hickory Forests), now retired, worked for the Missouri Department of Conservation from 1952 to 1989. During that time he spent 31 years working on wild turkey research, management, and restoration. He assisted in the development of a program for capture and transfer of wild turkeys for restocking to various parts of the state. In 1960, Lewis initiated the first spring hunting season in the state that has been successful ever since. He worked closely with U.S. Forest Service personnel in the development of a plan for coordinating timber-wildlife management on national forests. Lewis was the first recipient of the National Wild Turkey Federation's Henry S. Mosby Award.

JAMES E. MILLER (Population Influences: Predators) is the national program leader, Fish and Wildlife Extension Service, USDA. He holds B.S. and M.S. degrees in for-estry-wildlife management from the University of Florida. He was formerly a wildlife biologist with the USDI Fish and Wildlife Service and extension wildlife specialist with Arkansas Cooperative Extension Service. He is a certified wildlife biologist. He has held several offices in the Wildlife Society (TWS) and currently is the southeastern representative to TWS Council. Miller has been active in the National Wild Turkey Federation, having served as technical representative and as a director. For his contributions, he received the Federation's C.B. McLoud Award. He has produced more than 80 technical papers, many in varied national media. He contributed to international wildlife educational studies in Pakistan. In 1990, he received the USDA Extension Administrators Award for Excellence.

CHERYL MOLLOHAN (Merriam's Turkey) was born near Akron, Ohio, in 1959. She received a B.S. in wildlife biology from Arizona State University in 1981. In 1982, she began working for the Arizona Game and Fish Department in the Research Branch. Mollohan received an M.S. in environmental resources in agriculture from Arizona State University in 1985. Her master's thesis focused on black bear habitat in northern Arizona. From 1987 to 1990, she returned to school at Northern Arizona University, where she worked on a Merriam's turkey habitat project. In 1990, she returned to the Arizona Game and Fish Department, where she is currently a wildlife education specialist working with Project WILD.

JAMES C. PACK (Eastern Turkey in Eastern Oak-Hickory and Northern Hardwood Forests) is a biologist with the West Virginia Department of Natural Resources, Wildlife Section. Previously, he was district biologist, Virginia Department of Game and Fish; coleader national forest development project, and leader forest game research West Virginia Department of Natural Resources. Pack received a B.S. in forestry from West Virginia University and an M.S. in wildlife science from Virginia Polytechnic Institute and State University. His work experience has been primarily habitat research and management of forest game species, and he has worked with wild turkeys for 25 years.

DR. PAUL H. PELHAM (Physical Characteristics), now retired, received a D.V.M. from Cornell University and practiced veterinary medicine. He formerly was a director of the National Wild Turkey Federation, as well as president of the New York chapter, and was recognized for his contributions with the Foundation's Roger Latham Award. He has raised human-imprinted turkeys and studied their behavior and development for about 8 years. He has made numerous presentations concerning the wild turkey, particularly identifying turkeys by sex and age in the field.

DR. WILLIAM F. PORTER (Habitat Analysis and Assessment, Habitat Requirements) received a B.A. in 1973 from the University of Northern Iowa and a Ph.D. in 1979 from the University of Minnesota. In his doctoral research, he examined wild turkey populations in southeastern Minnesota and was one of the first to document the importance of agriculture to turkeys in northern latitudes. Currently he is professor of wildlife ecology at the State University of New York College of Environmental Science and Forestry in Syracuse. His research includes continuing studies of the population dynamics of wild turkeys as influenced by land use, weather, and hunter harvest.

DR. SANFORD D. SCHEMNITZ (Gould's Turkey) currently is a professor at New Mexico State University at Las Cruces. He previously was a faculty member at the University of Maine and at Pennsylvania State University. He has been a research biologist for 2 state agencies. He has a B.S. from the University of Michigan, an M.S. from the University of Florida, and a Ph.D. from Oklahoma State University, all in wildlife. He and his students, through their research, have gained most of the information that is known about the Gould's turkey. He has authored almost 100 scientific publications and edited the *4th Wildlife Techniques Manual*. Recently he completed 2 Fulbright wildlife lecture sabbaticals, to Nepal and Kenya.

HARLEY G. SHAW (Merriam's Turkey) is a wildlife consultant with General Wildlife Services, specializing in wildlife habitat evaluation, and is helping develop the *Merriam's Turkey Guidelines*. He is retired from the Arizona Game and Fish Department, where he was a research biologist for 27 years. Much of his previous research focused on mountain lions, deer, and the Merriam's turkey, particularly censusing, habitat suitability, and mortality. He received a B.S. from the University of Arizona and an M.S. from the University of Idaho.

JULIA I. SMITH (Systematics and Population Genetics) is involved in research focusing on the evolutionary processes that determine the structure and the dynamics of avian population differentiation. For her M.S. at the University of Oklahoma, she explored a hybrid zone between red-bellied and golden-fronted woodpeckers. Combining analyses of morphological and allozymic variation, she discovered a high frequency of hybrids. She is currently pursuing a Ph.D. at the University of

California–Berkeley. The objective of her dissertation is to detail, via a quantitative genetic analysis, the forces acting to preserve the pattern of morphological differentiation in song sparrows. This research will help to clarify the role of genetic diversity in maintaining patterns of morphological variation in vertebrates.

DR. PETER W. STANGEL (Systematics and Population Genetics) is director of the National Fish and Wildlife Foundation's Neotropical Migratory Bird Conservation Initiative. He received a B.S. in biology from Furman University in Greenville, South Carolina, and a Ph.D. in ecology from the University of Georgia. His research interests include the genetic structure of populations and the impact of management programs on the genetic variability and structure of bird populations.

DR. LARRY D. VANGILDER (Population Dynamics, Population Management) is a wildlife research biologist with the Missouri Department of Conservation, Fish and Wildlife Research Center, in Columbia. He received a B.S. and M.S. in wildlife from the University of Missouri–Columbia, and in 1981 a Ph.D. from Ohio State University. In 1985, he joined the Missouri Department of Conservation, where he was responsible for directing the wild turkey program, both research and harvest recommendations. He is presently conducting a 10-year wild turkey study in the Missouri Ozarks that involves radio marking and monitoring both hens and gobblers. His other research interests include population modeling, mortality and survival, and population dynamics.

EMILY JO WENTWORTH (Population Influences: Diseases and Parasites) is a wildlife biologist with the Georgia Department of Natural Resources (DNR), Game and Fish Division. Her primary responsibilities include liaison with the U.S. Forest Service, ruffed grouse research and surveys, peregrine falcon recovery, hard mast abundance and distribution, technical assistance, and nuisance abatement. She serves as the statewide Nongame Committee chairman, president-elect of the Georgia Chapter of The Wildlife Society, and board member of the Georgia Wildlife Federation. Prior to her work with the DNR, Wentworth was a research technician with Southeastern Cooperative Wildlife Disease Study and participated in research and diagnosis of diseases and parasites of a variety of mammals, reptiles, and birds, including wild turkeys. She earned B.S. and M.S. degrees from the University of Georgia, School of Forest Resources.

DR. LOVETT E. WILLIAMS, JR. (Florida Turkey), holds degrees from Florida State University and Auburn University and a Ph.D. in wildlife ecology from the University of Florida. He headed up the Florida Wildlife Research Bureau before he left the agency to enter private business in 1985. His books on the wild turkey include *The Book of the Wild Turkey*, *The Art and Science of Wild Turkey Hunting*, *Studies of the Wild Turkey in Florida*, and *Managing Wild Turkeys in Florida*. He produces Real Turkeys audiocassettes based on recordings of the wild turkey's calls, and he is co-owner of a hunting lodge in Glades County, Florida. He is currently conducting a study of wildlife management technology on private land as research associate with Clemson University. In recognition of his innovative research and substantial publications, Williams received the National Wild Turkey Federation's Henry S. Mosby Award.

DON E. WILSON (Rio Grande Turkey) is a wildlife biologist living in Maxwell, Texas. He received a B.S. in wildlife management from Texas A&M University in 1964. He has worked for the past 27 years for the Texas Parks & Wildlife Department: 8 years in the Texas Edwards Plateau with deer and Rio Grande turkeys, and 8 years in the Texas Oak-Prairie with white-tailed deer, bobwhite quail, pheasant, and waterfowl. Headquartered in Austin since 1980, he is the program leader for Upland Game. The program deals with 4 species of quail; Rio Grande, eastern, and Merriam's turkeys; prairie chickens; pheasants; chachalacas; rabbits; and squirrels. He has been actively involved in the restoration of eastern turkeys to East Texas.

GERALD A. WUNZ (Eastern Turkey in Eastern Oak-Hickory and Northern Hardwood Forests, Wild Turkeys Outside Their Historic Range), a native of Erie, Pennsylvania, resides in Milroy, Pennsylvania. He received a B.S. and an M.S. at Pennsylvania State University and worked for the Kentucky Department of Fish and Wildlife Resources for 8 years as project leader of bobwhite quail and game-farm habitat research studies. He retired from the Pennsylvania Game Commission after 30 years as wild turkey research and management project leader, specializing in forest habitat research. He published 25 research papers and more than 50 final reports and popular articles relating to wildlife research and management. He also served as consultant to several states, Canada, and Germany. Wunz was awarded the Henry S. Mosby Award for his long-term contributions to the wild turkey.

WILLIAM D. ZEEDYK (Gould's Turkey) was a biologist with the U.S. Forest Service from 1956 until 1990 and was director of wildlife and fisheries, Southwest Region, U.S. Forest Service, before recently retiring. He helped restore wild turkeys in 5 states and implement effective management. He served 3 terms as a National Wild Turkey Federation director, was chairman of the Directors' Research and Management Committee, and helped organize southeastern and western Federation chapters. He coauthored the summary of the *Fifth National Wild Turkey Symposium*. Zeedyk always promoted the ethical and sporting nature of turkey hunting and helped the wild turkey, turkey management, and sport hunting gain status in the West.

Index

Hunting
  baiting and decoys, use of, 184
  defensive, 395–96
  of Florida wild turkey, 215–17
  monitoring of eastern wild turkey in eastern and northern
      forests, 259–61
  mortality rates, 156–57
  processing the kill, 397–402
  reducing accidents, 184
  safety, 394–95
  statistics, 388
  strategies for providing quality, 181–84
  trophies and trophy scoring, 396–97
Hunting pressure, monitoring, 176–81
Hunting seasons and regulations
  fall, 180–81
  spring, 177–80
  states allowing spring, 6
Hunting techniques
  blowgun, 8
  for fall hunting, 393–94
  nets, 8
  pens, 8
  sarbacane, 8
  snares, 8
  for sport hunting, 390
  for spring gobbler hunting, 390–93
  used by Native Americans, 8
Hurricanes, impact of, 141–42

Idaho, turkeys in, 374
Imprinting and early experiences
  description of, 53–55
  domestic turkeys and, 60
Incubation
  description of, 51–53
  for Florida wild turkey, 228
Interplantings, 171

Jolly-Seber model, 152
Jump-peck, 68
Juveniles
  feeding habits, 70
  food, 69–70
  nutritional needs, 70
  sex determination, 42, 43
  water needs, 70

Kaplan-Meier method, 152, 153

Lacey Act (1905), 12
Large Indian Domestic, 7
Laying and incubation
  description of, 51–53
  for Florida wild turkey, 228
Legislation
  Farm Bill (1985), 304
  Lacey Act (1905), 12
  National Environmental Policy Act (1969), 188, 202
  National Forest Management Act (NFMA) (1976), 300–302
  Pittman-Robertson Act (1937), 12
Legs, 36
  age determination and color of, 41
Leucocytozoon smithi, 86, 109–10
Lice, 115–16
Line and strip transects, 172
Linnaeus, Carl, 6, 20
Livestock, Rio Grande wild turkey and relationship with, 320–21
Longevity, 98
Louse flies, 116
Luteinizing hormone (LH), 87, 88, 89

Maine, turkeys in, 368
Maintenance behavior, 59
Manitoba, turkeys in, 381
Mark-recapture methods, 171–72
Mating season. *See* Breeding season; Reproduction
Mayfield technique, 152–53
Melanin, 36
Meleagris gallopavo
  subspecies, 6–7
  use of the term, 20
Merriam's wild turkey (*Meleagris gallopavo merriami*)
  breed-strutting habitats, 336–37
  brood-rearing sites, 340–42
  climate, 332–33
  description of environment, 333–36
  fall and winter habitats, 343–47
  feeding-loafing-escape habitats, 343, 345
  food, 77–78
  future for, 348–49
  habitat management goals for, 347–48
  habitat requirements, 332–47
  introducing to other ranges, 383
  migration corridors for, 336
  naming of, 7
  nesting sites, 337–39
  origin of, 7, 23, 331
  population estimates for, 15, 16
  range of, 331
  roosting sites, 342–43
  spring habitats, 336–39
  summer habitats, 339–43
Metabolism, 92
Metatarsi, 36–37
Michigan, turkeys in, 369–70
Middle East, turkeys in, 365
Migration corridors, 336
Minnesota, turkeys in, 370
Missouri model, 159–63
Mites, 115
Molting, 32
  in developing poults, 40
  factors affecting, 91
  Florida wild turkey, 229–30
Molting pattern, age determination and, 40
Montana, turkeys in, 374
Mortality
  annual survival rates, 153–55
  causes of death, 155–56
  cause-specific rates, 155
  harvest, 156–57
  population dynamics and, 151–58
  poult, 56, 69
  poult mortality posthatching, 150–51
  rates, 98
  seasonal survival rates, 157–58
Mortality, methods used to study
  band recovery data, 151–52
  mark-recapture/mark-resighting information, 152
  Missouri model, 159–63
  radiotelemetry, 152–53
  Suchy model, 163–64
Movement, population dynamics and, 144
Multivariate data-analysis techniques, 3–4
Multivariate statistical analysis, 191–93
Mycoplasma gallisepticum
  breeding and, 86
  hatchability of eggs and, 89
Mycoplasmosis, 103–4

National Environmental Policy Act (1969), 188, 202
National Forest Management Act (NFMA) (1976), 300–302